ADMINISTRATIVE TRIBUNALS IN THE COMMON LAW WORLD

Administrative tribunals are a vital part of the public law frameworks of many countries. This is the 1st edited book collection to examine tribunals across the common law world. It brings together key international scholars to discuss current and future challenges.

The book includes contributions from leading scholars from all major common law jurisdictions – the UK, the USA, Canada, Australia, New Zealand, Ireland, Israel, Hong Kong, Singapore, India and South Africa. This global analysis is both deep and expansive in its coverage of the operation of administrative tribunals across common law legal systems. The book has two key themes: one is the enduring question of the location and operation of tribunals within public law systems; the second is the continued mission of tribunals to provide administrative justice.

The collection is an important addition to global public law scholarship, addressing common problems faced by the tribunals of common law countries, and providing solutions for how tribunals can evolve to match the changing nature of government.

Administrative Tribunals in the Common Law World

Edited by
Stephen Thomson
Matthew Groves
and
Greg Weeks

•HART•
OXFORD • LONDON • NEW YORK • NEW DELHI • SYDNEY

HART PUBLISHING

Bloomsbury Publishing Plc

Kemp House, Chawley Park, Cumnor Hill, Oxford, OX2 9PH, UK

1385 Broadway, New York, NY 10018, USA

29 Earlsfort Terrace, Dublin 2, Ireland

HART PUBLISHING, the Hart/Stag logo, BLOOMSBURY and the Diana logo are trademarks of Bloomsbury Publishing Plc

First published in Great Britain 2024

A catalogue record for this book is available from the British Library.

A catalogue record for this book is available from the Library of Congress.

Library of Congress Control Number: 2024940693

ISBN: HB: 978-1-50996-690-5
ePDF: 978-1-50996-692-9
ePub: 978-1-50996-691-2

Typeset by Compuscript Ltd, Shannon

FOREWORD

I am honoured to be asked to introduce this important work on tribunals in the common law world. My own credentials are somewhat dated. It is 12 years since, on my appointment to the Supreme Court, I stood down from my position as the first UK Senior President of Tribunals. Over the preceding seven years I had been tasked with providing judicial leadership for the radical reform programme for UK tribunals, following the 2001 Leggatt Report.[1] Leggatt had envisaged that role being taken by a High Court judge. But it was decided that to provide the greater weight and authority for these major reforms, a Court of Appeal judge should be appointed.

I was selected, I would like to think, because of my experience, as practitioner and judge, both of administrative law in general, and of tribunals dealing in particular with tax, land, social security and immigration. But, perhaps more realistically, I may have been the only candidate for the job. Tribunals were not seen as a glamorous area of the law. They had grown up over the best part of a century in response to particular needs and concerns, but without any coherent framework of law or practice. They were not seen by practitioners as a natural route to the higher reaches of the profession. They had received very little attention from academics. Tribunals may consider an enormous number of cases, but they do so largely under the radar of political and media attention.

The Leggatt vision, which I wholly endorsed, was that they deserved much more recognition. In terms of both numbers and importance to the parties concerned of their cases they were the match of any of the higher courts. Their defining characteristics were the specialist character of their jurisdictions, their ability to combine legal and non-legal expertise relevant to their subject-matter, and their accessibility. The reform programme, given statutory underpinning by the Tribunal, Courts and Enforcement Act 2007, created a uniform two-tier structure for all tribunals, divided by subject-matter into separate 'chambers' each headed by a senior judge as 'President', and under the overall leadership of the Senior President. The subsequent progress of the reforms is described elsewhere in this volume. For me two features stand out. The first was to give tribunals their own clear identity within the legal world. Critical to this were the overall structure, headed by a senior judge, the common nomenclature ('first tier', 'upper tribunal' etc)

[1] Sir A Leggatt, *Tribunals for Users, One System, One Service: Report of the Review of Tribunals* (HMSO, 2001). The prior history is described in more detail by Robert Thomas (ch 8).

and the unified set of procedural rules. The other was to put them on the same footing as the court judiciary. The legal members were to be described as tribunal 'judges'. Court judges were able to sit as members. High court judges regularly sat in the Upper Tribunals along with specialist members. They were appointed by the same Judicial Appointments Commission, and movement between the two systems was encouraged.

Reading the present volume, I have found it fascinating to see how our experience compares with that of other common law jurisdictions, faced with similar issues. One striking difference is the absence in the UK of any of the constitutional constraints, which feature in many of the chapters,[2] and have sometimes forced (to my mind) an artificial separation between the courts and 'administrative' tribunals. The only serious debate that I remember from those early days was how close we should be, and in particular whether the Senior President should be under the authority of the Lord Chief Justice. The then Lord Chancellor, Lord Falconer, was adamant that the Senior President should be independent. I had no strong views on the issue, but as it turned out my independence from the senior court judiciary proved a significant asset in enabling us to develop the tribunal system in our own distinctive way. Once the new system had settled down, it made sense (as Carol Harlow has described) for steps to be taken to bring the two systems closer together to create a 'single judicial family'.

As is discussed in the first chapter,[3] a common theme of the contributions to this volume from other jurisdictions appears to be a desire for reform of tribunal systems. This comparative study will do much to inform that debate. More generally I welcome it as focussing much-needed attention on a very important part of the legal system – indeed 'a coalface of administrative law and administrative justice'. As such it is long overdue.

Robert Carnwath
London
May 2024

[2] Thomson, Groves and Weeks (ch 1), discussing the 'considerable structural limitations' imposed upon tribunals by different constitutions. See, for example, in Ireland *Zalewski v Workplace Relations Commission* [2021] IESC 24: discussed by O'Donovan and Donson (ch 16).

[3] ibid.

CONTENTS

ABOUT THE CONTRIBUTORS

Michael Asimow is Professor of Law Emeritus at UCLA School of Law and Dean's Executive Professor of Law at Santa Clara Law School. He was previously a long-term visiting professor at Stanford Law School. He specialises in the study of administrative adjudication, both state and federal, as well as comparative. He co-authored a law school course book with Ron Levin, *State and Federal Administrative Law* (5th edn, West Publishing, 2020). Professor Asimow has served as a consultant to the Administrative Conference of the United States on several occasions. He is currently studying administrative prosecutorial discretion.

Chintan Chandrachud is a barrister at Brick Court Chambers, London. His practice focuses on commercial and public law. He is widely published on public law subjects and is the author of *The Cases that India Forgot* (Juggernaut, 2019) and *Balanced Constitutionalism: Courts and Legislatures in India and the United Kingdom* (OUP, 2017). He taught constitutional law at St Catherine's College and Christ Church, University of Oxford.

Kenny Chng is an Associate Professor of Law at the Singapore Management University Yong Pung How School of Law. His primary research interest is in constitutional and administrative law. Kenny has extensive publications and forthcoming articles in leading international and local academic journals in his areas of interest, including the *Law Quarterly Review, Legal Studies, Public Law, the International Journal of Constitutional Law, Judicial Review, the Journal of Private International Law, the Civil Justice Quarterly, the Hong Kong Law Journal, the Asian Journal of Comparative Law, and the Singapore Journal of Legal Studies*. His work has been cited with approval by the Singapore Court of Appeal.

Hugh Corder served as the Professor of Public Law from 1987 to 2019, and as Dean of the Faculty of Law from 1999 to 2008, at the University of Cape Town. He is now Emeritus Professor and a Senior Research Scholar at the same university. A graduate of Cape Town, Cambridge, and Oxford, he was a member of the committee which drafted South Africa's first Bill of Rights in 1993 and has played the leading role in administrative law reform initiatives since 1992. His research and writing focus on administrative justice and all aspects of judicial service. He has been a Fellow of the University of Cape Town since 2004.

Robin Creyke AO FAAL is an Emeritus Professor at the Australian National University, where she was a long-term academic. Robin has been a member of several tribunals and of organisations designed to ensure government accountability. She co-authored a foundation law text, *Laying down the Law* (11th edn,

LexisNexis, 2020), and an administrative law text, *Control of Government Action* (6th edn, LexisNexis, 2018), as well military law texts, *Veterans' Entitlements and Military Compensation Law* (4th edn, Federation Press, 2024), and *Military Law in Australia* (Federation Press, 2019). A specialist in dispute resolution by tribunals, she has also authored numerous articles and other material on tribunals and government, and administrative law in general.

Paul Daly holds the University Research Chair in Administrative Law & Governance at the University of Ottawa. Professor Daly's influential, bilingual, award-winning scholarly work on public law – dozens of books, peer-reviewed journal articles, book chapters and shorter pieces – has been cited more than 100 times, including by the Supreme Court of Canada, various other Canadian courts and tribunals, the High Court of Australia, the Irish Supreme Court and the New Zealand Supreme Court. Since September 2019 he has been a part-time member of the Environmental Protection Tribunal of Canada.

Fiona Donson is a Senior Lecturer at University College Cork, Ireland. She is currently Co-Director of the Traveller Equality and Justice Project and was formerly Director of the Centre for Criminal Justice and Human Rights. Her research engages with critical intersections of law, accountability and government including the interrelationship between human rights, public administration and citizen participation. Her publications include *Legal Intimidation* (Free Association, 2000), *Law and Public Administration in Ireland* (Clarus Press, 2015) (co-authored with Dr Darren O'Donovan) and *Traveller Law in Ireland* (forthcoming) (co-authored with Dr Samantha Morgan-Williams).

Elizabeth Fisher is Professor of Environmental Law at Faculty of Law and Corpus Christi College, University of Oxford. She has written widely in administrative law and environmental law including on the topic of tribunals. Recent relevant projects include Elizabeth Fisher and Brian Preston (eds) *An Environmental Court in Action: Function, Doctrine and Process* (Hart, 2022) and Elizabeth Fisher and Sidney Shapiro, *Administrative Competence: Reimagining Administrative Law* (CUP, 2020) (jointly awarded the American Bar Association Administrative Law Section's Scholarship Award 2021).

Matthew Groves is Alfred Deakin Professor of Law, in the Law School of Deakin University, Australia. He has published widely on public law, particularly administrative law. Matthew is co-author of M Aronson, M Groves and G Weeks, *Judicial Review of Administrative Action and Government Liability* (7th edn, Thomson Reuters, 2022), which is the definitive Australian work in the field. He has edited ten books, the most recent of which is M Groves and A Sthumcke, *Omubdsman in the Modern Age* (Hart, 2022). Matthew is also General Editor of the *Australian Journal of Administrative Law*.

Carol Harlow is Emerita Professor of Law and the London School of Economics and Political Science. Her many works on public law include *Law and Administration*

(4th edn, CUP, 2022) and *Process and Procedure in EU Administration* (Bloomsbury, 2014). She acted as Special Adviser to the House of Lords Select Committee on Inquiries in 2013 and was appointed as Queens Counsel (honoris causa) in 1996.

Swati Jhaveri Knowledge Management Consultant, Singapore International Arbitration Centre and Consultant, Peerpoint by Allen & Overy LLP. Swati is a Knowledge Management Associate in the Strategy and Development Department of the Singapore International Arbitration Centre as well as a Consultant with Peerpoint by Allen & Overy LLP. Prior to this, Swati held academic positions at the Faculty of Law of The Chinese University of Hong Kong and The National University of Singapore.

Eleana Kasoulide is a PhD student at the York Law School researching the experimental stage of introducing new digital public services. She is also a research assistant for the Administrative Fairness Lab working on projects that aim to improve public administrative processes.

Sarah Nason is Senior Lecturer in Administrative Law and Jurisprudence, Bangor University School of History, Law and Social Sciences. After legal practice training Sarah moved into academia in 2007, she has written widely on judicial review (inc *Reconstructing Judicial Review* (Hart, 2016, paperback 2019)) administrative law and administrative justice (Oxford University Press, Hart Publishing, Edward Elgar, *Modern Law Review*, *Journal of Law and Society*). Funders of her administrative justice and tribunals research include the ESRC, Nuffield Foundation, British Academy, and Welsh Government.

Darren O'Donovan is Senior Lecturer in Administrative Law at La Trobe Law School, Melbourne. Darren holds a BCL (Hons), and a PhD from University College Cork, Ireland, where he also lectured from 2009–2012. Darren has written extensively on rights, oversight and public administration, including the book *Law and Public Administration in Ireland* (co-authored with Dr Fiona Donson). Much of Darren's work has reflected upon the centrality of non-judicial review bodies and first instance decision-makers to delivering administrative justice.

Huw Pritchard is Lecturer in Law, Cardiff University School of Law and Politics. Huw has been a lecturer in devolved law and governance since 2015. His main areas of interest are the law of devolution in Wales and the UK and the devolution of justice. He is also interested in constitutional law, administrative justice and the effects of devolution on the law of health and social care. Huw was appointed to the Academic Panel of the Administrative Justice Council in 2018 and is secretary of the Public Law Wales Society.

Aisling Ryan is Research Fellow in the Administrative Fairness Lab at the University of York where she is working on developing a research agenda on the links between administrative fairness and health, including mental health. Aisling researches administrative justice, administrative law and access to justice with a focus on lower level administrative processes and first instance decision making. Aisling is qualified to practice as a solicitor in Ireland, England and Wales having previously trained and worked as an associate in one of Ireland's leading law firms. Aisling was appointed to the panel of adjudicators for the Residential Tenancies Board in 2021 and in this role adjudicates on landlord-tenant disputes. Sheteaches Administrative Law, Commercial Law and Equity.

Guy I Seidman is a professor at Reichman University (formerly IDC Herzliya) where he has been on the faculty since 1999. Professor Seidman specialises in administrative law, comparative law and legal history, and has written and taught in Israel, the United States and Europe. Professor Seidman is the co-author of *Deference* (Oxford University Press, 2019), *A Great Power of Attorney* (Kansas University Press, 2017), *The Constitution of Empire* (Yale University Press, 2017), *The Dynamism of Civil Procedure* (Springer, 2015) and *The Legal Aspects of Shaming* (Edward Elgar, 2023 forthcoming). Professor Seidman was educated in Israel (LLB, LLM, Tel-Aviv University) and the United States (LLM, SJD, Northwestern University).

Robert Thomas is a Professor of Public Law at the University of Manchester and works on administrative law and administrative justice. His publications include: *Administrative Justice and Asylum Appeals* (Hart, 2011); *Administrative Law in Action* (Hart, 2021); *Immigration Judicial Reviews: An Empirical Study* (Palgrave, 2021 co-authored with Joe Tomlinson); and *Public Law* (3rd edn, OUP, 2020, co-authored with Mark Elliott).

Stephen Thomson is an Associate Professor in the ANU College of Law at The Australian National University. He has published widely on domestic and comparative public law in several jurisdictions, particularly on matters of administrative law and constitutional law. Stephen is the author of *Administrative Law in Hong Kong* (CUP, 2018), *The Nobile Officium* (Avizandum/Edinburgh University Press, 2015) and the forthcoming *Administrative Law: A Very Short Introduction* (Oxford University Press), and co-editor of Stephen Thomson and Denis Edwards (eds), *Administrative Law (2nd Reissue)* in *The Laws of Scotland: The Stair Memorial Encyclopaedia* (LexisNexis, 2023). Stephen is the General Editor of the *Federal Law Review* and was previously a Legal Adviser to the Ombudsman of Hong Kong.

Joe Tomlinson is Professor of Public Law at the University of York. His research focuses on administrative law and justice. His work has been widely used in the courts (including the UK Supreme Court), by government officials, in Parliament, and in the charity sector. His most recent books – *Experiments in Automating Immigration Systems* (Polity, 2021 co-authored with Jack Maxwell) and *Immigration Judicial Reviews: An Empirical Study* (Palgrave, 2021 co-authored with Robert Thomas) –focus on the intersection of administrative law and immigration administration.

Greg Weeks is a Professor in the ANU College of Law at the Australian National University and a Member of the Administrative Appeals Tribunal. He has published widely on his research interests, which are primarily related to judicial review, state liability and remedies against public authorities. He is the author of *Soft Law and Public Authorities: Remedies and Reform*, (Hart, 2016) and a co-author of *Government Liability: Principles and Remedies* (LexisNexis, 2019) and *Judicial Review of Administrative Action and Government Liability* (Thomson Reuters, 6th edn, 2017 and 7th edn, 2022), Australia's leading administrative law text. Greg is General Editor of the *Australian Journal of Administrative Law*.

Hanna Wilberg is an Associate Professor at the University of Auckland. Her research and teaching interests lie mainly in administrative law, social security law, and the tort liability of public authorities. Her publications include Wilberg and Elliott (eds) *The Scope and Intensity of Substantive Review: Traversing Taggart's Rainbow* (Hart, 2015), a forthcoming book on *The Principles of Administrative Law in Aotearoa New Zealand* (Hart), and articles in leading United Kingdom, Australian and New Zealand journals. She has held visiting fellowships at the University of Cambridge and at Magdalen College, Oxford.

1

The Distinctive Nature of Tribunals

STEPHEN THOMSON, MATTHEW GROVES AND GREG WEEKS

The recent focus of administrative law scholarship has been dominated by two issues – one new and the other age old. The new issue is the impact of automation and artificial intelligence (AI). This fourth industrial revolution, the coming of a new digital age, will increasingly affect every aspect of public decision-making and administrative review, as well as how people interact with every part of the bureaucratic state.[1] Scholarship about automation and AI, much like those very processes, remains in its infancy.[2] The age-old question that has returned to the fore of administrative law scholarship is the quest for theoretical coherence. Some authors have traced historical factors,[3] others have a clearly contemporary focus,[4] while some question the existence or value of any overarching theory.[5] The quest for a theoretical foundation or coherence in administrative law has largely continued an odd feature of the body of scholarship, which has been to bypass or marginalise the role of tribunals. The focus of scholars upon judicial review is hardly surprising when it has been proclaimed as 'the most striking features of the development of the common law'.[6] Many, perhaps even most, theoretical accounts of administrative law pay no real attention to tribunals.[7] The same is often true of

[1] The digital age was described as the fourth industrial revolution by K Schwab, *The Fourth Industrial Revolution* (Penguin, Random House, 2017).

[2] The generational nature of this challenge is discussed in J Tomlinson, *Justice in the Digital State: Assessing the Next Revolution in Administrative Justice* (Bristol University Press, 2019) ch 1; and P Daly, J Raso and J Tomlinson, 'Administrative Law in the Digital World' in C Harlow (ed), *A Research Agenda for Administrative Law* (Edward Elgar, 2023).

[3] P Cane, *Controlling Administrative Power – An Historical Comparison* (CUP, 2016).

[4] See, eg, P Daly, *Understanding Administrative Lawin the Common Law World* (OUP, 2021).

[5] See, eg, J Bell, *The Anatomy of Administrative Law* (Hart Publishing, 2020); and J Weinrib, 'Maitland's Challenge for Administrative Legal Theory' (2021) 84 *Modern Law Review* 207. These doubts are not new: R Stewart, 'The Reformation of American Administrative Law' (1975) 88 *Harvard Law Review* 1667, 1807.

[6] *Mahon v Air New Zealand Ltd* [1984] AC 808, 816.

[7] The indices in Daly (n 4) and Bell (n 5) do not have a single entry for tribunals. In Harlow (n 2) the only indexed references to tribunals refer to the chapter of the editor. This point can hardly be a criticism of any of those books when two editors of this book co-author a volume well over 1,000 pages about judicial review alone. The other editor of this book did, however, devote 16 pages to tribunals in a jurisdiction where tribunals scholarship was almost non-existent: S Thomson, *Administrative Law in Hong Kong* (CUP, 2018) 304–19. S Thomson, *Administrative Law: A Very Short Introduction* (OUP, 2024 forthcoming) also includes a chapter on tribunals.

the teaching of administrative law, which tends to spend time on tribunals and judicial review processes in inverse proportion to their prevalence.[8]

The role of tribunals has not been ignored by public law scholars,[9] but the area remains the poor relation of judicial review. One reason, noted long ago by Rawlings, was 'not merely that courts are the centre of [public law] analysis' but that 'the analysis of other grievance mechanisms is court centred'.[10] In his study of immigration administration, Thomas noted that administrative law was 'principally conceptualised' as a body of judicially developed doctrines that tended to perceive administrative law as 'comprising the legal principles of judicial review which apply across the broad range of government and public bodies', which scholars then dissected 'in order to uncover their normative basis and how they are applied by the courts'.[11] The tendency of scholars to view the work of tribunals and other agencies through the prism of courts has two strands. A large part is the scholarly focus upon analysis of supervisory judicial review of tribunals and other forms of review, which means that doctrinal quests by scholars about the nature and operation of tribunals, ombudsmen and so on occur through a prism largely shaped by the judicial perspective. This may not be completely surprising given that administrative lawyers are, in the first instance, lawyers.

A subsidiary strand of this scholarship is the continued emphasis on whether and to what extent tribunals, inquiries and other processes can and should differ from those of the courts.[12] Scholars of tribunals also often face a more practical obstacle. Thomas recently lamented the widespread 'traditional reluctance to allow researchers to venture inside government'.[13] That problem has been a particular obstacle to research about tribunals because their operation, when compared to

[8] E Fisher, 'Administrative Tribunals: An Essay about the Legal Imagination of Administrative Law Scholars' in J Goudkamp, M Lunney and L McDonald (eds) *Taking Law Seriously: Essays in Honour of Peter Cane* (Hart Publishing, 2021) 259, 267 notes that most texts on administrative law place tribunals at the end, almost as an afterthought. Fisher has elsewhere pointedly referred to her reliance on judicial review as a focus on 'one area of administrative law scholarship': E Fisher, 'Imagining Method in Administrative Law Scholarship' in Harlow (n 2) 1, 1.

[9] Notable considerations of tribunals include: P Cane, *Administrative Tribunals and Adjudication* (Hart Publishing, 2009); R Thomas, *Administrative Justice and Asylum Appeals – A Study of Tribunal Adjudication* (Hart Publishing 2011); L Jacobs and S Baglay, *The Nature of Inquisitorial Processes in Administrative Regimes* (Routledge, 2013); and JRS Forbes, *Justice in Tribunals* (5th edn, Federation Press, 2019). This list would, of course, be incomplete without mentioning Dennis Pearce's magisterial *Administrative Appeals Tribunal* (5th edn, LexisNexis, 2020) which was inevitably consulted by practitioners in that body.

[10] R Rawlings, 'In the Jungle' (1987) 50 *Modern Law Review* 110, 110. An example is the tendency of administrative law values to emphasise procedure over substance: E Rock and G Weeks, 'Getting What You Want from Administrative Law' (2023) 108 *AIAL Forum* 88, 89.

[11] R Thomas, *Administrative Law in Action – Immigration and Action* (Hart Publishing 2022) 10.

[12] This is not necessarily a theoretical exercise, however, and can have significant practical implications. See, eg, S Thomson, 'Ombudsmen As Courts' (2022) 42(1) *Oxford Journal of Legal Studies* 76. The habit of tribunals to contribute to this practice is questioned in D Mullan, 'Tribunals Imitating Courts – Foolish Flattery or Sound Policy?' (2005) 28 *Dalhousie Law Journal* 1.

[13] See, eg, Thomas (n 11) vi. Cane also lamented 'logistical reasons' that prevented his planned empirical study of the effect of merits review: Cane (n 9) viii. Compare, however, S Halliday, *Judicial Review and Compliance with Administrative Law* (Hart Publishing, 2004).

that of courts, is less able to be fully understood by publicly available decisions and rules of procedure.[14] It would also prove a considerable obstacle to research about internal review, another relative wilderness in administrative law scholarship.[15]

The difficulties faced by scholars of tribunals sometimes arise because their processes are barely visible. O'Donovan and Donson note that tribunals typically pass under the radar of media and political attention and only burst into public consciousness when an occasional scandal occurs.[16] One consequence of the otherwise low profile of tribunals those authors identify in Ireland is a lack of any comprehensive assessment of Irish tribunals. Thomson, Wilberg and Seidman each note the difficulties in identifying all of the tribunals in the jurisdictions they each examine, which Thomson suggests is partly because there is 'no central, organising system of tribunals'.[17] Thomson noted that, in the course of his research on tribunals in Hong Kong – an exercise which had never been comprehensively undertaken by an academic (meaning there was almost no secondary literature on which to draw) – there were real difficulties associated with how to classify or list tribunals in the first place. In a needle-and-haystack exercise, Thomson manually trawled scores of primary and secondary legislation in the search for tribunals, compiling their powers and processes into a database. This was partly done with a view to providing a definitive list of tribunals in Hong Kong as part of that research. However, he found that a sizeable number of bodies sat at the margins of the function or definition of a tribunal, such as disciplinary panels and regulatory bodies with powers of adjudication and sanction. Where the definition of a tribunal ended, and other bodies and adjudicators began, became intractable and it was concluded that the production of a definitive list of tribunals would be a fairly futile exercise as the list could be open to dispute. If we struggle to produce a definitive list of tribunals in the first place, any study of the wider species is inevitably hampered.[18] Fisher also drew attention to the many and complex ways in which tribunals interface with other aspects of public law and the legal system.[19]

The difficulties in identifying and collating examples of tribunals are perhaps both a cause and effect of why none of the authors in this book seeks to define

[14] See, eg, T Henning and J Blackwood, 'The Rules of Evidence and the Right to Procedural Fairness in Four Quasi-Judicial Tasmanian Tribunals' (2002) 10 *Australian Journal of Administrative Law* 84 and J Blackwood and T Henning, 'Tribunals' Power to Control Their Own Procedures and the Requirements of Procedural Fairness' (2003) 11 *Australian Journal of Administrative Law* 5. This novel study about the internal workings of tribunals ended when one of the tribunals withdrew co-operation. That had a chilling effect on other Australian scholars.

[15] One exception to that rule is now over 20 years old: D Cowan and S Halliday, *The Appeal of Internal Review: Law, Administrative Justice and the (non-) Emergence of Disputes* (Hart Publishing, 2003).

[16] See O'Donovan and Donson, Chapter 17 in this volume. Chapter 7, by Groves and Weeks, recounts how this afflicted the Australian Administrative Appeals Tribunal, which was hardly known to the public until political and media attention focused upon claims that the tribunal was stacked with ill-suited political appointees.

[17] See Thomson, Chapter 12 in this volume.

[18] Though, as Corder notes in Chapter 16 of this volume, this exercise is not simply about definitional questions of what might constitute a tribunal but also the rights of appeal or review entailed.

[19] See Fisher, Chapter 6 in this volume.

clearly what a tribunal is. It is indeed a paradox of such a major international collaboration on tribunals that this book cannot – or will not – produce a global definition of a tribunal; though that difficulty has only been confirmed and compounded by the many experienced contributors to this volume. The default definition is often that tribunals are the obverse of a court,[20] though a negative definition is of course fairly unsatisfactory. Creyke concedes that tribunals are different from courts but argues that they are so diverse that 'location of a single underlying principle may not be achievable'.[21] The distinction between an underlying principle rather an all-embracing definition is a fine but important one.

The idea of tribunals as 'not courts' reflects the rigid Australian approach that flows from an equally inflexible approach to the separation of powers that divides judicial and administrative functions.[22] Groves and Weeks explain how this divides the form and powers of courts and tribunals, so that the functions of each are defined and constrained in equal measure by constitutional principles. According to this approach, the negative definition of a tribunal is a constitutional one. A tribunal is what a court is not and cannot be, does things that a court cannot do and cannot do things that a court does.[23] The opposite is true of the UK, where Thomas and Harlow each conclude that the court/tribunal distinction does not apply and arguably does not even make sense because UK tribunals are essentially also courts.[24] This conclusion is clearly right for UK tribunals but invites a question about the direction of such statements. Why is a court never proudly declared, on closer inspection, to be a tribunal?[25] We must also be mindful of the sometimes misleading nomenclature attached to institutions; not all tribunals are called 'tribunals', and not all bodies called 'tribunals' are, in fact, tribunals (they might, for example, be courts).[26] Some institutions may be tribunals which nonetheless have the capacity to exercise judicial power.[27]

[20] The same distinction is often drawn between the 'merits' of a matter and questions of law and is similarly 'hampered by the blancmange-like quality of the expression "merits review"': Sir A Mason, 'Judicial Review: a View from Constitutional and Other Perspectives' (2000) 28 *Federal Law Review* 331, 333.

[21] See Creyke, Chapter 2 in this volume.

[22] The hard distinction between courts and tribunals only applies at Commonwealth level in Australia, a fact which does not remove all jurisdictional difficulties from State and Territory tribunals; see G Hill, 'State Tribunals and the Federal Judicial System' in G Weeks and M Groves (eds), *Administrative Redress In and Out of the Courts: Essays in Honour of Robin Creyke and John McMillan* (Federation Press, 2019) 195.

[23] This blunt distinction can only be taken so far. A more comprehensive distinction would need to take account of the place of bodies such as ombudsmen. Parliaments also have some judicial functions, such as when exercising disciplinary and expulsion powers over members or deciding whether to remove judges for cause.

[24] See Harlow, Chapter 4 in this volume, who describes UK tribunals as 'more properly courts with limited jurisdiction'; See Thomas, Chapter 9 in this volume, who describes UK courts as 'de-facto administrative courts'.

[25] See, eg, the merits review work of Commissioners of the Land and Environment Court: E Fisher, 'The Administrative Law Expertise of the Land and Environment Court of New South Wales' in E Fisher and B Preston (eds), *An Environmental Court in Action: Function, Doctrine and Process* (Hart Publishing, 2022) 195, 199.

[26] See Thomson, Chapter 12 in this volume.

[27] See eg *Citta Hobart Pty Ltd v Cawthorn* (2022) 96 ALJR 476.

Fisher has elsewhere described tribunals as 'separation of powers misfits'[28] adding that 'while tribunals are distinct from the courts, they are not disconnected from them'.[29] Like all co-dependent relationships, the closer we look, the less healthy things seem. In the case of tribunals and courts, the value of any sharp distinction may not be clear and/or easy to draw but that does not deny the existence of the distinction. When a former Chief Justice of Australia rejected arguments that some grounds of judicial review appeared little different to fact-based merits review typical of tribunals, he acknowledged that the difference was 'not always clear-cut; but neither is the difference between night and day. Twilight does not invalidate the distinction between night and day'.[30] On this view, the many fuzzy lines or apparent similarities between courts and tribunals does affect the elementary distinction between the two.

A striking example of tribunals as 'separation of powers misfits' comes from the United States, where tribunals as they are known elsewhere do not exist. Where Fisher sees 'misfits', Asimow sees specialist tribunals such as the US Tax Court and Executive Office of Immigration and Review as 'outliers'. Tribunals as they are known elsewhere have little place in the US.[31] The default position within this approach is that decision-making and review occurs within agencies, with some level of judicial oversight.[32] If the traditional view of US constitutional structure is one of a fairly strict adherence to the separation of powers, as a matter of strict logic, it is hardly surprising that the executive subsumes the work of tribunals within executive agencies without much pretence of independence. Asimow's account of the *Administrative Procedure Act* of 1946[33] suggests it preserves much of the substantive work of tribunals within the administrative agencies of the executive branch.[34] If we can accept the UK accounts of tribunals as being little different from courts, can we not accept that Montesquieu's constitutional pendulum can also acceptably swing towards the executive? To outsiders, the apparently puzzling US approach suggests that tribunals or like bodies that are drawn within a strict conception of the separation of powers – so that administrative bodies lie entirely within the power matrix of administrative agencies – is a misfit of a different nature.

Some authors identify a functional taxonomy in their relevant jurisdiction, which goes some way to a general typology. The three categories that Chng and Jhaveri identify for tribunals in Singapore are: frontline administrative tribunals,

[28] Fisher (n 8). Similar claims have been made about other public law entities. See, eg, R Snell, 'Towards an Understanding of a Constitutional Misfit: Four Snapshots of the Ombudsman Enigma' in C Finn (ed), *Sunrise or Sunset? Administrative Law in the New Millennium* (AIAL, 2000) 188), suggesting that any problem might be more to do with constitutional doctrine than those entities themselves.

[29] See Fisher, Chapter 6 in this volume. Nason and Pritchard similarly conclude that the apparent erosion of longstanding distinctions between courts and tribunals can be seen as the decline of an outmoded view of the separation of powers.

[30] M Gleeson, 'Judicial Legitimacy' (2000) 20 *Australian Bar Review* 4, 11.

[31] See Asimow, Chapter 10 in this volume.

[32] ibid p 209.

[33] 5 USC §§551 to 706.

[34] Asimow, pp 214–217.

which make administrative decisions; adjudicative appellate review bodies, which review the decisions of bureaucrats; and regulatory disciplinary bodies, which implement professional and other regulators by way of disciplinary standards.[35] This panorama of 'decide', 'review' and 'implement' signals a wide range of functions that is possible through the same essential decisional model. Daly's four-fold model is quite similar. The four key tribunal functions he identifies within Canada are adversarial, inquisitorial, regulatory or mediative, or a mixture of more than one.[36] Daly also notes the considerable variation between tribunals in their procedures, composition and organisational structure.

An important and often neglected aspect of the variation noted by Daly is the different legislative frameworks that govern tribunals in different provinces or states within federated states. That stands in stark contrast to the amalgamation and procedural convergence that Groves and Weeks trace in Australia. They argue that the interplay between federal and state tribunal models has, over time and in a truncated way, edged towards a level of procedural similarity that is rare in Australia. Creyke identifies a different change in the operation of Australian tribunals in her suggestion that the judicial cloak that was originally cast over Australia's Administrative Appeals Tribunal (AAT), which saw judges conceive that body as one constituted on the judicial model,[37] has slowly been cast aside as the institutional place of tribunals has become more secure.[38]

The evolution of institutional practices occurs in different ways. Harlow and Thomas trace historical changes in UK tribunals. Harlow notes that the highly judicialised period heralded by the Franks report was followed by a period of less formalism.[39] Thomas identifies an enormous range of political and social influences that fashioned and refashioned tribunals that slowed considerably with the global financial crises and associated austerity.[40] The forces of change are not always social or political. Daly notes that the different view about the status of tribunals held by successive Chief Justices of Canada has the potential to affect the status of tribunals in a profound way.[41] The influence of individual judicial conceptions is equally important when the leading cases of a single judge provide an enduring doctrinal foundation. Groves and Weeks note that the first President of the AAT (Brennan J) delivered a landmark judgment about the character of merits review, which can only be fully understood by the complementary nature of a landmark judgment on judicial review that Sir Gerard Brennan delivered after his appointment to the High Court of Australia.[42]

[35] See Chng and Jhaveri, Chapter 15 in this volume.

[36] See Daly, Chapter 11 in this volume.

[37] Note the reflections on this issue of the AAT's inaugural President: Sir G Brennan, 'The Administrative Appeals Tribunal: Early Issues' (2001) 9 *Australian Journal of Administrative Law* 5.

[38] See Creyke, Chapter 2 in this volume.

[39] See Harlow, Chapter 4 in this volume.

[40] See Thomas, Chapter 9 in this volume.

[41] See Daly, Chapter 11 in this volume.

[42] The relevant decisions are *Re Drake and Minister for Immigration and Ethnic Affairs (No 2)* (1979) 2 ALD 634 (merits review) and *Attorney-General (NSW) v Quin* (1990) 170 CLR 1 (judicial review): discussed in Groves and Weeks, Chapter 7 in this volume, pp 137–9.

While some influences are readily apparent, the absence of an influence can easily pass unnoticed. Before we explain that absence, one English influence that continues to echo must be mentioned – the Franks Report[43] – which examined tribunals and inquiries in the United Kingdom and sparked enactment a year later of the *Tribunals and Inquiries Act 1958*. Craig alludes to the enduring influence of the report in his suggestion that its guiding taxonomy of tribunals and inquiries created an 'implicit assumption that all administrative institutions could be fitted into the pigeon-holes "inquiry" or "tribunal", with those terms bearing their Franksian meaning'.[44] Harlow and Thomas trace the many consequences of the Franks Report, but the ripples of that document extend well beyond British shores. Chandrachud, for example, notes that a Franks-like approach was quickly rejected in India.[45] The same is implicitly true in Hong Kong, which Thomson describes as having a 'pre-Franks' model.[46]

The possible influence of the Franks Report sits both comfortably but also awkwardly with a comparative analysis of administrative law. Two contributors to this book have elsewhere drawn attention to the comfortable or familiar aspect. In her volume analysing the evolution and often increasingly distinct nature of judicial review in common law jurisdictions, Jhaveri traced the divergence of individual national principles from their UK doctrinal origins.[47] One 'yardstick question' that volume used was the continued use of English judicial review principles.[48] Corder noted a separate but closely related issue long ago in his work on the reconstruction of administrative law and bureaucratic justice in post-apartheid South Africa. In a workshop that drew together public law scholars from the common law world,[49] Corder detected a growing transnational use of precedent by judges and lawyers across the Commonwealth in judicial review.[50] The transnational use of precedent has been a striking aspect of the continued doctrinal connections in judicial review across the common law world, even when that precedent is sometimes rejected by other jurisdictions,[51] but there is

[43] *Report of the Committee on Administrative Tribunals and Enquiries* (1957, Cmnd Paper 218).

[44] PP Craig, *Administrative Law* (9th edn, Sweet & Maxwell, 2021) 62.

[45] See Chandrachud, Chapter 13 in this volume.

[46] See Thomson, Chapter 12 in this volume p 258.

[47] This statement greatly simplifies the detailed and subtle analysis of the papers in S Jhaveri and M Ramsden (eds), *Judicial Review of Administrative Action Across the Common Law World* (CUP, 2021).

[48] S Jhaveri, 'What's So Common About "Common Law" Approaches to Judicial Review?' in Jhaveri and Ramsden (n 41) 3, 12.

[49] The workshop was stimulated partly by the need to devise a post-apartheid approach to administrative law but also with a goal to 'examine trends in administrative law, compare problems and solution, learn from each other and develop a collaborative agenda for the future': C Saunders, 'Apples and Oranges' (2006) *Acta Juridica* 423, 424.

[50] H Corder, 'Comparing Administrative Justice Across the Common Law World: A First Scan' (2006) *Acta Juridica* 1, 8.

[51] Such as the different reception, sometimes outright rejection, that English developments in substantive legitimate expectations received in other jurisdictions: M Groves and G Weeks, *Legitimate Expectations in the Common Law World* (Hart Publishing, 2017).

no such parallel in the use of precedent in tribunals. Precedent does not play the same organic function in the work of tribunals that it does in the courts. There is, therefore, no real common body of doctrine that can found and foster the work of tribunals in a way that bears parallel to supervisory judicial review. That lack of common precedent is surely a factor in the relative lack of scholarship on tribunals, both generally and particularly in the context of comparative research.

PART ONE

The Doctrine and Practice of Tribunals

2

History, Development and Future of Tribunals in Australia

ROBIN CREYKE

History and Development

Australia can be justifiably proud of its tribunal history. Australia included in its inheritance from Britain the practice of setting up bodies outside the court system to adjudicate on disputes or make decisions. Tribunals were among those bodies. Early tribunals in the United Kingdom were the Commission on Sewers and a body to hear complaints about excluding students from public universities.[1] Australia too set up tribunals early in its history to deal with disputes over matters such as dust diseases and coal. Over time, the dispute-handling landscape in Australia contained a polyglot mix of such bodies.[2] Many of these tribunals were developed by private sector organisations like racing clubs,[3] sporting clubs,[4] churches,[5] and education institutions.[6] Some were set up under executive power.[7] Many of these executive type bodies were subsequently regulated under legislation.[8] Others were hybrid public/private bodies handling disputes relating to matters such as superannuation,[9] initially the sole province of individual superannuation funds but later also dealt with under national

[1] *R v University of Cambridge ex parte Bentley* (1723) 1 Strange 557; 93 ER 698.

[2] See generally, JRS Forbes *Justice in Tribunals* (5th edn, The Federation Press Ltd, 2019).

[3] *Australian Jockey Club Act 1873* (NSW); *Racing Act 1976* (SA); *Racing Act 1958* (Vic). See also *Law v National Greyhound Racing Club Ltd* [1983] 1 WLR 1302.

[4] *Hughes v Western Australian Cricket Association Inc* (1986) 69 ALR 660.

[5] See, eg, *Plenty v Seventh-Day Adventist Church of Port Pirie* (1986) 43 SASR 121.

[6] See also *Concord Data Solutions Pty Ltd v Director-General of Education* [1994] 1 Qd R 343.

[7] Defence Honours and Awards Tribunal (DHAAT).

[8] See, eg, *Grammar Schools Acts 1860* (Qld); *University of Queensland Act 1985* (Qld); *Defence Act 1903* (Cth) pt VIIIC (DHAAT).

[9] *Attorney-General (Cth) v Breckler* (1999) 197 CLR 83.

legislation.[10] Others still were government-regulated from their inception such as the eponymous National Lighthouse Advisory Committee,[11] Repatriation Boards which determined claims and benefits by returned service personnel[12] and industrial relations bodies.[13]

In the face of this heterogeneous collection of bodies, Australia initiated a significant change to its tribunal landscape as part of the national reforms to administrative law in the 1970s and 1980s. This was to develop a new concept, a tribunal with jurisdiction to review decisions across public administration including in areas such as taxation, pensions, migration, planning, and occupational licensing. This inaugural multi-jurisdictional body – the Administrative Appeals Tribunal (AAT) – commenced work in 1976.

The move followed dissatisfaction with the limited remedies then available to people to challenge decisions by government, coupled with the post-war expansion of government regulation of the life of its citizens. As its title indicates, the AAT's remit was limited to appeals against decisions made by the public administration. The tribunal gradually acquired jurisdiction so that it now handles disputes between individuals and governments under more than 400 pieces of national legislation.[14]

The AAT has been in operation for close to half a century. Given that timespan, it is not surprising that the national government decided that revitalisation of the Tribunal is required.[15] The AAT has been replaced by the Administrative Review Tribunal: Administrative Review Tribunal Act, and the Administrative Review Tribunal (Consequential and Transitional Provisions (Nos 1 & 2) Acts 2024. The new body contains much that is familiar to users of the AAT model.

The establishment of the AAT marked a profoundly important step in tribunal development, not only in Australia but also in the common law world. A measure of the success of the AAT model is that the combined jurisdiction innovation for administrative tribunals was adopted in Victoria,[16] the Australian Capital Territory[17] and New South Wales.[18] Outside Australia, the administrative tribunal amalgamation model has been followed or proposed with

[10] *Superannuation (Resolution of Complaints) Act 1993* (Cth) s 14(2).

[11] Established under the *Lighthouses and Light Dues Regulations 1911* (Cth). The Committee copied Lighthouse Advisory Committees in Britain which developed out of an 1858 Royal Commission which looked at the current state of lighthouse provision in Britain.

[12] *Australian Soldiers' Repatriation Act 1917* (Cth).

[13] *Industrial Relations Act 1999* (Qld); *Industrial Relations Act 1979* (WA).

[14] *Report of the Statutory Review of the Tribunals Amalgamation Act 2015 (CTH) (Callinan review)* (2018) [6.24].

[15] The Hon Mark Dreyfus KCMP, Commonwealth Attorney-General, *Media Release* 'Albanese Government to Abolish Administrative Appeals Tribunal' (16 December 2022).

[16] Administrative Appeals Tribunal Act 1984 (Vic).

[17] Administrative Appeals Tribunal Act 1989 (ACT).

[18] Administrate Decisions Tribunal Act 1997 (NSW).

appropriate modifications, in other common law countries such as England,[19] Wales,[20] Scotland[21] and Canada.[22]

The advantages of the combined jurisdiction model at the national level led to further developments. Every Australian state and territory has introduced an expanded form of amalgamated tribunal, the last being Tasmania in 2020. The modification is the inclusion in the amalgam of much of the civil jurisdiction from lower-level courts.[23] Matters transferred involve private law actors in areas such as consumer complaints, credit, employment, rental and building issues.

A third category of matters involving human rights of individuals, such as discrimination and guardianship, are divided between federal, state and territory amalgamated tribunals according to the Australian division of powers in the national *Constitution*. Hence, discrimination and human rights topics are heard in all Australian tribunals, while guardianship is solely a state or territory matter.[24]

The benefits of locating civil and commercial matters in a tribunal, rather than a lower court, include the less formal style of hearing; the freedom to adopt, as appropriate, a more inquisitorial style of evidence gathering; the ability of members to bring their own experience and expertise to their decision-making in the matters under review; less need for legal representation; shared infrastructure and administrative services; the increased use of negotiated, not adjudicated, outcomes, and a speedier, less costly process.

Despite the existence of the amalgamated tribunals, single-issue tribunals have been retained in Australia. These fall into two categories: bodies the subject matter of which do not align easily with those included in an amalgamated body; or the multiple examples of low-volume decision-making or review bodies.

Typically, the first excluded category deals with disputes in areas such as workers' compensation, mental health, land and environment, copyright, national native title, dust diseases and competition and consumer matters. Their separate existence is justified due to special features of the matters they decide or the

[19] The Tribunals, Courts and Enforcement Act 2007 c 15 (Eng and Wales) set up a First Tier Tribunal with appeals to an Upper Tribunal. The system is administered by HM Courts and Tribunals Service.

[20] The administration of certain Welsh tribunals is administered by Wales under the Wales Act 2017. The Law Commission has since recommended that Wales should replicate the First Tier Tribunal and an Upper Tier Tribunal system for Welsh tribunals: Law Commission *Devolved Tribunals Wales Report* (Law Com No 403).

[21] The Scottish (Tribunals) Act 2014 set up a First Tier Tribunal and an Upper Tier Tribunal for those Scottish tribunals devolved to Scotland. The tribunal system is administered by the Scottish Courts and Tribunals Service.

[22] The Administrative Tribunals Support Service of Canada Act 2014 provides for administrative support for 11 Canadian federal tribunals. Ontario has established a cluster of 14 tribunals (*Adjudicative Tribunals Accountability, Governance and Appointments Act 2009, SO 2009, c 33, Sch 5*).

[23] J Pritchard 'Australian Civil and Administrative Tribunals: Challenges and Opportunities' (2020) 100 *AIAL Forum* 148, 153–56 (Pritchard).

[24] The division has been adopted by the Council of Australasian Tribunals (COAT). See COAT (2016) 1.

procedures they adopt.[25] For the most part they are not the subject of this chapter. The second category covers tribunals with boutique topics or low numbers, such as sporting bodies. Despite their continued existence outside the fold of amalgamated tribunals, these low-volume bodies are not unaffected by the jurisprudence of the major tribunals. If created by statute, frequently there is a right of appeal to the amalgamated tribunal, ensuring a degree of consistency in jurisprudence across all tribunals. Even if set up by agreement or contract, they generally rely on principles from the major tribunals as guidance for their own findings.

The radical change from reliance on courts to tribunals signalled a significant change in attitude by the executive. Governments are more comfortable with tribunals than courts because they have greater control over them. Although tribunals are relatively independent bodies, their members are usually statutory or Ministerial appointments; their findings lack the formal precedential strength of decisions by courts; the terms of members are more limited than judicial terms; and Ministers generally exercise a degree of control over funding and allocation of jurisdiction, as well as appointments. They are also useful if governments want to distance themselves from politically difficult decisions. The universal practice of having environmental bodies separate from government is a clear example. These advantages have seen government increasingly take advantage of the tribunal option for dispute handling.

The discussion which follows focuses on the two models of combined jurisdiction tribunals: the federal administrative review only body; and the state and territory civil and administrative tribunals, often referred to as 'CATS'. Despite that dual focus, there are frequent references to the federal model (the AAT) as it provided the template for the state and territory model. Together these combined jurisdiction tribunals in Australia play a predominant role in dealing with disputes or complaints by those dissatisfied by decisions adversely affecting them. As a key report on access to justice in Australia observed, as a consequence of these features, Australian tribunals have become one of the three pillars of the Australian justice system alongside courts and Ombudsman offices.[26]

Core Features of Tribunals

Australian tribunals have features in common. Typically, these have been described as:

> to create a less onerous process [than courts] for preparing and conducting hearings. The main objectives … are to deal with questions according to their substantial merits; to act as speedily and as informally as possible; to minimise the cost to parties; and to make appropriate use of the knowledge of members.[27]

[25] Report of the Commonwealth Administrative Committee Parliamentary Paper No 144 (1971) (Kerr Committee Report) [233].

[26] Productivity Commission *Access to Justice Arrangements* (Report No 72, 2014) Overview, 6.

[27] B de Villiers 'Accessibility to the Law – the Contribution of Super-tribunals to Fairness and Simplicity in the Australian Legal Landscape' (2015) 39 *University of Western Australia Law Review* 239, 259.

Some of these features are captured in the objectives of the tribunals; others emerge from the ambit of their decision-making; still others from their membership.

Tribunals are Designed to be Different from Courts

Among the advantages of dispute handling by tribunals is they are able to offer 'relatively convenient, informal and cheap processes whereby citizens can challenge adverse … decisions'.[28] This enables them to be a more accessible institution than courts for the provision of access to justice. Discernible in the reports which preceded the AAT model is the intention that tribunals' processes are to 'offer to the Australian public something that it did not have before' when seeking review by courts, that is, 'an appropriate degree of protection from bureaucratic error' through independent review by a tribunal exercising the same powers as the initial decision-maker: ART Act, s 54.[29] Although the aspiration as expressed was tied to decisions by government, this merits-review function is the standard measure for decision-making by Australian tribunals.

Their informal processes are designed to distinguish tribunals from courts by providing for the multiplicity of jurisdictions in which tribunals make decisions. They are a feature of Australian amalgamated tribunals. Particular processes may be required to accommodate matters to specific jurisdictions but the informal mode of operation is the starting point. An advantage of amalgamation is that it facilitates the aspiration for adoption of informal procedures. The informality feature is most apparent in relation to the joinder in the states and territories of their administrative and their civil and commercial jurisdictions. Operating in this manner was a marked departure for the civil matters transferred to amalgamated tribunals in the states and territories as discussed under 'Flexible procedures'. Although post-amalgamation statutory remnants of such procedures remain, generally, hearings of civil matters have embraced the less formal tribunal method of operation.

Alternative Modes of Dispute Resolution

The use of dispute resolution processes (often referred to as alternative or facilitated dispute resolution processes) is also symptomatic of tribunal proceedings. The extensive use made by tribunals of such processes is illustrated by the fact that from its inception, four out of five AAT matters were settled pre-hearing. With the accretion in 2015 of the migration and refugee, and the social services and child support jurisdictions, which did not adopt these forms of dispute settlement, the percentage of matters dealt with by these means plummeted to some 10% of

[28] The Hon Duncan Kerr Chev LH 'Challenges facing Administrative Tribunals – The complexity of legislative schemes and the shrinking space for preferable decision making' speech given at a COAT, Victoria, Twilight Seminar, 18 November 2013, 6.

[29] D O'Connor, 'The Model for the ART: The ART and Values 1' (2000) 27 *AIAL* Forum 6.

dispute settlements.[30] Nonetheless, this is changing following the commencement of the ART.[31] In the CATS, such distinctive procedures do not appear. All jurisdictions can access ADR.[32]

The advantages of these dispute resolution processes are that they are less costly, quicker, and less resource-intensive for both parties. They reduce the stress for applicants from participation in a hearing, preserve the confidentiality of the outcome and can minimise the damage to long-term relationships between a party and an agency, or between the parties involved. The use of such methods of dispute resolution has particular relevance for those relying on long-term support from governments, such as arise in cases of family breakdown, mental health or guardianship matters, for people with disabilities, or for those involved in contractual relationships or partnerships.

In a recent survey, 75% of the respondents nominated the need for alternative dispute resolution to be available across all types of matters.[33] The results indicate strong support for this feature of tribunal operations.

Flexible Procedures

A further distinctive feature is that, unlike courts, tribunals are not required to adhere to the formal rules of evidence.[34] As de Villiers explained, the reason for such provisions is the perception that:

> The atmosphere of the court room is intimidating; the conflictual nature of proceedings is scary; the procedures and protocols are complex and user-unfriendly; and the interaction between counsel for the respective parties can be frightening. All of these factors contribute to making the courtroom a place where ordinary people find themselves lost, often frustrated, and with a distinct sense of being out of control. This feeling of hopelessness is ironic, because ideally, a courtroom should be the place where individuals feel at ease, equal, protected and respected.[35]

The permission not to apply the rules of evidence is captured in the provision found in the legislation for many tribunals including the consolidated tribunals.[36] It is exemplified in the former AAT's provision that:

> 33 In a proceeding before the Tribunal:
>
> (1) (b) the proceeding shall be conducted with as little formality and technicality, and with as much expedition, as the requirements of this Act and of every

[30] AAT Annual Report 2021–2022, 22.

[31] See, eg, the Administrative Review Tribunal (Consequential and Transitional Provisions No 1) Act 2024 Sch 2.

[32] See, eg, the legislation for the amalgamated tribunals.

[33] Commonwealth Attorney-General's Department *Administrative Review Reform: Issues Paper* (2023) 17.

[34] For example, the Evidence Act 1995 (Cth) s 4.

[35] de Villiers (n 27) 258.

[36] Cth: Administrative Review Tribunal Act 2024 (Cth) (ART Act), ss 49–53; ACT: Civil and Administrative Tribunal Act 2009 (ACAT Act) ss 7, 8, 26; Civil and Administrative Tribunal Act 2013

other relevant enactment and a proper consideration of the matters before the Tribunal permit; and

(c) the Tribunal is not bound by the rules of evidence but may inform itself on any matter in such manner as it thinks appropriate.

The adoption of provisions such as these was a deliberate choice to avoid the more formal trappings of court proceedings. The exemption is also appropriate since members of tribunals may comprise those without legal qualifications untrained in the formal rules of evidence.[37] The exemption often reduces for the applicant the need for legal representation and the costs associated with such assistance. A similar provision is found in the legislation for most Australian tribunals.[38]

Reliance on flexible procedures has been challenged with the accretion to the state and territory tribunals of much of the lower courts' civil jurisdictions. A wholesale transfer of matters in the civil jurisdictions formerly handled by judicial processes, subscribing to the rules of evidence, and operating in adversarial mode is not intuitively sensible. Despite the apparently unworkable combination, the data available suggests that the 'marriage' with an administrative caseload is working.[39] The states and territories manage special requirements in their CAT Acts or in their legislation of the agencies or other bodies bestowing jurisdiction on the combined tribunal. The accommodation is a testament to the flexible approach tribunals adopt.

Despite their more flexible procedures, a base obligation is that tribunals follow procedurally fair processes. This is fundamental to their operation and any failure, if challenged, may lead to the decision being declared invalid. The public expects that procedural fairness will be provided in their dealings with tribunals. That understanding was confirmed by the 87% of respondents in the survey referred to earlier who ranked the importance of fairness of tribunal process in categories 1 to 3 from a possible ranking of 1 to 6.[40]

Inquisitorial Approach to Eliciting Evidence

Another feature of Australian tribunals is that members are able, where suitable, to adopt an inquisitorial approach in hearings. This mode of conducting proceedings,

(NCAT Act), s 38; NT: Northern Territory Civil and Administrative Tribunal Act 2014 (NTCAT) Act, ss 10, 53; Qld: Queensland Civil and Administrative Tribunal Act 2009 (QCAT Act), s 28; South Australian Civil and Administrative Tribunal Act 2013 (SACAT Act) s 8, SACAT Rules 2014, r 8; *Tasmanian Civil and Administrative Tribunal Act 2020* (TasCAT Act) s 10; *Victorian Civil and Administrative Tribunal Act 1998* (VCAT Act) s 98; WA: *State Administrative Tribunal Act 2004* (SAT Act) ss 9, 32.

[37] R Pepper and Amelia van Ewijk 'Making Sure that Curiosity Does Not Kill the CAT: the Use of Expert Evidence in Merits Review for a Where the Rules of Evidence Do Not Apply' (2019) 97 *AIAL Forum* 37, 40.

[38] Cth: ART Act, s 50: ACT: ACAT Act, s 8; NSW: NCAT Act, s 38(2); NT: NTCAT Act, s 52(3)(b); Qld: QCAT Act, s 28(3)(b); SACAT Act, s 39(1)(b), SACAT Rules 2014, r 8; TasCAT Act, s 79(b)(i); VCAT Act, s 98(1)(b); WA: SAT Act, s 32(2).

[39] Pritchard (n 23).

[40] Commonwealth Attorney-General's Department *Administrative Review Reform: Issues Paper* (2023) 10.

as compared with the traditional adversarial process usually applying in courts, allows the decision-maker to question parties to elicit evidence rather than relying on the parties to adduce evidential material. This is, in part, dictated by the nature of the tribunal hearings. An inquisitorial style, for example, is often an imperative in guardianship and mental health proceedings due to capacity issues of the subject person and the absence, in most cases, of a contradictor. As guardianship is one of the busiest jurisdictions in the combined state and territory tribunals, the ability of the tribunal members to operate in an inquisitorial manner is essential. Members' ability to frame questions and seek answers, their active, questioning role, mandates an approach to evidence gathering that has been approved by the High Court for use, when appropriate, in tribunal hearings.[41]

Objectives

The objects clauses in each of the relevant Acts lists the procedures intended to be applied to achieve the more timely, less formal and costly procedures intended as a mark of tribunals' intended difference from courts.[42]

The flexibility required of tribunal processes is evident in these objects. They also encapsulate aspirational elements such as to improve public administration, to provide processes which are not intimidating for applicants, particularly by offering multiple forms of communication and for settlement without a hearing. The objectives are a notable benefit of tribunals' operations given the spread of matters over which they adjudicate and the cross-section of the community which use their services.

A key aspect of their objectives is that tribunals, when appropriate, operate with minimal levels of formality. Even so, there are practical limits to this informality. The intention can founder on two realities: human frustration; and the breadth of matters included in the combined jurisdiction bodies. Initially, the architects of the AAT envisaged that coffee-table justice would be the tribunal hearing mode.[43] That vision was abandoned when the first ashtray was unleashed at a tribunal member by a disgruntled applicant. Most tribunals now use plastic not glass water jugs in hearings. The nature of the matter is also a determinant of the level of formality. Significant disputes involving valuable contracts, town planning, matters of security, the national interest or significant errors by public administration, require an appropriately senior level of decision-maker, legal representation and a more formal style of hearing. Tribunals' mode of operation has had to adapt to accommodate these realities.

[41] *Minister for Immigration and Citizenship v SZIAI* (2009) 259 ALR 429 at [18]; (2000) 83 ALJR 1123.

[42] Cth: ART Act, s 9; ACT: ACAT Act, s 6; NSW: NCAT Act, s 3; NT: NTCAT Act, s 10; Qld: QCAT Act, s 3; SA: SACAT Act, s 8; Tas: TasCAT Act, s 10; Vic: VCAT Act, s 98; WA: SAT Act, s 9.

[43] H Whitmore, 'Administrative Law in the Commonwealth: Some Proposals for Reform' (1972) 5 *Federal Law Review* 2.

Reasons for Decisions

Another common feature is the requirement that tribunal decisions be accompanied by reasons.[44] The obligation falls on the original decision-maker as well as the tribunal. The reasons statement by the decision-maker enables the recipient to understand the basis for the decision and whether there are grounds for seeking further review. The reasons, in turn, permit the tribunal to assess whether it has jurisdiction and the nature and issue for its decision. When the tribunal makes the initial decision, the reasons statement is the basis for any internal or judicial review. The importance of the reasons statement was emphasised in a recent survey in which some 72% of respondents nominated written reasons as their preferred method of receiving an AAT decision.[45] This requirement distinguishes tribunals from courts. In the absence of specific legislation, there is no such legal obligation on the courts,[46] although, in practice, many courts do provide reasons.[47]

Tribunal Membership

Another feature of tribunals which distinguishes them from courts is that their members are not confined to those with legal training, nor, generally, to those who hold judicial office. Tribunal members often have no legal qualifications but instead bring their expertise and experience in the many different areas – town planning, medicine, aviation, child welfare, disability – over which tribunals have authority to make decisions.

What qualifications members should possess has long been a matter of some controversy. Early proponents of tribunals saw the logic of having decision-makers with specialist expertise to match the multiple types of matters for dispute resolution.[48] Those with legal training often have a different perception. The Callinan review, for example, recommended that, with the possible exception of accountants for tax and commercial matters, all appointments to the AAT should be enrolled lawyers.[49] Justice Pritchard, President of the Western Australian State Administrative Tribunal (SAT), had a more nuanced view. While stating that 'it cannot be disputed that in many areas of the civil and merits review jurisdiction conferred on CATS, it is essential that members have legal training and experience', she also acknowledged that 'there is an important role for members who are

[44] For example, AAT Act, s 28.

[45] Commonwealth Attorney-General's Department *Administrative Review Reform: Issues Paper* (2023) 20. The Short Form Issues paper from which these figures are drawn had 287 respondents.

[46] *Public Service Board of New South Wales v Osmond* (1986) 159 CLR 656; *Wingfoot Australia Partners Pty Ltd v Kocak* (2013) 252 CLR 480.

[47] Kerr Committee Report [94], [390] at [8].

[48] ibid, rec 19.

[49] IDF Callinan AC *Report on the Statutory Review of the Tribunals Amalgamation Act 2015* (2018) (Callinan review) Measure 6 [1.8]. Callinan was a former Justice of the High Court of Australia.

not legally trained but who have specialist knowledge and expertise in fields of endeavour related to the work of CATS'.[50]

The Senate Standing Committee on Legal and Constitutional Affairs, in a 2023 report on the national administrative review system, referred to the conflicting views. The report quoted one submission that 'legal practitioners and judges are best suited to undertake the "complex and progressively difficult nature of work"'.[51] At the same time, the report noted another view that while legal qualifications are 'likely to equip members to make decisions' in the context of the highly complex matrix of legislation and policy' that tribunals face, 'members without legal qualifications but who have relevant "special knowledge and skills" nonetheless have the capacity to contribute enormously to the merits review jurisdiction'.[52] Although the report focused its recommendations on the processes, rather than the qualifications for appointment, the Senate Committee did recommend that 'memberships be broadly canvassed'.[53]

The Council of Australasian Tribunals (COAT), the principal body monitoring the operation of tribunals in Australia and New Zealand, while also focusing on the appointments processes recommended, in the context of devising appointments criteria, that 'the needs of the tribunal at the time, such as whether the tribunal requires particular specialist knowledge or skills in the membership' should be taken into account.[54]

On balance, while accepting that legal skills are essential to many areas of tribunal work, having a mix of qualifications is more consistent with the premise on which tribunals were established and the disparate areas over which they make decisions. Any move to remove non-legally qualified members from tribunals would be a retrograde step, not least because it helps deter the creeping legalism to which tribunals are prone.[55]

Principles

The core features of tribunals referred to in the previous discussion may be further distilled. Given the multiple forms in which tribunals appear, there is value in identifying a central defining principle or principles without which a body cannot be categorised as a tribunal.

[50] J Pritchard 'Australian Civil and Administrative Tribunals: Challenges and Opportunities' (2020) 100 *AIAL Forum* 158. Justice Pritchard is the President of Western Australia's State Administrative Tribunal and is also a judge on the Court of Appeal of the WA Supreme Court.

[51] Senate Standing Committee on Legal and Constitutional Affairs, 'The Performance and Integrity of Australia's Administrative Review System' (Interim Report, June 2022, confirmed as final in December 2022), submission of Dr J Donnelly at [4.79].

[52] ibid, submission of Professor Greg Weeks at [4.83]–[4.84].

[53] ibid, rec 4.

[54] COAT *Tribunal Independence in Appointments – A Best Practice Guide* (2016) 5.

[55] 'The role of VCAT in a changing world: the President's review of VCAT', Speech delivered to the Law Institute of Victoria, 4 September 2008 by Justice Kevin Bell – President, VCAT, 5.

Justification for identification of a principled basis underpins not only the identity of a body as a tribunal, but also helps decide which kinds of disputes are suitable for resolution by the tribunals process.[56] The issue is particularly critical for an amalgamated tribunal given the multiplicity of their jurisdictions.[57] Finding that principle may be elusive but to avoid some of the problems identified in this chapter decisions to amalgamate or to add to a combined jurisdiction tribunal will pay dividends if a principle or a cluster of principles can be identified. As the Law Commission in England and the Administrative Justice Council Welsh Committee in a report into tribunals for Wales, explained, 'there should be a common framework or principles to guide the establishment of new tribunals'.[58]

Variety of Views

There have been different responses to the challenge to develop such a principle or principles. Justice Pritchard adopted a sectoral approach to the issue. As she pointed out:

> The philosophy underlying a CAT's merits review jurisdiction might be to promote the best principles of public administration by identifying the correct and/or preferable decision at the time of the review. The philosophy underlying a CAT's small civil claims jurisdiction might be to resolve disputes using resources and time proportionate to the quantum and complexity of those disputes. In vocational regulation, the philosophy might be to promote the observance of professional standards of conduct, for the protection of the community. In guardianship and administration, a CAT's philosophy might be to adopt an inquisitorial role to ensure that those who required the protection of the legislation receive it, so far as their best interests require. Different CATS may have different views about how to encapsulate the underlying objects of particular aspects of their jurisdiction.[59]

In other words, the diversity of matters for decision and their concomitant variable modes of operations means that the location of a single underlying principle for tribunals may not be achievable. McCabe, an experienced Deputy President of the AAT, also denies that a single principle is discernible. As he observed:

> The dispute resolution and review functions which lie at the heart of the tribunal concept have few essential features apart from a measure of independence and an obligation to act judicially. … As a student of design might explain, their form should correspond to their function. If they have several different functions, they may require a number of different forms'.[60]

[56] Discussed later under 'Which tribunals should be included in an amalgamated model?'.

[57] R Creyke 'Tribunals – Carving out the Philosophy of their Existence: The Challenge for the 21st Century' (2012) 71 *AIAL Forum* 19; Pritchard (n 23) at 157.

[58] Law Commission (England and Wales) *Devolved Tribunals in Wales Report* (Law Com No 403, 2021) [1.39]. The Law Commission report cited a similar view in the 2010 report of the Administrative Justice and Tribunals Council Welsh Committee at [1.23].

[59] Pritchard (n 23) 157.

[60] B McCabe 'Perspectives on Economy and Efficiency in Tribunal Decision-Making' (2016) 85 *AIAL Forum* 40, 44.

Despite these responses, there remain practical needs for identification of principles. As Pritchard convincingly summed these up:

> Identifying the philosophical foundation for CATS permits a principled approach to decision about the procedures adopted by a CAT in the exercise of its diverse jurisdiction, and may also inform other decisions, such as those concerning its membership and composition, or the role and emphasis on ADR or FDR [facilitated dispute resolution] across all areas of its jurisdiction, or the extent to which technology can and should be used to resolve disputes. Furthermore, keeping that philosophical foundation steadily in focus acts as a reminder that CATS exist because they are able to offer an approach to the delivery of justice which is different from the approach taken in the courts. If the manner in which CATS operate does not continue to manifest that difference, the purpose for their existence may be called into question.[61]

McCabe is correct to identify as a principle that form must correspond with function; and it is self-evident that multiple functions involve multiple forms. At the same time, thought must precede form. To the extent that a tribunal, even with multiple functions, may benefit from thought about suitability, and Pritchard's assessment that multiplicity of principles must match the variety of functions identification of a principle or principles to guide such decisions is an important consideration.

Principles assist governments to make the initial decision whether a tribunal's decisions could usefully be included in an amalgamation, whether the matter is suitable at all for tribunal adjudication, or whether another institution could provide needed redress. The notion of coherence of structure and procedures advocated by the Law Commission (England and Wales) may be a pointer. What remains to be discovered is what distinguishes tribunals from courts.

Despite these doubts there are discernible principles in Australia which underpin the difference between tribunals and the courts: tribunals make decisions based on the merits of the case; and their procedures are less formal than those of courts.

Merits Review as a Core Principle

Hidden in plain sight; taught, but not explicitly described, in the legislation of any Australian tribunal, the concept deserves more explicit recognition. The failure to explain the concept of merits review more precisely is surprising given its historical link to the tribunal idea and because it is the key element of a tribunal's function. The notion was crystallised in the foundation Kerr Committee report which identified that the basic problems of the administrative law structure in Australia in the 1970s was that 'review cannot as a general rule, in the absence of special statutory provisions, be obtained [from courts] "on the merits"'. This, as

[61] Pritchard (n 23) 157.

the Committee concluded 'is usually what the aggrieved citizen is seeking'.[62] The principal distinction between tribunals and the courts that review their decision is merits review.

'Merit' has multiple but related meanings. The first two dictionary meanings are 'worth' or 'something that entitles to reward or commendation'.[63] Those two meanings are legislatively recognised in much tribunal legislation. Advertisements for membership of a tribunal are required to be based on 'merit', namely, that the candidate possesses the qualities and qualifications required to be a tribunal member.

A third dictionary meaning comes closest to its meaning as intended in the Kerr Committee report: 'merits' means 'the substantial right and wrong or a matter unobscured by technicalities – *the merits of a case*'.[64] In this sense the notion has no overt legislative acknowledgment in tribunals in Australia. It is arguably implicit in the statutory description of a tribunal's decision-making role, namely, to affirm, vary, or set aside and substitute the decision under review but is not made explicit in Australian tribunal legislation.[65] The significance of this statutory authority is lost if the reader does not understand how the decision being reviewed has been made.

Merits review in this sense captures the essence of administrative decision-making, including by tribunals. A tribunal as an original decision-maker or on review is able to make or remake the entire decision taking account of legal principles, the facts and lawful policy – the 'substance' of the dispute. In this sense, the 'worth' of a matter is explored in every aspect.

By contrast, the courts are generally limited to deciding whether the primary decision was made in accordance with procedures required by law, not what should have been the correct or preferable [initial] decision. In this sense, 'merits review' by tribunals significantly extends the review powers available to courts since they can provide the successful party with the decision initially sought. The indicium marks the boundaries between dispute resolution by tribunals and courts. In that context it is a foundational principle.

Flexible Procedures

The third of the dictionary meanings of merit(s) captures another seminal feature of tribunals, namely, their decision making is 'unobscured by technicalities'. As the earlier discussion of 'Tribunals' core features', particularly at 'Objectives', indicates another seminal principle distinguishing tribunals from courts is that

[62] Kerr Committee Report [58].
[63] *Macquarie Concise Dictionary* (9th edn, 2023) 968.
[64] ibid.
[65] See, eg, ART Act, s 103.

tribunals operate in a much less formal manner.[66] This aspect of 'merits review' is legislatively recognised. It is captured in the objectives of tribunals which typically require they operate in a manner which is not only fair but informal and quick;[67] they must act with minimal formality, according to equitable principles of fairness,[68] but are exempt from following the technical rules of evidence. This procedural flexibility distinguishes tribunals from courts and is also foundational. Together, merits review and a distinctive style of procedure are the key principles which distinguish tribunals from courts.

Challenges

Despite the benefits of tribunal dispute resolution, tribunals have their share of challenges. Ironically, these often reflect their success as a dispute resolution institution. At the same time, there are inherent dangers in these advantages, some of which will be discussed in the following material. The dangers are in part a reflection of the anomalous position of tribunals from a constitutional and an operational perspective.

Judicial or Other Model?

As one commentator has warned:

> Tribunals will only be tolerated by the judiciary if they can be made as court-like as possible. If they do so, however, they stand to lose the qualities, such as reduced level of formality, freedom not to abide by the strict rules of evidence and an ability to avoid aspects of the adversarial process, which were principal reasons for their creation.[69]

Despite the evident intention that the processes adopted in tribunals should not mirror those of the courts, full acceptance of this distinction did not emerge in the early years of amalgamated tribunals. As Justice Brennan, the first President of the AAT observed of the practice model first adopted:

> It is no secret that the AAT followed the judicial mould, nor that the period of my presidency was one in which that model was adhered to closely – perhaps too closely.[70]

[66] See at 'Core Features of Tribunal' under 'Flexible procedures' and 'Objectives'.

[67] See, eg, AAT Act, s 2A.

[68] See fn 38.

[69] R Creyke 'Overview' in *Administrative Tribunals: Taking Stock* R Creyke (ed) (ANU, Centre of International and Public Law, 1992) v.

[70] Sir G Brennan, 'Twentieth Anniversary of the AAT: Opening Address' in J McMillan (ed) *The AAT – Twenty Years Forward: Passing a Milestone in Commonwealth Administration* (Australian Institute of Administrative Law, 1998) 5.

Justifying his stand, Brennan argued:

> If the AAT be reproached for judicializing administrative decision-making, it can be said that the Act required decision-making by the AAT to become more acceptable than primary decision-making by adopting some juridical characteristics. Of course, the rules of evidence were not to be binding and the AAT's procedures could and should be as informal and flexible as the nature of the case permitted (s 33), but the basic requirements of the Act could not be short-cut by the adoption of a procedure that brought into the review process the summary, and sometimes unsatisfactory, aspects of administrative decision-making.

Nonetheless, as Brennan also observed:

> … a judicial model could not be adopted for the AAT without qualification. Courts declare and enforce existing rights and obligations; administrative decisions create or modify rights and obligations. Courts exercise their powers upon findings of fact made on evidence governed by legal rules; the AAT exercises its powers upon findings of fact, made by reference to wider sources of information. But courts and the AAT are both bound by, and bound to apply, the law and to apply it precisely. The major distinction between courts and the AAT is that, generally speaking, the courts are not concerned with administrative policy, while administrative policy is a core concern in some areas of AAT jurisdiction.[71]

McCabe supports Brennan's initial response, suggesting that even today the AAT operates in a judicial mode. As he pointed out, the judicial model was 'not the product of lack of imagination'[72] but 'consciously chosen because it was thought best adapted to the AAT's larger normative responsibility for promoting good government'.[73] Relying on the Kerr Committee report, he argued that from its inception the AAT was 'intended to operate on a court-like model'. He cites as support the requirements for:

- a highly skilled decision-maker, potentially in the form of a panel that included laypersons with relevant expertise, who proceeded judicially. Proceeding 'judicially' in this context means being objective, impartial and independent of the original decision-maker;
- a commitment to evidence-based decision-making, albeit that the strict rules of evidence would not necessarily apply;
- access to a suite of tools conventionally used by the courts to gather and evaluate evidence, including a summons power applying to documents and witnesses, evidence on oath and cross-examination;
- a hearing, which was conceived as a forum for a person affected by the evidence to present their case, test evidence, and make submissions in accordance with the rules of procedural fairness; and
- a published decision.[74]

[71] ibid, 9.
[72] McCabe (n 60) 47.
[73] ibid.
[74] B McCabe *Submission* in response to the Administrative Review Reform: Issues Paper, 3.

His advocacy for a judicial style model based on these requirements is not universally shared.

Cloaking the AAT with a judicial carapace was justified when it was first established given the hostility of public administration to the new body. It was a wise move at the time. Since then, as the AAT has acquired a reputation as a fair and sound decision-maker, a judicial cloak is no longer required.

Whatever the opposing views, the judicial model adopted 50 years ago, as Brennan hinted in the first of his extracts in this section, is no longer necessary as a default mode of ART – and indeed other tribunals' – operations. Today, tribunals can take advantage of the flexible mode of operations permitted under their legislation by adopting more nuanced processes. At times this will mean tribunal proceedings appear quite court-like; at other times, procedures can be more relaxed. Procedures are adopted to reflect the type of hearing or the special requirements of users. Today's approaches demonstrate that flexibility, a hallmark of tribunals, is a facet of their operations which negates a judicial model as the default style of their processes.

Which Tribunals Should Be Included in an Amalgamated Model?

How to decide which dispute-handling tribunals should be amalgamated or which new areas should be added to an existing tribunal's jurisdiction are issues which require analysis and decision, measured not only by principle but also against standards. National governments have progressively added jurisdictions to the list of matters for tribunal decision or review. This evidence increased confidence in their output. Early on Australia adopted a sensible approach to allocation of jurisdiction. Tribunal legislation provided that it is left to organisations or government agencies to nominate which decisions are to be reviewed and by which institution. The advantage of this process is that incorporation should be a matter of considered choice. For example, only a handful of Acts gave jurisdiction to the AAT when it was established. Twenty years later it had jurisdiction under some 360 pieces of legislation.[75] Nearly 50 years after it was established, the number now exceeds 400.[76] What is missing are the criteria used to decide which tribunals or topic areas should be amalgamated or allocated to an amalgamated tribunal.

In Australia, the reports preceding amalgamation generally list only pragmatic reasons for an amalgamation. A single point of entry, unification of support services, streamlining of processes and increased opportunities for

[75] Deirdre O'Connor, President of the AAT 'The Model for the ART: The ART and Values 1' (2000) 27 *AIAL* Forum 6.

[76] See AAT Annual Report 2021–2022.

members are listed as advantages of amalgamation. However, almost universally, the principal justification has been financial benefit. For example, the first reasons justifying the grafting onto the AAT in 2015 of the Migration Review Tribunal, the Refugee Review Tribunal and the Social Security Appeals Tribunal was 'to save money'.[77]

The absence of criteria based on principles heralds danger for the institution. As Bacon noted of the decision for initial amalgamation:

> These reforms are taking place in the absence of data about their likely implications and without a thorough understanding of the objectives that generalist versus specialist tribunal systems can realistically achieve. This ill-considered or 'over-hasty' trend towards amalgamation raises a number of questions which have not previously been addressed in academic or policy-making circles.[78]

The reports recommending amalgamation do not squarely address these questions, nor is there data available to assist with their answers.

The warnings give rise to a number of questions:

- Is a proposal to amalgamate or to add to a multi-jurisdiction tribunal appropriate?
- Against what principles were these decisions made?
- Is there an optimal size overall for an amalgamated tribunal?
- Is it necessary to have a roughly equivalent dispute-handling workloads for an amalgamated tribunal?
- Will there be adverse effects on resources and operational efficiency if a new jurisdiction is added?

The following discussion addresses some of these questions.

Suitability for Inclusion

The question of which matters are suitable for decision by tribunals arises for those making the initial decision to amalgamate as well as for a decision to incorporate a new jurisdiction into an existing tribunal. Underpinning both issues is whether the joinder of single-issue tribunals or the addition of the new matter are too disparate to co-exist without tension. As the Law Commission of England and Wales explained: '[T]ribunals should have a coherent structure.'[79]

[77] Gleaned from: second reading speech for the Tribunals Amalgamation Bill 2014; Australian Parliament, *Parliamentary Debates*, Senate, 3 December 2014, 10070 (Senator Fifield); and Tribunals' Reform Bill 2014 Divs 2 & 3.

[78] R Bacon 'Amalgamating Tribunals: A recipe for optimal reform' (PhD thesis, Faculty of Law, University of Sydney, 2004) 1.

[79] Law Commission (England and Wales) *Devolved Tribunals in Wales Report* (Law Com No 403, 2021) [1.39].

Although each single-issue tribunal or topic area within an amalgamated tribunal has characteristics that are germane to their particular jurisdiction, the tolerance for divergence within an amalgamated body is not unlimited. Stretched too far, the elastic breaks. Attention by governments to the elasticity issue should remain a requirement when deciding whether to set up an amalgamated tribunal.

An experienced New Wales tribunal chair and member warned of the amalgamation of tribunal registries in the United Kingdom:

> The tribunals that were brought into that structure were all like tribunals. They were all administrative decision-making tribunals. They all dealt with appeals from government decision-makers. They were not the disparate range of tribunals that we have in NSW or indeed that ended up in VCAT, QCAT et cetera. It is a slightly different creature.[80]

In other words, similarity of type of dispute is one indicator which needs to be taken into account when amalgamating tribunals.

Pointers to guide such decisions are whether the nature of the matters for decision of tribunals intended for inclusion, and their objectives and modes of procedure are sufficiently alike for the tribunals easily to co-exist. These issues have not ostensibly been prominent in the reports recommending inclusion.

In relation to the second issue – whether to add a new area of responsibility to an amalgamated tribunal – the responses of the Australian tribunals surveyed in a recent empirical study were that if there is consultation with tribunal heads prior to adding a new area, there need be no worry about whether the proposed new jurisdiction will be an appropriate 'fit'.[81] The report noted:

> Provided there are sufficient resources, and there is input about possible additions, taking on of new jurisdictions is manageable and the existing jurisdictions are able to be accommodated.[82]

That confidence is based on the proviso that adequate new funding has been provided.[83] Even without that proviso, the view may be unduly sanguine. Brennan warned against basing choices solely on impact on the individual:

> In selecting areas of jurisdiction for the AAT, the criterion cannot be merely the importance of an exercise of the relevant power to the individual. … The importance of a decision to the individual is one factor, but the critical factors are the elements that go into the making of a decision. The finding or evaluation of facts, the need for a clear application of legal principle and the scope and nature of any discretion that must be given require the most careful attention. The AAT has been immensely

[80] K Ransome (Chair of CTTT) evidence to NSW Standing Committee on Law and Justice, Parliament of NSW, *Consolidation of NSW Tribunals* Report 49, 2012, 26.

[81] R Creyke 'Australian Tribunals: Impact of Amalgamation' (2020) 26 Australian Journal of Administrative Law 206, 224.

[82] ibid.

[83] Discussed further at 'Resources'.

successful, and it would be regrettable if its utility were prejudiced by the conferring of jurisdiction in areas that are not appropriate for external review.[84]

His view focuses on the distinctive elements discussed earlier of tribunal decision-making. Beyond these suggestions there has been little attempt in Australia to define what are the indicia for amalgamation or for adding new areas of jurisdiction to a combined jurisdiction tribunal.

New Zealand has attempted the task, albeit by devising criteria in *Guidelines* to decide whether jurisdiction should be granted to a court or tribunal. The country does not have a combined jurisdiction tribunal, so the indicators were not designed for that purpose. Nonetheless, the list is instructive.

Features of the *Guidelines* indicating allocation of jurisdiction to a tribunal not a court were listed as:

- specialist expertise;
- speed;
- informality;
- investigative approach; and
- lower cost.

These practical objectives are already found in the objectives of all Australian tribunals. The criteria generally define in a practical sense how disputes are to be handled but go no further in identifying more fundamental principles.

More helpfully, the *Guidelines* do list criteria for allocation of jurisdiction to courts, rather than tribunals. These are when technical legal issues are involved, where sanctions are 'serious or significant', when the 'legal expertise of decision-makers is more important than specific or technical focus' and where 'the legal robustness of the proceedings [rather] than other factors such as low cost and speed' is key to the outcome for the parties.[85] By implication, if those factors are answered in the negative, the matters are more suitable for a tribunal. Another useful consideration in the *Guidelines* is whether there are more appropriate sources for the complaint or dispute-handling within other government or non-government bodies.[86] This too should be a consideration in Australia, replete as it is with multiple accountability bodies.

Adoption by Australia of suggestions such as these could highlight the need to focus on the initial allocation issue. Once again, however, these are largely practical considerations. The task of identifying more apposite criteria for those making policy decisions about what are the substantive criteria which determine

[84] Sir Gerard Brennan AC KBE 'Twentieth Anniversary of the AAT: Opening Address' in J McMillan (ed) *The AAT – Twenty Years Forward: Passing a Milestone in Commonwealth Administration* (Australian Institute of Administrative Law, 1998) 17.
[85] New Zealand Ministry of Justice *Tribunal Guidelines* 9–10.
[86] ibid, 10–13.

suitability to amalgamate tribunals, or to add new jurisdictions remains substantially unperformed.

Optimum Size of Tribunal

Existing indicators fail to shed light on the potential for issues to emerge if the size overall of the tribunal becomes unwieldy or any of its component areas are so large as to create an imbalance within the tribunal. As amalgamated tribunals increase their areas for review or addition, awareness of these potential problems becomes more pressing. Overall size matters. As the empirical report referred to earlier concluded:

> The larger tribunals … such as VCAT and QCAT referred to their concerns that if the tribunal takes on too many jurisdictions, [the] objectives [of amalgamation] will increasingly not be met. The example of the pressures and reputational impact on the AAT of the increasing backlog of migration cases reinforces this finding.[87]

In support of these concerns, the report also observed:

> A key finding is that successful amalgamation correlates with the size of the amalgamated tribunal. The smaller and more contained is the amalgamated tribunal, the more likely is it to achieve the benefits of consolidation. That was demonstrated by the smaller tribunals involved in the survey. They have generally been able to introduce uniform procedures, deploy their staff across all the tribunal's jurisdictions, and achieve the cohesion and unified rules and modes of operation which were the aims of amalgamation.[88]

These factors emphasise the value of limiting the size of the tribunal, a matter which is critical if an amalgamated tribunal is to operate as a cohesive whole. Overall size also needs to be considered to avoid overburdening the tribunal with too many cases to the detriment of the quality of its decisions and its reputation.[89] There is a paucity of data on this question. The information deficit should be rectified to devise guideline parameters for optimal size.

Imbalance in Workload

An aspect of the size issue is whether there is an imbalance in workload in one or more jurisdictions within a tribunal. Markedly different numbers of applications in an area of a tribunal's workload create the potential for 'certain matters [to] swamp any new tribunal, effectively drowning out … other matters from

[87] Creyke (n 81) 206, 231.
[88] ibid.
[89] See, eg, S Skehill 'The Hidden Dimension of Administrative Law: Internal and First Tier Review' (1989) 58 *Canberra Bulletin of Public Administration* 137.

receiving adequate attention'.[90] Such an imbalance also raises concerns that the higher application rate in some areas of a tribunal's jurisdiction may leach resources from and impose their processes on the smaller jurisdictions, thus failing to allow for their particular characteristics.[91] A related concern is that the marked imbalance in size of any constituent element of a consolidated tribunal could also come to 'dominate the culture and procedures' of the amalgamated tribunal.[92]

These warnings in relation to an imbalance in size of particular jurisdictions within a tribunal, and the adverse cultural effects were made in connection with the proposed amalgamation in 2012 in New South Wales of its existing Administrative Decisions Tribunal (ADT) with the Consumer, Trading and Tenancy Tribunal (CTTT).[93] The ADT was a body dealing only with administrative disputes; the CTTT was principally a body dealing with disputes in the civil and commercial areas formerly dealt with by lower-level courts. The CTTT was one of the busiest Australian tribunals with a caseload finalisation in 2012–2013, the final year of its independent operation, of just over 68,000;[94] the ADT in that period had a modest finalisation caseload of just over 13,000.[95] Despite the expression of these concerns the amalgamation went ahead and the two tribunals became the New South Wales Civil and Administrative Tribunal (NCAT). Data is not available to identify whether, and if so, what disadvantages have been produced by the imbalance in workload following amalgamation.

The variation in workload is illustrated by the grafting on to the AAT in 2015 of cases previously heard in the larger federal single-issue tribunals, the Migration Review Tribunal, the Refugee Review Tribunal and the Social Security Appeals Tribunal. The considerable delays which developed following amalgamation, particularly in the Migration and Refugee Division (MRD), became a matter of public notoriety. Prior to 2015, the caseload of the AAT was around 6,000 per annum. As at 30 June 2022, the number of applications on hand at the AAT was 67,720, of which 56,129 or 83% were MRD cases.[96] Consistently since 2015, the delays by the MRD in clearing its caseload have far exceeded that for other divisions.

The AAT's response to the backlog was that the lack of members allocated to that division was a substantial reason for their backlog. However, even with the appointment of new members, there is a 'reduced immediate capacity on a per head basis as the new appointees develop their knowledge and experience'.[97]

[90] NSW Legislative Council Standing Committee on Law and Justice 'Opportunities to consolidate tribunals in NSW' Report 49 (2012) [3.45]–[3.47], [3.53], [4.55]–[4.59].

[91] ibid [3.45], 28.

[92] ibid [3.44], 28.

[93] ibid [3.37], [3.45].

[94] 'Consumer, Trader and Tenancy Tribunal Annual Report 2012–2013', 6.

[95] Administrative Decisions Tribunal Annual Report 2012–2013, 48.

[96] AAT Annual Report 2021–2022: '2021–2022 At a Glance', 2.

[97] ibid, 223.

The tribunal denied that the needs of the MRD led to reduced resources in other divisions.[98] New members have been appointed in 2023 and 2024 to meet these concerns. Nonetheless, even if the number of members is increased, as the response indicates the impact of greater numbers of members takes time to make inroads into the unresolved cases. It is also not a given that a higher number of members to clear a backlog, if available, will be maintained. This creates the possibility that a backlog will again develop.

The issue emerged also in the Victorian Civil and Administrative Tribunal (VCAT). One of the busiest jurisdictional areas for the state and territory tribunals is residential tenancies. The backlog issues for VCAT arose in 2023 in the landlord and tenant jurisdiction. Some '10,700 bond and compensation applications and 2,200 compensation applications [were] waiting to be heard at that time'.[99] The result of such delays impacts adversely on the reputation of tribunals, one of the universal objectives of which is to be 'quick'.

The marked disparity in numbers of certain categories of disputes within amalgamated tribunals is also graphically illustrated by the finding by Pritchard that the civil and commercial jurisdictions of the state and territory combined tribunals comprise nine out of 10 of their applications.[100] Such a gross imbalance in workload, at first sight, supports the concerns raised in this section. It may be, however, that the problems indicated by such an extreme numerical disparity do not create a commensurate workload imbalance. Many civil and commercial disputes are resolved relatively quickly. As a consequence, the time taken to handle them is significantly less than more complex, often discretionary matters, in other jurisdictions.[101] A deeper analysis of the raw numbers is needed to assess whether the imbalance in size of specific jurisdictions in the state and territory tribunals creates a problem.

Despite these equivocal responses, imbalances exist and will continue to emerge. They need to be watched by the management of tribunals to forestall the development of problems from imbalances in size of workloads, or growing backlogs. Management should not shy from advising the government of the potential for issues which may emerge from taking on new jurisdictions which create too large an institution. Failure to do so has the potential to threaten the cohesion and effective operation of a combined tribunal and the achievement of the goals of amalgamation.

Resources

It is essential for adequate resources to be provided for tribunals, especially when new jurisdictions are added. The government's view is that combined tribunals

[98] ibid, 223–24.

[99] See www/theguardian.com/australia-news/2023/jul/18/leaking-sewage-and-no-water-victorian-renters-compensation-claims-stall-in-tribunal-backlog.

[100] Pritchard, n 23, 153–56.

[101] Discussions between the author and the President and Deputy President of QCAT, August 2023.

are a cheaper dispute resolution option than courts. This is based on the expectation that once amalgamation has occurred there will be a reduction in costs of the former single-issue tribunals and that this cost-saving will continue. Despite the expectation, the history of cost savings has not been sanguine. As a result, tribunals have been consistently underfunded which has undoubtedly had an adverse impact on their operations.

One reason is the continued accretion of new jurisdictions which inevitably require members with an ever-wider range of expertise. High volumes of cases in particular jurisdictions also increase the need for adequate numbers of members to service those areas. Inadequate numbers of members, as indicated earlier, leads to delays in clearing caseloads and generates public dissatisfaction. Deployment of members to manage high caseloads may be resisted by management as their expertise and experience is required in other areas. This tension is commonly experienced by tribunals.

The development of backlogs is a particular concern. In October 2022, the Victorian Civil and Administrative Tribunal (VCAT) had a backlog of 34,310 cases;[102] the Queensland Civil and Administrative Tribunal (QCAT) had 7,937 matters outstanding at the end of the 2022 financial year.[103] The backlogs in the migration and national disability insurance divisions of the AAT are well known. Lack of members inevitably means hearings are delayed. It is common knowledge that adverse media attention to a backlog puts pressure on the tribunal's leadership to stem the criticism by allocating a greater share of the funds to that area; it thus follows that there are fewer funds available for other jurisdictional areas. Delays in managing caseloads leads to public notoriety and impacts on the tribunal's reputation.

A related funding issue arises where there are different sources of funding for particular jurisdictions. If this results in differential salaries for members, the differences can affect members' morale, increase the likelihood of a siloing mentality, adversely affecting cooperation between members and the development of cohesion within the tribunal. As one report expressed it, there is: 'concern among some tribunals … that if the tribunals take on too many jurisdictions or take on jurisdictions with different funding models, there will potentially be resources problems'.[104] For tribunals with multiple sources of funding for its various streams of work such as VCAT and the ART, the problem can be a major one.[105]

The reality is that Tribunals regularly express concern about the absence of sufficient members to handle increasing caseloads in some areas and that their operations are hampered by lack of resources. Obtaining adequate resources is a constant theme in tribunals' annual reports and appears to be a chronic problem for all Australian tribunals. The issue is a live one and continues to be a challenge.

[102] See www.proquest.com/newspapers/vcat-unable-cope/docview/2719919999/se-2?accountid=12528.
[103] QCAT Annual Report 2021–2022, 13.
[104] AAT Annual Report 2021–2022, 224.
[105] ibid, 226.

Technology

The tribunals' flexibility stood them in good stead when, like other bodies in the community faced with COVID-19 lockdowns, they had to modify their *modus operandi* and operate largely online. In-person hearings became the exception; video or telephone interactions became the norm and ways of lodging documents via electronic portals were expedited. To achieve these changes required upgrading video conferencing systems, equipment and support.

The legacies of these developments have been mixed. To illustrate, the following extract from a recent NCAT annual report indicates the steps taken by tribunals to meet this challenge.

> **'Investment in technology**
>
> NCAT's ability to maintain its high clearance rate during the COVID-19 pandemic was a direct result of our focus on investing in technology and the Tribunal's ability to adapt to rapidly changing environments with its flexible practices and processes. During the reporting period, AVL technology was installed in additional hearing rooms, increasing NCAT's capacity to conduct virtual hearings across all Divisions and the Appeal Panel. NCAT's virtual hearing technology enabled the Guardianship Division, Occupational Division and Appeal Panel to conduct multi-Member hearings with Members and participants joining virtually from NCAT different locations. The Consumer and Commercial Division was able to adjust its group list processes to the new virtual hearing environment to ensure its Members could continue to hear matters in high volume. Many types of matters before NCAT benefitted from our investment in virtual hearing technology, including shorter interlocutory proceedings. New laptops were also distributed to all Members with the virtual hearing technology during the reporting period, allowing Members greater flexibility to conduct hearings from any location.[106]

This report is replicated in annual reports for others of the Australian cohort of amalgamated tribunals.

With the lessening of concern about the pandemic, tribunals have begun to operate in a manner more akin to the position pre-COVID. Nonetheless, some of the changes are permanent. There are now more online directions hearings and a greater use of online portals for receipt of documents. The upgrades to tribunals' communication technology undoubtedly facilitated the maintenance of some of the practices adopted during 2019–2021. So, too, has familiarity with the technology and facility with its management.

Interestingly, in a recent survey in relation to replacement of the AAT, respondents were almost evenly divided as to how easy or very easy were the processes offered by tribunals to engage in their proceedings. Just over 70% nominated a preference for written submissions for communication with the tribunal; 73%

[106] NCAT Annual Report 2021–2022, 5–6.

nominated a preference for participating via telephone; 75% for participating via video link; and 70% listed participation in person.[107] The comfort of operating online was also illustrated by findings in the survey of people for the purposes of devising the body to replace the AAT was illustrated by the fact that over 94 per cent favoured commencing an application by filling out an online form.[108]

The results are equivocal and need further analysis. What they do illustrate is that overall the public is comfortable with communication using an online medium but are equally comfortable with managing interaction with the tribunal in person. The resources available to amalgamated tribunals enabled them to invest in upgraded technology, but whether governments will continue to fund needed upgrades is yet to be seen.

Cultural Issues

The internal operations of a tribunal affect its culture including the harmonious relationship between members and staff. Cultural problems were identified in the Callinan Review.[109] They related to the AAT's migration divisions. Submissions from members complained that there were members in the General Division, the division comprising much of the work of the pre-2015 amalgamation of the AAT, who considered that the MRD work was less demanding than their own. As to which, in his summary, Callinan noted: 'Despite a perception on the part of some, the General Division is not superior to other divisions and does not, in my view, have any better ability to deal with particular matters.'[110] Nonetheless, the views which led to these complaints contained the seeds of divisional suspicion, inimical to development of a cohesive culture.

The problem is not confined to the AAT. For the state and territory tribunals, the different types of hearings between their administrative and civil arms may also affect culture. As one report noted:

> It is not just the imbalance in size which is of concern but also the different culture and practices between the two arms. Civil matters were formerly undertaken by courts; initial administrative decisions were made by the executive. These factors import parameters for decisions by the judicial and executive arms of government which are significantly distinct. To an extent, these differences have been retained for most combined tribunals in their legislation. There has been little analysis to date of the impact of this feature of their statutory frameworks.[111]

[107] Commonwealth Attorney-General's Department *Administrative Review Reform: Issues Paper* (2023) 18.
[108] ibid, 14.
[109] Callinan review [8.26]–[8.28].
[110] ibid, 21.
[111] R Creyke 'From Sewers to "Super" Adjudicators: What Next for Tribunals?' (2023) 107 *AIAL Forum* 31, 37.

Whether Adverse Impacts are Occurring is a Matter Which Needs Analysis

The reality, however, is that all institutions including tribunals can become hostage to cultural issues. That may occur on restructuring the body or at other times. As McCabe put it in relation to a restructure:

> The establishment of a [new general jurisdiction tribunal] inevitably precipitates cultural tensions as members and officers of former bodies settle into the new structure or cling to elements of the old one. A fresh culture must emerge. That process takes time. It must also be handled with care. Not all of the cultural traits of the former organisations will make the transition, and some of them must be actively avoided in the new body. Tribunal leaders have an obvious role to play in shaping what emerges. But individual members must also play their part.[112]

Whatever stage a tribunal has reached – whether at initial amalgamation or when new jurisdictions are added to an existing amalgamated tribunal – ensuring that a harmonious relationship exists within a tribunal imposes obligations on tribunal leadership and must be watched if issues of this kind are to be avoided.

Structural Issues

Administration

All tribunals need some internal structure for organisational purposes. The arrangements enable the tribunal to seek members with particular expertise, for funding, for internal administrative support and as an appropriate means of allocating workloads to suitable members. The legislation for Australian tribunals provides at a broad level for their original, review and, if appropriate, internal appeal powers.

The justification for having institutional divisions is:

> … a need to take account of the differential kinds of jurisdiction vested in the combined tribunal and to preserve essential features of former specialist tribunals. A desirable flexibility is achieved by providing for a divisional structure within the combined tribunal and the introduction of procedures and practices within each division to reflect the specific needs within particular divisions.[113]

The AAT, as recommended by the Bland Committee, has had statutory divisions from its foundation.[114] Nonetheless, some disquiet about the arrangement

[112] McCabe (n 60) 43.
[113] R Creyke 'Amalgamation of Tribunals: Whether 'tis better …', Chapter 11 in S Nason (ed) *Administrative Justice in Wales and Comparative Perspectives* (University of Wales Press, 2017) 316, 337.
[114] Final Report of the Committee on Administrative Discretions (Bland Committee Report) AGPS, 1973) [40].

emerged quite early in the history of the Tribunal. The Administrative Review Council (Council), the body set up in 1975 to monitor the administrative justice system in Australia, was tasked in 1987 with a report on the issue. At that time, there were four divisions within the Tribunal. The Council observed that:

> … divisional arrangements of the AAT may be seen as primarily a method of providing for ministerial consultation in connection with appointments to the AAT and ensuring that persons thus appointed constitute the Tribunal for the purpose of relevant cases.[115]

That observation reflected the fact that members could not be assigned to the Veterans' Appeals Division and the Taxation Appeals Division unless the Minister for Veterans' Affairs had consulted with veterans' organisations or the Attorney-General had consulted with the Treasurer, respectively.[116] The requirement for Ministerial approval of appointments to AAT divisions continued and became a requirement for allocation of members to all divisions. With the advent of the ART members are appointed to a Tribunal,[117] not a division, and the consultation provisions have significantly been lessened.[118]

There are other reasons for structuring a tribunal along subject matter divisions. The Council's findings in favour of divisions were that specialisation by members enhanced their expertise, increasing government and community confidence in the Tribunal's decisions, not least because the structure was known to the public and it gave a degree of predictability to members.[119]

Against these advantages, the Council found that the arrangement limited the flexibility of the Tribunal; increased the cost and disruption involved for members required to travel regularly for hearings to different registries around Australia which lacked lay members with appropriate expertise; created silos within the Tribunal; and led to variable quality decisions across the Tribunal when similar statutory tests in different Acts were decided inconsistently by members assigned to different divisions.[120] Ultimately the Council recommended that the AAT not include a divisional structure, a recommendation that was not then heeded.[121]

The Callinan review criticised the 'siloing' that had developed in the AAT which he found adversely affected the Tribunal's collegiality.[122] This led to an observation in the Issues Paper for the new federal administrative review body that the current divisional structure was 'rigid and an impediment to

[115] Administrative Review Council (ARC) *Constitution of the Administrative Appeals Tribunal* (ARC Report 29, 1987) [79].
[116] ibid.
[117] ART Act, ss 197–199.
[118] ART Act, Pt 8 Div 3.
[119] ibid [80]–[82].
[120] ibid [84]–[85]
[121] ibid rec 4, 24.
[122] Callinan review [8.26]–[8.28].

efficiency', again raising the question of whether formal divisions are an optimal arrangement.[123]

These criticisms have been heeded and instead of divisions, the ART Act refers to 'jurisdictional areas'[124] and the President is generally able to assign members to a jurisdictional area,[125] subject only to the circumstance in which the 'Minister' has recommended a particular assignment to the Governor-General.[126] This may only occur in 'exceptional circumstances' for members with 'skills, qualifications and experience' particular to a jurisdictional area.[127] Such circumstances are likely to be rare and these provisions have provided needed flexibility for the proposed new federal tribunal.

For the state and territory tribunals the issues arise in a stark form in relation to the two broad areas of jurisdiction – the civil and the administrative – in their combined tribunals. The legislation for about half of these tribunals provides distinct divisions for their civil as compared with their administrative matters.[128] At that broad level, the impact of the division is variable depending on the size of the tribunal. For the smaller jurisdictions – the ACT, and the Northern Territory, and Western Australia – the absence of statutory divisions appears to avoid the issue of silos.

The difficulties that may emerge with too rigid a division, whether provided for in legislation or as a matter of practice, is particularly acute in larger state and territory amalgamated tribunals. This is illustrated by what happened to the South Australian Civil and Administrative Tribunal (SACAT). The Tribunal had been established with functions allocated by statute to 'streams', rather than 'divisions'. There was a distinct division of functions and membership between members in each stream. The problems which arose were described in the 2017 statutory review of SACAT as follows:

> There are good and cogent reasons to reconsider the ongoing utility of the Streams. Their continuance will serve to preserve and possibly enhance the silo culture. … There is some evidence that Stream leaders develop an almost proprietorial interest in their staff and facilities and jealously guard against their transfer to or use by another Stream. There is budget competition for scarce resources without having regard to the overall requirements and interests of the organisation. Decisions are sometimes made within and for the purposes of one Stream without consideration of the possible adverse consequences on another Stream. The existence of Streams makes it difficult to transfer

[123] Commonwealth Attorney-General's Department *Administrative Review Reform: Issues Paper* (2023) Issue 5.

[124] ART Act 2024, s 196.

[125] ibid, ss 197–199.

[126] ibid, s 197.

[127] ibid, s 199(8)–(10).

[128] ACAT Act, Pts 4, 4A (civil and administrative matters); ACAT Regulations 2020 Pts 3.2–3.7 (Rules for six different jurisdictions); NCAT Act, s 16 (5 divisions including appeal division); NTCAT (no divisions); QCAT Act divs 2–4 (4 divisions); SACAT Act, s 27 (may provide for streams), SACAT Rules 2014, r 10 (3 streams); TasCAT Act, s 59 (2 divisions); VCAT Act (no divisions except original and review jurisdictions), VCAT Rules 2018, r 2.01 (5 divisions); SAT Act, s 11 (no statutory divisions). However, the *SAT Annual Report 2021–2022* refers to four streams.

> staff and inhibits the flexible deployment of staff. It also inhibits the across-fertilisation between different streams.[129]

The review supported its findings by the experience in Western Australia's SAT which had also operated under a strict structural division, but abandoned the structure because:

> It gave increased flexibility and members now have a greater variety of work. ... They found that adjustments could readily be made to meet demand thereby preventing underwork and overwork. The decision was good for collegiality, and from a cultural perspective it was better to have the staff as one team. The streams were maintained for listing and statistical purposes but not for organisational purposes.[130]

These findings indicate that providing a fixed divisional structure is less than optimal. For smaller tribunals with fewer members the Australian experience indicates there is no need for fixed, particularly statutorily specified, streams. For larger tribunals with high volume jurisdictions, the administration of the tribunal requires some form of divisional structure. The need for the orderly allocation of personnel and work required for administrative purposes must be balanced against the advantage of retaining a degree of flexibility in the structural arrangement. Statutory designation of divisions is not ideal. Deployment of members needs to be flexible to accommodate changes in funding, in workloads and for there to be a ready availability of members with appropriate expertise to avoid backlogs arising.

In Australia, just over half the amalgamated tribunals do not include a formal divisional structure, leaving it to an internal process or tribunal Rules to do so.[131] Nonetheless, in practice, members are appointed to a particular division. To avoid the issues identified in the SACAT review, a flexible arrangement is the best option. This can be achieved by using Rules or an internal administrative process, rather than fixed statutory divisions or streams to allocate members to particular jurisdictions, thus avoiding the need for Ministerial approval for allocation to members to each division. Heads of tribunals need flexible arrangements for deployment of members. This strategy encourages increased interaction between members and avoids the possibility of more rigid allocations. The rewards are increased employment satisfaction, the development and maintenance of morale and collegiality, and are administratively sensible.

Internal Appeals

Another structural issue is whether a tribunal should have a facility for internal review. Formerly, internal review was available in only one division of the AAT.[132]

[129] 2017 Statutory Review: South Australian Civil and Administrative Tribunal [SACAT] (the 'Bleby review') 50.

[130] ibid, 51.

[131] Exceptions are: ART Act, s 196; NCAT Act, s 16; SACAT Act, s 27; TasCAT Act, s 59.

[132] Social Security (Administration) Act 1999, s 179. Significantly, the ART Act has provided for a Guidance and Appeals Panel which permits more extensive internal appeals. Restrictions on appeals in some high-volume migration and refugee jurisdictions of the ART remain.

By contrast, in the states and territories all except VCAT, SAT, NTCAT and TasCAT have a right to internal review for all matters.[133] Options which include two tiers within tribunals have long been canvassed and deserve consideration.[134] Factors to be considered when introducing such an internal appeal system are: the nature of the issues; the needs and characteristic of people affected; the volume of cases; the need for increased consistency of tribunal findings; and the 'bureaucratic structures, methods and culture of the primary decision-making'.[135]

The inapplicability of even an informal doctrine of precedent within the tribunal system means that inconsistencies are more likely to arise between decisions of individual members. The advantage of an appeal panel is that it can provide more authoritative tribunal decisions by senior members. This limits the possibility of inconsistent decisions arising within the tribunal. Inconsistency leads to frustration on the part of those in the workplace or government agency seeking clarity and certainty by the relevant tribunal and detracts from a tribunal's reputation. Having a right to appeal to a panel is responsive to requests by unsuccessful applicants at first instance and provides better guidance to public administration in the face of inconsistent decisions at first instance in the tribunal.

One of the measures recommended for the AAT by the Callinan review was that its existing internal appeal facility for one division should be removed.[136] The reasons were that most first tier decisions were reviewed by another single member whose decisions are 'not necessarily or even likely to be better than another decision of another [member]'.[137] The review noted that retention of the right 'will likely continue to be a source of disharmony'.[138] The Law Council of Australia, at that time, expressed 'a degree of opposition to this measure' on the grounds that the justification for it had not been provided.[139]

Despite Callinan's recommendation that the existing right of appeal at the AAT be abolished, submissions for the purposes of the new federal administrative review body called for an extension, not a removal, of that right.[140] The Law Council's more recent submissions on the ART provide two circumstances in which an appeal would be valuable. The first was for second tier review by an experienced panel for all divisions other than the MRD and the General Division on certain migration matters; the second was for the President to have power to allocate a matter for review by an appeal panel.[141]

[133] ACT Act, ss 77–82; NCAT Act, ss 79–81; QCAT Act, ss 142–143A; SACAT Act, s 70.
[134] Skehill (n 93) 140.
[135] T Brennan 'The Hidden Dimension of Administrative Law: Internal and First Tier Review – II' (1989) 58 *Canberra Bulletin of Public Administration* 141.
[136] Callinan review, Measure 13.
[137] ibid [9.21].
[138] ibid 97.
[139] Law Council of Australia *Callinan Review: Past Reflections, Future Directions* (2019) 4.
[140] Commonwealth Attorney-General's Department *Administrative Review Reform: Issues Paper* (April 2023) Discussion Question 58.
[141] Visa cancellation and protection decisions in the Tribunal would be excluded since adding another step in the process would have furthered the opportunity to prolong time in Australia for those applicants whose presence is unlawful.

The second recommendation arose out of the events in Australia dubbed Robodebt.[142] An aspect of that significant breach in Australia's public administration emerged from institutional deficiencies within the AAT. At the AAT's first tier hearings of matters relating to the relevant recovery of payments by the social services department, the tribunal findings that the scheme was unlawful were concealed because first tier hearings were not publicly reported and the agency chose not to appeal the AAT decision. The Law Council submission suggested that the problems caused by that concealment would have been discovered earlier had the President been advised of the first tier's findings. Had that occurred some of the pernicious effects of the scheme could have been avoided. Those effects included the distress for affected social services recipients faced with often apparently large debts for overpayment and the significant financial impost on the Commonwealth for reparation for the unlawful payments when they were eventually found to be unlawful.

The Law Council accordingly recommended that an 'own motion' power be available to the President so that when systemic and unlawful decisions of this kind occur the President could direct that any like decision be directed to an appeal panel. The panel's decision *would be* reported. An effective pre-hearing triage process is required for identification of such decisions. That recommendation has been heeded and the ART Act 2024 does provide for an avenue of appeal within the ART.[143]

There are advantages and disadvantages in having an internal right of appeal. The value of such a process, consistent with the tribunal's objective of being accessible, is that it can respond to applicants who disagree with a tribunal decision, correct errors made by less-experienced members, or provide a more authoritative decision when there are inconsistent decisions at the first level. The use of members on the appeal panel also provides an opportunity for members to make decisions across the spectrum of matters heard by the tribunal which enhances members' overall job satisfaction.

A disadvantage is that the right of appeal requires additional members. An appeal panel, if it is to be justified, should comprise more than one member. There is little point in having one member on appeal reviewing a decision of another single member at first instance. The call for multiple members to sit on the panel may result in a reduction of members for other areas of work and cause delays in tribunal output. This may be an issue for smaller tribunals with fewer members.

[142] Robodebt is the simplified description adopted to identify a program operating between the Australian Taxation Office and the federal Department of Social Services which employed an algorithm to identify recipients of social security benefits who had failed properly to declare their earnings. The program was found to be unlawful and has been disbanded. A Royal Commission which was held in relation to the operation of the program was critical of the failure of federal public administrators to identify and notify the government of the illegality which had caused significant distress in the community.

[143] ART Act 2025 Pt 5.

It is also a factor of importance in cases at first instance where financial relief is being sought and speedy resolution of the issues is required as, for example, when social security payments are involved. Delays need not be experienced, however, if choices are made to allocate sufficient numbers of members to avoid such delays. As has been pointed out, 'dispute resolution processes can be effective for the expedient resolution of matters where [they are] applied strategically and [are] tailored to the caseload'.[144] Another potential disadvantage is that such an appeal may require more documents, more formal proceedings, and some additional costs for the parties, especially if they choose to have legal representation for the appeal.

These imposts must be balanced against the reduced time overall if the appeal panel can lead to a correct or preferable outcome, not just a finding of unlawfulness. The right to an internal appeal avoids the additional time and more costly correction of errors by a superior court. On balance, a right of internal review is a benefit for users and avoids the problem of inconsistent decisions which reduce respect for the tribunal. The arguments in favour of extending the right to a second internal review are persuasive and are likely to be effected for the ART.

Figures from the states and territories which have an internal right of review indicate that the numbers of matters heard by a second-tier panel are not excessive.[145] That means, that although hearing such reviews require additional members, the volume should be manageable. Part-time and sessional members can be called upon, or judicial members seconded from the courts and used strategically to meet any membership shortfall. The additional expenditure must be weighed against the considerable benefits to the reputation of the tribunal in providing more consistent decisions at the tribunals' primary level, as well as the wider benefits to decision-makers within government and the undoubted benefits for applicants seeking authoritative merits review.

Conclusion

As this history indicates, dispute resolution by tribunals has continued to evolve in Australia. Nonetheless, tribunals, particularly amalgamated tribunals, are still in their development phase. Looking back over the years of their operation in Australia provides insights into the benefits but also the challenges they face. These challenges can be surmounted provided better data is available on their operation,

[144] Commonwealth Attorney-General's Department *Administrative Review Reform: Issues Paper* (April 2023) 73.

[145] Concern about cost of a further tier of review is misplaced. The state civil and administrative appeals tribunals appeal rates for the 2021–2022 FY were as follows: ACAT: 44 (1,909 applications); QCAT: 343 (25,538 applications); NCAT: 813 (70,448 applications); SACAT: 724. These figures can at most be rough since appeals may be from decisions which were matters lodged in previous financial years. As less than 10 per cent of the applications to state CATS are in the administrative law field, the total number of appeals in 2021–2022: 1200) should be reduced by at least 90 per cent, that is to roughly 120 per annum.

standards are developed for their operation and, above all, principles are developed that can underpin what matters are best adjudicated by tribunals, and provide governments with better guidance as to which tribunals to amalgamate, at least when an amalgamated tribunal is in place or being contemplated. Attention to these matters will ensure that tribunals' place in the panoply of justice bodies performs the functions for which they are designed and assist the people for whom they provide services.

3

Tribunals as Part of the Administrative Justice System

SARAH NASON AND HUW PRITCHARD

This chapter considers the place of tribunals within the broader notion of 'administrative justice'. Many common law jurisdictions saw an apparent 'rise' of administrative justice corresponding with systemic tribunal reforms, including amalgamation, and the creation of oversight bodies, alongside, in some cases, the codification of administrative law and rights to administrative justice. Tribunals have since been challenged by austerity (impacting users, public bodies and tribunal budgets), a rise in other administrative review and redress mechanisms, declining systematic oversight, coupled with loss of political support for the notion of 'holistic' administrative justice, and digitalisation. This chapter focuses on common cross-cutting issues in tribunal reform, including amalgamation/rationalisation, 'creeping legalism', tribunals and multi-level governance, the relationship between tribunals and administrative law, oversight, and digitalisation. We conclude that conceptions or models of administrative justice that focus only on institutional structures or modes of adjudication may be of decreasing relevance, whereas those that focus on underpinning lived experiences of users and other actors, values, principles, and administrative law doctrines, will be more instructive to understanding tribunal developments.

Defining Administrative Justice

Administrative justice has been challenging to define. As part of this quest, the UK Administrative Justice Institute collated definitions each giving different emphases to administrative justice institutions, relationships and values.[1] Accordingly,

[1] UKAJI, 'What is Administrative Justice? A Discussion Paper' (3 March 2015): https://administrativejusticeblog.files.wordpress.com/2016/08/what-is-administrative-justice-a-ukaji-discussion-paper.pdf. UKAJI was established in 2014 with funding from the Nuffield Foundation to kickstart the expansion of empirical research on administrative justice in the UK. Since 2018, the Institute has been funded by Essex Law School, and is re-named the Essex Constitutional and Administrative Justice Initiative (CAJI).

administrative justice can be seen as: the interaction between citizen and state, from rule-making, to decision-making, to challenge, to resolution; decision-making by public bodies; citizen versus state conflicts; initial decision-making, dispute resolution and feedback processes related to the interaction between citizen and state; the means by which good administration is ensured for citizens; and the idea that citizens should be treated fairly by those in power and the processes that make this aspiration a reality.[2]

The editors of the *Oxford Handbook of Administrative Justice*, published in 2022, note the term administrative justice can be used descriptively, to identify decision-making and redress-providing bodies, and normatively, to elaborate a particular vision of rights and duties inherent in relationships between individual and state.[3] The editors also note that interest in administrative justice stems from interactions with administrative-type decisions of their state constituting the primary way citizens across the world experience justice. This is justice in 'small places'[4] and 'where the rubber meets the road for constitutionalism'.[5]

Various 'models' of administrative justice have been developed, questioned and refined over time. Jerry Mashaw's initial three models were developed from his empirical study of the processes of hearings and appeals before administrative law judges and federal courts in the USA concerning the denial of social security disability benefits.[6] He observed competing conceptions each with different legitimating values and goals, evidenced in different structures or organisational attributes, and with different cognitive techniques characterising decision-making. These models are now well known as bureaucratic rationality, professional treatment and moral judgment. Both critiquing and building on Mashaw's work, Michael Adler added a further three 'models', reflecting developments in so-called 'New Public Management', a UK term referring to the use of private sector techniques in the management of public sector administration. These models are managerialism, consumerism and markets.[7] Adler also adjusted some criteria in his typology to include modes of accountability as opposed to institutional structure/organisational attributes, and modes of redress, with the latter then introducing a criterion of external as well as internal accountability for decision-making.[8]

[2] Ibid.

[3] M Hertogh, R Kirkham, R Thomas and J Tomlinson (eds), *The Oxford Handbook of Administrative Justice* (Oxford University Press 2022) 'Administrative Justice as a Field of Study' xv–xxviii.

[4] M Doyle and N O'Brien, *Reimagining Administrative Justice: Human Rights in Small Places* (Palgrave 2019).

[5] Tom Ginsberg, 'Written Constitutions and the Administrative State: On the Constitutional Character of Administrative Law' in S Rose-Ackerman and P Lindseth (eds), *Comparative Administrative Law* (Edward Elgar 2010).

[6] J Mashaw, *Bureaucratic Justice: Managing Social Security Disability Claims* (Yale University Press 1983).

[7] M Adler, 'Fairness in Context' (2006) 33(4) *Journal of Law and Society* 615.

[8] See the chapter by Asimow, Chapter 10 in this volume, who adopts a five-fold model of adjudication.

Other typologies include Simon Halliday and Colin Scott's account using a normative cultural grid-group model as a tool for categorising good administration.[9] This led to four conceptions – fatalism, individualism, hierarchism and egalitarianism –useful in comparing approaches to administrative justice across diverse societies. These various approaches to modelling and typologies have been valuable to understanding administrative justice and its evolution. However, as Mashaw himself notes, the purpose of model construction is straightforward:

> [M]odels of administrative justice allow us to specify the dimensions of administrative justice that are of interest and to structure investigation either of particular administrative justice practices or the characteristic approaches of a society or legal culture. Whether a particular model or set of models, or a particular approach to building them, is useful depends upon what an analyst is trying to do.[10]

Other approaches to defining or conceptualising administrative justice have included the articulation of statements of values or principles,[11] or of rights to administrative justice.[12] The right to administrative justice has achieved constitutional status in African legal systems that have transitioned from dictatorship or authoritarianism to a form of democracy, though some appear to be backsliding on such commitments in practice. The right to administrative justice had been seen as important to achieving a fairer and more equitable distribution of socio-economic goods and services,[13] as well as being associated with moving from a so-called 'culture of authority' to a 'culture of justification'.[14] On this account public bodies are required to 'justify' their decisions with reasons of adequate quality. This shifts away from more traditional administrative law conception focused on jurisdiction and authority and demonstrates increasing recognition of the connections between administrative justice and social justice.[15] This shift is

[9] S Halliday and C Scott, 'A Cultural Analysis of Administrative Justice' in M Adler (ed), *Administrative Justice in Context* (Hart Publishing 2010).

[10] J Mashaw, 'Models of Administrative Justice' in M Hertogh, R Kirkham, R Thomas and J Tomlinson (eds), *The Oxford Handbook of Administrative Justice* (Oxford University Press 2022) 375, 393.

[11] Such as those produced by the UK Administrative Justice and Tribunals Council, and those produced by the Council of Canadian Administrative Tribunals/*conseil des tribunaux administratifs canadiens.*

[12] See, e.g., Article 47 of the Kenyan Constitution 'Fair administrative action' and Section 33 of the South African Constitution 'Just Administrative Action' – and note also Article 41 of the EU Charter on Fundamental Rights 'Right to good administration'.

[13] H Corder, 'A Right to Administrative Justice: 'New" or Just Repackaging from the Old?' in A Arnauld, K Decken and M Susi, *The Cambridge Handbook of New Human Rights: Recognition, Novelty, Rhetoric* (Cambridge University Press 2020).

[14] This phrase is attributed to Etienne Mureinik who perceived a shift in constitutional and administrative thought from a 'culture of authority' to a 'culture of justification': E Mureinik, 'A Bridge to Where? Introducing the Interim Bill of Rights' (1994) 10 *S Afr J on Hum Rts* 31, 32–33. It has been taken up and modified by D Dyzenhaus, 'Law as Justification: Etienne Mureinik's Conception of Legal Culture' (1998) 14 *S Afr J on Hum Rts* 11 and M Taggart, 'Reinventing Administrative Law' in N Bamforth and P Leyland (eds), *Public Law in a Multi-layered Constitution* (Hart Publishing 2003) 332.

[15] See, eg, J Gulland, 'Social Justice and Administrative Justice', in M Hertogh, R Kirkham, R Thomas and J Tomlinson (eds), *The Oxford Handbook of Administrative Justice* (Oxford University Press 2022) 245.

also evidenced in conceptual accounts of judicial review, and in doctrinal developments around proportionality and variable intensity of review.[16]

The UK Administrative Justice Institute also suggested 'there is value in considering how to reposition administrative justice as an overarching set of principles and values governing individuals' interactions with the state rather than as being one of the four "strands" of the justice system'.[17] Christian Gill similarly proposed that administrative justice can be seen as 'both a cross cutting and underpinning constitutional principle and a spectrum of procedures and mechanisms, operating in each branch of the constitution, to give force to those principles'.[18]

The editors of *The Oxford Handbook of Administrative Justice* considered their purpose to be 'to highlight and confirm the place of administrative justice as an important field of research and scholarship', whilst also illustrating 'the progress administrative justice has made to become an increasingly important area of international scholarship'.[19] These statements contrast with a trend, acknowledged by contributors to the collection, of administrative justice (or at least a so-called 'holistic' account of administrative justice) being on a downward trajectory from the perspective of political and policy interest. We might say that academic interest seems currently inversely proportional to political and policy interest. Whereas the introduction to the *Oxford Handbook* quotes the definition of an administrative justice system from the UK Tribunals Courts and Enforcement Act 2007 (TCEA), this provision was repealed just shy of 10 years before the *Handbook's* publication, alongside the abolition of the related statutory administrative justice oversight body the Administrative Justice and Tribunals Council (AJTC). The so-called decline of administrative justice, at a political and policy level in some jurisdictions, includes 'de-tribunalisation'.[20] Consisting of various reforms, either to abolish tribunal appeal rights entirely, replace them with other forms of more bureaucratic redress (such as administrative review), and/or to make remaining appeal rights more difficult to exercise – especially due to austerity related reductions in legal aid funding and the introduction of, or increases to tribunal fees. The policy context likely includes an ideology of shrinking the state, but also suggests short termism, given that 'holistic' administrative justice, including oversight, is seen as costly, whereas the savings it generates for the public purse take longer to

[16] See, eg, D Knight, *Vigilance and Restraint in the Common Law of Judicial Review* (Cambridge University Press 2018); H Wilberg and M Elliott (eds), *The Scope and Intensity of Substantive Review: Traversing Taggart's Rainbow* (Hart Publishing 2015).

[17] UKAJI (n 1).

[18] C Gill, 'The Evolving Role of the Ombudsman: A Conceptual Constitutional Analysis of the "Scottish Solution" to Administrative Justice' (2014) 4 *Public Law* 662, 667.

[19] *Oxford Handbook* (n 3) xvi.

[20] See, eg, R Thomas, 'Current Developments in UK Tribunals: Challenges for Administrative Justice' in S Nason (ed), *Administrative Justice in Wales and Comparative Perspectives* (University of Wales Press 2017), R Thomas and J Tomlinson, 'Mapping Current Issues in Administrative Justice: Austerity and the "More Bureaucratic Rationality" Approach' (2017) 39(3) *Journal of Social Welfare and Family Law* 380; and M Adler, 'The Future of Administrative Justice' in M Hertogh, R Kirkham, R Thomas and J Tomlinson (eds), *The Oxford Handbook of Administrative Justice* (Oxford University Press 2022) 623.

be realised. Reforms, in the UK at least, have reduced the number of appeals to tribunals in high-volume areas such as immigration and social security, and there have also been other parallel trends aimed at enhancing the judicial or legal 'status' of tribunal justice alongside a general blurring of boundaries between courts and tribunals. These reforms, which include rationalisation/amalgamation, so-called 'legalisation' or 'judicialisation', and which are now underpinned by digitalisation/online resolution, can lead to different understandings of the relationship between tribunal justice and wider administrative justice.

Administrative Justice and Tribunal Justice

In some jurisdictions, the phrase 'tribunal justice' is increasingly prevalent, often in contexts where it had previously been common to speak of administrative justice, including in systemic tribunal reforms.[21] It would be wrong to equate tribunal justice and administrative justice, albeit tribunals are the largest by-volume forum for administrative law adjudication in many common law jurisdictions. The conceptual development of administrative justice can, nevertheless, be associated with the establishment of oversight bodies in common law jurisdictions specifically tasked to oversee reforms that catalysed or cemented the developing constitutional position of tribunals. For example, the UK Council on Tribunals was established in 1958 to oversee the principled development of tribunals from administrative (or quasi-administrative) bodies not fully separable from government departments to their present position in the UK as part of the adjudicative and not the administrative branch of state. In Australia, an Administrative Review Council (ARC) was created with responsibility to oversee the development of a new tribunal process, 'merits review', within a newly Amalgamated Appeal Tribunal (AAT) that exercised powers constitutionally understood to be executive rather than judicial.[22]

Both the UK Council on Tribunals and the Australian ARC eventually gained broader oversight responsibilities beyond tribunal reform. The UK Council was later replaced by the AJTC which was 'to act as the hub of the wheel of administrative justice'.[23] The AJTC had a statutory remit to keep the range of mechanisms for delivering Proportionate Dispute Resolution under review and to consider ways to make the system accessible, fair and efficient.[24] This breadth of function necessitated producing a statutory definition of the UK's administrative justice system, the now-repealed definition cited in *The Oxford Handbook*.

[21] See, eg, in the UK, Carnwarth LJ, *Tribunal Justice – A Quiet Revolution* (The Holdsworth Address 2004–5) and 'Tribunal Justice: A New Start' (2009) *Public Law* 48.

[22] Administrative Appeals Tribunal Act 1975 (Cth) Part V. The ARC was functionally abolished without those statutory provisions being repealed. The entire AAT will shortly be abolished and replaced under new legislation. The chapter by Groves and Weeks in this volume explains that the ARC will be reconstituted as part of the scheme to replace the AAT.

[23] A Leggatt, *Tribunals for Users: One System, One Service* (The Stationery Office 2001) 7.49.

[24] Tribunals Courts and Enforcement Act 2007, Schedule 7.

In its first Annual Report, the AJTC set out its purpose, values and strategic objectives, extending the idea of administrative justice from being about tribunal systems and structures, to include the processes and substance of administrative decision-making.[25] It conceptualised administrative justice as a virtuous circle of good initial decision-making, appropriate avenues for redress and seeking continuous improvement through feedback.[26] However, in Australia, the Administrative Appeals Tribunal Act 1975 did not initially include a section stating the objectives of the Act and purpose of the AAT. An objects section was not inserted until 2005. Although the ARC had many functions (as listed in the original section 51 of the 1975 Act) that coalesced in practice as an instruction to keep the administrative law and justice system under review, there is no express reference to administrative justice.

Whilst the AJTC and Australian ARC experienced periods of comparatively high resourcing and influence (not least due to statutory requirements on the political branch to respond to their activities), they had their work cut out in monitoring increasingly diverse and non-hierarchical institutions, with inter-acting and overlapping roles. The growth of the 'integrity' branch[27] (including commissions and commissioners, auditors and other regulatory and/or promotive institutions) added a new dimension, as did the expansion of ombudsmanry.[28]

The AJTC and ARC as statutory whole-system oversight bodies have subsequently either been abolished or rendered practically moribund due to lack of funding and limited political support for administrative justice,[29] and a similar Administrative Review Council in South Africa, aimed at monitoring the development of the Promotion of Administrative Justice Act 2000, itself designed to give practical effect to the constitutional right to administrative justice, never fully took shape.[30]

A common factor in the debates around abolishing administrative justice oversight has been political support for conceptions of administrative justice wherein the government of the day is responsible for administrative justice policy,[31] with oversight bodies seen as providing expensive duplication of that role, and in which tribunals are tasked to focus only on the efficient resolution of disputes, in an increasingly judicialised way. When responding to proposals to abolish the AJTC, the UK Ministry of Justice argued that administrative justice policy is the

[25] AJTC, *First Annual Report* (The Stationery Office 2008).

[26] ibid.

[27] See eg, R Creyke, 'Administrative Justice – Towards Integrity in Government' (2007) *Melbourne University Law Review* 705.

[28] See, eg, B Thompson, R Kirkham and T Buck, *The Ombudsman Enterprise and Administrative Justice* (Routledge 2010).

[29] See S Nason, 'Oversight of Administrative Justice Systems' in M Hertogh, R Kirkham, R Thomas and J Tomlinson (eds), *The Oxford Handbook of Administrative Justice* (Oxford University Press 2022) 155.

[30] C Hoexter, *Administrative Law in South Africa* (Juta, 3rd edn, 2021).

[31] Public Administration Select Committee, *Future Oversight of Administrative Justice: The Proposed Abolition of the Administrative Justice and Tribunals Council* (HC 2010–12, 1621).

function of the Ministry itself, and that the AJTC would simply be duplicating it. In Australia, it was argued that the ARC's functions could be transferred to the auspices of the Attorney-General, by requiring it to assist the Attorney-General's Department and focus on 'matters of current Government priority'. As a matter of governing legislation, the Australian Attorney-General had always had comparatively greater say over the ARC's agenda than the UK Ministry of Justice had with respect to the AJTC.[32]

Tribunal Justice, Rationalisation and Legalism

The contribution of tribunal justice as a more specific subdivision of administrative justice may be seen in the statements of principle expressly adopted through legislation governing tribunals, especially at the time of their rationalisation. For example, in the UK, the TCEA requires tribunal professionals to have regard to the need for tribunals to be accessible, for their proceedings to be fair, quick and efficient, for members to be subject-matter or legal experts, and to have regard to 'the need to develop innovative methods of resolving disputes that are of a type that may be brought before tribunals'.[33] In Australia, section 2A of the 1975 Act requires that in carrying out its functions, 'the Tribunal must pursue the objective of providing a mechanism of review that: (a) is accessible; and (b) is fair, just, economical, informal and quick; and (c) is proportionate to the importance and complexity of the matter; and (d) promotes trust and confidence in the decision-making of the Tribunal'. However, this provision was a late addition, with the precise objectives of the AAT determined by its various presidents, and with its processes evolving through a series of key cases.

These characteristics of 'tribunal justice' have arisen in the context of amalgamation or rationalisation of tribunal jurisdictions, as a matter of efficiency, which has been a wider trend across the common law world. Tribunal amalgamation has been pioneered particularly in Australia, where all the states have amalgamated tribunals. The Federal AAT long had extensive jurisdiction, though its major amalgamation occurred in 2015 with the transfer of the Migration Review Tribunal, Refugee Review Tribunal, Social Security Appeals Tribunal and Australian Classification Review Board into its structures. Although the AAT has more recently suffered serious challenges and is in the process of being replaced, its successor will likely continue to operate as an amalgamation of subject-matter tribunal jurisdictions marked by a distinctive process of 'merits review'.

[32] How Attorneys-General had used these powers varied; the Attorney General at the time the ARC was effectively abolished had not engaged extensively with the ARC, such as by using statutory powers to give directions or engaging with matters of inquiry.

[33] TCEA, s 2(3).

Australia is not the only country to have experienced rationalisation/consolidation. In Canada, for example, although tribunals can be seen as markedly different to both Australia and the UK, including through retention of the descriptors quasi-judicial and 'administrative tribunal' (now an oxymoron as far as the UK is concerned) there has been 'clustering' of jurisdictions based on similar reasoning to UK rationalisation and Australian amalgamation. The 'cluster' concept is a more pragmatic 'half-way house' and various approaches to co-location and shared services have been adopted, noting the legislative distinctiveness of many of Canada's administrative tribunals.[34] There have also been rationalisation reforms of New Zealand's tribunals, which were said to number up to 100 different jurisdictions at the time the reforms were proposed.[35]

In the UK, rationalisation was achieved following Sir Andrew Leggatt's review of tribunals, reporting in 2001.[36] The Review noted that, at the time of writing, there were some 70 different tribunals in England and Wales, dealing with nearly 1 million cases per annum. Most tribunals were rationalised into a single system, their independence from sponsoring government departments re-emphasised and strengthened, and administration came to be through an amalgamated Tribunals Service. The reforms also improved training for members and aimed to empower 'users' to participate without the need for legal representation. In addition to the Leggatt recommendations, the then Government stressed the importance of proportionate dispute resolution and that the new service should be empowered to innovate, to consider alternative methods of dispute resolution and to stimulate improved decision-making to avoid disputes occurring. The subsequent TCEA rationalised the previous tribunals into a Tier and Chamber system. Employment Tribunals and Employment Appeal Tribunals remained outside the structure but are operationally integrated within the tribunals system. The previously distinct jurisdictions now comprise specific Chambers within the First-tier or Upper Tribunal depending upon their status as first instance or appellate bodies, the seniority of their members and the subject matter of their expertise.

[34] The Administrative Tribunals Support Service of Canada Act 2014 involved integrated administrative support for 11 federal tribunals. In British Columbia some social justice tribunals have been integrated and the Tribunal Administratif du Québec, in operation since April 1998, is organised into four sections (social affairs, real estate, territory and environment and economic affairs) and one division, namely mental health. In Ontario, the Adjudicative Tribunals Accountability, Governance and Appointments Act 2009 allows the government to group adjudicative tribunals into an organisation called a cluster when 'the matters that the tribunals deal with are such that they can operate more effectively and efficiently as part of a cluster than alone'. See L Sossin and J Baxter, 'Ontario's Administrative Tribunal Clusters: A Glass Half-Full or Half-Empty for Administrative Justice?' (2012) 12 *Oxford University Commonwealth Law Journal* 157 and P Daly, Administrative Law Matters – 'Administrative Tribunals – Structural Variability' and 'Administrative Tribunals: Adversarial, Inquisitorial, Regulatory and/or Mediative'. Available online at: www.administrativelawmatters.com/blog/2023/06/26/administrative-tribunals-adversarial-inquisitorial-regulatory-and-or-mediative/ These issues are discussed in the chapter by Daly in this volume.

[35] Chapter 8 in this volume by Wilberg explains that New Zealand's tribunal system remains fragmented and has not received significant scholarly analysis.

[36] Sir A Leggatt, *Tribunals for Users – One System, One Service* (Lord Chancellor's Department, 2001).

Thinking about these trends towards amalgamation more generally, some of the commonly stated benefits include systematising tribunal jurisdictions, improving coherence and reducing fragmentation including by avoiding the creation of new ad-hoc routes to redress, bolstering tribunal independence, increasing access to justice both through physical co-location and more accessible procedures and practices as well as shared learning across subject-matter jurisdictions, and enhanced adoption of Alternative Dispute Resolution (ADR) mechanisms. Other objectives of amalgamation or rationalisation include facilitating the use of technology, improved training, deployment, and career prospects for judges, members and other staff, and achieving potential economies of scale through shared rather than duplicated facilities and resources.[37] Although the proposed benefits of tribunal consolidation and rationalisation have been stated on numerous occasions, there remains little detailed research examining the extent to which such proposed benefits have been achieved. For example, some 17 years post-enactment of the TCEA 2007, we are not aware of any studies expressly assessing the impact of the new tribunal structure against common benchmark factors for and against rationalisation or amalgamation or examining whether the amalgamation of diverse fields of law, particularly in the Upper Tribunal Administrative Appeals Chamber, has led to watered down rather than concentrated legal and subject-matter expertise. The jurisdiction of the Upper Tribunal Administrative Appeals Chamber in terms of its list of jurisdictions is especially broad, with, as Lady Hale has put it, a risk that amalgamation of the 'very different jurisdictions in the new chambers will dilute rather than enhance the specialist expertise of their judges and members'.[38] However, in this volume, Robert Thomas argues that, in practice, it acts as a specialist public law court in in the field of social security law, with responsibility for a miscellany of other smaller jurisdictions that generate very few claims.

Robin Creyke's work does directly address the impact of reforms in Australia, though primarily from the perspectives of the tribunals themselves.[39] She concludes that amalgamation has not involved any feared loss of independence or reduction in fairness of processes and that the objectives of having limited formality and avoiding the creation of ad hoc new redress bodies, have been achieved. She further argues that amalgamated tribunals have heeded negative accessibility connotations stemming from the risk of having a single key physical centre, by making use of regional locations and members and with other more centralised members travelling on circuit. Although she found the evidence of whether amalgamated tribunals are indeed more financially economical than their fragmented predecessors to be 'equivocal', half of Creyke's survey respondents nevertheless considered it 'probable' that savings had been made.[40] Many respondents also

[37] R Creyke, 'Amalgamation of Tribunals: Whether 'tis Better … ?' in S Nason (ed), *Administrative Justice in Wales and Comparative Perspectives* (University of Wales Press 2017).

[38] *Eba v Advocate General for Scotland* [2011] UKSC 29 at [54].

[39] R Creyke, 'Australian Tribunals: Impact of Amalgamation' (2020) 26 *Australian Journal of Administrative Law* 206.

[40] ibid 226.

gave examples of increased efficiency in the deployment of judges and other staff, with less down time, improved training and enhanced career satisfaction, all seen as contributing to perceptions of increased professionalism. Creyke however, concludes: 'Whether an amalgamated tribunal costs less for government than the previous fragmented systems is not possible to assess',[41] in part due to the lack of baseline figures for comparison, and that many other variables (beyond structural changes) are likely to impact caseloads and practices; these include, for example, demographic, economic and legislative changes. Interestingly for those from other jurisdictions where consolidation of tribunals is less formalised and more variable, the area of concern identified by Creyke is whether there has been enough formal homogenisation of procedures. She concludes that tribunal experiences indicate 'a need to encourage governments to accept that most, if not all, procedures should be located in the legislation of the amalgamated tribunals, and variations should be kept to a minimum'.[42] However, in amalgamated tribunals where large jurisdictions such as immigration and/or social security constitute the overwhelming majority of cases, general rather than subject specific legislative or regulatory procedures are only likely to apply to a very small number of cases, and removing all or most variation seems unachievable.

With amalgamation and rationalisation driving tribunal reform, and systematisation and procedural harmonisation often key features, there is a belief that such modern 'tribunal justice' will be subject to increased 'legalism'. Margaret Doyle and Nick O'Brien for example refer to the influence of 'law's empire' or a 'pathology of legalism' as increasingly central to justice in public administration, at least when viewed from the perspective of tribunals.[43] So-called 'creeping legalism', particularly in combined civil and administrative tribunals, is said to be characterised by 'aspects of adversarial legal practices infecting the practices and procedures of an amalgamated tribunal'.[44] This is associated with the influence of members largely specialised in the civil jurisdictions. For example, a ten-year review of the Victorian Civil and Administrative Tribunal noted that:

> Within the community sector, there was a sense that the tribunal needed to get back to its roots. It was intended to provide quick, cheap and efficient justice for the general public. Yet many people think it had become too formal, with lawyers, expert witnesses and advocates dominating proceedings. It was often said the tribunal had allowed 'creeping legalism' to occur.[45]

Cross-deployment of members between civil and administrative jurisdictions within a combined tribunal, or indeed across separate courts and tribunals, is nowadays more prevalent. The more court-based training and experience of legal practitioner members may induce a natural tendency towards a more adversarial

[41] ibid 221.
[42] ibid 223.
[43] Doyle and O'Brien (n 4).
[44] Creyke, 'Tribunal Amalgamation' (n 37) 340.
[45] Justice K Bell, *President's Review of VCAT* (2009) 21.

approach that is not appropriate for particular subject areas of disputes, and which may require tempering by a strong informal counterculture. The rationales for cross-deployment and cross-ticketing are themselves variable, although often based on judicial career enhancement and added value, the use of these mechanisms is also associated with shorter term needs to manage large caseloads in high volume areas, such as employment, immigration and social security.

Although the UK does not yet have bodies classified formally as civil and administrative tribunals, the lack of more formalised distinctions between matters of private law and public administrative law means there may well be civil law disputes determined within 'administrative' tribunals, and it is not unusual that matters classed as 'administrative law' in one jurisdiction are classed as 'private civil law' in another. In practice, levels of formality, procedural rules, arrangements for legal representation, and the listing of judges and other members to determine cases, tends to differ across individual tribunals and courts within and across various justice systems.

The unification of court and tribunal judiciaries also potentially reduces the distinctiveness of the classificatory divide between courts and tribunals. In proposing to establish unified judicial leadership of the courts and tribunals judiciary for England and Wales both the government and the judiciary:

> are agreed that a unified leadership model could help deliver greater cohesion between the tribunals and the courts, as well as affording more flexibility in the system. A single, unified courts and tribunals judiciary in England and Wales will promote efficiency and consistency in our justice system, build an inclusive collegiate structure and increase opportunities for cross-deployment between the courts and tribunals.[46]

Practically, the proposals are to replace the existing office of Senior President of Tribunals with a new office that would be equivalent in standing to the current Heads of Divisions of the High Court within the England and Wales judiciary: these are, the President of the King's Bench Division (a Division which includes the Administrative Court), the President of the Family Division, and the Chancellor of the High Court. Many of the responsibilities of the Senior President of Tribunals would be legislatively transferred to the Lord Chief Justice of England and Wales, with a power to delegate them. Responsibilities relating to tribunals will then be delegated to the post holder of the reformed head of the tribunals' office, in the same manner as the Lord Chief Justice currently delegates responsibilities to other Heads of Division. The potential for a single England and Wales judiciary had been considered previously during the merger of HM Courts Services with HM Tribunals service, however, this was not progressed at the time, it seems in part due to concerns over the position of the devolved judiciaries. Brian Thompson reports that the Scottish judiciary was not consulted about the merger proposals.[47]

[46] Ministry of Justice, *Tribunals Leadership: Consultation on reform of the office of Senior President of Tribunals* (CP 829, 2023) 3.

[47] B Thompson, 'Opportunities and Constraints: Reflections on Reforming Administrative Justice Within and Across the United Kingdom' in S Nason (ed) *Administrative Justice in Wales and Comparative Perspectives* (University of Wales Press) 147, 161.

The Senior President of Tribunals currently has responsibilities over tribunals which deal with reserved issues of UK law and have UK-wide jurisdictions and structures. The new merged judiciary proposals carve out the Senior President of Tribunal's responsibilities insofar as they relate to judges and non-legal members working within reserved tribunals in Scotland and Northern Ireland. As the consultation proposals themselves note, it would be constitutionally undesirable for the Lord Chief Justice of England and Wales to have leadership responsibility for the judiciary in Scotland and Northern Ireland.[48]

The proposed reforms to the role of Senior President of Tribunals are part of a broader shared ambition, reaffirmed in July 2022, by the Lord Chancellor, the Lord Chief Justice of England and Wales, and the Senior President of Tribunals, to create 'One Judiciary'. It has been expressed that: 'The principal aim of One Judiciary is to bring the courts and tribunals closer together to make better use of resources and to demonstrate that judges, whether they sit in courts or tribunals, are part of a single judicial family.'[49] The risk of 'creeping legalism' appears to be acknowledged, with the government recognising, 'the unified tribunals system, has strong jurisdictional identity and expertise that benefits all who use the tribunals'[50] and any reform proposals should not weaken this. The aim is rather:

> to integrate the judiciaries – so that both tribunals and courts judicial office-holders can benefit – rather than to subsume the very different nature of tribunals practice and procedure into a courts model. This will protect the specialism of the tribunals while minimising inconsistencies across the jurisdictions.[51]

Nevertheless, the proposals for enhanced cross-deployment, and aligning judicial terms and conditions and ways of working, with oversight by the Lord Chief Justice of England and Wales, may indicate that the apparent distinctiveness of tribunals will further erode. The Courts and Tribunals Judiciary website openly acknowledges that tribunals are in fact courts:

> The tribunals are specialist courts whose judges and members hear a wide range of cases, such as tax, employment, and immigration and asylum. The Upper Tribunal and Employment Appeal Tribunal hear appeals challenging some tribunal decisions.[52]

The judicial reforms require primary legislation, which although anticipated, had not been announced at the time of writing, nor had the responses to the consultation yet been published.

Digitalising procedures is another development that further reduces distinctions between courts and tribunals. The 'one system, one judiciary' approach has also included seeking to create a 'single point of entry to the justice system'

[48] Ministry of Justice Consultation on Tribunals Leadership (n 46).
[49] Pursuing 'One Judiciary' by the Lord Chancellor, the Lord Chief Justice of England and Wales and the Senior President of Tribunals July 2022. Available at: www.judiciary.uk/pursuing-one-judiciary-by-the-lord-chancellor-the-lord-chief-justice-of-england-and-wales-and-the-senior-president-of-tribunals/.
[50] Ministry of Justice Consultation on Tribunals Leadership (n 46) 9.
[51] ibid.
[52] See www.judiciary.uk/courts-and-tribunals/tribunals/.

and that online access will be enhanced by 'developing a single online system for starting and managing cases across the criminal, civil, family and tribunal jurisdictions'.[53] To date the attempt to introduce a single 'Common Platform' into just one area of law, criminal law, has been beset by major problems, with rollout of other aspects of the online transformation programme persistently delayed.[54] It now appears likely that rather than seeking a single point of access and single procedure, development is proceeding through various procedures and platforms attuned to the needs of particular jurisdictions, but underpinned by the same principles, including accessibility, user friendliness, effectiveness and access to remedies. Within digitalisation programmes tribunals risk losing some of what has been considered their characteristic accessibility, and the 'vulnerability' of users in various jurisdictions such as social security, mental health and special educational needs often makes online procedures challenging or impossible to navigate. Administrative justice principles can be harnessed to ensure that 'digital by default' does not disadvantage particular individuals and groups.

Creyke's research also found that 'creeping legalism' and enhanced visibility, including online visibility, associated with amalgamation can also lead to some degree of enhanced status for tribunals. She anticipated that a single main tribunal building and website would increase public awareness of the tribunal as an avenue for dispute resolution, but her less expected finding was that the increased size and presence of an amalgamated body led to heightened government awareness of amalgamated tribunals, with the result that 'tribunals are now considered significant elements of the adjudicative architecture' and 'accorded equivalent status to the courts'.[55] She also found some evidence that this improved status feeds into greater accountability in government and other administrative decision-making and to more extensive acceptance of tribunal jurisprudence.

Part of the reasoning behind amalgamating tribunal structures, and the creation of upper tribunals designated as superior courts of record within the relevant jurisdiction, is to enable development of principled and consistent jurisprudence across tribunals which in many common law jurisdictions hear substantially more claims than the courts. In some jurisdictions, the higher tribunals can largely be seen as de facto public law courts. In the Australian context, Creyke has stated that a consequence of tribunal amalgamation is that it 'enhances the opportunity for uniform jurisprudence'.[56] In this vein, the creation of the England and Wales Upper Tribunal was said to provide an 'unprecedented opportunity to work towards a more coherent and distinctive system of tribunal justice, drawing together strands of the principles developed from various jurisdictions'.[57]

[53] Ministry of Justice, 'Transforming Our Justice System, By the Lord Chancellor, the Lord Chief Justice and the Senior President of Tribunals' (September 2016).

[54] Committee of Public Accounts, *Progress on the courts and tribunals reform programme* (HC 2022–23, 1002).

[55] Creyke (n 39) 228.

[56] ibid.

[57] Carnwarth LJ, 'Tribunal Justice' (n 21) 56.

In effect a separate body of tribunal doctrine, that, for various reasons including the specialism of the tribunal judiciary and its closeness to relevant policy, would be subject to less intervention by the 'ordinary' courts. Tribunal justice might normally be associated with the practical matters of efficiency, accessibility and proportionate dispute resolution laid out in underpinning legislation, yet here it seems more associated with the development of principles of administrative law. It had been said that the Upper Tribunal would 'lead on developing the law underlaying administrative justice'[58] and that it would 'come to play a central, innovative and defining role in the new system, enjoying a position in the judicial hierarchy at least equivalent to that of the Administrative Court'.[59] On the contrary, in this volume Robert Thomas argues that the work of the Upper Tribunal largely replicates that of its predecessor tribunals and that it is yet to issue any rulings on wider principles of administrative justice, to guide tribunals or administrative decision-makers. Nevertheless, there has been increased interest in tribunal decisions, with more extensive publication, including digital dissemination, and wider academic and practitioner discussion.

Tribunals and Administrative Law

Despite the narrative of 'creeping legalism', tribunals are still rarely analysed through the lens of doctrinal administrative law. Rather it is presumed that studying tribunals should be through methods of functional and/or socio-legal analysis. Liz Fisher argues that those who have sought to take, at times, a more normative and doctrinal legal focus to exploring the roles of tribunals, have been criticised for not adopting a sufficiently 'law in context' approach. As such, she proposes that 'tribunals are not the focus of sustained doctrinal discussion',[60] compared to matters including grounds of judicial review or general principles of administrative law, but often 'stand outside the norms of legal inquiry'.[61]

However, in more institutional and empirical studies when the normative or legal position of tribunals is analysed, this is also primarily against the yardstick of how court-like they are. Such reasoning is still common, but giving way to analyses that focus on the principles and context behind the attributes and functions of tribunals, as seen in the cases of *Cart v Upper Tribunal*[62] and *Eba v Advocate General for Scotland*[63] which examined the new amalgamated tier and chamber structure

[58] Tribunals Service, Transforming Tribunals: Implementing Part 1 of the Tribunals, Courts and Enforcement Act 2007 (CP 30/07, 2007) [131].

[59] ibid [178].

[60] L Fisher, 'Administrative Tribunals: An Essay about the Legal Imagination of Administrative Law Scholars', in J Goudkamp and M Lunney (eds), *Taking Law Seriously: Essays in Honour of Peter Cane* (Hart Publishing 2022) 269.

[61] ibid.

[62] *R (Cart) v The Upper Tribunal* [2011] UKSC 28.

[63] *Eba v Advocate General for Scotland* [2011] UKSC 29.

for England and Wales tribunals, and relevant Great Britain/UK Tribunals, under the TCEA (especially where an Upper Tribunal refusal of permission to appeal cannot be subject to any further appeals). This leaves dissatisfied litigants with only one option, to seek judicial review in the Administrative Court (part of the King's Bench Division of the High Court). However, as the Upper Tribunal is legislatively designated a 'superior court of record', prevailing opinion was that it would be immune from judicial review (specifically it would be immune from the inherent non-legislative supervisory jurisdiction of the Administrative Court). In the Court of Appeal in *Cart's* claim, Sedley LJ noted that the Upper Tribunal itself has a judicial review jurisdiction that had been specifically defined by an Act of Parliament, but that the High Court's judicial review jurisdiction stems from the common law. He concluded that 'far from standing in the High Court's shoes … the shoes the [Upper Tribunal] stands in are those of the tribunals it has replaced'.[64] The provisions of the TCEA which confer a limited legality review power on the Upper Tribunal are necessary precisely because the Upper Tribunal and High Court 'are not meant to be, courts of co-ordinate jurisdiction'.[65] Throughout the litigation, the Upper Tribunal was treated as a de facto court in its areas of specialism.

Both Laws LJ in the Divisional Court and Sedley LJ in the Court of Appeal had approached the issue of assessing the Upper Tribunal's susceptibility to judicial review via a normative examination of the High Court's inherent supervisory jurisdiction, with both accepting the continuing serviceability of a doctrinal distinction between jurisdictional and non-jurisdictional errors of law, at least as concerns specialist bodies. Laws LJ approved and applied the approach taken in the case of *R v Cripps ex parte Muldoon* as being to 'examine all the characteristics of the court [or tribunal] in question in order, not to dignify it with a name or status, but to ascertain whether in substance it should be subject to the judicial review jurisdiction'.[66] On the other hand, the UK Supreme Court sought to avoid reference to the doctrine of jurisdiction and its technicalities, with Lady Hale considering the key issue to be one of proportionate access to justice and that: 'Both tribunals and the courts are there to do Parliament's bidding. But we all make mistakes. No-one is infallible. The question is, what machinery is necessary and proportionate to keep such mistakes to a minimum.'[67]

The Supreme Court's approach in *Cart* and *Eba* has been characterised, and criticised, as being focused on 'law in context', the social facts of proportionate dispute resolution, to the point of favouring pragmatism at the expense of principle, even as a 'blasphemy' against doctrinal analysis, rejecting precedent on the matter of jurisdictional errors.[68] However, we take the view, espoused both by

[64] *(Cart) v Upper Tribunal* [2010] EWCA Civ 859 [19].
[65] ibid [20].
[66] [1984] QB 68, 87.
[67] *Cart* (n 64) [37].
[68] C Forsyth, 'Blasphemy Against Basics: Doctrine, Conceptual Reasoning and Certain Decisions of the UK Supreme Court', in J Bell, M Elliott, J Varuhas and P Murray (eds), *Public Law Adjudication in Common Law Systems* (Hart Publishing, 2016).

Sarah Nason[69] and by Joanna Bell (though each for slightly differently reasons) that pragmatic considerations taken into account by the Supreme Court, such as high caseloads, the relative merit/demerit of many of these claims, and costly delays in the system, were not, as Bell puts it, 'ideas from some extra-legal dimension'.[70] Rather, the considerations were carefully extracted from precedent, legislation and legal history. It was these matters that determined the role and status of the Upper Tribunal in this context, not how court-like or otherwise it is.

Another example, also drawn on by Fisher, is *Ku-ring-gai Council v Bunnings Properties Pty Ltd*.[71] This New South Wales Court of Appeal decision concerned a Land and Environment Court of New South Wales Commissioner hearing a merits review appeal against a refusal of consent to a development application. Fisher concludes that submissions before the Court about appropriate role and functions of the Commissioner tended to frame the issue in terms of the judicial or administrative nature of the Commissioner's powers. However, instead, and more broadly, the Court of Appeal judges considered a range of factors including the powers of Commissioners, of Councils, and the actual legal effects of the development application; a similar array of intersecting legal concepts to those considered by the UK courts in *Cart* and *Eba*. Fisher also highlights the comments of Spiegelman CJ in a similar case, that reasoning by analogy – whether proceedings are more like merits review in a tribunal or like adversarial litigation in a court – 'diverts attention from the power conferred by the statute and the rule' and that instead the 'focus should be on the principles that underlie the practice'.[72] The same can be said of focusing too closely on whether the practice of the tribunal can be demarcated as adversarial or inquisitorial, rather than considering what specific approach is most suited to the particular matters at issue, the composition of the tribunal, and underlying legislation and impacts of the case at hand.

R (Privacy International) v Investigatory Powers Tribunal[73] also involved analysis of complex legal architecture, with scope for reasonable disagreement between justices of the UK Supreme Court; with some justices focusing on the supposed court-like nature of the Investigatory Powers Tribunal, and/or its procedures and practices including the importance of confidentiality, whereas others raised concerns about institutional isolation and 'local law' if ouster were allowed to preclude further judicial review. These cases show that as a matter of legal analysis, the classification 'tribunal' means little on its own without further analysis of powers, procedures, and statutory context, going beyond a yardstick comparison with perceived traditional characteristics of courts as more formal and adversarial.

[69] S Nason, *Reconstructing Judicial Review* (Hart Publishing 2016).

[70] J Bell, 'Rethinking the Story of Cart v Upper Tribunal and Its Implications for Administrative Law' (2019) 39 *Oxford Journal of Legal Studies* 74, 84.

[71] *Ku-ring-gai Council v Bunnings Properties Pty Ltd* [2019] NSWCA 28; (2019) 236 LGERA 35.

[72] *Port Stephens Council v Jeffrey Sansom* [2007] NSWCA 299, 156 LGERA 125 [47].

[73] *R (on the application of Privacy International) v Investigatory Powers Tribunal* [2019] UKSC 22, [2020] AC 491.

Amalgamated or rationalised tribunal structures appear to make provision for procedures that go beyond traditional conceptual distinctions between appeal and review that have been anchored in heuristics about the separation of administrative and judicial power. In the TCEA structure, the First-tier and Upper Tribunal powers to review their own decisions, have been described as based on a 'curious amalgam'[74] between a first instance merits decision, factual appeal and legality review. The first Senior President of Tribunals, Carnwarth LJ, cited a distinctive advantage of tribunal justice within the new structure as being the capacity to transcend traditional conceptual distinctions between fact and law, and between merits and legality to do justice in individual cases. Seldey LJ, for example, described legal principles that might develop within the new rationalised tribunals structure as 'not quite lawyers' law'.[75]

We take a similar view to Fisher, that the juxtaposition of judicial and quasi-judicial justice, doctrine against pragmatic approaches to proportionate dispute resolution, and judicial versus executive/administrative powers, are heuristics that can obscure rather than illuminate our understanding of tribunals. Tribunals fashion their own reality. As Fisher puts it: 'Tribunals are not just passive actors in administrative law. They are not just objects to be governed. They are also active subjects in the process of making and evolving administrative law in their specific area of operation.'[76] She further considers that as '... adjudicative sites of dispute resolution and accountability [tribunals] are also stabilising forces that can address and manage both the dynamism and particularity of administrative law'.[77] The heuristics noted above are awkward, we might even say somewhat redundant, when set against this picture of tribunal particlarity.

Matthew Groves and Greg Weeks similarly stress that 'tribunals are not mere vessels powerless and thrown about by legislative change. They influence and respond to the world in which they operate, including the legislation that fashions and refashions them'.[78] Groves and Weeks note that a particular challenge for tribunals is the constantly changing environment in which they operate, and particularly that they must 'grapple with the relentless enactment and amendment of legislation over which they have review jurisdiction'.[79] Recent empirical research has disclosed the extent to which administrative law adjudication, both in courts and tribunals, turns more on interpretation of often subject-specific legislation, policy and guidance, than on the doctrines that occupy so much scholarly attention.[80] In this respect, whilst in practice there seems to be little evidence of

[74] P Cane, 'Judicial Review in the Age of Tribunals' [2009] *Public Law* 479, 492.
[75] *Cart* (n 64) [42].
[76] Fisher (n 60) 274.
[77] ibid 278.
[78] M Groves and G Weeks, 'Tribunals – Their Continued Evolution and Reform' (2020) 26 *Australian Journal of Administrative Law* 189, 190.
[79] ibid.
[80] Bell (n 70); J Bell, 'The Relationship Between Judicial Review and the Upper Tribunal: What Have the Courts Made of *Cart*?' [2018] *Public Law* 394; and J Bell and L Fisher, 'Exploring a Year of Administrative Law Adjudication in the Administrative Court' [2021] *Public Law* 505.

the Upper Tribunal having laid down overarching principles of tribunal or administrative justice, there are many instances of tribunals having developed specialist fields of administrative law through statutory interpretation in policy context. Resort to heuristics and neglect of more thorough legal analysis of tribunals is, we argue, in part a consequence of a general failure to take legislation seriously across administrative law scholarship in common law jurisdictions.

Tribunals, Politics and the Rise and Fall of Administrative Justice

As we have argued, the rationalisation or amalgamation of tribunals can be associated with enhanced legal status, coupled, however, with declining attention to more holistic administrative justice, and in this vein the UK's multilevel governance context of devolved nations provide interesting case-studies. Scotland, Northern Ireland and Wales generally have little responsibility over matters such as social security and immigration, as such they can avoid the challenges associated with high-volume tribunals; challenges that UK governments have tended to meet through increased bureaucratic administration, alongside reducing access to tribunals. Due to lower volumes of claims, the devolved nations have more scope for policy innovation and for retaining a more 'holistic' approach to administrative justice and tribunals.

The Leggatt Review did not extend to devolved tribunals, but it was nevertheless concerned as to whether the degree of coherence envisaged for the operation of a new tribunals system and service would be achievable across the range of tribunals that operated cross-border in the UK, whilst at the same time maintaining coherence with the devolved systems with which the rationalised tribunals would interact. Subsequently the devolved nations have pursued tribunal amalgamation, showing that the pull of such professionalising and consolidating trends remain strong even in much smaller jurisdictions. For example, the Tribunals (Scotland) Act 2014 created a new simplified statutory framework for tribunals in Scotland bringing together existing jurisdictions and providing a structure for the flexible development of new jurisdictions. This structure includes a First-tier Tribunal for Scotland and an Upper Tribunal for Scotland. The Lord President, who is head of the Scottish Judiciary, is also head of the Scottish Tribunals but delegates various roles to the President of Scottish Tribunals. Alongside this, a Review of Civil Justice led to changes in the civil courts, reform of the judicial review procedure, and the creation of a Scottish Courts and Tribunals Service effected by the Court Reform (Scotland) Act 2015. Notably alongside these reforms, the existence of STAJAC (the Scottish Tribunals and Administrative Justice Advisory Committee) as successor to the AJTC Scottish Committee, and its more 'holistic' approach to administrative justice, was short lived. However, more recently the Law Society of Scotland has consulted on the implementation, through legislation, of a principles-based approach to administrative justice,[81] with its work significantly echoing that conducted on behalf of the now abolished Committee for Administrative Justice and Tribunals in Wales (CAJTW). This seems characteristic of devolution, and multi-level governance more generally, enabling a degree of piggybacking and leapfrogging with respect to policy development.[82]

The Welsh Committee of the AJTC, and its successor body, the CAJTW, both recognised that a collection of 'Welsh' tribunals had developed ad hoc and piecemeal over the various phases of devolution.[83] We have elsewhere argued that the executive nature of devolution to Wales, and the continuation of the combined England and Wales legal jurisdiction, has proven interesting as a context to the development of administrative justice.[84]

When the first Government of Wales Act 1998 devolved subject fields to the then National Assembly for Wales, this included functions over tribunals associated with these fields, principally because, at the time, tribunals continued to be seen as part of the executive, established by government departments they were created to serve, rather than exercising judicial functions. As part of the most recent phase of devolution, moving Wales to a reserved powers model, the judicial nature of Welsh tribunals has been acknowledged; the Wales Act 2017 defines 'Welsh tribunals' and creates the office of the President of Welsh Tribunals (PWT) to provide judicial leadership. In this role the PWT has many of the same statutory responsibilities for the tribunals within their jurisdiction as does the Senior President of Tribunals for England and Wales tribunals, and for some Great Britain/UK reserved tribunals.

CAJTW recommended further reform of the tribunals system, and of broader administrative justice including the development of a set of Administrative Justice Principles for Wales, and such reform was also acknowledged and recommended by a Commission on Justice in Wales which reported in late 2019.[85] Following our own research, we proposed that the collection of Welsh tribunals and their administration and oversight, provides the nucleus in the DNA of a developing Welsh justice system.[86] This has been accepted by the Commission on Justice in Wales, which proposed that 'the Welsh tribunals and their administration should

[81] Law Society of Scotland, Administrative Justice Committee, Administrative Justice principles: a second discussion paper and consultation (August 2022). Available at: www.lawscot.org.uk/media/373508/administrative-justice-principles-discussion-paper-and-consultation-august-2022-002.pdf.

[82] Thompson, 'Administrative justice within and across the UK' (n 47).

[83] Welsh Committee of the AJTC, Review of Tribunals Operating in Wales (2010); CAJTW, Administrative Justice: A Cornerstone to Social Justice in Wales (2016). Available at: www.gov.wales/administrative-justice-cornerstone-social-justice-wales.

[84] S Nason and H Pritchard, 'Administrative Justice and the Legacy of Executive Devolution: Establishing A Tribunals System for Wales' (2020) 26(4) *Australian Journal of Administrative Law* 233.

[85] Commission on Justice in Wales, *Justice in Wales for the People of Wales* (October 2019). Available at: www.gov.wales/sites/default/files/publications/2019-10/Justice%20Commission%20ENG%20DIGITAL_2.pdf.

[86] Nason and Pritchard (n 84).

be seen and treated as part of Wales own emergent justice system'.[87] The England and Wales Law Commission has subsequently examined the Devolved Welsh Tribunals,[88] and the Welsh Government has issued a White Paper on proposals for reform,[89] largely following the recommendations set out by the Law Commission. The main elements of the proposed reform agenda include: a statutory framework for a single, unified and coherent tribunal system organised by type of jurisdiction with clear and consistent onward rights of appeal and capable of accommodating additional jurisdictions over time; statutory duties to uphold the independence of the new tribunal system and greater structural independence for the way in which it is administered; judicial leadership for the new tribunals system under the aegis of the President of Welsh Tribunals and Chamber Presidents and Deputy Presidents; clear and efficient processes for setting procedural rules for the new tribunal system, and consistent arrangements for appointing tribunal members and clear processes including for determining remuneration, deployment and dealing with complaints and/or disciplinary matters.

These reforms echo the trend towards judicialisation of tribunals. What makes the reforms in Wales so interesting is that Wales continues to be, according to many high-profile commentators,[90] the only nation in the world with primary legislative powers, held by an Assembly, now Senedd Cymru/Welsh Parliament, but with no separate legal jurisdiction over which to exercise those powers. The Wales Act 2017 contains many reservations under the 'Justice' heading, the reservation of the single legal jurisdiction of England and Wales includes courts, judges, civil and criminal proceedings, and judicial review of administrative action, with the legal profession, legal aid, arbitration, prisons and offender management also being reserved. We argue then, that the process of tribunal reform, including rationalisation, in Wales, is not just about the common goals of efficiency, effectiveness and shared-services etc, but is also about constitution building using what – some might say, little – control over institutions of justice, is held by the Welsh Government and Parliament. This is another example of how 'political' tribunal reform, including amalgamation and rationalisation can be. As Rachel Bacon put it in her doctoral thesis, 'government see the process of amalgamation as a way of 'making their mark' or increasing their control over smaller, specialist tribunals …'[91] As Robert Thomas states in relation to England and Wales and reserved Great Britain/UK tribunals, 'government through gov.uk now exercises more control over the information available about tribunals than

[87] Commission on Justice in Wales (n 85) [12.162].

[88] Law Commission, *Devolved Tribunals in Wales Report* (Law Com No 403; 2021).

[89] Welsh Government, *A New Tribunal System for Wales: White Paper* (2023).

[90] See, eg, Liz Saville-Roberts MP, Leader of Plaid Cymru at Westminster, *Hansard* Vol 612 col 766, 5 July 2016.

[91] Bacon, 'Administrative Law: Problems areas – reflections on practice'. Paper delivered at the annual conference of the Australian Institute of Administrative Law, 3–4 July 2003, 5, and quoted in Creyke (n 37) 321.

in the past when there was a better-funded advice sector and tribunals had their own websites'.[92]

In developing the Welsh reform proposals one of the most challenging matters has been the case for an Upper Tribunal for Wales given its potential capacity to lay down distinctive legal principles. Many respondents to the Law Commission's consultation on the matter agreed that a uniform approach to appeals would be desirable, where previously appeals have been to various bodies, primarily the England and Wales Upper Tribunal and the High Court. However, some respondents noted that even if appeal routes from devolved Welsh tribunals were harmonised, there would still be some divergence as compared to the various appeal routes from reserved tribunals operating in Wales. Some respondents favoured maintaining existing appeal routes on the basis that these were to specialist chambers of the Upper Tribunal for England and Wales dealing with a repetitive caseload in particular areas of expertise such as mental health, and aspects of taxation and property.

Despite divergence in Welsh legislation, it was primarily tribunal leads themselves who wished to maintain existing appeal routes to the Upper Tribunal to facilitate consistent development of legal principles. For example, the President of the Residential Property Tribunal for Wales stated: 'I do not believe that the Appeal Tribunal for Wales would be able to replicate the experience and learning of the Upper Tribunal, nor do I think at this stage, that it would be desirable to have two senior appellate bodies determining the same issues.'[93] The Mental Health Review Tribunal for Wales considered that appeals to the England and Wales Upper Tribunal should be retained due to seeking consistency of jurisprudence, but also due to cross-border issues: 'It is crucial for us to have the same appeal route as the First-tier Tribunal (Mental Health). Many of the decisions made on appeal from us revolve around human rights issues which equally affect patients in England. Also, many English patients are detained in Wales, so a system which potentially risks key decisions on appeal being decided differently in Wales to England would create chaos.'[94] It could be argued that the general sentiment of the tribunal judiciary responses, at least at the time, was that consistency with tribunal jurisprudence in developing principles of interpretation in particular subject areas of administrative law on an England and Wales basis, even in devolved policy areas such as health, property, and standards of local government administration, was more greatly emphasised than a developing body of 'Welsh' jurisprudence based on the interpretation of Welsh law (primary and secondary legislation, policy and guidance etc, created by the Welsh Parliament and Welsh Ministers an expressing a more distinctive set of human rights and social justice values).

[92] R Thomas, 'Current Developments in UK Tribunals: Challenges for Administrative Justice' in S Nason (ed), *Administrative Justice in Wales and Comparative Perspectives* (University of Wales Press, 2017) 184, 190.

[93] Law Commission (n 88) [4.20].

[94] ibid [4.19].

Other responses illustrated views of the relationship between the Upper Tribunal and the High Court. Some respondents, such as the Adjudication Panel for Wales, argued that appeals to the High Court ought to be maintained 'due to the complexity of the matters considered and the need for it to be perceived to be reviewed at a higher level by a suitably qualified judge of sufficient standing to win respect and deal with the human rights issues'.[95] Various submissions also raised accessibility issues, and these were primarily based on perceptions of upper appellate tribunals being more accessible to users than the High Court. In our own submission we acknowledged this, but also noted that legal aid funding for representation remains available, albeit in a very attenuated form, for some appeals and judicial reviews in the High Court, whereas such is unlikely to be available in an appeal or review to an upper appellate tribunal. We also emphasised that legal aid policy is reserved to the UK Parliament and Government, making it difficult for the Welsh Government and Welsh Parliament to provide legal aid funding for appeals to any Welsh appellate tribunal established.

Most respondents to the Law Commission's consultation supported the creation of an Appeal Tribunal for Wales, whilst noting that its caseload would initially be very small and would in practice duplicate expertise already available elsewhere. The Law Commission recommended creating an Appeal Tribunal for Wales, noting that whilst its initial jurisdiction would be quite minimal, it could be expected to grow over time, and the transfer of jurisdictions to it should be cautious and staged. The Law Commission noted that Welsh Government has no control over the operation of the Upper Tribunal, and the President of Welsh Tribunals cannot determine what the procedural rules for the tribunal should be. An Appeal Tribunal for Wales would serve only the devolved tribunals, would be subject to the President of Welsh Tribunals, and to the oversight of a recommended Tribunal Procedure Committee for Wales. Whilst responses to the Law Commission focused primarily on accessibility, efficiency, resources, expertise, avoiding duplication, different aspects of consistency in caselaw, and the currently very small number of appeals from devolved Welsh tribunals, Welsh Government's approach to structural tribunal reform has much more explicit underpinnings of constitutional principle and reform. As the Ministerial Foreword to the Welsh Government's White Paper notes, an Appeal Tribunal for Wales is emblematic, it will be the first appeal tribunal in Welsh legal history and is recommended to have the status of a superior court of record. Structural tribunal reform serves two aims for Welsh Government, the creation of a rationalised modern tribunal system with all the associated trappings of accessibility, independence and efficiency, alongside laying the foundations 'for a future where justice is devolved, and Wales administers its own wider system of courts and tribunals'.[96]

The multi-level governance context is an issue for tribunals in other jurisdictions, which can stem not only from areas of potentially shared competence over

[95] ibid [4.16].
[96] Welsh Government (n 89).

the subject-matter of disputes, but also in relation to different types of power. Most starkly this can be seen in Australia where State tribunal judges may exercise judicial powers, but Federal tribunal judges may not. Questions too remain over whether it is constitutionally permissible for a state tribunal in exercise of its ordinary functions involving the use of state judicial power to adjudicate a dispute between residents of different states, or where the Commonwealth is a party, or in which a party seeks to rely on Commonwealth legislation. A dense thicket of caselaw appears to cover these matters, cutting against the principles of accessibility and efficiency said to be at the heart of tribunal justice.[97]

It may be argued that the Welsh focus on tribunal justice also evidences the decline of administrative justice more generally, and of oversight. The CAJTW's final legacy report, before it was disbanded by Welsh Government, described administrative justice as a 'cornerstone to social justice in Wales' and included recommendations for other parts of the administrative justice system, yet few of these have been actioned. Drawing on the work of the AJTC, and a range of other oversight bodies across the common law world, as well as on the work of the Council of Europe, the CAJTW developed a set of *Administrative Justice Principles for Wales*. These principles recognise administrative justice as a fundamental right, and include provisions relating to decision-making, systems and procedures, and values and behaviours. Although Welsh Government acknowledged that the principles 'will provide a helpful source of guidance'[98] there has been no formal adoption of the principles or incorporation of these or similar principles into the working practices of the devolved Welsh tribunals. Notably, Welsh Government's *White Paper on A New Tribunal System for Wales* makes no mention of the term 'administrative justice'. Whilst the Law Society in Scotland seems to have taken up the mantle of pushing for a more expressly principles-based approach to administrative justice, this has now fallen out of favour in Wales.

The political nature of administrative justice then plays out in various ways in different jurisdictions, in stark cases it can even lead to the total failure of institutions.[99] For example, institutional reforms to increase the efficient functioning of the Australian AAT appear to have paved the way for a dramatic rise in seemingly politicised appointments leading to such a collapse in trust that the body in its present form is in the process of being replaced. The demise of the AAT highlights the need for appropriate attention to tribunal appointments and specifically to the necessary degree of independence (regardless of whether tribunal 'judges' are formally part of the traditional judicial or administrative branches of state, or

[97] See, eg, A Olijnyk 'Burns v Corbett: the latest word on State tribunals and judicial power' on AUSPUBLAW (19 April 2017). Available at: https://auspublaw.org/blog/2017/04/the-latest-word-on-state-tribunals-and-judicial-power/.

[98] Welsh Government, Response to CAJTW (March 2026). Available at: www.gov.wales/sites/default/files/publications/2018-11/welsh-government-response-to-cajtw-report.pdf.

[99] Chapter 12 in this volume by Thomson explains the significance of this issue to tribunals in Hong Kong.

some hybrid quasi-judicial classification). Groves and Weeks also consider that the debacle underscores the importance of wider administrative justice oversight, particularly that the situation within the AAT would not have been as extensive or have continued for so long had the Australian ARC continued to function.[100]

The need for thorough independent and expert oversight is important given innovations in public administration and in dispute resolution. Submissions to *The Australian Senate – Legal and Constitutional Affairs References Committee: The performance and integrity of Australia's administrative review system*, reporting in March 2022, supported re-establishing and re-funding the ARC, particularly noting the role the ARC could play in monitoring the use of emerging technology in administrative law, and that failures of the online compliance initiative (commonly known as 'Robodebt') could have been minimised had the ARC been operative. Groves and Weeks consider 'the costs of the failures of public administration consequent on having no independent source of advice to government about administrative law matters massively outweighed whatever saving was made by disestablishing the ARC'.[101]

The focus on 'tribunal justice' in the UK also obscures the problems of limited holistic oversight. For example, a study by Catherine Barnard and Amy Ludlow casts some doubt on both tribunal reform, including the success of the TCEA 2007 structure, and the achievement of administrative justice. After conducting empirical research into cases in the First Tier Social Entitlement Chamber, Barnard and Ludlow conclude that whilst at a high level the rationalisation of tribunals objectives may have been met, 'data suggest that practical success of this streamlining process is questionable especially when budgets are tight'.[102] They conclude that tribunals generally act comparatively informally, and show sympathy and understanding towards appellants, with the chances of success for appellants also high, but that this only provides 'tribunal justice' in the narrow sense. They consider that of greater concern are the failures that occur 'upstream' including with medical assessments, often contracted-out, that form the basis for initial decision-making. Their data suggests that right first time remains an aspiration not a reality, with 'significant ongoing obstacles to broader administrative justice and this has a serious impact on the lives and well-being of some of the most vulnerable in society'.[103] These findings suggest that whilst tribunals may now enjoy a greater sense of 'status' with increased prominence given to the concept of 'tribunal justice', the empirical shift in redress volumes from tribunals to administrative review means fewer people now receive their entitlements, and public accountability is weakened.

[100] M Groves and G Weeks, 'Tribunal Justice and Politics in Australia: The Rise and Fall of the Administrative Appeals Tribunal' (2023) 97(4) *Australian Law Journal* 278.

[101] C Barnard and A Ludlow, 'Administrative (in)justice? Appellants' experiences of accessing justice in social security tribunals' [2022] *Public Law* 406.

[102] ibid 419.

[103] ibid 426.

Conclusions

The cross-cutting themes of this chapter can be drawn together as areas for future research. One theme is the role of tribunals, and particularly upper appellate tribunals, in multi-level governance structures, whether resulting from devolution, federalism or other forms of organisation. This is related to a second theme of, what we consider to be, the eroding of traditional distinctions between courts and tribunals that can now be seen as based on out-dated notions of power separation. The more court-like tribunals become, in the traditional sense of laying down overarching and authoritative principles of administrative law, the more authoritative or 'senior' is their place in multi-level governance structures, and the more important it is to understand them as sites of doctrinal administrative law, rather than from a purely sociological or institutional perspective.

With the procedural harmonisation instigated by rationalisation and amalgamation now being accelerated by digitalisation and online dispute resolution, the distinctive space between courts and tribunals is further narrowing. Digitalisation generally and automated decision-making will continue to necessitate re-thinking our conceptions and models of tribunal and administrative justice.

It could be argued that more insightful approaches to tribunal justice lie within accounts that focus not on levels of formality, or the contrast between bureaucratic rationality (as administrative) and moral judgement (as legal), but rather on so-called 'scales' or 'ladders'. For example, in considering what makes a court, Martin Shapiro proposes two cross-cutting scales, one focusing on mode of adjudication (from mediator, to conciliator, to arbitrator, to judge) and a second examining whether the body is primarily concerned with individualised dispute resolution, or if it has a broader role of developing precedent and/or laying down principles of good administration for public bodies.[104] The same body may well be placed differently on these scales depending on the nature of the issue at hand, and crucially both the statute law and policy that governs the field.

Grainne McKeever notes that tribunals are hybrid political and legal institutions, with her work focusing on how, from the citizen participant's perspective, their experience is not dictated by the formal classification of tribunal or court modes of adjudication and procedures, but rather by lived experiences of delay, access to information, legal support and their own expectations.[105] The same can be seen in Barnard and Ludlow's study of the First-tier Social Entitlement Chamber. This body of work then further reinforces the conclusion that differences between tribunals and courts, particularly lower civil courts and administrative law tribunals, are more presumed than real.

Whilst understandably the promise of digital justice has focused on accessibility for citizens, what may yet be less explored is how digital and other technological

[104] M Shapiro, *Courts: A Comparative Political Analysis* (University of Chicago Press 1981).
[105] G McKeever, 'A Ladder of Legal Participation for Tribunal Users' [2013] *Public Law* 575.

advancements can be used to re-establish connections between tribunal justice and wider administrative justice. The large volumes of data created on all aspects of governance, including real-time data on the volume and subject-matter of tribunal claims, judicial reasons for deciding, and outcomes, could surely be harnessed to improve so-called 'right first time' decision-making and to identify wider policy and practice problems before these become endemic. Technology can facilitate more systemic learning, and over much shorter timescales.

We have not attempted in this chapter the daunting task of proposing yet further models or principles of administrative justice, the field is already crowded, but our conclusion is that those models that focus on rigid institutional differences between bodies that determine questions of law will be of decreasing use in modern administrative justice, whereas those based on underpinning lived experiences, values, principles and administrative law doctrines, ought to take centre stage and will help us better understand tribunals in the common law world.

4

Tribunals and Adversarial Process: Messages from History

CAROL HARLOW

> The whole ethos of tribunals is one of a fair and swift individualised adjudication in which appellants can participate directly via oral hearings or now online. Tribunals apply the same rules as caseworkers but decisions are taken by an independent judge before whom the appellant can appear in person, a feature that is likely to more instil confidence than the distanced, faceless, box-ticking culture prevalent in departmental casework routines.
>
> Robert Thomas, *Administrative Law in Action. Immigration Administration* (Hart Publishing 2022) 146

Introduction

Tribunals occupy a special place in English administrative law. They are an important part of our system of administrative justice. We tend to think of tribunals as court-substitutes, although today they are more properly specialist courts with limited jurisdiction. Embedded in the UK judicial system by the Tribunals, Courts and Enforcement Act 2007 (TCEA),[1] they have been swallowed up by the One Judiciary project, which aims to bring 'courts and tribunals closer together'.[2]

The message of history is more complicated. Tribunals grew up in the nineteenth century, emerging with the emergent administrative state as a way of resolving disputes between officials and members of the public. They evolved during the twentieth century into the main vehicle for the resolution of disputes

[1] Tribunal justice is a partly devolved function in the UK. The TCEA and this chapter cover English tribunals and those with a UK-wide jurisdiction.

[2] Statement by the Lord Chancellor, the Lord Chief Justice of England and Wales and the Senior President of Tribunals, 'Pursuing "One Judiciary"' (London, Ministry of Justice, 8 July 2022).

involving administrative bodies: a less costly, less formal, more accessible and speedier alternative to courts. Section 2 of this chapter provides a brief overview of the long and somewhat bumpy road travelled by English tribunals from their origins in early days as largely administrative in character to their present position as partners in a unitary justice system at UK level. Section 3 looks more closely at the key attributes of the tribunal as machinery for adjudication, comparing the adversarial model of justice which is the common law norm with the inquisitorial model commonly adopted in an administrative process, where the adjudicator is a managerial figure in charge of the proceedings with responsibility both for assembling evidence at the pre-trial investigatory stage and for managing the adjudication. Section 4 identifies a recent trend in modern public administration to turn to new forms of alternative dispute resolution which are, like an ombudsman investigation, inquisitorial in character. It is argued that growing recourse to automated public administration in the form of algorithmic decision-making, online justice, and artificial intelligence (AI), is likely to accelerate this trend. The chapter concludes by asking whether our long tradition of adversarial justice is sufficient to underpin an adversarial process as the default model of administrative justice or whether it is destined to be superseded by automated adjudicative processes operated by the administration.

Tribunals to Courts: A Long Journey

Early Days

The genesis of the tribunal in the common law world is usually taken to be the nineteenth century, which is conveniently also the generally accepted starting point for modern systems of administrative law.[3] For the legal historian Chantal Stebbings, tribunals were a necessary by-product of the industrial revolution, evolving in the period after the Napoleonic Wars when state regulation of the new industrialising society began in earnest.[4] Industrialisation and the beginnings of a road and railway network across the country triggered disputes that required 'frequent adjudication of a kind which the courts were unable to give',[5] while Factories Acts, public health legislation and a reconstituted Poor Law all gave rise to disputes which needed to be resolved quickly and cheaply. For a variety of reasons, these matters were considered unsuited for trial in the ordinary courts and better suited to resolution by 'experts'.

[3] C Carr, *Concerning English Administrative Law* (Oxford University Press 1941).

[4] C Stebbings, *Legal Foundations of Tribunals in Nineteenth Century England* (Cambridge University Press 2007) 6.

[5] RE Wraith and PG Hutchesson, *Administrative Tribunals* (Allen & Unwin 1973) 17. For a concise overview of the reforms, see O McDonagh, *Early Victorian Government 1830–1870* (Weidenfeld & Nicolson 1977).

Typical of English law, there was no general debate, no attempt at definition of the term 'tribunal' and no fixed adjudicative model. It was left to specific enabling legislation to contain provision for dispute resolution in each particular subject area. The outcome was a jumble of statutory bodies with dispute-handling functions, the majority with essentially administrative functions but a few with 'discrete, express and unambiguous dispute-resolution powers'.[6] There were no uniform provisions for appeal or jurisdiction and no established and consistent procedures; if not prescribed by statute, procedure was determined by those responsible for administering the system or by the deciding body itself and it was both informal and variable. Stebbings, however, notes a number of common features: a circumscribed statutory jurisdiction with mixed administrative and judicial functions, a lay membership, a practice of conducting oral hearings and often – though not invariably – a measure of independence. It is these miscellaneous, essentially administrative, bodies that she sees as the prototype of our modern statutory tribunals.[7]

The line generally taken both by Parliament and the courts was that dispute resolution arising out of administration was 'no more than an element … in a wider administrative process': in other words, although adjudicative in the broad sense of that term, it was considered administrative in style and form.[8] Since it was an administrative function, the common practice of embedding adjudicators within administrative agencies was not at that time a cause for concern.[9] When income tax was introduced in 1799, for example, the General Commissioners, already in place locally, were made responsible for assessment and collection, but the appellate jurisdiction was vested in a differently constituted Commission of Appeal, suggesting a measure of independence. Yet only five years later, the appellate jurisdiction was transferred to the General Commissioners transforming them into a 'mixed function' or 'hybrid' body that combined administrative and adjudicative functions.[10] In later years, as we shall see, this practice did become a cause for concern and an occasional subject of legal challenge as a threat to the important constitutional principle of judicial independence. But nineteenth-century courts were content to see statutory tribunals as administrative bodies with administrative characteristics, limiting their supervision to review through the prerogative writs.[11]

On other occasions, a more court-like approach might be adopted, exemplified in the case of railways. Disputes involving railway matters were initially resolved by the Court of Common Pleas, which unsurprisingly adopted a procedure that

[6] *Legal Foundations* (n 4) 6.
[7] ibid 282.
[8] ibid 62.
[9] P Cane, *Controlling Administrative Power, An Historical Comparison* (Cambridge University Press, 2016) 328.
[10] C Stebbings, 'The General Commissioners of Income Tax: Assessors or Adjudicators?' (1993) *British Tax Review* 1, 52.
[11] *Legal Foundations*' (n 4) 294, 306, 311.

echoed its own adversarial procedure but was 'less formal than a court of law and less rigid on such matters as locus standi and in deciding questions (eg, fairness of charge) which were matters of administrative policy rather than questions of law'.[12] The judicial flavour survived the transfer of dispute resolution to a succession of bodies significantly labelled by Professor Robson in his study of administrative tribunals, 'The Railway Courts'.[13] In the three-person Railway and Canal Commission, for example, one member was expert in railway matters but a second was always a lawyer, later a judge, who was the final arbiter of the law, and appeal lay from this court-like body to a 'real' court: the Court of Appeal. Robson found the structure confusing and 'uncharacteristic of an administrative tribunal of the English type'.[14] Hesitantly, he concluded that the Commission, despite the fact that it 'differed widely from an ordinary court of law' and 'embodied administrative elements to a high degree', bore a far closer resemblance to a court of justice than to an administrative tribunal.[15] It was, in other words, a court substitute.

Robson was not in general an admirer of courts or judges, whose attitudes and procedures he saw as cumbersome and old-fashioned.[16] Yet he deplored the growing practice of assigning important adjudicative decision-making 'to vast and faceless departments of state' with no appeal to the courts and without any body of guiding principle.[17] Robson was unswerving in his support for administrative machinery for supervision and control, advocating a Council on Tribunals with a supervisory role, capable of systematising tribunal adjudication, and a single administrative appeals tribunal to handle appeals.[18] The latter idea (which would come to fruition in Australia) was rejected by a (shocked) Franks Committee on the ground of constitutionality: it would 'involve a departure from the principle whereby all adjudicating bodies in this country, whether designated as inferior courts or tribunals, are in matters of jurisdiction subject to the control of the superior courts'.[19] This principle, energetically guarded by the courts,[20] has been an important factor in judicialisation.

[12] WA Robson, *Justice and Administrative Law* (3rd edn, Stevens 1951) 27.

[13] ibid 90. There is an unexpected echo here of Lord Hewart's celebrated anti-administration diatribe in *The New Despotism* (Ernest Benn 1929).

[14] ibid 98.

[15] Robson, (n 12) 95. Wikipedia describes the 1888 Railway and Canal Commission as a 'British court of record'.

[16] See WA Robson, 'The Report of the Committee on Ministers' Powers' (1932) 3 *Political Quarterly* 346, 360–61, where Robson castigates the failure of the judiciary to reform 'a fantastic procedure which has been obsolete for at least a century'. Robson gave evidence both to the Donoughmore Committee on Ministers' Powers, Cmnd 4050 (1932) and the Franks Committee arguing for an administrative appeal tribunal.

[17] *Justice and Administrative Law* (n 12) 90.

[18] Evidence to the Franks Committee (n 16) on Days 13 and 14.

[19] Report of the Franks Committee on Tribunals and Enquiries, Cmnd 218. [122].

[20] *Anisminic Ltd v Foreign Compensation Commission* [1969] 2 AC 147; *R (Cart) v Upper Tribunal* [2011] UKSC 28; [2012] 1 AC 663; *R (Privacy International) v Investigatory Powers Tribunal* [2019] UKSC 22; [2020] AC 491.

Franks and After

When the Unemployment Assistance Act 1934 set in place an autonomous National Assistance Board responsible for administration, there was much debate as to whether appeals from its decisions should be internal and administrative or external and lie to a tribunal.[21] Advancing an argument that is often heard today, the Minister of Labour asserted that 'neither Parliament nor public opinion' would tolerate a situation where the only appeal possible was from one official to another; appeal from public assistance committees should consequently 'go to an outside body'.[22] In the event, the 1934 Act set in place district appeal tribunals, comprising a chairman, who might or might not be legally qualified, plus two lay members, one selected from an employers' panel of members of trade associations, the other from a workman's panel nominated by trade unions. This 'welfare model' was to prove surprisingly enduring, although, as we shall see, in recent years it is frequently modified.

Yet, although the tribunals set up by the 1934 Act represented a first step in their recognition as machinery for adjudication, it would seem that the judicial role of the tribunals was at first played down.[23] A circular issued by the Board in 1934 underlined this, stating that a tribunal acts:

> in an administrative capacity exercising the same discretion upon the facts before it as the officers of the Board might exercise, but no more. It will really be expressing a second (and final) opinion on the case in its own right as a competent administrative body and will not be sitting in judgment upon the officer's determination.[24]

Two decades later, the Franks Committee, which was set up in 1955 to review the constitution and performance of tribunals and inquiries, made the same point, asserting that, although welfare tribunals 'exercise[d] adjudicative functions, in practice their task much resembles that of an assessment or case committee, taking a further look at the facts and in some cases arriving at a fresh decision on the extent of need'.[25] For Franks, which with hindsight can probably be criticised for not taking welfare tribunals sufficiently seriously, this role justified a degree of 'desirable simplicity of procedure' and precluded the need for further appeal on points of law.

Franks: A Watershed

Nonetheless, Wraith and Hutchesson call the Report of the Franks Committee 'a watershed between a recent past when tribunals were regarded as unavoidable

[21] See PT Stafford, 'Unemployment Assistance in Great Britain' (1937) 31 *American Political Science Review* 433 at 442–450.

[22] Sir Henry Betterton cited in T Lynes, 'Unemployment Assistance Tribunals in the 1930s' in M Adler and A Bradley (eds), *Justice, Discretion and Poverty, Supplementary Benefit Appeal Tribunals in Britain* (Professional Books 1975) 7.

[23] ibid.

[24] ibid 8.

[25] Cmnd 218 [182] and [179–183].

expedients and a future when they were coming to be accepted for what they really are – an important part of the judicial systems of the country'.[26] The Committee did not go so far as to endorse the inference in its terms of reference that tribunals were in fact courts 'other than the ordinary courts of law'. But it firmly rejected the government case that tribunals were part of the administration,[27] calling then 'machinery provided by Parliament for adjudication' with the function of providing cheap, accessible, untechnical, expeditious and expert decision-making such as courts were sometimes unable to provide. As such, they must observe basic adjudicative characteristics of *openness*, meaning that proceedings should be open to the public and decisions should be reasoned, *fairness*, which required a clear procedure enabling parties to know their rights, to present their case fully and know what case they must meet, and *impartiality*, meaning 'freedom from the influence, real or apparent, of Departments concerned with the subject-matter of their decisions'.[28] Franks deserves its brand name of 'watershed'. The Report's simple mantra of openness, fairness and impartiality proved durable and set in place standards and values for tribunals that would come to be seen as inseparable from the adjudicative function. They continue to govern our thinking today. Fairness is the 'overriding objective' for tribunal justice, tribunal hearings are, for the most part, open and accessible and impartiality in the sense of independence has finally been established, although not for many years.

The Post-Franks Era

Franks started tribunals on the path to judicialisation. In the post-Franks era, judicialisation owes much to the work of welfare lawyers. The degree of informality in Supplementary Benefit Appeal Tribunals (SBATs),[29] was soon to bring a raft of criticism.[30] Their proceedings were contrasted unfavourably with that of national insurance local appeal tribunals (NILTs), chaired by lawyers and described as 'usually a model of balancing informal expertise with order and legality', a disparity attributed, fairly or unfairly, to a lack of legal expertise in SBATs.[31] Ruth Lister, a non-lawyer, was highly critical in her study of London SBAT hearings of the way in which the Department ran proceedings, concluding

[26] Cmnd 218 [42].
[27] Cmnd. 218 [39–40].
[28] Cmnd 218 [42].
[29] National Assistance Appeals Tribunals replaced Unemployment Assistance Tribunals in 1948 and were in turn replaced by SBATs in 1966. They are now the Social Security and Child Support Tribunal (SSCST) in the Social Entitlement Chamber of the F-TT (see below).
[30] R Lister, *Justice for the Claimant: A Study of Supplementary Benefit Appeals Tribunals* (Child Poverty Action Group 1974); A Bradley, 'Reform of Supplementary Benefit Tribunals – The Key Issues' (1976) 27 *Northern Ireland Law Quarterly* 96; M Adler, E Burns and R Johnson, 'The Conduct of Tribunal Hearings' in *Justice, Discretion and Poverty* (n 20).
[31] N Lewis, 'Supplementary Benefits Appeal Tribunals' [1973] *Public Law* 257, 258.

that the threefold Franks criteria were not being met. Neither fairness nor impartiality could be guaranteed in proceedings held before a three-person panel where no one was legally qualified, hence heavily dependent for advice on the clerk and departmental presenting officer, both of whom were employees of the organising Department, the DHSS. An orderly framework for proceedings was necessary for fairness, set out in basic rules of procedure open to claimants, and a presidential structure should be adopted to underline the need for independence.[32]

A rising tide of criticism led the DHSS to commission a survey of SBATs from Professor Kathleen Bell, a sociologist, who recommended 'a planned programme of judicialisation' for an integrated system of SBATs and NILTs. Stage 1 of her three-stage programme for reform would strengthen existing tribunals by appointing legal practitioners as supervisors; Stage 2 would bring in legally qualified chairpersons; Stage 3 would introduce appeal on a point of law to the National Insurance Commissioners.[33] Throughout there would be an emphasis on training.

The Bell Report, itself an important stage in the move to judicialisation, was followed up with a piecemeal pattern of measures for reform. The Senior President was made a judicial appointment, the chairpersons were legally qualified, procedures were standardised and a procedural manual made available at hearings, and appeal lay to legally qualified Commissioners, whose important decisions were recorded. circulated and published. Reinforced by supervision, training and some outstanding appointments, these gradual reforms undoubtedly made social security tribunals more orderly, independent and fairer, but they also moved tribunals closer to courts. The key feature marking tribunals off from courts was not yet rectified, however: tribunals were not autonomous; they remained a departmental responsibility.

Tribunals as Courts

It took a new review, commissioned by the Lord Chancellor in 2000 from Sir Andrew Leggatt, a High Court judge, to end this position. Much like Franks, the Leggatt Committee was asked to 'review the delivery of justice through tribunals other than ordinary courts of law' and to ensure that 'fair, timely, proportionate and effective arrangements' were in place for the resolution of citizen/state disputes. This time the terms of reference went further, clearly marking out tribunals as court-like machinery for adjudication. They would operate within

[32] R Lister, 'Supplementary Benefit Appeal Tribunals: An Urgent Case for Reform' in *Justice, Discretion and Poverty* (n 20).

[33] K Bell, *Research Study on Supplementary Benefit Appeal Tribunals: Review of Main Findings: Conclusions: Recommendations* (HMSO 1975). National Insurance Commissioners were barristers of 10+ years standing, some very distinguished: see R Micklethwait, *The National Insurance Commissioners* (Stevens, 1976).

a framework that, 'together with the superior courts' would form 'a coherent structure for the delivery of administrative justice', an objective that Leggatt took to mean 'a system that is independent, coherent, professional, cost-effective and user-friendly'.[34] The stage was set for a centralised tribunal service, which would free tribunal administrators from departments by offering them a career structure and would link tribunals to courts by creating a tribunal judiciary. Not without protest from Departments, some of which, especially the Home Office, fought hard to keep control of their adjudicative systems, a single Courts and Tribunals Service within the Ministry of Justice was set up in 2006 and made responsible for administration. The legislation necessary for the restructuring reached the statute book as the Tribunals, Courts and Enforcement Act (TCEA) in 2007.

The TCEA provided for a two-tier appellate tribunal system covering the main (but not all) tribunals, in the care of a Senior President who is a senior member of the judiciary appointed by the Lord Chancellor. The First-tier Tribunal (F-TT) is a first instance general tribunal comprising seven chambers structured around subject areas. Appeal lies from the F-TT to the Upper Tribunal (UT), an appellate tribunal arranged in four chambers handling different subject areas and thence to the Court of Appeal and Supreme Court.[35] The UT is designated a 'superior court of record' with equivalent status to the High Court. Emphasising this new status, the re-organisation provided for 'tribunal judges' appointed and dismissible by the Lord Chancellor on the advice of the Judicial Appointments Commission and, significantly, with the same guarantees of judicial independence as High Court judges.[36] For the first time there was a degree of interchangeability and in recent years the UT has acquired a substantial judicial review jurisdiction.

The significant steps towards embedding tribunals in the judicial system were reinforced in 2011, when the Courts and Tribunals Services were merged. A further step came in 2016, with a joint statement from the Lord Chancellor, Lord Chief Justice and Senior President of Tribunals promising a single justice system with a single judiciary, trained, and serviced with adequate technology.[37] Since then, events have moved fast. The 'One Judiciary' programme aims to bring courts and tribunals closer together and demonstrate that judges, whether they sit in courts or tribunals, are 'part of a single judicial family'.[38] A single court system with a unified leadership structure is to be headed by the Lord Chief Justice of England and Wales and the Senior President's office downgraded to Head of

[34] Terms of Reference, Sir Andrew Leggatt, *Tribunals for Users, One System, One Service* (HMSO, 2001) 1.

[35] There are exceptions: see notably s 2 of the Courts and Judicial Review Act 2022, reversing *Cart* (above n 20).

[36] Under s 3(1) of the Constitutional Reform Act 2005.

[37] Ministry of Justice, *Transforming Our Justice System*, Statement by the Lord Chancellor, Lord Chief Justice of England and Wales and Senior President of Tribunals (15 September 2016) 5.

[38] Ministry of Justice, *Pursuing One Judiciary*, Statement by the Lord Chancellor, the Lord Chief Justice of England and Wales and Senior President of Tribunals (8 July 2022).

Division status.[39] Differences of function remain. Tribunals still examine facts and have jurisdiction to decide cases on the 'merits' while courts are the final arbiters of law. Essentially, however, all that remains of their origin is 'specialisation' in a limited sense of a circumscribed statutory jurisdiction and a margin of procedural flexibility. In all but name, tribunals are now courts.

Adversarial Justice: The Default Position

Given the influence of lawyers at every stage of the reform process, it is hardly surprising that the road to judicialisation was also a road to adversarial procedure. The adversarial model is, after all, the paradigm for judicial process throughout the common law world, and Michael Asimow, in a study of administrative adjudication in groups in Australia, the US and the UK together as common law countries where a lawyer-controlled proceeding before a relatively passive and independent adjudicator is the paradigm for administrative justice.[40]

Judges are not at liberty in an adversarial system to conduct 'own initiative' inquiries and are strongly discouraged from 'conceiving and deciding an issue not raised by the parties'.[41] As Stebbings notes in her study of early tax adjudication discussed above, this sense of the judge as neutral between parties who shape and conduct the proceedings marks an important dividing line between adversarial and inquisitorial models of justice. In inquisitorial procedure, the object of inquiry is to ascertain the facts and establish the truth. Many would agree with Jolowicz that it is a 'major defect of the adversary system that the judge has no duty to try to ascertain the truth'.[42]

Again, in inquisitorial procedure, the same person exercises investigatory and adjudicatory functions as part of a single process managed and controlled by an investigator/adjudicator with responsibility for selecting and assembling relevant evidence.[43] The adjudicator is a managerial figure with responsibility for controlling all stages of the investigation. The litigants have a much-reduced role and oral hearings assume less significance; they are, in other words, less participatory.[44]

[39] At the time of writing, this proposal was out to consultation: Ministry of Justice, *Tribunals Leadership: Consultation on Reform of the Office of Senior President of Tribunals*, CP 829 (11 May 2023).

[40] M Asimow, 'Five Models of Administrative Adjudication' (2015) 63 *American Journal of Comparative Law* 3, 4.

[41] *Shinelock Ltd v Revenue and Customs* [2023] UKUT 107 (TCC) [119] citing *Satyam Enterprises v Barton* [2021] EWCA Civ 287.

[42] JA Jolowicz, 'Adversarial and Inquisitorial Models of Civil Procedure' (2003) 52 *International & Comparative Law Quarterly* 281, 283; M Groves, 'The Duty to Inquire in Tribunal Proceedings' (2011) *Sydney Law Review* 211.

[43] Asimow, 'Five Models of Administrative Adjudication' (n 40).

[44] See for comparison of the two procedures, Jolowicz, 'Adversarial and Inquisitorial Models' (n 42); N Bedford and R Creyke, *Inquisitorial Processes in Australian Tribunals* (Australian Institute of Judicial Administration, 2006) 4–5.

No system is wholly adversarial or inquisitorial and there are some signs in recent times of a tendency towards convergence. It is generally accepted today, for example, that every well-functioning administrative justice system will be 'contradictory', which means that parties to the case must be kept properly informed and given an opportunity to comment and make representations, though not necessarily in oral proceedings. It is also generally accepted that an adjudicator should be 'impartial', though there may be disagreement over the form impartiality should take.[45]

Convergence is partly due to Anglo-American influence, spread through international institutions such as the European Court of Human Rights (ECtHR). The Parole Board for England and Wales, for example, is a semi-autonomous agency with tribunal-like characteristics which sits to decide on prisoners' suitability for release on licence. Following a ruling from the ECtHR,[46] that its 'important judicial functions' must be discharged by a body 'with the essential attributes of a court', the Parole Board, which for many years acted as adviser to the Home Secretary, now makes its own independent decisions which bind the Secretary of State.; The Board's procedures must be 'fair' and must ensure that a prisoner is able 'properly to participate in the proceedings of the Board'.[47] In practice, procedure is largely adversarial: parties can put questions to each other at an oral hearing, call and question witnesses and hear each other's witnesses and representations.[48] But the Board must also be 'independent and impartial' and its closeness to the Justice Secretary, who appoints and can dismiss the Board's members, has provoked well-merited challenges in the domestic courts.[49]

In the UK context, reforms to civil procedure introducing the concept of the managerial judge have also contributed to convergence.[50] Prior to the reforms, for example, it seems there was no case management in tax tribunals:

> The parties would have been expected on the day of the hearing to provide whatever evidence by way of documentation each thought was relevant: whether there was any exchange of evidence or the production of a statement of case or skeleton arguments was left to the parties to agree.[51]

[45] For a spirited defence of French 'republican' justice against the adversarialism of the European Court of Human Rights, see M Lasser, *Judicial Transformations, The Rights Revolution in the Courts of Europe* (Oxford University Press, 2009); J Massot, 'The Powers and Duties of the French Administrative Law Judge' in S Rose-Ackerman and P Lindseth (eds), *Comparative Administrative Law* (Edward Elgar 2nd edn, 2017) 435–8.

[46] *Weeks v UK* (1987) 10 EHRR 293.

[47] *R (Pearce v The Parole Board* [2023] UKSC 13 [3].

[48] Rule 24 of the Parole Board Rules 2019, SI 2019/1038.

[49] *R (DSD and others) v The Parole Board for England and Wales and others* [2018] EWHC 694 (Admin). *R (Wakenshaw) v Secretary of State for Justice* [2018] EWHC 2089 (Admin). But see now s 54(2)(c) of the Victims and Prisoners Act 2024, which limits the ministerial power of dismissal to cases where 'the Secretary of State considers it necessary to do so for the maintenance of public confidence in the Board'.

[50] Jolowicz, (n 42) 295 referencing as seminal Lord Woolf, *Access to Justice, Report to the Lord Chancellor on the Civil Justice System in England and Wales* (London, HMSO 1996).

[51] R Thomas, 'Tax Tribunals and Justice for Litigants in Person' in D de Cogan and P Harris (eds), *Tax Justice and Tax Law: Understanding Unfairness in Tax Systems* (Hart Publishing, 2020) 250.

The Procedural Rules of Tax Tribunals now recognise that case management is necessary and that different types of case may require different management regimes with different procedures. The Procedural Rules of the Immigration Chamber authorise tribunals to require a party to produce documents, information or evidence; state the issues on which it requires evidence or submissions and the nature of the evidence or submissions it requires; permit or require the parties to provide expert evidence; on its own initiative require any person to attend as a witness at a hearing and order any person to answer any questions or produce any documents in that person's possession or control which relate to any issue in the proceedings.[52] These provisions, if not precisely inquisitorial, are at least highly managerial in character.

Nonetheless, considerable scope remains for a clash of values. A Mental Health Review Tribunal (MHRT), for example, sits to determine whether someone should be detained in terms of the Mental Health Act 1983. It is made up of a legal chairperson, a medical member, usually a trained psychiatrist from the hospital where the appellant is to be detained and an 'expert member', who may be a social worker, probation officer or someone familiar with the mental health sector in other ways. It is arguable that such a tribunal is not – and perhaps never can be – impartial to the extent that adversarial proceedings require. This suspicion may well be accentuated by the ambiguity of the semi-inquisitorial procedures used by MHRTs. Patients are entitled to an oral hearing with legal representation and often free legal aid (adversarial) but there is a statutory obligation for one of the members, usually the medical member, to conduct a 'pre-hearing examination' of the patient; this can be conducted by video link with the patient's permission. The report is subsequently sent to the panel and circulated to the participants with the evidence contained in three prescribed written reports.[53] These inquisitorial structures and procedures have been questioned by lawyers on grounds of lack of independence. and impartiality.[54]

In *Gillies*,[55] the problem reached the House of Lords in a case involving the medical member of a Disability Appeal Tribunal, whose presence was challenged for potential bias because she had previously acted as adviser to the Benefits Agency, at that time an executive agency of the defendant Department of Work and Pensions. The House skirted round the problem by drawing a distinction between 'impartiality', defined as the tribunal's approach to deciding the cases before it, as independence or the structural or institutional framework which secured this impartiality 'not only in the minds of the tribunal members but also

[52] Rules 4(3)(d), 14(1)(a)(b)(c), 15(1)(a)(b) of The Tribunal Procedure (First-tier Tribunal) (Immigration and Asylum Chamber) Rules 2014, SI 2014/2604.

[53] N O'Brien, 'Personal Reflections on Life as a Mental Health Tribunal (MHT) Judge' *Tribunal Journal* (Judicial College 2023, Issue 2).

[54] G Richardson and D Machin, 'Doctors on Tribunals: A Confusion of Roles' (2000) *Public Law* 494, 507–8; J Peay, 'Mental Health Review Tribunals: Just or Efficient Safeguards?' (1981) 5 *Law and Human Behaviour* 161; C Turner, 'Seen to be Fair?' (2005) 50(11) *Journal of the Law Society of Scotland* 24.

[55] *Gillies v Secretary of State for Work and Pensions* [2006] UKHL 2; [2006] 1 WLR 731.

in the perception of the public.'[56] The impartiality of the tribunal would not be compromised by the member's specialist knowledge or experience; indeed, it was an asset available to the other tribunal members to draw upon when they were considering the evidence as a whole. This is arguably a questionable decision and is, in any case, out of line with popular opinion, where an increasing expectation of structural independence can be detected. Public opinion, in other words, is not satisfied that an adjudicator who is not structurally independent can be impartial.

Narelle Bedford and Robin Creyke concluded at the end of an extensive empirical study, that tribunals in Australia do not generally operate in an inquisitorial fashion, one reason being that tribunals are 'sited in an adjudicative system the final tiers of which traditionally operate in an adversarial fashion.'[57] Much the same could be said of the UK, where appeal also lies to the higher courts. Recent practice has been to paste inquisitorial features onto the basic adversarial model under the cover of soft adversarial language. Thus, the term 'enabling procedure' was invoked by the Leggatt Committee to cover active help from tribunals and tribunal chairpersons to unrepresented and inexperienced claimants in presenting their case, though Leggatt cautioned tribunals to retain their neutrality and maintain a proper. balance between the parties in the interest of 'fairness'.[58] And the Committee saw no reason to unsettle the double assumption (i) that tribunals should follow where courts had led and (ii) that this was what the public wanted. The Report simply states that 'This [adversarialism] is the style in which United Kingdom (UK) lawyers are trained, and to which both they and the general public are accustomed.'[59]

Participation, Orality and Adversarial Justice

Central to the concept of procedural justice in the adversarial model is the assumption that there will be a 'hearing', terminology indicative of oral procedure. The oral hearing has a participatory dimension reflected in the Tribunal Rules of Procedure, which provide that a tribunal *must* hold a hearing before making a final decision unless each party has consented or has not objected to the matter being decided without a hearing and the Tribunal considers that it is able to decide the matter without one. The Rules also require tribunals to deal with cases 'fairly and justly' and ensure that the parties are able to participate fully in the proceedings.[60]

[56] ibid at [38] (Lady Hale).

[57] Bedford and Creyke *Inquisitorial Processes in Australian Tribunals* (n 44) 64.

[58] Sir Andrew Leggatt *Tribunals for Users* (n 34) [7.2-6].

[59] ibid 85.

[60] Rule 2 of the Tribunal Procedure (Upper Tribunal) Rules, SI 2008/2698 (L25) or the Procedure Rules of the F-TT Chambers, which are largely standardised.

The importance placed by the courts on oral hearings was spelled out by the Supreme Court in the leading case of *Osborn*.[61] In making its decisions about prisoners' entitlements to release on licence, the Parole Board sits in panels.[62] Procedure is governed by a copious statutory and regulatory framework. To fill a gap, however, the Board chose to embellish the regulatory framework by issuing Guidance advising panels that, if an appellant requested a hearing, the panel should 'consider whether it is possible to decide the issues and release on the papers' – a severe restriction of the circumstances in which an oral hearing would be granted. It was held in the Supreme Court that the Board had breached the duty of procedural fairness and Article 5(4) of the European Convention on Human Rights. The Board should hold an oral hearing whenever fairness to the prisoner required one, bearing in mind the facts of the case and the importance of what was at stake. An oral hearing not only assists in the decision-making, but it also reflects 'the prisoner's legitimate interest in being able to participate in a decision with important implications for him, where he has something useful to contribute'.[63] To underline, Lord Reed, in a unanimous judgment, took the opportunity to list the circumstances in which an oral hearing might be necessary.

In the tribunal system, where legal aid was a rarity and legal assistance, exceptional even where permitted, the question of participation was largely a question of necessity. But the wider significance of the concept was underlined by Kathleen Bell in her review of social security tribunals (above). Bell saw participation by appellants in oral tribunal hearings as helping to 'foster civic competence, personal responsibility and active involvement rather than over-dependency on professionals and a belief that people are not able to cope'.[64] Lay members, she thought, encouraged individual participation by showing 'sympathetic understanding of the problem, listening, asking relevant questions, drawing out [the appellant] and generally helping to sort out the case'.[65] Reportedly, however, lay members found it hard to adapt to the increased judicialisation of tribunals and, confused as to their proper role, were progressively marginalised.[66] With the approbation of Leggatt,[67] lay members have virtually disappeared from tribunals to be replaced by legally qualified judges and members with 'special expertise'. Thus, the traditional 'community member' of an MHRT, whose function was obvious, has been replaced by the 'expert member' with 'added value' in the shape of knowledge and experience of the mental health sector.

[61] *Osborn v The Parole Board* [2013] UKSC 61.

[62] *R (Pearce) v The Parole Board* [2023] UKSC 13; [2014] AC 1115 [3] (Lord Hodge). The Parole Board was established by the Criminal Justice and Public Order Act 1994.

[63] *Osborn v The Parole Board* [2013] UKSC 61; [2014] AC 1115 [2] (Lord Reed).

[64] Bell, *Research Study* (n 33) 18.

[65] ibid.

[66] N Wikeley and R Young, 'The Marginalisation of Lay Members in Social Security Appeal Tribunals' (1992) 14 *Journal of Social Welfare and Family Law* 127; Annual Report of the Senior President of Tribunals, *Tribunals Transformed* (2010) [62]–[65].

[67] *Tribunals for Users* (n 34) [90–91].

Perhaps more important, Bell saw lay members as acting with juries and lay magistrates as representatives of the public, to create a sense of ownership of 'our' justice service and helping to provide an 'accountability check' on its operation.[68] In this way, the presence of non-professional members in tribunals exemplifies the concept of open justice. The role of the tribunal as part of a wider network of governmental accountability is an important one to which we return at a later stage.

It is, however, one thing to talk of participation in a hearing that involves 'taking a further look at the facts' or 'arriving at a fresh decision on the extent of need';[69] it is quite another for a tribunal user to manage an essentially legal process in the environment of contemporary public administration, which operates in a bureaucratic framework of complex and confusing rules and procedures, embedded in legal texts that are difficult to understand and navigate without professional assistance.[70] The appeals procedures may themselves be complex and confusing. Challenging a mental health decision, for example, was once likened by an experienced ombudsman to entering a 'labyrinth that warrants review'.[71] It involves comparing the merits of several in-house NHS complaints systems, a network of public (or possibly private) ombudsmen, and tribunals, all with different procedures and time limits. Appellants are moreover likely to be 'one shotters', with little idea of what will happen at a tribunal hearing: 'in some cases, they do not even realise that there will be a hearing and they are often confused by the paperwork they are sent'.[72]

There are many further barriers to participation. Cost is a major issue.[73] Tribunals are not necessarily cheap; indeed, the Supreme Court recently ruled that employment tribunal fees were so high as to interfere unjustifiably with the constitutional right of access to justice.[74] The issue of legal aid in tribunals has been endlessly debated, has occupied the time of numerous committees and is too well-known to require amplification here.[75] Yet the case for publicly funded legal assistance is strengthened today both by the increasingly legalistic style of public administration and also by the transmutation of tribunals into courts. In a time

[68] See for discussion, House of Commons Justice Committee, *Open Justice: Court Reporting in the Digital Age*, HC 339 (2022/3) [11].

[69] Franks Report, Cmnd 518, [182] describing the work of National Assistance Appeal Tribunals.

[70] C Harlow and R Rawlings, 'Proceduralism and Automation. Challenges to the Values of Administrative Law' in E Fisher, J King and A Young (eds), *The Fundamentals and Future of Public Law* (Oxford University Press 2019).

[71] A Abraham, 'Taking the Bull by the Horns' (2008) *Tribunals Journal*, Issue 1.

[72] M Adler and J Gulland, *Tribunal Users' Experiences, Perceptions and Expectations: A Literature Review* (Council on Tribunals 2003) [2.3].

[73] T Hickman, 'Public Law's Disgrace', UK Const L Blog (9 Feb 2017) and 'Public Law's Disgrace: Part 2', UK Const L Blog (26 Oct. 2017).

[74] *R (Unison) v Lord Chancellor* [2017] UKSC 51; [2020] AC 869 the sums due are tabulated at 884–885 [18].

[75] See for a full, if partisan, discussion, the *Justice* /All Souls Review, *Administrative Justice – Some Necessary Reforms* (Clarendon Press 1988) ch 9.

of financial stringency, however, when civil legal aid is shrinking fast and self-representation is becoming more common in courts, the extension of legal aid in tribunals is unlikely to be a top priority for government.

The problems facing would-be participants in adversarial proceedings are certainly not discounted by the courts. In a set of challenges mounted by Detention Action to the Home Office Fast Track Asylum Procedures, the essential steps in a fast-track asylum claim were enumerated. They included checking whether the general detention criteria were properly applied; making representations, where appropriate, that the appellant is unlawfully detained; taking instructions from the appellant, preparing his or her statement, checking it and having it signed; applying and arranging for bail if the representations are rejected; arranging for expert evidence and necessary translations; and last but by no means least, making an application where appropriate for the appeal to be transferred out of the Fast Track appeal procedure, and considering the Home Office response.[76] Onerous for a lawyer, these steps might have to be carried out by a detainee without legal assistance in a matter of days. Largely because the short time limits rendered it virtually impossible to prepare and present an adequate response to the Home Office case, the Fast Track Process was ruled 'structurally unfair' hence unlawful by the Court of Appeal. It is still in abeyance.

In *Kiarie and Byndloss*, the Supreme Court held that an out-of-country appeal may be unlawful if it is not 'effective'. An effective appeal requires an opportunity to give live evidence; to give evidence on screen would prejudice the appellant, as the tribunal would want to hear how he 'explained himself orally' and, more particularly, would want to assess whether he could 'survive cross-examination in relation to it'.[77] Lord Wilson's judgment contains a lengthy and informed discussion of the barriers to participation in out-of-country immigration appeals. Lawyer/client communication is likely to be difficult, preparations for the hearing costly and problematic and participation by the appellant at the hearing only possible with the aid of modern technology such as a video link or Skype. It was left for the F-TT to determine on a case-by-case basis whether an online appeal is likely to be effective.[78]

Towards Merger?

In recent years, ideas of administrative justice have been changing and the subject has undergone a substantial reconceptualisation. Emphasis has shifted from the

[76] *Detention Action v First-Tier Tribunal (Immigration and Asylum Chamber) & Others* [2015] EWHC 1689 (Admin) [23]–[38]; *The Lord Chancellor v Detention Action* [2015] EWCA Civ 840; [2015] 1 WLR 5341 [20].

[77] *R (Kiarie and Byndloss) v SSHD* [2017] UKSC 42; [2017] 1 WLR 2380 [61]–[75] (Lord Wilson).

[78] The criteria are set out in *Secretary of State for the Home Department v Nare* [2011] UKUT 443 (IAC) [21].

formal adjudicative stages of dispute resolution in courts and tribunals to a more user-orientated, 'bottom-up' approach. Influenced by the work of Jerry Mashaw in the United States, who was amongst the first to emphasise the importance of getting the initial decision right,[79] Michael Adler defines administrative justice as 'the justice inherent in administrative decision making', a generous definition capable of encompassing multiple layers of dispute resolution, different formats and different approaches.[80]

More pragmatically, government was looking for a holistic system of 'proportionate dispute resolution' that would embrace 'not just courts and tribunals but the millions of decisions taken by thousands of civil servants and other officials' and would be 'quick, cheap, simple and stress-free' for users.[81] As the Lord Chancellor put it in his Preface to the 2004 White Paper, *Transforming Public Services*: 'The public do not want to go to a Tribunal, they want their complaint or dispute resolved quickly and fairly.' The White Paper promised a user-orientated system taking as its starting point the types of problems and disputes people faced and the outcomes they wanted to achieve and focusing on the various options available to avoid or resolve disputes, their effectiveness in addressing peoples' needs and any gaps in provision.

A consumer-orientated, 'bottom up' approach is now a priority for public administration with 'Getting it right' as the first principle of good administration.[82] Every department or public body must nowadays have in place and advertise a system for handling complaints 'owned', designed and operated, or at least controlled by a specified department or public body, with publicly available particulars. Complaining has assumed a participatory dimension as a tool for communication with a vocabulary redolent of values associated with adjudication. Complaints are to be investigated thoroughly and 'fairly' to 'establish the facts of the case' and reviewed by 'someone not involved in the events leading to the complaint'. Good complaints handling requires acting 'fairly and proportionately', treating the complainant 'impartially and without unlawful discrimination or prejudice' and ensuring that decisions are 'proportionate, appropriate and fair'.[83]

Many public services now have in place systems of internal review of challenged decisions, which are coming to be seen as the first rung on the ladder of administrative justice. Some, such as the Revenue Adjudicator's Office, are genuinely

[79] JL Mashaw, *Bureaucratic Justice Managing Social Security Disability Claims* (Yale University Press 1983). RA Kagan, 'Varieties of Bureaucratic Justice, Building on Mashaw's Typology' in NR Patrillo (ed), *Administrative Law from the Inside Out* (Cambridge University Press 2007).

[80] M Adler, 'Understanding and Analysing Administrative Justice' in M Adler (ed), *Administrative Justice in Context* (Hart Publishing, 2010) 159. And see T Mullen, 'A Holistic Approach to Administrative Justice', ibid.

[81] Department of Constitutional Affairs, *Transforming Public Services*, Cmnd 6243 (2004) [1.5-6] (Lord Falconer).

[82] Principle 1 of the *Principles of Good Administration* and of *Good Complaint Handling* published on the website of the Parliamentary and Health Services Ombudsman (PHSO) and other public services ombudsmen.

[83] PHSO, *Good Complaint Handling*, (n 82).

adjudicative. The office is, according to its website, 'external to [HM Revenue and Customs] (HMRC) with the independent personal authority to review complaints' about HMRC But the Adjudicator, who manages the procedure, operates more like an ombudsman than a tribunal and attempts to mediate an agreed outcome (though this is not, of course, a uniquely inquisitorial trait).[84]

A less-adjudicative form of internal review is often no more than a reassessment on the papers by a second official. Such kinds of internal review, as a strictly administrative process, are likely to increase with the spread of automated decision-making within public administration. They claim to be 'quick, cheap and simple'. Almost certainly cheaper than a tribunal hearing, they are not necessarily easy to use and often ineffective An early review of the mandatory reconsideration process set up by the Department of Work and Pensions to reassess certain classes of welfare decision heard, for example, that claimants found the system 'overly complex' and, as with an adversarial process, often found difficulty in accessing advice and gathering evidence inside the short time limits imposed.[85] This makes it a matter of concern that internal review may discourage claimants from appealing to tribunals.[86] Tribunals, as an external and independent body, afford a more disinterested review of the administrative process and, perhaps because they involve an oral hearing, are more likely to decide for the claimant.[87]

The main alternative to a tribunal hearing is an ombudsman investigation, a statutory process managed by the ombudsman's office, which has the considerable advantage of being cost-free to the complainant. This is not the place for an extended account of ombudsman procedure other than to say that it is investigatory and inquisitorial and almost invariably documentary. Ombudsmen do not need a court order to access departments or public bodies, talk to officials and inspect official files. Formal hearings at which the parties are present and participate are a rarity. An investigation can be informal to the point that it is conducted through telephone conversations and (video) interviews – though this is a point of convergence; something similar may sometimes be true of tribunals.[88]

[84] See V Bondy and M Sunkin, *The Dynamics of Judicial Review Litigation* (Public Law Project 2009); V Bondy, L Platt and M Sunkin, *The Value and Effects of Judicial Review: The Nature of Claims, Their Outcomes and Consequences* (Public Law Project 2015).

[85] Social Security Advisory Committee, *Decision Making and Mandatory Reconsideration* (2016). And see V Bondy and L Mulcahy with M Doyle and V Reid, *Mediation and Judicial Review: An Empirical Research Study* (Public Law Project 2009). It should be noted that mediation is about to become mandatory as part of the small claims process: Ministry of Justice, 'Increasing the use of mediation in the civil justice system, Government response to consultation,' CP 897 (July 2023, updated Dec 2023).

[86] A point made many years ago by R Sainsbury, 'Internal Reviews and the Weakening of the Social Security Claimants' Rights of Appeal' in G Richardson and H Genn, *Administrative Law and Government Action* (Clarendon Press 1994).

[87] R Thomas, 'Mandatory Reconsideration: What Do The Latest Stats Tell Us?' (UKAJI website, 16 July 2018).

[88] Compare PHSO, 'How we look into complaints'. Available on the PHSO website together with 'Transforming our Justice System' (2016) [5.1].

Ombudsman investigations are, however, confidential and must be conducted in private and, although they are, in principle, 'contradictory', the part played by the complainant may be limited. This may raise a suspicion of a pro-administration bias, especially if the complainant has less input than the defending public body. This is a well-known breach of the principles of procedural justice and the English High Court once quashed an ombudsman's decision not to undertake a full investigation on the ground that it was based on a private interview with interested officials, notes of which should have been disclosed to the complainants for them to comment.[89] Ombudsman procedure is beginning to be the subject of complaints[90] and, even if these stem from a public misunderstanding of the ombudsman's role and what ombudsman schemes are set up to provide, they are nonetheless suggestive of a feeling that some of the elements crucial to administrative justice are missing. Somehow the adversarial model is 'fairer'.

Conclusion

Tribunals have been with us for a long time and it is generally assumed that they are here to stay. As this chapter has tried to show, however, the message from history is more nuanced. Over the centuries tribunals have undergone many changes. Today, tribunals are designated courts, under the control of courts, using modified adversarial procedure. We may, however, have reached a tipping point. In a period of rapid technological change and social unrest, the future of tribunals could be very different.

It would seem that barriers to participation in tribunal hearings may be mounting and that opportunities for participation are shrinking., Users of an expanding administrative justice system are consumers looking for 'relatively stress-free, speedy and affordable' methods of dispute resolution; they may be reluctant to become involved in legal proceedings because of the anticipated expense and complexity.[91] Internal reviews are already online procedures, sold to the public as quick, inexpensive and easy for the consumer to use. Requests for oral hearings in tribunals have declined markedly and, as the public becomes more accustomed to the new age of automation, signalling a move to administrative forms of dispute resolution, the shift to administrative process, favoured by administrators for its promise of economy and efficiency, is likely to accelerate. Experiments with online

[89] *R (Turpin) v Commissioner for Local Administration* [2001] EWHC Admin 503.

[90] N Creutzfeldt and C Gill, *Critics of the Ombudsman System: Understanding and Engaging Online Citizen Activists* (Oxford Faculty of Law, 2015); R Kirkham and P Wells, 'Evolving Standards in the Complaints Branch: The Ombudsman, Tribunals and Administrative Justice Section' (2014) 36 *Journal of Social Welfare and Family Law* 19.

[91] H Genn, B Lever and L Gray, *Tribunals for Diverse Users* (Department of Constitutional Affairs, DCA Research Series 1/06 (2006); H Genn 'Quick Cheap and Satisfying' (2006) *Tribunals Journal*, Issue 2; J Aitken, 'Alternative Routes to Fairness' (2019) *Tribunals Journal*, Issue 2?.

dispute resolution are under way, the intention apparently being to use oral hearings 'only when necessary'.[92] Presented as an aid to access, online justice might end by eroding the customary oral hearing and replacing it with a process that is less open, less autonomous and independent, and considerably less participatory.

Not every problem can easily be resolved by technology. Technology does not automatically unpick algorithmic decision-making – rather the reverse. It does not afford an opportunity to come face-to-face with and question official witnesses or provide a justice service for those without technical skills. As the power of government increases and its long arm stretches into more and more aspects of life, there is a greater need for accountability and a growing demand in an age of popular democracy for public participation by members in public affairs. These are outputs that we look to administrative justice to supply.

The adversarial model is not only what the 'general public are accustomed to', though this is in itself enough to 'constrain the possibilities of change'.[93] Our legal culture and system of administrative justice have been built up over the centuries on models of justice and citizen/state relationships that are adversarial in character. The adversarial model symbolises our concept of justice, creating an expectation on the part of the public that administrative justice too will embody judicial impartiality. Courts and tribunals are part of a service that is structurally independent of government and in which the public can actively participate. These are the true strengths of the adversarial model, which are likely to ensure it will survive.

[92] *Transforming Our Justice System* (n 13).

[93] Asimow, 'Five Models' (n 40) 28; G Teubner, 'Legal Irritants: Good Faith in British Law or how Unifying Law Ends Up in New Divergences' (1998) 61 *Modern Law Review* 11.

5

Delays and Backlogs as an Administrative Justice Problem: Reflections on the Case of the UK's Immigration and Asylum Tribunal

JOE TOMLINSON AND ELEANA KASOULIDE

Introduction

Backlogs and delays are ubiquitous, perennial and inherent challenges in modern administrative justice systems.[1] Public demand on decision-making systems – from frontline processing of decisions through to complaints, appeals and judicial review – can fluctuate, as can the resources government commits to supporting these systems. While it may seem unusual to think of public systems in such terms, large-scale public decision-making systems are precariously balanced between these two forces of supply and demand. When the balancing act fails, the result is that delays and backlogs emerge. The consequences can be significant for both efficient government and justice for individuals.

Despite the scale and public prominence of the issues and their potential for harmful effects, there is remarkably little scholarly thought directly addressing delays and backlogs in administrative justice systems.[2] It is difficult to explain why this is so. Perhaps the issue falls into the classic trap of public administration problems: that 'how law should be administered with enlightenment, with equity, with speed, and without friction, [is] put aside as 'practical detail' which clerks could arrange after doctors had agreed upon principles'.[3] Whatever the cause, this neglect is unfortunate and must be remedied.

[1] We use the term 'administrative justice system' to refer to all processes through which the public have decisions made about their rights and entitlement by public bodies, from 'frontline' decision makers to redress systems and the higher courts.

[2] Most of the literature we draw upon for this chapter is therefore from other disciplines, including other fields concerned with law and justice, but also much more broadly.

[3] W Wilson, 'The Study of Administration' (1887) 2(2) *Political Science Quarterly* 197, 198–99.

We suggest in this chapter that treating delays and backlogs as a significant matter of administrative justice in their own right provokes a number of questions and we seek to delineate four central issues. First: What is a 'delay'? What is a 'backlog'? How do we know when delays and backlogs are occurring? Second: What are the causes of delays and backlogs in administrative justice systems? Third: What are the harmful effects of backlogs and delays, both for citizens and good government? Fourth: What are the strategies for averting and responding to backlogs and delays? These are, we suggest, the four major questions at the centre of the challenge to advance understanding of this issue. It is through examining and developing the evidence we possess about each of them and reflecting on how we articulate the demands of administrative justice in this domain that we can hope to advance understanding of this significant challenge further.

As with any administrative justice inquiry, an important tension arises at the outset in trying to answer the questions we have posed in general terms: although there are common themes across different decision-making systems that are useful to connect, it is also difficult to generalise across different parts of the overall administrative justice system. As such, and in keeping with the theme of this collection, our focus in this chapter will be on reflecting upon these questions in the specific context of first-tier immigration and asylum tribunal appeals in the UK.[4] This tribunal has experienced a range of difficulties with delays and backlogs – in particular, an episode in 2016–2017 that was described by the then Chair of the Public Accounts Committee as 'shocking'.[5] It has also been impacted by multiple reform efforts in recent years, not least because it has become caught up in an increasingly contentious politics of immigration and asylum. Alongside our discussion of the experience within the tribunal, we make broader observations about the nature of delays and backlogs in administrative justice. Our aim is thus to contribute to the understanding of modern tribunals by addressing the issues of delays and backlogs in that particular context, while also pointing to broader questions of administrative justice that arise.

Definition

Preliminary Observations on Definition

All administrative justice systems involve people waiting for some amount of time and, in any system operating at scale, there will be multiple people waiting at any

[4] We do not introduce the context of the UK tribunals system in this chapter as Robert Thomas (Chapter 9 in this volume) covers that topic expertly. The formal name of the tribunal is the 'First-tier Tribunal (Immigration and Asylum)' but, for ease, we will refer it as simply 'the tribunal'.

[5] J Hyde, 'Immigration appeal delays "shocking" as backlog reaches 63,000' (*Law Society Gazette*, 22 December 2016). Available at: www.lawgazette.co.uk/practice/immigration-appeal-delays-shocking-as-backlog-reaches-63000/5059191.article (accessed 17 April 2023) (the article quotes Meg Hillier MP).

given time. Thus, it could be said, at least from one perspective, that all administrative justice systems are inevitably in a constant state of producing delays and backlogs. But what is usually of greater concern is, first, the length of time people are waiting because of the number of unresolved cases and, second, the metrics people apply to suggest inevitable waiting and caseloads have reached a point where they have become problematic delays and backlogs.

It is important, therefore, to note that the way that delays and backlogs are commonly spoken about in the context of administrative justice can conceal a multitude of underlying empirical positions and normative judgments. For instance, while the idea of a 'backlog' is commonly understood as an unresolved build-up of cases, some also use that term simply to mean all cases awaiting a decision.[6] Others use the term as a label to describe a factual position that also implies a normative assessment of systemic failure to process cases satisfactorily.[7] The position is similar with delay and it is often the case that something is treated as a delay when accessing a service takes longer than was originally anticipated or promised, or where the lapse in time is perceived to have been avoidable.[8]

While there is a connection between the terms 'delay' and 'backlog', they are used in different ways. 'Delay' is commonly used as a term to describe both the circumstances of individual cases or a systemic problem of many people waiting. 'Backlog' is a term used to describe a systemic position relating to overall caseloads. Backlogs can, of course, cause delays. And delays can also cause backlogs.

It is further worth noting that the use of the terms 'delay' and 'backlog' often frame how we see the wider issue of speed of processing as an administrative justice issue.[9] Slow processing, associated with delays and backlogs, is the focus of this chapter and the common problem in practice. However, decisions made too quickly are also liable to create problems of justice. For instance, hasty decision-making may be a sign, at least seen as a sign, of a failure to properly consider all factors relevant to a decision.

By drawing attention to these features of how delay and backlogs are commonly discussed, we do not seek to split hairs for the sake of it. Rather, it is to recognise that the interconnected matters of delays and backlogs are fluid, the

[6] For instance, see: PW Walsh and M Sumption, 'The UK's asylum backlog' (The Migration Observatory, 22 February 2023). Available at: https://migrationobservatory.ox.ac.uk/resources/briefings/the-uks-asylum-backlog/ (accessed 8 March 2023).

[7] For instance, see: Health and Social Care Committee, *Clearing the backlog caused by the pandemic* (HC 2021-12 599), paras 16–21; British Medical Association, 'NHS backlog data analysis' (BMA, 2023). Available at: www.bma.org.uk/advice-and-support/nhs-delivery-and-workforce/pressures/nhs-backlog-data-analysis (accessed 13 March 2023).

[8] T Sourdin and N Burstyner, 'Justice Delayed is Justice Denied' (2014) 4 *Victoria University Law and Justice Journal* 49, 53. For an example in relation to passports in the UK see: L Gilder, 'Why is my passport taking so long to arrive?' (BBC News, 2022). Available at: www.bbc.co.uk/news/explainers-62378144 (accessed 28 February 2023).

[9] A Valkeapää and T Seppälä, 'Speed of Decision-Making as a Procedural Justice Principle' (2014) 27 *Social Justice Research* 305.

common usage of the terms can conceal a number of underlying empirical and normative positions and they frame how we think about administrative justice dynamics in a certain way. They are useful terms that reflect substantively important systemic issues, but one of the central challenges in this domain is ensuring we speak about these problems in a way that increases clarity, rather than confusing the issues.

The question of definitions also has a practical facet: What are the appropriate measures for problematic delays and backlogs in any given process? Some parts of the public sector do adopt standards in this respect – now usually referred to in language inspired by New Public Management, such as 'service benchmarks'. But it is a noticeable feature of administrative justice scholarship that it has neither engaged in independently developing, appropriate, sophisticated measures of delay and backlogs, nor has it done much in terms of evaluating the standards which are used in practice.

Defining Delays and Backlogs in the Immigration Tribunal

The UK's first-tier immigration and asylum tribunal is perpetually dealing with a fluctuating caseload and the time taken to resolve cases varies over time. HM Courts and Tribunals Service ('HMCTS') publishes quarterly data, which allows us to examine trends over time. More specifically, this data allows us to look at the number of appeals lodged in the tribunal and the number of disposals over time, as well as any gap between the two, which may indicate delays or backlogs (see Figure 5.1). A 'snapshot' of outstanding caseloads is also taken at the end of March each year, giving us further insight into the issue (see Figure 5.2). This data also allows for further disaggregation between types of appeal and a more nuanced analysis of different time periods.

Figure 5.1 First-tier immigration and asylum tribunal appeals and disposals

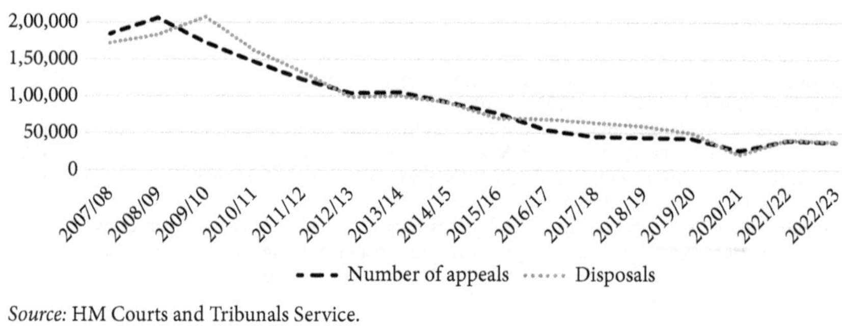

Source: HM Courts and Tribunals Service.

Figure 5.2 First-tier immigration and asylum tribunal's outstanding caseload at the end of the financial year

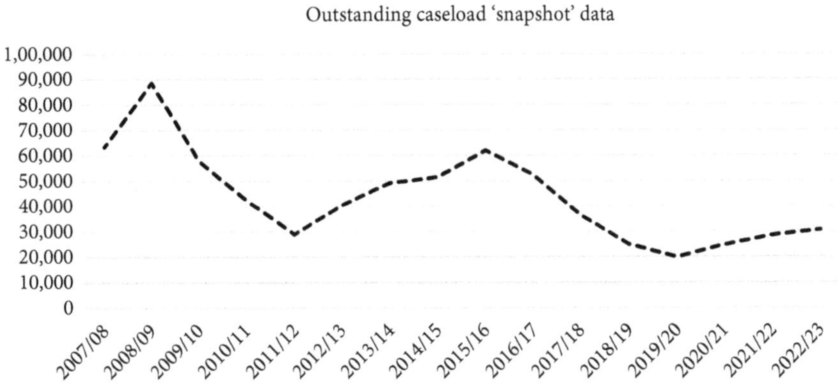

Source: HM Courts and Tribunals Service.

While anyone seeking to analyse delays and backlogs in the first-tier immigration and asylum tribunal will be assisted by the available data, it is noteworthy that there are no published official metrics of what constitutes either an acceptable or expected processing time for an appeal. Instead, discussions of delays and backlogs in the tribunal have mostly revolved around concerns of excessive delays and backlogs. One of the most prominent examples of this emerged in late 2016. Meg Hillier MP, Chair of the House of Commons Public Accounts Committee, stated the tribunal was the source of 'shocking' delays and that the 'response of the government has been pretty poor and it is having a devastating impact on people's lives … [p]eople are coming to my surgery who have not heard when their case will be or have been told to wait months'.[10] It is important to remember that the harms of backlogs and delays – to which we will turn later – do not just accrue in extreme situations and focusing on such situations can obscure the more routine but no less impactful experience of delays.

Causes

Preliminary Observations on Causes

One frequent observed cause of delays and backlogs is insufficient or inappropriately allocated funding.[11] A lack of funding has the potential to severely limit

[10] Figure 5.2 shows the backlog that developed during that period.

[11] See, eg, P Walley, 'Does the Public Sector Need a More Demand-driven Approach to Capacity Management?' (2012) 24(10) *Production Planning & Control* 877. For recent, topical examples from

the capacity of systems to handle incoming cases. Public resource allocation is also, of course, not necessarily determined or responsive to demand levels and resource allocation decisions are inevitably shaped by substantive political preferences.[12] Observations about resource in the context of delays and backlogs in the administrative justice system are typically about understaffing in particular, and how this can limit the capacity of systems to cope with demand.[13] It is also often the case that understaffing is not just a question of more or less staff, but can also relate to the quality of staff and their working environment – high-volumes of low-quality staff could be, in certain circumstances, more likely to produce delays and backlogs than lower numbers of high-quality staff.

Another commonly observed cause of delays and backlogs is an increase in the demand being placed on a system. This can be especially problematic when the relevant process is underprepared to respond, either due to lack of preparation or the uptick in demand being unforeseen. Administrative justice systems are susceptible to a wide range of environmental changes. For instance, in the UK and many other countries, it is widely predicted that increases in demand will continue in certain areas of the public sector because of the change in the demographic profile of the population. In particular, as the population ages and the working age population shrinks, it is broadly expected that a greater proportion of people are going to be relying on public systems. Increases in demand may also occur due to external factors such as tumultuous foreign affairs, as has been the case with the recent Syrian, Afghan, and Ukrainian refugee crises. The COVID-19 pandemic is another obvious recent example.[14] The pandemic increased the demand pressure for services, prevented the proper functioning of certain systems, restricted economic activity, and even stopped some services from operating to safeguard public health. It is worth noting that even where systems are relatively prepared and willing to increase their capacity to match an increase in demand, changes to deliver cannot usually be instantaneous and backlogs and delays may still occur or even worsen within the time it takes for a system to adapt.

the UK's public sector and justice system, see: A Tolhurst, 'The NHS is suffering a huge backlog of elective procedures due to the coronavirus pandemic' (Civil Service World, 2022). Available at: www.civilserviceworld.com/in-depth/article/all-the-major-covid-backlogs-government-must-get-a-grip-of-in-2022 (accessed 28 February 2023); L Dearden, '"Overwhelmed" justice system failing victims of crime, CPS chief warns' (Independent, 2 January 2023). Available at: www.independent.co.uk/news/uk/home-news/criminal-justice-system-delays-overloaded-b2250604.html (accessed 13 March 2023).

[12] See Walley (n 11) 885.

[13] For an example in the context of healthcare, see: S Flinders and S Scobie, 'Hospitals at capacity: understanding delays in patient discharge' (Nuffield Trust, 3 October 2022). Available at: www.nuffieldtrust.org.uk/news-item/hospitals-at-capacity-understanding-delays-in-patient-discharge (accessed 10 March 2023); The King's Fund, 'What's going wrong with A&E waiting times?' (The King's Fund, 26 May 2022). Available at: www.kingsfund.org.uk/projects/urgent-emergency-care/urgent-and-emergency-care-mythbusters (accessed 10 March 2023).

[14] See, eg, Greater Manchester Immigration Aid Unit, 'Wasted childhoods: the impact of COVID-19 asylum delays on children in the North-west of England' (2021). Available at: https://gmiau.org/new-report-wasted-childhoods-the-impact-of-covid-19-asylum-delays-on-children/ (accessed 13 March 2023); National Audit Office, *Investigation into the management of backlogs in driving licence applications* (HC 2022-09 851); Health and Social Care Committee, *Clearing the backlog caused by the pandemic* (n 7).

Some also argue that delays and backlogs can be attributed to 'failure demand' – extra demand created because there was a failure to 'get things right the first time'.[15] Examples of failure demand include not responding to an initial request that causes a person to make a further request or internal administrative errors causing duplication of work. Such 'failures' generate what has been referred to as preventable 'unwanted demand', redirecting resources from 'true demand' and creating backlogs and delays. In a sense, the idea of failure demand links very closely to the administrative justice agenda of 'getting decisions right the first time', which was particularly prominent during the early 2000s – both effectively stress the costs of initial decision-making errors and the need to avoid them.[16]

Substantive policymaking can also have major impacts on backlogs and delays. There are a variety of instances where government policy has been influential on the extent of backlogs, even if indirectly or by virtue of unintended consequences. For instance, cuts in legal aid in the UK have been observed to lead to an increase in people representing themselves in judicial processes and consequently more delays, on the basis that unrepresented claimants often need much more support from courts and tribunals.[17] Judicial interventions into public sector systems, and how public bodies respond to them, can also have the effect of generating surges in demand, and thus resulting in backlogs and delays. The UK's Supreme Court's decision in *R (UNISON) v Lord Chancellor*[18] was seen by many as a triumph for access to justice in the context of employment rights, but significant backlogs and delays in the employment tribunal soon followed.[19]

Causes of Delays and Backlogs in the Immigration Tribunal

There has been much discussion among practitioners about the causes of delays and backlogs in the first-tier immigration and asylum tribunal, but less scholarly

[15] G Morris and P Walley, 'Implementing Failure Demand Reduction as Part of a Demand Management Strategy' (2022) 42(1) *Public Money & Management* 22, 25; P Walley et al., 'Failure Demand: A Concept Evaluation in UK Primary Care' (2019) 32(1) *International Journal of Health Care Quality Assurance* 21, 24–26; J Laufs, K Bowers, D Birks, and S D Johnson, 'Understanding the Concept of "Demand" in Policing: A Scoping Review and Resulting Implications for Demand Management' (2020) 31(8) *Policing & Society* 895, 907–909.

[16] See, eg, Administrative Justice and Tribunals Council, *Right First Time* (2011).

[17] P Foster et al., 'Backlog Britain: How public sector delays spiralled to record levels' (*Financial Times*, 26 November 2022). Available at: www.ft.com/content/ffdbd69b-1c7e-4fb2-b10a-d62c644bb988 (accessed 28 February 2023); The Law Society, 'Family court system still facing significant backlogs and delays' (The Law Society, 16 December 2022). Available at: www.lawsociety.org.uk/contact-or-visit-us/press-office/press-releases/family-court-system-still-facing-significant-backlogs-and-delays (accessed 14 March 2023).

[18] [2017] UKSC 51.

[19] D Pyper and F McGuinness, *Employment Tribunals after R (Unions) v Lord Chancellor* (House of Commons Library Briefing Paper, No CBP 8296, 2018). See further: A Adams and J Prassl, 'Vexatious Claims: Challenging the Case for Employment Tribunal Fees' (2017) 80(3) *Modern Law Review* 412.

analysis.[20] Several causes can, however, be observed as being particularly relevant to the jurisdiction.

In terms of what may drive up demand for accessing the tribunal, the quality of initial administrative decision-making is likely an important factor – particularly given that such decision-making in the UK Home Office and related agencies is widely observed to be of variable quality.[21] Not all tribunal appeals suggest there is poor-quality decision-making – appeals may not have merit and, even when they do succeed, the successful appeal may be due to factors such as the availability of new evidence at the tribunal stage. Nonetheless, avoidable errors in decision-making by the UK's Home Office do occur and can drive up the workload of the tribunal. Systemically poor decision-making, of which there have been multiple episodes in recent years, can have significant impacts in this respect.[22] For instance, a systemic failure in decision-making around an English language test led to the tribunal hearing 9,277 appeals between April 2014 and March 2019.[23]

Another potentially important factor on the 'demand' side of the picture is the behaviour of litigants before the tribunal. For instance, appellants decide, in the first instance, whether to seek to access the tribunal and which points to raise. Government respondents may then take varying times to respond to an appeal and show more or less willingness to seek to compromise and settle the dispute. The way parties behave can have the effect of both speeding up or slowing down the disposal of appeals, affecting the time taken to resolve specific disputes and how many matters are in the tribunal's overall backlog.

On the 'supply' side, one of the major issues in the tribunal has been the number of judges made available to hear appeals. Judicial capacity in the UK is measured by the overall number of 'sitting days' available across the relevant period.[24] Judges in the tribunal can be 'salaried' and available for a fixed number of days or 'fee-paid' and available as a resource which can be more flexibly deployed. How many overall 'sitting days' are assigned to the tribunal each year is a matter of financial resourcing, predicting the demand the tribunal will face, and the availability of judicial personnel.[25] When the forecasting is inaccurate, the lack of judicial resources can have serious effects on backlogs and delays as there may

[20] There are some exceptions, see, eg, R Thomas, 'Immigration appeals and delays: On the verge of a crisis?' (UKAJI, 18 May 2017). Available at: https://ukaji.org/2017/05/18/immigration-appeals-and-delays-on-the-verge-of-a-crisis/ (accessed 26 June 2023).

[21] There is an enormous amount of commentary on this issue, as well as large number of reports from watchdogs which explore it in detail. For an excellent synthesis of that material, see: R Thomas, *Administrative Law in Action* (1st edn, Bloomsbury, 2022).

[22] On which, see: R Thomas, 'Analysing Systemic Administrative Justice Failures: Explanatory Factors and Prospects for Future Research' (2021) 43(3) *Journal of Social Welfare and Family Law* 339.

[23] For a detailed account of this failure and its impact on the tribunals and courts, see: J Maxwell and J Tomlinson, *Experiments in Automating Immigration Systems* (Bristol University Press, 2022), Ch 2.

[24] K Sadler, '"Sitting Days": How are they decided' (*Inside HMCTS*, 18 June 2021). Available at: https://insidehmcts.blog.gov.uk/2021/06/18/sitting-days-how-are-they-decided/ (accessed 26 June 2023).

[25] ibid.

not be enough judges to decide cases. An important part of the backdrop for the backlog 'crisis' of 2016–2017 was that the number of judges had been reduced by a third from 479 to 319.[26]

The wider policy environment is a particularly important factor for the immigration and asylum tribunal. Immigration and asylum are two of the most vexed political issues. Government policy is constantly changing, new primary legislation is often passed and the Immigration Rules are notoriously complex and subject to frequent amendment.[27] At the ground level, all this change results in fluctuations in the number and nature of appeals to the tribunal. This can true both of substantive changes to immigration policy – such as Brexit, which led to the creation of a new route to settlement in the UK that involved the creation of new appeal rights[28] – but also to changes to government policy on what forms of appeals are available in certain cases. In recent years, tribunal appeals have been removed by the UK government in many immigration contexts, and there has been a shift towards internal 'administrative review' systems.[29] This has placed fewer demands on the tribunal and there has been a significant drop in the overall number of appeals in recent years (see Figure 5.1).

Harms of Delays and Backlogs

Preliminary Observations on Harms

A key harm of backlogs and delays across the administrative justice system can be the health and wellbeing of individuals who are seeking to use them. It goes without saying that a backlogged healthcare system has a detrimental effect on health, but it can also be the case that severe delays in accessing any type of administrative justice can have health implications for people. For instance, the negative effect of delays on the health and wellbeing of asylum seekers awaiting decision is often observed. Asylum seekers find themselves in a state of limbo, unable to start building a new life in the UK or leave and seek protection elsewhere. As a result, many asylum seekers experience severe hopelessness, anxiety and depression which can

[26] For further analysis, see Thomas, 'Immigration appeals and delays: On the verge of a crisis?' (n 20).

[27] For a recent detailed investigation of this issue, see: Law Commission, *Simplification of the Immigration Rules: Report* (HC 14, 2020); Law Commission, *Simplification of the Immigration Rules* (Consultation Paper 242, 2019).

[28] For a detailed analysis of these issues in relation to the UK's withdrawal from the EU, see J Tomlinson, 'Justice in Automated Administration' (2020) 40(4) *Oxford Journal of Legal Studies* 708.

[29] R Thomas and J Tomlinson, 'A Different Tale of Judicial Power: Administrative Review as a Problematic Response to the Judicialisation of Tribunals' (2019) *Public Law* 537. See also: R Thomas, 'Immigration and Access to Justice: A Critical Analysis of Recent Restrictions' in E Palmer and T Cornford (eds), *Access to Justice: Beyond the Policies and Politics of Austerity* (Hart Publishing 2016).

then exacerbate or contribute to the development of other conditions.[30] In this sense, delays and backlogs can be a social determinant of health.[31]

Delays and backlogs could also adversely affect the public's perception of services and ultimately their views on and trust in government. Beyond the procedural justice literature, which has emphasised the importance of these perceptions,[32] other fields, such as marketing and service operation research, have long spoken of the negative effects long waits have on how customers evaluate the service they eventually receive.[33] Beyond perception, the actual quality of justice – i.e. outcomes – may be affected by backlogs and delays. Delays may cause the withdrawal of cases and applications or affect the nature of proceedings in a range of other ways.[34]

From the perspective of taxpayers and economic efficiency more generally, backlogs and delays can harm efforts to reduce public expenditure, not least because they can have consequential costs downstream. The classic example of this is in the healthcare setting where, for instance, undiagnosed or untreated diseases due to delays not only harm the health of the patient but also incur greater care costs for conditions that would have required fewer or different resources if treated earlier. But this dynamic is more broadly relevant in the context of administrative justice. For example, asylum seekers awaiting decisions, barred from working to support themselves and thus unable contribute to their maintenance, are often housed in accommodation provided by the state. In 2022, it was reported that the daily cost of providing accommodation to asylum seekers was £5.6 million, a number that might have been significantly lower had the system been less backlogged and people been granted their eventual status more quickly.[35] Furthermore, it has been suggested that long delays significantly hinder refugees' ability to integrate and find employment in their

[30] Walsh and Sumption, 'The UK's asylum backlog' (n 6). Refugee Council, 'New figures reveal scale of asylum backlog crisis' (Refugee Council, 2022). Available at: www.refugeecouncil.org.uk/latest/news/new-figures-reveal-scale-of-asylum-backlog-crisis/ (accessed 8 March 2023); D Neal, 'An Inspection of Asylum Casework' (2021). Available at: www.assets.publishing.service.gov.uk/government/uploads/system/uploads/attachment_data/file/1034012/An_inspection_of_asylum_casework_August_2020_to_May_2021.pdf (accessed 10 March 2023), paras 6.43–6.44; Refugee and Asylum Seeker Voice, 'The Waiting Game: The impact of delayed asylum decisions' (2018). Available at: www.refugee-action.org.uk/wp-content/uploads/2018/03/RAS-Voice-Web3.pdf (accessed 13 March) 2023, 2–3.

[31] Relatedly, see: H Genn, 'When Law is Good for Your Health: Mitigating the Social Determinants of Health through Access to Justice' (2019) 72(1) *Current Legal Problems* 159.

[32] See, eg, TR Tyler, *Why People Obey the Law* (Princeton University Press 2006). See also: K van den Bos, *The Fair Process Effect: Overcoming Distrust, Polarization, and Conspiracy Thinking* (Cambridge University Press 2023).

[33] See, eg, S Taylor, 'Waiting for Service: The Relationship between Delays and Evaluations of Service' (1994) 58 *Journal of Marketing* 56; K Sun, Y Liu, X Li, 'Make Waiting Not to Seem Like Waiting: Capacity Management of Waiting-area Entertainment' (2022) 50 *Operations Research Letters* 745.

[34] There has been extensive discussion of such issues in criminal justice: see, eg, Ministry of Justice and HM Courts & Tribunals Service, *Reducing the backlog in criminal courts* (HC 2021-08 732), paras 1.19–1.22.

[35] Home Affairs Committee, *Oral evidence: Channel crossings* (HC 2022-08 822), Q85.

new country, which can create a long-term financial (and social) effect for the government, taxpayers and the economy more broadly.[36]

Harms of Delays and Backlogs in the Immigration Tribunal

In the context of the first-tier immigration and asylum tribunal, almost all appeals relate to a fundamental aspect of how the appellants, and often their family, wish to live their lives. Furthermore, many appellants are often in positions where they are at risk or vulnerable in various ways. For instance, asylum appeals routinely consider matters of torture, trafficking and political persecution. Individuals who have had such traumatic experiences are often deeply affected by their experiences and the prospect of an appeal where their future immigration status is to be determined does not make life easier. As such, the effects of delays and backlogs in the jurisdiction can be profound. It must also be remembered that the tribunal will not be the start of an appellant's journey through the system; any delays in the tribunal must also be seen alongside the time taken, and delays experienced, at earlier stages of the process. For instance, currently, a person who succeeds in an asylum appeal in the tribunal will almost certainly have been waiting for years, not months, for the state to resolve their case.[37]

Given the nature of cases that arise in the tribunals, there is significant scope for delays in the process to affect the health of appellants. Furthermore, as noted above, any delays in tribunal appeals in this context can also have repercussions that sound in the economic sphere. For instance, in some circumstances, the government, by dint of its own restrictive rules, may be required to provide accommodation and care for an economically inactive person until a claim is resolved. Similarly, it has widely been observed that keeping people in limbo for long periods of time can, if they remain in the country, negatively impact their chances of effectively integrating with the UK labour market, as well as the wider community more generally.[38]

Harms flowing from delays and backlogs in the tribunal might also take more legal forms. Specifically, tribunal appeals are a key part of the machinery established to allow people to their legal rights, and tribunal rights themselves are

[36] See, eg, I Ruiz and C Vargas-Silva, 'What works for improving refugee outcomes in high-income countries? Policy insights for the UK' (2021). Available at: www.compas.ox.ac.uk/wp-content/uploads/What-Works-for-Improving-Refugee-Outcomes-in-High-Income-Countries-Policy-Insights-for-the-UK.pdf (accessed 13 March 2023) 10–11.

[37] Refugee Council, *Living in Limbo: A decade of delays in the UK asylum system* (2021), 17; C Yeo, 'Briefing: the state of the UK asylum system' (Free Movement, 20 June 2023). Available at: https://freemovement.org.uk/briefing-the-sorry-state-of-the-uk-asylum-system/#Asylum_backlog (accessed 25 September 2023); J Tyler-Todd et al., Delays to Processing Asylum Cases in the UK (CBP 03-2023 9737), 4.

[38] Refugee Council, 'Living in Limbo' (n 37) 14; M Marbach et al., 'The Long-Term Impact of Employment Bans on the Economic Integration of Refugees' (2018) 4 *Social Advances* 2–4; Walsh and Sumption (n 6).

established via statute. Backlogs and delays can, when excessive, have the effect of not only frustrating the enforcement of rights by individuals but of statutory frameworks more generally. Similarly, public policy on immigration and asylum can be frustrated: delays and backlogs in the tribunal can undermine both effective immigration control and prevent legitimate entry into the country. In the UK's contested politics of immigration, the politics of delays can play out in multiples ways but, as Robert Thomas has pointed out, '[i]rrespective of the political dimension, such delays pose risks to the legitimacy of the process and trust and confidence in it'.[39]

Management of Delays and Backlogs

Preliminary Observations on Management

Resource allocation, while often seen as a common cause of delays and backlogs, is, unsurprisingly, often presented as a common saviour. Sometimes, the proposal is for investment, i.e. making more resources available will help systems better meet demand in a timely manner.[40] However, other strategies in this respect focus on driving efficiency and getting more productivity out of existing resources. For instance, some argue that a way through which public funding limitations can be counteracted is through the incorporation and better understanding of private sector practices in relation to capacity, demand and queuing.[41] Some also promote the use of so-called 'lean strategies', such as making public services more 'customer-led' than 'supply-led' and transforming staff culture in a way that encourages the uncovering of wastefulness and failures in performance.[42]

Technological solutions are often proposed. For instance, arguments are made for remote hearings, interoperable and interconnected systems for the sharing of data, improved collection and utilisation of data, and the general digitalisation and automation of repetitive processes.[43] It is often suggested that better use of

[39] Thomas (n 20).

[40] See, eg, Health and Social Care Committee, (n 7), paras 69–71; Committee of Public Accounts, *Managing NHS backlogs and waiting times in England* HC 2023-05 729), paras 12–14; Ministry of Justice and HM Courts & Tribunals Service, *Reducing the backlog in criminal courts* (HC 2021-08 732), paras 2.20, 3.3, 3.18-3.19.

[41] See, eg, G Morris and P Walley, 'Implementing Failure Demand Reduction as Part of a Demand Management Strategy' (2022) 42(1) *Public Money and Management* 22; Z Radnor and S P Osborne, 'Lean: A Failed Theory for Public Services?' (2013) 15(2) *Public Management Review* 265; N Bhatia and J Drew, 'Applying Lean Production to the Public Sector' (2007) 3 *The McKinsey Quarterly* 97; J Shand, 'Backlogs and Bulges: Can Value Chains Fix the National Health Service Waiting List?' (Catalyst, 23 September 2023). Available at: www.catalyst.nejm.org/doi/full/10.1056/CAT.22.0252 (accessed 14 March 2023).

[42] Bhatia and Drew, 'Applying Lean Production to the Public Sector' (n 41), 2 and 4.

[43] Ministry of Justice and HM Courts & Tribunals Service, *Reducing the backlog in criminal courts* (HC 2021-08 732), paras 3.17–3.18; Public Services Committee, *Fit for the Future? Rethinking the*

technology may help increase efficiency and reduce delays by improving communication between departments, simplifying processes and supplying more data to inform better planning.[44]

There are also often calls for changes in policy or practice to combat backlogs and delays. For example, there have been recommendations for altering the way asylum cases are triaged, such as prioritising more straightforward cases, as well as improving communicatio'simpler'icials and those awaiting a decision.[45] Another suggestion in this context has been to dispense with interviews in certain cases.[46] Other strategies in this context might include changing substantive law or policy to create a 'simpler' system or to permit a form of 'amnesty' to allow a system to 'reset'.

Another potential strategy to alleviate the harmful effects of delays and backlogs is focusing on improving how users experience them even if they cannot be completely avoided. Managing the experiences of delay has been studied in various contexts including delayed flights, waiting for health services and general service operations.[47] Experience of time is susceptible to influence both by internal factors, such as human psychology and personality traits, and external factors, such as different environments and treatment from staff.[48] It has been found that several aspects of a waiting period, which may be irrelevant to the wait time itself, may cause people to feel that they are experiencing a longer delay than they think. Examples include having long pre-process waits, feeling anxious, not knowing or being uncertain of the duration of the wait and perceiving the wait as unfair.[49] There is an argument that, in some settings, working towards managing expectations, enabling better communication with users and generally investing in improving the wait experience could make wait times feel shorter and potentially

Public Services Workforce (HL 2022-07 48), paras 207–11; National Audit Office, *Investigation into the management of backlogs in driving licence applications* (n 14), para 1.9.

[44] Ministry of Justice and HM Courts & Tribunals Service, *Reducing the backlog in criminal courts* (n 43), paras 3.17–3.18; Public Services Committee, *Fit for the future?* (n 43), paras 28–34; Health and Social Care Committee, (n 7), paras 115–19.

[45] Neal, 'An Inspection of Asylum Casework' (n 30), paras 4.2–4.3; Refugee and Asylum Seeker Voice, 'The waiting game: (n 30), 6.

[46] Greater Manchester Immigration Aid Unit, 'Wasted childhoods: The impact of COVID-19 asylum delays on children in the North-west of England' (n 14), 4–5.

[47] N Y Kim and J W Park, 'A Study on the Impact of Airline Service Delays on Emotional Reactions and Customer Behavior' (2016) 57 *Journal of Air Transport Management* 19; G R Bitran, J C Ferrer, P R Oliveira., 'Managing Customer Experiences: Perspectives on the Temporal Aspects of Service Encounters' (2008) 10 *Manufacturing & Service Operations Management* 61; Sun, Liu and Li, 'Make Waiting Not to Seem Like Waiting (n 33) 745; H Chu, R A Westbrook, S Njue-Marendes, T P Giordano, and B N Dang, 'The Psychology of the Wait Time Experience – What Clinics Can Do to Manage the Waiting Experience for Patients: A Longitudinal, Qualitative Study' (2019) 19 *BMC Health Services Research* 459.

[48] J Baker and M Cameron, 'The Effects of the Service Environment on Affect and Consumer Perception of Waiting Time: An Integrative Review and Research Propositions' (1996) 24 *Journal of the Academy of Marketing Science* 338; M Wittmann, *Felt Time: The Psychology of How we Perceive Time* (Erik Butler tr, MIT Press 2015).

[49] Bitran, Ferrer and Oliveira, 'Managing Customer Experiences: Perspectives on the Temporal Aspects of Service Encounters' (n 47).

increase a willingness to wait.[50] Some straightforward ways of doing this could be proactively informing people of the delays, accompanied by a reason for the delay and even an apology, and giving them a better sense of where they are in the queue with regular updates. Depending on the administrative process and service in question, the ease with which these methods can be adopted will vary, as well as the part of the system responsible for adopting them. Although not remedying the root causes of backlogs and delays, taking into account how delays are experienced when designing administrative systems may still help in relieving some of the psychological burden experienced by people caught in backlogs and help improve public perception.

One strategy which has risen in prominence in recent years is to focus on better prediction techniques. Managing any administrative justice process involves some prediction of the demand systems will face and what resources will be required to meet it. Increasingly, government bodies employ civil service professionals whose job is to attempt to 'model' demand and make informed estimates about what resources are required, but their work is inherently complex and uncertain. While officials charged with this task might be able to look closely at previous case volumes and receive input from frontline officials, any prediction is, at a foundational level, sophisticated guesswork and may turn out to be wide of the mark.

Management of Delays and Backlogs in the Immigration Tribunal

HMCTS, the agency responsible for managing the administration of the first-tier immigration and asylum tribunal, primarily seeks to manage demand in the tribunal – and thus prevent backlogs and delays emerging – by modelling how many appeals are likely to be lodged. To do this, specialists in this area look at all the available evidence, including past caseloads and the wider context of the tribunal, and produce forecasts of the number of 'sitting days' that will be required in a particular jurisdiction.[51]

The task in respect of the first-tier immigration and asylum tribunal could be said to be particularly complex as the environment in which it operates has a number of changing variables that are liable to change quickly. For instance, changes in migration flows are difficult to predict, especially in the context of mass displacement crises. Substantive immigration law and policy are frequently changing, which can create new complexities, legal issues or routes of appeal. Most notably in recent years, changes to which decisions attract a right of appeal have affected the volume of appeals.[52]

[50] Chu et al., 'The Psychology of the Wait Time Experience' (n 47) 459.
[51] Sadler 'Sitting Days' (n 24).
[52] For a detailed analysis of this issue, see: R Thomas and J Tomlinson, *Immigration Judicial Reviews: An Empirical Study* (Palgrave Macmillan, 2021).

Forecasts produced for the tribunal then inform HMCTS resourcing considerations, with decisions being made by the Lord Chancellor, who must consider the forecasts alongside the level of outstanding work in jurisdictions and available judicial resources. This decision is then shared with the HMCTS Board, who then provide independent advice to the Lord Chief Justice and Senior President of Tribunals on whether the 'settlement is sufficient for the efficient and effective operation of the system'.[53] A discussion between the Lord Chancellor, the Lord Chief Justice and the Senior President of Tribunals follows, where the Lord Chief Justice and Senior President consider the Board's advice and respond to it. This process is representative of how the complex and technical task of prediction finds its way into a budgeting negotiation process which is inherently political but also engages judicial leaders.

Another development in the tribunal in the recent years is to seek to remove 'low level' administrative tasks from judges and assign them to qualified tribunal staff – known as 'Legal Officers'.[54] The everyday work of the tribunal involves judges dealing with many procedural and preparatory issues, to ensure appeals can be properly heard and dealt with. This is now increasingly seen as work that should not be consuming significant amounts of judicial time as it can be dealt with adequately and more efficiently elsewhere in the tribunal.

Conclusion

This chapter has sought to bring the issue of backlogs and delays from the periphery of administrative justice thought and treat it as an important topic worthy of scholarly inquiry in its own right. At the start of the chapter, we set out four major questions that we see as central to the challenge of advancing understanding of this issue, and we explored these questions through a discussion of the experiences of the immigration tribunal in the UK. Though we have examined one aspect of one part of one administrative justice institution, we have pointed to new directions for future administrative justice research on these issues, both in tribunals and other institutions.

Developing a greater understanding of the dynamics of this administrative justice problem no doubt leads us to familiar themes, such as the inevitably of complex trade-offs in the design of processes, decision-making quality and the importance of officials getting decisions 'right first time', and questions of procedural justice. But there is ample scope for less familiar areas to be explored in greater depth, including the role of predictive techniques in the delivery of administrative justice, subjective perceptions of time within processes, and the wider health, fiscal, and economic impacts of public sector delay.

[53] Sadler (n 24).

[54] HM Courts & Tribunals Service, *First-tier Tribunal (Immigration and Asylum Chamber) Reform: Interim Process Evaluation* (2022). Available at: www.assets.publishing.service.gov.uk/government/uploads/system/uploads/attachment_data/file/1109001/First-tier_Tribunal__Immigration_and_Asylum_Chamber__Reform_interim_evaluation_final_report.pdf (accessed 25 September 2023).

6

Paying Legal Attention to Specialist Tribunals

ELIZABETH FISHER*

As Peter Cane has stated, '[t]he paradigm administrative tribunal is a "specialist" adjudicatory body'.[1] Cane used the word 'paradigm' as 'a typical instance of something'.[2] In making this comment, Cane was, and is, correct. Most administrative tribunals in common law jurisdictions have some sort of 'specialist' dimension, even when part of a generalist administrative tribunal structure.

But 'paradigm' is a slippery word.[3] It can also refer to '[a] conceptual or methodological *model* underlying the theories and practices of a science or discipline at a particular time'.[4] While the '[t]he paradigm administrative tribunal is a "specialist" adjudicatory body', specialist administrative tribunals do not figure significantly in the models underlying the theories of doctrinal administrative law. In an earlier essay I argued that this is because administrative tribunals register in the administrative law imagination as functional 'non-legal' institutions.[5] Their legal nature and their legal contributions have thus been overlooked.

At the end of that essay, I genuflected towards another paradigm – another conceptual model – of administrative law. To develop it, I argued, there is a need to pay more attention to 'the dynamism and "definitional sensitivity" of specific legal arrangements of tribunals.[6] This is because the value of any conceptual model is how it reflects reality.[7]

* I would like to thank Mark Aronson, Chantal Bostock, Peter Cane, Ceri Warnock and the editors for comments on earlier drafts of this chapter. Any errors or omissions remain my own. The writing of this chapter was supported by Leverhulme Grant MRF-2021-071.

[1] P Cane, *Administrative Tribunals and Adjudication* (Hart, 2009) 91.

[2] Oxford English Dictionary (OED).

[3] D Shapere, 'Review: The Structure of Scientific Revolutions' (1964) 73 *Philosophical Review* 383, 384–5 critiquing the ambiguous use of the term by Thomas Kuhn.

[4] OED. My emphasis.

[5] E Fisher, 'Administrative Tribunals: An Essay about the Legal Imagination of Administrative Law Scholars' in J. Goudkamp, M. Lunney and L. McDonald (eds), *Taking Law Seriously: Essays in Honour of Peter Cane* (Hart, 2022).

[6] ibid 279.

[7] National Research Council, *Models in Environmental Regulatory Decision Making* (National Academies Press, 2007) 31.

This chapter is an exercise in paying such attention in relation to how specialist tribunals are governed by law. It is first and foremost an exercise in legal description in which I chart the complex legal structures of specialist tribunals and how those structures shape judicial review of them. But this chapter also reflects on the implications of the resulting map for how administrative law scholars conceptualise administrative law and the place of tribunals in it. While this chapter is directed at administrative law scholars, I limit its focus to environmental and planning tribunals (EPTs). Not only does this make the discussion more manageable, but it is through ongoing research in this field that the importance of paying attention to 'the dynamism and "definitional sensitivity" of specific legal arrangements became apparent to me.[8]

The structure of the chapter is as follows. First, I provide an overview of administrative tribunals and EPTs. Second, I explore some of the different facets and complexities that makes an EPT 'specialist'. Third, I consider how 'specialist' tribunals are subject to judicial review and provide examples of how the 'specialist' nature of a tribunal figures in doctrinal reasoning. Fourth, I consider the implications of this descriptive exercise for administrative law thought more generally. Paying attention to 'the dynamism and "definitional sensitivity" of specialist tribunals underscores the need for administrative law scholars to unpack ideas of specialisation, see the legal complexity of specialist tribunals, and reflect on what is commonly understood to bring coherence to judicial review reasoning. Pondering these three issues does not a different conceptual model make, but it does point to a different way forward.

There are three points to make before starting. Even with a narrowed focus on EPTs, my analysis is not exhaustive. Footnotes and examples are illustrative. The aim of this chapter is to provoke critical reflection about how administrative law scholars imagine and navigate administrative law worlds, rather than to provide a comprehensive account of EPTs.[9] Second, related to this, as the purpose of this chapter is to encourage administrative law thought to be more grounded in administrative law realities. I am thus not evaluating the merits of particular legal arrangements or particular doctrines concerning specialist administrative tribunals, although I do argue for a more nuanced approach to thinking about them. Third, due to space, this chapter touches on, but does not focus on, the substantive legal contributions that specialist administrative tribunals make to shaping the substance of the law.[10]

[8] E Fisher, *Risk Regulation and Administrative Constitutionalism* (Oxford, Hart, 2007) Ch 4; E Fisher, 'Administrative Law, Pluralism and the Legal Construction of Merits Review in Australian Environmental Courts and Tribunals' in L Pearson, C Harlow and M Taggart (eds), *Administrative Law in a Changing State: Essays in Honour of Mark Aronson* (Hart, 2008); E Fisher and B Preston (eds), *An Environmental Court in Action: Function, Doctrine and Process* (Hart, 2022).

[9] For a comprehensive conceptual account see C Warnock, *Environmental Courts and Tribunals* (Hart, 2020).

[10] Fisher, 'Administrative Tribunals' (n 5) 274–5. See the collection of essays in Part 2 of Fisher and Preston (n 8).

Specialist Administrative Tribunals and Environmental and Planning Tribunals: An Overview

Administrative tribunals are a 'neutral third actor'[11] that have the power to 'rehear' a decision[12] and/or to engage in some form of decision-making[13] or dispute resolution[14] that relates to an administrative decision. It is in these senses that administrative tribunals 'adjudicate'. As noted in the introduction, the norm has been the creation of 'specialist' administrative tribunals. As Chantal Stebbings notes of nineteenth-century tribunals, '[t]he nature of their duties was determined by the character of the legislation they were called on to implement'.[15] That remains the case today. Even when there has been amalgamation of tribunals, the 'specialist' nature of individual tribunal jurisdictions has usually been retained in different chambers.[16]

EPTs are a subset of specialist tribunals. These tribunals have been created in many common law jurisdictions to hear appeals, resolve disputes, or make recommendations that relate to administrative action concerning land use, natural resource development, environmental impacts, and/or environmental quality. EPTs can take many different forms, can govern different areas, engage in different processes and wield different powers.[17]

In Australia some form of EPT exists in most states.[18] The oldest and most high profile of these is the New South Wales Land and Environment Court (NSWLEC).[19] There also exists the South Australian Environment Resources and Development Court (SAERDC),[20] and in Queensland there is the Planning and Environment Court (QPEC)[21] and the Land Court.[22] Victoria, Western Australia, and Tasmania have separate planning and environment jurisdictions as part of their amalgamated tribunal structures.[23] New Zealand has an Environment Court (NZEC),[24]

[11] Cane (n 1) 10.

[12] See, eg, the Land and Environment Court Act 1979, s 17 (NSW) (LEC Act 1979 (NSW)).

[13] Eg, the Land Court of Queensland may be required to make a recommendation after a hearing in relation to a matter where there has been an objection. See the Mineral Resources Act 1989, ss 265 and 269 (Qld).

[14] Eg Part 4, Division 1, Planning and Environment Court Act 2016 (Qld) (PEC Act 2016 (Qld)) and LEC Act 1979 (NSW) ss 34 and 34AA. See M Walker, 'Alternative Dispute Resolution in the Land and Environment Court of New South Wales' in Fisher and Preston (n 8).

[15] C Stebbings, *Legal Foundations of Tribunals in Nineteenth Century England* (CUP, 2007) 147.

[16] R Carnwath, 'Tribunal Justice – a New Start' [2009] PL 48, 51 and R Creyke, 'Tribunal Amalgamation 2015: An Opportunity Lost?' (2016) 84 *AIAL Forum* 54, 56.

[17] G Pring and C Pring, *Greening Justice: Creating and Improving Environmental Courts and Tribunals* (Access Initiative, 2009).

[18] Fisher, 'Administrative Law' (n 8) for an outdated overview of some of these.

[19] For an overview see Fisher and Preston (n 8).

[20] Environment, Resources and Development Court Act 1993 (SA) (ERDC Act 1993 (SA)).

[21] PEC Act 2016 (Qld).

[22] Land Court Act 2000 (Qld).

[23] See www.vcat.vic.gov.au; www.sat.justice.wa.gov.au; and www.tascat.tas.gov.au/home, accessed 27 July 2023.

[24] Resource Management Act 1991, Part 11 (NZ).

and the UK has an 'environment' jurisdiction as one of the 16 jurisdictions of the First Tier (General Regulatory Chamber) Tribunal (First Tier GRCT).[25] The structure and nature of EPTs are not static and have evolved over time.[26] Some started out as separate tribunals but now exist within amalgamated tribunal structures,[27] while others have a formal, independent existence.[28] A legal system may have more than one type of EPT.[29] Given their different jurisdictions, the number of cases they hear can also be very different.[30]

EPTs have a long history,[31] but also have been heavily promoted in the last three decades.[32] Administrative tribunals tend to be separation of powers misfits,[33] but EPTs particularly so.[34] The formal legal architecture of these institutions often combine administrative and judicial elements in different and often ambiguous ways.[35] The work of EPTs is also often similar to the work of planning inspectors conducting administrative inquires[36] and some environmental 'tribunals' also explicitly wield judicial power.[37] The difference between an administrative tribunal and an inferior court can also be difficult to distinguish.[38] In this analysis I focus on when EPTs are exercising some form of 'rehearing' power.

[25] C Cole and C Hodges, 'A Critical Analysis and Review of the Procedure and Substance of Appeal Rights to the First-tier Tribunal (General Regulatory Chamber)' (Centre for Socio-Legal Studies, 2020) 26.

[26] B Preston, 'The Land and Environment Court of New South Wales: A Very Short History of an Environmental Court in Action' (2020) 94 *ALJ* 631.

[27] Eg, the Tasmanian Resource Management and Planning Appeal Tribunal was amalgamated into the Tasmanian Civil and Administrative Tribunal in 2020.

[28] Eg, NSWLEC; NZEC; and QPEC. Note while they may have formal independence, they are physically housed with other courts and tribunals. The NZEC is an example. See www.environmentcourt.govt.nz/contact-us/, accessed 27 July 2023.

[29] Eg, the Land Court and QPEC in Queensland.

[30] In 2021 the NSWLEC disposed of 527 cases across all jurisdictions by hearing and 926 pre-trial finalisations which include 529 cases finalised through ss34 and 34AA conferences or onsite hearings: The Land and Environment Court of New South Wales, *Annual Report 2021* (2022) 32–3. The SAERDC finalised 189 cases in both their civil and criminal jurisdictions: Government of South Australia, *Courts Administration Authority: 2021–22 Annual Report* (2022) 12. The Resource and Planning Stream of the Tasmanian Civil and Administrative Tribunal made 104 substantive decisions, including 32 final decisions and 72 arising from consent agreements. See Tasmanian Civil and Appeal Tribunal, *Annual Report 2021–22* (2022) 51.

[31] B Preston, 'Specialist Environmental Courts: their Objective, Integrity and Legitimacy'. Paper presented at the Enduring Courts in Changing Times Conference, Sydney, 8–10 September 2023; Warnock (n 9) 119–23.

[32] Pring and Pring (n 17).

[33] Fisher, 'Administrative Tribunals' (n 5) 263.

[34] Warnock (n 9) 76–90. In the Australian context, one of the reasons for this is that EPTs operate at the state level where the Australian Constitution's framework for separation of powers does not govern.

[35] ibid, 42–6 discussing the NZEC. Consider also the Land Court of Queensland. The Land Court Act 2000, s 4 (Qld) creates the Court as a 'specialised judicial tribunal' (s 4(1)) and a 'court of record' (s 4(2)).

[36] In England and Wales, 'merits appeals' are handled by the Planning Inspectorate (The Town and Country Planning (Determination of Appeals by Appointed Persons) (Prescribed Classes) Regulations 1997 (SI 1997/420)(UK) and related delegated legislation) while similar work is carried out by the NSWLEC in New South Wales (LEC Act 1979, s 17 (NSW)).

[37] Eg, the NSWLEC's Class 4 and 5 jurisdictions. See LEC Act 1979, ss 20–21 (NSW).

[38] *Kirk v Industrial Court of New South Wales* [2010] HCA 1; 239 CLR 531, 572–73 [68]–[69].

In exercising that merits review power, EPTs perform one of what Karl Llewellyn called 'law-jobs' – dealing with 'trouble cases' where 'offence, grievance or dispute' arises.[39] That 'law-job' is particularly important in planning and environmental law. Administrative decisions to authorise or not to authorise development or an activity inevitably give rise to conflict among a range of actors in affected communities.[40] As John Griffith noted in his analysis of the Franks Committee in 1959, in relation to planning decisions:

> We are dealing here with interference with property rights mainly compulsory purchase and clearance orders, development plans and planning applications. The citizen whose land is directly affected is on the defensive. ... He is protecting himself against the demands of the State: that he must sell his land, that he may not build on it. His reaction is a cry which has echoed down the valley of the generations: 'I've been robbed.'[41]

But planning and environmental decisions do not only engage property rights. They also impact on the quality and acceptability of the natural and built environment that communities live in. Ceri Warnock noted that:

> [t]here can be many impacted parties ... and so environmental disputes often transcend traditional bi-party conflicts. Disputes may concern 'the commons' or public resources, but environmental problems can also impact individual rights, including property rights. They may therefore have 'redistributive force', or allocate risk-burdens and address normative conflicts.[42]

The resolution of these disputes thus potentially involves a wider number of parties than seen in other areas of administrative law. Moreover, given that planning and environmental law is concerned with regulating to ensure the acceptability of future impacts, resolution of disputes often involve assessing facts, particularly future facts.[43]

The catalysts for creating EPTs, like the catalysts for creating generalist administrative tribunals, are not singular. As Harry Arthurs has pointed out about the creation of tribunals more generally, it may be because: traditional courts are not seen as fit for dealing with grievances; it is the deliberate promotion of informal adjudication; it is an evolutionary response to specific situations; or it is the product of an ideological agenda.[44] The creation of the NSWLEC was part of a comprehensive package of environmental law reform committed to promoting legal certainty in processes of dispute resolution.[45] In contrast the environmental jurisdiction of the First Tier GRCT has developed in a far more ad hoc way that has resulted in a

[39] K Llewellyn, 'The Normative, the Legal, and the Law-Jobs: The Problem of Juristic Method' (1940) 49 *Yale Law Journal* 1355,1375.

[40] E Fisher, 'Afterword: Law in UnExpected Places' in Fisher and Preston (n 8) 310–2.

[41] J Griffith, 'Tribunals and Inquiries' (1959) *MLR* 117, 128.

[42] Warnock (n 9) 155–6.

[43] ibid 152–5. See also L Fisher, 'Environmental Law as "Hot" Law' (2013) 25 *JEL* 347, 348–54.

[44] HW Arthurs, *'Without the Law': Administrative Justice and Legal Pluralism in Nineteenth Century England'* (University of Toronto Press, 1985) 191–3. See also Griffith, (n 41), 129–30.

[45] L Stein, 'The Place of the Land and Environment Court in the Planning System of New South Wales' in Fisher and Preston (n 8), 54–7.

piecemeal jurisdiction.[46] Furthermore, what makes a EPT 'specialist' varies. It is to this matter than I now turn.

The Specialist Nature of Administrative Tribunals

Like 'paradigm', 'specialist' is a word much deployed but not easy to define. It is often contrasted with the word 'generalist' but given that specialist administrative tribunals are the norm and that nearly all 'generalist' administrative tribunals are divided into specialist chambers, that is not illuminating. Part of the problem of definition is that there is no one single attribute that gives an administrative tribunal its specialist quality. As Justice Brian Preston, Chief Judge of the NSWLEC notes of that Court, it is 'like a cut and polished diamond' that has 'many facets'.[47] He thus maps that Court's roles, competence, expertise, functions, doctrines, and processes.[48] Other scholars provide different taxonomies. George Pring and Catherine Pring identify 12 'critical decisions' in 'building' an environmental court or tribunal.[49] Brian Opeskin identifies five different types of judicial specialisation and four different modalities for achieving such specialisation.[50] All of this underscores that there are indeed many 'facets' to specialisation. Here, for ease of analysis, I focus on the specialist competence of EPTs. That competence has two dimensions – authority and capacity.[51]

Tribunals need formal *authority* to act. Authority refers to the 'right to give orders, make decisions, and enforce obedience'.[52] A tribunal is 'specialised' because it is vested with authority to consider a limited set of cases which have 'common characteristics'.[53] But what those 'common characteristics' are, and how a tribunal is vested with authority in relation to them, can vary significantly. EPTs are a case in point.[54]

Different EPTs are given authority over disputes in different subject areas. The NSWLEC can hear merits review appeals in relation to a range of planning, environmental protection, and local government matters.[55] In contrast, the 'environment' jurisdiction of the First Tier GRCT does not include any jurisdiction

[46] Cole and Hodges (n 25) 6, 11.

[47] B Preston, 'The Many Facets of a Cutting-Edge Court: A Study of the Land and Environment Court of New South Wales' in Fisher and Preston (n 8), 1.

[48] ibid.

[49] Eg, Pring and Pring (n 17) 19–88; See also, 144–55; See also E Lees, 'Adjudication Systems' in E Lees and J Viñuales (eds) *The Oxford Handbook of Comparative Environmental Law* (OUP, 2019).

[50] B Opeskin, 'The Relentless Rise of Judicial Specialisation and its Implications for Judicial Systems' (2022) 75 *CLP* 137.

[51] This division is taken from thinking about the competence of public administration. See E Fisher and S Shapiro, *Administrative Competence: Reimagining Administrative Law* (CUP, 2020) 14–16.

[52] OED.

[53] Borrowing from Opeskin's definition, Opeskin 'The Relentless Rise' (n 50) 145.

[54] Also see Fisher, 'Administrative Law' (n 8).

[55] Sections 17–18 LEC Act 1979 (NSW).

in relation to planning matters but rather hears matters concerning 38 pieces of legislation including in relation to the greenhouse gas emission trading scheme, the single use carrier bag charge scheme and the nitrate pollution regime.[56]

The ways in which a tribunal is vested with jurisdiction in these different areas can be done in a variety of ways. For example, the NSWLEC is empowered to hear 'appeals, objections and applications under sections 4.55, 8.7, 8.8, 8.9, 8.16, 8.18, 8.21, 8.22, 8.23 and 8.25 of, and clause 35 of Schedule 5 to, the Environmental Planning and Assessment Act 1979'.[57] But legislation can also vest an EPT with other powers. Thus the NSWLEC is also empowered to 'have regard to this or any other relevant Act, any instrument made under any such Act, the circumstances of the case and the public interest'.[58] The SAERDC has 'the jurisdiction (including the jurisdiction to try a charge of an offence) conferred on it by or under this or any other Act'[59] but what an appeal involves is found in other legislation.[60] The First Tier GRCT is vested with different appeal powers under different pieces of legislation.[61] In appeals relating to the Wildlife and Countryside Act 1981, they can, among other things, make 'such other order as the Tribunal thinks fit'.[62] In contrast, the Single Use Carrier Bags Charge (England) Order 2015 empowers the Tribunal to 'take such steps as the Administrator could take in relation to the act or omission giving rise to the requirement or notice'.[63]

The specialist authority of an EPT will also be shaped by how it is legally constituted, empowered, and limited. Legislation can do that in different ways with differing levels of specificity, particularly given that many EPTs are part of amalgamated structures.[64] As seen above, EPTs are granted authority under specific legislative provisions. But there are also other ways in which the authority of a tribunal is shaped.[65] As seen above a tribunal can be empowered to 'rehear' a case in different ways.[66] The authority given to a tribunal will be shaped by which parties can appear before them,[67] procedural rules,[68] and what evidence an EPT

[56] See www.gov.uk/guidance/environmental-fines-or-notices-appeal-against-a-regulator, accessed 25 July 2023.

[57] S 17(d) LEC Act 1979 (NSW).

[58] S 39(4) LEC Act 1979 (NSW).

[59] S 7(1) SAERDC Act 1993 (SA).

[60] Compare s 205, Planning, Development and Infrastructure Act 2016 (SA) and s 55 Irrigation Act 2009 (SA). See also s 58 of that Act that also governs the constitution of the ERDC in relation to appeals under that Act.

[61] Some examples can be found in Cole and Hodges (n 25) 49–50.

[62] Para 16, Schedule 9A.

[63] SI 2015/776, art 16. Again, this is one of a number of powers granted by that Article.

[64] Compare LEC Act 1979 (NSW); Schedule 2, Pt 8 of Tasmanian Civil and Administrative Tribunal Act 2020 (TCATA 2020)(Tas); and the Tribunals Court and Enforcement Act 2007 (TCEA 2007)(UK) (which makes no mention of the jurisdiction of the General Regulatory Chamber).

[65] For a longer analysis see Fisher, 'Administrative Law' (n 8) 332–44.

[66] See s 43 and s 46 PEC Act 2016 (Qld).

[67] Compare s 202 Planning, Development Infrastructure Act 2016 (SA); ss 8.6–8.9, Environmental Planning and Assessment Act 1979 (NSW); and para 7, Part 8, Schedule 2, TCATA 2020(Tas).

[68] Compare s 38(1) LEC Act 1979 (NSW); Pt 3 and Land and Environment Court Rules 2007 (NSW) with the Tribunal Procedure (First-tier Tribunal) (General Regulatory Chamber) Rules 2009 (UK) (SI 1997/420). See also para 9, Part 8, Schedule 2, TCATA 2020(Tas).

can consider.[69] Specialist authority over cases having common characteristics is thus not granted by a singular legislative act of vesting power.

The second aspect of tribunal specialisation is the *capacity* of the tribunal to discharge the authority it has. To quote Justice Edelman of the Australian High Court, '[p]rocesses have no thought process'.[70] A tribunal needs the ability to hear the cases before it. One aspect of capacity is expertise – the set of thick and embedded knowledge and institutional practices by which a tribunal operates.[71] The most obvious expert capacity of an EPT is in terms of personnel and a hallmark of specialisation is that those carrying out adjudication have expertise in specific areas. Legislation allows tribunals to appoint non-lawyers in adjudicative roles with some legislation being quite prescriptive about the qualifications of those being appointed.[72] Legislation may also provide for the appointment of lawyers in adjudicative roles who have particular expertise.[73] That reflects the fact that EPTs need both legal and problem-specific expertise.[74]

But capacity, like authority, is not singular. It is also resources – institutional, financial, cognitive, and otherwise. It can include the information that a tribunal can consider and the processes and procedures by which it can consider it. It concerns who can participate in proceedings and the evidence they can provide. That capacity can be bolstered or hindered through the processes an EPT engages in. For example, the requirement to carry out a site visit ensures that the person adjudicating has first-hand knowledge of the site that an appeal concerns.[75] Likewise, as Jeff Smith and Sue Higginson note, the NSWLEC's ability to consider specific types of expert evidence is directly related to its public interest jurisprudence.[76] Much of the legislation that governs EPTs allows them flexibility in developing their own procedures to improve capacity. EPTs developing those procedures often do so in light of the types of disputes they are adjudicating upon. The NSWLEC's concurrent evidentiary procedures[77] and specific procedures in relation to disputes concerning aboriginal cultural heritage are cases in point.[78]

Capacity is also shaped in other ways. How the problems that a tribunal is adjudicating are understood will directly relate to what is understood to be the capacity to adjudicate upon them. Take, for example, the merits review of *Bulga Milbrodale Progress Association Inc v Minister for Planning and Infrastructure and*

[69] Compare s 21(1)(b) and s 22 SAERDC Act 1993 (SA) and s 38(3) LEC Act 1979 (NSW).

[70] *Oakey Coal Action Alliance Inc v New Acland Coal Pty Ltd* [2021] HCA 2; 272 CLR 33, 59 [81]. His Honour made this comment in discussing actual and apprehended bias.

[71] Fisher and Shapiro (n 51) ch 2.

[72] Eg ss 12–13 LEC Act 1979 (NSW); reg 4, Part 8, Schedule 2 TCATA 2020(Tas).

[73] Eg s 16 Land Court Act 2000 (Qld). Compare with s 8 LEC Act 1979 (NSW).

[74] Preston, 'The Many Facets of a Cutting Edge Court' (n 47) 11–12.

[75] S 34D LEC Act 1979 (NSW); s 10 SAERDC Act 1993 (SA).

[76] J Smith and S Higginson, '"Please Come In": Access to Justice in the Land and Environment Court' in Fisher and Preston (n 8) 266–7.

[77] Land and Environment Court of New South Wales, *Conference of Expert Witnesses Policy* (2015).

[78] M Davis, 'The Land and Environment Court of New South Wales and the Recognition of Indigenous Peoples' Rights' in Fisher and Preston (n 8).

Warkworth Mining Limited[79] in which the decision being reviewed was framed in the following way:

> The exercise of the power under s 75J to approve or disapprove the carrying out of the Project requires consideration, weighting and balancing of the environmental, social and economic impacts of the Project. The range of interests affected, the complexity of the issues and the interdependence of the issues, means that decision-making involves a polycentric problem.[80]

A consequence is that, as part of merits review, the following steps needed to be undertaken:

> identification of the relevant matters needing to be considered; secondly, fact finding for each relevant matter; thirdly, determining how much weight each relevant matter is to receive, and fourthly, balancing the weighted matters to arrive at a managerial decision.[81]

What each of those steps required was shaped by an analysis of the larger legal framework. The result was the Court was required to exercise capacity in assessing a range of impacts of the development that the decision being reviewed related to.

This discussion of EPT specialisation is by no means exhaustive. It illustrates just how complex the idea of specialisation is in the administrative tribunal context. There are three points that emerge from it.

First, EPTs are serving a function, a law job, in adjudicating disputes in the environment and planning context.[82] Like other administrative tribunals, EPTs are examples of what Arthurs described as 'state-sponsored legal pluralism'[83] – governments explicitly create tribunals to do something legally distinct (and usually relatively informal) – both in manner and form. Besides the fact that specialisation brings with it both benefits and risks,[84] just because a tribunal is specialist does not mean it is effective or it does its law job well. There are many facets to what makes a tribunal 'specialist'. The capacity of a tribunal should ideally relate to the authority of a tribunal, but it does not necessarily need to do so.[85] The capacity and authority of a tribunal should also bear a relationship to the type of disputes that a tribunal adjudicates upon[86] – but again that relationship is not guaranteed. These issues are complicated by the fact that there may not be agreement about what it means for

[79] [2013] NSWLEC 48; 8 ARLR 127; 194 LGERA 347.

[80] ibid at [31].

[81] ibid at [36].

[82] C Warnock, 'Reconceptualising Specialist Environment Courts and Tribunals' (2017) 37 *LS* 391, 397–400.

[83] Arthurs (n 44) 191.

[84] L Woods, L McNamara, and J Townend, 'Executive Accountability, and National Security' (2021) 84 *MLR* 553, 566–8.

[85] M Groves and G Weeks, 'Tribunal Justice and Politics in Australia: The Rise and Fall of the Administrative Appeals Tribunal' (2023) 97 *ALJ* 278, 283–8.

[86] C Warnock, 'Environment and the Law: The Normative Force of Context and Constitutional Challenges' (2020) 32 *JEL* 365.

a tribunal to do a job well. This is particularly when environmental and planning decision-making is controversial.[87]

Second, tribunals are serving a function and are not ordinary courts, but they are legal objects.[88] Legislation, delegated legislation and forms of soft law constitute and govern the work of tribunals in detailed ways. These different forms of law relate to both the authority and capacity of an EPT. Thus, as seen above, it is common for legislation to set out the powers an EPT has and the expertise of those sitting on a tribunal. The framework for some EPTs is more legible, legally or otherwise, than for others. The Land and Environment Court Act 1979 (NSW) sets out the NSWLEC's specialised nature in a relatively straightforward manner. The 'specialised' nature of the First Tier GRCT is far more elusive and ad hoc. As Charmaine Cole and Christopher Hodges note 'while almost half of the legislation creating the appeal rights to the GRC concern environmental regulations, this does not mean the rights or remedies in these regulations, or even the terms used to describe the rights are identical'.[89]

Third, and flowing on from these two points, what makes an EPT 'specialist' is a mix of the legal and non-legal. The non-legal is what is normally thought of when using the word specialisation. A specialist tribunal is understood as being 'specialist' in terms of a particular type of problem.[90] Specialisation is thus contrasted with law. For example, Cane has argued that the word 'generalist' in the administrative tribunal context privileges one form of specialism –'namely legal expertise, and one set of values namely legal values'.[91]

While that may be a common understanding, it ignores that a significant dimension to specialisation is legal. The 'special' nature of a tribunal's authority attaches to certain legislative provisions and much of the specialised nature of administrative tribunals derives from a tribunal's understanding of a particular administrative law regime.[92] As Preston notes of the NSWLEC's expertise, it requires a 'broad and deep understanding of what is law and what are the functions and processes of legal institutions charged with the responsibilities of administering law'.[93] More significantly, while specialist tribunals may be legally pluralistic, and the law they produce is 'local law',[94] their work is still infused with legal values and legal reasoning.[95]

[87] M Rackemann, 'How Green is my ECT? The Challenge of Impartiality and Objectivity' (2017) 29 *ELM* 88, 91.

[88] Fisher, 'Administrative Tribunals' (n 5) 271–4.

[89] Cole and Hodges (n 25) 6.

[90] C Okongwu and A Okposin, 'Specialised Environmental Courts and Tribunals as Legal Instruments for Sustainable Environmental Justice' (2021) 3 *International Review of Law and Jurisprudence* 93, 94 and L Baum, *Specialising the Courts* (University of Chicago Press, 2011) 2.

[91] Cane (n 1) 125.

[92] H Street, *Justice in the Welfare State* (2nd edn, Steven and Sons, 1975) 7.

[93] Preston, (n 47) 11.

[94] *Cart v The Upper Tribunal* [2011] UKSC 28, [2012] 1AC 663, 684 [42].

[95] Fisher, 'Administrative Tribunals' (n 5) 271–6.

Furthermore, as seen in the discussion of specialisation above, the legal and non-legal dimensions of specialisation permeate each other. EPTs always engage in merits review in a context framed and infused with law.[96] That law is not hermetically sealed. As Warnock has noted, in its merits review role, the NZEC 'cannot treat legal reasoning as an exercise immured from the factual context, and the court's form and its function helps frame its legal approach'.[97]

Law plays a role in building the architecture for an EPT, law pervades the reasoning of an EPT, and law governs the disputes that will inevitably emerge about a specialist tribunal's work.

Specialist Tribunals and Judicial Review

EPTs are performing a 'law job' in being a forum for grievances, but they will not resolve all grievances. Not only is their competence limited, but their decisions may give rise to further grievance. Some of this may relate to the general design and operation of an EPT,[98] but in most cases it will relate to individual decisions. Given that much of what an EPT does is permeated by law, it is inevitable that some grievances will raise questions about the existence of legal errors. And there is also a risk of legal error due to the legal work of a tribunal being 'developed in isolation'[99] particularly in 'highly technical and fast-moving area[s] of law'.[100]

Administrative tribunals thus form the large lower terraces of an administrative law ziggurat.[101] While tribunals are distinct from courts, they are not disconnected from them. Some tribunal architectures combine administrative tribunals and superior courts in the same structure, including some form of appeal from a first instance tribunal to a judge wielding judicial power.[102] Nearly all tribunal frameworks provide a route to legally challenge a tribunal decision in a court.[103] Tribunals are also subject to common law judicial review powers.[104] Attempts to oust a reviewing court's jurisdiction have tended to be interpreted narrowly by courts.[105]

[96] Fisher, *Risk Regulation and Administrative Constitutionalism* (n 8) ch 4.

[97] Warnock, (n 9) 163.

[98] Report of the Land and Environment Court Working Party (September 2001). Available at: www.lawlink.nsw.gov.au/report/lpd_reports.nsf/pages/lec-working-index, accessed 10 August 2023. See also the discussion in relation to the NZEC in Warnock (n 9) 46–51.

[99] *Privacy International, R (on the application of) v Investigatory Powers Tribunal* [2019] UKSC 22, [2020] AC 491, 549 [139].

[100] *Cart* (n 94) 684 [43].

[101] N Wikeley, 'Future Directions for Tribunals: A UK Perspective' in R Creyke (ed) *Tribunals in the Common Law World* (Federation Press, 2008) 176.

[102] Eg s 57A LEC Act 1979 (NSW) and s 11 TCEA Act 2007 (UK).

[103] Eg s 57 LEC Act 1979 (NSW); s 30 ERDC Act 1993 (SA);.

[104] *Cart* (n 94).

[105] *Privacy International* (n 99) 550 at [144].

Given the number of specialist administrative tribunals, and given the judicial review routes that exist, it is not surprising that many judicial review cases concern judicial review of a decision of an administrative tribunal or inferior court that has specialist aspects.[106] Judicial review of specialist tribunals is not marginal to judicial review practice but central to it. There is nothing surprising about this as specialist tribunals are usually set up in relation to regimes where the case load justifies the creation of a distinctive adjudicative body. While they perform a 'law job', they do not fully displace the 'law job' of courts in providing legal oversight. The opposite is true. They give rise to that legal work.

On occasion, judges and commentators describe courts in these cases giving significant leeway to a specialist tribunal because of its 'specialist' nature.[107] That leeway, restraint, or deference (the language varies from context and jurisdiction) can operate in different ways. It may be giving respect to a tribunal's interpretation of a statutory provision,[108] how the reasoning of a tribunal is scrutinised,[109] or how the tribunal's assessment of facts is reviewed.[110] Separate from this is that courts will determine whether judicial review is available in light of the rights of appeal set out in legislation.[111] It is tempting to see these cases as involving choices for the courts as between imposing 'law' on the work of tribunals or not. That is not what is occurring, however. The 'leeway' given to a specialist tribunal is the *outcome* of the legal reasoning that a court has engaged in. To get to that outcome courts are having to integrate the legally pluralist frameworks of tribunals with administrative law doctrine.

The grounds of legal challenge in cases concerning specialist administrative tribunals are as multifarious as the grounds of review concerning challenges to administrative decision-makers. What those grounds are, and the legal reasoning they give rise to, will depend on the specific legal culture.[112] With that said, what adjudication of these cases has in common is that courts are required to scrutinise the statutory, institutional, and contextual context carefully and integrate it with precedents. The Australian case law concerning jurisdictional and non-jurisdictional error, in which specialist tribunals and inferior courts commonly feature, is a good illustration.[113]

[106] Eg *Privacy International* (n 99); and *Kirk* (n 38).

[107] Michael Fordham, *The Judicial Review Handbook* (7th edn, Hart, 2021) at [13.4.5] and [42.1.5].

[108] See the cases discussed in M Aronson, M Groves, and G Weeks, *Judicial Review of Administrative Action* (7th edn, ThomsonReuters, 2021) at [5.150].

[109] *Brimbella Pty Ltd v Mosman Municipal Council* (1985) 79 LGERA 367, 368 and *Criminal Injuries Compensation Authority v Hutton & Ors* [2016] EWCA Civ 1305 at [56].

[110] *G v Scottish Ministers & Anor* [2013] UKSC 79 at [76].

[111] Fordham (n 107) at [36.3.2].

[112] V Malsukhum, *Legal Culture, Legality, and the Determination of the Grounds of Review of Administrative Action in England and Australia* (Singapore, Springer, 2021).

[113] Eg *Kirk* (n 38). Care needs to be taken with some of this case law as it concerns cases when an EPT is exercising some form of judicial review power. See, eg, *Timbarra Protection Coalition Inc v Ross Mining NL* [1999] NSWCA 8; 46 NSWLR 55; 102 LGERA 52.

But there are many other examples. For example, judicial reviewing courts are dealing with legal questions concerning the substantive understanding of the legislative tasks of a specialist tribunal.[114] The New Zealand (NZ) case of *King Salmon* is a case in point.[115] In that case the NZ Supreme Court concluded that the NZEC, in tandem with High Court precedents,[116] had come to interpret its legislative obligations under the Resource Management Act 1991 (NZ) (RMA) in a way that did not acknowledge the full nature of the legal architecture of that Act. Put in its simplest terms, over time the NZEC had developed a body of doctrine in which section 5 of the RMA (which set out the multifaceted concept of sustainable management) was understood to dictate an 'overall judgment' approach to decision-making that downplayed the texts and hierarchy of plans made under the Act. The Supreme Court, after a careful analysis of the statutory scheme, concluded that:

> Section 5 was not intended to be an operative provision, in the sense that it is not a section under which particular planning decisions are made; rather, it sets out the RMA's overall objective. Reflecting the open-textured nature of pt 2, Parliament has provided for a hierarchy of planning documents the purpose of which is to flesh out the principles in s 5 and the remainder of pt 2 in a manner that is increasingly detailed both as to content and location. It is these documents that provide the basis for decision-making, even though pt 2 remains relevant. It does not follow from the statutory scheme that because pt 2 is open-textured, all or some of the planning documents that sit under it must be interpreted as being open-textured.[117]

None of this was to negate the specialist nature of the NZEC, but rather to assess and understand that specialist nature in the context of the overall legal architecture of the RMA.[118] In doing that, this case reorientated legal understanding of the role and nature of the NZEC.[119]

As that case illustrates, reviewing specialist tribunals is often primarily an exercise of statutory construction (or deconstruction). That exercise accommodates not only primary legislation but may also take into account delegated legislation and guidance and other forms of documentation that exist.[120] Courts also need to consider the implications of legislative reform.[121]

[114] Eg *Kidd v Resource Management and Planning Appeal Tribunal* [2012] TASSC 60 (breach of s 24, Resource Management and Planning Appeal Tribunal Act 1993 (Tas)) and *Darkinjung Local Aboriginal Land Council v Minister Administering the Crown Land Management Act 2016* [2022] NSWCA 275, (2022) 254 LGERA 311 (interpretation of s 36(1)(c), Aboriginal Land Rights Act 1983 (NSW)).

[115] *Environmental Defence Society Incorporated v The New Zealand King Salmon Company Limited* [2014] NZSC 38.

[116] *New Zealand Rail Ltd v Marlborough District Council* [1994] NZRMA 70 (HC).

[117] *Environmental Defence Society Incorporated* (n 115) at [151].

[118] ibid at [150].

[119] *Eden-Epsom Residential Protection Society Incorporated v Auckland Council* [2022] NZ Env C 60 and *Port Otago Limited v Environmental Defence Society Incorporated* [2021] NZCA 638.

[120] See also *QCoal Pty Ltd v Isaac Regional Council* [2022] QCA 237 (2022) 254 LGERA 228 (planning schemes);.

[121] On the NZ context, see S Elias, 'Righting Environmental Justice' (Resource Management Law Association Salmon Lecture 2013), 14. Available at: www.rmla.org.nz/wp-content/uploads/2016/07/

Legal challenges also concern what an EPT is authorised to do as part of merits review.[122] Adjudicating upon these questions requires a form of mixed legal and institutional analysis on the part of a court.[123] This analysis needs to also accommodate the different forms of process that may fall under, or abut, a merits review.[124] Because an EPT is engaging in a form of merits review, the legal analysis must also encompass consideration of the primary decision-maker.[125]

EPTs, like other specialist administrative tribunals, have also been subject to challenges on grounds of procedural impropriety, including bias.[126] Commentators often raise concerns that such challenges raise concerns about 'juridifying' tribunals through imposing legal procedures on them.[127] Such an argument can miss the fact that courts, in considering these arguments, are often engaging in a careful evaluation of the institutional nature of a tribunal. For example, the case of *Bulga Milbrodale Progress Association Inc*[128] (discussed above) was judicially reviewed in *Warkworth Mining Limited v Bulga Milbrodale Progress Association Inc.*[129] It was argued that there were breaches of procedural fairness including in relation to the use of the concept of polycentricity to frame the analysis. The Court dismissed the appeal after a careful analysis of the legal and institutional context.

Arguments about procedural impropriety can also gloss over the legal complexity of the procedural questions raised. Take, for example, the Australian High Court case of *Oakey Coal Action Alliance Inc v New Acland Coal Pty Ltd.*[130] It concerned the legal consequences of apprehended bias in a decision of the Queensland Land Court in the carrying out an administrative function. After a hearing that lasted for nearly 100 days, Member Smith for the Court recommended refusal of an application for the extension of a coal mine.[131] That decision was legally challenged under the relevant judicial review legislation. Justice Bowskill of the Supreme Court of Queensland concluded that no apprehended bias was found, but it was concluded that there had been errors of law. The decision was referred to the Land Court for reconsideration, but with an order that the new decision-maker should be bound by the findings of the original hearing that did not relate to the errors of law and that some of the findings in relation to noise should stand.[132]

salmon_lecture_2013_cj_s_elias.pdf accessed 9 August 2023. For another example, see *NSW Commissioner of Police v Rabbits Eat Lettuce Pty Ltd* [2019] NSWCA 182; 371 ALR 719; 245 LGERA 1.

[122] *Al Maha Pty Ltd v Huajun Investments Pty Ltd* (2018) 233 LGERA 170; [2018] NSWCA 245.

[123] A discussion of this type of analysis can be found in Fisher, 'Administrative Tribunals' (n 5) at 265–7 of *Ku-ring-gai Council v Bunnings Properties Pty Ltd* (2019) 236 LGERA 35 [2019] NSWCA 28.

[124] *McMillan v Taylor* [2023] NSWCA 183 (challenge of a process involving a conciliation conference). See [57]–[65] in particular.

[125] *AQC Dartbrook Management Pty Ltd v Minister for Planning and Public Spaces* [2021] NSWCA 112; 105 NSWLR 152; 247 LGERA 318, [258].

[126] Eg *Gillies v Secretary of State for Work and Pensions*, [2006] UKHL 2, [2006] 1 WLR 781.

[127] For a discussion of some of this literature see C Harlow and R Rawlings, *Law and Administration* (4th edn, CUP, 2022) Ch 14.

[128] *Bulga* (n 79).

[129] *Warkworth Mining* [2014] NSWCA 105; 86 NSWLR 527; 307 ALR 262; 200 LGERA 375, [153].

[130] *Oakey Coal* (n 70).

[131] ibid [12]–[13].

[132] ibid [17].

At that point, two different courses of action happened. The first was that President Kingham of the Land Court did reconsider the decision and recommended that approval with conditions should be given. Second, Justice Bowskill's decision was appealed and cross appealed to the Court of Appeal. The cross appeal was successful, as the Court concluded that there had been apprehended bias, thus raising the question of remedy. The Court of Appeal decided not to set aside the decision for rehearing.[133] On appeal, the High Court of Australia disagreed. As it concluded:

> Kingham P did not behave in any way that gave rise to any apprehension of bias on her part. Through adopting findings and conclusions of Member Smith in accordance with the directions of Bowskill J, the process by which Kingham P arrived at the new recommendations she made nevertheless breached a condition of the exercise of the Land Court's jurisdiction to perform its administrative functions under the MRA [Mineral Resources Act] and the EPA [Environmental Protection Act.[134]

Reaching that conclusion required careful analysis of the legal framework, the role of the Land Court and the Supreme Court in that framework, and consideration of the role of the Land Court in the wider decision-making framework.

The discussion above about judicial review is the tip of an iceberg of case law. It has focused on a few cases in relation to one set of specialist tribunals. What it illustrates is that the legal analysis in these cases is requiring reviewing courts to often integrate the different legislative provisions that relate to a decision made by a tribunal along with an understanding of the institutional arrangement.[135] A court performing judicial review is required to sift through the different statutory provisions, and analogise with cases concerning specialist tribunals from other legal contexts,[136] This is a process of relating the horizontal grounds of review with the vertical context.[137]

What is significant is the reasoning process that courts are engaged in to do that. There are some examples where courts will state that issues of law are best left to specialist appellate tribunals and do not explain exactly why that is so. But there are many examples of where courts are not imposing 'conclusory labels'[138] and are working assiduously with the relevant legal and administrative material. Much of what they will focus on will be to do with the specialist authority of an EPT (in the sense discussed above), but it also relates to capacity.

[133] ibid [28].
[134] ibid [49].
[135] Eg *Broken Hill Cobalt Project Pty Ltd v Lord* [2022] NSWCA 271 (whether reasons are adequate required consideration of provisions of the Mining Act 1992 (NSW) and the LEC Act 1979 (NSW)) and *Sullivan v District Council of Riverton* (1997) 95 LGERA 150, 154 ('There is nothing in the Development Act which requires the consideration of the relevant issues in any particular order'.).
[136] *Secretary of Department of Environment, Energy and Climate Action v Hanson Construction Materials Pty Ltd* [2023] VSC 353, [25]–[36].
[137] M Aronson, 'Judicial Review of Administrative Action: Between Grand Theory and Muddling Through' (2021) 28 *AJAL* 6, 9.
[138] Aronson, Groves, and Weeks, (n 108) at [3.70]. *Jones v First Tier Tribunal* [2013] UKSC 19; [2013] 2 AC 48 at [16].

Take, for example, *King Salmon*.[139] As seen above, that case was about statutory construction of the authority of the NZEC under the RMA. As Warnock notes, the case also 'increases the importance given to public participation in the decision-making process by elevating the legal weight of plans made with full public input'.[140] Likewise, the questions about polycentricity and procedural fairness in *Warkworth Mining Limited* are directly concerned what type of evidence was considered in the merits review process and how it was assessed.[141] The issues to do with the consequences of apprehended bias in *Oakey Coal Action Alliance Inc* impacted upon what issues could be considered in the latter rehearing.[142]

Given the complexity of specialist tribunals it is also not surprising that such material can give rise to competing interpretations and arguments.[143] In working through this material, respect is paid to the specialist nature of the tribunal,[144] but that respect does not negate the need for a court to engage in legal and institutional analysis that accommodates the authority and capacity of a specialist tribunal.

Towards Different Paradigms of Administrative Law Thought

As stated in the introduction, the above has been an exercise in legal description. It has covered a lot of ground and so it is useful to sum up my analysis so far. Specialist administrative tribunals are a typical feature of administrative law landscapes. As Arthurs noted, 'there is an attachment [in the administrative law context], conscious or implicit, to a special system of law directed to a limited range of purposes and persons, with a limited range of powers, and with at least partial autonomy from the general legal system'.[145] EPTs are a subset of specialised administrative tribunals and they have been created to handle particular types of disputes. In performing their functions, the specialist nature of EPTs is multifaceted. It encompasses both authority and capacity. It has both legal and non-legal dimensions. While tribunals have a functional purpose, they do not necessarily operate functionally. Reforms can make matters worse.[146] EPTs, like all specialist tribunals, have given rise to a significant body of judicial review case law. A feature of that case law is the need for courts to engage in legal and institutional analysis.

[139] *King Salmon* (n 115).

[140] Warnock (n 86) 387. See also Elias (n 121) 6.

[141] *Warkworth Mining* (n 129) at [165]–[174].

[142] *Oakey Coal* (n 130).

[143] See the discussion of the nature of the Investigatory powers Tribunal in *Privacy International* (n 99) as discussed in Fisher, 'Administrative Tribunals' (n 5) 273–4.

[144] *Department for Work and Pensions v The Information Commissioner & Anor* [2016] EWCA Civ 758, [2016] WLR 1 at [30]–[36];.

[145] Arthurs (n 83) 193.

[146] R Bacon, 'A Study in Tribunal Amalgamation: the Importance of a Principled Approach' (2005) 12 *J of Social Security Law* 81 discussing the problems of unprincipled amalgamation.

Overall, the legal pluralism of specialist tribunals does not lead to a legal empty space. EPTs have been set up for functional reasons and are novel in legal form but law is doing a lot of work in relation to them. Review of them requires reviewing courts to engage in a form of legal analysis that integrates evaluations of a tribunal's authority and capacity with existing legal doctrines. What is distinctive in these cases is not so much the substance of the doctrine, but the *techniques* of doctrinal analysis. Specialist tribunals, as a 'typical instance' of tribunals, result in 'typical instances' of judicial review doctrine, when their decisions are subject to review. Legal pluralism is not in the margins. It is at the core of what judicial review is.

I appreciate that my exercise of legal description has limits. There is much that has been left out – for example how the architecture and practice of EPTs are shaped by different legal cultures.[147] I could also explore in greater depth how 'merits review' in any context is a complex legal construct.[148] I am also aware that the above description raises many questions about how administrative law scholars think about tribunals. Does the functional logic of EPTs still make sense in light of legal complexity of these tribunals? Given that legal complexity, how should judicial review of EPTs be evaluated? But raising these questions is exactly the point of my analysis. By paying legal attention to specialist tribunals, a new set of issues for administrative law scholars to think about emerge. Let me identify three here.

First, 'specialisation' and 'specialist' are descriptors that always need unpacking. That is both by those who think about them in functional terms and in the context of doctrinal exercises such as judicial review. Specialisation and specialist (and expertise for that matter) are not fixed concepts. They are multifaceted. Unpacking them requires consideration of authority and capacity. There is a lot of legal analysis involved in that unpacking. Even in one area – environment and planning – a specialist tribunal can take different forms, have different forms of authority, and different capacity. For those involved in the design, reform and review of specialist administrative tribunals there is a lot to think about.

Second, as I have discussed elsewhere, the analysis above highlights the need to revisit how tribunals are understood as functional objects they are non-legal.[149] That is an issue for all administrative tribunals, but it is particularly so for specialist tribunals. 'Specialisation' is seen as the 'hallmark of modern society'.[150] Specialist tribunals thus are seemingly part of a more efficient mode of governing.[151] Law is not seen as part of that mode. Indeed, for some, the 'judicialisation' of tribunals is seen as problematic.[152]

[147] E Fisher '"Jurisdictional" Facts and "Hot" Facts: Legal Formalism, Legal Pluralism, and the Nature of Australian Administrative Law' (2015) 38 *MULR* 968.
[148] Fisher, 'Administrative Law' (n 8).
[149] Fisher, 'Administrative Tribunals' (n 5).
[150] Baum (n 90) 1, 4.
[151] H Street, *Justice in the Welfare State* (2nd edn, Steven and Sons, 1975) 7–9.
[152] See the scholars discussed at Harlow and Rawlings (n 127) ch 14.

That reflects how administrative law thought is seemingly riven with an intellectual division that requires a choice to be made. The way in which that division is mapped varies. For example, it is characterised as involving divergences between red light theory and green light theories of intellectual thought[153] or between normativist and functionalist styles of public law thought.[154] Law is understood to be the province of the former and administration in the latter.[155] Tribunals, being separation of powers misfits, have never fit in easily to this analysis,[156] but have tended to be treated by scholars as functional adjuncts to administrative law. In being so, they have tended to be shuttered off from mainstream legal analysis. That has narrowed down how tribunals are imagined.

In part this is an artificial divide. Two different disciplinary paradigms are engaged in different intellectual exercises. As Allan has noted in the context of the ultra vires/common law debate: '[t]he "normativist" defence of the rule of law and separation of powers, based on arguments drawn from political theory, is rejected by a "functionalist" counterclaim, summarising the conclusions drawn by descriptive political science'.[157] But it also reflects the way in which functionalist styles of analysis reject legal positivism but provide no alternative account of law.[158] Law tends to be understood as about the delivery of social democratic policy.[159] That functional and non-legal understanding of tribunals is used both to praise them[160] but also to criticise them.[161] As Warnock has noted, instrumentalist frames can be 'highly exclusionary' in that they focus on ends and outputs.[162] What is missing from the analysis is the importance of law and legal reasoning. Paying attention to specialist administrative tribunals requires paying attention to their legal nature. None of this negates the importance of functional institutions like EPTs. Rather it makes clear they do not displace law.

This leads onto the third implication of my analysis above. Recognising the legal complexity of specialist administrative tribunals has implications for how law is understood. Paying attention to them requires richer forms of legal reasoning and legal analysis. This includes the decisions of tribunals themselves,[163] the legal architecture of tribunals, and judicial review doctrine. Legal pluralism is thus

[153] ibid ch 1.

[154] M Loughlin, *Public Law and Political Theory* (Clarendon Press, 1992).

[155] See also Fisher and Shapiro (n 51) Ch 1.

[156] J Farmer, *Tribunals and Government* (London, Weidenfeld and Nicolson, 1974) 166.

[157] TRS Allan, 'The Constitutional Foundations of Judicial Review: Conceptual Conundrum or Interpretative Inquiry?' (2002) 61 *CLJ* 87, 92.

[158] Loughlin (n 154) 245.

[159] D Dyzenhaus, *The Constitution of Law: Legality in Time of Emergency* (Cambridge, CUP, 2006) 124–5.

[160] T Daya-Winterbottom, 'Specialist Courts and Tribunals' (2004) 2 *Waikato L Rev* 21, 24.

[161] Rackemann, (n 87) 89. See also *Kirk* (n 38) [122] per Heydon J dissenting.

[162] Warnock (n 9) 74.

[163] For a discussion of the precedent value of tribunal decisions versus judicial review see R Creyke and J McMillan, 'Executive Perceptions of Administrative Law – An Empirical Study, (2002) 9 *AJAL* 163, 168.

interwoven with mainstream legal thought.[164] As Arthurs noted: '[a]dministrative tribunals are not necessarily courts writ small, any more than courts in the exercise of their reviewing function are merely administrative tribunals writ large'.[165] Both are doing forms of law and there is much legal work in relating them to each other, relating the specific to the generic, and relating legal pluralism to legal centralism. Indeed, this work could be argued to be the central task of administrative law.

That relates to a broader point. In recent years there have been those judicial review scholars who are anxious about what they see as a body of doctrine akin to 'Tennysonnian wilderness of single instances'.[166] The idea that in judicial review 'context is everything'[167] is a reason for analytical uneasiness.[168] There is also disquiet over ideas of deferential and intensive review.[169] And there are those that doubt that the intellectual robustness of particular doctrines.[170] Overall, there is a suspicion that judges are using law as a smokescreen for deciding cases on the basis of their own preferences.[171] The analysis above suggests the need to shift attention. This body of doctrine is not so much the product of idiosyncratic judging, but to do with the detailed particularities of different specialist administrative tribunal schemes both in terms of the authority and capacity a tribunal has. This illustrates not only that '[j]udicial review's vertical dimensions are both unavoidable and perfectly proper'[172] but that what coheres the treatment of those different vertical dimensions together is a style of administrative law reasoning.

That is particularly obvious in relation to specialist administrative tribunals because their authority and capacity are subject to detailed statutory frameworks. How a court crafts its review in light of particular regimes is more visible than in other contexts. Aronson has noted that legislation is often incomplete in the way it governs administrative action and there are no Brandeis briefs explaining administrative structures.[173] But specialist administrative tribunals, particularly in Australia, are part of detailed legislative frameworks.[174] A study of the judicial review case law in relation to EPTs illustrates how much judicial review doctrine is a set of techniques for assessing the legality of action in relation to legally pluralist schemes set out in legislation.

[164] See also Fisher '"Jurisdictional" Facts' (n 147).
[165] HW Arthurs, 'Rethinking Administrative Law: A Slightly Dicey Business' (1979) 17 *Osgoode Hall LJ* 1, 37.
[166] J Varuhas, 'Mapping Doctrinal Methods' in P Daly and J Tomlinson (eds), *Researching Public Law in Common Law Systems* (Edward Elgar, 2023) and A Hutchinson, 'Why I Don't Teach Administrative Law (and Perhaps Why I Should)' (2016) 53 *Osgoode Hall LJ* 1033, 1041.
[167] *R v Secretary of State for the Home Department, ex parte Daly* [2001] 2 AC 532, 548 at [28].
[168] J Varuhas, 'Taxonomy and Public Law' in M Elliott, J Varuhas, and S Wilson Stark (eds) *The Unity of Public Law?: Doctrinal, Theoretical, and Comparative Perspectives* (Hart, 2018) 51.
[169] D Knight, *Vigilance and Restraint in the Common Law of Judicial Review* (, CUP, 2018) 193.
[170] C Forsyth and I Ghosh, *Wade and Forsyth's Administrative Law* (12th edn, OUP, 2023) 211.
[171] Hutchinson (n 166).
[172] Aronson, Groves and Weeks (n 108) at [3.50].
[173] Aronson (n 137) 15.
[174] A point Aronson recognises, ibid 14.

Paying attention to specialist administrative tribunals thus underscores the need to pay attention to the processes of doctrinal legal reasoning and how courts unpack the 'specialist' nature of institutions.[175] As seen above, how a court approaches reviewing a specialist tribunal is less a single decision about how intensive or deferential review should be and more a product of engaging with the different aspects a tribunal's specialised nature.[176] None of that is to say the reasoning in all cases is equal. But more careful study of judicial review of specialist tribunals offers a way of deepening understandings of what work 'context' is doing in reasoning.[177] For the administrative lawyer immersed in doctrinal reasoning, none of the above is surprising. It is a reality of 'typical instances'. It also begs many questions about how courts are crafting their review and whether there are patterns to be seen in how courts approach and understand tribunal architectures. But that is my point. Specialist administrative tribunals raise many legal questions and paradigms of administrative law thought should reflect that.

Conclusion

Let me conclude with this. Writing this chapter required constant reference to different statutes and different cases. As I sat at my computer researching and writing, the books and notes I needed to refer to turned into tottering piles and the number of windows open on my screen multiplied. I engaged in close reading, and even closer re-reading. Not just of legal material, but of secondary sources that concerned the institutional logics of tribunals and the nature of the problems that tribunals were considering. I also needed to revisit legal doctrines and concepts in administrative law I thought I knew well. I pondered the Australian doctrine of jurisdictional error and thought again about procedural fairness. Paying attention to 'the dynamism and "definitional sensitivity"'[178] of the legal arrangements of specialist administrative tribunals is hard legal work. Even when is only analysing a small subset of tribunals.

Stating this fact is not a complaint on my part. Rather it underscores that thinking about, and writing about, specialist administrative tribunals as a scholarly task requires hands on engagement with a lot of law. Not only that, but it is also a very challenging task. That writing of this chapter drew on all my administrative law and scholarly skills, and then some. Thus, paying attention to specialist tribunals is not only about developing more robust scholarly models of administrative law thought. It is also ultimately about fostering our expertise as legal scholars.

[175] See this in relation to public administration in Fisher and Shapiro (n 51) chs 8 and 9.

[176] Besides the examples above see *C and S v Special Education Needs and Disability Tribunal & Anor* [2007] EWHC 1812, [18]–[24].

[177] See, eg, the work it is doing in *Shi v Migration Agents Registration Authority* (2008) 235 CLR 286, 295 at [25]; J Bell, ACL Davies and E Fisher, 'Tailored Judicial Review Doctrine, Tailoring Judicial Review Doctrine' [2024] PL, forthcoming.

[178] Cane (n 1) 279.

PART TWO

Tribunals in the Common Law World

7

The Unique Jurisdiction of Australian Merits Review Tribunals

MATTHEW GROVES AND GREG WEEKS

Introduction

Tribunals occupy a distinct position in Australia by reason of our quite rigid approach to the separation of powers. The Australian Constitution creates and allocates power into three main parts – legislative, executive and judicial – but the evolution and maintenance of this separation of powers doctrine has focused heavily on the protection of judicial power.[1] The effect on tribunals of that doctrinal journey has been profound. The powers and functions of Australian tribunals are determined by constitutional considerations but somewhat indirectly – constitutionally, tribunals are simply part of the executive. Judicial power may only be exercised by courts that are constituted in accordance with constitutional imperatives. Only courts can make authoritative and binding declarations of the law.[2] A tribunal is usually conceived negatively; it is what a court is not. In this sense, the province of tribunals is judicial leftovers – no small thing – but such a conception gives insufficient consideration to the fact that tribunals do many things that courts *cannot* do.

Foundational constitutional rules shaped conceptions of non-judicial bodies long before tribunals came into the fore of Australian law. Many of the early constitutional cases that yielded enduring rules were about industrial and other commissions, whose powers and functions often ran aground on the separation of powers doctrine.[3] The principles derived from those cases informed the creation

[1] This separation and protection of judicial power was extended to state courts in *Kable v DPP (NSW)* (1996) 189 CLR 51; *Kirk v Industrial Court of NSW* (2010) 239 CLR 531.

[2] *Huddart Parker & Co Pty Ltd v Moorehead* (1909) 8 CLR 330, 357. This principle means the orders of tribunals cannot be enforceable in the same manner as the orders of courts: *Brandy v Human Rights & Equal Opportunity Commission* (1995) 183 CLR 245.

[3] See, eg, *New South Wales v Commonwealth* (1915) 20 CLR 54 ('*Wheat Case*'); *Waterside Workers' Federation of Australia v JW Alexander Ltd* (1918) 25 CLR 434; *R v Kirby; Ex parte Boilermakers' Society of Australia* (1956) 94 CLR 254.

of Australia's first tribunal of general administrative jurisdiction in 1975 – the Administrative Appeals Tribunal (AAT). The design of the AAT was heavily influenced by constitutional limitations but also sought to exploit the obverse of those restrictions. The principles that confer courts with exclusive jurisdiction over questions of law also preclude their involvement in the substantive merits of any decision that gives rise to a question of law. The administrative power denied to the courts was the heart of the AAT's jurisdiction. One of the remedies conferred upon the AAT was the power to replace the decision under review with a new one made by the tribunal itself. This remedy became known as merits review and was characterised as the doctrinal opposite of judicial review. The nature and content of merits review has evolved with increasing sophistication, but that growth has never escaped its origins. Merits review can only be fully understood as something that judicial review is not. That distinction applies in the same way as the distinction between courts and tribunals described above.

The merits review function of the AAT was widely lauded as a quick, simple and efficient alternative to judicial review with significant remedial advantages over court orders. The success of the AAT was confirmed by its replication. Every state and territory created its own merits review tribunal.[4] Those tribunals were modelled on their federal counterpart but incorporated innovations that in turn influenced reforms to the AAT. The most significant change was amalgamation. The states amalgamated virtually all of their tribunals into a single 'super tribunal' of sorts.[5] The Commonwealth followed suit by incorporating migration, refugee and social security tribunals into the AAT.[6] This enormous new caseload has enlarged the AAT,[7] arguably even engulfed it. The consequences are still felt.[8] Before we examine those changes, it is useful to revisit the creation of the AAT.

The 'New Administrative Law' and the Modern Australian Tribunal

In the first 70 years of federation, Australian administrative law operated essentially as a copied version of English law, particularly in judicial review. The impetus for change began in the late 1960s with an acceptance that the highly technical

[4] The first was Victoria's *Administrative Appeals Tribunal Act 1984* (Vic).

[5] The first was created under the Victorian Civil and Administrative Tribunals Act 1998 (Vic). This was followed by State Administrative Tribunal Act 2004 (WA); Queensland Civil and Administrative Tribunal 2009 (Qld); Civil and Administrative Tribunal Act 2013 (NSW); South Australian Civil and Administrative Tribunal Act 2013 (SA); Northern Territory Civil and Administrative Tribunal Act 2014 (NT); Tasmanian Civil and Administrative Tribunal Act 2020 (Tas). Future references to these statutes are abbreviated to the initials of the relevant statute.

[6] By enacting the Tribunals Amalgamation Act 2015 (Cth).

[7] The amalgamation of federal tribunals incorporated specialist migration and social security tribunals into the AAT. Migration and social security applications comprise 46% and 29% of all AAT applications: Administrative Appeals Tribunal, *Annual Report 2021–22* (2023) 28.

[8] M Groves and G Weeks, 'Tribunal Justice and Politics in Australia: The Rise and Fall of the Administrative Appeals Tribunal' (2023) 97 *ALJ* 278, 284–285.

procedures governing prerogative writs were long overdue for reform.[9] The federal Solicitor-General of the day, Anthony Mason QC (later Chief Justice of Australia), suggested the establishment of a specialist group to review and recommend reforms.[10] The terms of reference of this group – the Kerr Committee – were to consider the jurisdiction of a proposed federal superior court to review administrative decisions, the procedure and substantive grounds of review, and the desirability of introducing legislation akin to the Tribunal and Inquiries Act 1958 (UK).[11] That reference to British innovations is apt to mislead because the focus of the Kerr Committee fell to the local constitutional constraints that would shape any reforms. The Committee decided that structures modelled on the French *Conseil d'Etat* and *tribuneaux administratifs*, which would require constitutional amendment and enormous cultural change, which were 'to be avoided at all costs.'[12]

The key solution suggested by the Kerr Committee was to establish a specialist tribunal with general review jurisdiction over federal administrative decisions. The proposed 'Administrative Review Tribunal' would be empowered to reconsider and remake administrative decisions. The Kerr Committee was acutely mindful that this task could not be vested in a court because key aspects of the proposed remedy and the methodology used to reach it lacked ingredients essential to the Australian conception of judicial power.[13] The two committees established to consider and refine the recommendations of the Kerr Committee reached largely similar conclusions,[14] which greatly reduced official resistance to large scale reforms. One of those later committees lamented the 'burgeoning proliferation' of specialist tribunals,[15] which tacitly strengthened the case to establish an administrative tribunal of wide jurisdiction.

The AAT was only one part of a complete reformation of Australian administrative law that also included creation of a federal Ombudsman, codification

[9] See, eg, D Benjafield and H Whitmore, *Principles of Administrative Law* (Law Book Co, 3rd edn 1966) 314 (criticising the 'highly dangerous effect' of the 'uncontrolled and unsystematic creation of ad hoc administrative bodies').

[10] Sir A Mason, 'Administrative Law Reform: The Vision and the Reality' (2001) 8 *Australia Journal of Administrative Law* 135, 136–7.

[11] The terms of reference were slightly amended to include the possibility that federal judicial review could occur either in a new specialist court or other courts exercising federal jurisdiction: Mason, ibid 137.

[12] Mason (n 10) 138. The Committee also examined the systems of the UK, New Zealand and America: [Australia] *Commonwealth Administrative Review Committee Report* (Parliamentary Paper 144/1971) ('the *Kerr Committee Report*') chs 2–5.

[13] Mason (n 10) 139. A member of the Kerr Committee acknowledged that most review cases would involve people wishing to 'challenge findings of fact which they consider to be wrong[ly]' made in discretionary decision-making: H Whitmore, 'Reform of Administrative Law' (1972) 5 *Federal Law Review* 5, 11. The review and remaking of such judgments do not involve a dispute or question of law which is one hallmark of judicial power. The remaking of administrative decisions by courts would also involve an impermissible judicial exercise of executive power.

[14] *Interim Report of the Committee on Administrative Discretions* ('the Bland Committee Interim Report') (Parliamentary Paper 53/1973); *Final Report of the Committee on Administrative Discretions* (Parliamentary Paper 316/1973); *Report of the Committee of Review of Prerogative Writ Procedures* ('the Ellicott Report') (Parliamentary Paper 56/1973).

[15] *Bland Committee Interim Report* 24. Most of that report was devoted to the ombudsman's office.

of judicial review and enactment of freedom of information legislation. When the federal scheme was commenced, there was no indication that the states and territories would follow suit by creating tribunals of broad jurisdiction,[16] although those jurisdictions largely adopted very similar comprehensive schemes of administrative review and accountability.[17] The collective impact of these and other procedural reforms was greater than their individual parts. A senior judge explained that one of the wider consequences of these systemic changes was the introduction of a 'new and distinctive' element to public governance, which he termed 'administrative responsibility'. That judge reasoned:

> What we now have, operating in parallel to the system of ministerial responsibility – both individual and collective – is a system that is appropriately characterised as 'administrative responsibility'… a system by which public servants have a direct responsibility for their conduct, not merely a derivative responsibility, through their minister and parliament.[18]

This new framework also fostered connections between institutions. The AAT was integrated into the federal judicial system in several ways. One was that the tribunal President was required to be a judge of the Federal Court of Australia.[19] Other members of that court may sit as Deputy Presidents of the AAT,[20] but the many judges appointed to these roles over the years have rarely presided in that capacity. Most Deputy Presidents are full time tribunal members who do not hold judicial office. The remainder of the tribunal is a hierarchical structure of senior members and members. Substantive decisions of the AAT were originally amenable to appeal in the Federal Court on a question of law.[21] When the AAT later assumed the jurisdiction of other federal tribunals, the right of review from AAT decisions was amended so that many less-complex decisions could be appealed to a lower court of federal jurisdiction.[22] Most of the AAT's procedural determinations are amenable to supervisory review.[23]

[16] In most instances, federal reforms flowed through to the states and territories. The exception was ombudsman legislation which had been introduced earlier by Western Australia (1971), South Australia (1972), Victoria (1973), Queensland (1974) and New South Wales (1974) and followed swiftly in Tasmania (1978) and the ACT (1983).

[17] The notable exception is the codification of judicial review, which has not occurred in Western Australia, New South Wales, South Australia or the Northern Territory.

[18] J Spigelman, 'Foundations of Administrative Law: Towards General Principles of Institutional Law' (1999) 58 *Australian Journal of Public Administration* 3, 7.

[19] AAT Act, s 7(1).

[20] AAT Act, s 7(2)(a). That provision now allows judges of the Federal Circuit and Family Court of Australia to sit as Deputy Presidents.

[21] AAT Act, s 44(1). Appeals must involve 'a question of law'. There is a large and largely arid body of doctrine on the difference between a question and an error of law.

[22] AAT Act, s 44AAA(1) allows an appeal to the Federal Circuit and Family Court of Australia of AAT decisions about child support dispute. The Federal Court can also transfer appeals to this lower court unless the decision was made by the President or a Deputy President of the AAT: s 44AA(1)(2). These provisions effectively divide appeal rights to the higher and lower federal courts according to the status of the AAT constituted to make the decision under appeal.

[23] This is possible under the Administrative Decisions (Judicial Review) Act 1977 (Cth) or the Judiciary Act 1903 (Cth) s 39B. The latter vests in lower federal court the original supervisory jurisdiction of the High Court of Australia entrenched in s 75(v) of the Australian Constitution.

The right of appeal from decisions of the AAT to the Federal Court was only one of many connections between these new elements of administrative governance and review. The Commonwealth Ombudsman was empowered to refer questions about administrative action to the AAT, which in turn could refer questions of law to the Federal Court.[24] The main connection drawn between each of these various institutions was the Administrative Review Council (ARC), which was created as a standing body to review all aspects of the federal administrative review system, including the practices of government agencies and officials and the scope of administrative review mechanisms.[25] The ARC was comprised of the Presidents of the AAT and the Australian Law Reform Commission, the Ombudsman and later also the President of the Australian Human Rights Commission and Commonwealth Information Commissioner as ex officio members, along with others appointed by the government of the day.[26] The Council conducted significant inquiries into important policy issues such as automated decision-making,[27] as well as providing a policy framework to determine which decisions should be subject to merits review.[28] The role of the ARC will become more apparent later in this chapter.

The Procedural Reforms of the AAT

The purpose of the AAT was long clear, at least in a superficial sense, but legislatively unclear. The AAT Act was enacted without any statement of purpose or objectives provision.[29] That omission was only corrected 30 years later when amending legislation provided that the tribunal's purposes were to provide a form of review that was accessible, fair, just, quick, informal, proportionate to the matter under review and to do so in a way that promotes public trust and confidence on the tribunal's decision-making.[30] This belated legislative statement of purpose

[24] Enabled respectively by the Ombudsman Act 1976 (Cth) s10A(1) and AAT Act s 45.

[25] AAT Act, s 51.

[26] ibid s 49(1). The latter two officers were added to the ARC upon enactment of the Australian Human Rights Commission Act 1986 (Cth) and the Australian Information Commissioner Act 2010 (Cth).

[27] Administrative Review Council, *Automated Assistance in Administrative Decision Making* (ARC Report 46, 2004). This report was ahead of its time.

[28] Administrative Review Council, *What Decisions Should be Subject to Merits Review?* (1999).

[29] The same is true of the codification of judicial review achieved by the Administrative Decisions (Judicial Review) Act 1977 (Cth). Unlike the AAT Act, this legislation still has no objectives provision. This may not be accidental. Mason suggested political and bureaucratic opposition to codifying judicial review could be overcome if the project was confined to 'simplification and clarification': Mason (n 10) 138. That simplicity may have included omitting wide ranging purposive provisions. Another possible answer is that Australian judicial review is so remedially focused that any other purpose is secondary at best. We do not fully accept such cynicism.

[30] AAT Act, s 2A, the first of which was inserted by Administrative Appeals Tribunal Amendment Act 2005 (Cth). The objectives of proportionality and public confidence were added by Tribunals Amalgamation Act 2015 (Cth).

acknowledged what was apparent from the disparate provisions of the AAT Act and the style of review that had evolved.[31] The absence of a clear statement of purpose in the AAT Act had a curious parallel with the content of the statute itself. The AAT Act contained a raft of innovative procedures for the lodging and hearing of cases yet was entirely silent on the mode of review. These curious omissions meant the AAT Act was awash with procedural detail but strangely obscure on the key questions of 'why' and 'how' reviews were to be conducted.

As a creature of statute itself, the AAT has no inherent jurisdiction and can only be conferred with jurisdiction by a statute to review decisions made or given effect under that statute.[32] This mechanism enables the AAT's jurisdiction to be conferred as part of the making or amendment of statutes, but also provides the legislature with a discretion constrained only by the Constitution to confer as much or as little review jurisdiction as the government of the day might wish. The Administrative Review Council published guidelines to inform the judgment of which decisions or powers should be subject to merits review.[33] The impact of those guidelines has not been subject to empirical study, though it is notable that AAT was conferred review jurisdiction under 500 statutes by 2023.

Two aspects of the AAT Act heralded an accessible approach to its jurisdiction. Each can have a great impact at the early stages of a claim. One was a standing requirement to govern representative and public interest bodies. Australian judicial review law remains wedded to a test of 'special interest',[34] which has proven restrictive to public interest bodies. Those litigants can only gain standing if they are able to satisfy a court that they have sufficient involvement with, or connection, the subject of the relevant decision. This standing test remains a significant obstacle to public interest judicial review claims but has never arisen in the AAT. The AAT Act provides that an 'organization or association of people, whether incorporated or not' will be deemed to have interests affected by a decision 'relates to a matter included in the objects or purposes' of that body.[35] This inclusive standing test for public interest bodies has not been replicated in state and territory bodies and, perhaps more surprisingly, was not repealed by the federal government when a more flexible approach to the standing of public interest groups evolved in judicial review.[36] Another aspect of the AAT Act relevant to early stages of a claim is

[31] The legislative articulation of the purposes of the AAT was probably sparked by the enactment a year earlier of the SAT Act (WA), which provided the first coherent legislative of purpose of such a tribunal. The VCAT Act 1998 (Vic) does not explain the purposes of that tribunal and s 1 simply explains that the Act is intended to 'establish a Victorian Civil and Administrative Tribunal'.

[32] AAT Act, s 25(1).

[33] Administrative Review Council, *What Decisions Should be Subject to Merits Review?* (n 28). This document has long provided de facto guidance to state and territory governments.

[34] *Australian Conservation Foundation v Commonwealth* (1980) 146 CLR 493. This case affirmed key elements of *Boyce v Paddington Borough Council* [1903] 1 Ch 109.

[35] AAT Act, s 27(2). This presumption does not apply if the body was formed, or its objects or purposes were amended to incorporate the subject of the decision, after the decision was made: s 27(3).

[36] That trend in judicial review cases began with *North Coast Environment Council Inc v Minister for Resources* (1994) 55 FCR 492.

the right to reasons for administrative decisions, which Australian common law continues to deny.[37] The AAT Act creates a right to reasons for decisions that can be reviewed by the tribunal and allows reasons to be sought even if no application for review is lodged.[38]

The procedures to lodge an application and prepare for a hearing in the AAT were strikingly simple.[39] When an application for review was lodged, the respondent agency was required to file and serve copies of all material relevant to the decision.[40] This obligation bypassed lengthy pre-trial preparation and often also enabled applicants to obtain internal policies and other soft law material previously hidden from public view.[41] That procedural simplicity was continued in the requirements to prepare for hearings. Both the applicant and the respondent agency had to lodge a simple statement that explained the key facts and contentions of the application.[42] These streamlined prehearing procedures were a striking contrast to the technical demands of judicial review claims.[43] Importantly, the procedures to lodge applications and prepare for hearings were simple enough that they could be completed by applicants who lacked legal representation or training.

The individual administrative responsibility we previously explained manifested in different ways in the AAT. Reasons for decisions issued under the new rights in merits and statutory judicial review were signed by a decision-maker. In merits review, individual officials began to appear in hearings and give evidence

[37] *Public Service Board (NSW) v Osmond* (1986) 159 CLR 656. This case was decided against the backdrop of statutory rights to reasons developing federally. It remains good law, largely because statutory rights to reasons are so common that the chance of a suitable vehicle to review *Osmond* reaching the High Court is remote.

[38] AAT Act, s 28(1). This provision enables decision-makers to contest a claim to reasons: s 28(1AA)–(1CC). It also enables people to seek better reasons by order of the AAT, if the ones provided are found inadequate: s 28(5)–(6). Similar rights exist in the Administrative Decisions (Judicial Review) Act 1977 (Cth), s 13.

[39] Another important procedural issue is the relatively low fee to file AAT applications. The fee before abolition of the AAT was $1,082: Administrative Appeals Tribunal Regulations 2015 (Cth) reg 20(1). The fee for most migration applications was $3,374. Both fees could be reduced by reason of hardship. The filing fee for an appeal from the AAT to the Federal Court was $11,890 (for corporations) and $5,505 (for all other parties): Federal Court and Federal Circuit Court and Family Court Regulations 2022 (Cth), Sch 2.

[40] AAT Act, s 37.

[41] Effectively working in tandem with the Freedom of Information Act 1982 (Cth) s 10, another example of federal administrative review legislation operating as a scheme.

[42] The early practice directions issued by the AT to govern these procedures was only one-and-a-half pages long. The last practice direction issued before abolition of the AAT was 19 pages long but was drafted in plain language and remained easy to follow: AAT, *General Practice Direction* (28 February 2019). Available at: www.aat.gov.au/AAT/media/AAT/Files/Directions%20and%20guides/General-Practice-Direction.pdf.

[43] An important ingredient to this simplicity was that applicants did not need to explain in detail why they sought to challenge a decision. Most applications lodged with the AAT simply stated that review was sought 'because the decision is wrong' and did not elaborate on that simple statement. It was long assumed that such simple statements were sufficient for the requirement that applications for review 'contain a statement of reasons for the application': AAT Act, s 29(1)(c). This long-standing assumption was largely upheld by the High Court in *Miller v Minister for Immigration, Citizenship and Multicultural Affairs* [2024] HCA 13.

on behalf of their agency.[44] The impact of officials appearing in merits review hearings has never been subject to empirical analysis, but anyone who has observed an AAT hearing could not doubt that the appearance and public questioning of officials about the justifications for a decision can dramatically affect the dynamics of hearings.[45]

Another neglected aspect of AAT hearings is the formalised nature of their informality. Informality is codified into merits review hearings in many ways. The AAT is not bound by the rules of evidence,[46] which means that related evidentiary notions such as the burden of proof cannot be imported into merits review hearings.[47] Exemption from the rules of evidence enables the AAT to receive material not admissible in courts, such as hearsay, but the inability of parties to test such material by cross examination means such material is usually given less weight than other material that is received in a hearing.[48] While informality is mandated by statute, its practical application varies markedly within the Tribunal. For example, an application for the AAT to reconsider the denial of a protection visa under the Migration Act 1958 (Cth) is heard by a member but the Minister whose delegate made the original decision plays no part in the hearing; frequently, the member and the applicant (and often an interpreter) are the only people present. By contrast, a member hearing an application to revoke the cancellation of a visa on character grounds under the same statute is often faced by legal representatives (frequently counsel) for both the applicant and the Minister in a hearing that has many of the trappings of judicial procedure, including opening and closing statements, arguments about the admissibility of evidence and so forth. The processes in these two types of proceeding reflect the range encompassed by the objective of informality.

The balance between informality and fairness is reflected in the guiding statutory principle that the AAT must also conduct proceedings with 'as little formality and technicality' and 'as much expedition' as 'a proper consideration of the matter before the Tribunal permit[s]'.[49] This tension between fairness and informality is an ongoing doctrinal one that does not engage more substantive and structural

[44] Ministers remain an exception. Australian governments vigorously contest attempts to force ministers to appear to give evidence, especially in judicial review claims: M Aronson, 'Minister's Signatures – What Do They Prove?' (2023) 30 *Australian Journal of Administrative Law* 10, 25–6.

[45] A related issue is the public nature of hearings, which enables the AAT 'to play its important systemic role as a tool of good government': *Williams & Members of the Companies Auditors and Liquidators Board* [2019] AATA 504, [25].

[46] AAT Act, s 33(1)(c).

[47] *Sullivan v Civil Aviation Safety Authority* (2014) 226 FCR 555; *Sun v Minister for Immigration and Border Protection* (2016) 243 FCR 220. In practice, if an issue is uniquely known to one party, adverse inferences may be drawn if the party refuses to bring that knowledge to the hearing: *McDonald v Director-General of Social Security* (1984) 1 FCR 354, 357.

[48] This is one of many principles affecting proof in tribunal hearings not subject to the rules of evidence: L Pearson, 'Tribunals: Evidence, Satisfaction and Proof' in G Weeks and M Groves (eds), *Administrative Redress In and Out of the Courts: Essays in Honour of Robin Creyke and John McMillan* (Federation Press, 2018) 217.

[49] AAT Act, s 33(1)(b).

questions of inequality and unfairness that occur outside tribunal hearings. Whatever statutory and procedural innovations may exist within the confines of merits review hearings, huge disparities exist between the people who challenge official decisions and the governments that defend them. These problems have not simply remained undisturbed by almost half a century of merits review in Australia, they have arguably grown in scale.[50] As innovative as merits review may be, the explanation of the concept in the next section shows that its effect beyond the walls of tribunal hearing rooms is unclear.

The Radical Reform of Merits Review

That the formation of the AAT signalled 'a new and substantially unprecedented regime of merits review'[51] appears obvious with the benefit of hindsight but was only hinted at when the AAT was first formed. The Kerr Committee explained that a new form of review was an important part of the reforms it envisaged because the 'basic fault of the entire structure' of existing administrative law was that 'review cannot as a general rule … be obtained "on the merits" – and this is really what the aggrieved citizen is seeking'.[52] Yet this central notion of merits review was not expressly adopted or defined by the AAT Act and was only hinted at by the novel remedial powers granted to the AAT. The most important power enabled the AAT to exercise 'all the powers and discretions' conferred upon the official whose decision is under review and enabled it to affirm, set aside or vary the decision under review, or make a wholly new one.[53] A related restriction provided that a decision under review would be altered only by the AAT once an application for review was commenced.[54] These provisions simultaneously vested decisional power in the AAT and removed it from the official who had made the decision under review.[55] The key remedial power granted to the AAT was otherwise remarkably 'uninformative' on how the tribunal was intended to exercise its review function.[56] As is typically the case in Australian law, that question about tribunals was answered by judges.

In the influential early case of *Drake*,[57] the Full Court of the Federal Court explained that the key question for the AAT was not whether the original

[50] M Groves, 'Equality of Arms in Administrative Review' (2023) 46 *Melbourne University Law Review* 726.

[51] *Frugtniet v Australian Securities and Investments Commission* (2019) 266 CLR 250, 257 [14] ('*Frugtniet*').

[52] *Kerr Committee Report*, [58].

[53] AAT Act, s 43(1).

[54] ibid s 26(1).

[55] ibid, s 43(1) enables the tribunal to remit matters to the original decision-maker. This rarely used power essentially revives the power of original decision-maker.

[56] M Allars, 'The Nature of Merits Review: A Bold Vision Realised in the Administrative Appeals Tribunal' (2013) 41 *Federal Law Review* 197, 197.

[57] *Drake v Minister for Immigration and Ethnic Affairs* (1979) 1 ALD 60.

decision-maker had made the 'correct or preferable decision', but what the Tribunal *itself* concluded was the correct or preferable decision after considering the material placed before it.[58] This reasoning shifts focus from what has happened in an agency to what should happen in the Tribunal and, in that sense, revealed that the Tribunal does not conduct 'appeals' as that term is usually understood. When *Drake* was returned to the AAT for rehearing, Brennan J (another future Chief Justice of Australia, then sitting as President of the AAT) explained that the different position of the Tribunal enabled it to take a different perspective on the same issues. Brennan J held that the AAT could reach a different decision to the original decision-maker by several means, such as by taking a different interpretation of the material presented, or a different (though legally permissible plausible) interpretation of the statutory discretions that could be exercised.[59] This decisional freedom did not simply enable the AAT to take a different view of facts or applicable legislation, which could be relevant to issues such as the scope of a discretionary power and whether the case at hand presented good reason for its favourable exercise, it also had important consequences for official policies and others forms of soft law.[60] While the AAT's decisional freedom enabled it to take a different approach to the application or variation of an official policy that was relevant to an application, Brennan J stressed that the importance of consistent decision-making meant the AAT should be 'cautious and sparing' in any departure from official or ministerial policies.[61] The AAT could therefore depart from official policies if a case presented 'cogent reasons' to do so, such as when 'injustice in a particular case' might occur if a policy was applied.[62]

The legacy of the *Drake* cases is twofold.[63] One is that the Full Court's decision that the Tribunal must reach the 'correct or preferable' decision on the merits of the application before it has become the orthodox explanation of merits review. The distinction between these alternatives is that '"correct" is more applicable to non-discretionary decisions, whereas "preferable" is more applicable to discretionary decisions'.[64] After this concept of correct or preferable had been applied widely in lower courts for almost 30 years, it was finally endorsed by the High Court.[65] The formula has also been expressly adopted by most of the statutes of state and

[58] ibid 68. It took almost three decades for the High Court to be presented with an opportunity to confirm that the AAT may decide issues as they stood at the time of its own decision, rather than when the decision was first made, unless legislation specified otherwise: *Shi v Migration Agents Registration Authority* (2008) 235 CLR 286 ('*Shi*').

[59] *Re Drake and Minister for Immigration and Ethnic Affairs (No 2)* (1979) 2 ALD 634, 644.

[60] Brennan J expanded on these points in an influential speech: FG Brennan, 'Anatomy of an Administrative Decision' (1980) 9 *Sydney Law Review* 1.

[61] *Drake (No 2)* (1979) 2 ALD 634, 644. See also 639–40. Sometimes the AAT is required to take departmental guidelines into account; see, eg, Ministerial Direction No 84 made under Migration Act 1958 (Cth) s 499.

[62] *Drake (No 2)* (1979) 2 ALD 634, 645.

[63] Their influence has been enormous. When this chapter was written, *Drake* had been cited in over 1,500 subsequent court and tribunal decisions and *Drake (No 2)* in nearly 1,300.

[64] *Laming v Racing Victorian Ltd* [2022] VSC 813, [93] (fn 108).

[65] *Frugtniet* (2019) 266 CLR 250, 271 [51]. See also *Shi* (2008) 235 CLR 286, 327 [142].

territory administrative review tribunals,[66] although not in the AAT Act itself.[67] The legacy of *Drake (No 2)* is equally important because of Brennan J's explanation of how the AAT could reach a different decision by considering exactly the same facts, policies and laws illuminated a key feature of merits review. Different minds can examine the same things and reach different conclusions. This possibility provided, in contrast to judicial review, a meaningful right of review based simply upon disagreement with a decision. It also provided a level of freedom to merits review officials that might be available to bureaucrats in theory only.

This account of merits review is not the only one. Just as merits review anticipates that different people may view the same issues and interpret them differently, the same is true of interpreting merits review itself. Cane argued that merits review was ultimately a thinly disguised form of judicial review.[68] His metaphor of merits review as a Trojan horse for judicial review arguably aligns with Brennan J's conception of the AAT as constituted on the judicial model.[69] This characterisation of merits review does not sit easily with the continued emphasis of the High Court upon the clear distinction between judicial and merits review.[70] Creyke considered the very opposite possibility in her analysis of the appellate jurisdiction of the Federal Court over decisions of the AAT, arguing that the boundaries between judicial and merits review were being slowly narrowed by the progressively wider interpretation taken by the courts to what might constitute an error of law for the purposes of appeals from the AAT.[71] Just as Cane argued that tribunals were assuming the review style of courts, Creyke argued that courts were doing the reverse.

Another concept important to merits review, established shortly after Drake, is the notion that the AAT stands 'in the shoes' of the original decision-maker.[72] That metaphor was long thought to explain that the AAT was granted the same

[66] See: State Administrative Tribunal Act 2004 (WA), s 27(1); South Australian Civil and Administrative Tribunal Act 2013 (SA), ss 34(4), 70(5); Northern Territory Civil and Administrative Tribunal Act 2014 (NT), s 46(1); Tasmanian Civil and Administrative Tribunal Act 2020 (Tas), s 75(1). The concept was not expressly adopted in the tribunal statutes of Victoria, New South Wales or the Australian Capital Territory but is regarded as applicable to those bodies. See, eg, *Secretary, Department of Environment, Energy and Climate Action v Hanson Constructions Materials Pty Ltd* [2023] VSC 353, [14]. The Queensland Civil and Administrative Tribunal Act 2009 (Qld) s 20(1) mistakenly requires the 'correct **and** preferable' decision to be made; cf *Shi* (2008) 235 CLR 286, 327 [140].

[67] But AAT Act, s 29AB empowers the AAT to require applicants to more clearly identify why they believe the decision under review is not the correct or preferable one.

[68] P Cane, 'Merits Review and Judicial Review: The AAT as Trojan Horse' (2000) 28 *Federal Law Review* 213. Sir Anthony Mason has suggested that the real target of Cane's criticisms was the High Court's 'excessively artificial concept of judicial power', a criticism Mason thought was 'by no means devoid of merit': Mason (n 10) 139.

[69] This conception has passed into history and may be best understood as an (ultimately successful) attempt by the AAT's inaugural President to ensure its survival.

[70] See, eg, *Bond v Australian Broadcasting Tribunal* (1990) 170 CLR 321, 341; *Minister for Immigration and Citizenship v SZMDS* (2010) 240 CLR 611, 636 [96]. The most influential articulation of that point was made by Brennan J himself in *Attorney-General (NSW) v Quin* (1990) 170 CLR 1, 35–36.

[71] R Creyke, 'Judicial Review and Merits Review: Are the Boundaries Being Eroded?' (2017) 45 *Federal Law Review* 627.

[72] *Minister for Immigration and Ethnic Affairs v Pochi* (1981) 3 ALD 139, 143.

powers available to primary decision-makers, but its limitations also became apparent. The High Court explained in Frugtniet that placing the tribunal in the shoes of the original decision-maker meant it held 'the same power or powers as the primary decision-maker, subject to the same constraints'.[73] On this view, standing in the shoes of the initial decision-maker both empowers and constrains. That constraint was influential in Frugtniet, which held that legislation precluding the original decision-maker taking account of spent convictions imposed the same limit upon the AAT. A distinct but closely related limit was identified in Makasa.[74] The Minister wished to cancel the applicant's visa after an earlier cancellation was overturned in the AAT.[75] The Minister essentially sought to exploit the notion of 'standing the shoes' by claiming that the AAT had taken off its decisional shoes when its decision was made, allowing the Minister to put them on again at that point. The High Court rejected that bold claim as one would reduce the AAT's role 'to a mockery' by allowing its decisions 'to be revisited by the primary decision-maker in the unqualified re-exercise of the same statutory power already re-exercised by the AAT'.[76]

These disparate features of merits review may help to flesh out the nature and limits of the concept but they send mixed signals about the relationship of the AAT to the executive and bureaucracy. An influential early decision of Brennan J as President of the AAT held that the Tribunal was intended to 'be constituted upon the judicial model, separate from, and independent of, the Executive'.[77] That statement included the curious rider that the function of the tribunal was 'to decide appeals, not to advise the Executive'.[78] His Honour's reasoning and the repeated affirmation of the independence of the AAT do not sit easily with more recent statements suggesting the Tribunal is part of a 'administrative continuum' that begins with agencies and departments and extends into the AAT.[79] The idea of an administrative continuum gains support from the many ways that the AAT and the agencies whose decisions it reviews are intermingled.

When the Tribunal metaphorically stands in the shoes of original decision-makers, it quite literally assumes many of their powers. A senior official of the

[73] *Frugtniet* (2019) 266 CLR 250, 271 [51]. Similar reasoning was adopted in *Shi* (2008) 235 CLR 286, 327 [142].

[74] *Minister for Immigration and Border Protection v Makasa* (2021) 270 CLR 430, 447 [50].

[75] Decisions to cancel visas or deport non-citizens have long served as a flash point between the AAT and executive government. One aspect of this ongoing saga is that the jurisdiction of the AAT and the ministerial powers to override AAT decisions are subject to relentless amendment and political arguments.

[76] (2021) 270 CLR 430, 447 [50].

[77] *Re Becker and Minister for Immigration and Ethnic Affairs* (1977) 1 ALD 158, 161.

[78] ibid.

[79] This notion originated in *Jebb v Repatriation Commission* (1988) 80 ALR 329, 333–4 and was approved in *Shi* (2008) 235 CLR 286, 300–1 [45] (Kirby J). In *SDCV v Director-General of Security* (2022) 96 ALJR 1002, [120]–[121] Gageler J made clear that courts exercising appellate jurisdiction over the AAT were not part of this continuum.

agency that made the decision under review usually becomes a party to the proceeding in the AAT.[80] While it has long been recognised that proceedings in the AAT are not adversarial,[81] the denial of adversarialism rarely moves beyond general statements to the effect that parties in AAT hearings are not adversaries in the traditional sense.[82] Some statutory requirements appear to clearly set aside adversarialism, such as the obligation of both parties to use their 'best endeavours to assist the tribunal to make its decision in relation to the proceeding'.[83] But these isolated provisions have not prevented a perception of 'creeping legalism' in merits review hearings which have 'become too formal, with lawyers, expert witnesses and advocates dominating proceedings'.[84] This is a criticism of adversarialism in all but name. What lies underneath such rhetoric is more than one form of division. Many applicants for merits review continue to see the decision-maker and wider government as an opponent, often justifiably so.[85] Officials and their agencies often perceive the AAT as their opponent.

The continued influence of adversarialism in merits review is hardly surprising in light of the domination of judicial power explained earlier in this chapter. That domination is not only a constitutional matter, but also a practical one. Virtually all key decisions about the nature of merits review are delivered by either appellate courts, judicial members of the AAT or one of its state and territory equivalents. It may seem odd that the nature and purpose of merits review in tribunals is articulated by courts and judges, but that oddity sits comfortably within Australia's constitutional hierarchy.[86] The strong judicial influence upon conceptions of merits review can also explain the otherwise strange suggestion of Brennan J that the functions of the AAT do not include advising the executive. What may seem counterintuitive for tribunal officials would seem natural to judges. How, then, is the bureaucracy expected to learn from the tribunals that review its decisions?

[80] *SDCV v Director-General of Security* (2022) 96 ALJR 1002, [120].

[81] An exception is when an onus of proof is cast by statute upon a party, such as in many taxation review proceedings: *Shord v Federal Commissioner of Taxation* (2017) 253 FCR 157, 188 [180]. In practice, such proceedings tend closely to resemble judicial proceedings.

[82] *Uelese v Minister for Immigration and Border Protection* (2015) 256 CLR 203, 221 [62]–[63]; *Applicant VEAL of 2002 v Minister for Immigration and Multicultural and Indigenous Affairs* (2005) 225 CLR 88, 98 [24].

[83] AAT Act, s 33(1AA). This duty 'does not impose a wider obligation on decision-makers to seek out themselves evidence which may bear on the decision, although it is to be expected that they would consider and facilitate any reasonable requests for assistance': *Shord v Federal Commissioner of Taxation* (2017) 253 FCR 157, 178 [132].

[84] K Bell, *President's Review of VCAT* (2009) 21. Concerns about creeping legalism should be compared to the recommendation of a former High Court judge that AAT members should generally be legally qualified: IDF Callinan QC AC, *Review: section 4 of the Tribunals Amalgamation Act 2015 (Cth)*, (2018).

[85] See C Holmes AC SC, *Report*, Royal Commission into the Robodebt Scheme (Commonwealth of Australia, 2023).

[86] Those inclined to a more pejorative description than 'odd' are keeping excellent company; see M Taggart, '"Australian Exceptionalism" in Judicial Review' (2008) 36 *Federal Law Review* 1.

One Deputy President of the AAT explained that the tribunal was 'not simply a dispute resolution mechanism' but:

> … is also a cultural institution designed to promote a bureaucracy-wide commitment to better decision-making for the benefit of all Australians. The Tribunal does that by modelling good decision-making behaviour in particular cases. Its decision-making creates norms and educates primary decision-makers and other stakeholders dealing with similar issues in the future.[87]

The normative, educative impact of the AAT and other merits review tribunals is ultimately a matter of speculation[88] because this has never been subject to sustained empirical inquiry.[89] There are, of course, many ways that tribunals can provide guidance, feedback and other signals to agencies, such as through their individual decisions, guideline decisions,[90] or various forms of dialogue that can help tribunals and agencies better understand each other.[91] The normative potential of these avenues is limited by the divisive, lingering effects of adversarialism, but the very nature of merits review also limits its educative potential. It is a fact-sensitive and non-judicial form of decision making that can depend heavily on the contextual judgment reached by an individual tribunal member contains. Those features of the doctrine help explain why notions of precedent do not generally apply to merits review decisions.[92] If tribunals are not bound to follow their own previous decisions, the extent to which they can form a sound foundation to educate administrative officials is inevitably weak.

The dilemma of the precedential value of tribunal decisions arose indirectly in the *Drake* cases but had been at the forefront of academic debate some years earlier in the context of the degree to which discretion should be controlled.[93] The reason that it remains hard to pin down is because the solution cannot easily be diluted into the form of a legal rule although the nature of the balance to be struck

[87] *Williams & Members of the Companies Auditors and Liquidators Board* [2019] AATA 504, [25].

[88] The 'educative effect' of the AD(JR) Act's enumerated grounds of review has long been almost an article of faith in Australian administrative law; see, eg, M Aronson, 'Is the ADJR Act Hampering the Development of Australian Administrative Law?' (2004) 15 *Public Law Review* 202, 214; cf S Gageler SC, 'Impact of Migration Law on the Development of Australian Administrative Law' (2010) 17 *Australian Journal of Administrative Law* 92, 105. Ultimately, that effect is also speculative and difficult to prove.

[89] The lack of such work is somewhat mysterious. See, eg, P Cane, *Administrative Tribunals and Adjudication* (Hart Publishing, 2009) viii, where the author explained that he abandoned a planned empirical study of the dissemination of knowledge about merits review in agencies 'for various logistical reasons'.

[90] Migration Act 1958 (Cth), ss 353B, 420B and 473FC ensured the Migration and Refugee Division (MRD) of the AAT had the power to make guidance decisions; however, these powers were almost never exercised.

[91] R Thomas, 'Administrative Justice, Better Decisions, and Organisational Learning' [2015] *Public Law* 111, 124–8.

[92] See, eg, *Kanashori (Migration)* [2023] AATA 663, [17]; *Drummond v Gordian Runoff Ltd (No 2)* [2023] NSWSC 731, [21]; *Director of Liquor Licensing v Kordister Pty Ltd* [2011] VSC 207, [107]. These and similar decisions hold that while merits review decisions do not create a precedent, considerations of comity may apply to merits review tribunals and their decisions.

[93] The main sources are discussed in G Weeks, *Soft Law and Public Authorities: Remedies and Reform* (Hart Publishing, 2016) 36–40.

is relatively easy to understand, if not always to apply. Tribunals generally aspire to broad consistency in their approach to like cases on the understanding that their statutory duty is still to determine each case on its merits.[94] To that end, they are at least aware of other cases decided on comparable facts under particular legislation. Indeed, given the high volume of cases in some tribunals, such awareness is both vital and hardly avoidable. The difference between this approach and the judicial doctrine of *stare decisis* is that it is self-imposed rather than a constraint on decision-making regulated by appellate courts.[95]

The Contagious Effect of the AAT and 'the CATs'

The AAT may have been the first truly generalist Australian tribunal, but its jurisdiction remained relatively limited because many migration, refugee, social security and military benefit cases were decided in other specialist federal tribunals. A recommendation of the ARC to amalgamate most of those tribunals failed in the late 1990s,[96] but that proposal was influential elsewhere. The trend to amalgamate tribunals and create what are often called 'super-tribunals' began in Victoria when that state's range of specialist tribunals were collapsed into a single administrative tribunal. This change saw Victoria move from having an AAT to a 'CAT' – the Victorian Civil and Administrative Tribunal (VCAT). The key goal of VCAT was to simplify a state tribunal system by creating a single large tribunal of wide and varied jurisdiction. The driving, but not exclusive purpose of this change was budgetary. A single large tribunal was much cheaper. Another purpose was more practical. Many small tribunals were costly to maintain as separate entities and often did not have a large enough number of cases to warrant a significant number of members and support staff.[97] Collapsing many smaller tribunals into a single larger one created economies of scale which, in turn, allowed lawyers, tribunal members and government officials to work as specialists in tribunals.

The other innovation of VCAT was to combine the review of government decisions with a range of fairly simple commercial or consumer disputes. This was the tail of the 'CAT' – its jurisdiction was both civil *and* administrative, something that the constitutional arrangements of States and Territories allows but which

[94] Brennan J warned that inconsistency risked the appearance of arbitrariness in decision-making: *Drake (No 2)* (1979) 2 ALD 634, 639. Examples of inconsistency in the results reached in merits review cases serve to emphasise this point; see eg *Segal v Waverley Council* (2005) 64 NSWLR 177.

[95] In Australia, this regulatory effect has been so pronounced that it has been cited as an example of the judiciary's 'formalist' tendencies; see M Aronson, 'Process, Quality, and Variable Standards: Responding to an *Agent Provocateur*' in D Dyzenhaus, M Hunt and G Huscroft (eds), *A Simple Common Lawyer: Essays in Honour of Michael Taggart* (Hart Publishing, 2009) 5, 23–8.

[96] This was one of several recommendations made in Administrative Review Council, *Better Decisions: Review of Commonwealth Merits Review Tribunals* (ARC Report 39, 1995).

[97] In the decade before VCAT was created, it was estimated that somewhere 200–300 tribunals, boards and like bodies existed in a state with a population of three million: A Robbins, *Administrative Tribunals in Victoria* (Victoria Law Foundation, 1982) 1.

the separation of powers doctrine makes impossible in a Commonwealth tribunal. That change simultaneously relieved lower courts from a huge number of smaller commercial cases, which gave overworked local courts some respite, but placed those cases in a less formal, non-judicial environment that was a more suitable and user-friendly venue. This blend of administrative and relatively minor civil cases has been adopted in all other states and territories, though with the puzzling jurisdictional differences that are a constant feature of Australian life. VCAT has jurisdiction over building, planning and environmental matters, yet these same issues in New South Wales are largely reserved for the specialist Land and Environment Court.[98] The growth of state and territory CATs is not simply a matter of economics, it is also about distance. The vast size of Australia compared to its population means that many public services must be concentrated in order to be viable.

The CATs drew heavily from the AAT model. Most have a Supreme Court judge as President,[99] which echoes the status of the AAT President as a judge of the Federal Court of Australia. Just as the AAT has Deputy Presidents, so do the CATs but with some difference. The Deputy Presidents of CATs are typically judges from the intermediate state courts who hold the tribunal role on a full-time basis for several years.[100] The procedures and powers of CATs were also clearly modelled on those of the AAT but the CATs have also yielded innovation. Two notable examples can be drawn from VCAT. The exemption from the rules of evidence that applies to all Australian merits review tribunals is qualified in VCAT. The tribunal is empowered to adopt some, or all, of the rules of evidence. This novel power is used regularly but the many cases using that power have not yielded a coherent guiding principle.[101] VCAT is also subject to what may be called an 'anti-*Drake*' provision, which makes clear that official policies that cover the subject matter of a case at hand *must* be applied by the tribunal in certain circumstances.[102] That novel direction applied to the predecessor to VCAT,[103] which was clearly designed to extinguish the latitude towards the application of official policy sanctioned by Brennan J in *Drake (No 2)*. Different forms of this provision have existed in Victoria for 40 years. We have not found a single example of their use, which suggests that the bureaucratic fear of *Drake (No 2)* is more imagined than real. That conclusion

[98] See Fisher, Chapter 6 in this volume.

[99] The last Australian jurisdiction to create a CAT provides the exception. The President of TASCAT needs only to be 'eligible for appointment as a magistrate': Tasmanian Civil and Administrative Tribunal Act 2020 (Tas), s 12.

[100] See, eg, VCAT Act 1998 (Vic), s 11(2) [referring to Vice Presidents of VCAT]; SAT 2004 (WA), s 112(3) [Each Deputy President must also be a District Court judge].

[101] D Wallace, 'The Victorian Civil and Administrative Tribunal and the Rules of Evidence' (2018) 25 *Australian Journal of Administrative Law* 171.

[102] VCAT Act, s 57. The policy must be certified by a government minister, have been published in the government gazette and VCAT must be satisfied that the applicant either knew of the policy or that people likely to apply for review of decisions governed by the policy could reasonably have been expected to know of the policy.

[103] Administrative Appeals Tribunal Act 1984 (Vic), s 25(3).

is arguably evidenced by the absence of anti-*Drake* provisions in other state and territory tribunal statutes.

The very foundation of the CAT model has influenced a key change to the AAT described in the next section. The CATs amalgamated many small tribunals into a single larger one. The mantras of efficiency and economies of scale that drove the formation of CATs provided the basis for a renewed and ultimately successful amalgamation of social security and migration tribunals with the AAT. This structural change may have hastened the demise of the AAT but was replicated in the post-AAT world.

The Fall and Rebirth of the AAT

The ARC proposed in 1995 that federal tribunals be amalgamated.[104] The key consequence of this proposal would have been to amalgamate the AAT with specialist migration tribunals which had a burgeoning caseload that greatly exceeded that of the AAT. The ARC reasoned that amalgamation would not simply save administrative costs but also concentrate staff and expertise and thus raise the quality of tribunal leadership and decision-making. These proposals faltered under strong political and public opposition to the perceived danger that the AAT would be swamped by the relentlessly growing migration caseload. Sir Anthony Mason later acknowledged the underlying concern about these proposals was that calls to 'reform' merits review are in truth calls for its emasculation.[105] Yet the ARC's proposals were revived 20 years later, by a government that had first gutted the ARC. The ARC remained on the statute books but stopped operation when it was defunded.[106] The quiet destruction of the ARC was justified on the specious budgetary grounds that to do so would 'reduce the size and complexity of government'.[107] The irony that, at the same time, an ARC report was invoked as a key basis to amalgamate the AAT and federal migration tribunals was clearly lost on those in government who thought that body failed to provide value for money.[108]

The Tribunals Amalgamation Act 2015 (Cth) folded the migration, refugee and social security tribunals into the AAT and created a federal super

[104] ARC (n 96).

[105] Mason (n 10) 143.

[106] The outgoing Labor government had previously appointed the ARC President to be Commonwealth Ombudsman, which made him an ex officio member of the ARC. However, a new ARC President was not appointed by that Labor government or its Coalition successor.

[107] Australian Government, *Budget Measures: Budget Paper No 2, 2015–16* (2015) 65. See also Parliament of Australia, 'Amalgamation of Merits Review Tribunals' (Budget Review 2014–15). See www.aph.gov.au/About_Parliament/Parliamentary_Departments/Parliamentary_Library/pubs/rp/BudgetReview201415/Tribunals.

[108] The amalgamation of many federal tribunals was originally recommended by the Administrative Review Council, *Better Decisions: Review of Commonwealth Merits Review Tribunals* (ARC Report No 39, 1995).

tribunal that was roughly equivalent to the State and Territory CATs, without civil jurisdiction.[109] One striking feature of this amalgamation was that most migration cases continue to be governed by the extremely lengthy and complex codified hearing rules, which mean that the otherwise uniform procedural rules of the AAT did not apply to what had become an overwhelming majority of cases heard by the AAT. A statutory review of the AAT required by the Tribunals Amalgamation Act 2015 (Cth) concluded that the objectives of amalgamation had not been met and that the AAT was not operating 'as a truly amalgamated body'.[110] The Callinan Report noted that the continued operation of quite different procedural rules for different jurisdictions reviewable by the AAT was almost inevitable and meant procedural uniformity within the AAT was 'difficult and probably undesirable'.[111] It also identified many surprising administrative problems. The large migration and refugee division was clearly underfunded,[112] which did not sit easily with the strong political emphasis the government of the day placed on migration and refugee issues.

The empirical study of Creyke into the impact of the amalgamation of tribunals, both in the AAT and in state and territory tribunals, found that amalgamation had, on balance, been beneficial.[113] Enlarged tribunals with a single point of contact were more visible to the public, which also led to better practices within tribunals, such as the more efficient use of resources and better training opportunities for staff.[114] But Creyke also documented many shortcomings of amalgamation, such as continued problems in combining existing IT systems into a single and effective system for the entirety of the new tribunal. Creyke also cautioned that the financial benefits expected from amalgamation were not readily apparent. The initial costs of amalgamation were significant and easily obscured by 'jurisdictional creep', in which tribunals were regularly given new jurisdiction without any corresponding funding.[115]

Creyke had earlier expressed concern about the loss of expertise that occurred with amalgamation,[116] when existing tribunal members and administrative staff would resign or be made redundant during the disruption of amalgamation.

[109] Some tribunals were excluded for apparently political reasons. The Veterans' Review Board, which considers claims for military pensions, was not amalgamated into the AAT, almost certainly due to the perceived politically powerful position of former members of the armed forces. The Australian Competition Tribunal or the Australian Copyright Tribunal were also not amalgamated within the AAT, most likely because of the highly specialised jurisdiction of each body.

[110] The Hon IDF Callinan AC QC, *Review: Section 4 of the Tribunals Amalgamation Act 2015 (Cth)* (Final Report, 23 July 2019) (*Callinan Report*) 26.

[111] Callinan Report (n 110) 162.

[112] ibid 166. The Report concluded that funding arrangement across the AAT were 'neither appropriate nor consistent': 27.

[113] R Creyke, 'Australian Tribunals: Impact of Amalgamation' (2020) 26 *Australian Journal of Administrative Law* 206.

[114] ibid 211, 216.

[115] ibid 229.

[116] R Creyke, 'Tribunal Amalgamation 2015: An Opportunity Lost?' (2016) 84 *AIAL Forum* 54.

The Callinan Review also expressed concern about the staffing of the AAT and recommended that the government 'should generally appoint qualified lawyers with proved capacity and experience in forensic analysis and opinion or judgment writing' who are also 'persons of good character, even temperament, courteous disposition and proved diligence'.[117] Neither Callinan nor Creyke dealt in any detail with problems in appointing members, the issue which led most directly to the demise of the AAT. The creation and operation of the AAT and other public law reforms made around the same time had strong bipartisan support,[118] which had wavered in earlier times with perceived cronyism in appointments to migration tribunals.[119] Bipartisan support for the AAT collapsed almost overnight when the conservative Coalition government appointed a large number of ministerial advisers, former parliamentarians and other people associated with the government of the day to the AAT just before an election in 2019.[120] That practice was repeated on the eve of the federal election in 2022.[121] The impact of these practices upon the AAT was catastrophic. The perception of crony appointments drew sustained political attack and scathing public criticism.[122] While the quality of the substantive work of the AAT was not subject to the same criticism, a parliamentary inquiry (albeit one that predictably split across party lines) made clear that the political standing of AAT had been damaged beyond repair.[123]

The AAT will be replaced by the Administrative Review Tribunal (ART), which was the name proposed almost 50 years earlier by the Kerr Report. The ART mostly follows the AAT without any real change. The jurisdictional basis for ART review, the right to reasons for reviewable decisions and the standing test essentially reproduce those that applied in the AAT.[124] As with the AAT, the new tribunal is not subject to the rules of evidence and parties to proceedings are

[117] Callinan Report (n 110) 127.

[118] The Kerr Committee was established by a Conservative government. Its work was implemented by a subsequent Labor government, which passed the AAT Act. The subsequent conservative government created the Federal Court, Commonwealth Ombudsman and freedom of information legislation. All this legislation received bipartisan support.

[119] Australian Parliament, Joint Standing Committee on Migration, *The Immigration Review Tribunal Appointments Process* (1994) (examining claimed ties between appointees to migration tribunals and the Labour government of the day).

[120] See, eg, Michael Koziol, 'Porter Gave Ex-adviser $250,000 Job' *Sydney Morning Herald* (25 February 2019) p 8 (noting that the Attorney-General had appointed one of his former advisers to the AAT).

[121] See, eg, M Robin, 'Michaelia Cash's Unbound Chutzpah Revealed in Latest AAT Appointments' *Australian Financial Review* (12 April 2022) p40 (noting that the Attorney-General appointed a former candidate of her party, who was not legally qualified, as a Deputy President of the AAT).

[122] Serious constitutional doubts were raised about the AAT appointments made just before the 2022 federal election: K Mason and L Katz, 'Questions of Secrecy and Validity Arising out of Senator Cash's Election Eve Appointments to the AAT' (2023) 97 *Australian Law Journal* 448.

[123] [Australia] Senate Standing Committee on Legal and Constitutional Affairs Committee, *The Performance and Integrity of Australia's Administrative Review System* (Interim Report, March 2022) Recommendation 3 (recommending the AAT be replaced with a new federal review tribunal). This Interim Report was confirmed as the final report of the Committee on 30 June 2022.

[124] Administrative Review Tribunal Act 2024 (Cth) (ART Act), ss 12, 23-4, 15.

required to use their best endeavours to assist the Tribunal.[125] In a striking echo of the AAT Act, the new statute assumes that the meaning of merits review is understood and says almost nothing about this guiding principle. The ART Act contains only oblique references to the 'correct or preferable' formula and does not seek to codify or define the foundational concept of merits review.[126] This legislative gap is desirable because it leaves a complex and useful body of doctrine undisturbed, but also enables the possibility of further doctrinal innovation in the meaning and scope of merits review.

The ART also adopts the same membership structure of a judge of the Federal Court as President, supported by layers of judicial and non-judicial Deputy Presidents, Senior Members and General Members. That longstanding membership structure has been supplemented with an express requirement that appointments are merit based.[127] Another notable reform requires the President to promulgate a code of conduct for tribunal members,[128] which provides a basis for the President to receive and consider complaints against tribunal members.[129] The ART is also guided by a Tribunal Advisory Committee which is required to consider and respond to trends in the work of the Tribunal and to take account of the views gained from its stakeholders.[130] The Advisory Committee will no doubt be assisted by a revived ARC, which includes the President of the ART as a standing member.[131]

The creation of the ART introduced several notable changes beyond the clear recognition of the role of merit in appointments. The nine divisions into which the AAT was organised became eight 'jurisdictional areas' of the ART.[132] The most significant part of this change was the division of the enormous Migration and Refugee Division into separate Migration and Protection jurisdictional areas.[133] A more significant change is that the President has the power to establish and abolish lists as sub-areas within each of these jurisdictional areas.[134] Each list is led by a Deputy President or Senior Member and these are effectively the central organisational units of the ART. The President may appoint members to one or

[125] ibid s 56(2).

[126] ibid s 56 (requiring parties to assist the ART in reaching the correct or preferable decision). Section 63(2) contains a similar duty.

[127] A merit-based process is stated to be a requirement for the appointment of the ART President (ART Act, s 205(2)(b)(1)), non-judicial Deputy Presidents (s 207(2)(b)(i)), Senior and General Members (s 208(2)(b)(i)) and the Principal Registrar (s 227(2)(b)(i)). It is not a stated requirement for the appointment of Judicial Deputy Presidents.

[128] ART Act, s 201(1). The Senate inquiry into the AAT criticised the lack of transparency about the standards expected of AAT members and any processes to receive and review complaints: Senate Legal and Constitutional Affairs References Committee (n 123) paras 3.61–67.

[129] ART Act, s 203.

[130] ibid s 236.

[131] ibid s 247(1).

[132] ibid s 196(1).

[133] Commensurate changes were made to the provisions of the Migration Act 1958 (Cth) to qualify the merits review procedures of the ART Act.

[134] ART Act, s 196(2).

more jurisdictional areas in the ART, a power that had rested with the Attorney General with regard to the AAT. The creation of a Guidance and Appeals Panel ('GAP') is another notable innovation.[135] The President may constitute a GAP of up to three members in relation to an eligible matter to perform either of two key functions.[136] The GAP has an appellate function where a decision at first instance may contain a material error of fact or law. The GAP is also able to issue a guidance decision, that will effectively provide an internal precedent on a particular issue, where a decision at first instance raises an issue of significance to administrative decision-making.[137]

None of these changes were radical but their overall impact could be. Federal tribunal members were not previously subject to a requirement of merit for appointment or a code of conduct after appointment. Since the ART President is empowered to decide which jurisdiction members will preside in and whether they will sit in the GAP, the extent to which politicians can dictate the operation of the ART by way of targeted appointments is greatly restricted. This partial but important reduction of political control is furthered by a small but crucial change to the ARC, which is now expressly enabled to investigate matters of its own motion.[138] The ARC could, in theory at least, investigate any repetition of the type of crony appointments that sparked the demise of the AAT. However, weaknesses remain in the revised system. For example, while the notion of merit is expressly mentioned in the criteria for appointment, that notion, like merits review itself, is not defined. Furthermore, the ARC could once again be left without a leader and thus disabled, or the government of the day could appoint a compliant President to the ARC.

Concluding Observations

Thirty years after the AAT had commenced operation, an analysis of tribunals concluded that they had become 'an integral and frontline element of the Australian justice system'.[139] That assessment was right in a very literal sense. Merits review tribunals were longstanding and their heavy caseloads indicated they operated as the first, and often only, port of call for many people wishing to challenge official decisions. The rise of the CATs suggested that a successful federal model had been transposed to the states and territories and that a happy ending of sorts had been reached. Newton's third law of motion – that for every action there is an equal and opposite reaction – spoiled that party. The amalgamation that was central to state and territory tribunals became politically harder to resist at the federal level.

[135] ibid Pt 5.
[136] ibid ss 40 and 41.
[137] ibid s 128(2).
[138] ibid s 249(2).
[139] N Bedford and R Creyke, *Inquisitorial Processes in Australian Tribunals* (Australian Institute of Judicial Administration, 2006) 66.

The budgetary justifications to amalgamate federal tribunals was conveniently extended to 'amalgamating' the functions of the ARC into the Attorney-General's Department. That was both intended and clearly understood to amount to the abolition of the ARC. The consequences of these changes were catastrophic.

The amalgamation of tribunals heralded a level of political control over tribunals that laid the foundation for crony appointments to the AAT. Those appointments might have been much harder to make if the ARC had remained in operation. The ARC would have been an obvious forum to discuss growing problems in the staffing and operation of the AAT, but also other problems such as the continued veil of secrecy over social security decisions and the grotesque bureaucratic negligence at the heart of the scandalous attempts to recover questionable social security debts (known as 'Robodebt').[140] Each of these changes amplified the effect of the other. The interconnected impact of changes to the AAT and ARC made clear that an integrated system of administrative review can become undone if more than one of its constituent parts comes under strain.

[140] There has been much written about the Robodebt scandal, including the report of a Royal Commission: C Holmes AC SC, *Report of the Royal Commission into the Robodebt Scheme* (2023). In summary, it was 'a shameful chapter in the administration of the Commonwealth social security system and a massive failure of public administration': *Prygodicz v Commonwealth of Australia (No 2)* (2021) 173 ALD 278, [5].

8

Administrative Justice Through Administrative Tribunals in Aotearoa: Exploring the Tensions and Trade-offs

HANNA WILBERG

This chapter offers an administrative justice framework for evaluating remedial avenues, and a sketch of how this might apply to administrative tribunals in Aotearoa New Zealand. My framework aims to identify the range of competing considerations and to emphasise the tensions between them and the consequent need for trade-offs. I start here with a brief introduction to both administrative tribunals and the administrative justice literature in this jurisdiction.

Aotearoa New Zealand still does not have any unified system of administrative tribunals. Rather, most administrative regimes include their own set of remedial avenues. These include informal internal review, more or less internal but formal review bodies, and specialist external tribunals. My discussion in this chapter extends to the latter two, and I will refer to both as tribunals: any formal body charged with reviewing administrative decisions within a particular regime, whether internal or external. On the other hand, since my interest is in remedial bodies, I do not discuss bodies that exercise an original decision-making function, even if they are called tribunals. My purpose is to evaluate the different features of remedial bodies in light of competing administrative justice criteria and considerations.

Examples of these remedial regimes in Aotearoa New Zealand include the following. Decisions about social security benefits are reviewed first by a Benefits Review Committee, and then on appeal by the Social Security Appeals Authority.[1] Decisions about accident compensation – commonly known as ACC[2] – are reviewed first by an independent reviewer appointed by the Corporation, and then

[1] Social Security Act 2018, Part 7.

[2] This stands for the Accident Compensation Corporation, which administers the scheme (currently constituted under Part 7 of the Accident Compensation Act 2001). However, it is used to refer to the scheme and to entitlements under it.

on appeal by the District Court.[3] Tax assessments can be challenged either in the Taxation Review Authority or in the High Court.[4] Immigration and refugee status decisions can be appealed to the Immigration and Protection Tribunal.[5]

There is only limited literature on administrative justice in Aotearoa NZ.[6] Tribunals have been examined by the Law Commission, but without a specific focus on administrative tribunals.[7] Various best practice guides are available for the design of remedial regimes.[8] Particular regimes that have been subjected to critique include the remedial regimes for ACC[9] and social security[10] decisions.

The first part of this chapter outlines my proposed administrative justice framework, which centres around three criteria. The remaining three parts then offer a sketch of how each of these criteria might apply to NZ administrative tribunals, highlighting the tensions and trade-offs with competing considerations.

An Administrative Justice Framework

Administrative Justice Objectives and Criteria

Administrative justice for my purposes comprises the principles or objectives according to which we should design and evaluate regimes for making and reviewing administrative decisions. I suggest there are several relevant sets of objectives and considerations, and many of these are at least potentially in tension with each other. Debates about administrative justice are best understood as debates about the necessary trade-offs.

[3] Accident Compensation Act 2001, Part 5.

[4] Tax Administration Act 1994, Part 8A. A disputes procedure is available under Part 4A prior to an assessment being issued.

[5] Immigration Act 2009, Part 7.

[6] M Pirini, 'The Citizen and Administrative Justice: Reforming Complaint Management in New Zealand' (2010) 8 *New Zealand Journal of Public and International Law* 239 is one of the few pieces discussing the system and issues arising.

[7] Law Commission, *Tribunals in New Zealand* (NZLC IP 6, Wellington, New Zealand, 2008). For a critique, see J Hopkins, 'Order from Chaos? Tribunal Reform in New Zealand' (2009) 2 *Journal of Australasian Law Teachers Association* 47.

[8] Ministry of Justice, *Tribunal Guidance – Choosing the right decision-making body – Equipping tribunals to operate effectively* (2015). Available at: www.justice.govt.nz/tribunals/; Government Centre for Dispute Resolution, *Best practice guidance on dispute resolution*, mbie.govt.nz; Legislation Design and Advisory Committee, *Legislation Guidelines* (2021 edition) http://www.ldac.org.nz/, ch 28.

[9] K MacKinnon, 'Redefining the Facts – Marginalising the Claimant?' in R Creyke (ed), *Tribunals in the Common Law World* (Annandale, NSW, The Federation Press, 2008) 122; Acclaim Otago (Inc), *Understanding the Problem: An Analysis of ACC Appeals Processes to Identify Barriers to Access to Justice for Injured New Zealanders* (9 July 2015); MR Dean, *Independent Review of the Acclaim Otago (Inc) July 2015 Report Into Accident Compensation Dispute Resolution Processes* (May 2016).

[10] K Morton et al, *Access to Justice for Beneficiaries: A Community Law Response* (Community Law Canterbury, October 2014), Part 2; M Stephens, *Social Security and Welfare Law in Aotearoa New Zealand* (Wellington, Thomson Reuters, 2019), ch 14.

The main objectives of administrative justice as commonly discussed in the literature[11] may be summarised as follows:[12]

(1) Get it right the first time.
(2) Put errors right with the minimum of difficulty for the affected person.
(3) Learn from errors.

The objective that directly concerns remedial avenues such as tribunals is the second of these objectives. It flows from the first objective: if public administration has failed in its responsibility to get it right the first time, it bears the onus to minimise the impact of that failure by putting the error right with the minimum of difficulty. The question is what types of remedial regimes best serve this objective.

In answering this question, the administrative justice literature tends to focus on accessibility. However, accessibility alone does not achieve the objective of putting errors right. Other distinct criteria are also reflected in commentators' assessments of different remedial options.

A fuller set of administrative justice criteria, I suggest, includes whether a remedial avenue such as a tribunal is –

- effective at putting errors right,
- accessible (lacking barriers to entry and use), and
- trustworthy (likely to give the complainant a fair go, both actually and as perceived by potential complainants).

Accessibility is especially important for the disadvantaged or vulnerable; the other two criteria are important for all who wish to challenge administrative decisions.

There are tensions between these criteria. For instance, some features that make a remedial avenue accessible may compromise trustworthiness or effective error correction. In particular, trustworthiness is commonly associated with the principles of natural justice, while accessibility is often promoted by informal procedures that may compromise some aspects of natural justice.[13]

Evaluating judicial review and other judicial avenues of recourse against these three administrative justice criteria reveals the reasons why the administrative justice literature has promoted alternative avenues of recourse. The judicial avenues have significant weaknesses in terms of two of the three criteria: their effectiveness in putting errors right, and accessibility. They therefore need to be accompanied by other avenues that make up for these shortcomings, such as tribunals. What is

[11] For a survey, see S Halliday and C Scott, 'Administrative Justice' in P Cane and H M Kritzer (eds), *The Oxford Handbook of Empirical Legal Research* (Oxford, Oxford University Press, 2010) 469.

[12] See T Mullen, 'A Holistic Approach to Administrative Justice?' in Michael Adler (ed), *Administrative Justice in Context* (Oxford, Hart Publishing, 2010) 383 at 386; summarising the objectives set out in the White Paper *Transforming Public Services: Complaints, Redress and Tribunals* (Cm 6243, 2004) at [1.5] and [1.7].

[13] Law Commission (n 7) at [6.4], also at [9.6].

the best combination of avenues for each administrative regime is a much more difficult question to answer, given the need for contestable trade-offs.

Further potentially competing objectives in assessing a remedial system also include wider public interest objectives. The objectives and criteria discussed so far primarily concern individual justice. In addition, they also reflect a secondary public interest in a system that treats individuals fairly and has legitimacy as a result.

However, there is a potential tension between these fair treatment objectives and criteria and other aspects of the public interest. The latter may be conceived of as potentially competing with administrative justice, or as forming part of a broader conception of administrative justice. These aspects of the public interest include the following:

- promoting the social goals of the particular regime,
- conserving public resources,
- proportionate dispute resolution.[14]

While some parts of the administrative justice literature are firmly focused on the fair treatment of individuals, other work associated with the 'green light' school of thought[15] also reflects a concern with implementation of each regime's positive rules and promoting its social objectives.[16] From that perspective, what counts as getting it 'right' turns both on what an individual should receive and on what is required to serve the social goals served by the relevant regime.

As regards cost and resources, the fair treatment objectives include limiting the cost and burden imposed on the individual seeking just treatment. There is, however, also a public interest in containing the cost and burden of the system's operation. This is at least potentially in tension with individual fair treatment.

Finally, the objective of proportionate dispute resolution serves both individual fair treatment and competing public interests.

Trade-offs are unavoidable in light of these tensions. Such trade-offs are clearly part of the practice of public administration and dispute resolution in the real world. Arguably, however, they are also valid aspect of the normative framework of administrative justice. We can strive for creative solutions that reduce the conflicts as far as possible and achieve good results on most criteria. However, tensions will remain. There is much room for debate about the best balance, and which criteria should be prioritised.

A final set of considerations that are brought to bear in these debates concerns constitutional principles. The rule of law and the separation of powers are often invoked in arguments about remedial avenues. In engaging with such arguments,

[14] White Paper (n 12) at [1.7] and Part 2.

[15] C Harlow and R Rawlings, *Law and Administration*, 4th edn (2022), ch 1.

[16] See, eg, J Mashaw, *Bureaucratic Justice: Managing Social Security Disability Claims* (New Haven and London, Yale University Press, 1983).

it is important to remember that the content and meaning of these principles is itself highly contestable.

A Range of Variable Features of Remedial Avenues

For the purposes of evaluating tribunals and other remedial avenues, and for designing new avenues, we need to identify relevant points of difference between them. The list of features that vary between judicial review, tribunals and other avenues includes the following:[17]

- scope of scrutiny: full merits review or supervisory review of legality
- type of remedies available:
  - substitution of decision or quashing and remitting
  - binding determination or non-binding recommendation
- expertise or experience, in at least three senses:
  - specialist legal knowledge or experience
  - expertise or experience in the subject area, such as medical expertise
  - representation of relevant interests
- degree of independence and impartiality
- type of procedure: adversarial or an alternative form (inquisitorial, investigative, active, enabling)
- degree of formality in other respects
- speed of resolution
- funding and resourcing
- public awareness and understanding of the avenue
- legal representation: whether it is allowed and whether it is funded (legal aid).

Each of these features relates to one or more of the three administrative justice criteria. Effectiveness at putting errors right depends on the scope of scrutiny and the types of remedies available, expertise or experience, and speed of resolution. Accessibility depends on the formality of the procedures, funding and resourcing, and public awareness, as well as again on speed. Trustworthiness depends on independence and fair hearings.

The remaining parts of this chapter take these three criteria in turn. I explore debates concerning the advantages and disadvantages of the features associated with each criterion in light of the competing criteria, the public interest objectives and relevant constitutional principles.

[17] For a shorter list of five main characteristics, see T Mullen, 'Access to Justice in Administrative Law and Administrative Justice' in Palmer and others (eds), *Access to Justice: Beyond the Policies and Politics of Austerity* (Oxford and Portland, Oregon, Hart Publishing, 2015) 95 at 99.

Effective at Putting Errors Right

Whether an avenue of recourse is effective at putting errors right can be considered in terms of three sets of features: the scope of scrutiny and the types of remedies available, expertise or experience, and speed of resolution. Non-judicial avenues tend to have significant advantages over judicial review where effectiveness is concerned.

Scope of Scrutiny and Types of Remedy: Merits Review vs Limited Supervisory Review

A power to deal with the merits, and to substitute the correct or preferable decision,[18] at least prima facie makes for the most effective error correction: all types of error can be fully put right.

Merits review is a central feature of almost all the non-judicial avenues of recourse and is one of the main features that distinguish them from judicial ones. In the case of the Ombudsman, merits review is combined with a remedial power that is limited to recommendations.[19] Administrative tribunals, in contrast, have a merits review power along with the power to make binding determinations. It is exceptional for a first appeal to an administrative tribunal to be a limited appeal.[20]

In contrast, the judicial avenues are generally limited to supervisory review of legality and procedure, and to remedies of quashing decisions and remitting them for reconsideration. That goes for both judicial review and appeals on questions of law,[21] which are the usual form of appeal to the general courts in this context.[22]

This section addresses two questions. First, the nature of merits review and what types of errors it corrects. Secondly, an evaluation of merits review: why it is necessary for effective error correction, and how it relates to competing objectives and considerations.

[18] The 'correct or preferable' formulation is used in relation to the Australian Administrative Appeals Tribunal (AAT): see *Shi v Migration Agents' Registration Authority* (2008) 235 CLR 286, 327 [140] (Kiefel J).

[19] Ombudsmen Act 1975, s 22(1) and (3).

[20] Examples include Legal Services Act 2011, s 52.

[21] M Rodriguez Ferrere, 'The Functional Convergence of Appeal and Judicial Review' [2016] *New Zealand Law Review* 157.

[22] See, eg, Social Security Act 2018, s 405; Accident Compensation Act 2001, s 162; Immigration Act 2009, s 245. For exceptions where general courts hear merits appeals from administrative authorities see, eg, Accident Compensation Act 2001, ss 149–161; Tax Administration Act 1994, Part 8A; Trade Marks Act 1953, s 27(6) and (7) and Trade Marks Act 2002, ss 170–173.

The Nature of Merits Review and What Errors It Corrects

The nature of merits review is a greatly understudied topic.[23] What is clear is that a merits review tribunal has power to substitute what it considers to be the correct or preferable decision. The power of such a tribunal is at least the same as that of a court hearing a general appeal,[24] but it usually goes further both in terms of procedure and substantive power.[25]

The provisions often lack specificity and are open to interpretation. Often, merits review is signalled simply by provision for substitutionary remedies: the review or appeal body may confirm, cancel or vary the impugned decision.[26] A merits tribunal often considers the matter afresh ('de novo').[27] It is often said to stand in the shoes of the primary decision-maker,[28] and may be provided with 'all the duties, functions and powers of the original decision-maker'.[29] Such provisions indicate that there is no onus on the appellant, unlike in a general appeal.[30] This is even clearer where it is provided that the tribunal must determine the matter without regard to the first instance decision.[31] Where further and new evidence may be heard, that means developments since the time of the original decision are relevant. In summary, the fullest form of merits review gives the reviewing body full power to consider all relevant law, facts and evidence at the time of its decision, and to reach what it considers to be the best decision.

What is less clear is how merits review deals, and should deal, with the types of complaints that are the focus of judicial review: complaints concerning unlawful reasoning process (such as irrelevant considerations) or unfair procedure.[32] In judicial review, such errors result in the decision being remitted for reconsideration. How merits review should respond to such complaints depends on how we conceive of effective error correction.

[23] One of the few instances of in-depth consideration: P Cane, *Administrative Tribunals and Adjudication* (Oxford and Portland, Hart Publishing, 2009) ch 5. Cane's take on merits review has, however, been controversial in Australia, as he acknowledges in the chapter.

[24] On which, see *Austin, Nichols & Co Inc v Stichting Lodestar* [2007] NZSC 103, [2008] 2 NZLR 141.

[25] See G Taylor, *Judicial Review: A New Zealand Perspective*, 4th edn (Wellington, LexisNexis NZ, 2018) at [4.05]–[4.06].

[26] See, eg, Social Security Regulations 2018, regs 247(2) and 254(1); Tax Administration Act 1994, ss 135(1)(a) and 138P(1)(b); Trade Marks Act 2002, s 173(a). Cf Accident Compensation Act 2001: s 145(1)(b) expressly refers to the 'substantive merits', while substitutionary review is provided for in ss 145(3)–(4) and 161.

[27] See, eg, Accident Compensation Act 2001, s 155(2); Social Security Regulations 2018, reg 253(1).

[28] That is usually said of the AAT: see Cane (n 23) at 145. See similarly, eg, concerning Benefit Review Committees: *Arbuthnot v Chief Executive of the Department of Work and Income* [2007] NZSC 55, [2008] 1 NZLR 13 at [19].

[29] See, eg, Social Security Act 2018, s 401; Trade Marks Act 2002, s 173(b); Tax Administration Act 1994, s 135(1)(b) and s 138P(1)(b). On the last of these, see *Tannadyce Investments Ltd v Commissioner of Inland Revenue* [2011] NZSC 158, [2012] 2 NZLR 153 at [50], [54], [55], [57].

[30] *Austin, Nichols & Co* (n 24) at [4], [13].

[31] Films, Videos and Publications Classification Act 1993, s 52(2). Similarly, see Accident Compensation Act 2001, s 145(1)(a).

[32] For discussion, see Cane (n 23) at 149–69.

If an unlawful reasoning process or unfair procedure has led to a decision that is not sound in substance, merits review can substitute a better decision. Arguably that is sufficient for correcting the error. Perhaps, however, the tribunal should also record the reasoning or process error that contributed to the decision-maker reaching the wrong decision. Conversely, if the decision is sound in substance, on merits review it will usually be upheld even if it was affected by a reasoning or procedural error. In that case, that error may not be corrected at all. However, the tribunal could still record that error in its decision.

Whether merits review should address reasoning or procedural errors by any of these means, in addition to determining the best outcome, has not been fully and authoritatively considered in Aotearoa NZ. Support can be found both for and against it, and of course it may depend on the particular powers of each tribunal. The Supreme Court in *Tannadyce* interpreted the merits review provisions in the tax regime as including power to adjudicate on any claimed ground of error whatsoever, as well as to determine the correct outcome.[33] It did not elaborate on what this would look like. However, the Supreme Court in *Austin, Nicholls & Co* commented that an appeal court hearing a general appeal is not required to pay explicit attention to the reasons of the body appealed from.[34] The comment was, however, addressed to a different issue: the point was to reject any requirement of deference to those reasons.

Where reasoning errors are concerned, what is clear is that most merits review tribunals can reach the best decision for any reasons they consider relevant and appropriate – they do not need to rely on the original decision-maker's reasons.[35] Conversely, it is also clear that a successful applicant cannot appeal against the reasons for a decision.[36] The question is only whether, in an appeal by an unsuccessful party, a merits tribunal can, in addition to determining the best outcome, examine the original decision-maker's reasons and record that they were erroneous. *Tannadyce* seems to indicate that the answer, at least in some contexts, is yes.

Turning to procedural unfairness, the Court of Appeal in *Ramsay* appears to suggest in obiter that merits tribunals cannot always address this.[37] At least on some occasions, however, merits review tribunals have recorded breaches of natural justice in their decisions. For instance, the Social Security Appeal Authority did so when Benefits Review Committees (BRCs) adopted a procedure of deciding some review applications on the papers and in their decisions identifying their members only by pseudonyms. The purpose of this practice was to protect members from clients who were assessed as disruptive and potentially violent, but the Authority did not accept that this concern justified such an 'alarming' practice.[38]

[33] *Tannadyce* (n 29) at [54]–[57].

[34] *Austin, Nichols* (n 24) at [5].

[35] *Arbuthnot* (n 28) at [16]–[17].

[36] ibid [25].

[37] See *Ramsay v Wellington District Court* [2006] NZAR 136 (CA) at [32] – it is not clear whether the doubts about the availability of a natural justice challenge relate to the District Court's merits review jurisdiction, or rather to appeals on questions of law at the next stage of the process.

[38] *An appeal against a decision of a Benefits Review Committee* [2015] NZSSAA 102 at [25]–[32].

Evaluating this, the ability to record errors of reasoning or procedure is important, in cases where such errors are likely to be repeated unless and until the tribunal records them as erroneous. One of the functions of appeals is to supervise the authority being appealed from (which may be a primary decision-maker or a first instance review body).[39] The problem with BRC members hiding behind pseudonyms is an extreme example of the problematic practices or policies that may creep in when there is a lack of legal supervision of public decision-making regimes. Supervision could also, of course, take the form of judicial review. However, in contexts involving vulnerable applicants, recourse to judicial review is unlikely due to its inaccessibility.[40]

Finally, some merits review tribunals are expressly provided with a choice of remedies, including the judicial review remedy of remitting a decision to the authority appealed from, rather than determining the correct or preferable decision.[41] The question is under what circumstances it is appropriate for them to deploy that option. It could be used in response to reasoning or process errors. However, this would be unnecessary and inappropriate if the hearing and reasoning carried out by the merits review body has repaired and hence cured any procedural or reasoning process defect in the original decision.[42]

Whether this is so may depend on the nature of the defect and on the procedures of the merits review body. The question was addressed by the Supreme Court in *H (SC 52/2018) v Refugee and Protection Officer*, albeit for the different purpose of determining whether to give effect to an exclusive remedy clause that requires recourse to the Immigration and Protection Tribunal before accessing the courts' jurisdiction on appeal or judicial review. The Court held that a merits appeal to the Tribunal would not cure a fundamental breach of natural justice in the original decision: this was one of the statutory regimes under which applicants have a right to a fair hearing at both levels.[43] This was at least in part because the first instance decision-making process included statutory safeguards that were missing from the tribunal's process. It may also have been due partly to the importance of the decision – determining refugee status.

In other contexts, however, lawful reasoning and procedure by the merits tribunal can cure the defect in the first instance decision.[44] In such cases, it is likely inappropriate for that merits review tribunal to remit the decisions to the first

[39] Law Commission (n 7) at [8.2].

[40] It is also sometimes precluded by an 'exclusive remedy' type of privative clause. However, such clauses have been held ineffective to preclude challenges on grounds that are not available through the statutory avenue of recourse: see *Ramsay* (n 37) at [32], *Tannadyce* (n 29) at [57]–[59].

[41] See, eg, Social Security Regulations 2018, reg 254(3) and (4). Contrast, eg, Immigration Act 2009, s 198(3).

[42] Cane (n 23) at 150, 151. See also Taylor (n 25) at [4.05].

[43] *H (SC 52/2018) v Refugee and Protection Officer* [2019] NZSC 13, [2019] 1 NZLR 433 at [43], [67]–[70], [74], [78]. For the general proposition that some regimes entitle applicants to no less than two fair hearings, see *Calvin v Carr* [1980] AC 574 (PC) at 592.

[44] On curing generally, see *Nicholls v Registrar of the Court of Appeal* [1998] 2 NZLR 385 (CA) at 435–37.

instance decision-maker: determination of the substantive issue by the tribunal is a more expeditious way of arriving at the same outcome.[45]

How Merits Review Relates to the Relevant Competing Objectives and Considerations

The second question to be addressed in this section is why merits review is crucial for the administrative justice objective of putting errors right, and how it relates to competing public interest objectives and constitutional considerations.

The administrative justice criterion of effectively putting errors right requires at least one opportunity to have the merits reviewed in the context of most administrative regimes.[46] Errors obviously do happen and are especially likely in areas where there is a high volume of front-line decisions.[47] Judicial review has very limited scope for correcting errors of evaluative assessment and judgment. Without a full opportunity to challenge such errors, individuals would have to live with unjust decisions and administrative regimes would fail to achieve their social purposes as fully as they should. Merits review is therefore important for administrative justice both in the narrower individual sense and in the broader public interest sense. Errors may still persist after one or two opportunities to revisit the merits. At that point, however, the strong arguments for merits review tend to be outweighed by concerns about finality and about proportionate allocation of resources.[48]

Turning to constitutional principles, there are potential separation of powers concerns about merits review tribunals, but these are sometimes overstated. In other jurisdictions, there have been extensive debates about whether such tribunals are judicial or administrative (executive) in nature.[49] If those two functions are seen as strictly separate and distinct, then merits review is an oxymoron: the exercise of public power is an executive or administrative function, while resolving disputes, including grievances against government, is a judicial function. Yet merits review can be both.

However, the strict separation of branches of government with distinct and mutually exclusive functions, as insisted on in some jurisdictions such as Australia, is not the version of the principle that operates in the UK or Aotearoa NZ.[50] The sharp dichotomy between functions is illusory – for instance, applying general norms to individual cases is both an executive and a judicial function.[51]

[45] See *Tannadyce* (n 29) at [55]; *Ramsay* (n 37) at [31].

[46] Law Commission (n 7) ch 8.

[47] Cane (n 23) at 179, 228.

[48] See Law Commission (n 7) at [8.4].

[49] Cane (n 23) ch 2 charts the history of the debate; ch 1 notes that in the UK, tribunals are increasingly treated as judicial, while in Australia, the Constitution requires them to be classified as administrative.

[50] See Law Commission (n 7) at [2.8], [2.14]. See also C Warnock, 'Environment and the Law: The Normative Force of Context and Constitutional Challenges' (2020) 32 *Journal of Environmental Law* 365 at 385–86; Cane (n 23) at 13–14, 32.

[51] Cane (n 23) at 106–07.

The substantive concern underlying separation of powers is to avoid concentrations of power and conflicts of interests that risk abuse of power, and to promote integrity by appropriate constraints and checks on exercises of power.[52] Rather than presenting it as a constitutional puzzle, then, the problem with tribunals can be restated in terms of a choice of forms of accountability. On the one hand, since the decisions of merits review tribunals direct and shape the administration of the relevant regime, arguably they ought to be subject to bureaucratic supervision that feeds into political accountability. On the other hand, since they play an important role in holding authorities to account, arguably they ought to be independent from the authorities whose decisions they supervise. Independence goes to trustworthiness, one of the administrative justice criteria. Which of these two options is to prevail ultimately comes down to a contestable value judgement, but it also depends on the nature of the tribunal's jurisdiction.

For instance, a lack of political accountability matters most obviously where a merits review body has power to deal with the merits of general rules (either administrative guidelines or delegated legislation), as opposed to power merely to grant exemptions from those rules in individual cases, or merely to review their consistency with empowering legislation. The NZ Environment Court, unusually, does have a merits review jurisdiction in relation to statutory instruments of a broad policy nature.[53] The lack of political accountability in that context has been considered problematic. It therefore calls for other appropriate checks and constraints, such as in this case procedures involving wide participation.[54] Most merits tribunals, such as the Social Security Appeal Authority, deal primarily with individual decisions. In that context, the need for and appropriateness of political accountability is questionable.

Finally, a further reason for the limits to merits review in all the judicial avenues is that courts usually lack the specialist expertise and experience that would qualify them to review the decision on the merits and to substitute their own conclusion. In that respect too, tribunals are relevantly different, as we will see in the next section.

Expertise or Experience

Turning to expertise or experience, this section first outlines different types of expertise and experience and where they are found, and then explores reasons for and against having expert or specialist remedial avenues. In Aotearoa NZ most administrative tribunals are set up to ensure some form of specialised expertise or experience.[55] The NZ court system, in contrast, lacks a specialist administrative law court.

[52] Warnock (n 50) at 386; Cane (n 23) at 15, 32.
[53] Discussed by Warnock (n 50).
[54] See Warnock (n 50) at 379–88.
[55] See, generally, Law Commission (n 7) ch 4.

Specialised expertise or experience is found in all tribunals that form part of a particular regime. By definition internal review tribunals have specialised experience, but special expertise or experience is also a feature of external tribunals such as the Social Security Appeal Authority or the Immigration and Protection Tribunal. Given the specialised nature of such tribunals' jurisdictions, their members will receive training and build up expertise in that legal regime and experience with its practical operation.[56]

In addition, some tribunals include non-legal expert members. For instance, Medical Boards under the Social Security Act are composed entirely of medical practitioners and persons with qualifications or experience in vocational training and rehabilitation.[57] When hearing Accident Compensation appeals, a District Court Judge may appoint an 'assessor' with relevant expert knowledge if the appeal involves 'matters of a professional, technical or specialised nature'.[58] The Assessor sits with the Court as extra member, but the Judge alone determines the appeal.[59]

There is also sometimes an element of interest representation,[60] but there are no clear examples of this currently in New Zealand. Benefits Review Committees under the Social Security Act include, in addition to two Ministry staff members, one member appointed by the Minister to represent 'the community's interest'.[61] However, it is thoroughly unclear what is meant by the community's interest in this context, given that the community includes both taxpayers and social security beneficiaries.

Turning to evaluation, the chief advantage of expertise or experience is that it equips a tribunal to handle merits review, thus enabling effective error correction. Expert or experienced tribunal members are better placed to determine the correct or preferable decision in the circumstances.[62] They are less likely to misunderstand the regime or its social goals and the context in which it operates, or to be misled by questionable arguments or evidence.[63] In addition to producing better decisions, specialised experience also makes a tribunal more efficient, as it does not need time to familiarise itself with the regime before it can address the issues arising.[64]

This advantage is particularly marked for tribunals that are expected to adopt an enabling approach to assist unrepresented applicants, as many administrative

[56] For instance, members of the Social Security Appeal Authority are not required to have any particular qualifications (see Social Security Act, s 401 and Sch 8), but they do acquire specialist experience in the social security regime.

[57] Social Security Act 2018, Sch 9, cl 1(2).

[58] Accident Compensation Act 2001, s 157.

[59] Accident Compensation Act 2001,ibid s 158.

[60] See N Wikeley and R Young, 'The Marginalisation of Lay Members in Social Security Appeal Tribunals' (1992) 14 *Journal of Social Welfare and Family Law* 127 at 132–33 for a historical UK example.

[61] Social Security Act 2018, Sch 7, cll 2(a) and 3.

[62] See, generally, SH Legomsky, *Specialized Justice* (Oxford, Clarendon Press, 1990) at 8–13.

[63] This point is distinct from an expectation that specialist tribunals will be more *committed* to the social goals than the general courts – that is a more contingent effect.

[64] Legomsky (n 62) at 17. Query the doubts about this in Cane (n 23) at 125.

tribunals are.[65] Expertise or specialised experience equips the tribunal to more readily identify relevant law and evidence for itself, and therefore to assist claimants in that regard.[66] By facilitating such an enabling approach without compromising the quality of decision, expertise or experience contributes indirectly to accessibility.

The most commonly noted disadvantage is that expert or specialised tribunals can be less independent.[67] The reasons include that appointments of expert members can be facilitated by involving the authority whose decisions they review,[68] some specialist tribunals are administered by those authorities, and ease of interaction with that authority may assist tribunal members in building and maintaining their expertise.[69] Where independence is diminished by such features, that affects trustworthiness, one of the other the administrative justice criteria. It also raises constitutional concerns about the separation of powers and the rule of law: concerns about accountability and checks and balances.[70] However, the loss of independence does not necessarily accompany expertise and specialisation: these can be achieved without most of the features that compromise independence.

A further potential disadvantage is the fragmentation of the administrative justice system that results from a proliferation of specialist tribunals. This jungle[71] can make it difficult for claimants to access review and appeal rights.[72] However, this could be addressed by providing navigational assistance at the entry point.[73]

A potential concern about a lack of coherent development of general principles[74] also can be addressed. Specialist tribunals can be integrated into an overall system that includes appeals on questions of law to generalist courts or tribunals.[75] Such proposals have not yet been actioned in Aotearoa NZ, although most regimes include an appeal to the High Court on questions of law.

Not everyone, however, considers the development of pockets of 'local law' to be a disadvantage.[76] For scholars of the 'green light' school persuasion, such

[65] See below under Informal procedure.

[66] For this aspect of an enabling approach, see S Green and L Sossin, 'Administrative Justice and Innovation: Beyond the Adversarial/Inquisitorial Dichotomy' in LA Jacobs and S Baglay (eds), *The Nature of Inquisitorial Processes in Administrative Regimes: Global Perspectives* (Farnham, Surrey, Ashgate Publishing, 2013) 71 at 73, 90–1.

[67] Green and Sossin (n 66) at 108.

[68] ibid at 99.

[69] Law Commission (n 7) at [5.23]–[5.24].

[70] This was Dicey's reason for insisting on general courts rather than specialist tribunals for controlling exercises of public power: Albert V Dicey, *Introduction to the Law of the Constitution* 8th edn (London, Macmillan and Co) (first published 1885) at 198.

[71] Harlow and Rawlings, *Law and Administration* (n 15) ch 10 (the word has been dropped in the current 4th edn).

[72] Pirini (n 6) at 257.

[73] ibid at 259–60 proposes a one-stop-shop.

[74] *R (Cart) v Upper Tribunal (Public Law Project Intervening)* [2011] UKSC 28, [2012] 1 AC 663 at [42]–[44] expressed a concern about specialist tribunals developing 'local law'.

[75] See, eg, the UK system under the Tribunals, Courts and Enforcement Act 2007, broadly following the recommendations of *Tribunals for Users: One System, One Service. Report of the Review of Tribunals chaired by Sir Andrew Leggatt* (March 2001).

[76] For discussion of the general pros and cons of specialisation, integration and amalgamation, see R Creyke, 'Australian Tribunals: Impact of Amalgamation' (2020) 26 *Australian Journal of Administrative Law* 206; Cane (n 23) ch 4.3.1.

pluralism flows from a desirable functional approach to administrative law, which recognises the different goals served and the different contexts of different administrative regimes.[77]

Speed

As the old adage has it, justice delayed is justice denied. In terms of the objectives and criteria of administrative justice, delay in disposing of a successful challenge diminishes the effectiveness of putting the error right: the person has had to live without the benefit for the duration of the delay and, in some contexts, there can be irreversible loss. Delay in holding hearings furthermore impairs accessibility. Speed is therefore relevant to two of the criteria of administrative justice.

One of the purposes of more informal procedures in tribunals is to promote speedier resolution than in the courts. However, this can be achieved only if tribunals are adequately resourced.[78] Furthermore, tribunal procedures are often investigative in nature, to aid accessibility.[79] That calls for additional resources: the more investigative the procedures, the more impossible it is for an avenue to function effectively and with due despatch unless it has the required resources. Regrettably, unacceptable delays, apparently due at least in part to lack of resourcing, are common in some of our alternative remedial avenues.[80]

In addition to proper resourcing, tribunals need to adopt systems that will facilitate effective use of their resources and hence speedy resolutions.[81] This can be promoted by the legislative design of those avenues, but also by appropriate monitoring and incentives.[82] Arguably time limits for disposal of cases should be a feature of most tribunals, but these are often missing.[83] The Accident Compensation Act 2001 does impose a time limit for scheduling a hearing, which is enforced by deeming a favourable decision to have been issued if that time is exceeded.[84] Such a provision would be beneficial in other regimes. A time limit for issuing a decision after hearing could also be imposed and enforced in the same way. One way of promoting speedy resolution of complaints or challenges is to provide early informal interventions. These can take the form of an initial internal

[77] See, eg, HW Arthurs, 'Rethinking Administrative Law: A Slightly Dicey Business' (1979) 17 *Osgoode Hall Law Journal* 1, esp at 29, 32–33, 41.

[78] See, eg, Law Commission (n 7) at [9.10], [9.11], [9.16]–[9.17].

[79] Further discussed under the next heading.

[80] For instance, I have seen instances where Benefits Review Committees under the Social Security Act 2018 took six months to schedule hearings for challenges to decisions about temporary hardship support. For delays in ACC reviews, see Dean report (n 9) at 27.

[81] See, eg, Leggatt Report (n 75) at [8.4]–[8.6] on case management in tribunals.

[82] Law Commission (n 7) at [9.7] calls for monitoring and reporting obligations.

[83] Eg there are no legislated timeframes for Benefits Review Committee or Social Security Appeal Authority hearings.

[84] Accident Compensation Act 2001, s 146.

review,[85] early neutral evaluation,[86] or both.[87] Such informal interventions can resolve a significant proportion of complaints quickly and informally.

To serve the purpose of speedy resolution, however, these initial procedures must offer truly informal resolution.[88] They should require no separate application, but rather should be conducted on the papers as an automatic response to an applicant raising concerns about a decision or filing an appeal with an external tribunal. Arguably it is also advantageous if they do not involve a hearing, although that can be argued either way.

This type of informal intervention can be done without any special statutory authority: all statutory powers can be exercised again to correct an error or omission in an earlier exercise.[89] Examples are found in the social security and ACC regimes: internal reviews are carried out whenever a review application is filed.[90]

However, both regimes additionally include internal review tribunals created by statute that do not operate in such a beneficial fashion. The legislated first instance review by a Benefits Review Committee is essentially internal[91] and fairly informal. But it requires complainants to apply for it,[92] the application very rarely succeeds unless the complainant attends a hearing or sends a representative,[93] and it can involve very significant delays. Similar points can be made about first instance reviews under the Accident Compensation Act 2001.[94]

Where recourse to such a formalised internal procedure is made a compulsory step before accessing external review, as is the case with Benefit Review Committees[95] and ACC reviews,[96] the effect is the opposite of promoting speedy resolution. Complainants are required to invest time and effort in this internal review (which has low success rates),[97] delaying access to a more trustworthy external tribunal. If such compulsory internal review avenues are nevertheless to be used, enforceable time limits are especially important.

[85] See Law Commission (n 7) at [9.29]–[9.34]; Leggatt Report (n 75) at [9.6]–[9.8].

[86] M Adler, 'Tribunal Reform: Proportionate Dispute Resolution and the Pursuit of Administrative Justice' (2006) 69 *Modern Law Review* 958 at 976–77.

[87] An offer of mediation is another option – that is the practice adopted by ACC.

[88] Also, there should be no more than one level of internal review: Law Commission (n 7) at [9.33].

[89] Legislation Act 2019, s 46.

[90] See 'Reviews and Appeals' in the online *Manuals and Procedures*. Available at: https://workandincome.got.nz/map/Inocme-support/core-policy. The Law Commission (n 7) at [9.32] fn 571 reports that in 2006/07, 23% of challenged decisions were overturned on this informal internal review. On ACC, see Dean report (n 9) at 9, 34.

[91] On its lack of independence, see below at n 144.

[92] Social Security Act 2018, s 391.

[93] Community Law Canterbury (n 10) at 98.

[94] Accident Compensation Act 2001, ss 134–135; and see Acclaim Otago (n 9) at para 144.

[95] Social Security Act 2018, s 395.

[96] Accident Compensation Act 2001, ss 133(5) and 149.

[97] In social security matters, higher success rates have been reported for the informal administrative review (around one third) than for the Benefits Review Committee hearing that follows (around 10%): Community Law Canterbury (n 10) at 86, 99 (these percentages are for complete success; a further proportion of cases result in the decision being varied at both stages).

Accessibility

Turning to accessibility, the main features that may make for a good avenue on this second criterion are informal and enabling procedure, adequate funding and resources, and public awareness of the remedial avenue. Speed, discussed under the previous heading, is also relevant here.

Tribunals have the potential to offer much greater accessibility than courts, and that is one of the main reasons for establishing them.[98] However, that potential is not always realised in practice. Alongside lacking political will, the reasons for this also include disagreement on priorities and trade-offs between competing objectives.

Informal Procedure and Departures from the Adversarial Model

Most tribunals are provided with a measure of procedural flexibility.[99] More informal procedure can mean a lack of formal protocols as to attire, venue, language and other conduct, and a lack of complex rules governing the documents to be filed and the order of proceedings. Usually it also includes allowing helpful material, regardless whether it would be admissible as evidence in a court of law.[100] Finally, it can include a departure from the adversarial model, on which more below. Aside from informal procedure, some tribunals are also required to focus on the substantive merits and to disregard legal technicalities.[101]

Alternatives to the adversarial model are variously described as inquisitorial, investigative, active, and enabling.[102] These labels lack a clear and settled meaning. Some departure from the adversarial model along these lines, however, is a common feature of tribunals.[103] A measure of investigative or enabling initiative is commonly adopted by tribunals that are empowered to regulate their own procedure,[104] and some tribunals are expressly required or empowered to take

[98] See Law Commission (n 7) at [2.27]–[2.28], [2.41]–[2.43], [3.1]–[3.2]; *Chief Executive of the Ministry of Social Development v Genet* [2016] NZHC 2541 at [18]–[19], [26].

[99] See Law Commission (n 7) at [6.1]–[6.22].

[100] See, eg, Social Security Regulations 2018, reg 253(6); Accident Compensation Act 2001 ss 141(4) and 156(1).

[101] See, eg, the Human Rights Review Tribunal: Human Rights Act 1993, s 105.

[102] See, eg, Leggatt Report (n 75) at [7.2]–[7.5]; Law Commission (n 7) at [6.16]–[6.20]; Green and Sossin (n 68) 71; N Bedford and R Creyke, *Inquisitorial Processes in Australian Tribunals* (The Australasian Institute of Judicial Administration, 2006).

[103] For details of the enabling model, see, eg, Green and Sossin (n 75) at 73, 83–84; Leggatt Report (n 75) at [7.5].

[104] For examples of such a power, see Immigration Act 2009, s 222(4); Social Security Act 2019, s 403(1) and Sch 8, cl 10D.

such approaches.[105] They will usually explain the process to applicants and answer questions about it.[106] They may take an active part in identifying issues and missing evidence;[107] they will usually be ready to identify relevant law that may have been missed by the parties; some will make their own factual enquiries; and they may engage in questioning the parties and witnesses. Some tribunals are specifically empowered to take some of these steps, such as to seek further information.[108] Conversely, the original decision-making authority is often under an obligation to assist the tribunal with information.[109]

The advantages of these types of informal, non-adversarial procedures include that they may render legal or other representation less necessary. That, in turn, would be one way of dealing with the cost barrier to accessibility. It might also serve the public interest in reducing demands on public resources and might be part of proportionate dispute resolution.

However, there are concerns that, in many contexts, even with an enabling approach, unrepresented complainants do not tend to fare well.[110] Lack of representation may thus compromise achievement of the other two administrative justice criteria: effective error correction and trustworthiness. I will return to this under the trustworthiness heading.

A common objection to an enabling or investigative approach is that it threatens the neutrality and impartiality that is essential for an adjudicative body.[111] When raised by the respondent authority, this cannot usually be a valid objection. At least in contexts such as social security and ACC, there is an integral imbalance of power[112] and a resulting need for levelling the playing field.[113] NZ courts have acknowledged the appropriateness of departures from the adversarial model in such contexts.[114] However, complainants may have a valid concern about trustworthiness where an enabling approach is relied on to replace legal representation. As already noted, I will return to the issue of representation under that heading.

[105] See, eg, Immigration Act 2009, s 218(2); Accident Compensation Act 2001, s 140(e). Investigative powers can also be achieved by providing that the Commissions of Inquiry Act 2008 applies (see, eg, Social Security Act 2018, Sch 8, cl 12): s 4C of that Act provides such powers.

[106] The Social Security Appeal Authority (SSAA) provides an opportunity for this by way of a pre-hearing telephone conference. See www.justice.govt.nz/assets/Documents/Publications/Overview-Hearing-process-SSAA.pdf.

[107] In the SSAA, the pre-hearing telephone conference is also used for this: ibid.

[108] See, eg, Immigration Act 2009, ss 228–229.

[109] ibid s 229(1); Social Security Regulations 2018, reg 249.

[110] See, eg Community Law Canterbury (n 10) at 100–01, 104, 106, 113–15, 117; MacKinnon (n 9) at 122.

[111] See, eg, A Zuckerman, 'No Justice Without Lawyers – The Myth of an Inquisitorial Solution' (2014) 33 Civil Justice Quarterly 355 at 357–63; Justice H Winkelmann, 'Access to Justice – Who Needs Lawyers?' (2014) 13 Otago Law Review 229 at 237–38, 241 (the first passage relates to courts, but in the later passage the comments are said to apply also to tribunals with inquisitorial approaches).

[112] See Law Commission (n 7) at [6.16].

[113] Green and Sossin (n 75) at 92.

[114] See, eg, *Genet* (n 98) at [14]–[16]. See also *Claydon v Attorney-General* [2004] NZAR 16 (CA) at [66] (concerning the employment tribunal).

Cost and Resourcing

Cost barriers to accessibility can be addressed directly by public funding.[115] Unlike courts, many tribunals do not charge fees. They are funded by the Ministry of Justice, by the Crown generally,[116] or by the respondent authority.[117] There are also provisions requiring a respondent authority to cover the expenses of the applicant's attendance at a hearing, regardless of outcome.[118]

To the extent that representation is considered necessary, public funding for it takes a variety of forms. Legal aid is sometimes available for representation in tribunals and also for pre-hearing advice.[119] Civil legal aid is usually a repayable loan, but that debt can be waived on grounds of financial hardship.[120] Community Law Centres are funded to provide pre-hearing advice, but generally not to offer representation.[121] Public funding is sometimes available for organisations offering lay advocacy, but it is very limited.[122]

Rules for the award of costs can also be adjusted to help address cost barriers. In some tribunals, for instance, costs may be awarded even to unsuccessful complainants, and good faith complainants are protected against adverse cost awards.[123] Costs awards have also been made available for lay advocates providing representation or pre-hearing advice, even where they otherwise offer their services for free.[124]

There is little doubt that funding advocacy and advice promotes administrative justice. The difficulty is simply that such funding is very limited. This reflects the competing public interest in containing the cost of redress systems, and the lack of political will to prioritise the needs of vulnerable groups who lack a strong voice.

Public Awareness and Understanding of Avenues of Redress

The best remedial avenues will be of little use if people aggrieved at decisions are not aware of them, what they do and how to access them. This is the one aspect

[115] See generally Law Commission (n 7) at [3.5]–[3.10], [3.20]–[3.21], [7.37]–[7.41], table 2.
[116] See, eg, the Social Security Appeal Authority: see Social Security Act 2018, Sch 8, cll 6–7.
[117] See, eg, ACC reviewers: Accident Compensation Act, s 137.
[118] See, eg, Social Security Regulations 2018, reg 251.
[119] Legal Services Act 2011, s 7(1)(e)(v), (g), (i)–(j), s 7(5)(f)–(g), s 12(1).
[120] ibid ss 18, 21, 42–43.
[121] According to the Community Law Canterbury (n 10), the Ministry of Justice in 2013 reduced funding for legal representation, preferring a focus on early resolution. More recent budgets have included funding for a pro bono clearing house: see https://tearature.co.nz/about/#.
[122] On ACC, see Dean report (n 9) at 54–55. For social security, see Community Law Canterbury (n 10) at 143; Law Commission (n 7) at [6.39]. The total funding available through the CSF is $300,000 (excl GST) per year: MSD answer to question under the Official Information Act 1982, dated 11 July 2022.
[123] See, eg, Social Security Regulations 2018, reg 255(2); Accident Compensation Act 2001, s 148(2).
[124] *Genet* (n 98).

of accessibility where the judicial avenues currently have an advantage. Tribunals tend to be less well known. Much could be done to improve public awareness and understanding of them.[125]

There needs to be a duty on public authorities to advise applicants of their review and appeal rights.[126] Some legislation does impose such duties, but there are significant gaps.[127] In addition, tribunals need to publish guides on how to access them, and there is room for improvement in that regard. A further proposal, already touched on, is to tame the confusing 'jungle' of different avenues of redress. Arguably, it is also necessary to go beyond providing written information. An example of doing this, albeit at a fairly late stage of the process, is the Social Security Appeals Authority's practice of scheduling a pre-hearing telephone conference at which questions can be answered.[128] Finally, it is important that all tribunals have a system for publishing their significant decisions. Claimants and their advocates need to be able to look up what they can expect of a tribunal. Again, there are significant gaps in this regard.

Trustworthiness

Trustworthiness is the third criterion. The trustworthiness of an avenue of recourse may be assessed at least partly in terms of its compliance with the administrative law principles of natural justice or procedural fairness: its independence and impartiality, and whether it affords complainants a fair hearing in the circumstances. This is the one criterion on which judicial avenues are stronger than tribunals. The difficulty for tribunals is that features designed to promote accessibility and effectiveness at putting errors right can compromise independence and other aspects of natural justice. There is much room for debate as to the optimal compromise. In striking this balance, it is important to remember that the administrative law principles of procedural fairness are highly flexible and context sensitive.[129] The perceived tensions with other administrative justice features are unnecessarily exaggerated if we start from an assumption that all tribunals must adopt procedures modelled on courts.

[125] See Law Commission (n 7) at [3.11]–[3.13], [3.18], [3.22]–[3.25]; Community Law Canterbury (n 10) at 60–61.

[126] Law Commission (n 7) at [3.12]. Though notification by the primary decision-maker may be perceived as casting doubt on the independence of the review body: see, eg, a quote in G McKeever, 'A Ladder of Legal Participation for Tribunal Users' [2013] *Public Law* 575 at 585.

[127] For example, the Social Security Act 2018 imposes such a duty only in relation to some specific types of decisions: see ss 106, 252(2)(h). It is, however, MSD's usual practice to include such advice in all decision letters: Stephens (n 10) at 391.

[128] See www.justice.govt.nz/assets/Documents/Publications/Overview-Hearing-process-SSAA.pdf.

[129] *Daganayasi v Minster of Immigration* [1980] 2 NZLR 130 (CA) at 140–41; *Drew v Attorney-General* [2002] 2 NZLR 58 (CA).

Independence

Concerns about independence are among the main issues with tribunals.[130] For courts, in contrast, independence is one of their main strengths. The most independent among the non-judicial avenues are the Ombudsmen. They are appointed by the Governor-General and are designated officers of Parliament, thus avoiding any suggestion of accountability to executive government.[131] However, even here concerns have been raised. Parliament is, of course, to a large extent, controlled by the executive in our system. Furthermore, Ombudsmen are appointed for a fixed term with the possibility of renewal. They may perhaps worry about being denied renewal should they perform their role too assertively; this was allegedly behind the non-renewal of Nadja Tollemache's appointment in 1992.[132]

The concern about lack of security of tenure is at least as strong for most tribunals, even the external ones.[133] Tribunal members are usually appointed for a renewable fixed term of up to five years.[134] The Law Commission reported a consensus against tribunal members' appointments being permanent, up to retirement age, as for judges.[135] It is not necessarily clear why. One alternative is to have a long fixed term with no renewal – the Auditor-General, for instance, is appointed for a single term of seven years.[136] If the present system is maintained for tribunals, then the minimum safeguard should be to expressly allow non-renewal only on limited prescribed grounds.[137]

However, external tribunals are at least relatively independent from the department or other body whose decisions they review.[138] Appointment tends to be by the Governor General on the recommendation either of the relevant Minister[139] or of the Minister of Justice,[140] often after consultation with the relevant Minister[141] or the Minister of Justice.[142] Administrative support tends to be the responsibility of the Ministry of Justice.[143]

[130] See, eg, Ron Ellis, *Unjust by Design: Canada's Administrative Justice System* (2013); Matthew Groves and Greg Weeks, 'Tribunal Justice and Politics in Australia: The Rise and Fall of the Administrative Appeals Tribunal' (2023) 97 *Australian Law Journal* 278.

[131] Ombudsmen Act 1975, s 3.

[132] Mai Chen 'New Zealand's Ombudsmen Legislation: The Need for Amendments After Almost 50 Years' (2010) 41 VUWLR 723 at 751.

[133] See Law Commission (n 7) ch 5 and also ch 4.

[134] See eg, Legal Services Act 2011, Sch 3, cl 1; Immigration Act 2009, Sch 2, cl 1; Taxation Review Authority Act 1994, s 6(1); Social Security Act 2018, Sch 8, cl 2.

[135] Law Commission (n 7) at 5.19, 5.21.

[136] Public Audit Act 2001, Sch 3, cl 1.

[137] See Leggatt Report (n 77) at [7.7].

[138] Leggatt, ibid ch 2 considers this important.

[139] See, eg, Legal Services Act 2011, s 64(1).

[140] See, eg, Taxation Review Authorities Act 1994, s 5(4).

[141] See, eg, Immigration Act 2009, s 219(3). The chair of the Immigration and Protection Tribunal is appointed on the advice of the Attorney-General, after consultation with both Ministers: s 219(2).

[142] See, eg, Social Security Act 2018, Sch 8, cl 1(2).

[143] See www.justice.govt.nz/tribunals for a list of tribunals administered by the Ministry of Justice (only some of these are administrative tribunals).

For internal review tribunals, in contrast, even that independence from the department under review is missing. Consider, for example, the Benefits Review Committees provided by the Social Security Act 2018.[144] Two members of each panel of three are Ministry of Social Development employees appointed by the Chief Executive, albeit they must have no prior involvement in the case. The third member is appointed by the Minister of Social Development to represent the community's interest. That third member has little more independence than the employees: the person holds office on the terms the Minister sees fit.

The ACC regime features a peculiar attempt at independence. The Act requires first instance review applications to be made to the Corporation and requires the Corporation to 'engage' independent reviewers.[145] The Corporation has sought to achieve that independence by contracting out to a private entity.[146] It is difficult to see how this results in greater independence, given that the entity has an interest in retaining its contract with ACC.[147]

Turning to evaluation, the question is whether the lack of independence can be justified by reference to competing objectives or criteria. In relation to external tribunals, there is a potential argument for some qualifications to independence. That is not because of the need for specialisation – as already noted, this can be achieved without significantly compromising independence.[148] However, it may be considered important for a merits review tribunal to exhibit some commitment to the particular regime's social goals. Such commitment may be promoted by a measure of political or bureaucratic supervision. This might perhaps be facilitated by reduced security of tenure, but that is a questionable method. In any event, this argument is controversial – the mainstream position tends to be that we expect neutrality from administrative tribunals with a merits review jurisdiction, no less than from other adjudicative bodies. It is not at all clear, therefore, that this type of argument has played any role in the rejection of security of tenure for NZ's administrative tribunals.

Turning to internal review, while this inherently entails lack of any real independence, it has at least two potential advantages. One possible advantage of a truly internal review is that those involved in that review can learn from the errors they uncover.[149] Secondly, internal reviews can also be of great benefit in terms of their speed, accessibility and effectiveness at putting errors right. This second advantage applies *if* internal review deals quickly and informally with more obvious errors, without putting any additional burden on complainants. Internal review of that nature is better categorised as part of the agency's internal quality management systems than as part of the remedial regime.[150]

[144] Social Security Act 2019, Sch 7, cll 2, 3 and 6.

[145] Accident Compensation Act 2001, ss 133–134, 137–139.

[146] See www.fairwayresolution.com.

[147] For concerns, see the Dean report (n 9) at 25, 28–29.

[148] See above under 'Expertise and experience'.

[149] See David Cowan and others, 'Reconsidering Mandatory Reconsideration' [2017] *Public Law* 215 at 224–25, 226, 231.

[150] For the tension between these competing categorisations, see Harlow and Rawlings (n 15) at 552–53. According to the Supreme Court, Benefits Review Committees are not judicial authorities but

As noted earlier, however, several internal review tribunals do not operate in such a beneficial way.[151] They do put significant additional burdens on complainants. At the same time, complainants often experience them as failing to give proper consideration to review applications and as rubber stamping the decisions under review.[152]

It is highly problematic if recourse to such formalised internal procedures is made a compulsory step before accessing external tribunals, as is the case with Benefit Review Committees and ACC reviewers.[153] If the compulsory first instance body is not trusted due to its lack of independence,[154] then complaints may not be made at all. Those who do complain will be too dispirited to apply for a further level of review afterwards.[155] In the UK, for instance, a dramatic drop in numbers of social security appeals was tentatively attributed to the introduction of mandatory internal reconsideration.[156]

Right to a Hearing

As noted, the principles of procedural fairness are context-dependent, and a balance needs to be struck between this and competing administrative justice considerations. However, there are many aspects of the right to a hearing that need not and should not be compromised in tribunals. These include the right to adequate notice, and to disclosure of adverse material for comment. Where informality and procedural flexibility result in muddled proceedings that infringe these rights, administrative justice is no longer served either, because the applicant has not had an effective opportunity to challenge the decision in question.[157]

Among the questions that do call for balancing and compromise are whether there should be an oral hearing and whether legal representation should be allowed. An example of a context in which an oral hearing is arguably not desirable is first instance internal review, as noted under the previous heading. In exceptional contexts, proportionate dispute resolution may even favour external tribunals disposing of matters on the papers.[158] Most tribunals usually hold oral hearings

rather stand in the shoes of the primary decision-maker: *Arbuthnot v Chief Executive of the Department of Work and Income* [2007] NZSC 55, [2008] 1 NZLR 13 at [28].

[151] See above under 'Speed'.

[152] See Community Law Canterbury (n 10) at 90, 104; Acclaim Otago (n 9) at paras 150–51.

[153] Social Security Act 2018, s 395; Accident Compensation Act 2001, ss 133 (5) and 149.

[154] The lack of trust may be justified: while the Ministry of Social Development's informal internal reviews were reported to have overturned 23% of decisions in one year, Benefits Review Committees then overturned a mere 9% of the remaining challenged decisions: Law Commission (n 7) at [9.32] fn 571.

[155] Acclaim Otago (n 9) at para 134; Pirini (n 6) at 253; Law Commission (n 7) at [9.33]–[9.34].

[156] Mullen (n 17) at 119–22; see also P Gray, *The Second Independent Review of the Personal Independence Payment Assessment* (HMSO, March 2017) at 45.

[157] ACC review hearings have reportedly been affected by problems of this nature: see Acclaim (n 9) at 150–51.

[158] An instance where this is arguably appropriate is found in the Films, Videos and Publications Classification Act 1993, s 53.

but have a discretion to dispose of matters on the papers.[159] This should be used with great caution. In contexts such as social security, there is much evidence that appeals have better prospects when the appellant attends.[160] Holding a hearing therefore promotes effectiveness at putting errors right. Yet in areas such as social security, it is common for applicants not to attend hearings and for reviews therefore to be effectively disposed of on the papers.[161]

The question of representation is a very difficult one, because it involves acute tensions between the three administrative justice criteria. It should be noted that representation in many tribunals may take the form of lay representation as well as legal representation,[162] and experienced lay representatives can sometimes be better than lawyers who do not understand the regime in question.[163] However, in areas involving disadvantaged or vulnerable complainants, it is very common for applicants not to be represented at all.[164] That is at least partly because, as we have seen, funding for representation is very limited.[165]

In the administrative justice literature, it has often been assumed that representation is less necessary in tribunals, due to their informal procedures and enabling approaches.[166] The main arguments for seeking to render representation unnecessary in this way concern accessibility: it would remove the need to find a representative, as well as the potential cost barrier. At the same time, part of the attraction for policy makers undoubtedly is the saving to the public purse.

The NZ commentary, on the other hand, tends to assume that representation is necessary for a fair hearing,[167] reflecting the trustworthiness concern. It should be noted, however, that judicial review case law recognises no general right to legal representation as part of a fair hearing. According to *Drew*, whether representation is required at an administrative hearing depends on a range of factors including the nature of the body, the importance of the interests at stake and whether representation is necessary for an effective hearing in the circumstances.[168]

That last factor in *Drew* engages the first of the administrative justice criteria: effectiveness at putting errors right. This can be a strong reason for representation. In many contexts, unrepresented applicants may struggle to marshal the evidence and legal arguments required to win a meritorious case. This is a concern, for instance, in ACC reviews that turn on medical expert evidence.[169]

[159] See, eg, Social Security Act 2018, Sch 8, cl 10A.
[160] See, eg, Community Law Canterbury (n 10) at 98.
[161] ibid.
[162] This is permitted, for instance, in the Social Security Appeal Authority (Social Security Regulations 2018, reg 252(b)) and in ACC reviews (Accident Compensation Act 2001, s 142).
[163] See, eg, Hazel Genn and Yvette Genn, *The Effectiveness of Representation at Tribunals* (Lord Chancellor's Department, 1989), chs 2, 3 and 6.
[164] See, eg, Community Law Canterbury (n 10) at 114; also Acclaim Otago (n 9) at [417] on legal representation in appeals to the District Court in ACC matters.
[165] See above under Cost and resourcing.
[166] As noted in Cane (n 23) at 252.
[167] See, eg, Acclaim Otago (n 9).
[168] *Drew* (n 129) at [45]–[66], [70]–[75], [79]. The lists of factors are at [64] and [71].
[169] See MacKinnon (n 9).

On the other hand, this concern may be addressed by means other than representation. An enabling approach alone, however, will not be sufficient in all contexts. That is partly because such assistance at the hearing or even at a pre-hearing conference comes too late in the process.[170] More fundamentally, while a tribunal can assist complainants to some extent, its position prevents it being single-mindedly devoted to the complainant's case in the way that a representative would be.[171] Furthermore, where a tribunal takes an active role in identifying and eliciting relevant evidence, its questioning of the complainant may end up being perceived as cross-examination.[172] For all these reasons, it will often be necessary to have good pre-hearing advice as well as a tribunal with an enabling approach, as the minimum required for an effective hearing in the absence of representation.[173]

If these are the minimum requirements, that greatly reduces the ability to contain the cost to the public purse by avoiding representation. An enabling approach and pre-hearing advice both depend on adequate resourcing.

Conclusion

From an administrative justice perspective, tribunals serve the objective of putting errors right with the minimum difficulty for the affected person. Their main advantages over the judicial avenues in that regard, at least potentially, are their greater effectiveness at putting errors right and their greater accessibility. However, they can have weaknesses in terms of trustworthiness. Two further sets of considerations also influence the design, operation and evaluation of tribunals. First, there are the broader public interest objectives of proportionate dispute resolution, conserving public resources, and promoting the social goals of the particular regime. Secondly, constitutional principles must be considered.

Administrative tribunals in Aotearoa NZ do achieve the desired greater effectiveness at putting errors right, through offering merits review by specialist or specialised tribunals. A question deserving of more attention is whether merits review can address complaints about practices or policies involving unlawful reasoning processes or unfair procedures. Constitutional concerns about separation of powers and independence in relation to specialisation and merits review feature in overseas literature but have not carried much weight here. A further advantage of specialised tribunals is that they are more likely to understand the social goals of the regime in which they operate.

[170] ibid.

[171] Zuckerman (n 111) at 367–69, 371.

[172] Cane (n 23) at 242 (footnote 123), 243.

[173] Some overseas studies have found that unrepresented claimants can have good success rates, but only with pre-hearing advice: see Genn and Genn (n 163) chs 2–3; M Adler, 'Self-Representation, Just Outcomes and Fair Procedures in Tribunal Hearings: Some Inferences from Recently Completed Research' (Senior Presidents Conference for Tribunal Judges, 20 May 2009) at 5. See also Mackinnon (n 9) at 138.

However, effective error correction also requires speedy resolution. This is often compromised through inadequate resourcing and problematic design. Compulsory recourse to formalised internal review is a particular design problem impacting on speed.

Realising tribunals' potential for greater accessibility is a significant challenge. Informal and enabling procedures are widely used in Aotearoa NZ. However, without adequate resourcing for the tribunal, and without representation or at least good pre-hearing advice (again a resourcing issue), true accessibility remains to be achieved. There are also issues with public awareness and understanding of tribunals.

Trustworthiness is the area of potential weakness for tribunals. The problems can be minimised by appropriate design, but NZ tribunals have a long way to go in this regard. External tribunals could be made more independent, and internal review with its inherent lack of independence too often functions as a barrier to accessing external tribunals. The lack of resourcing for representation or at least pre-hearing advice, already noted above, also affects the availability of a fair hearing and hence trustworthiness.

Hopefully greater academic attention to administrative justice through tribunals, as represented by the present volume, can contribute to progress on all these fronts.

9

UK Tribunals: Structure, History, Constitutional Status and Practice

ROBERT THOMAS

'Tribunal' carries a range of meanings. In the UK, tribunals are low-level specialist administrative courts that decide appeals against individualised administrative decisions concerning people's entitlements and rights. Tribunals operate in areas including: social security; immigration and asylum; tax; school admissions and exclusions; mental health; special educational needs and disability; parking; care standards, war pensions and armed forces compensation; criminal injuries compensation; and so on. Low-level does not mean inferior. Tribunals are essential. They undertake the bulk of administrative law adjudication. They are also an institutional site at which law and administration blend into each other. The development of tribunals is intimately connected to that of the British state and the expansion of its functions.

This chapter examines UK tribunals. It considers their structure, history, constitutional position and practical operation. It examines how tribunals have evolved. Tribunals were originally administrative, but they are now judicial and part of the formal judicial system. This then leads to a discussion of the constitutional position of tribunals and whether they contravene the principle of the separation of powers. The chapter also considers aspects of contemporary tribunal practices and the wider administrative systems in which they operate.

Three general points are advanced. First, tribunals are deeply embedded within the specific social, political and administrative contexts in which they operate and can only be understood in this way. In the UK, government is not legally required to introduce appeal rights, but has often done so as a result of the social need for them and the inadequacy of other means of redress. Tribunals operate as a self-imposed legal constraint that government applies to itself. Second, the constitutional position of tribunals has shifted considerably. They were once viewed with deep suspicion by both lawyers and judges, but they have been brought within the formal judicial system. This has occurred as a result of wider social, political and legal-cultural changes. Tribunals do not contravene the separation of powers and have not been viewed as being particularly problematic in this respect since the 1950s. Tribunals have gained acceptance and expanded because they perform an important social function: providing reasonably accessible, fair and efficient justice. However – and this is the third point – over recent years, the practical problems with tribunals and the wider systems in which they operate have become increasingly acute. People sometimes experience difficulties in accessing tribunals. There are also extensive concerns about the variable quality of initial government decisions. These problems have arisen as part of the wider austerity-driven environment of administrative justice.[1] The resolution of these problems is largely for government, although it has little desire to improve matters.

Another initial point concerns the place of tribunals within administrative law scholarship. Tribunals are not part of the mainstream; 'the tribunals chapter is at the back of the admin law textbook'. When administrative law analysis does consider tribunals, the focus is typically judicial control of tribunals by the courts rather than what tribunals themselves do. However, for much of the twentieth century, tribunals were the principal administrative law institution, as reflected in the literature of the time.[2] Tribunals were synonymous with administrative law in the sense of the law-adjudication that took place within administration. It was only with the major texts of the 1960s that courts became the central scholarly preoccupation.[3] Nonetheless, there has been a minor tradition of researchers looking beyond the law reports and doing the legwork necessary to explore the law in action as it occurs within tribunals. Unlike judicial review, tribunals cannot really be studied from conventional internal-doctrinal-theoretical approaches.[4] Empirical and contextual methods are naturally adopted. The differences here reflect a deeper tension about whether the animating idea of legal scholarship should be a search for conceptual legal coherence or an examination of the effectiveness of legal institutions. Studies of tribunals often adopt the latter approach and for good reason. Tribunals generate many interesting and complex problems of law and administration that do not fit into a court-based model of administrative law. It is therefore necessary to examine what tribunals do, how they do it, their impacts and effects, their interrelationship with government and how people access justice and whether they receive it.

[1] E Palmer, T Cornford, Y Marique and A Guinchard (eds), *Access to Justice: Beyond the Policies and Politics of Austerity* (Hart, 2016); R Thomas and J Tomlinson, 'Mapping Current Issues in Administrative Justice: Austerity and the "More Bureaucratic Rationality" Approach' (2017) 39 *Journal of Social Welfare and Family Law* 380.

[2] WA Robson, *Justice and Administrative Law* (Macmillan, 1928); FJ Port, *Administrative Law* (Longmans, 1929) Chapter V; JAG Griffith and H Street, *Principles of Administrative Law* (Pitman, 1951) Chapters IV and V; CK Allen, *Administrative Jurisdiction* (Stevens, 1956). The *British Journal of Administrative Law* (1954–1957), later incorporated into *Public Law* (1958–) covered tribunals and approached administrative law as including, in part, judicial decisions not made by courts.

[3] S de Smith, *Judicial Review of Administrative Action* (London, 1959); HWR Wade, *Administrative Law* (OUP, 1961).

[4] C McCrudden, 'Legal Research and the Social Sciences' (2006) 122 *Law Quarterly Review* 632.

UK Tribunals

UK tribunals are adjudicatory bodies, *de facto* administrative courts.[5] Government takes individualised decisions on people's rights and entitlements, matters of acute and direct importance to the people involved.[6] There is an obvious inequality between the state and the individual. Many of the people concerned – benefit and asylum claimants, children with special educational needs – are often in a relationship of dependency on the state.[7] Decisions by front-line caseworkers within government are part of a huge caseload – often backlogs – of millions of decisions. Caseworkers work under enormous pressure to make decisions quickly and often in conditions that are far from ideal. They want to make good-quality decisions, but their endeavours are heavily constrained by the wider systems, processes, environments and cultures in which they work. Sometimes caseworkers will meet applicants face to face but, increasingly, they do not. In the benefits context, the first occasion on which claimants meet face-to-face with those deciding on their benefit entitlements will be at a social security tribunal hearing – the third stage of the decision process following an initial decision and administrative review. More generally, the demands placed upon government often exceed its institutional competence.

Government knows it will get decisions wrong. A safety-net is required. Government does not care much about individual decisions; they raise no wider policy implications. What remedy is appropriate? People do not want to go to court to resolve their problem. In any event, the inadequacies of judicial review are all too obvious. It is legalistic, costly, full of delay and largely inaccessible.[8] It excludes fact-finding and does not enable people to participate in the decision-making process. At best, a successful judicial review would only secure an administrative reconsideration of the challenged decision, thereby adding further delay. The courts also lack capacity.[9] What is required is an institutionalised process through which an independent person reconsiders the decision afresh on issues of both fact and law and then makes a reasoned decision from which there is an onward

[5] For a survey, see M Elliott and R Thomas, *Public Law* 5th edn (OUP, 2024) Ch 16. There is an important distinction between adjudicative and policy-oriented tribunals. All UK tribunals fall into the first category. Some take initial decisions, eg Mental Health Tribunals.

[6] G Richardson and H Genn, 'Tribunals in Transition: Resolution or Adjudication?' [2007] *Public Law* 116 advance a three-fold typology of tribunal cases: (i) human rights cases (eg mental health, asylum); (ii) rule-based entitlements to material benefits (eg social security, criminal injuries compensation); and (iii) resource-constrained entitlements to an assessment or to a consideration (eg school admissions and special educational needs).

[7] The paradigmatic administrative justice scenario concerns a person whose benefit claim is refused.

[8] T Hickman, 'Public Law's Disgrace' *UK Constitutional Law Blog* (9 February 2017).

[9] Whenever the High Court has received a high volume of judicial reviews against individualised decisions, caseload pressures have prompted the court to limit access either by tightening up on the permission threshold, as happened with homelessness cases in 1980s, or by shifting the caseload elsewhere, as happened with immigration judicial reviews during 2008–2013 or by requesting government to oust judicial review as per *Cart* [2011] UKSC 28; Judicial Review and Courts Act 2022, s 2.

challenge in case of error. Tribunals are almost always the preferred remedy against individualised decisions. Their effectiveness depends on whether they provide an adequate and proper safeguard by providing an accessible, fair and efficient process that results in good-quality decisions. Without tribunals, there would be no legal redress regarding the vast majority of individual decision-making. Since they were introduced in the early twentieth century, tribunals have always been used in social security schemes precisely because of the procedural inadequacies and legal–cultural attitudes of the courts.[10]

Most tribunals are now part of the First-tier Tribunal (Ft-T) and Upper Tribunal (UT) structure established in 2008.[11] These 'capital T' tribunals are part of the formal judicial system. The Tribunals, Courts and Enforcement Act 2007 placed tribunals on a new statutory basis and embedded them fully within the formal judiciary in terms of appointments, protections concerning judicial independence and structure.[12] They are always chaired by a legally qualified judge. Tribunal judges are appointed in the same way as a court judge. Some tribunal judges are salaried, but most are fee-paid.[13] Sometimes tribunal judges sit alongside non-legal members. Social security appeals tribunals have medical and disability members depending on the type of case being heard. Both the Ft-T and the UT have various chambers; the chamber structure largely mapped onto pre-existing tribunals.[14] The same body – HM Courts and Tribunals Service – provides administrative support to both courts and tribunals. Outside this structure, there are a range of other tribunals and local government appeal panels, some of which are comprised of non-legal members.[15]

First instance tribunals – principally fact-finding and rule-application bodies – are amongst the 'decision factories' of the legal system.[16] The UT decides onward challenges against Ft-T Tribunal decisions on error of law grounds. It also clarifies legal and other issues of wider application and undertakes some judicial review work. While the 2007 Act established the broad statutory framework for the Ft-T

[10] B Abel-Smith and R Stevens, *Lawyers and the Courts* (Heinemann, 1967) 111–21.

[11] Tribunals, Courts and Enforcement Act 2007; R Carnwath, 'Tribunal Justice – a New Start' [2009] *Public Law* 48 (Carnwath was the first Senior President of Tribunals).

[12] Constitutional Reform Act 2005, s 3; Tribunals, Courts and Enforcement Act 2007, s 1. Similar structures have been adopted for devolved tribunals in Scotland and Wales, though not Northern Ireland.

[13] Salaried judges have their home jurisdiction, but some sit in others, often as a break from a relentless diet of the same type of cases. Fee-paid judicial appointments enable flexible deployment in light of variable caseloads. There is more similarity between lower-level tribunal and court judges than between the latter and the higher judiciary.

[14] Courts and Tribunals Judiciary, *Tribunals Organisation Chart*. Available at: www.judiciary.uk/wp-content/uploads/2022/04/tribunals-chart-updated-January-2023.pdf. Anomalies remain: N Wikeley, 'Justice in the Welfare State – Tribunals in the Modern Era' (2022) 29 *Journal of Social Security Law* 74, 79–83.

[15] For instance, school admission and exclusion panels are non-legal, even though exclusion panels (in England) are limited to a judicial review function not an appellate one: Education Act 2011, s 4.

[16] Tribunal caseloads are large compared with the higher courts, but small compared with the enormous caseloads of major casework departments (eg tax, social security and immigration).

and UT, the jurisdiction of specific tribunals is determined by the relevant statute. In a sense, the differentiated nature of the tribunal 'system' reflects the departmental structure of UK central government. There is no specific department within government with overall responsibility for tribunals policy. Similarly, there is no generalist tribunal with a broad-ranging jurisdiction across the entirety of public administration, nor is there a general right of appeal against administrative decisions. Despite the apparent jurisdictional breadth implied by its name, the Upper Tribunal (Administrative Appeals Chamber) (UTAAC) is a de facto specialist public law court that has one very large jurisdiction (social security) and a miscellany of smaller jurisdictions (special educational needs; information rights; transport; mental health; and criminal injuries compensation). Tribunals have always specialised in particular contexts. This enables them to build up their knowledge and expertise. It also promotes efficiency.

The UK has no concept of merits review as exists in Australia.[17] Instead, statute creates rights of appeal against specified administrative decisions or on specified grounds.[18] The decision whether to have appeal rights is a policy matter for the relevant government department. 'Appeal' is understood in contradistinction to judicial review. Tribunals decide appeals *de novo* on issues of fact and law. Their decisions are legally binding, unless successfully challenged. Familiar concepts – legality and merits; the grounds and intensity of review – are irrelevant.[19] Much more important is knowledge and understanding of substantive decision-making. Social security tribunals must understand the effects of different types of health conditions upon a person's functional capacity. Asylum tribunals make judgements concerning, for instance, social attitudes toward gay men in Iran and the effectiveness of laws in Sierra Leone prohibiting female genital mutilation and how they are enforced in practice.[20] They must decide whether an asylum claimant is telling the truth. Appellants typically come from an entirely different culture, will give oral evidence through a translator, will possibly be a victim of torture and there will be no corroborative evidence. School admission panels must weigh up a child's case to be admitted to a school with the needs of those already there. This requires local knowledge about routes to schools, travel distances, social and family contexts and school capacity. Appeals concern complex human situations and personal circumstances upon which have been superimposed detailed and intricate rules and associated caselaw. Tribunals must exercise judgement to arrive at the 'right' decision – whatever that might be.[21]

[17] See Groves and Weeks, Chapter 7 in this volume.

[18] See, eg, Social Security Act 1998, s 12; School Standards and Framework Act 1998, s 94; Nationality, Immigration and Asylum Act 2002, s 82; and Children and Families Act 2014, s 51.

[19] Another important procedural difference between judicial review and tribunals is that the former has a permission requirement; only claims deemed arguable can proceed to a substantive judicial review hearing. Tribunals do not have a formal permission filter, although there are informal filters, such as whether people decide to appeal.

[20] R Thomas, *Administrative Justice and Asylum Appeals* (Hart, 2011).

[21] Given that decision-making is judgemental, this raises questions as to what the notion of the 'right' decision actually means. See ibid.

When viewed collectively from a horizontal perspective, tribunals comprise a distinct system. At the same time, the tribunal structure is more a federation of different tribunals than a truly unified system. While tribunals are now separate from their parent government departments, there is an inherent relationship between the two. Tribunals are built into the vertical administrative schemes (eg social security, immigration, etc) and only operate within them. This context conditions tribunals in myriad ways. Consider procedures. Procedural fairness is a central value of tribunal justice, although it manifests in different ways. Social security appellants are typically unrepresented. The Department for Work and Pensions (DWP) hardly ever sends presenting officers to hearings. Its approach is to hand over decision-making entirely to tribunals. By default, tribunals are inquisitorial. By contrast, immigration and asylum operates in a more contentious context. When the Home Office refuses an application, it will usually maintain that refusal regardless of any representations. Home Office presenting officers regularly attend hearings to defend initial 'reasons for refusal' letters, even when appeals could be conceded. Appellants are usually legally represented. Tribunal procedures are then adversarial, almost verging into more of a criminal trial.[22] By contrast, to decide low-value appeals against parking tickets, the Traffic Penalty Tribunal has for many years operated an online interactive portal to which people can upload evidence from their smartphone to have their appeals decided quickly. These procedural differences arise under the overriding objective that tribunals must deal with cases fairly and justly.[23]

Another wider consideration is that the vertical systems within which tribunals operate are subject to wider pressures. For instance, in the 2010s, social security appeal receipts increased dramatically. The Department for Work and Pensions had contracted out the medical assessments for disability benefits (which then informed its initial decisions) to a private provider, but the quality of such assessments was poor. The contractor then exited its contract at short notice for reputational reasons. In turn, HM Courts and Tribunals Service (HMCTS) and the tribunal had significantly underestimated the volume of appeals and lacked capacity to hear and decide them. Overall, the system descended into chaos.[24] There were huge delays and backlogs for appellants, many of whom eventually had their appeals allowed. Similar problems have arisen with immigration appeals when, for instance, the Upper Tribunal (Immigration and Asylum Chamber) (UTIAC) decided that a certain type of immigration decision did not attract a right of appeal,

[22] R Thomas, 'From "Adversarial v Inquisitorial" to "Active, Enabling, and Investigative": Developments in UK Tribunals' in L Jacobs and S Baglay, (eds) *The Nature of Inquisitorial Processes in Administrative Regimes:* (Farnham, Ashgate, 2013).

[23] The overriding objective is contained within tribunal procedure rules. Procedural fairness is particularly important in terms of ensuring people can effectively participate in their tribunal appeals and whether procedures need to be adjusted appropriately given a person's individual needs and characteristics. See *AM (Afghanistan) v Secretary of State for the Home Department* [2017] EWCA Civ 1123.

[24] House of Commons Work and Pensions Committee, *Employment and Support Allowance and Work Capability Assessments* (HC 302 2014-15).

which was later overturned by the Court of Appeal.[25] In the meantime, many appeals had built up, in addition to the ordinary run of other appeals resulting in backlogs. Matters such as caseloads, appeal forecasts and judicial deployment dominate the in-trays of senior judge-managers.

An important feature of the tribunal structure is the UT, the second-tier appellate body. It was established to rationalise the previously incoherent and confused system of onward rights of challenge.[26] The UT has also served as something of a convenient dumping ground for the low-level, routine and fact-specific judicial review caseload work which the overloaded Administrative Court lacks the appetite and resources to undertake.[27] There were some initial suggestions that the UT would perform a wider and distinctive role in the overall tribunal system. Procedural coherence would be complemented by 'jurisprudential coherence'.[28] As a strong and dedicated appellate body, the UT would take the 'lead on developing the law underlying administrative justice'.[29] In addition to rule-interpretation, the UT would develop norms and standards of general application to all tribunals thereby yielding long-term and sustained benefits for administrative justice more broadly.[30] The new structure would be more than just a federation of existing tribunals. Regular interchange amongst judges would ensure consistency of approach to administrative justice. The UT would not merely replicate the Administrative Court but would bring additional benefits.

Anyone might then expect that the UT would take the lead by issuing landmark rulings to develop tribunals law and standards and to improve initial decision-making, but this has not happened. Instead, the UT works entirely through its respective specialist chambers. It has never, as a corporate entity, issued rulings on wider principles of administrative justice to guide tribunals let alone government decision-making departments. Most of the UT's work is rule application and interpretation. It does not perform a wider role in improving administrative justice. In legal-formal terms, the Upper Tribunal is a superior court of record and thereby has an equivalent standing to the Administrative Court, although few people really think this as a matter of substantive legal-cultural reality.[31]

[25] *Sala v Secretary of State for the Home Department* (EFMs: Right of Appeal: Albania) [2016] UKUT 411 (IAC); *Khan v Secretary of State for the Home Department* [2017] EWCA Civ 1755, [2018] 1 WLR 1256. The UTIAC's *Sala* decision was widely seen as flawed.

[26] H Woolf, 'A Hotchpotch of Appeals – the Need for a Blender' (1988) 7 *Civil Justice Quarterly* 44.

[27] Tribunals, Courts and Enforcement Act 2007, ss 15–21. The Administrative Court is part of the High Court and hears judicial review claims from England and Wales. Most of the judicial review caseload transferred to the UTIAC was the routine and repetitive immigration judicial reviews against non-appealable initial decisions. See R Thomas and J Tomlinson, *Immigration Judicial Reviews* (Palgrave Macmillan, 2021). UT Chamber Presidents are High Court judges.

[28] G Hickinbottom, 'Tribunal Reform: A New Coherent System' [2010] *Judicial Review* 103, 107–09 (Hickinbottom was then the UTAAC chamber president and is now a Court of Appeal judge).

[29] Tribunals Service, *Transforming Tribunals: Implementing Part 1 of the Tribunals, Courts and Enforcement Act 2007* (CP 30/07, 2007) [131]. This document was published by the Labour Government (1997–2010).

[30] Hickinbottom (n 28) at 108; Carnwath (n 11).

[31] Tribunals, Courts and Enforcement Act 2007, s 3(5).

There are various explanations for this state of affairs: the dominance of a conservative legal culture amongst senior judicial leaders; the perceived dangers of taking an innovative approach; a less conducive governmental context since 2010; and a new politics of judicial review prompting the judiciary to take a formal approach to insulate itself from criticism.

The UT remains important, however. Its core appellate function is deciding onward challenges on error-of-law grounds. There is an inherent elasticity as to what is an error of law and when an appellate tribunal ought to intervene. The UT also exerts significant influence through its interpretation of the specialist rules and has produced an extensive body of decisions. Much of this is highly formalistic, although it can have significant impact. For instance, the UTAAC ruled that social security appellants do not lose their right of appeal to a tribunal when they have applied out of time for an internal administrative review, which is compulsory before an appeal. The UT (Immigration and Asylum Chamber) decides points of immigration law and issues country guidance decisions.

As regards the relationship between the UT and the higher courts, the Supreme Court has articulated an attitude of respecting the UT's decisions unless it has clearly decided incorrectly. The higher courts should adopt a pragmatic approach to the dividing line between law and fact and allow tribunals to exercise their expertise to best effect; appeal courts should not venture too readily into matters best left for specialist tribunals.[32] However, the tests here are inherently malleable and the higher courts can and have intervened when they have chosen to do so. It might be thought that this relationship raises questions about higher courts deferring to tribunals on questions of law and the degree to which tribunals can develop their own legal interpretations of legislation, but this has not happened. This is because the First-tier and Upper Tribunals are themselves courts and operate as such when it comes to statutory interpretation. The UK has (thankfully) avoided the types of debates that have dominated the US and Canada.[33]

Overall, tribunals operate overwhelmingly within a court-focused model of autonomous law based upon the separation of law and politics, legal formalism and procedural fairness.[34] Tribunals are focused on getting through their caseloads. They are not concerned with undertaking a responsive law approach of diagnosing institutional problems or improving government or forging ahead by developing new standards of administrative justice. Consider this. During the 1990s and 2000s, tribunals increasingly developed something of an inferiority complex compared with the 'proper courts'. Immigration Adjudicators repeatedly argued that they should be 'Immigration *Judges*'.[35] From this perspective, the 2007

[32] *AH (Sudan) v Secretary of State for the Home Department* [2008] 1 AC 678 [30] (Baroness Hale); *Jones v First-tier Tribunal and Criminal Injuries Compensation Authority* [2013] UKSC 19 [16] (Lord Hope).

[33] See Daly, Chapter 11 in this volume.

[34] P Nonet and P Selznick, *Law & Society in Transition* (Transaction, 1978) Chapter 3.

[35] An emotional need eventually satiated by the Asylum and Immigration Tribunal (Judicial Titles) Order 2005 (SI 227/2005).

Act was a great success for tribunals as it brought them fully within the established model of the courts.

The Growth and Development of Tribunals

We now consider how tribunals have developed and why. This topic is inextricable from wider changes in the British state and society, in particular the shift from a limited to a positive state and successive changes in the state's functions and its administrative structures.

Regulatory bodies called tribunals existed in the nineteenth century, but the foundations of modern tribunals were laid in the early twentieth century.[36] During the mid-nineteenth century, the notion of a limited state was in the ascendant. Dicey's constitutional theory and his rejection of administrative law were based upon this assumption. However, it was precisely during this period that the role of government and administration was changing. The state was increasingly intervening to address urgent social problems.[37] Under the 'new liberalism', the state came to be seen as an instrument to promote the people's welfare.[38] In 1906, the Liberal Government won a landslide parliamentary majority to improve conditions for working-class and under-privileged people.[39] Its programme of social reform covered areas including: old-age pensions; National Insurance; public health; tax; education; local government; and housing and town planning. All the associated administrative schemes involved individualised decision-making and factual evaluation. There was a need to combine the quick and effective adjudication of disputes with the implementation of the new social policies. Various 'tribunals' were established as part of the administrative machinery.[40] They had a mixed legal and lay membership, were separate from the common law courts and were created to combine justice with efficiency.[41] An embryonic administrative law was emerging based, not on the common law, but on the new social legislation. This was creating, piecemeal, a new legal framework within which government could implement its policy goals of which tribunals were a key part.

[36] C Stebbings, *Legal Foundations of Tribunals in Nineteenth Century England* (CUP, 2006).

[37] AJ Taylor, *Laissez-faire and State Intervention in Nineteenth Century Britain* (Palgrave, 1972).

[38] M Freeden, *The New Liberalism* (OUP, 1978).

[39] I Packer, *Liberal Government and Politics, 1905–15* (Palgrave, 2006) Chapter 7.

[40] The label 'tribunals' risks implying a much more consciously designed system than actually existed. 'Tribunals' were known by various titles – commissioners, boards, courts of referees, umpires, appellate body etc. As RE Wraith and PG Hutchesson noted, 'the nomenclature of the subject is chaotic' *Administrative Tribunals* (Allen and Unwin, 1974) 43.

[41] E Barker, 'The "Rule of Law" in *Church, State and Society* (Methuen, 1930) 178–90; R Thomas, 'The Development of Administrative Law in the United Kingdom (1890–1910)' in G della Cananea and S Mannoni (eds), *Administrative Justice fin de siècle: Early Judicial Standards of Administrative Conduct in Europe (1890–1910)* (OUP, 2021) 275–80.

The legal establishment was highly sceptical of tribunals. For Dicey, the conferral of judicial powers upon officials who sat on tribunals diminished the role of the common law courts and marked a decline in reverence for the rule of law.[42] There were concerns that tribunals could be subject to ministerial interference, although there was no evidence of this and efforts were made within government to separate adjudication from administration and politics.[43] Criticism also came from those who opposed the policies that the tribunals were adjudicating upon.[44] The *administrative* tribunals were seen as creatures of the executive and therefore inherently inferior to the courts; in practice they mostly did a reasonably good job.

Tribunals were used for pragmatic reasons.[45] Judicial review, as we now know it, did not exist. The common law provided few useful remedies for people against administration and often shielded it from scrutiny.[46] Moreover, given their narrow social background, judges were often antagonistic to the new social policies. By contrast, tribunals were considerably more familiar than the courts with the technical aspects of administration and ground-level social facts. By the late 1920s, a conservative-legal reaction asserted itself. Hewart saw the growth of delegated legislation and tribunals as a trend toward administrative despotism.[47] The civil service response was that tribunals were anomalous and unsystematic, but also necessary; 'work must get done'.[48] As a pragmatic matter, administrative adjudication through tribunals was essential and vastly preferable to the delays and costs of the higher courts. Moreover, tribunals were applying a new type of law quite unknown to the courts: neither common law precedents nor rules of private law, but evolving regulatory standards concerning medical treatment, sanitation, housing and education, which took their substance from changing social environments and needs. These issues were not amenable to formal judicial procedures, rigid rules and fossilised precedent. It was administrative law in the making with its 'fluid tendencies and tentative traditions'.[49] After World War II, tribunals proliferated.

[42] AV Dicey, 'Introduction to the Eighth Edition' in *Introduction to the Study of the Law of the Constitution* 8th edn (Macmillan, 1915) xxxviii.

[43] 'Encroachments of the Executive' *The Times* (4 May 1911); WA Robson, *Justice and Administrative Law* (Stevens, 3rd edn, 1951) 581–87.

[44] 'Appeals under the Finance Bill' *The Times* (8 July 1909); 'The Exaltation of the Executive' *The Times* (2 September 1909). Criticism of tax tribunals came from wealthy landowners who opposed land taxes whereas early benefits adjudication – the courts of referees – aroused little controversy; they were local bodies and some members were drawn from the same social class as those who appeared before them: Wraith and Hutchesson (n 40) 33–35.

[45] Following the discouraging the experience of workmen's compensation and the courts, government deliberately bypassed the courts in favour of tribunals.

[46] JH Morgan, 'Remedies Against the Crown' in GE Robinson, *Public Authorities and Legal Liability* (University of London Press, 1925).

[47] G Hewart, *The New Despotism* (Benn, 1929); M Taggart, 'From 'Parliamentary Powers' to Privatization: The Chequered History of Delegated Legislation in the Twentieth Century' (2005) 55 *University of Toronto Law Journal* 575, 576–80.

[48] S Leathes, 'The Alleged "New Despotism"' *The Daily Telegraph* (10 October 1929).

[49] F Frankfurter, 'The Task of Administrative Law' (1928) 75 *University of Pennslyvania Law Review* 614, 619.

The Labour Government set about creating the welfare state.[50] Government now assumed responsibility for people's well-being in ways that would have been unimaginable only a decade earlier. Many major social services were created. The government was concerned that a conservative judiciary might sabotage its programme. It was therefore natural to continue to have tribunals decide disputes in areas including social security, industrial injuries and health amongst others.[51]

Nonetheless, tribunals certainly had their weaknesses. Their ad hoc growth had resulted in an unsystematic structure. There were no procedural rules, merely departmental practice and custom. The policies which tribunals applied were created within broad skeletal statutory frameworks and entirely controlled by departments. They remained publicly unknown and undiscoverable. Tribunals sat in private. Decisions were not published.[52] Until *Shaw*, tribunals were only reviewable for jurisdictional error.[53] Having extended the scope of judicial review to errors of law on the face of the record, Denning highlighted another anomaly: tribunals did not give reasons for their decisions. If they gave no reasons, then there was no record for a court to review. Accordingly, tribunals needed to give reasoned decisions.[54] While tribunals were administrative, they were the means through which judicial procedures were used and integrated within administration. The 'administrative judges' in the tribunals were a mix of officials and lay people appointed by the relevant department and practising lawyers appointed by the Lord Chancellor. They were de facto independent and had security of tenure. Traditions of legal procedure were pervasive. The degree of judicialisation varied depending upon the service involved and the balance of contextual forces in play.[55]

Overall, tribunals attracted little attention, although social concerns about bureaucracy had been accumulating. The Crichel Down affair (1954) led to an outpouring of these anxieties.[56] Jolted into action, the two main political parties both wanted to enhance people's remedies, to protect 'the little man' against the new administrative state.[57] The government established the Franks committee to consider tribunals. The report viewed tribunals as part of the wider tension between authority and the individual, state and society. Efficient and fair administration had to be balanced. People needed confidence in tribunals. Franks therefore

[50] P Hennessy, *Never Again: Britain 1945–51* (Penguin, 2006).

[51] RSW Pollard (ed), *Administrative Tribunals at Work* (Stevens, 1950); R Micklethwait, *The National Insurance Commissioners* (Stevens, 1976).

[52] KB Smellie, 'Some Aspects of English Administrative Law' (1927) 5 *Public Administration* 276, 286–89.

[53] *R v Northumberland Compensation Appeal Tribunal, ex parte Shaw* [1952] 1 KB 338.

[54] A Denning, 'Law in a Developing Community' (1955) 33 *Public Administration* 1, 7–8 and his contributions to House of Lords debates on the Tribunals and Inquiries Act 1958, which required tribunals to give reasons for their decisions: *Hansard* HL Debs vol 208, cols 601–06 1 April 1958.

[55] WJM Mackenzie and JW Grove, *Central Administration in Britain* (Longmans, 1957) 393–98.

[56] WA Robson, 'Administrative Justice and Injustice: A Commentary on the Franks Report' [1958] *Public Law* 12.

[57] R Thomas, '*Ridge v Baldwin*: Executive and Judicial Approaches to Administrative Law before and during the Quartet Years' in TT Arvind et al (eds) *Executive Decision-Making and the Courts: Revisiting the Origins of Modern Judicial Review* (Hart, 2021).

recommended principles – fairness, openness and independence – that tribunals give reasons for their decisions and onward appeals to the higher courts.[58] The new Councils for Tribunals provided wider oversight. Robson's proposed general administrative tribunal to decide onward appeals perturbed senior officials who vehemently disliked the notion that all government decisions could potentially be appealed.[59] It was also rejected by Franks. At the same time, Franks reflected and reinforced a new spirit that government needed to provide people with open, fair and impartial remedies against administration. Tribunals were no longer aberrations, but a useful set of institutions that needed to be brought into some sort of order.

Following Franks, two new tribunals were created: mental health (1959) and immigration (1971). Tribunals were now 'one of the most important institutions of government'.[60] However, in the 1970s, a new and critical attitude emerged. Given pressing social issues of poverty and inequality, social security tribunals were heavily criticised. Their weaknesses included: ad hoc procedures; the subjective discretion of panels; tribunals' unclear structural position; and the chaotic nature of the whole 'system'. Part of the new welfare rights movement, the literature was empirical, realist, critical and reformist.[61] For '90 per cent of people 90 per cent of the time, tribunals are *the* courts and social security tribunals are the most important courts'.[62] However, these 'slums' of the tribunal system – 'the lowest form of tribunal life' – were incapable of performing their minimal role satisfactorily. Their real purpose was to shield government from criticism and to provide a symbolic figleaf of legality.[63] What was needed were better personnel, procedures and the separation of tribunals from government. Judicial procedures prevented unrepresented people from understanding let alone participating effectively in their appeals. This created a need for reform. Social security appeals were amalgamated and improved in the 1980s and again in the late 1990s.[64] Immigration tribunals were similarly later criticised for lacking cultural awareness.[65] In the 1980s, the

[58] Franks Committee, *Report of the Committee on Administrative Tribunals and Enquiries* (Cmnd 218, 1957); Tribunals and Inquiries Act 1958.

[59] TT Arvind and L Stirton, 'The Curious Origins of Judicial Review' (2017) 133 *Law Quarterly Review* 91, 104.

[60] JA Farmer, *Tribunals and Government* (Weidenfeld and Nicolson, 1974) ix.

[61] N Lewis, 'Supplementary Benefits Appeal Tribunals' [1973] *Public Law* 257; M Adler and AW Bradley (eds), *Justice, Discretion and Poverty: Supplementary Benefit Appeal Tribunals in Britain* (Professional Books, 1975).

[62] H Calvert, 'Appeal Structures of the Future' in Adler and Bradley ibid at 201.

[63] H Rose, 'Who Can De-label the Claimant?' in Adler and Bradley (eds) ibid 150; *Hansard* HL Debs vol 353, col 511 (Lord Gardiner) (9 July 1974); T Prosser, 'Poverty, Ideology, and Legality: Supplementary Benefit Appeal Tribunals and their Predecessors' (1977) 4 *British Journal of Law and Society* 39.

[64] AW Bradley, 'Recent Reform of Social Security Adjudication in Great Britain' (1985) 26 *Les Cahiers de droit* 403; N Wikeley 'Burying Bell: Managing the Judicialisation of Social Security Tribunals' (2000) 63 *Modern Law Review* 475.

[65] S Juss, *Discretion and Deviation in the Administration of Immigration Control* (Sweet & Maxwell, 1997).

introduction of consumerism into public services was reflected in school choice and school admission appeal panels.[66] Concerns were raised about the appointment of tribunal adjudicators by the same government departments that took the initial decisions being appealed against. Given the increased number of asylum judicial reviews (tiny in comparison with later volumes), a right of appeal was conceded.[67] The overall system remained ad hoc and unstructured.

By the end of the 1990s, various factors coalesced in favour of structural reform of tribunals. The Human Rights Act 1998, in particular the right to a fair trial under Article 6 of the European Convention of Human Rights (ECHR), required access to an independent and impartial decision-maker to determine a person's civil rights. A legal-cultural shift occurred. The appointment of tribunal members by parent government departments was no longer acceptable. The then Labour Government framed tribunal reform as part of its constitutional modernisation and public services reform agendas. Tribunals had come of age. The notion of a 'Tribunal Judge' was no longer an oxymoron. The Leggatt Report (2001) recommended a new tribunal system that would meet the needs of users, not the other way round.[68] This was accompanied by governmental and policy changes. The old Lord Chancellor's Department had long focused upon the senior judiciary, but the new Ministry of Justice would prioritise people's real-world problems.[69] Responsibility for managing tribunals was transferred from policy departments to the Ministry of Justice. In addition to the Ft and UT structure, the Council on Tribunals became an enhanced Administrative Justice and Tribunals Council (AJTC). On the ground level, tribunals became more managerial and focused upon their performance and efficiency.

This, then, was the major reform of tribunals. Everything seemed encouraging. For the first time, a government was giving administrative justice equal prominence alongside criminal and civil justice. Administrative justice was broadly defined. It was not confined to tribunals, but encompassed the entire system including initial decision-makers, those reconsidering decisions, ombuds, other complaints handlers, the tribunals and the courts, and how the system which they produce as a result of their individual roles functions as a whole.[70] The AJTC focused upon promoting proportionate justice and improving initial decisions.[71] The tribunals judiciary became more diverse and representative of contemporary society than the court judiciary. There was a developing community of academics,

[66] Education Act 1980, s 7.

[67] Asylum and Immigration Appeals Act 1993, ss 8–9.

[68] A Leggatt, *Tribunals for Users, One System, One Service* (London, 2001); Department for Constitutional Affairs, *Transforming Public Services: Complaints, Redress and Tribunals* (Cm 6243, 2004); M Adler, 'Tribunal Reform: Proportionate Dispute Resolution and the Pursuit of Administrative Justice' (2006) 69 *Modern Law Review* 958.

[69] R Percival, 'The Challenge of Public Law Law Reform: Reflections on a Failed Law Commission Project' (2019) 41 *Journal of Social Welfare and Family Law* 372.

[70] Tribunals, Courts and Enforcement Act 2007, Sch 7, para 13(4).

[71] AJTC, *Right First Time* (2011) and *Putting it Right* (2012).

policymakers and those working in tribunals and the broader administrative justice landscape.[72] The mood music toward tribunals and administrative justice was positive.

But then the global financial crisis (2007–2009) was followed by austerity (2010–).[73] The political and economic context changed entirely and decisively. Publicly funded legal aid was significantly cut. The short-lived AJTC was abolished.[74] Government policy in the two principal tribunal contexts – social security and immigration – became distinctly hard-line and hostile. Some appeal rights were abolished altogether. Departmental budgets were cut. The quality of primary decisions deteriorated.

The development of tribunals is far more intricate than this overview suggests. One feature that stands out is that the major expansion of procedural fairness that followed the expansion of administrative power had been driven principally by government, not the courts. Tribunals were used to judicialise the administrative process. This reality has often been eclipsed by the myths of administrative law, one being the symbolic value attributed to a handful of big cases far beyond their limited substantive impact on administration. While *Ridge v Baldwin* is frequently cited for reinvigorating procedural fairness, its impact upon government was limited.[75] Instead, it was principally through tribunals that an institutionalised form of procedural fairness was integrated within and across large swaths of governmental administration. More recently, the courts have played an important role in reviewing the systemic unfairness of tribunal procedures and emphasising the importance of oral hearings and of access to justice.[76] Nonetheless, the expansion of procedural fairness within administration has more often been driven by government itself through the mechanism of tribunals than imposed externally by the courts.

Tribunals and the Separation of Powers

Tribunals are often viewed as occupying an awkward constitutional position situated somewhere between government and the judiciary. They do not easily fit into conventional constitutional thought. What, then, is the constitutional status of UK tribunals?

[72] M Adler (ed), *Administrative Justice in Context* (Hart 2011).

[73] M Adler, 'The Rise and Fall of Administrative Justice – a Cautionary Tale' (2012) 8 *Socio-Legal Review* 28.

[74] C Skelcher, 'Reforming the Oversight of Administrative Justice 2010–2014: Does the UK Need a New Leggatt Report?' [2015] *Public Law* 215. A non-statutory body, the Administrative Justice Council, was established in 2018 and is chaired by the Senior President of Tribunals.

[75] Thomas (n 57).

[76] *Detention Action v Secretary of State for the Home Department* [2015] EWCA Civ 840; *Osborn v Parole Board* [2013] UKSC 61; *R (Unison) v Lord Chancellor* [2017] UKSC 51.

Tribunals may seem a little obscure from a separation of powers perspective, but that concept is itself more than a little ambiguous and contested.[77] The separation of powers is a principle of classic liberal constitutionalism to prevent the over-concentration of power and thereby protect liberty. Accordingly, the legislature makes the law (legislation), the executive administers it while the judiciary adjudicates disputes by applying the law. The separation of powers is, though, a conceptual construct. It is only one way of thinking about administrative law – and an amorphous and old one. It dates from the eighteenth century need to control the monarch and the emergent executive by having judicial and legislative bodies. Since then, there have been fundamental and irrevocable social and political changes which have entirely changed the structure and nature of administrative governance and increased its responsibilities far beyond what was previously imaginable. Tribunals developed as a consequence of this. From one perspective, tribunals are viewed as separation of powers 'misfits'.[78] However, the problem is not tribunals; they are real working institutions that people depend upon. The problem is the anachronistic principle of the separation of powers, which no longer provides an adequate conceptual framework from which to understand and analyse administrative law.

Like 'tribunals', the 'separation of powers' is polysemic; its meaning varies not only between different jurisdictions, but also within them and over time.[79] The UK has no formal separation of powers whereas Australian public law draws a rigid distinction between courts (which are judicial) and tribunals (which are administrative); courts and tribunals are seen as fundamentally different institutions.[80] From an Australian perspective, the Upper Tribunal seems like a heretical mix of court/tribunal that is both judicial and administrative. However, in the UK, it was natural to have the UT as the successor body of previous second-tier appellate tribunals. Further, transferring some judicial review work from the courts to the UT was simply a practical way of reducing caseload pressures. It raised no issue of constitutional principle.

The notion that tribunals were problematic in separation of powers terms held some sway in the UK until around the 1950s. The debate about the propriety of tribunals reflected different schools of public law thought.[81] From the common law perspective of the Diceyan legacy, tribunals were inherently suspect because they were not ordinary courts, but formally part of government, and therefore not

[77] C Möllers, 'Separation of Powers' in R Masterman and R Schütze (eds), *The Cambridge Companion to Comparative Constitutional Law* (CUP, 2019).

[78] E Fisher, 'Administrative Tribunals: An Essay about the Legal Imagination of Administrative Law Scholars' in J Goudkamp, M Lunney and L McDonald (eds) *Taking Law Seriously: Essays in Honour of Peter Cane* (Hart, 2021) 263.

[79] The language of executive and judicial 'branches' is inapposite in the UK; it implies a far firmer constitutional framework from what actually exists.

[80] M Groves and G Weeks, 'Origins and Adaptations in Australasia' in S Jhaveri and M Ramsden (eds), *Judicial Review of Administrative Action Across the Common Law World* (CUP, 2021).

[81] M Loughlin, *Public Law and Political Theory* (OUP, 1992).

independent. However, from a functionalist perspective, tribunals reflected the expanding role of government and the associated administrative law thereby being generated. From this perspective, the separation of powers no longer reflected the more fluid realities of an increasingly administrative government and the role of tribunals within it. The idealistic nature of the separation of powers was at odds with what actually happened. As Robson argued, judges often administered and administrators often judged. The separation of powers with its associated judicial-administrative dichotomy had simply outlived its usefulness.[82]

The debate played out through the Donoughmore and Franks committees.[83] Donoughmore was the principal forum for a polemical and ideological debate about administrative law. The report ended up distinguishing between administrative and judicial decisions (both with and without the prefixes 'quasi' and 'true'). However, its legalistic and hair-splitting conceptual distinctions made little sense and now seem almost incomprehensible from a contemporary standpoint.[84] The basic problem was that 'judicial' and 'administrative' are indeterminate in the abstract; they only assume meaning depending on the context. The Donoughmore report itself had no practical impact.[85]

There was a basic choice here: either the legal establishment could seek to impede the growth of administration and tribunals, or it could recognise the need to adjust itself and its mindset in light of changing social conditions. At the same time, government could recognise the need for a better integration of judicial procedures into the tribunals. While the principle of the separation of powers is often used in its tripartite sense, it is also used to refer to the need for checks and balances over the exercise of power. The need for such control is important. As government was exercising more power, there was a need for tribunals; there was also a need for tribunals to be better organised, consistent and for them to be kept in check by appropriate judicial oversight.

As we have seen, by the 1950s, things had moved on. The Franks report recognised tribunals to be a 'permanent feature of our society'.[86] It also accepted that the administrative-judicial distinction did not provide a valid criterion on which to allocate decisions to government or tribunals.[87] Over time, the functionalists' arguments came to be accepted. The practical arguments for tribunals reinforced the importance of their social function. A new synthesis was achieved. When the Leggatt report (2001) considered the allocation of cases to tribunals, it advanced pragmatic criteria: the ability of unrepresented users to participate in proceedings

[82] Robson (n 43), ch 1 and at 16: 'The legendary separation of powers [is] an antique and rickety chariot … so long the favourite vehicle … for the conveyance of fallacious ideas'. See also JAG Griffith, 'Tribunals and Inquiries' (1959) 22 *Modern Law Review* 125, 129.

[83] The Donoughmore committee focused principally on delegated legislation.

[84] Franks avoided Donoughmore's exegesis, although its own conceptual explanation was somewhat tautologous: Franks (n 58) at [26]–[33].

[85] Wraith and Hutchesson (n 40) 37–38.

[86] Franks (n 58) at [44].

[87] ibid at [27]–[30].

and the need for specialist tribunals with expertise in the social context and in administrative law (meaning the relevant legislation and rules). Other factors are, of course, relevant: cost; timeliness; caseload; departmental attitudes; and social and political forces.

At the same time, Leggatt reasserted a much narrower conception of the separation of powers, meaning judicial independence. This has obviously been internalised by the judiciary itself and also tribunals. As noted above, during the 1980s and 1990s, tribunals became increasingly concerned about their 'inferior' status and relationships with their parent departments. Tribunals could not be perceived publicly as independent unless they joined the formal judiciary. As we have seen, this was achieved by the 2007 Act.

Tribunals have then experienced 'several evolutionary changes'.[88] The meaning of 'tribunal' has also changed over time.[89] No-one today seriously argues that tribunals – or delegated legislation for that matter – are separation of powers misfits. That would elevate constitutional dogma above the realities of modern government and social needs. A perennial theme in the development of administrative law is that thinking about the subject needs to take account of and be nourished by the realities of administrative-legal practice and the wider social and economic forces in play. The type of sterile 'conceptualist wrangling' about functions and institutions that animated the 1930s has long since been jettisoned.[90] It distracts from understanding how social and political forces drive the development of administrative law and what tribunals actually do. The principal focus is no longer the place of tribunals within any wider constitutional 'order', but rather their practical effectiveness.

Two general points can be distilled from this. First, tribunals have persisted and expanded because there is a real social need for them. Their increased use reflects changing social attitudes and political circumstances. This was the decisive factor behind the introduction of tribunals as regards mental health, children with special educational needs, immigrants and asylum claimants. The decision whether to tribunalise a particular area of administration has not been determined based on a priori conceptual classifications of whether a particular matter is administrative or judicial, but upon an overall assessment of what is expedient, all things considered. Constitutional concepts must be useful in serving social needs; if not, then they must be discarded or modified.

A second and related point is that the use of tribunals gives us some insight into the wider notion of legality in an administrative state. The 'Rule of Law' is often viewed as an overarching aspect of constitutional government which derives from a higher-order normative theory. But this approach does not apply to tribunals.

[88] G Drewry, 'The Judicialisation of "Administrative" Tribunals in the UK: From Hewart to Leggatt (2009) 29 *Transylvanian Review of Administrative Sciences* 45, 47.

[89] The phrase '*administrative* tribunals' is no longer used.

[90] JAG Griffith '*Justice and Administration* Revisited' in JAG Griffith (ed), *From Policy to Administration: Essays in Honour of William A Robson* (Allen & Unwin, 1976) 203.

There is no higher overarching legal requirement for government to establish appeal rights to tribunals. Tribunals are legally constituted by primary legislation, which embodies government policy and the balance struck between the range of competing arguments for and against. In short, tribunals have been created as a pragmatic remedy when social needs and political forces require people to have access to a fair process through independent and specialist tribunals. The legality provided by tribunals is best understood as a self-imposed form of legality that government applies to itself and its own decisions as a result of social and political forces. It is not the result of an overarching higher-level legal norm.

Social security tribunals could, in theory, be abolished. However, that would be virtually unthinkable – not because it would be unlawful or unconstitutional – but because of the acute personal, social and policy need for such appeals. The institutional failings of government are well-known. We know that government caseworkers take poor decisions, that the people affected are often vulnerable and powerless and that the decisions are immensely important to their lives. We also know that judicial review would be an entirely inadequate remedy. The role of tribunals in ensuring lawful administration is the result of internalised social attitudes people have about how they should be treated by the state and what the most appropriate remedy is. However, none of this implies that all is perfect with tribunals and how they work. To understand why, we need consider how they operate in practice.

Tribunals in Practice

Tribunals are very much an evolving area of legal practice. This section highlights four important issues, which could and should be examined in more detail.

The first concerns tribunal decision-making, particularly the handling of evidence. The vast majority of tribunal decision-making occurs at the first-tier level and involves fact-finding, applying the relevant legal rules and standards and the challenges of substantive decision-making highlighted above. It is therefore important to investigate how tribunals handle evidential materials and make decisions. While judges are trained in the law, their most important task is the handling and assessment of evidence. The daily problem for tribunals is: how much weight is to be given to the evidence? Both fact-finding and the application of legal rules and standards are inherently judgemental and discretionary tasks. Analysing tribunal decisions to identify wider trends could tell us much about the realities of judicial behaviour.

There is extensive scope for investigating cognitive biases in judicial decision-making, especially the handling and assessment of evidential materials, a matter some judges are very interested in.[91] This provides a twist on the conventional

[91] E Cunliffe, 'Judging, Fast and Slow: Using Decision-making Theory to Explore Judicial Fact Determination' (2014) 18 *International Journal of Evidence and Proof* 139; Lord Leggatt, 'Would you

administrative law concepts of impartiality and the rule against bias. Another evidential problem concerns medical evidence and how it can best be provided and considered. In the social security context, medical assessments are undertaken by an outsourced contractor integrated within the initial decision-making process. Tribunals include a medical member who takes the lead in questioning appellants. The core problem has been the poor quality of the medical assessments upon which primary decision-makers rely heavily, which has then led to a high rate of allowed appeals. By contrast, in the asylum context, medical evidence (eg, whether the scarring on a person is consistent with torture) is commissioned by representatives and often seen by tribunals more as party evidence than independent expert evidence. There is scope to examine whether this method of presenting medical evidence and its quality can be improved, eg through having specialist doctors for disability benefit assessments or having jointly commissioned expert reports in asylum cases.

A second issue concerns the role and impact of the UT in interpreting legal rules. The regulations governing tax, immigration and benefits are hyper-detailed, intricate and technical.[92] They also embody basic policy tensions, which pervade their interpretation and application. Tribunals do not produce common law precedents, but the common law now accounts for a very small proportion of all laws. Tribunals adjudicate upon and interpret legislation and there is now a surfeit of published tribunal decisions.[93] These decisions can have a significant impact upon government. For instance, various UTAAC decisions interpreting disability benefit regulations prompted the DWP's large-scale corrective 'LEAP' exercises to review millions of previously decided benefit claims to ensure those who qualified under the new interpretations received their full entitlements.[94] Statutory interpretation accounts for much of the work of the higher courts as well as tribunals, but receives little academic attention.[95] Similarly, statutory interpretation by tribunals deserves study. There is considerable scope to analyse this body of legal materials to determine the legal and policy influence of the Upper Tribunal and the choices it makes when interpreting legislation. Analysing how tribunals interpret legal rules would also generate insights into their relationship with government and the higher courts.

The two remaining issues will be considered at greater length. They concern improving the quality of initial governmental decisions and administrative review. Tribunals are part of a wider system of decision-making. A number of interconnected administrative-legal issues swirl around the operations of government

believe it? The relevance of demeanour in assessing the truthfulness of witness testimony' (2022). Available at: www.supremecourt.uk/docs/at-a-glance-keynote-address-lord-leggatt.pdf.

[92] N Harris, *Law in a Complex State* (Hart, 2013).

[93] T Buck, 'Precedent in Tribunals and the Development of Principles' (2006) 25 *Civil Justice Quarterly* 458. Upper Tribunal decisions are available online.

[94] R Thomas, 'Legal Entitlements and Administrative Practices: LEAP Exercises and Benefits Administration' (2022) 29 *Journal of Social Security Law* 49.

[95] J Bell and E Fisher, 'Exploring a Year of Administrative Law Adjudication in the Administrative Court' [2021] *Public Law* 505.

departments, their policies and institutional behaviours. For present purposes these comprise: the quality of primary and review decision-making; departments' relationships with tribunals; the role of tribunals in improving primary decisions; the actual practices of administration; and how they entangle people who have no choice but to interact with government.

It is generally accepted that tribunal decision-making is of a higher standard than that of primary decisions. Tribunal success rates are high. However, appeals cannot in practice take the place of better-quality primary decisions. Having a high volume of appeals allowed by tribunals seems undesirable and dysfunctional. It suggests that something is going wrong at the initial level and people are being forced into appeals to correct bad primary decisions. This unnecessarily raises costs, delays and caseloads. Moreover, the combination of this with the position of claimants and the need to lodge appeals can in practice operate as an informal gate-keeping mechanism. Government can then make poor refusal decisions and rely upon people's unwillingness to appeal who then potentially lose their entitlements.

These are all long-standing issues. The Franks Committee considered tribunals; it was decidedly not invited to inquire into the 'closed, dark and windowless procedures' of administrative decision-making.[96] The matter is of immense importance. Government takes millions of decisions per year, but their quality is variable and often poor. All decision-making starts and most of it ends at the base of the pyramid. There is often an attitude within government that it should focus on processing caseloads and any errors can be picked up by tribunals. But this high-risk approach overlooks the fact that challenging decisions through internal reviews and then tribunals can be a stressful process for people who are often experience vulnerable circumstances, many of whom simply give up.

Having previously argued for government to engage in organisational learning from tribunal decisions, I am now more pessimistic about the prospects for improving primary decision-making.[97] There is an established ritualistic pattern to the debates. There are criticisms of the poor quality of initial decisions. Select committees and others urge government to learn appropriate lessons and thereby save the avoidable costs and delays of appeals. The answer is, of course, to get it right first time; easy to advocate, but difficult to achieve. Government responds by arguing that it has robust procedures and training in place. It argues that the headline figure of allowed appeals is misleading; appeals are allowed because appellants submit new evidence which changes their factual basis. In reality, decision-making staff have been progressively deskilled.[98] Being a government caseworker

[96] Griffith (n 82) at 127; Lord Cooper, 'Administrative Justice' (1954) 32 *Public Administration* 165, 171 (noting the 'obscurantism which disfigures many of the efforts of the Executive to discharge, as amateurs, judicial functions').

[97] R Thomas, 'Administrative Justice, Better Decisions, and Organisational Learning' [2015] *Public Law* 111.

[98] D Martin, 'Making Tax and Social Security Decisions: Lean and Deskilling in the UK Civil Service' (2017) 32 *New Technology, Work and Employment* 146.

is a low-pay, low-status job with high turnover. Despite these endemic problems, governmental defensiveness papers over the cracks and nothing really changes. The matter then subsides until the whole issue is revived and repeated without any further enlightenment. In the meantime, grinding casework within departments and tribunals continues with good, bad and indifferent decisions being churned out while departmental budgets are targeted for 'efficiency' savings. The end result is a repetitive pattern of institutional dysfunctionality and blame-shifting.

Leggatt had envisaged that the new structurally independent tribunals would enter a dialogue with government departments to improve their decision-making.[99] After all, tribunals are uniquely placed to tell government what they think about the standard of primary decisions, but these ambitions never really materialised. There was an inherent tension that Leggatt had glossed over. Leggatt had recommended that tribunals become fully judicial bodies – and hence subject to all the formal stringencies of judicial independence – while also expecting them to engage in discussions with government about their decisions. Yet, government is a permanent party to all appeals; having tribunals assisting one party to do better looks distinctly odd. Leggatt saw no impropriety in this respect, but that is just not how things have worked out in practice.

Tribunals now have no wider role in improving the quality of initial decisions or the processes through which they are taken. On a daily basis, tribunals send their decisions to departments but they end up within individual case files; they are not analysed to identify wider lessons. Officials making benefit decisions never know whether these are overturned on appeal. Indeed, the role of tribunals has diminished. Social security tribunals used to produce annual reports on the standards of primary decision-making, but this fell away on grounds of cost and governmental inaction and indifference.[100] There was also a cost-driven shift away from an internal culture of 'adjudication' within the DWP in favour of administrative processing, tighter rule-based entitlements and the department's withdrawal from the tribunal process.[101] Exasperated tribunals occasionally raise concerns, but to what real effect?[102] Bringing the tribunals within the formal judicial system has limited their ability to engage constructively with government to improve decision-making. Ombudsmen have increasingly entered the gap that has arisen. In 2021, the Northern Ireland Public Services Ombudsman issued a major own-initiative

[99] Leggatt (n 68), ch 9; Department for Constitutional Affairs (n 68) at [6.32]–[6.34].

[100] See, eg, the annual reports by the President of the Social Entitlement Chamber of the First-tier Tribunal on the standards of initial decisions throughout the 2000s.

[101] R Sainsbury, 'The Social Security Chief Adjudication Officer' [1989] *Public Law* 323; N Warren, 'The Adjudication Gap' (2006) 13 *Journal of Social Security Law* 110.

[102] *SM v Secretary of State for Work and Pensions* (JSA) [2021] UKUT 179 (AAC): 'Tribunals and courts have repeatedly sought to emphasise the importance of claimants being able to understand the basis for decisions which affect their benefit entitlement. In this case the claimant was told that the basis for stopping the benefit entitlement was: "This is because: the law says we cannot pay you". That was an entirely inadequate communication and was part of a series of inadequate communications and gaps in communication.'

investigation finding systemic maladministration in disability benefit decision-making because of the failure by the department to request further evidence from claimants' health professionals. The tribunals had complained of the problem but were unable to make any real progress. By contrast, the Ombudsman undertook an extensive and detailed investigation resulting in various positive changes.[103] These efforts reflect a more responsive law approach of institutional diagnosis and systemic improvement that is far beyond the ability of tribunals and the courts.

There are other ideas floating around: 'polluter pays' and the professionalisation of caseworkers within government. The theory behind 'polluter pays' is that government departments that make poor-quality decisions pollute the legal system by requiring people to appeal, thereby shifting the costs elsewhere. The failure of government to invest in good-quality decision-making creates a form of moral hazard. The costs of poor decisions are then passed onto the people concerned who either simply accept them or challenge them through tribunals, with the stress and uncertainty involved. The answer is to require government to bear these costs, which should, in turn, motivate it to improve the quality of its decisions. To date, the government has been unwilling to adopt a 'polluter pays' approach or to engage with the Administrative Justice Council on these issues. In 2017, Ernest Ryder, then Senior President of Tribunals, highlighting the high rate of allowed benefit appeals (75%), called for the DWP to be charged for having its poor initial decisions overturned by tribunals. Unsurprisingly, this was viewed as an unwelcome intervention by government and the episode prompted some mild, behind-the-scenes, executive-judicial friction. The episode illustrates a thin-skinned and bunker-like governmental mindset.[104]

Professionalising casework staff would be very welcome, but the direction has been all the other way. In 2022, the Home Office was recruiting asylum casework staff from supermarkets and MacDonalds and giving them two days training.[105] Some decision-making has been outsourced to private contractors with predictably poor outcomes.[106] The basic problem is that improving primary decisions requires commitment and effort by government. It will always be a long, hard organisational slog for minimal political return; ministers have no interest in operations. To expect the DWP or the Home Office unilaterally to improve their decision-making is simply to restate the endemic and lethargic nature of the problem.

[103] Northern Ireland Public Services Ombudsman, *Personal Independence Payments and the Value of Further Evidence* (2021). See also Public Services Ombudsman for Wales, *Homelessness Reviewed* (2021).

[104] E Dugan, 'A Senior Judge has suggested charging the Government for every "no-brainer" benefits case it loses in court' *Buzz Feed News* (9 November 2017).

[105] 'Revealed: Supermarket staff recruited to make 'life and death' asylum decisions' *The Guardian* (5 November 2022); 'Tough asylum cases handled by new Home Office staff, say insiders' *BBC News* (23 November 2022). See generally R Thomas, *Administrative Law in Action: Immigration Administration* (Hart, 2022).

[106] R Thomas, 'Does Outsourcing Improve or Weaken Administrative Justice? A Review of the Evidence' [2021] *Public Law* 542.

A concurrent development has been greater governmental reliance upon internal administrative review as a mandatory stage either before tribunals or an alternative. In theory, such reviews should provide an effective way of reconsidering primary decisions without the expense and delay of going to tribunals, but does it? At best, the answer is 'only sometimes' but often it is 'no'. A quick paper-based review by a senior officer can correct errors, such as the wrong immigration rule having been applied, without waiting months for an appeal hearing. Yet, administrative review suffers from the same systemic weaknesses that afflict initial decision-making.[107] Reviewers are not necessarily any senior or more experienced than initial caseworkers. They labour under the same pressures. Immigration practitioners report waiting a year for decisions on immigration reviews. Both sets of caseworkers work in the same department and imbibe the same institutional culture. Administrative review is often seen both as a means of largely confirming decisions already taken and as being inherently inferior to tribunal adjudication. One concern with social security 'mandatory reconsiderations' is that many claimants whose applications for reconsideration are turned down, will not then appeal, despite potentially succeeding if they did so. The decisions involved – for instance, on disability benefits –have significant implications for people in terms of giving them much-needed financial support. In this way, the current operation of mandatory reconsideration can further disadvantage some of the most vulnerable people in society who often lose out on their entitlements because they lack the confidence and knowledge about how the system works. The preferable solution would be to revert to the previous position in which primary refusal decisions upheld on reconsideration proceed automatically to tribunals.

Administrative review now occupies something like the same ground that tribunals inhabited many decades ago, an ambiguous no-man's land, but with little chance of improvement. If government is to rely upon administrative review procedures, then they should be of sufficient quality and robustness. The public should have confidence in them. Government quality assurance systems to pick out poor initial decisions do not necessarily work as effectively as they should. A Law Commission law reform project to examine and improve administrative review procedures stalled because of governmental resistance.[108]

While tribunals have shifted from the administrative to the judicial, there has been no corresponding integration of judicial skills, techniques and mindset into governmental casework cultures and systems. Instead, a mentality of mass administrative processing is pervasive and encased within a protective wall of governmental defensiveness. Those 'closed, dark and windowless procedures'

[107] R Thomas and J Tomlinson, 'A Different Tale of Judicial Power: Administrative Review as a Problematic Response to the Judicialisation of Tribunals' [2019] *Public Law* 537; T Mullen, 'Internal Review Systems and Administrative Justice' in M Hertogh, R Kirkham, R Thomas and J Tomlinson (eds), *The Oxford Handbook of Administrative Justice* (OUP, 2022).

[108] R Thomas and J Tomlinson, *Submission of a law reform project to the Law Commission* (2016); Law Commission (HC 640 2017-19) 13–14.

remain largely impregnable. The unwillingness of government to let in any light is a sign of weakness, not strength. Doing so would risk giving the whole game away and raise many unwelcome questions about the variable quality of primary decisions – matters which cannot be addressed without significant additional investment, a highly remote prospect.[109] In other words, if government itself lacks confidence about its own operations – but, of course, cannot publicly admit it – then it is just as trapped within the established structure and system as claimants are. It is generally accepted that the quality of primary decision-making needs to improve – but it is not going to and for reasons that are not going to change anytime soon.

All of which, of course, reinforces the need for tribunals. Yet, accessing them has become progressively more difficult. Some appeal rights have been withdrawn or downgraded.[110] Many immigration appeals were abolished in 2014 because 'too many' people had been using them. For the Home Office, the appeals system was 'a never-ending game of snakes and ladders' that was 'not fair to applicants' because of delays and costs.[111] There are well-recognised problems concerning limited advice and representation given how publicly funded legal advice and representation has been decimated.[112] The move toward using compulsory mediation before tribunals in certain contexts (eg special educational needs and disability (SEND)) is highly contested.[113] Access to justice is also influenced by social and other factors. Appellants to the SEND Tribunal are mostly middle-class; appeal rates of those from lower socio-economic status are significantly smaller.[114]

Administrative processes and behaviours can also limit access to tribunals in obscure but pervasive ways. The informal filtering effects of mandatory reconsiderations have been noted. Public bodies can also delay taking initial decisions or delay actioning appeals. Local authorities have delayed forwarding housing benefit appeals against their decisions to social security tribunals, thereby preventing access to justice. In the SEND context, delays and a lack of signposting by local authorities have meant that some people have lost their appeal rights altogether.

[109] The only viable investment government is likely to make will be to save money through, e.g. algorithmic based decision-making or by moving from discretionary based standards to rule-based decisions and thereby dispensing with tribunal appeals, as has occurred in the immigration context.

[110] Before 2011, there were appeals against permanent school exclusions in England; since then, panels can only review exclusion decisions on judicial review principles. In the rest of the UK, there continue to be appeals.

[111] Home Office, *Immigration Bill factsheet* (2013); R Thomas, 'Immigration and Access to Justice: A Critical Analysis of Recent Restrictions' in Palmer et al (n 1).

[112] S Hynes, *Austerity Justice* (Legal Action Group, 2012); S Kirwan (ed), *Advising in Austerity* (Policy, 2017).

[113] Mediation has been used principally in the SEND context: S Riddell, N Harris, E Smith and E Weedon, 'Dispute Resolution in Additional and Special Educational Needs: Local Authority Perspectives' (2010) 25 *Journal of Education Policy* 55.

[114] O Drummond, 'The Access to Justice Barriers for Tribunal Users: A Comparative Case Study on Special Educational Needs Tribunals' (Northern Ireland Assembly, Knowledge Exchange Seminar Series, 2016); AJ Marsh, 'Special Educational Needs and Disability Tribunals in England, 1994–2019' (2022) 37 *Research Papers in Education* 797.

Such problems have been addressed by ombudsmen.[115] In the homelessness context, some councils have prevented people from challenging refusal decisions by not issuing refusal letters; without one, there is no formal decision to challenge. This type of 'gatekeeping' activity is a procedural means of rationing access to substantive resources (ie temporary housing). Appeals against benefit sanctions are largely ineffective.[116] The length of time such appeals take to be heard often exceeds the duration of the sanctions imposed meaning that claimants gain nothing from appealing.[117] Some people find tribunals intimidating.[118]

The higher courts, the Upper Tribunal and ombudsmen have, in turn, responded to protect access to justice in various ways.[119] This collective effort has been significant, but has also been limited in its effects. The force of both government policy and its institutional behaviours are largely impervious to wider improvement and correction. The overall result is that when people do access tribunals, they receive administrative justice in a narrow sense, but are often failed by a wider system of poor decisions and reviews, the difficulties of preparing cases/representation and tribunal delays.[120] Overall, these types of administrative injustice reinforce larger-scale social and economic inequalities and weaken the effectiveness of tribunals. There is little political will from or capacity within government to improve matters. The overall tribunal system carries on, but the pervasive sense is that access to justice has been weakened.

The one ray of sunshine in an otherwise gloomy sky is the HMCTS court reform programme and associated digitisation; moving tribunals online to improve their accessibility and efficiency. In theory, this is potentially beneficial, although the effects of online appeals and virtual hearings are contested.[121] There is empirical

[115] R Thomas, 'The English Local Government and Social Care Ombudsman: Systemic Administrative Justice and Bureaucratisation' (Parts 1 & 2) [2023] *Public Law* 240; 424.

[116] Benefit sanctions are imposed when a claimant has not complied with a requirement, such as attending a job training programme or a job interview. See M Adler, *Cruel, Inhuman or Degrading Treatment? Benefit Sanctions in the UK* (Palgrave Macmillan, 2018).

[117] House of Commons Work and Pensions Committee, *Benefit Sanctions* (HC 955 2017–19) [108]–[113].

[118] C Selman, *Benefit Sanctions* (Public Law Project, 2022).

[119] *Detention Action* (n 77) (detained asylum fast-track appeal process systemically unfair); *R (Mohibullah) v Secretary of State for the Home Department* (TOEIC – ETS – judicial review principles) [2016] UKUT 00561 (IAC) (abuse of power by the Home Office by requiring student migrants to use out of country of appeal over the preferable in-country appeals); *Unison* (n 77) (employment tribunal appeal fees undermined access to justice); *R (CJ) v Secretary of State for Work and Pensions* (ESA) [2017] UKUT 324 (AAC) (late applications for 'mandatory reconsideration' did not prevent a subsequent appeal given the importance of access to justice). On the contribution of ombudsmen, see Thomas (n 115).

[120] R Thomas, 'Analysing Systemic Administrative Failures: Explanatory Factors and Prospects for Future Research' (2021) 43 *Journal of Social Welfare and Family Law* 339; C Barnard and A Ludlow, 'Administrative (In)justice? Appellants' Experiences of Accessing Justice in Social Security Tribunals' [2022] *Public Law* 406.

[121] J Tomlinson and B Karemba, 'Tribunal Justice, Brexit, and Digitalisation: Immigration Appeals in the First-tier Tribunal' (2019) 33 *Journal of Immigration, Asylum and Nationality Law* 47; J Tomlinson, *Justice in the Digital State* (Policy Press, 2019).

work underway to evaluate online justice and how it impacts upon users and judicial decision-making. It can reasonably be expected that, over time, online procedures and hearings will be refined and adapted. However, they are unlikely to provide the single big solution (as the Ministry of Justice initially thought) to address the substantial weakening of access to justice caused by legal aid cuts and the other problems highlighted above.

Conclusion

This chapter has provided an overview of UK tribunals by considering their historical development, constitutional place, and aspects of their practical operation. What, then, could be the way forward? By way of conclusion, three general areas of inquiry can be highlighted for future comparative research.

First, there is important historical work within each jurisdiction to be done to understand how tribunals have developed and why. What is critically important here is how the need for specific tribunals arose because of the social, economic and political forces which prompted the government to bureaucratise a particular area. There is archival and other research that could be pursued about how tribunals were created, the types of policy debates that conditioned them, how they have developed over time and how they operated. This type of scholarship can yield a number of insights to enable us to understand where we currently are and why.

Second, there is scope for legal analysis of tribunals, including the relationship between appellate tribunals and the higher courts, the law governing the institutional framework of tribunals, their powers and how they are exercised all raise important doctrinal questions about tribunals. Another matter concerns how tribunals themselves interpret and apply the detailed rules and regulations in their specific areas and their contribution to the development of this law and the impacts upon government and society. There is a wealth of materials to work with here.

Third, there is a continuing need to undertake research into how specific tribunals actually operate. It is important to study how administrative law works in practice. It is an artefact of legal values, social needs, political forces, institutional behaviours and the organisational means of implementing policy. Administrative law is certainly not just an exercise in abstract legal logic; it also concerns how government implements its policies and the impacts upon people's lives. Values such as fair process and participation must be realised in real-world conditions, which in turn influence their meaning. Administrative and tribunal systems must be made to work if they are to be effective. In this context, administrative lawyers have an important role to play in studying and evaluating how tribunals and related processes operate in practice. This type of research is important because tribunals are at the coalface of administrative law. Tribunals and policymakers are themselves interested in such research and it can have impact outside the academy. We need both top-down doctrinal and theoretical studies and ground-level up empirical studies and the point at which the two meet. Undertaking this type of work reveals the subtleties and complexities of how administrative law works in practice and the challenges of trying to balance fairness to the individual and wider public interests. It is important in terms of trying to find out what the problems are within tribunals and what could be done to address – or at least ameliorate – them.

10

Administrative Adjudication in the United States

MICHAEL ASIMOW

This chapter concerns administrative adjudication in the United States. Unlike most other English-speaking countries, the US does not rely primarily on tribunals to provide administrative hearings. Instead, the default system for both federal and state governments is a combined-function design. Under that model, a government agency adopts regulations and prosecutes violations of the governing statute and regulations. That agency then adjudicates the resulting disputes. Although the US default is the combined-function agency, its administrative adjudication system is quite varied and includes numerous tribunals. This chapter provides a general overview of that system.

This chapter sets out a theoretical approach to agency adjudication to assist the reader in distinguishing between the many design variations found in adjudicatory systems throughout the world, including both the combined-function and tribunal models. It then discusses the combined-function agency model. It sets out a typology of three different types of US combined-function administrative adjudication and discusses the US Administrative Procedure Act and the history of combined-function agencies. Finally, it discusses US tribunals.

The volume of decisions arising out of administrative adjudication is vastly greater than those resolved by courts. The outcome of most administrative disputes (such as disputes over benefit claims or minor penalties) is not very important to the government, but every one of them is vitally important to the private party who has challenged the government. For these reasons, administrative adjudication is deserving of scholarly attention. Comparative law helps scholars and policymakers to better understand their own administrative adjudicatory systems and furnishes them with ideas for transplanted procedures that might improve those systems.[1]

[1] See O Tamir, 'Our Parochial Administrative Law' (2024) (forthcoming Vol 97 *Southern California Law Review*).

Five Models of Administrative Adjudication[2]

All schemes of government regulation and distribution of benefits generate disputes between the government and private parties. These disputes may concern a rejected application for government benefits, a rejected application for a particular land use or approval of marketing a new drug, a sanctioning decision such as a civil monetary penalty or the withdrawal of a licence, or some other regulatory action that compels a private party to take an action or refrain from an action. Administrative law must prescribe a system of adjudication that resolves such disputes in an accurate and efficient manner and in a way that generates confidence that the process was fair.

By the term 'administrative adjudication', I mean the entire system for resolving *individualised* disputes between private parties and government administrative agencies.[3] This process starts with an administrative investigation leading to the agency's preliminary or 'front-line' decision, continuing through the process by which a private party challenges the front-line decision in a process that gives rise to an initial decision, agency-level reconsideration of the initial decision, and concluding with judicial review.[4] The systems in place for resolving individualised disputes differ around the world and are difficult to compare. Adjudication must be distinguished from rulemaking that involves agency action of *generalized* rather than individualised applicability. Rulemaking is conducted according to an entirely different set of legal constraints that vary extensively throughout the world.[5]

This part of the chapter sketches a theoretical approach to institutional design that may help the reader untangle the maze of adjudicatory systems in use around the world. It relies on three phases, four variables, and five possible models that incorporate different arrangements of these variables.

Most administrative adjudicatory systems have three phases:[6]

- *Initial decision*: this phase is the first agency proceeding that affords a private party an opportunity to present its case by challenging the front-line

[2] The first section of this chapter draws heavily on the author's previous work. See M Asimow, 'Five Models of Administrative Adjudication' (2015) 63 *American Journal of Comparative Law* 3 ('*Five Models*'), which discusses the theoretical approach to comparative institutional design in greater detail.

[3] This chapter uses the term 'agency' as it is used in US law, meaning a governmental unit (other than a court or a legislature) having delegated power to affect legal rights and obligations through rulemaking, adjudication or similar functions. The term includes governmental units with various titles used throughout the world including commissions, ministries and departments.

[4] In many countries, adjudicatory decisions by government agencies are referred to as 'administrative acts', 'orders', 'decisions,' or 'unilateral acts'.

[5] See M Asimow, G Bocksang, M Cirotteau, Y Dotan, N Mahboubi and T Perroud, 'Ex Ante Administrative Review of the Legality of Regulations: A Comparative Approach' (2020) 68 *American Journal of Comparative Law* 332.

[6] Actually, adjudication often has four phases rather than three. The three mentioned in the text are usually preceded by a preliminary investigation and a 'front-line' decision by the agency staff. In the preliminary investigation phase, the agency staff investigates whether an applicant should receive a

determination made by agency staff. The initial decision is legally binding unless it is challenged at a higher level.

- *Administrative reconsideration*: most administrative schemes include an opportunity for administrative reconsideration of the initial decision. Reconsideration can be performed by higher-level personnel of the same agency that made the initial decision or by a different agency.
- *Judicial review*: most administrative schemes include provision for the private party to seek review of the initial decision or the reconsidered decision in a court.[7]

There are four key variables. Each requires a design choice. The first and second variables relate to the initial decision and reconsideration phases. The third and fourth relate to the judicial review phase.

1. Is the adjudicating body a combined-function agency or a separate tribunal? In a combined-function design, the same agency combines investigation, prosecution, initial decision-making and reconsideration. In a tribunal system, a separate tribunal conducts the reconsideration but does not make initial decisions or engage in investigation or prosecution.
2. Is the proceeding adversarial or inquisitorial? Adversarial proceedings resemble the trial-type process employed in US or UK criminal cases. This process consists of a lawyer-controlled proceeding before a relatively passive and independent judge. In an adversarial system, the initial decision-making function is sharply distinguished from the investigation phase of the case. Inquisitorial administrative proceedings resemble Continental European, some Asian, or Latin American criminal process. In an inquisitorial administrative system, investigators assemble a dossier and come to a conclusion about how a dispute between government and a private party should be resolved. The initial decision phase is conducted by the staff members of the same agency that investigated or prosecuted the case. It provides the private party with a written or oral opportunity to change the minds of the investigators. Similarly, an inquisitorial reconsideration proceeding is controlled by

benefit or a licence or whether it should be targeted for a sanction or other regulatory order. The staff make a front-line decision to deny the benefit or licence or to impose the sanction or other regulatory order. This ends the case if the private party accepts the front-line decision. This sequence of investigation and front-line decision might be called 'phase zero'. See M Asimow, 'Greenlighting Administrative Prosecution' (2023) 75 *Administrative L Rev* 227 ('*Greenlighting*') for discussion of the division of authority between agency investigators, and prosecutors and the heads of the agency during phase zero. This chapter will have little to say about phase zero, given that it is highly discretionary, relatively unconstrained by legally required procedures, not meaningfully subject to judicial review, and specific to particular administrative schemes. See *Greenlighting* at 243–45. When the chapter refers to the 'three phases' of administrative adjudication, it excludes phase zero.

[7] For purposes of this chapter, the term 'judicial review' includes 'appeal'. Many countries distinguish between the two, treating 'appeal' as a judicial remedy provided by statute and 'judicial review' as a non-statutory remedy.

the investigative and prosecutorial staff. No system is purely adversarial or purely inquisitorial. Nevertheless, procedures can be arrayed on this axis and will tend to fall nearer the adversarial or inquisitorial poles.

3. Is judicial review open or closed?[8] In an open system, either party can introduce new evidence in court (in addition to the evidence introduced during earlier stages) or the court can request the parties to produce new evidence. Either party can offer new arguments that were not advanced at earlier stages and the government can offer new reasons for its actions. In other words, in an open system, the record does not crystallise until the judicial review stage. In a closed system, the parties cannot introduce new evidence, new reasons, or new arguments. The record crystallised either at the initial decision or reconsideration stage.
4. Does a reviewing court have generalised jurisdiction or is it a specialised administrative court?[9]

These variables can be shuffled to provide five models of administrative adjudication, each of them in use in different jurisdictions. Each of the five models involves a change in a single variable from previously described models. Each jurisdiction tends to rely *primarily on one of the three phases* (that is, initial decision, reconsideration, or judicial review) to achieve a fair and accurate result. Efficiency concerns require jurisdictions to make this choice. Jurisdictions cannot afford to invest resources equally in two, much less all three, of the phases. The phase that each jurisdiction chooses to receive the most resources is likely to be the phase that private parties regard as providing their best chance to win the case.

At this point, I introduce some methodological reservations. First, the approach discussed in Part I of this chapter oversimplifies the details of the adjudication schemes under discussion. Oversimplification is an inevitable flaw of model building in social science. It is necessary to abstract complex systems to compare and contrast them with examples in other countries.[10] I hope that my oversimplified description of these various adjudicatory systems does not distort their essential nature. Second, for political and historical reasons, the administrative adjudication systems of any given jurisdiction cannot all be described by a single model. As discussed below, for example, the US has a dominant or default model, but each of the four other models can be found somewhere in US administrative law.

[8] See *Five Models* (n 2) 20–27; M Asimow and Y Dotan (2016) 'Open and Closed Judicial Review of Agency Action' 64 *American Journal of Comparative Law* 521.

[9] See *Five Models* (n 2) 24–27.

[10] The value of any model of administrative justice depends on 'what an analyst is trying to do'. Jerry L Mashaw, 'Models of Administrative Justice' in M Hertogh, R Kirkham, RThomas and J Tomlinson (eds), *The Oxford Handbook of Administrative Justice* (OUP, 2021) 375, 393. The purpose of this chapter is to illuminate the design choices that are reflected in different systems of administrative justice around the world and to permit comparisons between them.

Model 1 – Adversarial Hearing/Combined Function/Limited Judicial Review

Model 1 is the default US design. A single agency investigates the case and makes the initial decision and performs reconsideration. The initial decision occurs after an *adversarial* hearing presided over by a hearing officer ('HO') who renders the initial decision.[11] The HO works for the agency that is a party to the dispute, rather than being independent of that agency.[12] The HO is expected to apply established agency policy as expressed in regulations, guidance documents or precedential adjudicatory decisions. As discussed below,[13] combined-function agencies have an internal separation of functions, meaning that investigators and administrative prosecutors cannot participate in the decisional process (except as witnesses or prosecutors).

The reconsideration phase occurs at a higher level of the same agency that rendered the initial decision and is performed either by the heads of the agency or a delegated reviewer or review panel. Especially when the reviewers are the agency heads, they are empowered to substitute new findings of fact or new legal interpretations or adopt new policies that have retroactive effect.[14] Courts of general jurisdiction review the legality and reasonableness of the agency decision.[15] Judicial review is closed (meaning neither side can introduce new evidence, arguments, or reasons).

Model 2 – Inquisitorial Hearing/Combined Function/Limited Judicial Review

Model 2 is the same as Model 1, except that the initial decision and the reconsideration are inquisitorial rather than adversarial. There is no separation of functions,

[11] In US practice, the HO is frequently referred to as an administrative judge or an administrative law judge (ALJ) or by some other title (such as Immigration Judge or Patent Judge). In most countries, however, an administrative HO would not be referred to as a 'judge' since this title is enjoyed only by decision-makers in the judicial system. In the US, administrative judges are 'functionally comparable' to judges in the judicial system. An administrative HO's powers 'are often, if not generally, comparable to those of a trial judge … More importantly the process of agency adjudication is currently structured so as to assure that the hearing examiner exercises his independent judgment on the evidence before him, free from pressures by the parties or other officials within the agency' – *Butz v Economou* (1978) 438 US 478, 513 (citations omitted).

[12] For discussion of the independence of administrative HOs in combined-function agencies as compared to judges in the judicial branch, see J Moliterno, 'The Administrative Judiciary's Independence Myth' (2006) 41 *Wake Forest LR* 1191.

[13] See text at n 28.

[14] The federal Administrative Procedure Act provides: 'On appeal from or review of the initial decision, the agency has all the powers which it would have in making the initial decision …' 5 USC. §557(b).

[15] 5 USC §706.

meaning the same person or persons exercise investigatory, prosecutorial and adjudicatory functions. Proceedings at the initial decision level are considered part of the investigation. The decision-maker is active rather than passive and assists unrepresented parties. Closed judicial review takes place in a generalised court. This model describes a substantial segment of US administrative adjudication.[16] It is also employed in cases decided at the level of the European Union (EU) institutions, but not in cases decided by EU member states.

Model 3 – Tribunal System[17]

Model 3 is like Model 1, except that the reconsideration decision is made by a *tribunal*. A tribunal is an agency engaged only in adjudication that is separate from and independent of the agency that investigated and prosecuted the case and made the initial decision. The tribunal model is used in numerous jurisdictions whose legal system is derived from the UK and is the model described in most of the chapters of this book. Some tribunals, like those in Canada,[18] are specific to the agency that made the initial decision; some, like those in the UK or Australia,[19] reconsider initial decisions by many agencies. As discussed in Part III of this chapter, the US administrative adjudicatory system includes tribunals, particularly at the state level.

Model 4 – Open Judicial Review

The initial decision and reconsideration phases are like Model 2, meaning that the initial decision and reconsideration stages are inquisitorial. However, judicial review is *open*, meaning that the reviewing court can consider new evidence, reasons and arguments, and the court is empowered to substitute its judgment for that of the agency on factual and discretionary issues as well as legal issues. This model is employed in mainland China, Japan and Argentina, among many other jurisdictions.[20]

[16] See M Asimow, 'The Last Frontier: Fair Procedure in Informal Adjudication' (2024) – *Michigan Journal of Environmental and Administrative Law*. Available at: https://ssrn.com/abstract=4738364.

[17] In some jurisdictions, the word 'tribunal' is used to refer only to courts. This chapter uses the term to refer to an adjudicative administrative body that is not a court and is independent of the agency that made the initial decision.

[18] See L Jacobs, 'A Wavering Commitment? Administrative Independence and Collaborative Governance in Ontario's Adjudicative Tribunals Accountability Legislation' (2010) 28 *Windsor Year Book of Access to Justice* 285, 294–97; L Sossin and S Hoffman, 'The Elusive Search for Accountability: Evaluating Adjudicative Tribunals' (2010) 28 *Windsor Year Book of Access to Justice* 343.

[19] See M Asimow and J Lubbers, 'The Merits of Merits Review: A Comparative Look at the Australian Administrative Appeals Tribunal' (2010) 28 *Windsor Year Book of Access to Justice* 261, 262–70; and Groves and Weeks, Chapter 7 in this volume.

[20] See *Five Models* (n 2) 20–24.

Model 5 – Specialised Administrative Courts

The initial decision and reconsideration phases are like Model 2, but the court that conducts judicial review is separate from the general court system and it decides only administrative law cases. This model is employed in France, Germany and numerous other jurisdictions in Europe, Asia and Latin America.[21]

Obviously, the four variables could be manipulated to produce more than five models. However, these five models describe the most frequently encountered adjudicatory systems in use today.

Perhaps an example will clarify how the five models might work in resolving a typical administrative adjudicatory dispute. Suppose that the Ministry of Transport ('MT') in Country C licenses ferry operators. The MT regulations and the specific licenses contain provisions relating to safety and environmental protection. One such provision prohibits ferries from disposing of waste by dumping it into the water. Cap operates a licensed ferry service. MT receives a complaint from Ed (a former employee of Cap), investigates the matter, and charges Cap with dumping waste into the water. This is MT's front-line decision.[22]

The *initial decision* process gives Cap an opportunity to challenge the frontline decision. Ed states that he saw Cap dump waste into the water. Cap states that he fired Ed for incompetence the previous year and Ed has a grudge against him. Cap denies that any dumping ever occurred and testifies that all waste has been disposed of properly. Several of Cap's employees testify that they never saw any illegal dumping and that company policy prohibits it. The official responsible for making the *initial decision* determines that Cap dumped waste in violation of the terms of his licence and recommends that Cap's licence be revoked (as opposed to paying a financial penalty). A reconsideration decision upholds the initial decision. Cap seeks *judicial review.* On judicial review, there are no issues of law or procedure. There are only two issues. First, who is telling the truth as a matter of fact – Cap or Ed? Second, if the dumping charge is upheld, what should the penalty be?

- *Model 1*: MT is a combined-function agency, meaning that it is responsible for investigation, prosecution, adjudication and reconsideration. At the initial decision phase, MT conducts a trial-type, adversarial hearing presided over by an HO who works for MT but has not been involved in the investigation and prosecution of Cap's case. The HO decision revokes Cap's licence. Cap has an opportunity to seek reconsideration at a higher level of MT, such as the agency head. The reconsidering official upholds the HO's decision. MT's decision is reviewed by a court of general jurisdiction in a closed proceeding. The court must sustain MT's decision (both the factual conclusions and the discretionary

[21] ibid 24–27.

[22] See n 4 for discussion of front-line decisions.

choice of penalty) if it is 'reasonable' in light of the record made at the initial decision stage.[23] This is the default model in the US.

- *Model 2*: Model 2 is the same as Model 1 except that the initial decision and reconsideration phases are inquisitorial rather than adversarial. The initial decision consists of a hearing that is treated as part of the agency investigation. It is conducted by MT investigators and prosecutors rather than by an HO. The reconsideration process is informal and is also conducted by MT staff or agency heads. This model occurs frequently in the US but is not the default.
- *Model 3*: Model 3 is the same as Model 1, except that reconsideration is provided by a tribunal that is independent of MT. The tribunal makes a written merits decision after an adversarial trial-type hearing. Model 3 occurs occasionally in the US but is not the default.
- *Model 4*: Model 4 is the same as Model 2 except that judicial review is open rather than closed. This means that the initial decision and reconsideration phases do not crystallise the record. The reviewing court has the power to receive new evidence or arguments from either side, and MT can introduce additional reasons for its discretionary decision. The court makes a merits decision, meaning that it has power to substitute its judgment on factual or discretionary issues for MT's judgment. Model 4 occurs in the US but is relatively infrequent.
- *Model 5*: Model 5 is the same as Model 4, except that review takes place in a specialized administrative court rather than a court of general jurisdiction. Few courts in the US are specialised but there are exceptions, such as the Court of Appeals for Veterans Claims.

The Default US Model: Combined Functions

Historical Development of the US Combined-Function Model

The default adjudicatory design used in the US is described by Model 1: an agency with combined functions conducts an adversarial trial-type hearing and renders the initial decision. The same agency reconsiders the initial decision (either at the agency head level or through a delegated reviewer or review board). Judicial review of the agency decision is closed and takes place in a court of general jurisdiction.

The Struggle to Regulate the Railroads

The US combined-function model developed as part of the struggle to regulate the railroads during the late 1800s and early 1900s. Various market failures made some

[23] See *Five Models* (n 2) 11–13.

form of regulation imperative. Both railroads and shippers pressed for federal regulation which resulted in the creation of the Interstate Commerce Commission ('ICC') in 1887.[24]

The original version of the ICC was largely toothless, and what few teeth it possessed were soon pulled by the courts.[25] By 1920, however, the ICC emerged as the prototypical combined-function economic regulatory agency. It had broad authority to regulate the railroads, including the power to adopt regulations, set and modify railroad rates, and disapprove mergers. In addition to its regulatory authority, the ICC adjudicated enforcement cases brought by shippers against railroads charging violation of ICC regulations, such as accusations that railroads charged an unreasonable rate or failed to follow rate tariffs.

The ICC was a classic example of a Model 1 adjudicating system. It exercised *combined functions*, meaning that it adopted regulations, approved or disapproved railroad rates, and investigated and prosecuted violations of statutes or regulations. It then resolved disputes through an internal adjudicatory process conducted by an HO, followed by reconsideration conducted by the five agency heads. The ICC even adjudicated private disputes between railroads and shippers, although such private disputes could also be adjudicated in courts. The losing party could seek closed judicial review in a court of general jurisdiction.

Congress followed the ICC model when it created the Federal Trade Commission ('FTC') in 1914.[26] The FTC was a policing agency with power to investigate, prosecute and adjudicate claims of unfair competition and antitrust violations. Legislatures adapted the combined-function model to countless regulatory and benefit-disbursing agencies at the federal, state and local levels throughout the twentieth century and continue to do so in the twenty-first.

Between 1906 and 1920, the ICC began to use its staff as hearing officers (HOs) to conduct the initial decision phase in railway rate cases. HOs presided over adversarial, trial-type hearings at which private lawyers opposed ICC staff counsel, or at which private lawyers for shippers and carriers opposed each other. The HOs wrote detailed initial decisions that became final and binding unless reconsidered by the five agency heads. The same HO design was copied in many other regulatory agencies including the FTC.[27]

The Administrative Procedure Act

During the depression era of the 1930s, federal combined-function regulatory agencies proliferated as part of President Franklin D Roosevelt's *New Deal*. Federal

[24] See R Rabin, 'Federal Regulation in Historical Perspective' (1986) 38 *Stanford Law Review* 1189, 1197–236. The ICC was abolished in 1995 and some of its functions were taken over by other agencies. ICC Termination Act of 1995, Pub L 104-88 §1 (1995).

[25] ibid.

[26] ibid at 1216–29.

[27] See DJ Gifford, 'Federal Administrative Law Judges: The Relevance of Past Choices to Future Directions' (1997) 49 *Administrative Law Review* 1, 4–5.

combined-function agencies regulated labour relations, banking, securities, energy, communications, agriculture and other sectors of the economy that had previously been regulated at the state level. Congress also created Social Security and other federal benefit agencies that were also designed to exercise combined functions. In the early 1930s, the Supreme Court overturned several federal regulatory schemes on constitutional grounds. By the late 1930s, however, the Supreme Court reversed direction and consistently upheld the constitutional validity of federal agencies that combined the various functions. Business interests (championed by the American Bar Association) protested mightily against the broadened scope of federal regulatory scheme and the combined-function agencies, but to no avail.

The lengthy and bitter battle to contain federal regulatory agencies was interrupted by the Second World War. After the War, Congress finally ended the political struggle by enacting the Administrative Procedure Act ('APA') of 1946,[28] which passed Congress by unanimous vote. The APA was a massive compromise that satisfied neither business nor government but was agreed as the best feasible outcome.[29] The APA prescribed the procedures for federal agency adjudication and rulemaking. It preserved the system of judicial review that existed before 1946[30] and contained detailed treatment of the standards courts would use to review administrative decisions and rules. The rulemaking process included an opportunity for public notice of proposed rules and an opportunity to comment on them.[31] All the states have enacted APAs, but there is a good deal of variation between them as well as between state and federal APAs.

For adjudication, the federal APA prescribed a detailed and rather formal process of agency trial-type hearings.[32] The APA preserved the system of combined functions and did not require that adjudication be performed by tribunals or that judicial review be conducted by administrative courts. Agencies retained the power to prosecute, investigate and decide the resulting disputes through a system of adversarial trial-type hearings and agency-head reconsideration.

The rationale for entrusting the reconsideration function to the heads of the agency that had conducted the investigation and prosecution and made the initial decision was that agency adjudication was often used to establish agency policy. The agency heads could retroactively establish new policy when they issued their final decision. Of course, agency policy could (and perhaps should) be made through the adoption of prospective rules rather than case-by-case adjudication, but rulemaking was relatively unfamiliar in 1946. In any case, the use of the adjudication function to make general policy was well established in 1946[33] and

[28] 5 USC §§551 to 706.

[29] GB Shepherd, 'Fierce Compromise: The Administrative Procedure Act Emerges from New Deal Politics' (1996) 90 *Northwestern University Law Review* 1557.

[30] 5 USC §§701–706.

[31] 5 USC §553.

[32] See 5 USC §§554, 556, 557.

[33] See *Securities and Exchange Commission v Chenery Corp* (1947) 332 US 194.

Congress wanted to preserve the control of regulatory agencies over the adjudication function.[34]

Decision-maker Impartiality Under the APA

The combined-function model in which the same agency is both prosecutor and judge inherently raises issues relating to impartiality of the adjudicative process. These are issues that do not arise to the same extent under a tribunal system where the adjudicators are independent of the prosecutors. The APA dealt with the issue of impartiality in carefully drafted compromise provisions.

Protection of the Independence of HOs

The APA's adjudication provisions prescribe adversarial trial-type hearings. The hearings are conducted by HOs who work for the prosecuting agency and make the initial agency decisions. In 1978, the HOs governed by the APA received a new and cherished title – Administrative Law Judges (ALJs).

The most important innovation of the APA's adjudication provisions was an elaborate set of protections of ALJ independence within the agency structure. The APA drafters intended that ALJs would be the primary fact finders in the adjudicatory process and should be secure from influence exerted by prosecutors or the agency heads.

Although ALJs are employed by the prosecuting agency, they must be organisationally separated from agency investigators and prosecutors.[35] Once hired by an agency, ALJs enjoy life tenure without any probationary period. They are highly compensated, relative to other government employees. They cannot be removed except for good cause. Cases involving the discharge of ALJs for good cause are heard by ALJs working for a separate agency, the Merit Systems Protection Board. ALJs cannot be given tasks other than deciding cases and must be assigned to cases by rotation so far as practicable. Unique among federal employees, ALJs are not subject to performance evaluation.[36] Federal ALJs are well organised and often take collective action to protect their turf.

Some administrative law scholars have argued that ALJs are overprotected.[37] There is a serious issue of the constitutionality of the provision that prevents the executive branch from discharging ALJs without cause. This issue may be decided by the Supreme Court in 2024.[38] Agencies such as Social Security have engaged

[34] See DJ Gifford, 'Adjudication in Independent Tribunals: The Role of an Alternative Agency Structure' (1990) 66 *Notre Dame L R* 965, 976–81, 992–94.

[35] ALJs 'cannot be responsible to or subject to the supervision or direction of an employee or agent engaged in the performance of investigative or prosecuting functions for an agency' – 5 USC §554(d)(2).

[36] See 5 USC §§3105, 5372, 7521.

[37] A Scalia, 'The ALJ Fiasco – A Reprise' (1979) 47 *University of Chicago Law Review* 57.

[38] See discussion of the *Jarkesy* decision in text at n 62 below.

in long-term battles with their ALJs over management issues, such as decisional quotas.[39] The American Bar Association has proposed the creation of a Social Security tribunal to remove the ALJs from control by the agency that administers the programme to end the bickering.[40]

Protection of the Adversarial Hearing

The APA contains several provisions designed to protect the adversarial trial-type character of the initial decision process.[41] The Act requires ALJs and other agency adjudicatory decision-makers to be impartial, meaning free of conflict of interest, animus toward the parties or prejudgment of adjudicatory facts.[42] Adjudicatory decision-makers may not receive ex parte (meaning off-the-record) communications from persons outside the agency; if such communications occur, they must be placed on the record.[43] A more specific ex parte communication provision prohibits ALJs from consulting a person or party (including any other agency staff member) on a fact in issue, unless the discussion is on the record.[44]

The APA requires internal separation of functions, meaning that agency staff 'adversaries' (prosecutors, investigators and advocates) in a case are excluded from serving as decision-makers in that case or furnishing off-the-record advice to ALJs or agency heads. Only staff members who have not served as adversaries in a given case can provide such advice.[45] The APA also establishes the 'exclusive record' principle, meaning that decision-makers can consider only evidence that was introduced at the hearing, not information learned through their own experience or personal investigations.[46]

This elaborate system of neutrality-protection can have only limited efficacy. All agency decision-makers – both ALJs and especially agency heads – are likely to possess 'institutional bias', meaning they support the agency's regulatory mission and want to uphold the hard work of its investigators and prosecutors.[47] Agencies are sometimes 'captured', meaning they have been essentially taken over by the

[39] See MH Taylor, 'Russian Roulette in an Administrative Law Context: The Déjà Vu of Decisional Disparities in Agency Adjudication' (2007) 60 *Stanford Law Review* 475, 485–90; Gifford, Adjudication in Independent Tribunals' (n 34), 1005–19.

[40] Resolution 201 (2021). See www.americanbar.org/content/dam/aba/administrative/house_of_delegates/ebook-of-resolutions-with-reports/2021-annual-resolution-ebook.pdf. For discussion of a separate Social Security tribunal, see PR Verkuil and JS Lubbers, 'Alternative Approaches to Judicial Review of Social Security Disability Cases' (2003) 55 *Administrative Law Review* 731.

[41] See 5 USC §§554, 556, 557.

[42] 5 USC §556(b). See L Virelli, 'Integrity in Agency Adjudication,' in American Bar Association, *A Guide to Federal Agency Adjudication* Chapter 10 (3rd edn, 2023).

[43] 5 USC §557(d).

[44] 5 USC §554(d)(1).

[45] 5 USC §554(d). See M Asimow, 'When the Curtain Falls: Separation of Functions in the Federal Administrative Agencies' (1981) 81 *Columbia Law Review* 759.

[46] 5 USC §556(e).

[47] See *Greenlighting* (n 4), 251.

industries they are supposed to regulate.[48] In the reconsideration process, agency heads may be subject to confirmation bias, because they have approved an earlier decision to prosecute and then must decide whether to uphold an ALJ decision resulting from that prosecution.[49] If the heads decide to overturn an ALJ's decision against a private party, that would suggest that they were wrong to have approved the prosecution in the first place and consequently wasted agency resources pursuing the case. Nobody likes to admit a blunder.

Types A, B and C Adjudication

Newcomers to US federal administrative law often assume that the APA describes all of it. This is more or less true of rulemaking, freedom of information and judicial review, but it is emphatically not true of adjudication. In order to understand the federal US administrative adjudicatory system, it is necessary to distinguish three different types of agency adjudication that I refer to as Types A, B and C adjudication.[50]

Type A involves adjudicatory disputes governed by the APA, as described above. To oversimplify a complex question,[51] the APA adjudication system applies *only* where the agency's governing statute requires it to apply. As a result, most federal agency adjudication is *not* covered by the APA. There is little logic to which agencies are subject to the APA and which are not.

Numerous important federal regulatory agencies conduct Type A adjudication. Most of these agencies provide Model 1 procedure, meaning they conduct adversarial trial type hearings presided over by ALJs. Agency heads reconsider the ALJ decisions and make the final agency decision. Most Type A regulatory agencies are 'independent' of executive control, meaning that the President cannot remove their agency heads except for good cause.

The vast majority of Type A adjudications are Social Security disability disputes that do not fit Model 1. Social Security ALJs are a part of the agency that manages the disability benefits programme. Social Security cases are inquisitorial rather than adversarial and thus properly described by Model 2. In Social Security

[48] There is a vast literature on the subject of agency capture. See, eg, RE Barkow, 'Insulating Agencies: Avoiding Capture Through Institutional Design' (2010) 89 *Texas Law Review* 15.

[49] See *Greenlighting*, (n 4), 251–56.

[50] The A-B-C typology originated in a report by the author to the Administrative Conference of the United States ('ACUS'), a federal agency that considers and recommends governance proposals: M Asimow, 'Adjudication Outside the Administrative Procedure Act' (2016) 81 *Fed Reg* 94, 314 ('*ACUS Type B Report*'). It has been employed in subsequent ACUS reports and recommendations and in numerous academic articles. See, eg, M Asimow, 'The Last Frontier: Fair Procedure in Administrative Adjudication,' n 16; ES Bremer, 'The Exceptionalism Norm in Administrative Adjudication' (2019) *Wisconsin Law Review* 1351, 1405–09.

[51] J Lubbers, 'Constitutional and Statutory Foundations,' in *A Guide to Federal Agency Adjudication* 253–55, n 42.

hearings, the government is not represented and the ALJ is responsible for developing the record and then deciding the case. Especially when claimants are not represented by lawyers, ALJs must make sure their interests are protected. Initial decisions by Social Security ALJs are reviewed by an internal review board called the Appeals Council rather than by the agency head.

Type B adjudications involve *evidentiary hearings required by statute* that are *not* covered by the APA because no statute requires the APA to apply.[52] Most Type B adjudication is Model 1. Type B proceedings resemble Type A proceedings and are often just as adversarial and as formal as Type A's. Agency-specific *procedural regulations* generally require that the agency's Type B adjudication complies with the same neutrality-protective principles that are set forth by the APA, including absence of bias, exclusive record, prohibition of ex parte outsider communications and internal separation of functions. Reconsideration is provided by higher level staff or review boards or by the agency heads.

The presiding officers at Type B evidentiary hearings are *not* ALJs. Hearings are presided over by staff members called administrative judges ('AJs') with varying titles, including Patent Judges or Immigration Judges. AJs lack the thicket of independence-protecting statutory provisions enjoyed by ALJs. Examples of Type B proceedings are those conducted by the Patent Trial and Appeal Board, the Environmental Review Board, the Board of Contract Appeals, the Board of Veterans' Appeals, the Immigration Court[53] and many others.

Type C adjudication occurs where *no statute requires the agency to conduct evidentiary hearings*.[54] Most Type C agencies exercise combined functions. Their proceedings are inquisitorial, so they fall within Model 2 rather than Model 1. Type C adjudicatory disputes are generally resolved through informal document exchange and oral argument, sometimes with public legislative-type hearings. Often agency investigators and prosecutors in a case serve as the initial decision-makers in the same case. Some important Type C functions include new drug approvals, bank licensing, land use planning approvals, scientific grant-making and many immigration decisions. Type C adjudication ranges from economically consequential disputes down to quite trivial disputes (the prototype trivial dispute involves the allocation of campsites by rangers at national forest campgrounds). Type C adjudications undoubtedly outnumber Types A and B adjudications combined.[55]

Judicial Review of Agency Adjudicatory Decisions

The APA did not significantly change the rules relating to judicial review of agency adjudicatory decisions. In general, all adjudicatory decisions (whether Types A, B

[52] Type B proceedings are described in the *ACUS Type B Report* (n 50).
[53] The Immigration Court is further discussed in text at nn 71–77.
[54] See Asimow (n 16).
[55] See M Asimow, 'Federal Administrative Adjudication Outside the Administrative Procedure Act' (2019) ch 5; Asimow, (n 16).

or C) are subject to judicial review. Federal or state courts of general jurisdiction provide closed judicial review. In other words, neither party to judicial review can introduce evidence or arguments that were not introduced at the agency level and the agency cannot supply additional reasons for its decision.[56] The courts must uphold an agency's fact findings if they are reasonable, based on the entire record of proceedings before the agency, and must uphold the reasonable exercise of discretionary authority.[57] In the federal system, the court must also uphold a reasonable agency interpretation of an ambiguous statute or regulation,[58] but state courts usually have full power to decide legal issues.

The Initial Decision as the Most Important Level of Administrative Adjudication

As mentioned above, a jurisdiction tends to rely heavily on one of the three phases of adjudication to reach a correct and fair result. In Model 1 jurisdictions like the US, that phase is the *initial decision.* Far fewer resources are invested in reconsideration or judicial review, which are designed as a check against an unreasonable or legally flawed initial decision. Lawyers concentrate most of their efforts at the initial decision phase, since it is relatively unlikely that an initial decision will be overturned because of errors at the initial decision or reconsideration phases.

The Attack on Combined-Function Agencies

Currently, combined-function agencies are under sustained attack from academic and judicial conservatives. These attacks are based on the separation of powers and due process provisions of the Constitution as well as political opposition to government regulation of the economy. For example, the Supreme Court invalidated the decisional process of the Patent Trial and Appeal Board because its HOs rendered decisions that were not subject to reconsideration by the agency head.[59] The Securities and Exchange Commission ('SEC') invalidly appointed its ALJs because the appointments were by lower-level staff rather than by the agency heads.[60] The court invalidated the structure of the Consumer Financial Protection

[56] See *Securities and Exchange Commission v Chenery Corp* (1947) 332 US 194.

[57] 5 USC §706.

[58] *Chevron USA, Inc v Natural Resources Defense Council* (1984) 467 US 837; *Auer v Robbins* (1997) 519 US 452. The *Chevron* methodology that requires a court to defer to an agency's reasonable interpretation of ambiguous statutory language is under sustained attack and might be overruled by the Supreme Court during the 2023–24 term. *See Loper Bright Enterprises v Raimondo*, 45 F4th 359 (DC Cir 2022), *cert granted*, 143 S Ct 2429 (2023).

[59] *United States v Arthrex, Inc* (2021) 141 S Ct 1970.

[60] *Lucia v Securities and Exchange Commission* (2018) 138 S Ct 2033.

Board because the President could not remove the one-person head of the agency without cause.[61]

Lower courts have been even more aggressive in attacking combined-function agencies. In the *Jarkesy* case[62] the Federal Court of Appeal in New Orleans invalidated an SEC adjudicatory decision imposing a monetary penalty for securities fraud on a regulated hedge fund operator and investment advisor. The grounds were that (i) the respondent was denied a jury trial to which he was entitled under the Seventh Amendment to the Constitution, (ii) the non-delegation doctrine prohibited giving the SEC power to decide whether it should proceed through internal adjudication or through seeking the same remedy in a federal court, and (iii) the SEC's ALJ's are unconstitutionally protected from being removed without cause. All these holdings represent a sharp break from established law.[63] Whether the US Supreme Court will follow any or all of the *Jarkesy* holdings remains to be seen, but the decision is momentous and indicates the level of hostility in conservative legal circles to combined-function regulatory agencies.

Tribunals in the US

The design of every jurisdiction's administrative adjudicatory system resists being compressed into a single model. There are exceptions to every generalisation. The design of a particular adjudication system is shaped by historical circumstances, legal culture and political struggle, rather than by legal theory or by mechanically following existing models. In the US, for example, there are numerous Model 3 tribunals, meaning adjudicating agencies that provide reconsideration of agency initial decisions that are independent of agency prosecutors or agency personnel that manage benefit programmes.[64] In addition, there are examples in the US of open judicial review (Model 4) and specialised administrative courts (Model 5) but these variations from the norm are not discussed in this chapter.[65]

United States Tax Court

The Internal Revenue Service ('IRS') is the federal tax collecting agency. It audits tax returns and asserts tax deficiencies. Most tax deficiency disputes are settled by

[61] *Seila Law LLC v Consumer Financial Protection Bureau* (2020) 140 S Ct 2183.

[62] *Jarkesy v Securities and Exchange Commission* (5th Cir 2022) 34 F 4th 446. The Court of Appeals declined rehearing by a vote of 10-6. (5th Cir 2022) 51 F 4th 644. The Supreme Court has granted a petition for certiorari in the *Jarkesy* case and is expected to issue a decision during 2024.

[63] See *Atlas Roofing Co v Occupational Safety & Health Review Comm'n* (1977) 430 US 442 (holding that the right to a jury trial does not apply to civil penalties imposed by administrative agency).

[64] See Gifford (n 27).

[65] See *Five Models* (n 2) at 14–15.

the IRS' Office of Appeals, but some disputes remain. Although there are alternative venues, almost all these cases are resolved by the Tax Court, because taxpayers can litigate the tax issues before paying the disputed tax. The Tax Court is esteemed by tax professionals for its expertise, fairness and efficiency in resolving cases. It is independent of the IRS and thus should be considered a Model 3 tribunal.

The Tax Court consists of 19 judges who preside over adversarial evidentiary hearings in tax cases. The judges are appointed by the President and subject to confirmation by the Senate and can only be removed for good cause.[66] The Tax Court also appoints Special Trial Judges who hear small tax cases under a less formal procedure.[67] Appeals of Tax Court decisions go to the Federal Court of Appeal located in the taxpayer's home area. These appellate courts provide closed review of Tax Court decisions and apply a clearly erroneous standard to the review of its fact findings. Decisions of the Special Trial Judges are not subject to judicial review.

Until 1942, review of IRS tax decisions was provided by an internal unit of the IRS called the Board of Tax Appeals. In 1942, Congress created an agency called the Tax Court that was separated from the IRS. In 1969, the Tax Court became a 'legislative court' under Article I of the Constitution, which is a somewhat anomalous status.[68] Although the Supreme Court referred to the Tax Court as a 'court of law'[69] it is not within the judicial branch nor is it subject to the authority of the bodies that establish procedures for the federal courts.[70] Its budget is provided annually by Congress separately from any other court or agency.

Executive Office of Immigration Review

The Executive Office for Immigration Review ('EOIR')[71] consists of the Immigration Court ('IC') and the Board of Immigration Appeals ('BIA'). EOIR adjudicates a wide range of cases involving immigration law, including asylum claims and issues relating to removal of undocumented aliens. EOIR employs hundreds of Immigration Judges ('IJs').

EOIR engages only in adjudication and is thus a Model 3 tribunal. The IC and BIA are organisationally separate from the immigration investigators and

[66] 26 USC §§7443, 7453.

[67] 26 USC §§7443A, 7463.

[68] See W Baude, 'Adjudication Outside Article III' (2020) 133 *Harvard Law Review* 1511, 1563–67; *Kuretzky v Commissioner* (DC Cir 2014) 755 F 3d 929.

[69] *Freytag v Commissioner* (1991) 501 US 868.

[70] See L Lederman, 'Tax Appeal: A Proposal to Make the United States Tax Court More Judicial' (2008) 85 *Washington University Law Review* 1196 (criticising the insularity and lack of transparency of the Tax Court); BJ Hellwig, 'The Constitutional Nature of the United States Tax Court' (2016) 35 *Virginia Tax Review* 269.

[71] See Note, 'Courts in Name Only: Repairing America's Immigration Adjudication System' (2023) 136 *Harvard Law Review* 908 (hereinafter *Courts in Name Only*); ACUS Type B report (n 50).

prosecutors, who work for Customs and Border Protection ('CBP') which is a unit of the cabinet-level Department of Homeland Security ('DHS'). CBP renders initial decisions in immigration cases using Type C adjudication.[72] IC conducts adversarial Type B trial-type hearings that provide *de novo* merits reconsideration of CPB's initial decisions. BIA provides appeals from IC decisions.

Although EOIR was separated from the immigration enforcement agency (now CBP) in 1983, it does not satisfy generally accepted standards of tribunal independence. EOIR is an agency of the Department of Justice ('DOJ'), headed by the Attorney General of the United States. The DOJ is a prosecutorial agency and the Attorney General (a member of the President's cabinet) is the nation's chief prosecutor. The DOJ selects the IJs and sometimes has done so through politicised criteria.[73] Obviously, immigration issues are politically salient and US presidents need to seem tough on immigration. The Attorney General's control over EOIR reflects that political policy.[74]

The EOIR agencies are highly dysfunctional with overwhelming backlogs of undecided cases. The IJs are overworked and subject to decisional quotas. There are enormous decisional variations between various IJs.[75] BIA usually provides single-judge reconsiderations, most of which rubber-stamp the IC decision under review. IJs are vulnerable to at-will dismissal if the DOJ disapproves of their rulings; obviously at-will removal severely compromises the independence of the IJs.[76] Academic commentators have urged that the IC and BIA become a true tribunal, free of the influence of prosecuting agencies, but this is unlikely to occur.[77]

State and Local Benefit Tribunals

US states administer a wide variety of employment benefit programmes, including unemployment compensation and workers' compensation (which provides compensation for injuries incurred in the course of employment). Agencies administer these programmes and collect a tax or an insurance premium imposed on employers. Applications for both unemployment and workers' compensation can be denied, while benefits can be revoked for various reasons. Most states utilise tribunals that are independent of the agency administering the programme. The tribunals provide a process of reconsideration of initial decisions rendered by

[72] *Courts in Name Only* (n 71); J Ramji-Nogales, AI Schoenholtz and PG Schrag, 'Refugee Roulette: Disparities in Asylum Adjudication' (2007) 60 *Stanford Law Review* 295, 305–10 (2007); Taylor (n 39), 482–83.

[73] *Courts in Name Only* (n 71), at 910–11.

[74] ibid at 912–17.

[75] Ramji-Nogales (n 72); Taylor (n 39).

[76] NS Tashovski, 'Immigration Judge Independence Under Attack: A Call to Re-Evaluate the Current Method of IJ Appointment and Create a Separate Immigration Court System' (2022) 19 *Hastings Race & Poverty Law Review* 173, 177–91.

[77] *Courts in Name Only* (n 71).

the administering agencies that deny or revoke benefits.[78] The tribunals conduct adversarial hearings and have large caseloads. Generally, judicial review of the decisions of these benefit tribunals lies in courts of general jurisdiction on a closed record.

Federal Tribunals: Mine Safety and Occupational Safety

Several federal statutes create administrative systems that provide for occupational health and safety as well as mine health and safety. These statutes create independent tribunals to provide reconsideration of initial decisions imposing penalties on employers rendered by the agencies that administer these systems and prosecute violations of their regulations. The Occupational Safety and Health Review Commission ('OSHRC') reviews initial decisions relating to worker safety made by the Occupational Safety and Health Administration ('OSHA').[79] The Mine Safety and Health Review Commission reviews initial decisions of the Mine Safety and Health Administration. Congress created this split-enforcement model as a political compromise because employers feared lodging the adjudicatory function in the same agency as the enforcement function.[80]

An early article studied the split-enforcement model.[81] It concluded that the separation of enforcement and adjudication created serious turf battles between the enforcement and adjudicating agencies, although these have abated since a Supreme Court decision required courts to defer to legal interpretations of the enforcement agency rather than those of the adjudicating agency.[82]

Conclusion

The US administrative adjudication system at state and federal levels is complex and contains numerous design variations. It is fair to say that the combined-function model is the default arrangement, whether the agency adjudication is Type A (meaning it is covered by the APA), Type B (meaning the agency is required to provide evidentiary hearings but is not covered by the APA), or Type C (meaning the agency does not employ evidentiary hearings and generally uses inquisitorial rather than adversarial procedure).

[78] Thus California, Florida, New Jersey and New York all make use of independent tribunals to provide reconsideration of initial decisions denying benefits in workers' compensation and unemployment compensation cases.

[79] See Gifford (n 34) at 1000-03.

[80] GR Johnson, Jr, 'The Split-Enforcement Model: Some Conclusions from the OSHA and MSHA Experiences' (1987) 39 *Administrative Law Review* 315.

[81] ibid.

[82] *Martin v Occupational Health & Safety Review Commission* (1991) 499 US 1441.

Under the combined-function system, an agency investigates and prosecutes a case and makes the frontline decision denying a benefit application or a licence or imposing a regulatory sanction. The same agency then makes the initial decision in the case and provides reconsideration of that decision. In Type A and B adjudication, statutes or regulations impose a complex system of internal separation of functions to counteract the potential institutional bias inherent in a combined-function system.

The US employs some tribunals that are independent of the agency that engages in law enforcement or in administration of benefit programmes. These tribunals adjudicate disputes about federal taxation, immigration, worker and mine safety and state employment benefits. These US tribunals have worked well and generally are approved of by their stakeholders. The Immigration Court is an exception; it is dysfunctional and is controlled by Department of Justice prosecutors (even though it is separate from the immigration enforcement agencies).

Tribunals have been widely viewed as successful models for the adjudication of disputes between government and private parties. In contrast, US combined-function agencies inspire little confidence and are currently the subject of sustained legal and academic criticism. This suggests that the US should continue to experiment with independent tribunals to provide reconsideration of agency initial decisions.

11

Administrative Tribunals in Canada: Constitutional Subordinates or Equal Partners?

PAUL DALY

Introduction

Shortly before 8pm on 29 January 2017, Alexandre Bissonnette stormed into the Grand Mosque of Quebec. Armed with a Glock pistol and a semi-automatic rifle, he entered the prayer room and opened fire, killing six worshippers and injuring five. He fled the scene but later gave himself up to police. In the days and weeks leading up to the attack, Bissonnette had avidly consumed extremist Islamophobic content on the Internet. As unattractive an accused as could be imagined, Bissonnette pleaded guilty to six counts of first-degree murder and six counts of attempted murder. Under the law on the books at the time, the sentencing judge was compelled to impose consecutive sentences of 25 years without possibility of parole: Bissonnette was thus to be jailed for 150 years, with no prospect of early release.

The question that occupied the sentencing judge, the Court of Appeal and, ultimately, the Supreme Court of Canada was whether the mandatory imposition of consecutive sentences amounted to 'cruel and unusual treatment or punishment' in contravention of the Charter of Rights and Freedoms.

Unanimously, the Supreme Court held that sentences of longer than 25 years without the possibility of parole constitute cruel and unusual punishment, a violation of s 12 of the Charter. For Wagner CJ, the core problem was that such sentences 'are degrading in nature and thus incompatible with human dignity', on the basis that an offender is denied 'any possibility of reintegration into society, which presupposes, definitively and irreversibly, that they lack the capacity to reform and re-enter society'.[1] Therefore, for any sentencing regime to be constitutional, it must allow for the possibility of parole after 25 years, as to which the

[1] 2022 SCC 23, para 76.

Parole Board is the 'ultimate arbiter'.[2] Although Wagner CJ did not put the point in these terms, the effect of his analysis is to create a constitutional right of access to an administrative tribunal, which will determine independently and impartially whether and on what conditions an offender should be released.[3]

It is useful at this point to consider Wagner CJ's comments about the possibility that the royal prerogative of mercy – a discretionary power to commute sentences, exercisable by the Attorney General – could be used to alleviate the harsh consequences of long sentences and thus serve as a constitutional safety valve. As a 'release mechanism based on compassion and on the existence of humanitarian grounds', the prerogative created 'no realistic possibility of parole for offenders serving a sentence of imprisonment for life for which there is no other review mechanism'.[4] As such, the prerogative of mercy could not function as a safety valve to ensure justice in a potentially unjust regime.

Bissonnette presents a striking contrast between an independent and impartial tribunal (the Parole Board), constitutionally necessary to avoid a conclusion that a lengthy sentence constitutes cruel and unusual punishment, and a ministerial discretion (the royal prerogative of mercy), incapable of remedying systemic problems in an administrative regime because of its exceptional, highly discretionary nature. Independent and impartial tribunals are good; executive discretion is to be distrusted.

But *Bissonnette* is thereby in tension with the Supreme Court's jurisprudence on the constitutional position of administrative tribunals. For in the leading case of *Ocean Port Hotel*, Wagner CJ's predecessor as Chief Justice of Canada, Beverley McLachlin, insisted that administrative tribunals have no constitutional status at all. Unlike courts, administrative tribunals lack 'constitutional distinction from the executive', as they are 'created precisely for the purpose of implementing government policy'.[5] Because of this 'primary policy-making function',[6] it is properly 'Parliament or the legislature that determines the nature of a tribunal's relationship to the executive'.[7] Indeed, given administrative tribunals' subordinate status, their enabling statutes are conclusive as to the degree of independence members enjoy in any given instance: 'The statute must be construed as a whole to determine the degree of independence the legislature intended.'[8]

On the one hand, in *Ocean Port Hotel*, administrative tribunals are seen as – effectively – a branch of the executive. On the other hand, in *Bissonnette*, an administrative tribunal is seen as the antithesis of executive discretion, capable of playing a valuable role at arm's length from the political branches. Canadian law on

[2] ibid para 138.
[3] ibid para 147.
[4] ibid para 118.
[5] *Ocean Port Hotel Ltd v British Columbia (General Manager, Liquor Control and Licensing Branch)*, 2001 SCC 52, [2001] 2 SCR 781, para 24.
[6] ibid para 24.
[7] ibid para 22.
[8] ibid para 20.

administrative tribunals is marked by this tension, with their subordinate constitutional status conflicting with their role as independent and impartial adjudicators of disputes between citizens and the state.

In this chapter, I explore this tension. In Part I, I provide a general overview of administrative tribunals in Canada, describing their infinite variety, highly variable procedures and structures and flexible appointment mechanisms. In Part II, I develop the *Ocean Port Hotel* line of thinking on the subordinate constitutional position of administrative tribunals. The focus here is on administrative tribunals as institutions. There is a link between Parts I and II, because the variety of administrative tribunals seems to have contributed to judicial reluctance to impose constitutional requirements of independence that might limit legislative creativity. However, notwithstanding the reticence of the judiciary to robustly protect the independence of administrative tribunals as institutions, the importance of administrative tribunals in the Canadian legal system is nonetheless manifest. In Part III, I introduce the important legal principles that give administrative tribunals a more elevated status than the jurisprudence on their constitutional position suggests. Indeed, administrative tribunals are in many ways equal partners of courts of law in the interpretation and application of legal norms. In this Part, the focus is more on the members of administrative tribunals than on administrative tribunals *qua* institutions. I will conclude by offering some critical analysis on the tension: the tension could be resolved, I argue, by granting administrative tribunals constitutional status but it is not necessary to resolve the tension; Canadian administrative tribunals can continue to be constitutionally subordinate but equal partners to courts of law in the interpretation and application of legal norms. The position is unattractive as a matter of principle but sustainable as a matter of practice.

An Overview of Administrative Tribunals in Canada

It has been said that administrative tribunals are like Cleopatra: age cannot wither them, nor stale their infinite variety.[9] This is certainly true of Canada. A variety of adjudicative bodies can be grouped under the heading of administrative tribunals, their procedures and structures vary significantly from province to province, and the regimes for appointment and reappointment of members are also highly variable.

Types of Adjudicative Body

Any Canadian lawyer would freely admit that an administrative tribunal can have adversarial, inquisitorial, regulatory or mediative functions, or any mix of these four.

[9] G Hogan, D Gwynn Morgan and P Daly, *Administrative Law in Ireland* (Roundhall, 2019) 6–10.

Sometimes a tribunal is *adversarial*, with two parties pitted against each other. The classic example in Canadian law is the labour relations tribunal, featuring employers on one side and employees on the other. Another familiar example is the human rights tribunal, entities that have the authority to hear and determine claims of discrimination. In both instances, a government actor might be a party, as government is sometimes an employer and sometimes alleged to have engaged in discriminatory conduct. However, the essence of the tribunal's role is to independently and impartially adjudicate a dispute between two parties 'to find facts, to interpret and apply the law to the facts before it, and to award appropriate remedies' through a hearing process with 'much the same structure as a formal trial before a court'.[10]

Other tribunals are better described as *inquisitorial*, with an adjudicator eliciting evidence from a party to make an informed judgement about the party's status. The classic example here is provided by the first-instance decision-makers at the Immigration and Refugee Board, who have the authority to make determinations about refugee and immigration status. As has been explained, '[t]he role of members of the Refugee Division at a hearing is characterized as inquisitorial since they not only hear the evidence which is presented before them but must also inform themselves sufficiently about the applicants and the conditions in their country of origin'.[11] The Chair of the Immigration and Refugee Board has exercised his statutory authority to issue guidelines about the conduct of first-instance refugee hearings and has explained the inquisitorial nature of the process in unequivocal terms. Refugee adjudicators 'may inquire into anything they consider relevant to establishing whether a claim is well-founded' and, accordingly, 'define what issues must be resolved in order for them to render a decision' and '[decide] and [give] directions as to how a hearing is to proceed'.[12] Indeed, refugee adjudicators are empowered to seek out evidence to ensure a fair determination of a refugee claim.[13] Simply put, the adjudicator has 'the task of probing the legitimacy of claims'.[14]

Still other tribunals can be characterised as *regulatory* in character. The most obvious examples come from various fields of economic activity, where prices or rates are fixed, for instance the energy, telecommunications and agricultural sectors. Regulatory tribunals will sometimes 'have a function that is investigative, prosecutorial and adjudicative' as it is only bodies equipped with these three powers 'that can be expected to regulate adequately complex or monopolistic industries

[10] *Bell Canada v Canadian Telephone Employees Association*, 2003 SCC 36, [2003] 1 SCR 884, para 23.

[11] *Sivasamboo v Canada (Minister of Citizenship and Immigration)* [1995] 1 FC 741 (TD) 757.

[12] Immigration and Refugee Board, *Chairperson Guidelines 7: Concerning Preparation and Conduct of a Hearing in the Refugee Protection Division* (December, 2006; Amended December, 2012), §§2.1, 2.2.

[13] Immigration and Refugee Board, *Instructions for Gathering and Disclosing Information for Refugee Protection Division Proceedings* (September, 2008; Amended December, 2012).

[14] *Thamotharem v Canada (Minister of Citizenship and Immigration)*, 2007 FCA 198, [2008] 1 FCR 385, para 35.

that supply essential services'.[15] Regulatory tribunals will often have a mixture of functions, some purely regulatory, some inquisitorial or adjudicative. The Canadian Nuclear Safety Commission, for instance, determines whether licences should be granted and also adjudicates on the imposition of administrative monetary penalties for breaches of licence conditions or regulatory requirements.[16] Similarly, the Canadian Radio-television and Telecommunications Commission has rate-setting jurisdiction but may also adjudicate disputes between regulated entities.[17]

Lastly, some tribunals are *mediative*, in the sense that their role is to avoid the adjudication of disputes. The leading example is British Columbia's Civil Resolution Tribunal. Originally envisaged as a 'voluntary tribunal',[18] successive 'waves' of legislative reform have created an extensive online dispute resolution jurisdiction.[19] The 'mandate' of the CRT is set out in s 2 of the *Civil Resolution Tribunal Act* and emphasises accessibility, efficiency, informality and flexibility.[20] As the inaugural Chair of the CRT stated, this innovative body 'inverts the traditional public justice process model by assuming that disputes can be resolved consensually, with the right assistance and expertise'.[21] In brief, the CRT's online Solution Explorer allows individuals to determine whether they have a justiciable dispute within the CRT's jurisdiction. The next stage offers the parties an opportunity for negotiation; if these efforts fail to bear fruit, an expert facilitator is appointed who can use a variety of communications methods to lead the parties to a consensual settlement. If settlement cannot be achieved, the matter is prepared (with the ongoing assistance of the expert facilitator) for a tribunal hearing.[22]

The CRT is just the clearest manifestation of the access-to-justice *Zeitgeist* in Canadian administrative law.[23] Many, if not most, administrative tribunals now offer alternative dispute resolution services, to avoid having to adjudicate matters.[24] Of course, there is never anything new under the sun. Despite the apparent novelty of alternative dispute resolution, mediative approaches have long been adopted in supply management for agricultural products. In Canada, government intervention in agriculture is pronounced, with prices for a variety of dairy, meat

[15] *Newfoundland Telephone Co v Newfoundland (Board of Commissioners of Public Utilities)*, [1992] 1 SCR 623, 634–5.

[16] *Nuclear Safety and Control Act*, SC 1997, c 9, ss 40, 65.01 *et seq.*

[17] See, eg, Broadcasting Decision CRTC 2023-22, *Complaint by Bell Media against Videotron alleging undue disadvantage and preference regarding the distribution of VRAK and Z.*

[18] British Columbia, *Hansard*, 39th Parl, 4th Sess, 8 May 2012 at 11686 (Hon S Bond).

[19] P Daly et al, *A Comparative Analysis of Online Dispute Resolution* (International Legal Aid Group, 2019) 64.

[20] SBC 2012, c 25.

[21] S Salter, 'Online Dispute Resolution and Justice System Integration: British Columbia's Civil Resolution Tribunal' (2017) 34 *Windsor Yearbook of Access to Justice* 112, 123.

[22] ibid 120–21; Daly et al., *A Comparative Analysis of Online Dispute Resolution* (International Legal Aid Group, 2019) 72–8.

[23] *Access to Civil & Family Justice: A Roadmap for Change* (Ottawa, October, 2013) 2.

[24] See, eg, the enabling provision in the *Statutory Powers Procedure Act*, RSO 1990, c S.22, s 4.8. See also *Administrative Tribunals Act*, SBC 2004, c 45, s 28.

and vegetables set by official agencies. In some instances, binding law provides that prices shall be negotiated between industry stakeholders.[25]

Variable Procedures

That administrative tribunals perform different functions implies that the procedures used will vary. What suits an adversarial tribunal is less likely to work for an inquisitorial or regulatory tribunal and decidedly unlikely to facilitate the efforts of a mediative tribunal. Sure enough, Canadian courts have recognised that as a matter of common law the requirements of procedural fairness will vary from tribunal to tribunal, looser at the 'executive end of the spectrum' where the 'primary purpose is to develop, or supervise the implementation of, particular government policies' but tighter at the 'judicial end of the spectrum' where the primary purpose 'is to adjudicate disputes through some form of hearing'.[26]

Accordingly, whereas the demands of procedural fairness press heaviest on adversarial tribunals, others have more flexibility: an inquisitorial tribunal has significant autonomy as far as the order of presentation of evidence is concerned,[27] for instance, and the requirements in relation to reasonable apprehension of bias are more relaxed for sectoral representatives who serve on regulatory tribunals.[28]

Statute law also recognises the variability of administrative tribunals. When one turns to statutory requirements, there is again significant variability. Evidently, each and every administrative tribunal might have particular provisions relating to procedure in its parent statute. However, even framework legislation designed to deliver a degree of uniformity leaves significant scope for deviation from prescribed statutory baselines; as one might expect in a federation, the frameworks themselves vary significantly from province to province. Federally, there is no framework legislation at all, with federal administrative tribunals left entirely to their own devices.

Let us start on the east coast, with Ontario's Statutory Powers Procedure Act.[29] Section 3(1) establishes the scope of the SPPA, applicable to 'a proceeding by a tribunal in the exercise of a statutory power of decision … where the tribunal is required … to hold or to afford to the parties to the proceeding an opportunity for a hearing before making a decision'. The term 'tribunal' is also defined by reference to the concept of a 'statutory power of decision'. Whether 'an opportunity for a hearing' is required is determined as a matter of common law. This 'formula'[30]

[25] See, eg, *R.R.O. 1990, Reg. 402: Chickens – Marketing*, art 17.

[26] *Bell Canada v Canadian Telephone Employees Association*, 2003 SCC 36, [2003] 1 SCR 884, para 21.

[27] See eg, *Thamotharem v Canada (Minister of Citizenship and Immigration)*, 2007 FCA 198, [2008] 1 FCR 385.

[28] See eg, *Newfoundland Telephone Co v Newfoundland (Board of Commissioners of Public Utilities)*, [1992] 1 SCR 623.

[29] RSO 1990, s 22.

[30] D Mullan, *Administrative Law* (Irwin Law, 2001), 215.

turns on whether the tribunal must act quasi-judicially.[31] Accordingly, any administrative tribunal in Ontario that is required to hold a hearing is subject to the SPPA. The SPPA sets out a series of baseline requirements in respect of notice (s 6), public hearings (s 9), representation (s 10), admissibility of evidence (s 15), judicial notice (s 16) and written decisions (s 17). However, significant discretion is built into the SPPA, expressly and implicitly. Several provisions expressly contemplate the exercise of discretion by administrative tribunals on a case-by-case basis, in relation to adjournments (s 21) and cross examination (s 23(2)). Other provisions contemplate administrative tribunals making their own rules of procedure to provide for more flexible forms of hearing – in writing (s 5.1) or electronically (s 5.2) – and less rigid approaches to disclosure (s 5.4), costs (s 17.1) and reconsideration of a final decision (s 21.2(1)). Put simply, the SPPA is a template but one that allows for significant modifications by administrative tribunals to suit their own purposes.

On the west coast there is an even more permissive statute in British Columbia, the *Administrative Tribunals Act*.[32] For the purposes of this statute, an administrative tribunal is simply 'a tribunal to which some or all of the provisions of this Act are made applicable'.[33] Section 11 vests administrative tribunals with the discretion to 'make rules respecting practice and procedure to facilitate the just and timely resolution of the matters before [them]'. The *Administrative Tribunals Act* also contains a power to make practice directives.[34] There is even a power to make powers: a tribunal may, 'to facilitate the just and timely resolution of an application' make any order 'in relation to any matter that the tribunal considers necessary for purposes of controlling its own proceedings'.[35] Admittedly, there are other more prescriptive provisions relating to matters such as the compulsion of witnesses and disclosure (s 34), the examination of witnesses (s 38) and adjournments (s 39), but even here the provisions vest considerable discretion in the tribunal.[36] Again, there is significant scope for the tribunal to shape its procedures to its own ends.

Lastly, amongst the provinces, it is worth considering, the *Act respecting administrative justice*,[37] the framework statute for the civil law province of Quebec. In civilian style, the legislation begins by prescribing general principles.[38] First, procedural fairness: 'The procedures leading to an individual decision to be made by the Administration, pursuant to norms or standards prescribed by law, in respect of a citizen shall be conducted in keeping with the duty to act fairly'.[39]

[31] *Re Abel et al and Advisory Review Board* (1980) 119 DLR (3d) 101 (Ont CA).
[32] SBC 2004, c 45.
[33] ibid s 1.
[34] ibid s 13. Some practice directives, in relation to time limits, must be made but the tribunal 'is not bound by its practice directives in the exercise of its powers or the performance of its duties' (s 12(2)).
[35] ibid s 14(c).
[36] ibid ss 34(3), 38(2), 39(2).
[37] CQLR c J-3.
[38] See F Houle, 'A Brief Historical Account of the Reforms to the Administrative Justice System in the Province of Québec' (2009) 22 *Canadian Journal of Administrative Law and Practice* 47, 50–1.
[39] ibid s 2.

Second, procedures and relevant information must be communicated clearly to the citizen.[40] Then, more specifically, the citizen has a right to be given notice of adverse decisions (s 5), to disclosure (s 6), to make representations (s 7) and to written reasons (s 8). And more specifically again, in respect of administrative tribunals, adjudication must be impartial (s 9), involve a hearing (s 10) including meaningful participation by the parties (s 12) and be followed by written reasons (s 13). However, the precise specification of the content of these rights is left to administrative tribunals, which are obliged to set out 'simple and flexible rules devoid of formalism, with respect, prudence and promptness, in accordance with the norms and standards of ethics and discipline governing its agents and with the requirements of good faith'.[41] Although the template differs in Quebec – following the civilian style – the ultimate result is the same: administrative tribunals have significant autonomy and flexibility when shaping their procedures.

Variable Organisational Structure and Composition

A similar story can be told about the organisational structures for administrative tribunals. The starting point is that each administrative tribunal is a discrete statutory creation, with its own legislative mandate and suite of powers. All matters of 'composition and structure' of administrative tribunals are the preserve of the legislature[42] and, as such, each tribunal is somewhat ad hoc. To take one example amongst many, the Immigration and Refugee Board is constituted by the *Immigration and Refugee Protection Act*, which exhaustively describes its composition and structure.[43] Nonetheless, there have been some legislative interventions seeking to ensure a level of consistency at the level of organisational structure and composition.

Organisational Structure

In Ontario, the guiding principle of the *Adjudicative Tribunals Accountability, Governance and Appointments Act, 2009*[44] is 'clustering'.[45] The provincial cabinet is empowered to group administrative tribunals together where 'the matters that the tribunals deal with are such that they can operate more effectively and efficiently as part of a cluster than alone'.[46] The idea was to promote 'flexibility and dynamism,

[40] ibid s 4.
[41] ibid s 4(1).
[42] *Ocean Port Hotel Ltd v British Columbia (General Manager, Liquor Control and Licensing Branch)*, 2001 SCC 52, [2001] 2 SCR 781, para 24.
[43] SC 2001, c 27, Part 4.
[44] SO 2009, c 33, Sch 5.
[45] The British Columbia legislation also provides for clustering though it seems that no administrative tribunals in the province have been clustered as yet: *Administrative Tribunals Act*, SBC 2004, c 45, s 10.1.
[46] ibid s 15.

with clusters afforded the freedom to develop their own organizational cultures and institutional mandates tailored to the particular needs, demands and capacities of the tribunals' users groups and memberships'.[47] Synergies across administrative tribunals with similar subject-matter expertise were expected to emerge, improving 'the quality of services offered to the public by sharing resources, expertise and administrative and professional support'.[48] In practice, however, the experience has been decidedly mixed. Initially, several clusters were created – one for environment and land use, one for social justice and one for public safety – but now there is only one large cluster known as Tribunals Ontario.[49] The province's tribunal structure has been beset by delays[50] and allegations of sub-par decision-making:[51] these are perhaps not attributable to the clustering principle but equally the clustering principle did little to prevent them.

Quebec, meanwhile, adopted a super-tribunal model.[52] The *Act respecting administrative justice* establishes the Administrative Tribunal of Quebec, organised into four divisions. The social affairs division deals with 'matters of income security or support and social aid and allowances, of protection of persons whose mental state presents a danger to themselves or to others, of health services and social services, of pension plans, of compensation and of immigration.'[53] Matters relating to real property, such as calculation of compensation for expropriation and of land values for municipal taxation, are the preserve of the immovable property division.[54] The territory and environment division is responsible for land-use and waste management decisions.[55] The economic affairs division, meanwhile, has jurisdiction over 'decisions concerning permits, licences, certificates or authorizations to carry on a trade or a professional, economic, industrial or commercial activity'.[56] Notice, however, that not every administrative tribunal in Quebec falls under the aegis of the Administrative Tribunal of Quebec. Labour relations, human rights and professional discipline each have their own bespoke administrative tribunal structure. In the end, despite the different starting points – clustering in one province, a super-tribunal in the other – Quebec and Ontario have ended up in similar positions, organisationally speaking.

[47] L Sossin and J Baxter, 'Ontario's Administrative Tribunal Clusters: A Glass Half-Full or Half-Empty for Administrative Justice?' (2012) 12 *Oxford University Commonwealth Law Journal* 157, 160.

[48] Kevin Whitaker, *Final Report of the Agency Cluster Facilitator for the Municipal, Environment and Land Planning Tribunals* (Minister of Government Services, 2007) 6.

[49] O Reg 126/10: *Adjudicative Tribunals and Clusters.*

[50] Tribunals Ontario, 'Tribunals Ontario Statement on Ombudsman Ontario's Investigation into Delays at the Landlord and Tenant Board' (4 May 2023).

[51] Tribunal Watch Ontario, 'The Human Rights Tribunal of Ontario: What Needs to Happen' (15 January 2023).

[52] R Ellis, 'Super Provincial Tribunals: A Radical Remedy for Canada's Rights Tribunals' (2002) 15 *Canadian Journal of Administrative Law and Practice* 15, 19.

[53] *Act respecting administrative justice*, CQLR c J-3, s 18. The mental health functions are performed by a division within the social affairs division known as the mental health division: ss 19, 22, 22.1.

[54] ibid s 32.

[55] ibid s 34.

[56] ibid s 36.

At the federal level, there is a statutory umbrella organisation known as the Administrative Tribunals Support Service of Canada. The statute creating the organisation is somewhat skeletal but nonetheless clearly expresses its *raison d'être* as the 'provision of the support services and the facilities that are needed by each of the [specified] administrative tribunals to exercise its powers and perform its duties and functions in accordance with the rules that apply to its work'.[57] The ATSSC does not have any operational control over tribunals – 'the chairperson of an administrative tribunal continues to have supervision over and direction of the work of the tribunal'[58] – but provides logistical support, such as web servers, secretarial services, teleconferencing facilities, legal analysis and review of draft decisions. It is probably not necessary to have statutory authority for an umbrella organisation of this nature – British Columbia's equivalent is an agency within the Ministry of the Attorney General[59] – as the ATSSC plays a coordinating and resourcing role and does not seek to control the day-to-day operations of administrative tribunals.

Composition

As with organisational structure, the composition of administrative tribunals is largely prescribed by the statute constituting the tribunal, as a brief survey of federal administrative tribunals illustrates. To take the Immigration and Refugee Board as an example again, the Board is overseen by a chairperson and '[such] other members as are required to ensure the proper functioning of the Board'.[60] The Board is divided into four sections, with first-instance and appellate tribunals given jurisdiction over refugee and immigration matters. The chairperson and appellate members are appointed by the federal cabinet for seven-year periods.[61] By contrast, first-instance members are appointed as members of the civil service.[62] Other federal administrative tribunals have different terms, methods of appointment and status. To take a random selection, the chairperson and vice-chairpersons of the Canada Industrial Relations Board are appointed by the federal cabinet for five-year terms[63] whereas ordinary members – who must be evenly split between employer and employee representatives[64] – can only serve three-year terms,[65] though there is expression provision for reappointment;[66] members of the Transportation Appeal Tribunal of Canada are all appointed by

[57] *Administrative Tribunals Support Service of Canada Act*, SC 2014, c 20, s 376, s 10.
[58] ibid s 14.
[59] See Government of British Columbia, 'Tribunal Transformation' (13 May 2023) describing the Tribunal and Agency Support Division.
[60] *Immigration and Refugee Protection Act*, SC 2001, c 27, s 152.
[61] ibid s 153(1)(a).
[62] ibid ss 169.1(2), 171(2).
[63] *Canada Labour Code*, RSC 1985, c L-2, s 10(1).
[64] ibid ss 9(2)(c), (d).
[65] ibid s 10(2).
[66] ibid s 12(1).

federal cabinet for seven years and may be reappointed;[67] and the Environmental Protection Tribunal of Canada draws its members from a 'roster' appointed by the Minister of the Environment (who is the protagonist in matters heard by the Tribunal) for renewable three-year terms.[68] Interestingly, there is no obvious difference between the appointment and reappointment provisions of these tribunals, which are adversarial or inquisitorial, and those of federal tribunals with regulatory functions.[69]

Government discretion in making administrative tribunal appointments and reappointments is close to absolute. Federally, there are no statutory constraints at all relating to appointment and reappointment. However, there is provision for security of tenure. One constant is that members can only be removed during their term for cause, which involves a procedurally demanding 'personalised inquiry'[70] into the factual basis for removal (though the federal cabinet is due significant deference on whether, as a matter of substance, removal is appropriate[71]).

Provincially, the most spectacular example of constraint-free discretion is found in Saskatchewan's Interpretation Act, s 20(1) of which permits an incoming government to immediately terminate, without cause, any appointment to an administrative tribunal.[72] When an incoming government duly terminated the appointments of the chair and vice-chair of the provincial labour relations tribunal, the Saskatchewan Court of Appeal reluctantly concluded that the government had acted lawfully, aptly describing this provision as 'extraordinary but clear'.[73]

Even where statutory constraints are provided for, they may, in practice, turn out to be paper tigers. Consider Ontario's *Adjudicative Tribunals Accountability, Governance and Appointments Act*.[74] Section 14(1) provides for a competitive, merit-based appointment process, including the development of criteria relating to subject-matter expertise and aptitude for adjudication. The responsible minister must, in addition, publish the criteria for this process.[75] However, the quality of tribunal appointments in Ontario has been subject to criticism, with the relative open-endedness of the statutory appointment criteria a particular target of critics: a vast pool of candidates will be capable of meeting these vague criteria, giving the provincial government a relatively free hand in making appointments.[76] In addition, the statutory criteria apply only to appointment not to reappointment and there is no statutorily-mandated term of appointment (such that a member can

[67] *Transportation Appeal Tribunal of Canada Act*, SC 2001, c 29, ss 6(1), (2).

[68] *Canadian Environmental Protection Act, 1999*, SC 1999, c 33, ss 243, 245.

[69] See, eg, *Canadian Radio-television and Telecommunications Commission Act*, RSC 1985, c C-22, s 3; *Nuclear Safety and Control Act*, SC 1997, c 9, s 10; *Canadian Energy Regulator Act*, SC 2019, c 28, s 10, ss 26, 28.

[70] *Vennat v Canada (Attorney General)*, 2006 FC 1008, [2007] 2 FCR 647, para 166.

[71] *Shoan v Canada (Attorney General)*, 2018 FC 476, para 91.

[72] SS 1995, c I-11.2.

[73] *Saskatchewan Federation of Labour v Saskatchewan*, 2010 SKCA 27, para 53.

[74] 2009, SO 2009, c 33, Sch 5. See also *Administrative Tribunals Act*, SBC 2004, c 45, s 2.

[75] ibid s 14(3).

[76] Tribunal Watch Ontario, 'Statement of Concern about Tribunals Ontario' (14 May, 2020).

be appointed for a very short period of time). Generally speaking, appointments to administrative tribunals are seen by provincial governments as opportunities for political patronage or (albeit less often) for furthering ideological or partisan agendas.[77]

Amongst the Canadian provinces, Quebec is an outlier. Members of the Administrative Tribunal of Quebec are appointed until retirement age subject to good behaviour,[78] which is overseen by an independent administrative justice commission that operates at arm's length from the government.[79] Other administrative tribunal members are not so lucky. Uniquely, however, Quebec has a quasi-constitutional guarantee of tribunal independence, meaning that the reappointment and removal processes are subject to strong procedural and substantive guarantees. No other province has made similar provision for the protection of the independence of administrative tribunals.

I have described the variety of organisation and practices of administrative tribunals in Canada at some length in part to give the reader a suitable overview (as befits a contribution to an edited contribution of this nature). But my description also provides important context for the discussion in the next Part of the constitutional status of administrative tribunals in Canada. Put simply, the variability of administrative tribunals has contributed to judicial reluctance to put administrative independence on any sort of constitutional footing.

The Subordinate Constitutional Position of Administrative Tribunals

There are three aspects to the subordinate constitutional position of administrative tribunals in Canada. By subordinate, I mean that administrative tribunals have no distinct constitutional status: they are subordinate to courts of law, in that courts of law have constitutionally enshrined guarantees of judicial independence; they are subordinate to the executive, in that they are seen primarily as instruments for giving effect to policy choices; and they are subordinate to legislatures, in that statute sets out the structure and composition of administrative tribunals.

In the first subsection, I will address the relative constitutional position of administrative tribunals and courts of law. In the second subsection, I will turn to the relationship between administrative tribunals and the political branches of government.

[77] See, generally, R Ellis, *Unjust by Design* (University of British Columbia Press, 2013). Admittedly, the same has often been alleged in respect of judicial appointments, both federally (*Democracy Watch v Canada (Attorney General)*, 2023 FC 31) and provincially (Michel Bastarache, *Rapport de la Commission d'enquête sur le processus de nomination des juges de la Cour du Québec, des cours municipales et les membres du Tribunal administratif du Québec* (Les publications du Québec, 2011).

[78] *Act respecting administrative justice*, CQLR c J-3, s 38.

[79] ibid Title III.

The Absence of a Constitutional Guarantee of Administrative Tribunal Independence

In order to understand the constitutional principles (or lack thereof) relating to administrative independence, it is necessary to begin with judicial independence.

Canadian judicial officers benefit from a constitutional guarantee of judicial independence. Their security of tenure, financial security and administrative autonomy is grounded in the constitution: they can only be removed through a process at arm's length from the government of the day; their salaries are set by governments on recommendations (not to be lightly deviated from) by an independent commission; and they must have the necessary resources to run their affairs free from day-to-day interference by the executive.[80]

This constitutional guarantee was litigated extensively in the 1980s and 1990s. In a first wave of cases in the 1980s, the courts concluded that judges exercising criminal jurisdiction benefited from a constitutional guarantee of independence: the *Charter of Rights and Freedoms* promises accused persons the right to trial before an independent and impartial tribunal and provides that individuals shall not be deprived of their liberty otherwise than by an independent and impartial tribunal. By the end of the 1990s, it was established that *all* judicial officers benefited from this constitutional guarantee, based in the Preamble and judicature provisions of the Constitution Act, 1867.

The details of the judicial independence cases do not concern us here other than to provide useful context for an analysis of the constitutional position of administrative tribunals. The case law on judicial independence posed an obvious question: if administrative tribunals were performing similar functions to courts, should they not also benefit from a constitutional guarantee of independence? Indeed, in a couple of decisions, the Supreme Court of Canada posited that the same hallmarks of independence applied in principle to administrative decision-makers: security of tenure, financial security and administrative autonomy.[81]

The issue arose squarely in *Ocean Port*. Here, the Liquor Appeal Board of British Columbia upheld a finding that a bar had failed to respect the conditions of its licence – by, variously, permitting minors, fights and intoxication on the premises and allowing patrons to leave with alcohol in their possession – and imposed a licence suspension. Ingeniously, the bar appealed on the basis that the Board lacked the necessary guarantees of independence. The British Columbia Court of Appeal adopted this clever argument: because members of the Board were removable at pleasure, they did not have the necessary security of tenure to decide cases independently.

[80] See generally *Ref re Remuneration of Judges of the Prov. Court of PEI; Ref re Independence and Impartiality of Judges of the Prov Court of PEI*, [1997] 3 SCR 3; M Valois, *Judicial Independence: Keeping Law at a Distance from Politics* (LexisNexis, 2013).

[81] *Canadian Pacific Ltd. v Matsqui Indian Band* [1995] 1 SCR 3; *2747–3174 Québec Inc Quebec (Régie des permis d'alcool)*, [1996] 3 SCR 919.

However, the Supreme Court of Canada agreed with the province that the Court of Appeal's reasoning 'elevated a principle of natural justice to constitutional status'.[82] There is, rather, a fundamental distinction between courts of law and administrative tribunals: 'the requirement of judicial independence developed to demarcate the fundamental division between the judiciary and the executive', protecting judicial impartiality, 'both in fact and perception' by 'insulating them from external influence, most notably the influence of the executive'.[83] By contrast, administrative tribunals 'lack this constitutional distinction from the executive' and, as a 'general rule', there is no constitutional requirement of independence: 'Thus, the degree of independence required of a particular tribunal is a matter of discerning the intention of Parliament or the legislature and, absent constitutional constraints, this choice must be respected.'[84] Although the infinite variety of Canadian administrative tribunals did not feature overtly in this analysis, its influence can be keenly felt: to constitutionalise administrative tribunal independence would be to limit the 'choice' of the legislature. As a result, administrative tribunals have neither constitutional status nor constitutionally enshrined protection for independence.

This principle was pushed to its logical conclusion in *Saskatchewan Federation of Labour v Government of Saskatchewan*.[85] We saw earlier the provision in the provincial *Interpretation Act* providing for the replacement by an incoming government of the members of various administrative bodies. Here, members of the Labour Relations Board were put out to pasture (albeit that many of these had been appointed by the previous government just a few months before the election) and new members were ushered in. As we saw, the Order-in-Council accomplishing this was challenged, but the Saskatchewan Court of Appeal held that the statutory authority to fire administrative decision-makers appointed by a previous government was clear. In this case, the enabling provision in the Interpretation Act was itself challenged as unconstitutional, on the basis that it violated the unwritten constitutional principle of adjudicative independence. The Court of Appeal considered that *Ocean Port* was a full answer to the constitutional argument: 'in light of reasons for judgment in *Ocean Port*, the unwritten constitutional principle of judicial independence grounded in the preamble to the *Constitution Act, 1867* cannot be seen to extend to the Saskatchewan Labour Relations Board, including the chairperson and vice-chairpersons of the Board'.[86]

Even where administrative independence is grounded in the Constitution, the guarantees for administrative tribunals are less than those for courts of law. The leading case is *Walter British Columbia*.[87] Controversy arose about the remuneration of

[82] *Ocean Port*, para 19.
[83] ibid paras 23–24.
[84] ibid.
[85] 2013 SKCA 61.
[86] ibid para 56.
[87] 2019 BCCA 221 [*Walter*].

the Chairperson of the British Columbia Review Board. Each Canadian province has a Review Board to make or review dispositions in respect of accused persons found Not Criminally Responsible by reason of Mental Disorder or unfit to stand trial. For many years, the Chairperson of the British Columbia Review Board was paid well below the minimum rates set out by the Treasury Board for 'group 4 tribunals', of which the Review Board was one.[88]

The Review Board has an important characteristic which distinguishes it from the liquour licence and labour relations adjudicators whose claims foundered in *Ocean Port* and *Saskatchewan Federation of Labour*. The Review Board deals with matters of personal liberty. It determines how long and under what conditions accused persons found Not Criminally Responsible spend in state detention. Section 7 of the Charter of Rights and Freedoms is squarely engaged by the Review Board's work. Once s 7 is engaged, the 'principles of fundamental justice' are also engaged and '[t]o that extent there … appears to be no doubt the BC Review Board requires independence to properly discharge its mandate.[89]

However, the conclusion of the British Columbia Court of Appeal in *Walter* was that the Review Board 'does not exercise judicial functions that relate to the bases upon which the principle of judicial independence is founded'.[90] As Willcock JA explained, whereas the constitutional principle of judicial independence is designed to safeguard superior court judges who exercise judicial functions of the highest importance, tribunal independence has a different source: 'principles of fundamental justice which call for the independence of a decision-maker as an essential part of procedural fairness'.[91] There is thus 'a distinction between the highest level of administrative independence, which may be constitutionally required for certain tribunals, and judicial independence', based on the fact that 'the judiciary, unlike administrative tribunals, has a constitutional obligation to maintain at all times a distance from the executive'.[92] Accordingly, tribunal independence is 'context specific':[93] 'the courts must adopt a flexible approach to the question of what constitutes procedural fairness in the administrative context'.[94] The Chairperson of the Review Board is entitled to 'some guarantee' of independence but not enough to underpin a declaration that the Treasury Board directive is unconstitutional as applied to his office.[95]

Indeed, the independence of administrative tribunals is inherently flexible, designed to accommodate the infinite variability described in Part I. When the Supreme Court of Canada recognised that the independence of administrative

[88] ibid paras 2–9.
[89] ibid para 61.
[90] *Walter* (n 87) note 247, para 88.
[91] ibid para 69.
[92] ibid para 70.
[93] ibid para 109.
[94] ibid para 110.
[95] ibid para 112.

tribunals – security of tenure, financial security and administrative autonomy – is a principle of natural justice, 'where the tribunal is functioning as an adjudicative body settling disputes and determining the rights of parties', it also took pains to point out that 'a strict application of these principles is not always warranted'.[96] It is necessary to have regard to the 'functions' being performed by the tribunal: 'The requisite level of institutional independence … will depend on the nature of the tribunal, the interests at stake, and other indices of independence such as oaths of office'.[97] In *Walter*, the British Columbia Court of Appeal distinguished between the 'rigorous and elaborate' guarantees of judicial independence and the 'context specific' protection for administrative independence.[98] The 'high degree' of judicial independence does not apply to administrative tribunals, even when the *Charter* is engaged.[99] The reason for the distinction is that the higher protection of judicial independence is 'a natural outgrowth of the commitment to the separation of powers between and among the legislative, executive and judicial branches of government' but administrative tribunals 'do not require judicial independence for the same purpose and to the same extent'.[100] Even in Quebec, where tribunal independence is entrenched in the province's quasi-constitutional charter of rights, a contextual approach prevails.[101]

The 'apparent conclusiveness'[102] of *Ocean Port Hotel* has been questioned by academic commentators[103] and courts,[104] who point to subsequent decisions as suggesting that some adjudicative functions are protected by 'constitutional constraints'. These commentators and courts point first to *Bell Canada*, where the Supreme Court held that some tribunals are adjudicative: their primary purpose is dispute resolution and they do not exercise policy-making functions. But the ratio decidendi of *Ocean Port Hotel* related to a body which was 'first and foremost a licensing body'.[105] Accordingly, Dr Ellis observes, '*Ocean Port* was decided on the basis of the Court's view that the Board was a licensing body; as a doctrinal authority, therefore, *Ocean Port* must remain a decision about a body exercising a licensing function'.[106]

These commentators and courts point then to *Ell*, the Supreme Court of Canada's extension of constitutional protections to Justices of the Peace on the basis of the 'important role' they play in assisting 'the provincial and superior courts

[96] *Canadian Pacific Ltd v Matsqui Indian Band*, [1995] 1 SCR 3, para 80.
[97] ibid para 83.
[98] *Walter* (n 87) para 101.
[99] ibid para 107.
[100] ibid para 109.
[101] *Association des juges administratifs de la Commission des lésions professionnelles c. Québec (Procureur général)*, 2013 QCCA 1690, paras 27, 40.
[102] *McKenzie v Minister of Public Safety and Solicitor General et al*, 2006 BCSC 1372, para 132.
[103] Ellis, *Unjust by Design* (n 77).
[104] *McKenzie* (n 102).
[105] *Ocean Port Hotel Ltd v British Columbia (General Manager, Liquor Control and Licensing Branch)*, 2001 SCC 52, [2001] 2 SCR 781, para 33.
[106] Ellis (n 77) 224.

in fulfilling the judiciary's constitutional mandate'.[107] As the British Columbia Supreme Court observed, in *Ell*, 'the Court held that a class of adjudicators other than superior or provincial court judges were constitutionally required to be independent in the exercise of their duties'.[108]

It is true that the Supreme Court has never determined whether other classes of adjudicators who are not s 96 judges are constitutionally protected. But these arguments were squarely before appellate courts in *Saskatchewan Federation of Labour* and *Walter* and were squarely rejected. In both instances, the Supreme Court declined to hear the appeals. For now, the broad reading of *Ocean Port* remains conclusive.

Administrative Tribunals Relative to the Legislature and Executive

As is clear from the previous subsection, administrative tribunals are subordinate to the courts. They do not benefit from any constitutional guarantee of their status. Their position relative to legislatures and executives is no stronger.

As to legislatures, in *Ocean Port Hotel*, the Court suggested that the degree of independence of administrative tribunals is *dependent* on choices made by the legislature. It is the legislature 'that determines the degree of independence required of tribunal members' and 'the nature of a tribunal's relationship to the executive'; the role of the courts is to construe the relevant statutory provisions 'to determine the degree of independence the legislature intended'.[109] Administrative tribunals' independence, then, depends entirely on legislative intent: statute dictates the 'degree of independence required' in any given instance.

As far as the executive is concerned, politicians exercise control over the structure and composition of administrative tribunals unless statute provides otherwise. This is entirely consistent with the fundamental proposition, underpinning the analysis in *Ocean Port Hotel*, that administrative tribunals exist only to give effect to policy.[110] In a recent case (brought in contract in an attempt to circumvent the parsimonious judicial approach to administrative tribunal independence), the Ontario Superior Court held that it was plain and obvious that an action brought by tribunal members who had not been reappointed by a new government of a different political hue to its predecessor was doomed to fail. Morgan J commented

[107] *Ell Alberta*, 2003 SCC 35, [2003] 1 SCR 857, para 26.

[108] *McKenzie v Minister of Public Safety and Solicitor General et al.*, 2006 BCSC 1372, para 139.

[109] *Ocean Port Hotel*, paras 20–22.

[110] There is an obvious point of comparison with Australia here, in that it has long been the case that the role of the Administrative Appeals Tribunal is to decide each matter on its merits and not merely to apply policy. That said, the use of 'policy' by Canadian courts is quite loose and, indeed, question-begging. Unfortunately, the literature on this issue is sparse. See R Macauley and J Sprague, *Practice and Procedure Before Administrative Tribunals* (Carswell, Looseleaf), s 3.2(e)(i).

in expansive terms on the extent of executive choice to shape the structure and composition of administrative tribunals:

> There is nothing illegitimate in a new government making appointments to administrative agencies, boards, and tribunals which take into account its own policy choices and political inclinations. Government representatives such as the Cabinet members that make the appointments in issue are required to ensure that the appointments are made in compliance with applicable legislation; beyond that, however, there is nothing more to restrict the exercise of discretion. In fact, to strip all politics from the decision would render meaningless the statutory delegation of this discretion to political representatives … In these circumstances, factoring political considerations into an appointment or reappointment decision is not prohibited and, indeed, is considered neither inappropriate nor unprincipled.[111]

It is notable that Morgan J made these comments about extensive executive discretion in a province where statute requires a competitive, merit-based appointment process. Even where there has been legislative intervention to cabin executive discretion, political actors still dominate administrative tribunals.

Legal Principles that Recognise the Important Role of Administrative Tribunals

As explained in the previous Part, administrative tribunals occupy, *qua* institutions, a subordinate constitutional role, with neither constitutional guarantees nor common law requirements imposing meaningful limitations on legislative and executive pre-eminence over administrative tribunals; in addition, administrative tribunals are, constitutionally speaking, not on a par with courts of law.

However, there are several legal principles that do, in fact, elevate the status of administrative tribunals. Most importantly, administrative tribunals are often entitled to deference on questions of law, giving them interpretive power on a par with courts of law. In addition, administrative tribunals in Canada have significant power to consider questions of constitutionality and grant appropriate remedies. Lastly, administrative tribunal members are strongly protected from pressure that might be exerted by colleagues and hierarchical superiors.

Deference on Questions of Law

Unlike other common law jurisdictions (but in common with the United States), Canada embraces deference on questions of law. Indeed, since the reformation of Canadian administrative law in the *Vavilov* decision in 2019, a presumption of deference applies whenever a legislature creates an administrative decision-maker.

[111] *McAnsh v Ontario* 2023 ONSC 3537, paras 65–66.

The origins of deference in Canadian law are firmly rooted in administrative tribunals, specifically, labour relations boards. Powerful critiques of the Supreme Court of Canada's overly interventionist approach in the area of labour relations (often diagnosed as reactionary judicial conservatism when faced with progressive legislative policy) led to the adoption of a deferential approach to judicial review.

The leading case is *Canadian Union of Public Employees v New Brunswick Liquor Corporation*,[112] which involved the interpretation of a prohibition on replacing 'striking employees with any other employee'. Henceforth, when the courts reviewed the decision of specialized administrative tribunals the judge was not to undertake a *de novo* review but rather should ask whether the tribunal's interpretation was 'so patently unreasonable that its construction cannot be rationally supported by the relevant legislation and demands intervention by the court upon review'.[113]

Several other Supreme Court decisions in cases involving labour relations boards soon made it clear that on matters central to the mandate of an administrative decision-maker, a manifestly unreasonable error would have to be identified to justify judicial intervention.[114] As has been said, '[i]t is impossible to disentangle *New Brunswick Liquor* from the historical treatment of labour relations decision-making in Canadian administrative law'.[115]

Deference on questions of law puts courts and tribunals on as equal a footing as possible. As Rosalie Abella, one of the Supreme Court's leading advocates of deference to administrative tribunals pithily put it, deference means that both courts of law and administrative tribunals are 'equally responsible for, and capable of, interpreting the applying law within their separate, assigned legal spheres'.[116] As far as interpretation of law is concerned, administrative tribunals are not subordinate to courts of law.

There are some caveats to insert here. Most notably, the commitment of Canadian courts to deference has ebbed and flowed, and some administrative tribunals (most notably human rights tribunals) have not benefited from deference as much as others.[117] For another thing, in *Vavilov*, the Supreme Court of Canada extended its historical solicitude to administrative tribunals to any and

[112] [1979] 2 SCR 227 [*New Brunswick Liquor*].

[113] ibid at 237.

[114] *Syndicat des employés de production du Québec et de l'Acadie v Canada Labour Relations Board* [1984] 2 SCR 412, 422. See generally B Langille, 'Judicial Review, Judicial Revisionism and Judicial Responsibility' (1986) 17 *Revue générale de droit* 169.

[115] P Daly, 'Canadian Labour Law after *Vavilov*' (2021) 23 *Canadian Journal of Labour and Employment Law* 103, 107.

[116] 'Canadian Administrative Law: The Case for Judicial Humility' (2020) 75 *RJ* 168, 169.

[117] See, eg, two cases separated by a generation and significant developments in administrative law thinking but coming to striking similar conclusions about human rights tribunals' relative ability to interpret the law: *Canada (Attorney General) v Mossop*, [1993] 1 SCR 554 and *United Nurses of Alberta v Alberta Health Services*, 2021 ABCA 194. See generally C L'Heureux-Dubé, 'The "Ebb" and "Flow" of Administrative Law on the "General Question of Law"' in M Taggart (ed), *The Province of Administrative Law Determined* (Hart, 1997).

all decision-makers exercising statutory authority (at least presumptively) whilst at the same time prescribing a more demanding standard of reasonableness review;[118] however, the 'new normal' of *Vavilov*[119] has been felt less by administrative tribunals, than by non-adjudicative decision-makers (such as ministers and front-line officials), and it has been remarked that '*Vavilov* does not constitute a significant change in the law of judicial review with respect to the review of the reasons of administrative tribunals'.[120] Much more could be said about *Vavilov* and the arc of deference in Canadian administrative law, but for present purposes it is sufficient to say that many administrative tribunals have the power to interpret the law, are subject to deferential judicial review, and cannot reasonably be described as subordinate to the courts.

Indeed, the 'equal responsibility' mentioned above applies to the implementation of Canada's normative commitments on the domestic and international plane. Domestically, administrative tribunals have a role in giving effect to the values underpinning the *Charter of Rights and Freedoms*[121] and, as discussed in the next subsection, applying constitutional provisions. A recent strand of jurisprudence puts administrative tribunals front and centre in achieving reconciliation between the Crown and Canada's First Nations, requiring them to discharge the Honour of the Crown in some instances by consulting with and accommodating Indigenous peoples,[122] and enabling them to interpret their statutory mandates to take account of the imperative of reconciliation.[123]

Internationally, the Supreme Court of Canada has recently made clear that international law 'should be considered' whenever interpreting a statute that 'purports' to implement a treaty 'in whole or in part'.[124] In interpreting statutes, the interpreter must consider text, purpose and context: international law 'is relevant at the context stage of the statutory interpretation exercise'.[125] 'Textual ambiguity' is not a pre-condition to considering international law, as statutory context 'includes any relevant international legal obligations'.[126] As reference to international law is permitted where 'the circumstances of the case'[127] justify reference to international law as part of the overall context, administrative tribunals have a role

[118] *Vavilov*, paras 24, 72.
[119] Daly (n 115) 118.
[120] *Radzevicius v Workplace Safety and Insurance Appeals Tribunal*, 2020 ONSC 319, para 57.
[121] *Doré v Barreau du Québec*, 2012 SCC 12, [2012] 1 SCR 395, paras 54–58; *Taylor-Baptiste v Ontario Public Service Employees Union*, 2015 ONCA 495, paras 54–58; *Gordon v British Columbia (Superintendent of Motor Vehicles)*, 2022 BCCA 260, para 59. See generally, P Daly, 'The *Doré* Duty: Fundamental Rights in Public Administration' (2023) 101 *Canadian Bar Review* 297.
[122] See generally, *Clyde River (Hamlet) v Petroleum Geo-Services Inc*, 2017 SCC 40, [2017] 1 SCR 1069; *Chippewas of the Thames First Nation v Enbridge Pipelines Inc*, 2017 SCC 41, [2017] 1 SCR 1099.
[123] See, eg, *Fort McKay First Nation v Prosper Petroleum Ltd.*, 2020 ABCA 163, paras 40, 57, 68; *AltaLink Management Ltd v Alberta (Utilities Commission)*, 2021 ABCA 342, at paras 55, 65, 114, 117, 120, 123.
[124] *Society of Composers, Authors and Music Publishers of Canada v Entertainment Software Association*, 2022 SCC 30, para 44.
[125] ibid.
[126] ibid para 45.
[127] ibid para 46.

to play in giving effect to Canada's international obligations. This is because administrative decision-makers *must* consider text, purpose and *context* in interpreting statutes.[128] The requirement to consider context is therefore an invitation to insert international law into the statutory interpretation exercise, and to insert administrative tribunals into the concretisation of Canada's international obligations. This, as with deference on questions of law, is inconsistent with administrative tribunals having subordinate constitutional status.

Constitutional Matters

The *locus classicus* of the contemporary approach to administrative tribunals' jurisdiction over constitutional issues is found in the aphorism of Justice Beverley McLachlin (as she then was) issued in dissent in *Cooper v Canada (Human Rights Commission)*: the constitution is 'not some holy grail which only judicial initiates of the superior courts may touch'.[129] Rather, as the Supreme Court held less than a decade later (endorsing Justice McLachlin's *Cooper* dissent), once an administrative decision-maker is vested with the express or implied power to determine *any* question of law, it is empowered to determine constitutional questions, barring express legislative exclusion of the authority to consider constitutional questions.[130] Accordingly, most administrative decision-makers have the jurisdiction to determine whether a provision of 'law' is consistent with the Constitution and to treat unconstitutional provisions as having no force and effect under section 52 of the Constitution Act, 1982 (the so-called supremacy clause). And where the authority to consider constitutional matters is restricted by legislation, the restrictions are narrowly construed.[131]

In *R v Conway*,[132] Justice Abella extended the Supreme Court's generous approach to administrative decision-makers' ability to consider questions of constitutionality to the issuing of constitutional remedies. Section 52 is only one of the constitution's remedial provisions: the other is section 24, which permits a 'competent' court to issue a remedy for an individualised violation of the Constitution. To the question 'is an administrative decision-maker a "competent" body for issuing constitutional remedies', Justice Abella provided as resounding a 'yes' as possible, in a passage worth quoting at length:

> Over two decades of jurisprudence has confirmed the practical advantages and constitutional basis for allowing Canadians to assert their Charter rights in the most accessible forum available, without the need for bifurcated proceedings between superior courts

[128] ibid para 118.
[129] [1996] 3 SCR 854, para 70.
[130] *Nova Scotia (Workers' Compensation Board) v Martin; Nova Scotia (Workers' Compensation Board) v Laseur*, 2003 SCC 54, [2003] 2 SCR 504, paras 36, 41.
[131] See, eg, *Rio Tinto Alcan Inc v Carrier Sekani Tribal Council*, 2010 SCC 43, [2010] 2 SCR 650, paras 66–75.
[132] 2010 SCC 22, [2010] 1 SCR 765.

> and administrative tribunals. … If … expert and specialized tribunals with the authority to decide questions of law are in the best position to decide constitutional questions when a remedy is sought under s. 52 of the Constitution Act, 1982, there is no reason why such tribunals are not also in the best position to assess constitutional questions when a remedy is sought under s. 24(1) of the Charter. … Building on the jurisprudence, therefore, when a remedy is sought from an administrative tribunal under s. 24(1), the proper initial inquiry is whether the tribunal can grant Charter remedies generally. To make this determination, the first question is whether the administrative tribunal has jurisdiction, explicit or implied, to decide questions of law. If it does, and unless it is clearly demonstrated that the legislature intended to exclude the Charter from the tribunal's jurisdiction, the tribunal is a court of competent jurisdiction and can consider and apply the Charter – and Charter remedies – when resolving the matters properly before it.[133]

This 'threshold question' is posed in terms as friendly as possible to administrative decision-makers: it maximises the scope for the granting of Charter remedies.

However, the administrative decision-maker must go on to determine 'whether the remedy sought is the kind of remedy that the legislature intended would fit within the statutory framework of the particular tribunal.'[134] In *Conway* itself, the remedy of an absolute discharge would be inconsistent with the statutory framework and was, accordingly, unavailable (absent a challenge to the constitutionality of the statutory framework itself).

Nonetheless, in terms both of constitutional supremacy and constitutional remedies, administrative tribunals are seen as partners of courts of law in applying the Constitution of Canada. Indeed, in its recent decision on the effect of declarations of unconstitutionality in *R v Sullivan*,[135] the Supreme Court of Canada further elevated the status of administrative tribunals relative to courts of law. Here, Kasirer J located the normative force of a declaration of unconstitutionality in the *reasons* a court gives for finding that a law is incompatible with the Constitution, rather than in the *judgment* the court issues on foot of those reasons.[136] It is a simple matter of *stare decisis*.[137]

From the perspective of administrative tribunals, the collapsing of the distinction between reasons and judgment is significant. The hallmark of the difference between a superior court and an administrative tribunal has been that a superior court can issue an authoritative declaration of unconstitutionality, effective against the world at large, whereas an administrative tribunal can only conclude that an unconstitutional provision cannot be applied in the context of a particular matter.[138] Put another way, superior courts have general authority to declare

[133] ibid paras 79–81.
[134] ibid para 82.
[135] 2022 SCC 19.
[136] ibid para 63.
[137] ibid paras 44, 68.
[138] *Nova Scotia (Workers' Compensation Board) v Martin* [*Martin*]; *Nova Scotia (Workers' Compensation Board) v Laseur*, 2003 SCC 54, [2003] 2 SCR 504, para 31; *R v Lloyd*, 2016 SCC 13, [2016] 1 SCR 130 para 15.

laws unconstitutional, but administrative tribunals may only decline to give effect to unconstitutional laws in specific cases. This hallmark has been eliminated by *Sullivan*. Both superior courts and administrative tribunals can give reasons for concluding that a law is unconstitutional. The normative force of these reasons is a matter of *stare decisis*, not the status of the body delivering the reasons. Whatever is special about a superior court's reasons relating to the unconstitutionality of a law comes from the doctrine of *stare decisis*, not its institutional status. The effect is to enhance the status of administrative tribunals relative to the superior courts. True, an administrative tribunal's reasons for finding a law to be unconstitutional will not bind a superior court, but they may be persuasive, especially where a tribunal demonstrates through its legal analysis that it has particular expertise in respect of the operation of the law in question. Indeed, a superior court's *reasons* have only persuasive force outside the province, further eroding the distinction between superior courts and administrative tribunals. Rather than playing a role subordinate to that of courts of law, administrative tribunals are viewed as partners in the application of the Constitution of Canada.

Adjudicative Independence

Even though administrative tribunals as institutions do not benefit from robust protection for independence, *members* of administrative tribunals are protected as individuals. Canadian courts have held that the 's/he who hears must decide' principle protects administrative tribunal members from pressure from colleagues and hierarchical superiors.

The leading case is *IWA v Consolidated-Bathurst Packaging Ltd.*[139] Here, an administrative tribunal allowed general policy discussions amongst board members to take place after the hearing of individual cases but before final decisions were reached. The individuals affected by the decision had no knowledge of the discussions, still less the opportunity to respond to them. Gonthier J. noted that 'nothing' in the governing statute gave 'the chairman, the vice-chairmen or other Board members the power to impose his opinion on any other Board member'.[140] Holding such general policy discussions as a means to achieve consistency in decisions was nonetheless held to be permissible. The goal was evidently to promote consistent decision-making across differently-constituted panels of the decision-maker and greater congruence between the general policy views of the Board and the decisions of individual panels: 'Those affected by administrative decisions are entitled to expect that like cases will generally be treated alike and that outcomes will not depend merely on the identity of the individual decision maker'.[141] However, Gonthier J. cautioned, 'this *de jure* situation must not be

[139] [1990] 1 SCR 282.
[140] ibid 333.
[141] *Canada (Immigration and Citizenship) v Vavilov* 2019 SCC 65, [2019] 4 SCR 653, para 129.

thwarted by procedures which may effectively compel or induce panel members to decide against their own conscience and opinions'.[142] Accordingly, participants in the high-level discussions could not lawfully descend into the factual minutiae of individual cases. Discussion of cases could proceed only subject to three safeguards. First, hierarchical superiors within the administrative tribunal cannot impose consultation, which must be requested by the adjudicators. Second, the consultation could only touch questions of policy and law, with adjudicators given exclusive authority in relation to fact finding. Third, 'even on questions of law and policy, the decision-makers had to remain free to take whatever decision they deemed right in their conscience and understanding of the facts and the law, and not be compelled to adopt the views expressed by other members of the administrative tribunal'.[143]

These principles extend to any sort of review or discussion of a member's draft reasons prior to a final decision being taken,[144] and to any internal guidelines that aim to encourage consistency and coherence on procedural[145] or substantive matters.[146] In all instances, administrative tribunal members must 'remain completely free to reach their own conclusions, based on the facts of each particular case'.[147] The effect is to create a zone of autonomy for administrative tribunal members, as individuals. Political influence over an administrative tribunal as an institution is acceptable, but any sort of influence over administrative tribunal members is unlawful. This robust protection for administrative tribunal members indicates that their role as adjudicators is valuable and worth protecting. It elevates their status. Indeed, it is indistinguishable in this regard from judicial independence. The law on the adjudicative independence of members of administrative tribunals is therefore difficult to reconcile with the proposition that administrative tribunals have subordinate constitutional status.

The theme of this Part has been that notwithstanding the jurisprudence on the constitutional position of administrative tribunals, there are several legal principles that recognize the importance of these bodies. They are partners with the courts in the elaboration of Canadian law and individual members of administrative tribunals are robustly protected by guarantees for their personal adjudicative independence. Parts II and III have therefore taken us full circle, back to the tension described in the Introduction between the *Bissonnette* decision – with its emphasis on the importance of independent tribunal adjudication – and the

[142] [1990] 1 SCR 282, 333.

[143] *Ellis-Don Ltd v Ontario (Labour Relations Board)* 2001 SCC 4, [2001] 1 SCR 221, para 29.

[144] See, eg, *Shuttleworth v Ontario (Safety, Licensing Appeals and Standards Tribunals)* 2019 ONCA 518, para 39.

[145] See, eg, *Thamotharem v Canada (Minister of Citizenship and Immigration)* 2007 FCA 198, [2008] 1 FCR 385, para 51.

[146] See, eg, *Canadian Association of Refugee Lawyers v Canada (Immigration, Refugees and Citizenship)* 2020 FCA 196, [2021] 1 FCR 271, para 65.

[147] *Canadian Association of Refugee Lawyers v Canada (Citizenship and Immigration)* 2019 FC 1126, para 59.

Ocean Port Hotel approach to the constitutional status of administrative tribunals. Can this tension be explained and, if so, can it be resolved? It is to those questions that I turn in the Conclusion.

Conclusion

There is significant tension between the two branches of jurisprudence on Canadian administrative tribunals described in Parts II and III. On the one hand, administrative tribunals occupy a subordinate constitutional position, with a much lower status in the legal order than courts of law and subject to legislative and executive whim. On the other hand, administrative tribunals are seen as equal partners in the interpretation and application of legal norms, with their members benefiting from strong guarantees for their adjudicative independence.

Can this tension be explained? Can it be resolved? Does it need to be resolved?

As I have suggested at various points, judicial reluctance to extend constitutional guarantees to administrative tribunals is probably attributable to the infinite variety described in Part I. Judges seem fearful that if administrative tribunals were to enjoy constitutional status, the freedom of legislatures and executives to shape administrative tribunals to achieve their political ends would be compromised. Put simply, to constitutionalize administrative tribunals would be to restrict their variability and governments' ability to implement policy. That is my explanation for the tension.

This judicial reluctance is not based on solid premises, however. For one thing, it would derive an 'ought' – administrative tribunals *should* not have constitutional guarantees of independence – from an 'is' – administrative tribunals *are* infinitely variable and engaged in implementing policy. This is bad philosophy and does not make for good law either. For another, independence can be constitutionalised without imposing uniformity: in Quebec, administrative independence has quasi-constitutional status but operates in a context-sensitive manner whenever an administrative tribunal is interpreting and applying law; the effect of constitutionalising administrative independence would simply be to impose basic conditions relating to salary setting, appointment and reappointment, and control of resources. Just as the guarantee of judicial independence operates differently for superior courts, provincial courts and justices of the peace, so too a guarantee of administrative independence would be operationalised with due regard for the infinite variety of administrative tribunals. Resolving the tension would not be a particularly difficult jurisprudential task. As far as their supposed 'policy' role is concerned, many administrative tribunals are engaged not in the development of political priorities but in the interpretation and application of the law: this is the daily fare of those with adversarial and inquisitorial functions and regular practice for those with regulatory functions as well. Independence could attach to those functions without compromising the ability of executives to set 'policy'.

That leads me to my final question, whether the tension needs to be resolved. Although I would favour the constitutionalisation of the independence of administrative tribunals, and short of that legislative reforms to enshrine tribunal independence in statute law,[148] I recognise nonetheless that Canadian law can continue to potter on without resolving the tension I have identified. This is because the analyses in Parts II and III relate to different aspects of administrative tribunals: the institutional and the individual. Institutionally speaking, as described in Part II, administrative tribunals are subordinate to courts of law, the executive and legislatures. But in individual cases, administrative tribunals can be equal partners in the interpretation and application of legal norms, with *members* subject to robust protection for their independence. As a matter of theory, the dissonance between the institutional and the individual is difficult to defend. As a matter of practice, however, the contrasting positions can co-exist, as they have co-existed for decades now. Given the apparent absence of judicial appetite to query the *status quo* and relative lack of interest politically in legislative reform, the co-existence seems likely to continue for decades more.

[148] R Ellis, 'An Administrative Justice Fix – A Model Act' (2022) 35 *Canadian Journal of Administrative Law and Practice* 53.

12

Administrative Tribunals in a Hybrid Regime: The Case of the Hong Kong Special Administrative Region

STEPHEN THOMSON[1]

The Hong Kong Special Administrative Region ('HKSAR') of the People's Republic of China ('PRC')[2] has had a tumultuous few years. In 2019, public protests against a proposed law providing extradition arrangements between the HKSAR and Mainland China, Macau and Taiwan[3] transmogrified into rioting and a partial breakdown of public infrastructure. Major road and rail links were blocked, public spaces were vandalised and university campuses were transformed into battlefields between students and police with exchanges of tear gas and makeshift explosives. In January 2020, the embryonic COVID-19 pandemic arrived in Hong Kong which came to adopt some of the world's most stringent border closures, quarantine regimes and mask mandates.[4] Also in 2020, the Standing Committee of the

[1] I would like to thank Simon Young and my co-editors Matthew Groves and Greg Weeks for comments on a draft of this chapter, Daisy Cheung for discussions on the institutions of mental health law in Hong Kong, and the Secretariats of the Administrative Appeals Board, Appeal Board (Town Planning), Immigration Tribunal, Mental Health Review Tribunal, Municipal Services Appeals Board, Torture Claims Appeal Board and Transport Tribunal for helpful information specific to their respective tribunals. The views expressed in the chapter, and any errors, are my own.

[2] Sovereignty over Hong Kong passed from the UK to the PRC on 1 July 1997 in accordance with the Sino-British Joint Declaration of 1984 (Joint Declaration on the Question of Hong Kong, 19 December 1984). The PRC incorporated Hong Kong as a Special Administrative Region under Article 31 of the PRC Constitution. The HKSAR holds the paradoxical position of being one of the most autonomous regions in the world (with more substantive legislative, executive and judicial powers than many federal states and territories), but with a very flimsy constitutional guarantee of autonomy by international standards. Its continued autonomy effectively depends on self-restraint by the central authorities of the PRC, with the HKSAR's primary constitutional instrument, the Basic Law, no definitive brake on unconstitutional acts – see eg S Thomson, 'The New Constitutional Disorder: The Unlawful Application of Mainland Chinese Law to Hong Kong' (2018) 54 *Texas International Law Journal* 115. On a day-to-day basis the Basic Law does serve as a constitutional document, but its essential status and durability are perilous.

[3] Fugitive Offenders and Mutual Legal Assistance in Criminal Matters Legislation (Amendment) Bill 2019.

[4] The anti-extradition bill riots and the COVID-19 pandemic were connected by an ironic twist of fate, with face coverings banned in relation to the former (Prohibition on Face Covering Regulation

National People's Congress enacted the National Security Law for Hong Kong.[5] With national security offences being vaguely expressed, prosecutions featuring a presumption against bail and cases being tried by designated 'national security' judges, the list of which is secret, the Law introduced a new era of erosion for individual rights and the rule of law. To compound the territory's difficulties, its democratic credentials were drastically reduced in 2021 with geographical constituencies reduced from a 50% to 22.2% composition in the Legislative Council, functional constituencies reduced from 50% to 33%, and the creation of an Election Committee constituency – facilitating enlarged executive control over election results and legislative output – comprising 44.4% of the Council.[6] Hong Kong's slide down the global ranking of democracies saw it drop from a 'flawed democracy' into the 'hybrid regime' category.[7]

In this maelstrom of events, administrative tribunals may appear to be comparatively insignificant institutions. Appeals against licensing and planning decisions seem to pale in comparison to a crackdown on free speech, alleged police brutality,[8] and the progression of the Legislative Council's journey to being

2019 (cap 241K)) and then mandated some nine months later in relation to the latter (Prevention and Control of Disease (Wearing of Mask) Regulation 2020 (cap 599I)). This became one of the world's longest-running mask mandates in the COVID-19 pandemic. See further S Thomson, EC Ip and M Ramsden, 'Hong Kong Special Administrative Region, People's Republic of China: Legal Response to COVID-19' in J King and OLM Ferraz et al (eds), *The Oxford Compendium of National Legal Responses to COVID-19* (Oxford University Press 2021).

[5] The Law of the People's Republic of China on Safeguarding National Security in the Hong Kong Special Administrative Region (中华人民共和国香港特别行政区维护国家安全法) (enacted by the Standing Committee of the National People's Congress on 30 June 2020 under the Decision of the National People's Congress on Establishing and Improving the Legal System and Enforcement Mechanisms for the Hong Kong Special Administrative Region to Safeguard National Security (28 May 2020)).

[6] Decision of the National People's Congress on Improving the Electoral System of the Hong Kong Special Administrative Region (11 March 2021); Amendment by the Standing Committee of the National People's Congress of Annex I and Annex II to the Basic Law of the Hong Kong Special Administrative Region (30 March 2021). These figures are rounded to the nearest 0.1% so do not add exactly to 100%. Easy as it is to criticise these electoral arrangements under PRC sovereignty, they are a colonial legacy. The Legislative Council only had its first elected members in 1985, its membership having previously been appointed in its entirety, though the constituencies were not geographical but 'functional' (i.e. constituencies were based not on territorial units but professional ones – for example, an engineering constituency, a trade union constituency and so on) (see SNM Young & A Law, 'Privileged to Vote: Inequality and Anomalies of the FC System' in C Loh and Civic Exchange, *Functional Constituencies: A Unique Feature of the Hong Kong Legislative Council* (HKU Press 2006) 59–110). Geographical constituencies were only introduced in 1991 in the dying days of the British colonial administration's governance of Hong Kong. The Election Committee constituency was originally created in 1995 under the colonial administration. See, generally, SNM Young, 'The Decision of the National People's Congress on Improving the Electoral System of the Hong Kong Special Administrative Region' (2021) 60(6) *International Legal Materials* 1163.

[7] The Economist, *Democracy Index 2022*. Available at: www.eiu.com/n/campaigns/democracy-index-2022/#:~:text=The%20Democracy%20Index%20is%20based,political%20participation%20and%20political%20culture.

[8] See Amnesty International, 'Hong Kong: Arbitrary arrests, brutal beatings and torture in police detention revealed' (19 September 2019). Available at: https://www.amnesty.org/en/latest/press-release/2019/09/hong-kong-arbitrary-arrests-brutal-beatings-and-torture-in-police-detention-revealed/.

a rubber-stamp parliament. Yet it is not as black and white as that. Persons whose businesses, properties and daily lives are directly impacted by the decisions of such tribunals as the Administrative Appeals Board, the Appeal Tribunal (Buildings) and the Torture Claims Appeal Board would be unlikely to regard tribunals as somehow insignificant, and these bodies continue to form an integral part of Hong Kong's administrative law system. Moreover, as the course of political and constitutional history has embarked on a fairly wild ride in Hong Kong, its administrative tribunals have, for the most part, remained for decades in a state of constancy. There have been no systematic reforms or plans for modernisation, which may be unsurprising considering that they seem barely to have featured in professional discourse. In almost 50 years they seem only to have been the dedicated subject of two scholarly studies (bar a handful of student dissertations)[9] and concerns tended to be muted and expressed sporadically, as by a Legislative Council ad hoc group in 1990 (whose concerns substantially went unheeded).[10] Whether classed as a 'flawed democracy' or a 'hybrid regime', the truth is that Hong Kong has long had authoritarian forms of government. The objective of this chapter is to set out the history, framework and constitutional position of administrative tribunals in Hong Kong and consider the extent to which the territory's history of authoritarian/hybrid models of governance has shaped those tribunals.

The History of Administrative Tribunals in Hong Kong

There is no comprehensive account of the history of administrative tribunals in Hong Kong. Tribunals are seen in many legal systems to develop in line with the changing demands of government and society, and different jurisdictions have faced varying challenges and needs at different times. Hong Kong's highly centralised form of colonial administration aimed at the maintenance of political control, coupled with small government and fiscal frugality until the 1950s, meant that public bodies themselves were a 'relatively late development'.[11] As explained by Ian Scott:

> The colonial government was strongly disinclined to develop social policy programmes for two reasons. First, the prevailing philosophy was that government should be kept

[9] M Bharwaney, 'Administrative Tribunals in Hong Kong' (1976) 6 *Hong Kong Law Journal* 189; S Thomson, 'Clutter and Cobwebs: How Administrative Tribunals in Hong Kong Can Learn From the UK' (2017) 36 *Civil Justice Quarterly* 363. Administrative tribunals are given briefer treatment in eg J Chan, 'The Judiciary' in J Chan and CL Lim (eds), *Law of the Hong Kong Constitution* (3rd edn) (Sweet & Maxwell 2021), EC Ip, *Law and Justice in Hong Kong* (4th edn) (Sweet & Maxwell 2022) 217–20, S Jhaveri, M Ramsden and A Scully-Hill, *Administrative Law in Hong Kong* (2nd edn) (LexisNexis, 2013) 47–62, and by this author in S Thomson, *Administrative Law in Hong Kong* (Cambridge University Press 2018) 304–19.

[10] R Fan, comments at second reading of Municipal Services Appeals Board Bill 1990 (9 May 1990). Available at: www.legco.gov.hk/yr89-90/english/lc_sitg/hansard/h900725.pdf.

[11] I Scott, *The Public Sector in Hong Kong* (2nd edn) (HKU Press 2022) 8–9.

> small and its functions should be limited. Business leaders believed that any social policy programmes could only be funded by increased taxes, to which they were fiercely opposed. Second, the British government put pressure on the Hong Kong authorities to balance the budget and there was little slack for expenditure on social policy. Instead, the government monitored [service] providers to prevent schools from becoming hotbeds of political dissent or condoning unhygienic health practices causing epidemics.[12]

It was only in the 1950s that the welfare state began to emerge in Hong Kong, prior to which social services were largely provided by churches and charitable organisations.[13] Initially, provision was seen in relation to housing,[14] and this need was in large measure attributable to the Chinese Communist Revolution in 1949 which saw migration into Hong Kong increase fourfold in six years.[15] The expansion of social services was also seen as a means of redressing the colonial administrations' legitimacy deficit.[16] With an emphasis on political control in this colonial outpost, endemic corruption was also an increasing concern. Matters came to a head in the early 1970s when Peter Godber, the Chief Superintendent of the Royal Hong Kong Police Force, was found to have millions of Hong Kong Dollars in unexplained wealth; he subsequently fled the territory only to be arrested in England and then extradited to Hong Kong in 1975. The scandal resulted in the establishment of the Independent Commission Against Corruption – now constitutionally enshrined[17] – as part of Governor Sir Murray MacLehose's anti-corruption drive which was so effective that it had to be scaled back or 'risk … the collapse of the whole system of public order'.[18] Getting matters under control in political terms, and not antagonising the local population,[19] were priorities over the social welfare of that population.

Hong Kong's need for structured accountability through administrative tribunals was thus similar to and dissimilar from that in other jurisdictions: similar in that tribunals emerged in response to changing societal pressures and needs; dissimilar in that they emerged at a comparatively late stage and not necessarily motivated by an altruistic sense of state responsibility for individual welfare. Key dates thus included the establishment of the Housing Authority in 1973 to build and manage public housing estates and the establishment of the Hospital Authority in 1990 to manage public hospitals. With the expansion of public services and assumption of government responsibility came a concomitant desire for accountability. Additional accountability channels were opened. The Office of the Unofficial Members of the Executive and Legislative Councils ('UMELCO') (the predecessor

[12] ibid 168. See also J Chan, 'From Colony to Special Administrative Region' in Chan and Lim (n 9) 13.
[13] Scott, *The Public Sector in Hong Kong* (n 11) 167.
[14] ibid 9 and 12.
[15] ibid 13.
[16] ibid 9 and 13–14.
[17] Basic Law, art 57.
[18] F Welsh, *A History of Hong Kong* (Harper Collins, 1997) 493.
[19] The local population was by no means a categorical supporter of the British colonial administrations, as demonstrated by the Hong Kong riots of 1967.

to the Ombudsman) was established in 1963,[20] allowing members of the public to complain or make representations about any matter of public interest or to lodge individual complaints against government departments; previously grievances about public administration could only be pursued by petitioning the Governor or the Legislative Council through Unofficial Members at sittings of the Legislative Council.[21] A programme of partial democratisation was embarked upon in the 1980s, including some District Board members being elected by universal suffrage, the electoral franchise for the Urban Council being extended to universal suffrage and the opening up of some seats in the Legislative Council to election for the first time in the colony's history.[22] The Commissioner for Administrative Complaints, now the Ombudsman, was established in 1989,[23] largely (but not exclusively[24]) absorbing the maladministration jurisdiction of OMELCO.[25] With more general support by the 1970s by Hong Kong residents for colonial rule in contrast to the prospect of Chinese Communist rule,[26] the Sino-British Joint Declaration having already been signed in 1984 – sealing Hong Kong's destiny under Chinese sovereignty – and capped by the totemic Tiananmen Square incident in 1989 which caused grave concern in Hong Kong,[27] perhaps a sense of poignancy and nostalgia fell upon the final colonial administrations such that real concern for the welfare of the local population did emerge.

One of the oldest administrative tribunals which is still in existence is the Board of Review (Inland Revenue Ordinance), established in 1947 under the administration of Governor Sir Mark Young.[28] The Appeal Tribunal (Buildings) was established in 1956 under the administration of Governor Sir Alexander Grantham.[29] However, many of the key extant tribunals in Hong Kong were

[20] UMELCO was renamed as the Office of Members of the Executive and Legislative Councils ('OMELCO') in 1986.

[21] Legislative Council, *A Companion to the History, Rules and Practices of the Legislative Council of the Hong Kong Special Administrative Region*, Ch 15. Available at: www.legco.gov.hk/general/english/procedur/companion/chapter_15/chapter_15.html, para 15.5.

[22] AHY Chen, 'A Tale of Two Islands: Comparative Reflections on Constitutionalism in Hong Kong and Taiwan' (2007) 37(2) *Hong Kong Law Journal* 647, 661–62.

[23] This proposal had been in the pipeline for some 20 years – Hong Kong Branch of Justice, *Report on the Feasibility of Instituting the Office of Ombudsman in Hong Kong* (1969).

[24] Instances of maladministration can still be taken up through the Legislative Council Redress System – see Legislative Council, *A Companion to the History, Rules and Practices of the Legislative Council of the Hong Kong Special Administrative Region*, Ch 15. Available at: www.legco.gov.hk/general/english/procedur/companion/chapter_15/chapter_15.html, para 15.16 and Thomson, *Administrative Law in Hong Kong* (n 9) 330–1.

[25] Commissioner for Administrative Complaints Ordinance (cap 397) (Ord 67 of 1988); now the Ombudsman Ordinance (cap 397).

[26] AHY Chen, 'A Tale of Two Islands: Comparative Reflections on Constitutionalism in Hong Kong and Taiwan' (2007) 37(2) *Hong Kong Law Journal* 647, 658.

[27] See WD Bowie, 'The Effect of the Tiananmen Square Massacre Upon Negotiations for the Draft Basic Law of the Hong Kong Special Administrative Region' (1990) 8(2) *Dickinson Journal of International Law* 245; and C Chan, 'Thirty years from Tiananmen: China, Hong Kong, and the Ongoing Experiment to Preserve Liberal Values in an Authoritarian State' (2019) 17(2) *International Journal of Constitutional Law* 439.

[28] Inland Revenue Ordinance (Ord No 20 of 1947) (cap 112).

[29] Buildings Ordinance (1956) (cap 123).

established in the 1980s and 1990s. The Transport Tribunal was established in 1979,[30] and the Immigration Tribunal in 1980,[31] under Governor Sir Murray MacLehose. Several important tribunals were created under the administration of Governor Sir David Wilson, including the Mental Health Review Tribunal in 1988,[32] the Securities and Futures Appeals Panel in 1989,[33] the Municipal Services Appeals Board in 1990,[34] the Appeal Board (Town Planning) in 1991[35] and the Insider Dealing Tribunal in 1991.[36] The Administrative Appeals Board was established in 1994 under Governor Chris Patten.[37] Several of these tribunals replaced appeals to the Governor or Governor-in-Council[38] and thus putatively enabled more independent scrutiny and accountability of government. For example, the Mental Health Review Tribunal replaced the Hospital Order Appeal Tribunal which, in the case of offender patients, made recommendations on appeals ultimately decided by the Governor-in-Council. While other tribunals have continued to be created after the Handover in 1997, such as the establishment of the Torture Claims Appeal Board in 2012 under Chief Executive Leung Chun-ying,[39] the 'model' of the administrative tribunal framework in Hong Kong had by the time of the Handover been constructed and there have been few innovations to that overall framework under 26 years of Chinese-backed administrations.

The System of Administrative Tribunals in Hong Kong

It is difficult to give a precise number or list of administrative tribunals in Hong Kong because of definitional challenges and because there is no central, organising

[30] Road Traffic Ordinance 1979 (cap 220) (now the Road Traffic Ordinance (cap 374)). The Tribunal became operational in 1981 with the introduction of the contract hire-car scheme, and its first hearing held on 21 September 1981.

[31] Immigration (Amendment) (No 2) Ordinance 1980 (Ord No 62 of 1980), inserting s 53F into the Immigration Ordinance (cap 115).

[32] Mental Health (Amendment) Ordinance 1988 (Ord No 46 of 1988), inserting s 59A into the Mental Health Ordinance (cap 136). The Tribunal did not come into operation until December 1989. It replaced the Hospital Order Appeal Tribunal, which appeared to serve an advisory function in relation to appeals to the Governor-in-Council. See further D Cheung, 'Mental Health Law in Hong Kong: The Civil Context' (2018) 48(2) *Hong Kong Law Journal* 461.

[33] Securities and Futures Commission Ordinance 1989 (Ord 10 of 1989) (cap 24). This tribunal was replaced by the Securities and Futures Appeals Tribunal.

[34] Municipal Services Appeals Board Ordinance (Ord No 58 of 1990) (cap 220).

[35] Town Planning (Amendment) (No 2) Ordinance 1991 (Ord No 101 of 1991), inserting s 17A into the Town Planning Ordinance (cap 131).

[36] Securities (Insider Dealing) Ordinance 1990 (Ord No 62 of 1990). This tribunal was replaced by the Market Misconduct Tribunal established in 2003 under Chief Executive Tung Chee-hwa – Securities and Futures Ordinance (cap 571), s 251 (LN 12 of 2003).

[37] Administrative Appeals Board Ordinance (No 6 of 1994) (cap 442).

[38] For example, the Appeals Tribunal (Buildings Ordinance) was preceded by appeals to the Governor-in-Council under the Buildings Ordinance (cap 123) (of 1936) ss 157–159.

[39] Immigration (Amendment) Ordinance 2012 (Ord No 23 of 2012), inserting s 37ZQ into the Immigration Ordinance (cap 115).

system. As is often the case with tribunals, a workable definition may begin from a negative proposition: that tribunals are not courts and are not part of the judiciary.[40] Though they generally hear appeals against executive decisions and do not exercise a review jurisdiction, they can typically consider points of law, fact or the merits of the impugned decision. Many, perhaps most, were established by legislation, but some – again depending on institutional definitions – are non-statutory in nature. While some entities (such as the Administrative Appeals Board and the Municipal Services Appeals Board) can uncontroversially be considered to be administrative tribunals, others are in a more ambiguous position including various regulators (such as the Communications Authority) and disciplinary bodies (such as the Disciplinary Tribunal (Electricity Ordinance)). Thus, the production of a precise number or list of administrative tribunals would very much depend on how they are defined in the first place.

Nevertheless, leaving aside those more ambiguous cases, Hong Kong's administrative tribunals (or entities performing their function) may be considered to fall into three main categories. The first and primary category comprises the bulk of administrative tribunals, often designated as 'appeals boards', which hear appeals against executive decisions. These form the backbone of the analysis that follows. The second category technically does not comprise administrative tribunals at all, but courts which may be considered to be acting in the capacity of an administrative tribunal when hearing statutory appeals from certain tribunals. There is commonly a provision for appeal on a point of law (typically to the Court of Appeal),[41] but sometimes for appeal on a point of fact or law (again, typically to the Court of Appeal),[42] or a general appeal which does not appear to be confined to fact or law and thus could potentially include merits. The latter may be an appeal from the original decision-maker[43] or from an administrative tribunal.[44] The final category comprises the Chief Executive or Chief Executive-in-Council ('CEIC') (which are distinct legal entities[45] despite their treatment in some cases to the contrary[46]) acting in the capacity of an administrative tribunal.[47] This latter route may have defective procedural safeguards and may in part be unlawful.[48]

[40] See below at [261–265]. Of course, they are part of the judiciary in the United Kingdom (see Harlow and Thomas, Chapters 4 and 9 in this volume), but even there they are seen as distinct from (general) courts.

[41] Eg, appeals from the Banking Review Tribunal to the Court of Appeal (Banking Ordinance (cap 155) s 101H).

[42] Eg, appeals from the Market Misconduct Tribunal to the Court of Appeal (Securities and Futures Ordinance (cap 571) s 266).

[43] Eg, appeals from the Collector of Stamp Revenue to the District Court (Hotel Accommodation Tax Ordinance (cap 348), ss 7(3) and (4)).

[44] Eg, appeals from the Appeal Board on Closure Orders (Immediate Health Hazard) to the Court of First Instance (Public Health and Municipal Services Ordinance (cap 132), s 128D(16)).

[45] See, eg, Country Parks Ordinance (cap 208), ss 17(9) and (10).

[46] Eg, *Gurung Bhakta Bahadur v Director of Immigration* [2001] 3 HKLRD 225.

[47] See, eg, Government Rent and Premium (Apportionment) Ordinance (cap 125) s 21; and Hong Kong Airport (Control of Obstructions) Ordinance (cap 301) s 10.

[48] See Thomson, 'Clutter and Cobwebs' (n 9) 379–83.

Some courts are labeled as 'tribunals' but are distinctly part of the judiciary;[49] one administrative tribunal – the Obscene Articles Tribunal – is part of the judiciary despite condemnation by the Judiciary, the Hong Kong Bar Association and the Law Society of Hong Kong,[50] and the HKSAR Government has yet to implement its proposal to remove the Tribunal's administrative functions.[51]

This section focuses, however, on 'ordinary' administrative tribunals. The statutory framework is piecemeal and there is no overarching system regulating administrative tribunals.[52] Typically, a statute which regulates particular subject matter will establish a tribunal to hear appeals in relation to that subject matter. There is one general tribunal, the Administrative Appeals Board, established in 1994,[53] which hears appeals on a wide array of topics, from an appeal against a determination that a person is unsuited to acting as a childminder[54] to an appeal against a decision relating to the approval of a genetically-modified organism.[55] It sits alongside a large number of specialised tribunals such as the Appeal Board (Bedspace Apartments), the Appeal Board (Town Planning) and the Banking Review Tribunal. Tribunals in Hong Kong generally operate on what may be described as a pre-Franks model, with little, if any, independence from government. In fact, tribunals are often operationally and financially dependent on the government department relevant to the tribunal's subject matter: for example, the Appeal Board (Town Planning) is administered by the Development Bureau and the Immigration Tribunal is administered by the Security Bureau.

The lack of independence from government is most prominently seen in the appointments system.[56] Tribunal members are typically appointed – and removed – by the Chief Executive, who often determines their remuneration, while others are usually appointed by the heads of government departments who are themselves accountable to, and capable of removal by, the Chief Executive.[57] The UK Franks Report had meanwhile regarded it as 'undesirable in principle that the

[49] Eg, the Competition Tribunal and the Lands Tribunal.

[50] Legislative Council, 'The Role of the Judiciary in the Adjudication System under the Control of Obscene and Indecent Articles Ordinance' (LC Paper No CB(2)863/11-12(03)). Available at: www.legco.gov.hk/yr11-12/english/panels/ajls/papers/aj0130cb2-863-3-e.pdf.

[51] Government of the Hong Kong SAR, 'Press Release: Review of Control of Obscene and Indecent Article Ordinance' (13 February 2015) (no longer accessible). See Commerce and Economic Development Bureau, 'Review of the Control of Obscene and Indecent Articles Ordinance' (CTB/A 235-5/1) (January 2013). Available at: www.legco.gov.hk/yr14-15/english/panels/itb/papers/itb20150309-ctba23551cpt1-e.pdf.

[52] Standardisation across tribunals was considered (and rejected) by the Administration in Department of Justice, 'Procedural Matters of Appeal Boards' (July 2011) (LC Paper No CB(2)2413/10-11(01)). Available at: www.legco.gov.hk/yr10-11/english/panels/ajls/papers/ajcb2-2413-1-e.pdf.

[53] Administrative Appeals Board Ordinance (cap 442), LN 428 of 1994.

[54] ibid Sch 1, item 33; Child Care Services Ordinance (cap 243), s 15B(2).

[55] ibid Sch 1, item 67; Genetically Modified Organisms (Control of Release) Ordinance (cap 607), s 10(1)(a).

[56] None of this analysis is intended to suggest a lack of professionalism or expertise on the part of individual tribunal members.

[57] Basic Law of the Hong Kong SAR, art 55.

appointment of … chairmen and members of tribunals should rest solely with the Ministers concerned'.[58] Hong Kong legislation tends to provide for no or vaguely expressed qualifications for appointment – 'such persons as he thinks suitable' is a common provision – contrary to the UK Leggatt Report's recommendation that statutory criteria for appointment be 'sufficiently explicit to form a clear basis for recruitment material and for training'.[59] In Hong Kong, vacancies are in general not expressly advertised and appointments standards and processes are opaque. There is no security of tenure for tribunal appointees who are typically appointed to short two or three-year periods, with statutes usually providing for a power (but no duty) to reappoint. Some statutes do not make any provision on the term of appointment. One aspect in which a number (but not all) of Hong Kong's administrative tribunals are more in line with Franks principles[60] is that persons are often eligible for appointment as chairmen only if they are qualified for appointment as a District Court judge. Nevertheless, the view of one judge was that the Chief Executive's degree of control over tribunal appointments and lack of security of tenure 'raises no more than a highly theoretical possibility of influence'.[61]

The flip side of an absence of security of tenure is the potential for high turnover of tribunal membership and the HKSAR Government has long expressed a commitment to a 'healthy turnover of members of advisory and statutory bodies'.[62] Two policies have in this regard been adopted by the HKSAR Government since the early 2000s: the 'six-board rule' under which a non-official (non-Government) member should not serve concurrently on more than six advisory and statutory bodies, and the 'six-year rule' under which a non-official member should not serve in any one capacity on a board for more than six years.[63] The most recently published figures, which cover statutory and advisory bodies in addition to administrative tribunals, reveal that 12 members were in breach of the six-board rule (a significant reduction from the early 2000s[64] but a figure now remaining relatively persistent) and 212 members were in breach of the six-year rule.[65] The latter is a

[58] Report of the Committee on Administrative Tribunals and Enquiries (1957) Cmnd 218 ('Franks Report'), para 45.

[59] Lord Chancellor's Department, Tribunals for Users: One System, One Service – Report of the Review of Tribunals by Sir Andrew Leggatt (March 2001) para 7.23. On the Franks and Leggatt Reports, see Thomas, Chapter 9 in this volume.

[60] Franks Report (n 58), para 55.

[61] *Television Broadcasts Ltd v Communications Authority* [2016] 2 HKLRD 41 (CFI), [103] (Godfrey Lam J). Godfrey Lam J was the first President of the Competition Tribunal, from 2013–2021.

[62] Home and Youth Affairs Bureau, 'Advisory and Statutory Bodies' (21 March 2023). Available at: www.hyab.gov.hk/en/policy_responsibilities/District_Community_and_Public_Relations/advisory.htm.

[63] ibid.

[64] Hong Kong Democratic Foundation, 'A Study on the Advisory and Statutory Bodies in Hong Kong – A Brief Report' (20 May 2003). Available at: www.hkdf.org/a-study-on-the-advisory-and-statutory-bodies-in-hong-kong-a-brief-report/.

[65] Home and Youth Affairs Bureau, 'ASB Six Year Board Rule' (21 March 2023), Available at: www.hyab.gov.hk/file_manager/en/documents/policy_responsibilities/others/ASB_six_year_board_rule.xlsx.

substantial reduction on recent years, with the main 'offender', the Appeal Tribunal (Buildings), having reduced from 149 members in breach of the six-year rule in 2017[66] to 80 members. It is worth noting the potential for politically-motivated or politically-aligned tribunal appointments, given overlap in the membership of some tribunals and the powerful Election Committee and, to a lesser extent, the fact that some tribunal members are Hong Kong deputies to the National People's Congress.[67] There is no general supervisory oversight of either the appointments system or the tribunals system other than by courts for legality.

There is no uniform procedural model adopted by tribunals (nor did the Franks Report recommend that[68]), but there are some common provisions on matters of procedure and powers. Chairmen commonly have the power to determine the practice and procedure of the tribunal insofar as not provided in, and not inconsistent with, the governing statute.[69] Many, but not all, tribunals have statutory provision for a hearing – those that do sometimes make no provision on whether that hearing should be held in public.[70] The tribunal or its chairman sometimes have the power to decide that a hearing shall be held in private,[71] with some tribunals having private hearings as the default statutory position.[72] Some statutes provide for a right to appear and be legally represented at tribunal proceedings; occasionally some other authorised representative is permitted.[73] It is sometimes provided that counsel and solicitors have no entitlement to be heard before a tribunal.[74]

Tribunals typically have the power to require evidence to be brought before them, for documents and materials to be produced and for witnesses to be summoned to give evidence at a hearing. Most, but not all, have the power to administer oaths. Some, but not all, have the power to award costs. Failure to comply with the directions of a tribunal may result in a finding of contempt, with penalties being imposed by the Court of First Instance[75] or, occasionally, by the tribunal itself.[76] While all tribunals have the power to confirm or revoke an impugned decision, most also have the power to vary it. Some tribunals are empowered to substitute their own decision for the impugned decision. A small number have other substantive powers conferred upon them, such as the power of the Air Pollution Control Appeal Board to award compensation[77] and the power

[66] Thomson (n 9) 369.
[67] ibid.
[68] Franks Report (n 58) para 63.
[69] Eg, Administrative Appeals Board Ordinance (cap 442), s 21(1).
[70] Eg, Electricity Ordinance (cap 406), s 46.
[71] Eg, Administrative Appeals Board Ordinance (cap 442), s 17.
[72] Eg, Immigration Ordinance (cap 115), Sch 1A, para 10.
[73] Eg, Buildings Ordinance (cap 123), s 52.
[74] Eg, Accreditation of Academic and Vocational Qualifications Ordinance (cap 592), s 13(4).
[75] Eg, Environmental Impact Assessment Ordinance (cap 499), s 19(9) and (10).
[76] Eg, Securities and Futures Ordinance (cap 571), s 221. There is a general right of appeal to the Court of Appeal against a finding of contempt – High Court Ordinance (cap 4), s 50. See further Thomson (n 9) 373.
[77] Air Pollution Control Ordinance (cap 311), s 33(6).

of the Mental Health Review Tribunal to discharge a patient.[78] Contrary to the Franks recommendation on the giving of reasons,[79] there is no general requirement for tribunals in Hong Kong to give reasons for their decisions.[80] A number of statutes do provide that reasons must be given by the tribunal, but some make no such provision. Few tribunals make their decisions publicly available and easily accessible. Tribunals are subject to judicial review and have been reviewed on a range of grounds including failure to comply with statutory procedure,[81] error of law,[82] failure to give reasons[83] and unreasonableness through a failure to take into account all relevant considerations.[84]

Are Hong Kong's Administrative Tribunals Constitutionally Compliant?

Categorisation of functions as administrative, judicial or quasi-judicial may have fallen out of fashion in judicial review but is fundamental to the architecture of a system of administrative tribunals. The Franks Committee famously regarded tribunals as part of the machinery for adjudication rather than the machinery of administration,[85] and that informed many of the structural and procedural expectations of tribunals. The Court of Appeal regarded the Municipal Services Appeals Board, a fairly typical tribunal, as having a 'quasi-judicial character' with its governing statutory provisions 'geared towards an adversarial process'.[86] The quasi-judicial character of tribunals is also supported by the general, though not unqualified,[87] principle that they should ordinarily adopt a neutral stance when challenged in an application for judicial review.[88]

Whether tribunals are 'judicial' or 'quasi-judicial' is of much more practical significance than mere academic speculation. Judicial power is constitutionally vested in 'courts'[89] and cannot be exercised by executive bodies,[90] a feature of

[78] Mental Health Ordinance (cap 136), s 59E.
[79] Franks Report (n 58) para 98; implemented in the UK by the Tribunals and Inquiries Act 1958, s 12.
[80] Nor is there any general requirement for public bodies to give reasons for their decisions – see Thomson (n 9) 257–64.
[81] *Building Authority v Appeal Tribunal (Buildings)* [2016] 1 HKLRD 1381.
[82] *Cathay Pacific Airways Ltd v Administrative Appeals Board* [2008] 5 HKLRD 539.
[83] *B v Torture Claims Appeal Board* [2015] 1 HKLRD 681.
[84] *Sabinano II Marcel R v Municipal Services Appeals Board* [2014] HKCFI 382.
[85] Franks Report (n 58) para 40.
[86] *Orrico Philippe v Municipal Services Appeals Board* [2015] 4 HKLRD 111, [20].
[87] *Wong Sin Hua Felix v Insider Dealing Tribunal*, HCAL 129/1999.
[88] *Dato Tan Leong Min v Insider Dealing Tribunal* [1999] 2 HKC 83, 99-100; *Orrico Philippe v Municipal Services Appeals Board* [2015] 4 HKLRD 111, [12]-[33]; *J v Torture Claims Appeal Board* [2022] HKCFI 510, [15].
[89] Basic Law of the Hong Kong SAR, art 80.
[90] *Yau Kwong Man v Secretary for Security* [2002] 3 HKC 457.

constitutional design also found in other systems such as Australia.[91] The independent exercise of judicial power 'free from any interference' is constitutionally guaranteed.[92] Judges, contrary to tribunal members, must be appointed by the Chief Executive on the recommendation of the Judicial Officers Recommendation Commission.[93] They enjoy constitutionally-enshrined security of tenure protections.[94] If tribunals are performing judicial functions, that may in itself be unconstitutional;[95] if tribunal members are, in law, judges, without enjoying constitutionally- and legally-mandated judicial protections, then doubly so.

The miscategorisation or fluidity in the categorisation of institutions in this space is not as implausible as may at first appear. Three examples illustrate this point. First, as noted, some of the functions of the Obscene Articles Tribunal are administrative in nature, yet the Tribunal is part of the Judiciary (though this is the obverse of the above scenario and not necessarily unconstitutional). Second, the Mental Health Review Tribunal was administered by the Judiciary from its establishment in 1989 until 2018 when, at the request of the Judiciary, administration was transferred to the then Food and Health Bureau (a government department) – bucking the trend of tribunals moving from the executive to the judiciary. Third, the Chief Executive's Office previously communicated to this author[96] that the Chief Executive or his delegated authority acts in a 'quasi-judicial capacity and as such would comply with the rules of natural justice' when determining statutory appeals and objections. Yet there seems to be no general legal guarantee of a hearing before the Chief Executive when he acts in the capacity of an administrative tribunal, as a hearing seems only to be generally provided for in an appeal to the CEIC otherwise than by way of petition (and thus not in an appeal to the Chief Executive or to the CEIC by way of petition).[97] Moreover, though the Chief Executive's Office regarded the Chief Executive as acting in a 'quasi-judicial capacity', statute clearly provides for the CEIC *not* to be acting in such a capacity:

> The Chief Executive in Council, when considering any appeal or objection to him (whether by way of petition or otherwise, and whether such appeal or objection is made by virtue of any Ordinance or otherwise) shall act in an administrative or executive capacity and not in a judicial or quasi-judicial capacity and shall be entitled to consider and take into account any evidence, material, information or advice in his absolute discretion.[98]

[91] Commonwealth Constitution, s 71. See J Stellios, *Zines and Stellios's The High Court and the Constitution* (7th edn) (Federation Press 2022), Ch 10; and Groves and Weeks, Chapter 7 in this volume. Yet the courts have cautioned against the over-assimilation of the Hong Kong and Australian constitutional positions with regard to administrative tribunals – *Luk Ka Cheung v Market Misconduct Tribunal* [2009] 1 HKLRD 114, [34]–[36].

[92] Basic Law of the Hong Kong SAR, art 85.

[93] ibid art 88; Judicial Officers Recommendation Commission Ordinance (cap 92).

[94] Basic Law of the Hong Kong SAR, arts 89 and 93.

[95] See *Stock Exchange of Hong Kong Ltd v New World Development Co Ltd* (2006) 9 HKCFAR 234.

[96] Email from Chief Executive's Office (2016).

[97] Administrative Appeals Rules (cap 1A).

[98] Interpretation and General Clauses Ordinance (cap 1), s 64(4).

Again, the Chief Executive and CEIC are distinct legal entities, but it would be a curious difference if the latter hears appeals and objections in an administrative or executive capacity, but the former hears appeals and objections in a quasi-judicial capacity. Moreover, the stakes are high for the constitutionality of administrative tribunals in general, as Article 10 of the Hong Kong Bill of Rights includes the following provision:

> In the determination of any criminal charge against him, or of his rights and obligations in a suit at law, everyone shall be entitled to a fair and public hearing by a competent, independent and impartial tribunal established by law.[99]

This matter was under the microscope in the Court of First Instance in *Television Broadcasts Ltd v Communications Authority*.[100] The Communications Authority ('CA') is a statutory regulator of the broadcasting and telecommunications sectors. It issued a decision finding that Television Broadcasts Ltd ('TVB') had violated competition provisions in the Broadcasting Ordinance[101] ('BO') and ordered TVB to end these infringements, implement compliance directions and pay a penalty of HK$900,000. Under section 34 of the BO, an aggrieved licensee had a statutory right of appeal by way of petition to the CEIC. TVB availed itself of that right of appeal, with the CEIC deciding, at TVB's request, to suspend the appeal procedure pending the outcome of TVB's judicial review application. The aspect of the judicial review application of primary relevance to this discussion is TVB's contention that neither the CA nor the CEIC constituted an independent and impartial tribunal under Article 10 of the Bill of Rights.[102] The Court of First Instance held that the CA was not an independent and impartial tribunal under Article 10 due to the 'comingled role'[103] of performing a 'judicial' function in ruling on infringements of the BO and performing the role of the executive's policy adviser on the broadcasting market:

> [A]n objective observer may legitimately doubt whether it could decide the issues solely on their legal and factual merits with the detachment and objectivity required by Article 10, uninfluenced by any policy considerations which in my view have no role to play in the adjudication of "guilt" or "innocence" in terms of contravention of the statutory prohibition in ss. 13 and 14.[104]

[99] Hong Kong Bill of Rights, art 10 (Hong Kong Bill of Rights Ordinance (cap 383), s 8). Article 10 of the Bill of Rights reflects art 14 of the International Covenant on Civil and Political Rights which is applicable in Hong Kong by virtue of art 39 of the Basic Law.

[100] [2016] 2 HKLRD 41 (CFI).

[101] Cap 562.

[102] TVB had separately contended that it was unconstitutional for the BO to vest a judicial function in the CEIC, but the court held that TVB had abandoned this ground having failed to advance any submission in support of it – [2016] 2 HKLRD 41, [58]. In *Yau Kwong Man v Secretary for Security* [2002] 3 HKC 457, it was held that s 67C of the Criminal Procedure Ordinance (cap 221) was unconstitutional as it was inconsistent with art 80 of the Basic Law by purporting to vest judicial power in the Chief Executive.

[103] [2016] 2 HKLRD 41, [118].

[104] ibid.

There are difficult problems of definition here: is a body in the position of the CA an administrative tribunal? Article 10 was clearly regarded as engaged in this case in relation to the CA, but it arguably has the character of a regulator rather than a tribunal in the orthodox sense. The CEIC did, in this case, act in the capacity of a more orthodox administrative tribunal, however, and the court found that the CEIC also did not meet the requirements of Article 10. Yet the court confined this analysis to the 'unique' provisions of the BO:

> There are a number of provisions in the law of Hong Kong that create appeals to the CEIC but they generally relate to matters pertaining to the formulation of policy or the exercise of administrative or policy-oriented discretion. In providing for an appeal to the CEIC from a finding of infringement of legal prohibition and an order affecting contracts with third parties and imposing financial penalties, however, s. 34 of the BO appears to be unique. It is unclear to what extent the CEIC, without acting at least in a quasi-judicial capacity, which it is proscribed by s. 64(4) [of the Interpretation and General Clauses Ordinance] from doing, can [at least when hearing an appeal by way of petition] dispassionately evaluate the evidence, objectively find facts, correctly determine the law and apply the law to the facts found in the determination of the legal rights and obligations of TVB, without regard to considerations arising from policy, expediency or public interest.[105]

It is unclear to what extent the appeal mechanisms to the CEIC under the BO is or was 'unique', but they do not appear to be numerous, noting statutory rights to appeal to the CEIC by way of petition where the Director of Lands decides not to determine Government rent or premiums,[106] where the Director-General of Civil Aviation decides to prohibit the use of any light exposed to the sky,[107] and where the Director of Agriculture, Fisheries and Conservation refuses to grant or revokes a licence in relation to the slaughtering of poultry for export.[108] The Hong Kong courts have taken a contextual approach to the question of categorising entities as courts or tribunals:

> [T]he mere resemblance of a process to the judicial process to ensure fairness cannot be the acid test for deciding whether the decision maker was exercising the judicial power of the state. Ultimately, one has to examine the nature, function and character of the decision in question in order to determine whether it involves the exercise of the judicial power of the state which by law reserves exclusively for the judiciary.[109]

The obligation to act 'judicially' may thus be taken to indicate the mandatory observation of procedural fairness standards rather than the categorisation of the

[105] ibid at [127]. As the court noted, in an appeal to the CEIC otherwise than by way of petition, the CEIC may state a case for the opinion of the Court of Appeal on any question of law (Administrative Appeals Rules (cap 1A), rr 2 and 13) but this did not apply to an appeal under s 34 of the BO which was an appeal by way of petition.

[106] Government Rent and Premium (Apportionment) Ordinance (cap 125), s 21.

[107] Hong Kong Airport (Control of Obstructions) Ordinance (cap 301), s 10(3).

[108] Poultry (Slaughtering for Export) Regulations (cap 139E), reg 114(2).

[109] *Lee Yee Shing Jacky v Board of Review (Inland Revenue Ordinance)* [2011] 6 HKC 307, [68] (Lam J).

entity as a court.[110] Moreover, the courts have indicated a disinclination to strike down the whole system of administrative tribunals as unconstitutional, signaling a pragmatic approach that was directly contrasted with the approach adopted in Australia:

> It is plain that in a modern society like Hong Kong, administrative tribunals and bodies have an important role to play. This is not a new phenomenon. It was already the case before the Basic Law was promulgated. Given the theme of continuity, it would be very surprising if the effect of the Basic Law, upon its proper interpretation, were to outlaw these administrative tribunals and bodies for ousting the jurisdiction or usurping the judicial functions of the courts of judicature of the HKSAR. Or put another way, the Basic Law should be interpreted in such a way as to enable, so far as violence is not done to the principle of the separation of powers as understood in the tradition of the English common law, the continued existence and development of administrative tribunals and bodies. This calls for a flexible and realistic, as opposed to an idealistic, approach to the doctrine of the separation of powers, and a purposive and contextualised interpretation of the scope and meaning of 'judicial power' in the Basic Law, rather than following indiscriminately the strict interpretation adopted by the Australian courts towards their own Constitution, which was written under very different circumstances in order to serve its own unique purposes.[111]

This does not mean that the courts will not find individual tribunals or instances of their jurisdiction or operation to be unconstitutional – indeed they have done precisely that in relation to the Chief Executive fixing the minimum term of imprisonment of a young person convicted of murder[112] and the Communications Authority[113] – but the probability of a court deeming Hong Kong's entire system of administrative tribunals to be unconstitutional is very low for pragmatic reasons if no other.

The Role of Administrative Tribunals in a Hybrid Regime

The term 'hybrid regime' is often applied to a system that embodies a mixture of democratic and authoritarian characteristics. Such systems are regarded as occupying a 'grey zone' between full democracies and classic authoritarian regimes,

[110] See, eg, *Orrico Philippe v Municipal Services Appeals Board* [2015] 4 HKLRD 111, [19], in which the joint judgment of the Court of Appeal stated that 'the common law rules on natural justice would embrace the notion that those who appeal to the [Municipal Services Appeals Board] are entitled to expect their appeals to be heard by an impartial board and the rule against apparent bias is applicable' even where art 10 of the Bill of Rights was not engaged. See also the discussion in *Town Planning Board v Oriental Generation Ltd* [2014] HKCA 548, [48]–[59]. On the classification of ombudsmen as courts or non-courts and difficulties in determining what is a 'court', primarily in a UK context, see S Thomson, 'Ombudsmen as Courts' (2022) 42(1) *Oxford Journal of Legal Studies* 76.

[111] *Luk Ka Cheung v Market Misconduct Tribunal* [2009] 1 HKLRD 114, [36] (A Cheung J).

[112] *Yau Kwong Man v Secretary for Security* [2002] 3 HKC 457.

[113] *Television Broadcasts Ltd v Communications Authority* [2016] 2 HKLRD 41 (CFI).

described by a range of labels including 'illiberal democracies', 'defective democracies', 'partly free', 'electoral authoritarianism' and 'soft authoritarianism'.[114] According to the 2022 version of *The Economist's* 'Democracy Index', Hong Kong has the lowest democratic score of any of the jurisdictions included in this volume and is the only one to be classed as a hybrid regime:[115]

Global Ranking (2022)	Jurisdiction	Regime type	Overall score (2022)
2	New Zealand	Full democracy	9.61
8	Ireland	Full democracy	9.13
12	Canada	Full democracy	8.88
15	Australia	Full democracy	8.71
18	United Kingdom	Full democracy	8.28
29	Israel	Flawed democracy	7.93
30	United States	Flawed democracy	7.85
45	South Africa	Flawed democracy	7.05
=46	India	Flawed democracy	7.04
70	Singapore	Flawed democracy	6.22
88	Hong Kong	Hybrid regime	5.63

To be clear, the author has reservations about such scoring systems and in particular their potential to be highly reductionist.[116] However, they are far from worthless and what is probably most significant is the direction of travel up or down the rankings for a particular jurisdiction.[117] General standards of administration and justice materially improved in Hong Kong, such that the territory

[114] See, eg, L Diamond, 'Thinking About Hybrid Regimes' (2002) 13(2) *Journal of Democracy* 21; S Levitsky and LA Way, 'The Rise of Competitive Authoritarianism' (2002) 13(2) *Journal of Democracy* 51; M Bogaards, 'How to Classify Hybrid Regimes? Defective Democracy and Electoral Authoritarianism' (2009) 16(2) *Democratization* 399; and A Stroh, S Elischer and G Erdmann, 'Origins and Outcomes of Electoral Institutions in African Hybrid Regimes: A Comparative Perspective', German Institute of Global and Area Studies report (2012). Available at: www.jstor.org/stable/cf3f04f1-4b66-30e1-b15b-97da97f69577?seq=4). In the Hong Kong context, see EC Ip, *Hybrid Constitutionalism: The Politics of Constitutional Review in the Chinese Special Administrative Regions* (Cambridge University Press 2019).

[115] It is not the first time that Hong Kong has been downgraded to a hybrid regime: it carried this status in the 2008, 2010 and 2011 versions of the *Index*. The *Index* was published for the first time in 2006, but Hong Kong may have fared considerably worse in the rankings had it been in currency before the partial democratisation beginning in the 1980s, or even after it. Hong Kong is also 'the oldest continuously functioning legal system in East Asia' save for the brief Japanese occupation of Hong Kong from 1941–1945 and is the only common law jurisdiction in the region – EC Ip, *Law and Justice in Hong Kong* (4th edn) (Sweet & Maxwell 2022) 4–5.

[116] See, eg, R Barros, 'On the Outside Looking In: Secrecy and the Study of Authoritarian Regimes' (2016) 97(4) *Social Science Quarterly* 953.

[117] In this regard, it is also insightful to note that Hong Kong ranked 18 out of 139 jurisdictions globally in Reporters Without Borders' first *World Press Freedom Index* in 2002 whereas, in the most recent,

was at its most democratic and protective of individual rights in the late 1990s and 2000s, straddling the milestone date of 1 July 1997 when sovereignty over the region transferred from the UK to the PRC. However, all but the most politically motivated of commentaries would conclude that Hong Kong's rule of law and democratic credentials have significantly deteriorated in recent years.[118] Regardless of the attribution of a specific numerical score, Hong Kong, in its present state, meets generally accepted definitions of a hybrid regime.

In truth, Hong Kong has long been subject to authoritarian models of government, including the vast majority of its time as a British colony, albeit an unusual blend of authoritarianism and laissez-faire administration.[119] Hong Kong's hybrid regime has been argued not to be an accident of history, but 'deliberately established as such by the framers of the Basic Law … under the auspices of China'. The Hong Kong and Macau Special Administrative Regions[120] are 'run by corporatist regimes, under ruling circles known as "Establishment Coalitions" without any comprehensive, competitive elections, headed by indirectly elected Chief Executives exempt from rigorous checks and balances by partially elected legislatures dominated by loyalists'.[121] However, Hong Kong has undergone a rapid process of further authoritarianisation, particularly since the COVID-19 pandemic. As noted at the outset of this chapter, the enactment of the National Security Law for Hong Kong has effected a systematic erosion of individual rights and the rule of law in Hong Kong and electoral reforms in 2021 have drastically reduced the democratic credentials of the territory's legislature, the Legislative Council. What was once an authoritarian but laissez-faire administration of the territory has, in key ways, become authoritarian in a more conventional sense, namely with higher levels of intrusion into personal liberty. Authoritarianism in terms of political control has remained as a foundational organising model of the Hong Kong polity.

It is worth considering what role administrative tribunals might play in a hybrid regime. Democracy and the rule of law (which are, of course, neither synonymous nor intrinsically linked[122] – this fact is borne out by Hong Kong itself which had a comparatively strong rule of law tradition despite weak democratic credentials)

2023 edition, it is ranked 140 out of 180 jurisdictions, below countries such as Angola, Colombia and Uzbekistan – Reporters Without Borders, *World Press Freedom Index 2023*, Available at: https://rsf.org/en/index?year=2023.

[118] For a flavour of this, see US–China Economic and Security Review Commission, *2021 Annual Report to Congress* (2021) Ch 5; and Thomson, 'The New Constitutional Disorder' (n 2) 115. But for a range of perspectives, see C Chan and F de Londras, *China's National Security: Endangering Hong Kong's Rule of Law?* (Hart Publishing 2020).

[119] Ip, *Hybrid Constitutionalism* (n 114), 68.

[120] Sovereignty over Macau passed from Portugal to the PRC on 20 December 1999 in accordance with the Sino-Portuguese Joint Declaration of 1987 (Joint Declaration on the Question of Macao, 13 April 1987). The PRC incorporated Macau as a Special Administrative Region under Article 31 of the PRC Constitution.

[121] Ip (n 114), 14–15.

[122] See, eg, I Bond and A Gostyńska-Jakubowska, 'Democracy and the rule of law: failing partnership?', Centre for European Reform report (2020). Available at: www.cer.eu/sites/default/files/pbrief_ruleoflaw_17.1.20.pdf.

tend to invoke characteristics such as openness, transparency and enhanced procedural fairness. One may expect a system with strong democratic and rule of law credentials to have more robust standards of public administration in its tribunals system; the converse also applies. Yet this does not lead to defined conclusions about, for example, the location of tribunals in a constitutional structure. Australia and the UK are among the world's most democratic states but administrative tribunals are part of the executive in the former[123] and the judiciary in the latter.[124] Though rule of law protections may be better protected where tribunals are part of the judiciary than the executive, the primary reason for federal tribunals being part of the executive in Australia is that tribunals (in contradistinction to courts) are constitutionally prohibited from exercising judicial power;[125] a shared characteristic with Hong Kong's constitution.[126] It is therefore not as straightforward as arguing that, if only tribunals in Hong Kong were moved out of the executive and into the judicial branch, concerns about their effectiveness as an accountability mechanism would be alleviated.

In any event, such a move would be likely to reduce political control over the system of administrative appeals. This would appear incongruent with the two most likely roles of administrative tribunals in a hybrid regime. On the one hand, tribunals may be operated as a tool for advancing the objective of political control by allowing for pro-administration, pro-establishment interests to be promoted in appeals against administrative decisions, particularly where, as in Hong Kong, tribunal membership appointment powers are vested in the head of government, or officials directly appointed by, and accountable to, the head of government. On the other, they may be a way of advancing the government's legitimacy objectives by either being, or appearing to be, a channel for seeking accountability in public administration but one which does not result in a diminution of political control.[127] They may thus be a compromise between a system of administrative tribunals which maximises the administrative justice imperative and one which does not weaken the government's political control. Perhaps the language deployed by Colonial Secretary Sir Hugh Norman-Walker on the 1969 report recommending the establishment of an ombudsman in Hong Kong – which he and Governor Sir David CC Trench opposed – is revealing: '[m]ight not the existence of such an institution, which would inevitably come to have an appellate flavor, serve to create rather than to close a gap between the Government and the governed?'[128] This was suggested to be the action of a 'self-protective bureaucracy'.[129]

[123] See Groves and Weeks, Chapter 7 in this volume.

[124] See Harlow and Thomas, Chapters 4 and 9 in this volume.

[125] Commonwealth Constitution, s 71.

[126] See above at 264–265.

[127] Though administrative tribunals are not courts, consider T Ginsburg and T Moustafa, 'The Functions of Courts in Authoritarian Politics' in T Ginsburg and T Moustafa (eds), *Rule by Law: The Politics of Courts in Authoritarian Regimes* (Cambridge University Press 2012) 1–22.

[128] *Hong Kong Hansard Session 1969/70*, 1 October 1969, p 11.

[129] J Rear, 'One Brand of Politics' in K Hopkins (ed), *Hong Kong: The Industrial Colony* (Oxford University Press 1971); N Miners, *The Government and Politics of Hong Kong* (2nd edn, Oxford University press) p 137.

There are thus risks associated with overstating the theoretical underpinning of the location and role of administrative tribunals in the Hong Kong legal system. There is no strong evidence for a system of design, rather one that has emerged as tribunals have been established on an ad hoc basis to deal with needs specific to individual sectors and circumstances. There may also have been resistance to the establishment and development of tribunals within the colonial administrations if the above is any indicator of attitudes prevailing as late as the 1960s and 1970s. Not only have tribunals barely featured in academic literature,[130] the Law Reform Commission of Hong Kong has, since its establishment in 1980, published no reports on tribunals or administrative justice.[131] They seem largely to have been absent from constitutional and administrative law discourse, and a lack of reforms, such as the Franks- and Leggatt-style reforms pursued in the UK, would be fairly unsurprising given the comparative apathy shown towards tribunals in Hong Kong.

What can be fairly deduced is that the PRC's increasing assertiveness in the governance of Hong Kong, the turn towards more conventional authoritarianism with higher levels of intrusion into personal liberty, and the new National Security regime which is emblematic of the security paranoia of authoritarian governments,[132] combine to make meaningful reform to the administrative tribunal system in Hong Kong less likely than it has been for decades. While tribunals could be a modest target for reforms within the public law sphere, anything that would or could result in a weakening of political control – or an increase in political transaction costs – is likely to be avoided. The fact that administrative tribunals in Hong Kong were, whether by design or observation, not likely to result in a diminution of political control is a convenient inheritance to a PRC in which political control, direct or indirect, is everything.[133]

Conclusion

Administrative tribunals in Hong Kong appear to be a comparatively late development by the standards of many common law jurisdictions, with a number of key tribunals emerging in the 1980s and 1990s. This is consistent with the underlying

[130] See above at 253.

[131] In fact, it has not even published dedicated reports on matters of constitutional law or administrative law.

[132] See US-China Economic and Security Review Commission, *Annual Report to Congress 2021*, Ch 5 ('Hong Kong's Government Embraces Authoritarianism'). Available at: www.uscc.gov/sites/default/files/2021-11/Chapter_5-Hong_Kongs_Government_Embraces_Authoritarianism.pdf.

[133] See, eg, SV Lawrence and MF Martin, 'Understanding China's Political System' (Congressional Research Service Report for Congress, 2013). Available at: https://sgp.fas.org/crs/row/R41007.pdf; AY So, 'The Rise of Authoritarianism in China in the Early 21st Century' (2019) 45(1) *International Review of Modern Sociology* 49; and E Smith, 'On the Informal Rules of the Chinese Communist Party' (2021) 248(S1) *The China Quarterly* 141.

pattern of colonial government in Hong Kong whereby administration was relatively light touch, the welfare state developed according to the needs and pace of local conditions, and democratic and administrative reforms were hurried through as the handover of sovereignty to the PRC approached. The development of accountability mechanisms against the government did not seem to be much of a priority for the British colonial administrations, with their emphasis on political control, and this is also seen in the long road towards the establishment of the Commissioner for Administrative Complaints, later the Ombudsman, in Hong Kong.

Yet with the Handover, so much has changed, and so little. The HKSAR continues to operate the 'system' of administrative tribunals in the colonial mould with little appetite shown for any kind of improvement or modernisation. While tribunals have played an important role in the lives of people who have been subject to their decisions both pre- and post-Handover, they have been a subject of relative disinterest and apathy. Compared to the likes of judicial review or even the Ombudsman, they have barely featured in academic, law reform or political discourse. And when it comes to law reform and political discourse, why should they? For Hong Kong has long been subject to authoritarian models of government and that continues to be the case, albeit – and moreover – with a recent turn towards a more classical form of authoritarianism. The PRC, whose hand in Hong Kong affairs is only growing, is unlikely to pursue any strategy that would or could result in a diminution of political control. Accordingly, tribunals are likely to remain under the administration of government departments, the methods for appointing their members are likely to remain opaque, there is unlikely to be any truly independent oversight of tribunals, and the courts have made it clear that there are no systemic constitutional problems with tribunals. In addition, given the tumultuous developments in Hong Kong over the past few years, it is not unreasonable to conclude that the region ultimately faces much greater problems. Yet whereas tribunals might once have been a modest target for reform, that seems a diminished prospect. Despite being an integral part of Hong Kong's landscape of administrative law and administrative justice, tribunals will likely continue to operate in relative obscurity and pose no major accountability threat to the government in a perennially hybrid regime.

13

Administrative Tribunals in India

CHINTAN CHANDRACHUD[1]

Background

The Indian courts bear the responsibility of delivering justice to millions of litigants each year. The dockets of courts at all levels have increased exponentially. The number of pending cases in the Supreme Court has risen from a few hundred in the year of its founding (1950) to 70,000 in 2023.[2] The High Courts and district courts are in an analogous position. There are over 50 million cases pending before the courts at all levels.[3] The burden of litigation that courts confront is exacerbated by the expense involved at all stages,[4] together with the difficulties in promoting the settlement of disputes by consent of the parties. These failings famously prompted Mendelsohn to describe the Indian legal system as pathological more than four decades ago.[5]

'Docket explosion' is not a new problem, and the search for solutions is almost as old as the problem itself. As far back as 1924, the Civil Justice Committee chaired by George Claus Rankin, a judge of the Calcutta High Court, received evidence as to the significant delays in the judicial system in British India.[6] One of the senior lawyers giving evidence noted pithily that 'there is delay, in some cases very great delay, in the disposal of suits and appeals'.[7] The Committee recommended a series of reforms to address backlogs in the system.

[1] I am grateful to Ishika Garg for providing excellent research assistance. All errors are mine.

[2] B Debroy, 'Justice Delivery in India – A Snapshot of Problems and Reforms' (2008) Institute of South Asian Studies Working Paper 47/2008, 6; Information obtained from the website of the Supreme Court of India. Available at: https://main.sci.gov.in/statistics, accessed 15 August 2023.

[3] P Thakur, 'Pending cases have now crossed 5 crore, House told' *The Times of India*. Available at: https://m.timesofindia.com/india/pending-cases-have-now-crossed-5-crore-house-told/articleshow/101998790.cms, accessed 15 August 2023.

[4] Daksh, 'Access to Justice Survey' (2015–2016) pp 14–17. Available at: https://dakshindia.org/wp-content/uploads/2016/05/Daksh-access-to-justice-survey.pdf, accessed 12 September 2023.

[5] O Mendelsohn, 'The Pathology of the Indian Legal System' (1981) 15 *Modern Asian Studies* 823–63.

[6] Report of the Civil Justice Committee, 1924–1925.

[7] ibid Appendix 2 – Oral Evidence, Volume III, p 5.

In its 14th Report, published in 1958, the Law Commission of India conducted a remarkably comprehensive study of the issues that plague the effective administration of justice in India.[8] Specifically, it looked into the question of whether the creation of tribunals for particular subject areas (such as administrative law) would be suited to the Indian context. Having examined similar tribunals in other jurisdictions, the Commission concluded that the creation of a general administrative body akin to the French model was ill advised.[9] Its reasons reflected a deep mistrust for executive-minded adjudication.

In spite of this, the Commission saw merit in establishing tribunals which would decide cases involving government officials seeking redress for the breach of the rules regulating their conditions of service. This conclusion was driven by the ever-increasing volume of cases of that nature that were flooding the courts. Perhaps conscious of the fact that the suggestion to create tribunals was bold and unprecedented at the time, the Commission was careful to clarify that the new administrative tribunals would not displace the writ jurisdiction of the High Courts of various Indian states. The Commission also recommended that the tribunals be presided over by a chairperson who is qualified to be a High Court judge.[10]

The movement for the creation of specialised administrative tribunals gained momentum from a 1969 Committee chaired by Supreme Court Justice JC Shah. Having analysed the pendency of writ petitions filed by various classes of litigants, including government officials, before the Supreme Court and High Courts, the Committee concluded in favour of setting up independent administrative tribunals to deal with specific subject matters.[11] However, this came to be quickly undone with the constitution of the 6th Law Commission in 1971. Under the chairmanship of Justice PB Gajendragadkar, the Commission's 58th Report instilled apprehension against the creation of a separate framework of tribunals in India.[12] This apprehension is not to be misunderstood as a distrust in the potential benefits of a system of tribunals. Quite to the contrary, the Commission explicitly highlighted the positive impact that such a system can have on addressing the rapidly multiplying backlog of cases before the courts.

The concern that the Report focused on was as follows. In the opinion of the members of the Commission, to allow the writ jurisdiction of the High Courts and the 'special leave petition' jurisdiction of the Supreme Court[13] to continue in parallel to the powers of the tribunal was impractical. Such simultaneous

[8] First Law Commission of India, 'Reform of Judicial Administration' (Report No 14, 26 September 1958). Coincidentally, this came only a year after the Franks Report in Britain: *Report on Administrative Tribunals and Enquiries*, August 1957, Cmd. 218.

[9] First Law Commission of India, 'Reform of Judicial Administration' (Report No 14, vol 2, 26 September 1958) 694.

[10] ibid.

[11] JC Shah, 'Report of the High Court Arrears Committee' (vol 1, 1972) 70.

[12] Sixth Law Commission of India, 'Stature and Jurisdiction of the Higher Judiciary' (Report No 58, 1974).

[13] Article 136 of the Indian Constitution empowers the Supreme Court to grant special leave to appeal against any judgment of any court in India.

jurisdiction would fail to meaningfully reduce the burden on the courts. At the same time, the majority of the Commission members found it improper to restrict the jurisdiction of the Supreme Court and the High Courts. This was attributable to fears that granting exclusive jurisdiction to tribunals for certain matters could mean that unscrupulous litigants would seek to abuse the extensive powers of tribunals by capitalising on their relative informality. That led to the ultimate, even if reluctant, recommendation against the establishment of separate tribunals.[14] The idea of establishing specialised tribunals was shelved for the next few years.

The Establishment of Tribunals

On 25 June 1975, a national emergency was imposed in India under Prime Minister Indira Gandhi, purportedly to counter imminent internal and external threats to the State. It is widely accepted that the real reason for the declaration of this 21-month period of emergency was to safeguard Gandhi's position and ensure that she remained in office. The period immediately preceding the emergency set the tone for the 21 months that followed. The most startling episode for the legal community during this period was the appointment of AN Ray as the 14th Chief Justice of India on 26 April 1973. His appointment was in defiance of the convention of appointing the most senior judge of the Supreme Court as its Chief Justice. Ray's appointment superceded that of Justice Shelat, who was next in line to become the Chief Justice, and two other senior Judges of the Court. Ray had found in favour of the government, while his three senior colleagues that had been overlooked had ruled against it, in the famous 'basic structure' case.[15] Ray's appointment established a justifiable feeling of mistrust in the independence of the judiciary, which began to be seen as a politically influenced institution rather than as a bulwark of democracy and the rule of law.

Arguably in a bid to restore confidence in the judicial system,[16] in 1976 a committee was set up under the Chairmanship of Swaran Singh, one of India's longest-serving Cabinet Ministers. Amongst other matters, the Committee revisited the question of whether specialised tribunals should be established. It recommended the establishment of tribunals for three distinct areas to improve the efficiency of the Indian judiciary.[17] These areas were: 'service matters' (involving the conditions of service of public sector employees); industrial and labour disputes; and matters relating to revenue, land reforms, procurement and distribution of foodgrains and other essential commodities.

[14] Sixth Law Commission of India, 'Stature and Jurisdiction of the Higher Judiciary' (Report No 58, 1974).

[15] *Kesavananda Bharati v State of Kerala*, AIR 1973 SC 1461. See, generally, A Sengupta and JV Ojha, 'Judicial Appointments in India: From Pillar to Post' (2020) 10 *Constitutional Court Review* 43, 44–45.

[16] Anusha Ramesh, 'Tribunalisation of India's Competition Regime' (2016) 9 *NUJS Law Review* 259.

[17] 'Swaran Singh Committee Report' (1976) 2 SCC (Jour) 45.

This recommendation revived the phase that immediately followed the First Law Commission's 14th Report. Where the suggestions of the Swaran Singh Committee differed from those of the First Law Commission is in relation to the interplay between the jurisdiction of the tribunals and that of the courts. The 14th Report of the First Law Commission had suggested that the writ jurisdiction of the High Court continue in parallel with the jurisdiction of the tribunals. It did this as a safeguard for cases where tribunals proved to be ineffective.[18] However, the continuance of such parallel jurisdiction was considered problematic by the members of the 6th Law Commission. They believed that allowing High Courts to continue to hear claims in areas demarcated for tribunals would mean that the 'docket explosion' problem would remain unresolved. The Report of the Swaran Singh Committee identified middle ground between the two extremes of depriving the courts of jurisdiction on the one hand and giving the courts and tribunals parallel jurisdiction on the other. It recommended that following the creation of tribunals, the writ jurisdiction of both the High Courts and the Supreme Court should no longer be available for those matters for which the newer facility has been formed. At the same time, the Committee was conscious of the fact that tribunals, being a new addition to the Indian adjudicative landscape, should not be left entirely unchecked. It therefore advised that the special leave petition jurisdiction of the Supreme Court should remain available.

While the Swaran Singh Committee identified a compromise between the two existing positions on the roadmap for tribunals in India, apprehensions were raised in relation to its political credibility. The Committee was, after all, constituted in the context of the emergency. During the emergency, the Indian judiciary was criticised for having compromised its independence. Although the Committee might have been set up to paint the judiciary in a more favourable light, it had the opposite effect.[19] The recommendation to exclude the writ jurisdiction of the High Courts was seen as an attempt to muzzle them.[20] This criticism was significant considering the critical subject matter that would form part of the Tribunals' jurisdiction.

Nevertheless, the Report had the support of the ruling party[21] and its recommendations were adopted through the Constitution (Forty-Second Amendment) Act of 1976 (the '42nd Amendment'). Through this amendment, a new Part XIV-A was added to the Constitution.[22] This consisted of two important provisions – Articles 323-A and 323-B. The former provided for the creation of administrative tribunals whose primary function is to settle disputes relating to the employment

[18] First Law Commission of India, 'Reform of Judicial Administration' (Report No 14, vol 2, 26 September 1958) 694.

[19] Anusha Ramesh, 'Tribunalisation of India's Competition Regime' (2016) 9 *NUJS Law Review* 259.

[20] AK Thiruvengadam, 'Tribunals' in S Choudhry, M Khosla and PB Mehta (eds), *The Oxford Handbook of the Indian Constitution* (OUP, 2015), 412–31.

[21] BD Dua, 'A Study in Executive-Judicial Conflict: The Indian Case' (1983) 23 *Asian Survey* 463.

[22] The Constitution (Forty Second Amendment) Act, 1976, §46.

and service of government officials. The latter gave both the state-level and central legislatures the power to constitute tribunals with jurisdiction over other matters, such as property and tax. While covering the recommendations of the Swaran Singh Committee in relation to the three distinct areas for tribunals in India, Article 323-B(2) also empowered the legislature to establish tribunals for election cases as well as rent control cases, which went beyond the recommendations of the Committee.[23]

In 1977, there was a shift in the political landscape and a new party came to power at the centre. The Janata Party ('JP') was determined to reverse the policy changes ushered in by Indira Gandhi's government. Members of the JP wanted to erase everything that the 42nd Amendment to the Indian Constitution stood for. They were especially opposed to the creation of tribunals, since they believed that these institutions would be subject to manipulation by the executive. While the JP succeeded in undoing a number of other provisions introduced by the 42nd amendment, Part XIV-A remained unaffected. The Congress Party's majority in the Rajya Sabha, the Upper House of Parliament, meant that the clause seeking to reverse the introduction of Part XIV-A did not garner sufficient support. After navigating choppy waters right from the 1950s, tribunals had finally found a stable position in the Indian constitutional landscape.

Situating Tribunals Within the Judicial Architecture

The Indian Constitution established a unitary judicial structure with the Supreme Court at the top. The Supreme Court is the final court of appeal in civil and criminal cases and is the authoritative interpreter of the Constitution. Its judgments are binding on all other courts and tribunals. Twenty-five high courts, representing the states and union territories of India, form the second tier of this hierarchy. High courts exercise appellate and original jurisdiction. Below the High Courts are the district courts for the (c. 700) districts in India.

Within this framework, administrative tribunals either sit alongside or below the High Courts. In some cases, appeals from tribunals or regulatory bodies are made to an appellate tribunal, with appeals from the appellate tribunal going directly to the Supreme Court. For example, orders made by the Securities and Exchange Board of India are appealed to the Securities Appellate Tribunal,[24] with a further appeal to the Supreme Court. In others, appeals from decisions of a tribunal are made to the High Court, with further appeals then being made to the Supreme Court. For example, appeals against decisions of the Appellate Board under the Copyright Act are made to the relevant state High Court.[25]

[23] The Constitution of India, 1950, Art 323-B(2).
[24] Securities and Exchange Board of India Act 1992, ss 15K and 15T.
[25] Copyright Act 1957, s 72.

Over the last two decades, there have been approximately 20 to 30 tribunals in place under central legislation, although there are disagreements over the exact number (arising from disagreements about whether particular bodies can properly be regarded as tribunals). There are also a number of tribunals established by state legislation. Some tribunals (such as the Armed Forces Tribunal) resolve disputes between citizens and the state, others (such as the Debt Recovery Tribunal) resolve disputes amongst citizens, and still others (such as the Electricity Appellate Tribunal) resolve disputes in both categories.[26]

In India, tribunals have been conceived of as quasi-judicial bodies established by law to decide disputes related to specific subject matter.[27] As Justice Hidayatullah explained in *Harinagar Sugar Mills Ltd v Shyam Sundar Jhunjhunwala* (1962) 2 SCR 339:

> With the growth of civilization and the problems of modern life, a large number of administrative Tribunals have come into existence. These Tribunals have the authority of law to pronounce upon valuable rights; they act in a judicial manner and even on evidence on oath, but they are not part of the ordinary Courts of Civil Judicature. They share the exercise of the judicial power of the State, but they are brought into existence to implement some administrative policy or to determine controversies arising out of some administrative law. They are very similar to Courts, but are not Courts.

Statutes establishing tribunals usually provide that proceedings before the tribunal are to be regarded as judicial proceedings (with the attendant criminal sanctions such as perjury); that tribunals will have all the powers of a civil court (including to summon witnesses, order the production of documents, and receive evidence on oath); and that orders of the tribunal are to be enforceable in the same way as orders of a civil court. However, tribunals have the power to regulate their own procedure, and are (at least in theory) not bound by strict rules of procedure or evidence that would apply in civil proceedings. In practice, it is a frequently aired complaint that tribunals follow the same approach to procedure and evidence as civil courts and are therefore (unsurprisingly) bogged down by the same inefficiencies.[28]

Tribunals may comprise a single panel/bench, or (in the case of tribunals with a heavy caseload) multiple panels. They are usually staffed by judicial members

[26] AAP Kumar and R Das, 'The State of the Nation's Tribunals: Introduction and Part 1', Vidhi Centre for Legal Policy, June 2014, pp 10–11.

[27] See Law Commission of India, Report 272, 'Assessment of Statutory Frameworks of Tribunals in India', October 2017, [1.6]; *Associated Cement Companies Ltd v PN Sharma* (1965) 2 SCR 366 ('… both the courts and the Tribunals are constituted by the state and are invested with judicial as distinguished from purely administrative or executive functions …'); *Kihoto Hollohan v Zachillhu* 1992 Supp (2) SCC 651 ('Where there is a lis – an affirmation by one party and denial by another – and the dispute necessarily involves a decision on the rights and obligations of the parties to it and the authority is called upon to decide it, there is an exercise of judicial power. That authority is called a Tribunal, if it does not have all the trappings of a court').

[28] AP Kumar and R Das, 'The State of the Nation's Tribunals: Introduction and Part 1', Vidhi Centre for Legal Policy, June 2014, p 2.

(i.e. retired judges or senior lawyers) and technical members (domain experts recruited from a ministry/government department or from the private sector). This is a major deviation from the courts, where legal training and/or experience is a prerequisite for judgeship. As will be seen, that has proved to be a cause for complaint rather than celebration. The quality of tribunal decisions is frequently called into question, and tribunal decisions are often overturned by the High Court and/or Supreme Court.[29]

The Evolution of Tribunals

Although some tribunals had already been established prior to independence,[30] the Indian Constitution as originally enacted did not make any specific provision for tribunals. The only reference to tribunals was in Articles 136 and 227, which stated that the Supreme Court and High Courts respectively would have the power to review decisions of tribunals.[31] However, drawing upon India's long tradition of self-government at the village level, Article 40 required the state to organise village panchayats and give them power and authority to function as units of self-government. The judicial branches of these panchayats were known as *nyaya* or *adalati* panchayats. While nyaya panchayats were established and became operational in principle, they failed to attract significant support over time, ceding ground to the courts. Their caseload declined so substantially that they became moribund by the mid-1970s.[32]

As noted above, outside of the panchayat context, tribunals first found a place in the Constitution with the introduction of Part XIV-A. The years that followed were punctuated by litigation focusing on the constitutional validity of the introduction of specialised tribunals. Most of these cases challenged the very rationale behind the benefits of tribunals and sought to reintroduce old suspicions of the executive-mindedness of tribunals.[33] The provocation for such disputes was the enactment of the Administrative Tribunals Act of 1985, which finally authorised the creation of tribunals as envisioned under Articles 323-A and 323-B. Until then, these articles only provided a mechanism for the creation of tribunals but did not

[29] ibid p 2.

[30] Notably, the Income Tax Appellate Tribunal, established in 1941 pursuant to s 5A of the Income Tax Act 1922.

[31] AK Thiruvengadam, 'Tribunals' in S Choudhry, M Khosla and P Bhanu Mehta (eds), *The Oxford Handbook of the Indian Constitution* (OUP, 2015), 413.

[32] J Krishnan and others, 'Grappling at the Grassroots: Access to Justice in India's Lower Tier' (2014) 27 *Harvard Human Rights Journal* 501, 504; CS Meschievitz and M Galanter, 'In Search of Nyaya Panchayats: The Politics of a Moribund Institution in R Abel (ed), *The Politics of Informal Justice: Comparative Studies*, Volume 2 (Academic Press, 1982), 47. Nyaya Panchayats were ultimately replaced by gram nyayalayas: see the Gram Nyayalayas Act 2008.

[33] AK Thiruvengadam, 'Tribunals' in S Choudhry, M Khosla and PB Mehta (eds), *The Oxford Handbook of the Indian Constitution* (OUP, 2015), 412–31.

actually set the wheels in motion. The 1985 statute provided for the establishment of tribunals to deal with disputes relating to the appointment and terms of service of persons appointed to public services and posts in connection with the affairs of the Union or of any State or of any other authority within the Indian territory.[34] Specifically, it provided for the constitution of a Central Administrative Tribunal ('CAT') at the centre and a State Administrative Tribunal ('SAT') at the state level for every Indian state.[35] The CAT is responsible for the adjudication of matters regarding the recruitment and conditions of service of personnel in Indian public services.[36] Similarly, the SATs are entrusted with resolving disputes affecting the recruitment and service conditions of the respective state government officials.[37] With the enactment of this statute, the 'threat' of the existence of tribunals became very real.

The Early Phase (1985–1997)

With the passage of the Administrative Tribunals Act came the first challenge to the constitutionality of establishing tribunals. In *SP Sampath Kumar v Union of India*,[38] a five-judge bench of the Supreme Court was faced with the question of the constitutionality of Section 28 of the Act, which ousted the writ jurisdiction of the Supreme Court and High Courts in areas which lay within the tribunals' domain. This challenge rested on the argument that such an exclusion of jurisdiction was in violation of the petitioners' constitutional rights to judicial review. The Supreme Court considered two questions: *first*, whether the exclusion of jurisdiction meant that the Act violated the Constitution by negatively impacting judicial review, which forms a part of the Constitution's basic structure; and *second*, whether the tribunals established under the Act were an appropriate substitute for the High Courts that had previously been dealing with cases that would now be considered by tribunals. The leading judgment on both these issues was authored by Justice Ranganath Misra, who later served as Chief Justice of India.

On the first question, Justice Misra considered the docket explosion in the Indian courts as a special circumstance which could be taken into account in determining whether it was appropriate to exclude the writ jurisdiction of Supreme Court and the High Courts in favour of speedy alternative institutional mechanisms to resolve disputes.[39] In his opinion, the creation of such institutions did not adversely affect the role of judicial review enshrined in the Constitution.[40]

[34] The Administrative Tribunals Act 1985, Act No 13 of 1985 (Indian Parliament), Preamble.
[35] ibid s 14.
[36] ibid.
[37] ibid s 15.
[38] *SP Sampath Kumar v Union of India*, (1987) 1 SCC 124.
[39] ibid para 15.
[40] ibid para 17.

That conclusion faced significant criticism amongst the legal community at the time.[41] It was based on the fact that the writ jurisdiction of the High Courts had been held to be a part of the basic structure of the Constitution, and was thus not to be lightly excluded for the purpose of creating 'effective alternative institutional mechanisms'.[42] In recognition of this argument, a subsequent Supreme Court judgment raised doubts about Justice Misra's conclusion.[43] In that case, the Court clarified that judicial review forms an inalienable part of the basic structure of the Constitution. While not explicitly overruling *Sampath Kumar*, the Court clarified that Justice Misra's judgment should not be seen to justify the view that tribunals are 'substitutes' of High Courts. Several High Courts then relied upon that view. For instance, the High Court of Andhra Pradesh held that any provision in the nature of Section 28 of the Act which ousted the writ jurisdiction of High Courts and Supreme Court would violate the basic structure of the Constitution.[44]

Justice Misra took a deferential approach to the second question. Instead of arriving at any definitive answer as to whether the tribunals created under the Act are analogous to the High Courts, he expressed his earnest expectation that the Act would be amended in the future to ensure that tribunals prove to be 'worthy successors' of and 'real substitutes' for the High Courts.[45] He also issued directions that could be referred to by the legislature as the yardstick for matters such as the manner of appointment of the members of the tribunals, their qualifications, tenure, and the like. On the question of tenure of members, Justice Misra expressed his dissatisfaction with section 8 of the Act. Under section 8, the term for the chair or members of tribunals would be the earlier of five years from the date of assumption of office and the attainment of retirement age.[46] He noted that this provision may act as a disincentive for those 'competent people belonging to younger age groups who would have more than five years to reach the prevailing age of retirement'. For this reason, Justice Misra suggested that the Legislature consider expanding this term to a relatively longer one in future amendments. To leave such important questions up to the chance of the law being amended in the future seemed to signal that the Court did not take the petitioners' allegations sufficiently seriously. The perils of the Court's approach are obvious given that even three decades after the suggestion to increase the tenure of tribunal members and chairpersons, the Act still only provides for a five-year term. However, the objections raised in the *Sampath Kumar* petition form a part of a chapter in history

[41] Dr Dinesh, 'The Administrative Tribunals Conundrum: A Figleaf for "Executive" Adjudication?' (2021) 8 *Journal of Campus Law Centre* 129; AK Thiruvengadam, 'Tribunals' in S Choudhry, M Khosla and P Bhanu Mehta (eds), *The Oxford Handbook of the Indian Constitution* (OUP, 2015), 412–31.

[42] ibid.

[43] *RK Jain v Union of India* AIR 1993 SC 1769.

[44] *Sakinala Harinath and Ors v State of Andhra Pradesh and Ors* 1993 (3) ALT 471.

[45] *SP Sampath Kumar v. Union of India*, (1987) 1 SCC 124, paras 17–18, 23.

[46] The Administrative Tribunals Act 1985, Act No 13 of 1985 (Indian Parliament), s 8.

that was not so easily closed. These issues would soon be re-litigated in *L Chandra Kumar v Union of India*.[47]

In *L Chandra Kumar*, a seven-judge bench of the Supreme Court conclusively decided the issues that were addressed unsatisfactorily in *Sampath Kumar*. Similar to *Sampath Kumar*, the Court in *L Chandra* upheld the constitutionality of the system of administrative tribunals. However, in relation to the question of the exclusion of the writ jurisdiction of the Supreme Courts and the High Courts, the bench reached the opposite conclusion to that in *Sampath Kumar*. For the judges in *L Chandra*, there was no doubt that all decisions of the tribunals created under Articles 323-A and 323-B of the Constitution would be subject to the writ jurisdiction of the relevant High Court. This would ensure that baseless claims are filtered out by tribunals before they reach the High Court.[48] Logically then, there would be a lower volume of cases flooding the High Courts. The High Court would also benefit from having a reasoned decision before it rather than deciding the issues de novo.[49]

To ensure that tribunals could serve as an effective first-stage substitute for High Courts, the Court in *L Chandra* made some (non-binding) recommendations. First, it suggested that an independent agency be set up to monitor the administration of tribunals to avoid their malfunctioning. Second, the Court suggested that the tribunals created under the Act consist of an appropriate balance of both judicial and non-judicial members. In order to maintain the independence of tribunals, the Court also suggested that the selection committee for appointing members of tribunals include a Supreme Court judge. The *L Chandra* Court concluded by stating that the suggestions that it had made in respect of tribunals 'need to be considered in detail by those entrusted with the duty of formulating the policy in this respect'.[50]

Post-L Chandra Kumar (1998–2016)

With the question of the constitutionality of tribunals finally having been settled, subsequent litigation revolved around ensuring the efficient functioning of the tribunals that had been set up following the 1985 Act. These tribunals extended well beyond the matters originally envisaged by Articles 323-A and 323-B, with the establishment of the Railway Claims Tribunal, the Intellectual Property Appellate Board and the Telecom Disputes Settlement and Appellate Tribunal, among others.[51] Still further examples include the National Company Law Tribunal ('NCLT') and

[47] *L Chandra Kumar v Union of India* AIR 1997 SC 1125.

[48] ibid para 91.

[49] ibid.

[50] *L Chandra Kumar v Union of India* AIR 1997 SC 1125, para 98.

[51] These tribunals were established under the Railway Claims Tribunal Act of 1987, the Indian Trademarks Act of 1999, and the Telecom Regulatory Authority of India Act of 1997 respectively.

the National Company Law Appellate Tribunal ('NCLAT'). The NCLT is a quasi-judicial authority that has primary jurisdiction over civil corporate disputes under the Companies Act, India's principal company law statute. The NCLAT was set up as an appellate tribunal mainly for hearing appeals against judgments and orders of the NCLT. The selection committee constituted to appoint members to both the NCLT and NCLAT was to be composed of secretaries of governmental ministries such as the Ministry of Law and Justice and the Ministry of Labour.[52]

In *Union of India v R Gandhi*,[53] the Supreme Court considered the constitutional validity of the establishment of the NCLT and the NCLAT. One of the issues before the Court concerned the independence of these tribunals. A five-judge bench of the Supreme Court concluded that the composition of the selection committee compromised its independence. The Court observed that the selection committee for the appointment of the members of the tribunals included the secretary of the governmental department which sponsored the funding and other needs of the tribunals. This undermined the ability of the tribunals to function independently of the department's influence. Instead, the Court ordered that the Chief Justice of India, or their nominee, chair the selection committee. In order to ensure the independence of the tribunals, the bench also mandated the concurrence of the Chief Justice of India for the removal or suspension of the Chairperson of the tribunals. In terms of improving the efficiency of these tribunals, the Court in *R. Gandhi* suggested that, as far as possible, members should have the same rank, experience or level of competence as High Court judges. Further, the Court ordered that the non-judicial members of these tribunals who are appointed for their technical expertise must be selected from a pool of officers who hold the rank of either Secretaries or Additional Secretaries in their respective departments.

The theme of independence of tribunals was soon explored by the Supreme Court again in relation to a challenge to the National Tax Tribunal Act 2005, which established the National Tax Tribunal ('NTT') to adjudicate upon taxation-related disputes.[54] Under the 2005 Act, the central government could conclusively decide crucial administrative matters such as the location, jurisdiction and constitution of benches of the NTT, the transfer of its members, and so on.[55] The Supreme Court found that those powers were an attempt to interfere with the functioning of the NTT, impacting its independence. This problem was particularly acute in light of the fact that the central government itself would be a party to a majority of the taxation disputes before the tribunal. The Court also raised concerns in relation to the composition of the selection committee for the members of the NTT. Under the Act, the committee consisted of more executive members than judicial members. These provisions risked the executive aggrandisement of power.

[52] The Companies Act 1956, Act No 01 of 1956 (Indian Parliament), s 10FX.
[53] *Union of India v R Gandhi* (2010) 11 SCC 1.
[54] *Madras Bar Association v Union of India* (2014) 10 SCC 1.
[55] The National Tax Tribunal Act 2005, Act No 49 of 2005 (Indian Parliament), s 5 (repealed).

The Court also came down heavily against provisions in the Act which allowed for the reappointment of members upon the expiry of their initial term, concluding that this would impair the ability of members who seek reappointment to arrive at impartial decisions.[56] For those reasons, the Court struck down the 2005 Act as unconstitutional.

The phase that followed *L Chandra Kumar* was primarily focused on improving the efficiency of the functioning of tribunals through attempts to standardise mechanisms such as the appointment of its members, their qualifications, and the like. The idea was to enhance the independence of tribunals in a way that allows them to effectively supplement the traditional judicial system. For instance, in 1993, Debt Recovery Tribunals ('DRTs') were constituted to ensure the speedy redressal of disputes for lenders and borrowers.[57] These tribunals were found to be unconstitutional by the Delhi High Court for violating the principle of judicial independence.[58] While this decision was pending in appeal before the Supreme Court, the Central Government framed rules for the formation of a selection committee including the Chief Justice of India for the appointment of the Presiding Officer of the DRTs.[59] This was presumably done to avoid allegations of executive interference in appointments and violations of the principle of judicial independence. Following the introduction of these rules, the Supreme Court upheld the validity of DRTs, relying on *L Chandra Kumar* in support of its analysis.[60]

New Era (2017 Onwards)

The last decade echoed growing calls for securing the independence of tribunals. However, the measures for reform did not live up to these demands. In fact, the reforms proposed in the five years since 2017 appear to undermine the existing jurisprudence on the constitutionality and independence of tribunals in India. The Supreme Court's decisions in *L Chandra Kumar* and *R Gandhi* served as the touchstone for litigants to bring constitutional challenges to these new reforms. The first such challenge was to the introduction of Part XIV of the Finance Act, 2017 ('2017 Act'),[61] which is the annual fiscal statute enacted by the Indian Parliament to give effect to the financial proposals of the Central Government. The Tribunal, Appellate Tribunal and Other Authorities (Qualifications, Experience and Other

[56] *Madras Bar Association v Union of India* (2014) 10 SCC 1, para 132.

[57] Recovery of Debts Due to Banks and Financial Institutions Act, Act No 51 of 1993 (Indian Parliament), s 3.

[58] *Delhi High Court Bar Association v Union of India* AIR 1995 Del 323.

[59] The Debts Recovery Tribunal (Procedure for Appointment as Presiding Officer of the Tribunal) Rules 1998, r 3.

[60] *Union of India v Delhi High Court Bar Association* (2002) 4 SCC 275.

[61] The Finance Act 2017, Act No 07 of 2017 (Indian Parliament), Part XIV.

Conditions of Service of Members) Rules, 2017 ('Tribunal Rules, 2017') that were framed under this Part of the 2017 Act were also challenged.[62]

Under Part XIV of the 2017 Act, eight tribunals that had been established under different statutes were abolished and their jurisdiction merged into seven existing tribunals. For instance, the Cyber Appellate Tribunal and the Airports Economic Regulatory Authority[63] were both abolished[64] and their powers transferred to the Telecom Disputes Settlement and Appellate Tribunal established under the Telecom Regulatory Authority of India Act, 1997.[65] Part XIV also amended the parent statutes of 19 central tribunals in relation to the service conditions of its chairpersons and members. It provided that the qualification, appointment, salary, removal and other conditions of service would, going forward, be governed by Section 184 of the 2017 Act.[66] This provision enables the Central Government to make rules regarding the qualifications, appointments, salaries, removal, and other conditions of service. The Tribunal Rules 2017 were notified by the Central Government pursuant to Section 184. The aim of these rules and of the amendments to various central statutes was to organise tribunals based on functional similarity and provide uniformity to the service conditions of the members. Interestingly, the Rules prescribed a vague qualification requirement for the appointment of members: specialist knowledge of 'certain subjects which in the opinion of the Central government is useful'. They also established a search-cum-selection committee (with minimal judicial involvement) for the appointment of members.[67]

In *Rojer Mathew v South Indian Bank Ltd*, the Supreme Court was asked to determine the constitutional validity of Part XIV of the 2017 Act (in particular, section 184) and the Tribunal Rules, 2017.[68] It was argued that section 184 should be struck down for excessive delegation, because it conferred upon the Central Government the carte blanche power to make rules on the terms and conditions of service of the members of various tribunals in the absence of any guidance from Parliament. Interestingly, while recognising this absence of guidance by Parliament, the majority opinion observed that the law laid down in *L Chandra*, *R Gandhi*, and other cases decided by the Supreme Court of India would provide sufficient 'guidance' to the Central Government in notifying rules under Section 184.[69] Though he delivered a largely concurring opinion on other points, Justice Deepak

[62] Tribunal, Appellate Tribunal and Other Authorities (Qualifications, Experience and Other Conditions of Service of Members) Rules, 2017.

[63] These tribunals were set up under the Informational Technology Act, 2000 and the Airports Economic Regulatory Authority of India Act, 2008 respectively.

[64] The Finance Act 2017, Act No 07 of 2017 (Indian Parliament), s 169; The Finance Act 2017, Act No. 07 of 2017 (Indian Parliament), s 170.

[65] ibid.

[66] The Finance Act 2017, Act No 07 of 2017 (Indian Parliament), s 184.

[67] Tribunal, Appellate Tribunal and Other Authorities (Qualifications, Experience and Other Conditions of Service of Members) Rules 2017, Schedule.

[68] *Rojer Mathew v South Indian Bank Limited* (2020) 6 SCC 1.

[69] *Rojer Mathew v South Indian Bank Limited* (2020) 6 SCC 1, ¶223.

Gupta strongly disagreed with the majority view. In his opinion, the law laid down by the Courts in previous cases could not provide sufficient guidance as the Central Government had previously failed to conform with the guidelines in those cases.[70] For Justice Gupta, the Tribunal Rules 2017 were themselves a paradigm example of such non-conformity.[71]

In *Rojer Mathew*, the Rules that were notified in pursuance of Section 184 of the 2017 Act were struck down in their entirety for violating the guidelines prescribed in *L. Chandra* and *R. Gandhi*. Specifically, it was found that the qualifications prescribed for the appointment of members were vague.[72] The qualification requirement of persons having specialist knowledge of 'certain subjects which in the opinion of the Central government is useful' was especially ambiguous, and allowed excessive room for executive discretion. The Court also observed that the majority of the search-cum-selection committee members should be judges.[73] If the Central government had considered the case law, it would have found that this requirement was strongly sounded by the Supreme Court when it analysed the NTT. Therefore, while Part XIV of the 2017 Act was upheld in its entirety, the Tribunal Rules of 2017 were declared unconstitutional.

However, history tends to repeat itself when it comes to the tussle between the demands for the independence of tribunals on the one hand and the desire of the executive to control the composition of tribunals on the other. Just four years after the Tribunal Rules 2017 were struck down, the government promulgated the Tribunals Reforms (Rationalization and Conditions of Service) Ordinance 2021. This Ordinance included provisions addressing the composition of the search-cum-selection committees for the selection of members of 15 Tribunals. Despite the ruling in *Rojer Mathew*, this Ordinance once again empowered the central government to notify, in its discretion, the qualifications and other terms and conditions of service for the Chairperson and members of these tribunals. These provisions were (unsurprisingly) struck down by the Supreme Court within four months of the Ordinance being promulgated.[74]

The story does not end here. About a month after sections of the Ordinance were struck down, Parliament enacted the Tribunals Reforms Act 2021. This Act was strikingly similar to the parts of the 2021 Ordinance that were struck down. A challenge to the constitutionality of this Act is currently pending before the Supreme Court.[75] Even if this statute is struck down, history tells us that it may emerge again, albeit in a slightly different form.

[70] ibid ¶377.
[71] ibid.
[72] ibid ¶160.
[73] ibid ¶175.
[74] *Madras Bar Association v Union of India* (2022) 12 SCC 455.
[75] The challenge is pending in a case being reported as *Madras Bar Association v Union of India* under Writ Petition (Civil) No 1018 of 2021.

Problems with Tribunals

The structure of administrative tribunals was put in place after a long history with the result that tribunals came to be saddled with high expectations. They have failed to meet those expectations for predominantly two reasons: *first*, an unfortunate lack of independence in their operation; and, *second*, the rise of administrative concerns in their operation due to a lack of uniformity in regulation.

As for the lack of independence, this is evident right from the appointment of the members of the tribunal to their removal from office. Most selection committees are dependent on secretaries of the departments which sponsor the functioning of the tribunal.[76] This is despite the ruling of the Supreme Court in relation to the NCLT and NCLAT, where it was found that a selection committee for the appointment of the members of the tribunals would be unable to function independently if it comprised of the secretary of the governmental department which sponsored the funding and other needs of the tribunals.[77] When departments are involved in the day-to-day workings of the tribunals, a clear conflict of interest arises when decisions made by such departments are challenged before those very tribunals. In spite of the judiciary's repeated insistence on allotting a majority of the positions on selection committees to judges, most tribunals today consist of significantly more executive members than judicial.[78]

The removal mechanism of members shines no better as a ray of hope for the independence of tribunals. Unlike the impeachment process followed across jurisdictions including India for the removal of judges of the Supreme Court and the High Courts, the removal of the members of tribunals lies within executive discretion. Most statutes constituting tribunals do not lay down any provisions for the removal of their members, paving the way for arbitrariness in the exercise of discretion. To ensure that members are not discarded arbitrarily, some safeguard akin to a judicial inquiry needs to be put in place. The absence of such safeguards is only one part of the host of problems that plague the independence of tribunals.

As to administrative problems, these arise largely from a systemic non-uniformity in regulation.[79] There are deep discrepancies across tribunals in areas such as the tenure of members. Some tribunal members have a short tenure of

[76] For example, the selection committee for the Telecom Disputes Settlement and Appellate Tribunal includes secretaries from the Department of Telecommunications and Ministry of Civil Aviation. Similarly, the selection committee for the Securities Appellate Tribunal includes secretaries from the Department of Economic Affairs and the Department of Revenue.

[77] *Union of India v R Gandhi* (2010) 11 SCC 1.

[78] For instance, see the Appellate Tribunal for Electricity ('ATE') constituted under the Electricity Act of 2003. As per s 78 of this Act, the members of the ATE are to be appointed by a selection committee. Four out of six of the members of the selection committee as per s 78 are either to be appointed by the central government or are secretaries of executive departments. Section 78 of the Electricity Act lays down no requirement for the presence of judicial members on the search-cum-selection committee.

[79] A Ghosh, D Sanyal, R Chandrashekar and R Sekhar, 'Reforming the Tribunals Framework in India: An Interim Report' (*Vidhi Centre for Legal Policy*, April 2018).

three to five years, which hampers the cultivation of domain expertise. The Supreme Court has recommended a five-to-seven-year tenure to remedy this.[80] Retirement age is another area where such discrepancies exist. While the retirement age for tribunal chairpersons is between 62 and 70, it varies from 62 to 65 for other members. There is no reason why an individual cannot be a member of a tribunal at 66 but can still be its chairperson at 66. Such administrative inconsistencies contribute to larger problems of pendency in tribunals, which goes to the very reason for which they were established. A shortage of personnel in these tribunals, in combination with the increasing pendency, has led to an overworked body of members, contributing to inefficiencies in decision-making.

In view of these difficulties, many have advocated the abolition of tribunals altogether. With tribunals becoming so entrenched in the Indian judicial system over the past 50 years, any attempt at abolition would be highly impractical, as it would require a cumbersome rearrangement of redress mechanisms by further increasing the workload of the judiciary (which already has 50 million cases pending before it).[81] Instead of abolishing the system, reforms can be introduced which attempt to improve the functioning of tribunals in a way that brings them closer to their originally envisioned design. Inspiration can be drawn from other jurisdictions that have faced similar difficulties.

Moving Forward

In order to re-imagine the tribunal system in a way that addresses the concerns surrounding its functioning, there are two major categories of reforms that can and should be put into effect. As a first step, it is important to better streamline the working of tribunals; mergers along the lines of what was suggested by the Leggatt Report in the UK,[82] can be considered in the Indian context. Merging tribunals based on subject matter can be used as a way of enhancing operational coherence. Tribunals dealing with similar subject matter can be merged into a single division with separate benches for original and appellate jurisdiction. For example, tribunals such as the Film Certification Appellate Tribunal and the Intellectual Property Appellate Board both deal with questions of licensing and certification and can be merged into a single division. The merger of tribunals under the Finance Act 2017 was (by contrast) somewhat haphazard, having been undertaken without sufficient regard for similarity in subject matter.

[80] *Union of India v R Gandhi* (2010) 11 SCC 1, para 55.

[81] See P Thakur, 'Pending cases have now crossed 5 crore, House told' *The Times of India*. Available at: https://m.timesofindia.com/india/pending-cases-have-now-crossed-5-crore-house-told/articleshow/101998790.cms, accessed 15 August 2023.

[82] 'Tribunals for Users- One System, One Service: Report of the Review of Tribunals by Sir Andrew Leggatt' (*The National Archives*, March 2001). Available at: http://webarchive.nationalarchives.gov.uk/20060214102004 and www.tribunals-review.org.uk/ (last accessed 10 September 2023).

In addition to those reforms, a somewhat more radical second step is necessary. Recent scholarship has mooted the idea of establishing a National Tribunals Commission ('NTC') that can help address both administrative and independence-related concerns that tribunals confront today.[83] A body in the nature of an NTC would also be in line with the idea of a single independent agency that was envisioned in *L Chandra Kumar* to monitor and supervise the administration of tribunals. Further, in *R Gandhi*, the Court had mandated that the administrative control over all tribunals should lie with the Ministry of Law and Justice. However, tribunals continue to be under the administrative control of the very ministry they will frequently be passing orders against. For instance, the Ministry of Communications continues to exercise administrative control over the Telecom Disputes Settlement and Appellate Tribunal. Such control raises suspicion in relation to the ability of tribunals to act impartially and be seen as acting impartially.[84]

The NTC can be entrusted to create sub-committees that can crystallise qualification requirements for appointment, processes of removal of members, retirement ages, and the like. Instead of different nodal ministries governing these areas, an independent statutory body like the NTC would better speak to the aim of achieving the independence of tribunals. The majority of NTC members should be judges, which would reduce the prospect of executive interference.

These reforms would constructively address some of the problems that tribunals face today and go some distance in the transformation of the justice delivery system in India. Tribunals are now so deeply entrenched in the Indian legal landscape that abolishing them is unviable. However, reform – perhaps even root and branch reform – is both achievable and necessary.

[83] A Ghosh, D Sanyal, R Chandrashekar and R Sekhar, 'Reforming the Tribunals Framework in India: An Interim Report' (*Vidhi Centre for Legal Policy*, April 2018).

[84] Ministry of Communications, Advertisement No 15-02/2019 (20 May 2020). Available at: https://tdsat.gov.in/admin/notice/uploads/Final_Advt_upload.pdf, accessed 29 August 2023.

14

Administrative Tribunals in Israel

GUY I SEIDMAN[1]

Introduction

Administrative law is one of the less-regulated parts of Israeli law. It is mostly made up of a mesh of principles, woven together in court decisions. Even by these standards, administrative tribunals (ATs), the officials within the executive who employ adjudicative power, are unique. Little public interest and limited judicial oversight have made ATs some of the least documented and transparent entities of the Israeli government. This is not because ATs are unimportant – the estimated size of their docket and the subject matter they deal with suggests that this is hardly the case; rather it is because of the way ATs were set up in Israel. Following the English tradition, ATs were established in a haphazard, case-by-case fashion and viewed as an 'internal adjudication unit' within a specific government unit.[2] As such they were thought of as more 'technical' and 'quasi-judicial', less professional than the general court system. It did not help that Israeli ATs enjoyed scant attention from legal scholars or from the Israeli Supreme Court, the apex of the general court system.

The current situation of ATs in Israel is not fully clear and far from ideal. The definition of what constitutes an AT is vague, as is the precise number of entities that currently operate as ATs, the size of their dockets, the number and content of their decisions and real-life impact. Since the 1990s, Israeli statutes have focused on around 30 ATs, listing them, regulating their working in part and allowing appeals from them to the general court system. Even these identified tribunals operate with

[1] I am grateful for comments from Israeli Justice Ministry advocates Yuval Roitman and Michal Reshef, my colleagues Assaf Porat, Yair Sagy and Hillel Sommer and the research assistance of Tom Armon. The opinions stated in this chapter are mine, readers' comments are welcome at gseidman@runi.ac.il. The translations from the Hebrew are mine, unless otherwise stated.

[2] I have previously written on Israeli ATs in a comparative law perspective, see: GI Seidman, 'A Hard Look at Common Law Administrative Tribunals' (2021) 11(2) *Oñati Socio-Legal Series* 409–44. Available at: https://opo.iisj.net/index.php/osls/article/view/1186; I am grateful for this opportunity to expand on that article and present the Israeli ATs in more detail. On the English tradition, see C Stebbings *Legal Foundations of Tribunals in Nineteenth Century England* (Cambridge University Press 2006, 2009).

limited transparency and what lies beyond them is truly unknown: formal statutory powers suggest there could be dozens more 'unlisted' ATs, undocumented, unreported and with little public oversight. This status quo is unsatisfactory. *All* ATs require – and deserve – more prominence. ATs handle massive caseloads impacting human and civil rights and significant, protected interests. Their workings should be better known to the public and the parties on whose rights they rule should have the right to appeal to the general court system. Indeed, Israel's Freedom of Information Law of 1998 ostensibly requires all judicial and quasi-judicial entities[3] to provide residents and citizens of Israel with information 'not concerning the content of a legal proceeding'[4] and publish an annual report with information about its responsibilities and activities.[5]

This requirement has not become the general rule, although it has to be said that two of the newest tribunals, dealing with refugee and asylum seekers and with state COVID-19 financial aid, have received significant press coverage, civil society interest and some litigation and are providing some information about their workings.

This chapter relates the story of ATs in Israel in the following three sections: Part II: Structure, details the formal place of ATs within the structure of Israeli government, somewhere between the executive branch and the judiciary; Part III: Origins, explains how the messy AT landscape in Israel was formed and why, by 1975, the need to reform was clear to all; Part IV: Reforms, looks into the changes made to AT in the 1990s and assesses their impact; Part V: Since 2000, details more recent developments and concludes the chapter with a call for further reforms.

Structure: Between the Executive and the Judiciary

The First World War ended four centuries of Ottoman-Turk rule over Palestine. The British occupied the land in 1917–1918 and ruled it until 1948 under a 1920 mandate from the League of Nations.[6] The mandate is our legal starting point. Under its authority came the Palestine Order-in-Council, 1922,[7] the British statute 'which is the Magna Carta, as it were, of Palestine'.[8] Signed by King George V in

[3] The Freedom of Information Law, 5758–1998 holds that every citizen or resident of Israel has the right to receive information from a public authority under this act (§1). The definition of a 'public authority' includes courts, tribunals and any other entities with adjudicative legal powers, (§2).

[4] Under the definition of a 'public authority' (§2). Under section §14(a)(11) the law does not apply to the proceeding before any quasi-judicial authority charged with deliberating a person's medical condition.

[5] §5. Nor have I found these tribunals within the official list of 'public authorities' published in the annual report.

[6] See Mandate for Palestine – League of Nations (12 August 1922).

[7] See ECF – Economic Cooperation Foundation: Palestine Order in Council, 1922 – English.

[8] N Benwtich, 'The Law and the Courts of Palestine' (1924) 2 *Cambridge Law Journal* 37, 38.

Council, the 1922 Order allowed the transition from military to civilian rule and the setting up of government institutions, including courts.

As a first step, the 1922 Order carried over the law as applied under the Ottomans (§46). This hodge-podge of religious (mostly Muslim) and secular (mostly French-civil) law was extensively replaced with English law within a few years.[9] The British had little patience with the limited, mostly lay judicial system they found in place. Thus, they moved fast and established, in the 1922 Order (§§39, 40 & 43), a three-tiered general court system. In addition, '[t]he British expanded the jurisdiction of state courts and strengthened state control over religious courts and other informal tribunals'.[10]

A century later, this structure remains at the core of the Israeli court system. It provides that civil and criminal cases begin at the Magistrates' (first tier) or the District Courts (second tier) depending on the sum of money sued or the severity of the alleged offence. Under §51 of the Courts Law [Consolidated Version], 5744–1984, the current threshold for filing at the Magistrates' Court as a first instance is a civil suit for up to 2.5 million shekels (ca. 650,000 USD) or a criminal matter punishable with up to 7 years' incarceration. Civil matters of higher value and the more serious criminal cases start at the District Court. Since Israeli law permits only one appeal by right the result is that cases first filed at the Magistrates' Court are appealed to the District Court, and cases begun at the District Court can be appealed, by right, to the Supreme Court, which thus becomes the main appellate instance. Under the 1922 Order the Supreme Court had a third, original, jurisdiction: sitting as a High Court of Justice ('HCJ'), designated as the first and only instance for administrative review. The logic for this was likely the existence, during the mandate, of a higher judicial authority with final decision power – the Privy Council (§44 of the 1922 Order).[11] This link to Britain was severed in 1948, yet the court structure remains much as the British set it up.

Beside the general court system exist three two-tiered specialised tribunal systems. The first, initially set up during Ottoman times and carried over through the British mandate, is a set of religious tribunals – one for each state recognised religious order. These have jurisdiction over family law matters of persons of their denomination.[12] Established under the Military Justice Law, 5715–1955, a second

[9] On this, see the writings of N Bentwich, mandatory Attorney General of Palestine, 1920–1931: ibid. fn 8 and N Bentwich 'The Legal System of Palestine under the Mandate' (1948) 2(1) *Middle East Journal* 33; N Bentwich 'The Legal System of Israel' (1964) 13 *International & Comparative Law Quarterly* 236. See also A Likhovski, 'In Our Image: Colonial Discourse and the Anglicization of the Law of Mandatory Palestine' (1995) 29 *Israel Law Review* 291; A Likovski, *Law and Identity in Mandate Palestine* (University of North Carolina Press 2006) 23.

[10] Likhovski (2006), 23.

[11] And the majority of British – rather than 'native' Jewish or Arab – Justices at the Supreme Court. For the background to this arrangement, see Y Sagy, 'For the Administration of Justice: on the Establishment of the High Court of Justice of Israel' (2004) 28 *Iyunei Mishpat – Tel-Aviv University Law Review* 28, 225–97 (in Hebrew) and Y Sagy, 'The Missing Link: Legal Historical Institutionalism and the Israeli High Court of Justice' (2014) 31 *Arizona Journal of International & Comparative Law* 703.

[12] See, in comparative perspective, R Benhalim, 'Religious Courts in Secular Jurisdictions: How Jewish and Islamic Courts Adapt to Societal and Legal Norms' (2019) 84 *Brooklyn Law Review* 745.

system is that of the military tribunals.[13] These deal with servicemembers' wrongdoings (not offences against national security), yet their jurisdiction is significant, given the prominent role of the military in Israel and its reliance on mandatory conscription for both men and women. The third system comprises t labour tribunals. Instituted in 1969 under civil law influence, this is a specialised system with jurisdiction on varied issues of employment and anti-discrimination laws.[14] *These are not ATs*. They are substantially made up of full-time, professional judges similarly appointed as the judges of the general court system. Only the military judges are part of the executive branch, but they enjoy de facto functional independence. The military courts are also the only tribunal of the three from where a direct appeal, by permission, can lie to the Supreme Court; the only way to challenge decisions of the religious and labour courts is by petition to the Supreme Court sitting as an HCJ.

The relevant statute in force is Basic Law: The Judiciary (1984).[15] Israel's formal Constitution is an ongoing project, legislated one topical chapter at a time. Such 'Basic Laws' stand normatively above 'regular' statutory acts of the Knesset.[16] Basic Law: The Judiciary is the constitutional segment regulating entities with powers of adjudication. Two sections are of particular interest. Both reiterate the structure set out in the 1922 Order, but with interesting wrinkles. The Basic Law does clarify, somewhat, what entities in Israel can be vested with adjudicatory powers. It distinguishes between 'courts' and all other entities. The term 'courts' is essentially reserved for the three tiers of the general court system.[17] However, '[t]he power of adjudication is also vested in the following: (1) A religious court (beit din); (2) Another tribunal; (3) Another authority – And all as prescribed by law'. Given that *Beit-Din* is the Hebrew word for 'tribunal', what we can glean from the Basic Law is this: first, that there are, in total, three categories of adjudicatory bodies: courts, tribunals (such as the three preeminent ones mentioned) and 'another', nameless, authority; second, that all provisions for adjudicatory authority must be made by statute (which is what the term 'by law' means in this context). What differentiates a tribunal from a court and makes 'another authority' still different from each? The Basic Law provides no answer – nor does any other Israeli law, which suggests that the Basic Law was referencing, constitutionally enshrining, the existing adjudicative bodies existent at the time.

[13] See, in detail: M Finkelstein and Y Tomer, 'The Israeli Military Legal System – Overview of the Current Situation and a Glimpse into the Future' (2002) 52 *Air Force Law Review* 137 and LM Schenck 'Article: Appendix: Fact Sheet on Israeli Military Justice' (2020) 14 *NYU Journal of Law & Liberty* 48.

[14] See G Mundlak, 'The Israeli System of Labor Law: Sources and Form' (2009) 30 *Comparative Labor Law & Policy Journal* 159.

[15] Available at: https://m.knesset.gov.il/EN/activity/documents/BasicLawsPDF/BasicLawTheJudiciary.pdf (Knesset website translations used in this chapter).

[16] See S Navot, *The Constitution of Israel: A Contextual Analysis* (Bloomsbury 2014).

[17] Basic Law: The Judiciary, §1(a); the section also lists a fourth option – to my knowledge, yet unused – to establish '(4) Another court designated by law as a court of law' (ibid).

Another pertinent provision is §15 of the Basic Law, covering the Supreme Court.[18] The Supreme Court jurisdiction is extensive. It hears appeals from the District Courts in civil and criminal law cases[19] and, under §15(c), sitting as an HCJ, 'it shall deliberate matters, in which it deems it necessary to provide relief for the sake of justice, and are not under the jurisdiction of another court or tribunal'.[20] The Supreme Court is here granted, as a court of equity, unique powers. It can act if an issue arises that is not under the original jurisdiction of any other courts – traditionally, public law petitions alleging government wrongdoing – and the Court is of the opinion that granting a hearing is 'necessary to provide relief for the sake of justice'.[21] The complementing section §15(d) elaborates on this grant of authority. The Supreme Court has the power of *Habeas Corpus*, to 'release of persons unlawfully detained or imprisoned',[22] the power to grant writs of *mandamus* and *prohibitio* against any 'persons holding public office under the law'.[23] The Supreme Court is also granted more limited powers over 'courts … tribunals, and … bodies and persons with judicial or quasi-judicial authority under the law'.[24] Here again we find the tripartite distinction of adjudicative bodies in Israel – courts, tribunals and 'others'. We also see that the Israeli Supreme Court is, institutionally, the 'one court to rule them all', as any case may reach it, by one route (civil, criminal and, nowadays, administrative appeal) or another (petition to the HCJ).

Furthermore, while the wording of §15(c) suggests that the HCJ has only residual authority, i.e., if a statute grants an AT the power to hear an administrative case the Supreme Court cannot take it up in first instance but only in review of the tribunals' decision, the Supreme Court has carved out the power to hear, at first instance, all administrative cases.

This covers the jurisdictional foundation for both the setting up of ATs in Israel and the general court system's oversight of ATs. The details, however, are less clear. Though one would like to be able to explain how Israeli law defines ATs or the exact rationales for setting them up; in practice it is difficult to determine how many ATs currently operate in Israel or how well they function. To explain why this is the case, we now go back in time.

[18] 'Other powers of the Supreme Court, not detailed in this section, and 'the established, powers, seat and jurisdiction areas' of all other courts shall be set by statute (§§15(e) and 16), this statute being, for the most part, The Courts Law [Consolidated Version], 5744–1984.

[19] The language of Basic Law: The Judiciary, §15(b) is mandatory – the Court 'shall hear appeals' and it is understood to apply to final – rather than interim – decisions of the District Courts. The Courts Law [Consolidated Version], 5744–1984, §41 allows for appeals, by permission, in additional cases.

[20] Basic Law: The Judiciary, §15(c).

[21] These words supersede the word 'shall' in the same section, making clear the Court does not have discretion whether to accept such cases.

[22] Basic Law: The Judiciary §15(d)(1); essentially, the Writ of Habeas Corpus.

[23] ibid §15(c)(2).

[24] ibid §15(c)(3); also granted even more limited power to order religious courts – §15(c)(4).

Origins: 1968–1975 CE

There is limited historical evidence suggesting that some ATs were formed during the less legally cohesive rule of the Ottoman Turks (1517–1918). What is abundantly clear is that, until Israel's independence in 1948, most ATs, and the legal tradition surrounding them, were created by the British authorities during their rule of Palestine (effectively 1917 to 1948). As English law concerning ATs did not provide clear rules or a uniform design for ATs, there is little surprise that the ad hoc, practical approach towards ATs was also applied in Palestine and carried over into the nascent State of Israel. It then took a full two decades for a call for reform to arise. It came from an academic, well informed about the condition of ATs in Israel and the legal reform of ATs in England, but also steeped in the more analytic, orderly civil law tradition.

That person was Prof Yitzhak Hans Klinghoffer. Born in Galicia in 1905, he acquired doctorates in political science (1927) and law (1930) at the University of Vienna. After the Second World War, he was recommended by his teacher, Hans Kelsen, for the Hebrew University's school of law. Arriving in 1953, he merged the logic of civil law with the common law mosaic of cases, advancing a systematic, analytic method for Israeli administrative law. In 1957, he published the first book on administrative law in Israel. Klinghoffer undertook various public positions, even serving as a member of the Knesset, Israel's Parliament.[25] Klinghoffer made his call for reform in the Knesset and, although he was member of the (then) opposition liberal party, his position as the 'father' of administrative law in Israel meant that what he said was taken very seriously.[26]

The Knesset discussed a report on the workings of the ministry of justice. Klinghoffer devoted part of his speech to the state of ATs in Israel.[27] Speaking of 'the multitude of administrative tribunals in our country' he explained that '[t]hese are bodies which functionally handle litigation, *i.e.*, adjudicate controversies, mostly between the individual and the government, but from an organizational-structural perspective, are not counted within the judiciary'. He noted the lack of uniformity in tribunals' makeup, operating procedure and the availability of review of court review. 'Almost every statute' he observed, 'set up for its own purposes one or even several types of administrative tribunals'. This, he noted, is:

> not by some general scheme but in a specific form, improvised, happenstance, that the legislator sets up for that matter, without giving his mind to whether the difference between the many patterns of tribunals is really necessary. This condition cannot continue without correction.[28]

[25] I Zamir, 'In Memoriam: Prof. Y. H. Klinghoffer' (1990) 20(1) *Mishpatim* 5 (official translation) (in Hebrew).

[26] I Zamir, 'Law Review Volume Dedicated to Prof. Itzhak H. Klinghoffer on his Retirement from Teaching at the Law Faculty' (1974) 5 *Mishpatim* 491 (in Hebrew).

[27] The 295th sitting of the 6th Knesset, 12 July 1968, 2228, at 2248.

[28] ibid 2248.

What is there to be done? Given the opposition of the judiciary, Klinghoffer noted that the establishment of one, central administrative tribunal in Israel seemed unlikely (this is still the case today) – and so, 'perhaps', he suggested, putting on his eminent 'professorial cap', 'the ministry of justice would consider following the way taken by English [UK] legislator in passing, in 1958, the Tribunals and Inquiries Act'. He then detailed the workings of the English Council on Tribunals, suggesting setting up such a body in Israel.

The referral to the UK was most apt. As noted, it was the British mandate that instituted the method for establishing ATs in Israel, using the British ad hoc approach. Now England was reforming its ways, but with the mandate over, such reform could not be directly applied in the now-independent Israel. As my teacher, Prof Baruch Bracha noted in 1986, English law had set up hundreds of tribunals, not part of the general court system, which were meant to 'absorb' the influx of cases arising from friction and disagreements between citizen and the rising welfare state. ATs were meant to settle relatively simple, often technical disputes, in a fast and informal procedure. Thus arose 'a compilation of entities with limited powers of adjudication, with almost no organisational common denominator or hierarchy'[29] and subject to the review of the general court system. At least until the end of the 1950s, ATs grew in the UK 'with no guiding hand and no controlling criteria regarding their makeup, powers and work. Tribunals were set up separately, in response to the needs of specific statutes and not as part of a methodical system of administrative adjudication'.[30] The growing realisation of this condition resulted, in the UK, in the famous Franks Report.[31] Presented to Parliament in 1957,[32] some of the recommendations were then given statutory force in the Tribunals and Inquiries Act 1958.[33] This included setting up the Council on Tribunals which, with powers of research, advice and report, helped to tighten the review of ATs and streamline their procedures.[34]

In Israel, where the situation of ATs was similar to that of the UK before the reform, the need for better regulation of ATs was clearly understood by 1968. Hence, a promising start: within three weeks of Klinghoffer's speech(!), the Minister of Justice appointed a committee. It was asked to opine and make recommendations on a wide range of issues concerning 'the operation of quasi-judicial authorities operating under statute (including appellate committees)'. Headed by a Supreme Court Justice, its 17 high-ranking members came from the judiciary, the legislature, legal practice and academia. The latter group included Professors Klinghoffer and his eminent 'student' Itzhak Zamir who, at 92, remains today the doyen of Israeli administrative law.

[29] B Bracha *Administrative Law Volume 1* (Nevo 1986) 99.

[30] ibid.

[31] The Report of the Committee on Administrative Tribunals and Enquiries, published August 1957 (Command Paper No 218).

[32] Administrative Tribunals and Enquiries (Report) (*Hansard*, 31 October 1957).

[33] Its successors were – The Tribunals and Inquiries Act 1971, and the Tribunals and Inquiries Act, 1992, currently in force.

[34] Bracha (n 29) at 99.

The committee held 24 plenary meetings and many more in committee. Yet the report only arrived in 1975 and, even then, offered limited recommendations and extensive dissenting opinions.[35] The same year, Prof Zamir, a committee member and its rapporteur, published a book titled *Adjudication in Administrative Cases*,[36] dedicated to 'my teacher, Prof. Y. H. Klinghoffer'. The 'good' news is that these two sources combined to provide valuable data and analysis on the state of administrative adjudication in Israel in 1975, including suggestions for reform. The less cheerful news is that a reform took until the 1990s to arrive and remains incomplete. Moreover, on the informational front, we have a more limited factual picture of ATs in Israel today than we had in 1975.

The 1975 committee report is highly informative. It found that by 1970 about 200 ATs had been set up by statute. Of these, the committee exempted 23,[37] asking the government for information on the remaining 177 and receiving data on 106. The report designated around 35 ATs as 'most active', i.e. handling over 20 matters per year, while an additional 58 ATs were found to 'exist only on paper. While the statute mandates that they be set up, they were never established, and if they were formed, they had nothing to deliberate'.[38]

The report explains that, during the British mandate, ATs were set up in two ways: the setting up of special adjudicatory instances, separate from the administrative apparatus (around 15 such tribunals were still in operation in 1975); or the granting of a right to appeal an administrative decision *within* the administration before a higher-ranking official, mostly the British High Commissioner, during the Mandate. After independence, setting up special tribunals became the norm. With the Israeli welfare state came a plethora of laws that required government to provide more services but also gave it more power to interfere in citizens' lives. The result was a necessary increase in friction between citizens and the government. The legislature thought it undesirable and impractical to authorise the general court system to deal with the many controversies that now arose and chose to set up a chain of specialised instances, each with its own rules set by statute. The main reasons given for setting up ATs were the high volume of disputes, the specialisation required of the adjudicators, the flexibility required in the application of social-policy statutes, the increasing public participation in adjudication, including self-representation and ATs' fast, affordable and efficient dispute resolution.[39]

The committee went the way of the Franks committee. It gave up on trying to find a single, academic definition for 'quasi- judicial authorities', admitting that the

[35] Including one by Prof Zamir – *Report of the Committee for the matters of Quasi-Judicial Authorities* (Jerusalem, 1975). The report notes that it was Klinghoffer's comment – rather than a stalled Justice Ministry of Justice's draft proposal for an ATs statute of 1958, that was the catalyst for setting up this committee (ibid, 4).

[36] I Zamir 'Adjudication in Administrative Cases' (1975, Hebrew).

[37] The example given was that of the Knesset sitting in appeal over election results; p 2.

[38] *1975 Report*, 2; listed in Appendix 3.

[39] ibid 3–4.

task was too elusive to be useful. Rather, it chose two functional tests which largely ask how similar such authorities are to 'real courts', then applied the tests to the many ATs in Israel. The first test was whether the entity has the authority to rule on controversies between two rival sides, in essence, serving as a third, independent party in the dispute between citizen and state; the second test was whether the entity sits in review of an initial administrative decision made by a first instance regarding citizens' rights.[40]

The committee did not consider several categories of adjudicatory entities to be ATs. These included, first, all three major tribunal systems – religious, military and labour. These are not 'quasi' but a 'real' judicial system and fully regulated by statute. Second, any appellate entity not created by law but stemming from the authority's voluntary willingness to reconsider its decision. Third, disciplinary tribunals and entities empowered to withdraw professional licenses. The reason given was that these entities make first instance decisions. Perhaps a better rationale is that they are more regulated by law and closer to the first category of major tribunals. Fourth, investigations under the Commissions of Inquiry Law, 5729-1968 and similar acts, because such entities do not have the power to rule on controversies but to investigate events and are not always required to even submit recommendations.[41]

Zamir's 1975 book is wider in scope. It takes a view across the entire administrative adjudication system from the Supreme Court at the top all the way down to ATs. The book foreshadows the 1990s reforms: first, in its clear understanding that the Supreme Court cannot remain the first instance forum in almost all administrative cases: the caseload is too great and it no longer makes sense to allow most petitions to begin directly at the highest court in the land. The necessary result was that the administrative caseload was redirected from the Supreme Court to the lower courts, mostly to the District (Appellate) Courts. In addition, the operation of at least some of the ATs – the other entity with original jurisdiction to conduct administrative adjudication – has been more clearly regulated, with recourse to the general court system available by appeal or petition.

What is perhaps most striking in Zamir's discussion of ATs is how frank and untroubled he is about the state of disarray of Israeli ATs in 1975.[42] He begins with what 'is well known' and uncontested: 'that many statutes, wherein the legislature grants new powers to an administrative agency, also regulate the setting up of administrative tribunals, to review the carrying out of this power'.[43] Then things begin to unravel:

First, how does one identify an AT? 'Sometimes they are called in the name appellate committees … or some other name, such as determination committee …

[40] This means that an appeal to a more senior office holder than the one who made the initial decision does not constitute an AT. See: 1975 Report, 5–6.

[41] See *1975 Report*, 7–8; Commissions of Inquiry Law, 5729-1968, SH 548 28 (Hebrew).

[42] Frankly, little has changed. Had Zamir viewed things differently, perhaps more would have been achieved, given his prominence as an academic and service as Attorney General (1978–1986) and Justice of the Supreme Court (1994–2001).

[43] Zamir (n 36) at 3.

Usually there is no meaning and no importance to the difference in name.'[44] If nomenclature is not dispositive, how then does one determine what is an AT? The answer is that sometimes ATs are only recognisable by their function. He cites to this effect a 1972 Israeli Supreme Court case, which held that 'there are many judicial institutions that fall within tribunals, even if they are not called that'[45] and then set some indicators for a tribunal – which may look familiar from the never-quite-successful-efforts to define the 'quasi-judicial'. These trappings are (i) that the functionary in question 'was equipped with all the tools needed to fulfil a judicial role' – in that case, he was given the powers of a magistrate of the peace and required to generally follow the rules of evidence – and (ii) that we are not dealing with a personal investiture with judicial power but rather with an official who is operating as part of an institution, to whom the authority was given, and has the markings of continuity and permanence.[46]

Second, what data is available about ATs? Zamir is quite untroubled when saying that 'it is hard to conclusively determine the number of ATs, because the number changes with the definition of tribunal, or the number of matters adjudicated before them, since there is no one to collect such data systematically'.[47] What he can say with certainty is that there are over 100 types of ATs, some of them 'have many branches, and that they deliberate thousands of appeals annually'.[48] Furthermore, while the Supreme Court has retained the power to hear *all* disputes between citizens and the government, it mostly refuses to hear cases set by law for hearing by ATs, meaning that 'it is fact that a large part of the litigation in administrative matters, perhaps even most litigation, and in any case, more than the litigation before the HCJ, is held before Ats'.[49]

Reforms: 1991–2000 CE

The years passed by. Committees were formed, reports filed, statutes drafted, all to no avail. 'Over the last years several proposals were made', wrote Zamir in the 1987 preface to the third printing of his 1975 book, 'but they remained frozen motionless'.[50] Prof Klinghoffer passed away in early 1990, missing by a mere 18 months the first major reform to affect ATs: in July 1991, the government proposed the Administrative Tribunals Act. While not the comprehensive code hoped for and only applicable to a small number of ATs, the Act nonetheless

[44] ibid at fn 1.
[45] Zamir (n 36) 3 and fn 1 and CA 44/72 *Shem Tov c Pribar*, PD 26(1) 617, 619 (per curiam).
[46] Shem Tov, 619.
[47] Zamir (n 36) 3.
[48] ibid.
[49] ibid 4 and fnn 5–6.
[50] Preface to the third printing, December 1987.

significantly clarified the law, identifying the main ATs active in Israel and providing a scheme for their form and function.

When we combine the explanatory section of the government bill proposal,[51] the frank words of then Justice Minister Dan Meridor introducing the proposal to the Knesset[52] and Prof Daphne Barak-Erez's first blush commentary on the newly legislated act,[53] we get a clear view of the condition of Israeli ATs in 1992 and the reform enacted.

First, Israel follows the UK model in bifurcating the adjudicative authority of *courts* and *tribunals*. 'The courts', says Meridor, 'are the regular, accepted, classic, institution that sorts out disputes among citizens and between citizen and the authority'.[54] The rule of law principle, notes Barak-Erez, 'comes into effect with the subordination of administrative authorities to the world of regular courts'.[55] She views this as the effective rejection of the French approach, in which administrative adjudication is entrusted to a separate court system. 'However, life experience has taught us, that the courts cannot be the sole arbiters in all conflicts between citizen and authority'.[56] And so, in Israel

> as in other states – a special system has evolved, whereby intermediary bodies are set up that are not the actual administrative authority and are not a court. They are called appellate committee … and various similar names. *We chose to call them by one name: administrative tribunals*.[57]

Second, why set up ATs? Several familiar reasons are given: (i) the simplified procedures ATs use make it easier for citizens to litigate, even unrepresented, with the authorities and makes the entire process fast, efficient and affordable; (ii) it is useful to be able to use adjudicators who are professionals in specific fields, e.g. medicine or agriculture – people well versed in the issues under dispute; and (iii) given the extensive role of the modern state, many disputes occur between citizen and authority; setting up ATs to handle them eases the pressure on the general court system.[58]

Third, why was a reform needed? Setting up each AT by a separate, 'organic' statute, without comprehensive, systematic planning, resulted in an uneven system

[51] Draft Bill Administrative Tribunals, HH 2073 334 (Isr) of 17 July 1991.

[52] In the 'first reading' of the bill: DK, 12th Knesset, 325 (1991)(Isr)(23 July 1991), 5254, 5283 et seq. Meridor, who was from Klinghoffer's party, which was now long in power, made a clear reference to the fact that the issue was initially raised before the Knesset by Prof Klinghoffer in 1968, and did so as this was a way 'to do justice with a man who is no longer with us' Klinghofer; ibid 5283.

[53] Law professor and former Dean of Tel-Aviv University's law faculty, now Justice of the Israeli Supreme Court, Barak-Erez is likely the most prominent contemporary administrative law scholar in Israel. For her commentary see: D Barak-Erez 'Administrative Law' in *Yearbook on Israeli Law* 1992–1993 (A Rosen-Zvi, ed., 1994, Tel-Aviv) 197–203.

[54] ibid 5283 (emphasis added).

[55] Barak-Erez (n 53) 199.

[56] ibid.

[57] Knesset hearing (n 52) at 5283 (emphasis added).

[58] ibid 5283 and see the explanatory notes.

on many core issues. Such differences are not easy to justify. In essence ATs lacked regulation:

> These tribunals were similar in terms of their basic characteristics, but a general order for their operation was never put in place. The HCJ has set in its rulings some basic principles regarding their operation … but more remains hidden than is revealed.[59]

ATs themselves were also hard to observe. Justice Minister Meridor spoke of 'many tens of committees'[60] and, later in the legislative process, MP Itzhak Levy, presenting the bill for final reading before the Knesset on behalf of the parliamentary committee, spoke of 'several dozens, perhaps close to-100 administrative, tribunals in different names'.[61]

What was to be done? As a first step, the Minister of Justice appointed an AT Council in 1985. Initially chaired by retired Supreme Court President Moshe Landau, then by Prof Zamir, the Council prepared the bill proposal. The Administrative Tribunals Act, 1992-5752[62] formally set up an AT Council comprising up to 15 members. Appointed by the Minister of Justice, its role was to counsel ministers on all matters pertaining to ATs, conduct studies, make public information about ATs and hand the Minister of Justice an annual report.[63] In 2012, a Justice Ministry draft bill proposed cancelling the council. The draft (to my knowledge, never enacted in law) explained that the council became redundant once it had helped the Attorney General draft an internal guiding rule on the principles of setting up ATs because the intensity and dynamism of the legislative process did not make consultation feasible.[64] The pertinent parts of the 1992 Act deal with ATs.

- *Nomenclature*: the 1992 Act defines as a tribunal or AT as 'any instance set up by a minister or other administrative authority which has adjudicatory power, whether it is called tribunal, appellate committee … or any other name' (§1).
- *Applicability*: the 1992 Act sets up a general framework for the operation of ATs. It does not apply to all tribunals, nor does it replace all current statutes. Rather, it applies to the entities listed in its appendix (initially 15, now expanded to around 30) and is set as a '*lex generalis*', one that does not overrule any *lex specialis* authorising a specific AT.[65]
- *Legal Authority*: the 1992 Act makes clear that a tribunal must be set up by statute (§2). Securing tribunal members' independence, §3 declares that in

[59] Barak-Erez (n 53) 199.

[60] Knesset hearing (n 52) at 5283.

[61] Referring to these ATs 'attached to the authorities … A service that the authorities provide the citizen, within which it is possible to appeal some kind of authority decision. This is the essence of administrative tribunals.' (DK, 12th Knesset, 386 (1992)(Isr)(18 February 1992), 3047, 3079–80.

[62] SH 1385 90 (Isr.) 2 ('the 1992 Act'). Available at: www.nevo.co.il.

[63] ibid §§49–52.

[64] Guidance Rule 2.3203 of 2003; The draft bill is available at: www.nevo.co.il/law_word/law11/41281.doc (in Hebrew).

[65] See Knesset hearing (n 52) at 5283; also §4 of the 1992 Act.

matters of adjudication they are only subordinate to the law, i.e. not their administrative superiors.[66]

- *Noteworthy provisions*: First, the 1992 Act seeks to limit the possibility that tribunal members find themselves in a state of conflict of interests. Thus, a person cannot be appointed as a tribunal member if she is in a frequent professional, business or other relationship with the administrative agency on whose decisions she may sit in appeal; this includes being an employee or elected official of that agency or having left such a position under one year before appointment to the tribunal (§§9–10). Similarly, a tribunal member cannot sit where she might be found to be, directly or indirectly, in a conflict of interest (§15). Second, tribunal members are appointed to three-year terms and can be reappointed. Once they start hearing a case, they can complete deliberation up to six months after their term has expired. The panel can sit even if one member, who is not the chair, is in absentia or has left the hearing, unless the sides do not agree to this or the chair has decided to postpone the hearing (§§8, 16–17, 19). Third, while ATs have the power to call witnesses and appoint experts, they are not bound by legal rules of evidence or procedure, unless otherwise provided by statute. The tribunal is to conduct its process 'in the manner it deems best for doing justice' (§§20–21, 28–29; cite: 21). However, the 1992 Act does provide a baseline: a litigant may be represented before the tribunal; the appeal is to be in writing and include all relevant documentation, but the argument before the tribunal can be oral; a tribunal will sit in public, with limited exceptions such as state security, protecting minors or trade secrets (§§22–23, 25–26). Fourth, an AT can give interim decisions and give force to a compromise reached by the sides; the AT will explain in writing and sign its final decision; it can decide by majority, and where the opinions are split, the chair will determine the outcome (§§34, 36, 40–41). Fifth, the 1992 Act links ATs and the general court system. It allows sitting judges to chair AT panels (§5) and states that a panel chair will either be a sitting judge or a person qualified to be appointed as a Magistrates' Court Judge (i.e. a lawyer with five years' experience) (§7).[67] Furthermore, the 1992 Act provides an appeal by right from an AT's final decision to a single judge of a District Court; further appeal to the Supreme Court is possible by permission. If the AT's chair was a District Court judge, an appeal by right lies to the Supreme Court. Interim decisions can be appealed by permission (§45).

A second major reform arrived with the new millennium: *The Administrative Affairs Courts Act, 5760-2000* ('AACA').[68] This Act expanded the powers of District (appellate) Courts in administrative adjudication. The main idea was to reduce

[66] This section essentially reiterates §2 of Basic Law: The Judiciary, which holds that '[w]hoever is vested with the power of adjudication shall not be subject to any authority regarding matters of adjudication, except for that of the law' (official translation).

[67] The Courts Law [Consolidated Version], 5744–1984, §4.

[68] The Administrative Affairs Courts Act, 5760-2000 SH 1739 192 (Isr). Available at: www.nevo.co.il (AACA).

pressure on the Supreme Courts' HCJ docket, given that few cases merit a direct first instance hearing in the highest court in the land. However, the Act now gave the District Courts a triple role: as appellate court over boards of appeal and quasi-judicial bodies, as first tier court for administrative claims, and as a replacement for the Supreme Court in designated categories of petitions, hitherto heard before at the HCJ.[69]

How does the AACA supplement the 1992 Act? The answer centres on §5 of the AACA, which contains three key provisions:

- §5(1) gives the right to challenge, before the District Courts, the decisions of 63 administrative entities listed in its Appendix A in all matters except those pertaining to promulgation of regulations. Without such a vested right, such administrative decisions could only be challenged by petition to the Supreme Court sitting as an HCJ. Having said this, it is also true that the Knesset could have, in principle, chosen to create specialised ATs and vest them with precisely this authority; had the Knesset done so, the appeal by right from the ATs would go the District Court, but under the new AACA regime, an appeal by right lies from the final judgment of the District Court to the Supreme Court (§11).
- §5(2) allows an appeal – not a challenge, an appeal – against 28 administrative deciding bodies listed in Appendix B. This is of note because the use of the Hebrew word for appeal suggests a distinction between the two groups and a recognition that these are quasi-judicial entities. And indeed, it seems that many of these 28 deciding bodies could fairly be characterised as ATs, and yet they are *not* recognised as such, and *not* listed in the appendix to the 1992 Act.
- §5(3) allows for the filing, in the District Court, of monetary lawsuits against agencies in matters listed in Appendix C, which are currently twofold: public procurement or class action lawsuits. This section clarifies the legal situation in Israeli law, but it less relevant to AT.

§5 appears to have clarified the three types of administrative adjudication powers now given to the district courts, and this is a great service to Israeli law. It does little, however, to clarify the legal situation of Israeli ATs.

Since 2000: Summary, Two Notes, a Conclusion, and a Call for Reform

What has happened during the past two decades in Israeli administrative law regarding ATs? An honest summary, to the best of my knowledge, would be that not much has changed.

[69] §1 of the Act & Government Draft Bill The Administrative Affairs Courts Act, 5759-1999, HH 2821 2 (Isr). Available at: www.nevo.co.il.

There is little Supreme Court case law of note pertaining to ATs and what we find in the newest academic tomes shows little change. Indeed, three major academic textbooks on Israeli administrative law published in recent years show this quite clearly. Starting with the two prominent Academic-Justices: in the most recent (2010) edition of his administrative law treatise, Prof Zamir notes that the 1992 Act only applies to a minority of ATs and that while ATs have some advantages over courts such as affordability, speed and depth of specialised knowledge, they also have the disadvantage of being a satellite body of the executive branch.[70] He states that ATs are 'not considered part of the judiciary and do not enjoy a[n] independent and prestigious status like the court. Therefore, review by an administrative tribunal is not the equivalent of review by court', which he views as 'the real thing'.[71] In her most recent (2017) treatise dealing with ATs,[72] Prof Barak-Erez similarly notes that AT review cannot be considered as fully independent judicial review. ATs can only be considered 'relatively independent' because of the limited protection of independence that tribunal members enjoy: true, the Basic-Law states that in matters of adjudication they are only subordinate to the law, but judges are subject to a more prominent appointments process and serve in the judiciary until retirement – not so tribunal members, who operate within the executive or with significant links to it.[73] Barak-Erez provides a brief sketch of the 1992 Act, admitting that it does not comprehensively cover all the issues regarding the operation of ATs, and that issues not covered by it 'receive from time to time a judicial answer, referencing the object for the setting up of these tribunals'.[74] She notes that the Supreme Court case law strives to 'fill in the blanks' in the very incomplete statutory scheme of the 1992 Act, but the examples are of modest impact. Prof Yoav Dotan makes similar observations in his recent book (2022).[75] He notes that the 1992 Act does not cover most ATs and that ATs are less independent than courts both because they are 'indisputably' part of the executive branch and because tribunal member include experts and sector representatives.[76]

There are, I believe, some developments of note. The starting point is the expansion of the number of ATs covered by the 1992 Act. The list of ATs in the appendix to the Act has grown from 15 to over 30. There has been a deliberate work of pruning (one of the original 15 ATs is gone), retrofitting (some of the ATs added predate the 1992 Act) and updating (adding to the list ATs created after 1992). I believe

[70] I Zamir *Administrative Power Volume 1* (2nd edn, Nevo 2010), Chapter 6: Judicial Review, 101, 109–10).

[71] So much so that Zamir thinks that the availability of review before an AT does not satisfy the basic right to access a court, so that court review must be either an alternative avenue or an appeal against ATs decisions. ibid 110.

[72] D Barak-Erez *Administrative Law – Vol. 4: Procedural Administrative Law* (2017).

[73] ibid Chapter 32, §32.2, 7 & fn 8; Chapter 34, §34.55, 191–92.

[74] ibid Chapter 34, §34.59, 199–200.

[75] Y Dotan *Judicial Review of Administrative Discretion Volume 1* (Nevo 2022).

[76] The latter point also explains the relative advantage that ATs have over court as administrative review instances. ibid Chapter 1, 39–41.

much deliberation and thought had gone into these changes. The precise policy considerations have not been made public,[77] but they may have to do with the Ministry of Justice trying to bring under the rules of the 1992 Act (imperfect and incomplete as they are) the 'major' ATs – in terms of their caseload, their societal and economic impact, the significance of the rights and interests they adjudicate and the public interest in them. Furthermore, there is also a clear indication that the Ministry of Justice is willing to take direct responsibility for making at least some ATs more transparent to the public.

To understand these changes, let us step back in time to 1959. One of the major ATs listed in the appendix to the 1992 Act is the Water Tribunal, established by the Water Act 1959.[78] An extensive Act for its time, it dealt with one of young Israel's greatest challenges: regulating the use of water, a precious resource of limited supply in an arid country to ensure supply to households, industry, and agriculture. Major waterworks and desalination plants have somewhat alleviated the situation since then, but water scarcity remains an issue. The Water Act empowers the Minister of Justice to form water tribunals and appoint its members: generally, three member panels comprising a judge and two public representatives (§141). The tribunal is given extensive powers in the Water Act and is said to have the full authority of a District – ie the appellate – Court. This means that there is an appeal by right from it to the Supreme Court (§§143, 146), although the general rule under the 1992 Act would have the appeal come before the District Court. Make no mistake, this is a very important tribunal that deals with vital decisions regarding water use. Zamir singles out the water tribunal as one that deals with a large number of legal disputes between citizens and administrative agencies[79] and its decisions have come before the Supreme Court for review on numerous occasions. A 1959 decree of the Minister of Justice created one single water tribunal in Haifa. Seated in the District Court of Haifa, it has jurisdiction over all of Israel.[80] Periodic announcements in the official record announce the identity of the judges who head the tribunal and the persons on the list from which public representatives are appointed. This, however, seems to be the extent of information available to the public about this tribunal.[81]

Now consider a more recent AT, established in the National Firefighting and Rescue Authority Act 2012.[82] While the Water Act can potentially impact a vast number of individuals and corporations – we are all consumers of water – and the AT established thereby wields extensive powers, the 2012 Act is different. It does

[77] I do not think that the Attorney General's Guidance Rule 2.3203 of 2003 (note 64) provides any clues as to the changes to the list.

[78] The Water Act, 5719-1959, SH 288 169. For an unofficial but complete translation see: www.pseau.org/outils/ouvrages/israel_water_law_5719_1959_en.pdf.

[79] Zamir (n 70) 95.

[80] See צו המים (הקמת בית דין לעניני מים) – ויקיטקסט (Available at: www.wikisource.org)(Hebrew).

[81] See בית הדין לענייני מים | הרשות השופטת (Available at: www.gov.il).

[82] SH 2381 702 of 8 August 2012. Israel – National Firefighting and Rescue Authority Law of 2012. (Available at: www.ilo.org).

not even cover all the potential dealings with the National Firefighting and Rescue Authority ('NFRA'). In fact, it addresses a single, not very common scenario, yet one with the potential for great friction with the public as it can be seen to infringe on many civil and human rights. It is where an organiser of a public event, the kind that requires fire precautions, requests the NFRA to allocate fire personnel and equipment for a fee to maintain safety at the event. Once an NFRA officer has decided for or against the request (§§36–37), 'a person' (of whatever standing) may seek review before the NFRA District Commander. That decision alone can be brought before an appellate committee, and this committee, finally, is the AT at hand (§38). Committee members, appointed by the Minister for National Security, include the NFRA commissioner or his deputy (chair), an employee of the Ministry of National Security and a jurist-civil servant, qualified to be appointed as a Magistrate's Judge, appointed by the Minister of Justice (§38(c)). Any decision of the appellate committee to allocate firefighters and equipment requires the consent of the chair (§38(e)). Decisions of the appellate committee can be appealed before a District Court sitting as an administrative affairs court.[83] No data is publicly available on the actual operation of this AT, yet it is noteworthy because the NFRA provides a wide array of public services for a fee, especially fire inspections and reviews, and for these likely much more common, if more mundane decisions, the NFRA Act does not provide a review mechanism by an AT.

Now let us look at two prominent examples of much more recent ATs, each dealing with a high-profile, sensitive topic of great public interest: the first concerns immigration, refugee and asylum policy; the second concerns COVID-19 employment assistance.

In Israel, as in many countries, immigration, refugee, and asylum policies have become highly polarising public issues in recent years. With a strong preference for Jewish 'Olim', Israel is less welcoming to any other immigration. This is especially the case with Palestinians entering Israel, where demographic concerns mix with national security concerns. Lawful entry into Israel is regulated by the Entry into Israel Law, 5712-1952 ('EIIL').[84] With strong security control of its sea and land borders and the existence of few legal entry points into the country,[85] Israel has traditionally maintained firm control over physical arrivals into its jurisdiction.

Historically, most illegal entrants came from the Palestinian territories, often in search of employment, some with nefarious intent. To counter this, the EIIL contains provisions criminalising providing such a 'foreign resident' with transportation, residence or employment, with supervisory powers entrusted with the courts, not an AT (§12).

[83] §38(f). This AT is currently listed as number 26 in the appendix to the 1992 Act.

[84] SH 111 354. For an unofficial but complete translation see: Refworld | Israel: Law No 5712-1952, Entry into Israel Law.

[85] See: www.iaa.gov.il/en/land-border-crossings/jordan-river/passengers-entering-israel/.

Since the 1980s, as Israel eased visa requirements for tourists and foreign workers, a second category developed – persons who entered Israel lawfully but outstayed their visa. In more recent years (mostly 2007–2012) an influx of around 65,000 African nationals entered Israel via the long desert border with Egypt; most then sought refugee status.[86] Add this to the lawfully employed foreigners (143,000 Palestinians and 115,000 others) around 25,000 African entrants still in Israel and tens of thousands of other illegal residents,[87] and the complexity of the issue in Israel becomes clear.

Israel's official preference, stated in the EIIL, is to remove illegal residents from the country, preferably of their own volition (§13(a)). Otherwise, they would be detained and removed by a decree of the Minister of the Interior (§13(b)). As Israeli governments piled up the measures to achieve this goal, so did the challenges by civil society groups – legal challenges before the courts and public challenges to both the Israeli public and the international community. Over time, the result has been the setting up of two ATs under the EIIL.

Following a challenge by the Association for Civil Rights Israel before the High Court of Justice, an AT was established in 2001 to review the detention of persons illegally staying in Israel. Tribunal members are persons 'qualified to be appointed as a Magistrate Judge and versed in the laws of entry to Israel and exit therefrom'. They are appointed by a three-member committee: the director general of the Ministry of Justice (chair), a jurist civil servant 'versed in the laws of entry to Israel and exit therefrom' and a jurist member of the public (EIIL §13(k)).[88]

As the number of persons Israel now terms 'foreign people' staying in the country rose, so did the number of legal petitions. In 2008 alone, 2,159 petitions were filed before the administrative affairs courts 'creating a major burden on the court system and the State attorney's office'.[89] By late 2008, the Ministry of the Interior formed, with the consent of the Attorney General, an internal, appellate committee; essentially a voluntary AT. In 2010, the government proposed amending the EIIL to upgrade the voluntary AT to a statutory one. The government explained that this would save resources and improve the quality of administrative decisions.[90]

[86] Though the Israeli government views most of them as migrants seeking economic opportunities. The influx ended as Israel fortified its border with Egypt. See: https://en.wikipedia.org/wiki/African_immigration_to_Israel.

[87] See: www.gov.il/BlobFolder/reports/zarim__2022/he/zarim2022.pdf; www.ice.co.il/research/news/article/936720 (Hebrew).

[88] Another AT for the review of the detaining of Infiltrators was set up in 2012 at the height of the influx of African nationals as a temporary measure under the more severe much earlier law meant to pervert Arabs, especially Palestinians, from 'infiltrating' Israel – the Prevention of Infiltration (Offences and Jurisdiction) Law, 1954, SH 161 160, 26 August 1954, and was declared, in part, unconstitutional, by the Israeli Supreme Court; see: חוק למניעת הסתננות (עבירות ושיפוט) – ויקיפדיה (wikipedia.org); www.hotline.org.il (Hebrew).

[89] Draft Bill Entry Into Israel Act (Amendment No 20) (Foreigners' Tribunal) 5771-2010, HH (Gov't) 550 312 (Isr), at 312.

[90] ibid 312.

Thus was created an Appellate Tribunal on matters of entry, residence, citizenship and exit from Israel, with much the same terms at the 2001 AT.[91]

And here is the punchline: while human rights organisations decried the fact that fewer than 1% of refugee status requests are granted,[92] or, in 2014, that '[t]he Detention Review Tribunals … have been active in Israel for the past 12 years. They operate far from the public eye, within the wards of immigration detention facilities',[93] something has changed: the two ATs operating under the EIIL[94] have become much more publicly visible: contact and other information is available on the Ministry of Justice website,[95] and an annual report sheds light on the tribunals' working.[96]

Finally, a good demonstration of agility in setting up an AT, the specificity of its jurisdiction and the public interest in its efficient working concerns the Economic Assistance Program Law (Novel Coronavirus) (Temporary Order), 5720-2020.[97] One of dozens of statutes making adjustments to life under COVID-19, this Act tried to reduce the high unemployment of the time by offering private employers monetary incentives.[98] The head of the Israeli Employment Service ('IES') was authorised to make decisions on the distribution of money grants under this law and on demands for the recouping of grants in cases of overpayment. The Act provides for review of these decisions before tax authority personnel authorised by the IES Head (§20), then an appeal before an AT – a two-member appellate committee of which the Minister of Justice was to set up one or more. The chair of this AT was to be a civil servant qualified to be appointed to the Magistrate's Court; the other, a public representative, appointed by the Minister of Finance, with knowledge and expertise in accounting, economics or any other pertinent field (§21). The only COVID-19-related Act to create an AT – currently number 29 in the appendix to the 1992 Act – this AT is well presented on the Ministry of Justice website[99] and files annual reports.[100]

[91] The sole difference is that any retired judge is qualified for appointment as a tribunal member. (EIIL §13(w)).

[92] See: HIAS-Asylum-Report-0.06-HEB.pdf. Available at: www.unhcr.org) (Hebrew).

[93] The Detention Review Tribunals, December 2014 report of the Israeli NGO Hotline for Refugees and Migrants 4. Available at: www.hotline.org.il.

[94] Both are mentioned – as well as the AT operating under the 1954 Prevention of Infiltration Act, which is currently listed as number 22 in the appendix to the 1992 Act.

[95] בתי הדין לאוכלוסין והגירה. Available at: www.gov.il (Hebrew) (including information about the adjudicators).

[96] For the most recent (2021) report see: www.gov.il (Hebrew).

[97] SH 2835 298 of 29 July 2020.

[98] See, in detail, the government bill proposal: Draft Bill Economic Assistance Program Law (Novel Coronavirus)(Temporary Order), 5720-2020, HH (Gov't) 1311 168 (Isr) of 1 June 2020.

[99] See: ועדת ערר לענייני קורונה – השתתפות בהוצאות קבועות לעסקים Available at: www.gov.il (Hebrew).

[100] For the most recent (2021) report see: www.gov.il (Hebrew).

To conclude, in recent years the Ministry of Justice has shown its responsiveness to some of the criticisms concerning ATs – adding more ATs to the 1992 Act regime and making some AT operations more transparent, allowing public oversight. There is much more work to be done. Many of the ATs – even those listed in the appendix to the 1992 Act – remain opaque. Given the Ministry of Justice's involvement in tribunal members' appointment, a full account of the number of ATs and their composition would be an important if long delayed first step. A second step would be a fuller public reporting of their workings – in not open proceedings, at least detailed, routinely-published annual reports. A third step should be a clearer analytic rationalisation, preferably by internal instruction of the Attorney General, possibly by an update to the 1992 Act, and hopefully with input from the public, academia and the courts, as to what subject matters, public and private interests could or should be subject to ATs rather than general system of court adjudication.

15

Reimagining Tribunals and Administrative Justice in Singapore

KENNY CHNG AND SWATI JHAVERI

Introduction

Relative to the UK[1] and Australia,[2] but in common with other post-colonial common law jurisdictions like Hong Kong,[3] Singapore does not have a consolidated system of administrative tribunals. Singapore's 'tribunals' landscape is made up of a dispersed and diverse set of bodies that adjudicate disputes between citizen and state relating to different subject matter, with each tribunal being constituted and deriving their power under different legislation.[4] This landscape has inhibited a holistic discussion of administrative tribunals in public law scholarship in Singapore.

This chapter seeks to deepen the conversation on tribunals and their contribution to administrative justice in Singapore.[5] It will take a deeper look at the

[1] Comprising a unified system of administrative justice dispensed through a First-Tier and Upper Tribunal with subject-matter-specific chambers.

[2] Comprising, previously the Administrative Appeals Tribunal ('AAT') which was abolished by the incumbent government in December 2022. See M Groves and G Weeks, 'Tribunal Justice and Politics in Australia: The Rise and Fall of the Administrative Appeals Tribunal' (2023) 97 *ALJ* 278 for a discussion on the recent abolition of the AAT. The AAT will be replaced by a new – again, unified – federal administrative review body which is the subject of a public consultation ending on 12 May 2023 (see *Administrative Review Reform: Issues Paper: Designing a New Federal Administrative Review Body that is User-Focused, Efficient, Accessible, Independent and Fair*, Attorney-General's Department, Australian Government, April 2023.

[3] See, S Jhaveri, M Ramsden and A Scully-Hill, *Administrative Law in Hong Kong* (LexisNexis, 2nd edn, 2013) pp 47–62; S Thomson, *Administrative Law in Hong Kong* (Cambridge University Press, 2018), pp 304–19 and Thomson, Chapter 12 in this volume.

[4] For example, see the Land Acquisition Appeals Board, constituted under s 19 of the Land Acquisition Act 1966; the National Council on Problem Gambling, which is constituted under the Casino Control Act 2006 and hears appeals from the Committee of Assessors relating to exclusion orders or visit limits on gambling-related premises which have been imposed on a person upon the application of a family member; and the Reviewing Tribunal constituted under the Foreign Interference (Countermeasures) Act 2021 ('FICA'), which hears appeals against orders issued by the Minister to combat hostile information campaigns under the FICA.

[5] Chief Justice Sundaresh Menon, 'The Role of Tribunals in the Delivery of Justice: Charting a Course for the Future', Keynote Address at the Inaugural Tribunals Conference: Advancing Access to

specialist features of administrative tribunals in the Singapore context, providing an overview of the personnel, processes and powers of these tribunals. As it looks into these features of tribunals, the chapter seeks to explore the question of why tribunals have developed in a piecemeal rather than comprehensive way. It will argue that the reason is that the emphasis in Singapore has been on the development of specialised tribunals staffed by experts in the subject-matter under consideration, as compared to experts (in the form of judges) of adjudicative procedure. Therefore, unlike the unified system of administrative justice dispensed via the tribunal system in the UK, tribunals in Singapore are not embedded in the judicial infrastructure but are part of the overall executive and administrative machinery of particular areas of government under the relevant governing legislation. In this way, Singapore shares characteristics with systems like the US where administrative adjudication of disputes between citizens and government takes place within subject-matter specific agencies, with the point of departure being the absence of an overarching legislative framework for administrative adjudication and rulemaking akin to the Administrative Procedure Act 1946 in the US.[6]

From this conclusion, the chapter goes on to consider the relative positioning of tribunals – performing specialist administrative decision-making in an adjudicative format while being formally embedded in the executive branch of government – in the broader constitutional landscape of Singapore. In doing so, it engages in a broader conversation on the separation of powers in Singapore.[7] Public law thought and scholarship in Singapore has developed significantly over the years, having been in a more nascent state of development previously. However, any opportunity to look at an underexplored topic or theme – in this case tribunals – provides an opportunity to assess how the broader constitutional landscape can further evolve. This chapter on tribunals will, accordingly, also be used to reimagine constitutional thought, especially on the separation of powers. While the separation of powers has undergone significant academic criticism in recent times for its failure to reflect the reality of the distribution of power and the

Justice Through a Quality Tribunals System (on file); R Magnus, 'Transparent, Fair and Impartial: a Snapshot of Tribunals in Singapore' (2004) 84 *Australian Law Reform Commission Reform Journal* 33; and D Cremean, *MP Jain's Administrative Law of Malaysia and Singapore* (4th edn, 2011, LexisNexis), 163–76 and 193–97.

[6] See JL Mashaw, *Creating the Administrative State: The Lost One Hundred Years of American Administrative Law* (Yale University Press, 2012) Chapter 14 for a discussion on the development of the system of administrative agencies' rulemaking and adjudication powers and the passing of the Administrative Procedure Act 1946. See also Asimow, Chapter 10 in this volume.

[7] The continuing utility of the 'separation of powers' as a framework for classifying and analysing public power has been the subject of much discussion: see EL Rubin, *Beyond Camelot: Rethinking Politics and Law for the Modern State* (Princeton University Press, 2005) who argues that the metaphor of three 'branches' of government (and of the separation of powers) is obsolete, and that government should be viewed instead as a 'network'. However, as the discussion in this chapter demonstrates, the traditional tripartite separation of powers framework still pervades constitutional discourse in Singapore. This is a theme that we will pick up on in this chapter.

range of power holders beyond the traditional tripartite structure,[8] it still captures the imagination of the courts and constitutional thought in Singapore – which thus far have been the most prominent voice on the identity and nature of administrative tribunals.

While tribunals are typically seen as acting in a similar way to courts – adjudicatively and with considerations of due process and procedural integrity in mind – they are also institutionally different and distinct from courts; largely located within or under the executive branch of government. This raises the question: in the Singapore context, where do we locate tribunals within the separation of powers? Can they reasonably be absorbed within the traditional tripartite separation of powers that occupies current constitutional thought in Singapore, or is their existence indicative of a more complex multi-branch conception of separation of powers that needs to take root? In answering these questions, this chapter will show how a judicially led discourse using a tripartite conception of the separation of powers in Singapore is incomplete in capturing the full breadth of accountability mechanisms that exist: in this case, administrative justice mechanisms like tribunals. The chapter will conclude with a discussion on how the separation of powers discourse needs to evolve to capture the more sophisticated landscape of administrative accountability and checks and balances in Singapore.

The Singapore Model of Administrative Adjudication and Tribunals: Technocratic Specialised Justice

Administrative tribunals in Singapore can be said to fall into the following broad categories:

(a) *Front-line administrative tribunals*: Tribunals in this category are responsible for making administrative decisions including licensing decisions. This includes, for example, the Copyright Tribunals, Liquor Appeal Board, Hotel Licensing Board, National Parks Board and Public Utilities Board.
(b) *Adjudicative, appellate review bodies*: This includes tribunals that review administrative decisions, including the Income Tax Board of Review, Valuation Review Board, Goods and Services Tax Review Board, Anti-Dumping Tribunal, Land Acquisition Appeals Board, and Reviewing Tribunals established under the Foreign Interference (Countermeasures) Act 2021.

[8] One part of the critique of this doctrine as it operates in Singapore is that several distinct conceptions of the doctrine are evident in judicial thought and that there is a need to more clearly articulate the Singapore version of the separation of powers: S Jhaveri, 'Localising Administrative Law in Singapore: Embracing Inter-branch Equality' (2017) 29 *SAcLJ* 828; J Neo, 'Autonomy, Deference and Control: Judicial Doctrine and Facets of Separation of Powers in Singapore' (2018) 5 *Journal of International and Comparative Law* 461.

(c) *Regulatory disciplinary bodies*: Tribunals in this category are responsible for implementing regulatory standards through disciplinary actions. In most other jurisdictions this would include financial services and market misconduct tribunals. In Singapore, these functions are undertaken by the Monetary Authority of Singapore – the main regulatory body – a point that is returned to later in this section's discussion. Beyond this, the main regulatory disciplinary bodies relate to the various professions (lawyers, doctors and accountants).

Category (c) is beyond the scope of this chapter. The discussion that follows focuses on categories (a) and (b).

At a conference in April 2022, the State Courts and Singapore Academy of Law considered, for the first time, the role of tribunals in Singapore's overall justice system.[9] This is the closest Singapore has come to a holistic consideration of the tribunals system. This can be contrasted with extensive reform pursued elsewhere.[10] As observed by Chief Justice Sundaresh Menon in his opening remarks at the conference:

> [the] ecosystem has thus far developed in a largely organic fashion. Tribunals are established mostly on an ad hoc basis – as and when necessary to meet a particular need – and in this way, the system has gradually expanded over the years. This relatively unplanned approach to the development of our tribunals may have worked well when the tribunals network was still relatively small and compact. But as that network matures and grows in size, we may, in time, need to confront and address important conceptual questions as to whether that network needs to be coordinated and organised …[11]

The focus of the conference, however, was not only administrative tribunals but also those that handle citizen-citizen disputes. So how does this observation apply to administrative tribunals that handle state-citizen disputes? Given Singapore's reputation and standing as a hub for legal services[12] and its regional and global standing as a centre of commerce,[13] it might be considered exceptional that Singapore has not devoted a similar level of attention as elsewhere to the role of tribunals in facilitating its legal and economic standing. However, as the discussion in the next section will demonstrate, this is because: (i) Singapore prioritises the

[9] *Advancing Access to Justice Through a Quality Tribunals System*, 26–27 April 2022, State Courts of Singapore and Singapore Academy of Law Journal.

[10] Akin to the Kerr, Ellicott and Bland Reports in Australia and the Franks Report 1957 and subsequent reform exercise in the UK culminating in the Tribunals, Courts and Enforcement Act 2007.

[11] Chief Justice Sundaresh Menon, 'The Role of Tribunals in the Delivery of Justice: Charting a Course for the Future', 26 April 2022 (on file).

[12] See *World Justice Project's 2022 Rule of Law Index*. Available at: https://worldjusticeproject.org/rule-of-law-index/global/2022/Singapore, last accessed 17 October 2023.

[13] See, eg, Singapore's ranking under the 2023 Index of Economic Freedom published by the Heritage Foundation. Available at: www.heritage.org/index/country/singapore#:~:text=Singapore's%20economic%20freedom%20score%20is,the%20world%20and%20regional%20averages. Singapore is the world's freest economy.

development of technocratic specialist tribunals over generalist adjudicative tribunals to achieve its ambitions as a legal and economic hub; and (ii) a consequence of this approach to government generally is that ministries, statutory boards and government agencies manage state-citizen disputes in-house within the relevant ministry rather than outsourcing them to tribunals, with the relevant specialisation based in the technocratic manpower of the ministry.

This section will first consider the aspects of specialism within the tribunals system in Singapore. The features of specialism with tribunals in Singapore are shared by tribunals elsewhere. The discussion, will, however, go on to analyse how the in-house approach to dealing with administrative disputes has specific issues: (i) an absence of a general appreciation of tribunals as more independent – but still specialised – fora for administrative justice; and (ii) gaps in administrative accountability in certain subject areas and domains.

Technocratic Specialisation: Personnel, Procedures and Powers

In common with the set-up of administrative tribunals elsewhere, there are three main indicators of specialism with tribunals in Singapore: (a) personnel; (ii) procedure; and (iii) powers of the tribunal. In this respect, administrative tribunals share characteristics of tribunals elsewhere. However, in the Singapore context, these features of specialism are more clearly aligned with the general design of government in Singapore – which centres around technocratic and expedient government.[14] This section looks at these three features across the landscape of tribunals in Singapore as a manifestation of the ideas of technocratic and expedient governance.

Membership of the tribunals listed above is not just drawn from the legal community – lawyers and judges – but also specialists and professionals. Taking the Appeals Board (Land Acquisition) as an example, an appeal is determined by a judge and such further persons selected from a Panel of Assessors appointed under section 26 of the Land Acquisition Act 1996: the latter can be populated by architects and engineers.[15] Other examples include the Income Tax Board of Review which can be populated with accountants and other

[14] See, M Barr, 'The Singapore School: Technocracy or Less: China's Singapore Model and Authoritarian Learning' in S Ortmann (ed) *China's "Singapore Model" and Authoritarian Learning* (Routledge, Taylor & Francis, 2020) pp. 54–71; M De Visser and P Straughan, 'Singapore: Technology and Transition' in V Ramraj (ed), *COVID-19 in Asia: Law and Policy Contexts* (Oxford University Press, 2021).

[15] The current list of assessors is available at: www.sgdi.gov.sg/ministries/minlaw/departments/appeals-board-(land-acquisition), last accessed 24 October 2023: it includes members with a background in sustainable building design, general architecture, mortgage valuations, project management, design and engineering, real estate and urban studies, real estate securitisation, asset management, property tax and urban planning and design.

tax specialists,[16] the Liquor Appeals Board which draws on the police force for its membership due to the public order aspect to liquor control in Singapore[17] and the Hotel Licensing Board which draws on the Tourism Board, Singapore Police Force, Singapore Civil Defence Force and Urban Redevelopment Authority for its membership.[18] Where the issues within the remit of the relevant tribunal are legal questions on the interpretation and application of legislation, membership is drawn from the legal community. This is the case, for example, with the Copyright Tribunal which is populated by judges and legal practitioners. This in itself is indicative of a technocratic approach to staffing – the issues under deliberation inform membership of the tribunal. In some instances, this may require legal expertise and in others more domain-based expertise.

In terms of procedure, again in common with the experience elsewhere, legislation will frequently make express that tribunals are not bound by the rules of evidence and have latitude in the conduct of proceedings.[19] While tribunals have a significant amount of freedom to design their process,[20] it is interesting to note that a number still follow judicialised procedures. For example, a circular issued by the Income Tax Board of Review describing its own procedures[21] provides for the exchange of documents between parties, legal submissions to the Board, pre-trial and pre-hearing conferences and hearings. This is reflective of the fact that an appeal on a tax assessment pursuant to s 79(1) of the Income Tax Act 1947 will largely involve complex issues of factual evidence and the application of legal provisions to that evidence.

On the issue of specialism, depending on the vantage point adopted, tribunals can be seen as having 'broader' or 'narrower' powers. When compared with the courts, tribunals' powers are broader in that they are not restricted by the boundaries of legality as applied in the context of judicial review. There is freedom to reconsider the merits of the case. It is open to them to review the technical, expert and polycentric nature of disputes – all of which are ostensibly outside the scope of judicial review. However, when considered against the powers of the original Minister or body that made the decision, the position is more nuanced.

[16] The current list is available at: www.sgdi.gov.sg/ministries/mof/departments/itbr, last accessed 24 October 2023. The Board comprises the chairperson, deputy chairperson and other members who are qualified persons appointed by the Minister for Finance to hear and decide income tax appeals – this currently includes tax advisors and planners, chief investment officers, corporate governance officers and tax leaders from the banking sector.

[17] This is currently situated within the Singapore Police Force. Available at: www.police.gov.sg/Join-SPF/Volunteer-Schemes/SPF-Boards-and-Councils, last accessed 24 October 2023. The Deputy Superintendent of Police is designated as the Officer-in-Command of Licensing, Public Entertainment and Liquor Licensing Division.

[18] See www.sgdi.gov.sg/ministries/mti/statutory-boards/hlb, last accessed 24 October 2023.

[19] See, eg, Regulations 37–38 of the Countervailing and Anti-Dumping Duties Regulations in relation to the Anti-Dumping Tribunal.

[20] See B Reddy & J Tan (eds) *Law and Practice of Tribunals in Singapore*, (Singapore Academy of Law Academic Publishing, Monograph Series, 2019), Chapters 3 and 5.

[21] See Income Tax Board of Review, Circular No 4 dated 4 May 2023.

For example, the Income Tax Board of Review can issue rulings that are binding on the underlying statutory board – in this case the Inland Revenue Authority of Singapore. The Land Acquisition Appeals Board is free to consider the adequacy of compensation awarded for the compulsory acquisition of land. However, decisions by the Anti-Dumping Tribunal are not similarly binding – the Minister simply has to consider the determination by the Tribunal when making a fresh decision. In this way, the Anti-Dumping Tribunal's powers are similar to that of courts in issuing judicial review remedies.

Issues with a Specialist versus Unified System of Tribunals

The discussion in the next section provides an overview of the specialism inherent in the tribunal system in Singapore: as a contrast to the generalist and unified tribunal structure like the UK and Australia. These aspects of specialism are not unique in themselves. It is when we factor these against the broader framework of the work of government and the administrative branch that we get a fuller picture of tribunals.

This chapter recognises that there is a significant amount of administrative accountability taking place outside of the tribunals system within the ministries and statutory bodies themselves. A key example of this is in the financial services sector. This remains one of the most highly regulated sectors of any jurisdiction. In most common law systems, regulatory discipline in this sector takes the form of standard setting and standard enforcement. On the latter, this is done through a matrix of tribunals and review boards. The Treasury Department in the UK recognised in its *Review of Enforcement Decision-Making at the Financial Services Regulators* that:

> Firms and individuals must have confidence that they can challenge the findings of the regulators before objective and independent decision-makers. The government has concluded that an executive-led model may not offer the perception of independence and objectivity required for contested decision-making. This review therefore recommends that the PRA establish an independent contested case decision making committee … But the government also recognises that some of those who are subject to enforcement action may prefer to challenge the regulators in a tribunal environment, where they can call evidence and cross-examine witnesses, rather than engaging with the regulators' decision-making procedures for contested cases. And so this review recommends that the regulators put in place a new, clearly signposted, expedited process to permit this.[22]

In the Singapore context, these powers are not vested in bodies like the Market Misconduct Tribunal in Hong Kong or the Financial Services and Markets

[22] HM Treasury, *Review of Enforcement Decision-Making at the Financial Services Regulators*, December 2014.

Tribunal in the United Kingdom. Rather it is the regulatory body itself – in this case the Monetary Authority of Singapore – that holds the relevant regulatory powers under the Monetary Authority of Singapore Act 1970 and the Financial Services and Markets Act 2022. This is symptomatic of a broader issue: the focus on developing technocratic specialism within the government and administrative branch is on the expertise of the manpower within the ministries and statutory boards themselves: without supplemental work by tribunals. Indeed, this means that emphasis is placed on internal modes of handling disputes such as ministerial appeals and internal appeals mechanisms. Examples of this in key sectors include: financial regulation as mentioned above, national and public security issues,[23] land use and housing planning.[24] Behind this lies the political reality of Singapore where ministers and heads of government portfolios are drawn not from political careerists but from private and external domains and areas of expertise.[25] The consequence of this state of affairs is that tribunals will remain specialist versus aggregated under an umbrella structure and supplemental to the internalised modes of handling areas of contention between citizen and state – this in turn bears consequences for true administrative accountability through a system of tribunals located externally from the executive actors themselves.

The Dynamic between Tribunals and Judicial Power in Singapore

In light of the discussion above, where we observed that tribunals sit formally within the executive branch, but exercise adjudicative, review and appellate functions, how do we locate administrative tribunals within the existing separation of powers in Singapore? The answer to this question is not entirely clear.

Article 93 of the Singapore Constitution vests judicial power in Singapore in 'a Supreme Court and in such subordinate courts as may be provided by any written law for the time being in force'.[26] The Singapore Court of Appeal (the final appellate court in Singapore) in *Mohammad Faizal bin Sabtu v Public Prosecutor* ('*Mohammad Faizal*'), elaborating on this provision, held that Article 93 vested judicial power in Singapore *exclusively* in the Supreme Court of Singapore and the Subordinate Courts – and *not* in any other entity which is not a 'court'.[27]

[23] Under various legislation: Protection from Online Falsehoods and Manipulation Act, Societies Act, Public Order Act 2009.

[24] Under the Planning Act 1998.

[25] 'Singapore's Technocratic Paternalism and How Behavioural Economics Justifies More of the Same' (2021) *Liberalism Unveiled*, 80–111.

[26] Constitution of the Republic of Singapore, art 93.

[27] *Mohammad Faizal bin Sabtu v Public Prosecutor* [2012] 4 SLR 947 at [17].

What, then, is a 'court'? The Court of Appeal explained that a 'court' would 'include any statutory body or tribunal having the characteristics of a court'.[28] What would the 'characteristics of a court' be? The court's elaboration on this crucial point was unfortunately rather sparse – at most, what one can glean from the court's reasoning was that a 'court' possessing the 'characteristics of a court' would be staffed by independent judges instead of laymen and thereby 'qualified to exercise judicial power'[29]

Accordingly, the Court of Appeal appeared to be of the view that the analytical focus in determining which kind of body comprises a 'court' is dependent on whether the members of the body in question enjoy judicial independence. Much can be said about the court's reasoning in this regard. For one, it appears somewhat formalistic (and perhaps even tautologous) to say that whether a body is a 'court' turns on whether the personnel comprising the body are 'judges' – one might think that more should turn on the nature of the power being exercised.[30] For instance, drawing from Australian jurisprudence, one way in which the distinction between courts and non-courts is drawn is based on whether the body in question has the power to enforce its orders – only courts have such a power.[31] In addition, as Stephen Thomson has suggested, one could go beyond an inquiry of whether the body in question has 'judicial characteristics' to also consider whether the body exercises the judicial power of the state.[32] Thomson identified a set of definitional criteria that would point towards the identification of a body as exercising the judicial power of the state: for instance, principally serving the function of dispute resolution, exercising the power of the state in resolving disputes, binding parties regardless of whether they consent, inter alia.[33]

In the absence of similar broader reasoning in Singapore on what constitutes a 'court', the reasoning of the Singapore Court of Appeal is arguably exclusionary of a number of administrative tribunals: which might be considered 'courts' in other jurisdictions (eg, Australia based on the reasoning discussed in the preceding paragraph). The members of administrative tribunals are often not judges. Laymen possessing specific expertise in a certain subject matter frequently feature in such tribunals. Their independence is not secured under Part VIII of the Singapore Constitution. Yet, it is quite clear that administrative tribunals do undertake aspects of the judicial function as defined in *Mohammad Faizal*: '[t]he judicial function entails the courts making a finding on the facts as they stand, applying the relevant law to those facts and determining the rights and

[28] ibid.

[29] ibid.

[30] For further discussion on how the form/substance distinction relates to Singapore constitutional and administrative law, see K Chng, 'Form and Substance in Singapore Constitutional and Administrative Law' (2020) 15(2) *Asian Journal of Comparative Law* 363.

[31] *Brandy v Human Rights and Equal Opportunity Commission* (1995) 183 CLR 245.

[32] S Thomson, 'Ombudsmen as Courts' (2022) 42(1) *Oxford Journal of Legal Studies* 76 at 82.

[33] ibid at 83.

obligations of the parties concerned for the purposes of governing their relationship for the future'.[34]

Given this, how should one square the practical reality of the work of administrative tribunals with the fact that the judicial power in Singapore is vested only in 'courts' staffed by independent 'judges'? A principled resolution of this issue would necessitate an analysis of what the concept of 'judicial power' means. Peter Cane's work on the nature of the 'judicial power' provides a useful framework for analysing the issues behind this question.[35] It should be emphasised at this juncture that this chapter is not drawing upon Cane's argument in a prescriptive manner – in other words, the chapter does not argue that Cane's analysis of the judicial power is *the* approach to understanding the relationship between tribunals and courts. Indeed, aspects of Cane's arguments fit uneasily with legal doctrine on the separation of powers as it has developed in some common law jurisdictions – most notably, Australia.[36] Nevertheless, Cane's work presents a useful analytical device for examining the separation of powers dynamic in the context of the relationship between tribunals and courts, especially in light of Singapore jurisprudence on this topic and at least helps to throw up questions for consideration in the Singapore context. It is, accordingly, being used as an analytical construct.

Cane identifies several different approaches to understanding the boundaries of 'judicial power'. Two of them are particularly relevant for present purposes and can be located in the reasoning of the Singapore courts. First, an 'essentialist' approach; and second, a 'reviewability' approach. The essentialist approach defines judicial power by reference to the functions of courts; for instance, as the Court of Appeal in *Mohammad Faizal* held, the judicial function involves a combination of fact-finding, identification of law, and the application of the law to the facts to resolve disputes. With the reviewability approach, the question is whether the decisions of the body in question are susceptible to review by a judicial body.

The approach which one adopts to define the concept of 'judicial power' has direct implications for how a particular body is identified. An essentialist approach would incline towards concluding that judicial power is exclusive to courts, as formally labelled in a jurisdiction's constitution or legislation establishing courts, and that the work of tribunals would possibly encroach upon the judicial power vested in 'courts'. This would thereby necessitate a sharp – and formal – distinction between tribunals and courts to avoid impermissible overlaps. A reviewability approach, on the other hand, would be much more forgiving of an overlap in function between tribunals and courts. Indeed, this approach would incline one towards thinking that judicial power is not necessarily exclusive to

[34] *Mohammad Faizal bin Sabtu v Public Prosecutor* [2012] 4 SLR 947 at [27].

[35] P Cane, *Administrative Tribunals and Adjudication* (Hart Publishing 2009) 83–85.

[36] For example, Cane's essentialist approach would cohere uneasily with Australian practice, since the AAT in Australia performed many of the functions traditionally prescribed to courts.

courts, and that tribunals and courts are capable of inhabiting a similar space. As Cane observed, the US Supreme Court has provided some support for this approach, given that it has allowed Congress to confer judicial power on non-judicial bodies, subject to the qualification that judicial bodies maintain supervisory oversight over the work of such non-judicial bodies.[37]

The Position of the Singapore Courts

Armed with these analytical devices to help us understand the ways in which 'judicial power' can be conceived, we turn then to observe that elements of both the 'essentialist' and 'reviewability' approaches can be identified in the perspective that the Singapore courts have adopted towards the judicial power.

It is clear that the essentialist approach is currently quite dominant in the court's jurisprudence on this issue. The Court of Appeal decision in *Mohammad Faizal*, referenced earlier, made clear that Article 93 of the Singapore Constitution vested judicial power *exclusively* in the Supreme Court of Singapore and the Subordinate Courts, and defined the judicial power principally by reference to specific functions undertaken by courts: fact-finding, identification of law, and the application of the law to the facts to resolve disputes.[38] Both features of such reasoning are emblematic of the essentialist approach.

Consistent with an essentialist approach, it is instructive to observe that in the face of judicial review challenges arguing that the judicial power had been impermissibly contravened, the Singapore courts have focused on the functions undertaken by courts. A useful example is the recent High Court decision of *Koh Rong Gui v Public Prosecutor* ('*Koh Rong Gui*').[39] In this case, a challenge was made to a specific feature of the sentencing framework for criminal offences in Singapore. In Singapore, an offender can be sentenced to a Mandatory Treatment Order ('MTO'), provided that a government-appointed psychiatrist has assessed that the offender in question is suitable for an MTO. An MTO would require an offender suffering from a treatable psychiatric condition to undergo psychiatric treatment for a certain specified period of no longer than 36 months. In *Koh Rong Gui*, the offender in question sought to be sentenced to an MTO, but the government-appointed psychiatrist assessed him to be unsuitable for an MTO. A judicial review challenge was subsequently made against the MTO sentencing regime, arguing, *inter alia*, that the separation of powers had been infringed. This was on the basis that the relevant provisions of the Criminal Procedure Code provided that the determination of the government-appointed psychiatrist was conclusive as to whether an offender was suitable to be sentenced to an MTO.

[37] Cane, *Administrative Tribunals and Adjudication* (n 35) 5, 50, 84.
[38] *Mohammad Faizal bin Sabtu v Public Prosecutor* [2012] 4 SLR 947 at [17].
[39] *Koh Rong Gui v Public Prosecutor* [2021] SGHC 259.

This, allegedly, was an impermissible intrusion upon the courts' sentencing discretion, which was a function falling within 'judicial power'.

The High Court held that there was no encroachment by the government-appointed psychiatrist upon judicial power. The court reasoned that it was permissible for 'the Legislature to statutorily designate a fact-finder other than the courts', and noted that the Court of Appeal had in various cases found legislation conferring fact-finding functions on government officers to be constitutionally unobjectionable.[40] With that in mind, the court noted that the government-appointed psychiatrist's function under the challenged provisions was indeed a fact-finding one, and the psychiatrist was best-placed to determine the factual questions under his jurisdiction. This included whether a psychiatric condition was treatable or whether there was a contributory link between an offender's psychiatric condition and the offence he committed.[41] Since these factual questions fell properly within the 'appropriate institutional competence' of the appointed psychiatrist – and *not* a judge – the challenged provisions could not amount to a trespass upon the judicial power on this basis.[42]

The approach taken by the High Court in *Koh Rong Gui* is paradigmatic of an essentialist approach towards the judicial power. Indeed, the High Court's reasoning in essence was that the fact-finding *function* in itself was not exclusive to courts exercising judicial power. Such functions could therefore validly be assigned to other decision-makers without infringing upon the judicial power in the Singapore Constitution.

The Court of Appeal decision in *Mohammad Faizal* itself provides another useful example of this approach in action. In *Mohammad Faizal*, it was argued that the provision of mandatory minimum sentences in the Misuse of Drugs Act 1973 amounted to an infringement of the judicial power, on the ground that the provision of such sentences in legislation interfered with the discretion of the judiciary to prescribe sentences to offenders. In addressing this argument, the Court of Appeal characterised the issue as such: was the power to prescribe sentences a function exclusively within the province of the judiciary?

The Court of Appeal answered in the negative. It held that the power to *prescribe* the punishment for offences was a *legislative* power – given that the Legislature had been vested with the power to make laws of general application, this power also extended to the prescription of punishments for offences defined in legislation.[43] Accordingly, 'no written law of general application prescribing any kind of punishment for an offence, whether such punishment be mandatory or discretionary and whether it be fixed or within a prescribed range, can trespass onto the judicial power.'[44] Judicial power, in contrast, required the courts

[40] ibid at [23].
[41] ibid at [24].
[42] ibid at [33].
[43] *Mohammad Faizal bin Sabtu v Public Prosecutor* [2012] 4 SLR 947 at [44].
[44] ibid at [45].

to 'inflict the legislatively-prescribed punishments on offenders, exercising such discretion as may have been given to them by the Legislature to select the punishments which they think appropriate.'[45]

Again, the approach taken by the Court of Appeal in *Mohammad Faizal* can be characterised as an essentialist approach towards defining judicial power, insofar as the court's analytical focus was on which *functions* lay properly within the scope of judicial power and which did not. Overall, it is interesting to observe that the Singapore courts have taken into account a variety of different considerations in their application of an essentialist approach. Indeed, the Singapore courts' take on the essentialist approach can be described as a blend of 'form' and 'substance', insofar as they have drawn formal distinctions to define a 'court' *and* at the same time delved into the substance of what an exercise of power entails – such as the fact-finding power – to determine whether it fell within judicial power. The Singapore courts have also taken into account elements of history in deciding which functions fall properly within judicial power.[46] Accordingly, one might conceivably argue that a uniquely Singaporean perspective towards the essentialist approach has emerged – one that might perhaps be characterised as a multi-dimensional essentialist approach.

Linking this discussion to the topic at hand, the dominance of the essentialist approach towards defining judicial power bears obvious implications for the relationship between administrative tribunals and judicial power in Singapore. Through the lens of an essentialist approach, it is clear that many of the functions performed by administrative tribunals in Singapore come very close to those performed by courts and that this would be seen as normatively problematic. Accordingly, should this approach be adopted, there would arise a prima facie tension between administrative tribunals and the judicial power in Singapore which would then have to be resolved by a specific articulation of how exactly the function of tribunals differs from that of courts.

Yet, complicating the picture somewhat is the emergence of a reviewability approach towards the judicial power in Singapore.[47] As described earlier, a reviewability approach would not hold an allocation of judicial functions to a non-judicial body to be impermissible in itself, but would require instead that decisions of the non-judicial body must be susceptible to review by a judicial body.

[45] ibid.

[46] In *Mohammad Faizal bin Sabtu v Public Prosecutor* [2012] 4 SLR 947, the court performed a historical survey of Commonwealth jurisdictions and concluded that 'there exists little historical and doctrinal support for the proposition that the sentencing power … is essentially and/or exclusively a judicial power' – see [36].

[47] Insofar as a reviewability approach can be understood as reflecting the endurance of judicial power as a supervisory check on exercises of executive power, this emergence of a reviewability approach tracks neatly with what Swati Jhaveri has described as a move towards 'judicial co-equality' in Singapore – see S Jhaveri, 'The Evolution of Administrative Law in Singapore: From Adoption to Autochthonous Adaptation' in S Jhaveri and M Ramsden (eds), *Judicial Review of Administrative Action Across the Common Law World: Origins and Adaptation* (Cambridge University Press 2021) 219.

An indication of such an approach can be found in the Court of Appeal decision in *Prabagaran a/l Srivijayan v Public Prosecutor* ('*Prabagaran*').[48] In this case, a feature of the sentencing regime for drug-related offences in Singapore was challenged. Amendments to the Misuse of Drugs Act 1973 in Singapore had accorded the courts the discretion to sentence drug offenders to life imprisonment instead of capital punishment, provided, *inter alia*, that the Public Prosecutor had issued a certificate stating that the offender had 'substantively assisted' the Central Narcotics Bureau in disrupting drug trafficking activities.[49] One of the arguments raised in *Prabagaran* was that the Public Prosecutor's power to grant such certificates of substantive assistance amounted to an infringement of the court's judicial power because the Public Prosecutor would effectively have the ability to select the sentence to be meted out to an offender, thereby impermissibly intruding upon the court's sentencing discretion.

The Court of Appeal found that there had been no infringement of the court's judicial power. One feature of the court's reasoning in this regard is particularly salient for present purposes. The court held that the Public Prosecutor's power to grant certificates of substantive assistance was permissible on the ground that his discretion was not unfettered; rather, the Public Prosecutor's discretion was 'circumscribed by the legislative purpose' underlying the amendments to the Misuse of Drugs Act 1973.[50] Implicit in such reasoning is a reviewability perspective towards the judicial power – indeed, one way of understanding the court's reasoning here is that there was no contravention of judicial power because it remained for the court to review exercises of the Public Prosecutor's discretion to grant certificates of substantive assistance on the ground of the purpose of the legislation, inter alia. In other words, insofar as the reviewability approach provides that there is no contravention of the judicial power in the exercise of a particular power as long as the court retains supervisory jurisdiction over the exercise of that power, the Court of Appeal appeared to be adopting such reasoning here in its holding that the Public Prosecutor's discretion to grant certificates of substantive assistance did not intrude upon the judicial power.

The High Court decision in *Koh Rong Gui* supplies an even clearer example of the reviewability approach to defining 'judicial power'. In addition to the argument discussed earlier, the applicant further argued that under the MTO sentencing regime, the 'final and conclusive' decision of the government-appointed psychiatrist on the suitability of an offender for an MTO was an infringement of the court's judicial power on the basis that this limited the supervisory jurisdiction of the court.

The High Court held that this too was not an infringement of the judicial power. In so holding, a crucial point that the court made was that the provision in question did not 'go so far as to preclude judicial review in general, such

[48] *Prabagaran a/l Srivijayan v Public Prosecutor* [2017] 1 SLR 173.
[49] Misuse of Drugs Act 1973, s 33B.
[50] *Prabagaran a/l Srivijayan v Public Prosecutor* [2017] 1 SLR 173 at [72].

that a wrong decision by an administrative decision-maker cannot be called into question'.[51] Comparing the provision at hand to other statutory provisions which on their face seek to exclude judicial review entirely, the court noted that the wording of the provision at hand did not contain such language and therefore could not amount to an infringement upon the judicial power.[52]

This reasoning, taken to its logical conclusion, would mean that if a statutory provision sought to exclude judicial review in general in its entirety, this could give rise to a contravention of the court's judicial power. While this reasoning was directed at an ouster clause rather than a tribunal *per se*, it is nevertheless indicative of how the Singapore courts have conceived the boundaries of the judicial power in a manner that would be applicable in principle to tribunals as well. Indeed, returning to the context of tribunals, this reasoning is suggestive of a reviewability approach towards the judicial power; on this view, the crux of whether there had been an infringement upon the judicial power would hinge upon whether the work of a particular decision-maker was reviewable by a court.

The acceptance of a reviewability approach towards the judicial power would also have direct implications for the relationship between administrative tribunals and judicial power in Singapore. In contrast to an essentialist approach, a reviewability approach would introduce far less tension between administrative tribunals and the judicial power. Indeed, if reviewability is the touchstone of whether there had been an infringement upon the court's judicial power, then there would be less direct conflict between the work of administrative tribunals and the work of courts – because most decisions of administrative tribunals in Singapore are susceptible to judicial review.

This is not to say, however, that a reviewability approach would do away with *all* tension between administrative tribunals and the judicial power. Issues may still arise in relation to tribunal decisions which are not susceptible to judicial review; in other words, where a legislative ouster clause excludes judicial review of certain tribunal decisions. An example of such a clause would be s 104 of the Foreign Interference (Countermeasures) Act 2021 ('FICA'), which seeks to limit judicial review of decisions made by the Reviewing Tribunal constituted under the FICA to procedural grounds only. While a separate exploration of the precise definitional boundaries of reviewability under FICA is outside the scope of this chapter,[53] this does not undermine the conclusion that a reviewability approach towards the definition of judicial power would pose fewer problems for the relationship between administrative tribunals and the judicial power in Singapore than would the essentialist approach.

[51] *Koh Rong Gui v Public Prosecutor* [2021] SGHC 259 at [39].

[52] The relevant provision, s 339(9) of the Criminal Procedure Code 2010, read: 'Any report made by the appointed psychiatrist shall be taken to be final and conclusive as to the matters referred to in subsection (3)(a), (b) and (c).'

[53] On this topic, see *Nagaenthran a/l K Dharmalingam v Attorney-General* [2019] 2 SLR 216; Thio LA, 'Ousting Ouster Clauses: The Ins and Outs of the Principles Regulating the Scope of Judicial Review in Singapore' (2020) *Singapore Journal of Legal Studies* 392; Kenny Chng, 'Reconsidering Ouster Clauses in Singapore Administrative Law' (2020) 136 *Law Quarterly Review* 40.

Navigating this Dynamic in Singapore

In the absence of clarity on whether the essentialist or reviewability approach will retain traction going forward and focusing for the present on how the judiciary can navigate this dynamic between administrative tribunals and judicial power, there are various options that the Singapore courts could adopt. First, the Singapore courts could continue to adopt the essentialist perspective towards the judicial power and apply it towards administrative tribunals. On this approach, in order to avoid the conclusion that all administrative tribunals are improperly exercising judicial power, it would become crucial for the courts to identify how exactly the function of administrative tribunals differs from that of courts. One possibility would be to draw upon Australian jurisprudence as an inspiration; that is, to hold that tribunals are concerned with merits review and that merits review of executive decisions is not a proper judicial function. The plausibility of this approach then would hinge on how clearly one can demarcate the functions that ought to be properly allocated to the judiciary and those which can be exercised permissibly by administrative tribunals – an endeavour that may potentially require the drawing of formalistic distinctions of the kind about which Lord Carnwath expressed concerns in the UK Supreme Court decision of *R (on the application of Privacy International) v Investigatory Powers Tribunal*, as his Lordship commented on the *Anisminic Ltd v Foreign Compensation Commission* approach to ouster clauses.[54]

Second, the Singapore courts could adopt a reviewability approach. On this view, administrative tribunals do not, ipso facto, infringe upon judicial power, as long as the decisions of administrative tribunals remain reviewable by the courts.[55] The primary difficulty with this approach would be how it would address situations where judicial review of certain decisions of administrative tribunals is indeed ousted by legislation – for instance, as mentioned earlier, decisions of the FICA Reviewing Tribunal are susceptible to judicial review only on narrow procedural grounds. One way to address this difficulty would be to hold that the complete ouster of judicial review is unconstitutional in itself as a violation of the judicial power – such a proposition can find support from recent Court of

[54] *R (on the application of Privacy International) v Investigatory Powers Tribunal and others* [2019] UKSC 22; [2019] 2 WLR 1219 at [128]–[129]; *Anisminic Ltd v Foreign Compensation Commission* [1969] 2 AC 147; [1969] 1 All ER 208.

[55] This is the case with respect to the majority of administrative tribunals: eg, s 35 of the Property Tax Act 1960 (2020 Rev Ed) allowing appeals to the High Court from a decision of the Valuation Review Board and also allowing the Chief Assessor or the Comptroller of Property Tax (s 35(1) to appeal to the High Court from a decision of the Valuation Review Board on any question of law or of mixed law and fact (s 35(3)); s 81(2) of the Income Tax Act 1947 (Rev Ed 2023) allowing appeals by an assessed citizen to the High Court from a decision of the Income Tax Board of Review; s 29(2) allowing appeals by a Collector of Land Review or an assessed citizen to appeal to the Court of Appeal from decisions of the Land Acquisitions Appeals Board.

Appeal jurisprudence as well as academic commentary.[56] More broadly, this proposition would reflect a certain approach towards how judicial power interfaces with the separation of powers in Singapore; namely that there would be a violation of judicial power if another institution (such as an administrative tribunal) abrogated or usurped the judicial power entirely, but that there would *not* be an infringement of the judicial power in situations where the power is merely being shared with the courts.

A third option that has been hitherto unexplored in the Singapore context would be to adopt a values-based approach – ie, to focus on whether values undergirding the allocation of judicial power to the courts have been infringed.[57] It is tentatively suggested here that this approach seems most desirable as a matter of principle. This is primarily because it would bring into the open the considerations which themselves undergird the other two approaches. Indeed, any principled demarcation of the functions which are properly allocated to the judiciary and any analysis of the extent of reviewability that is sufficient to satisfy the requirements of the judicial power would be premised on fundamental values such as the rule of law, judicial independence, and the requirements of administrative justice – values which would be the primary analytical focus under a functionalist approach. Accordingly, a functionalist approach would have the virtue of clarity and, more importantly, candour and transparency of reasoning insofar as these deeper debates are brought out into the open for discussion.

To conclude this section on the place of tribunals in the separation of powers and, in particular, judicial power as one of three branches of power – we have observed that structurally and de jure, administrative tribunals are not positioned under the 'judiciary' or seen as 'exercising judicial power' under the Constitution. At the same time, they de facto exercise power which bears a close resemblance to judicial functions exercised by courts. This section has identified and described salient portions of Singapore jurisprudence which have implications on how we might resolve this tension. We have also proposed a set of conceptual possibilities with which this tension can be engaged.

A broader question that is thrown up from this discussion is whether – in tandem with resolving the tension between administrative tribunals and the judiciary, as well as that between administrative justice and judicial power – we should consider alternative structural locations within the constitutional landscape. Indeed, while tribunals share *some* of their power with courts, they also exercise powers beyond typical judicial powers as exemplified in Section 2. Accordingly, this chapter concludes by considering, in particular, whether discussions in other jurisdictions on tribunals as a 'fourth' or 'new branch' of government have any

[56] See *Nagaenthran a/l K Dharmalingam v Attorney-General* [2019] 2 SLR 216; Chan SK, 'Judicial Review – From Angst to Empathy: A Lecture to Singapore Management University Second Year Law Students' (2010) 22 *SAcLJ* 469.

[57] Cane describes this as a 'functionalist' approach – see Cane (n 35) 83–85.

purchase in the Singapore context in acknowledging the richer scope and form of work carried out by tribunals.

Conclusion: Seeding Fourth Branch Thinking in Singapore and the Real Place of Tribunals on Singapore's Separation of Powers

The courts have been concerned with the question of under which of the three branches tribunals should be classed. Bearing in mind the earlier discussion on the specialism inherent in Singapore's tribunal system, it is clear that this does not complete the discussion on where tribunals fit within the separation of powers. Functionally, the separation of powers is a tool for designing and carving up government powers to prevent a concentration and risk of abuse of power.[58] The discussion in this section emphasises how administrative tribunals perform – in equality with the judiciary – a checking function on government power.

As highlighted at the outset of this chapter, Singapore does not have a consolidated system of administrative tribunals. Singapore's 'tribunals' landscape is made up of a dispersed and diverse set of bodies that adjudicate disputes between citizen and state relating to different subject matter, with each tribunal being constituted and deriving their power under different legislation.[59]

While disparate and dispersed, this chapter demonstrates that tribunals are a crucial component of the framework of administrative justice in Singapore. They provide parties affected by government decisions with an avenue for redress that is cheaper, more accessible and broader (in terms of merits review)[60] than judicial review via the courts.[61] The work of tribunals can therefore also relieve pressure

[58] CL de Secondat, Baron de Montesquieu, *The Spirit of the Laws* (1748) Book XI Chap IV, in *The Complete Works of M. De Montesquieu (1777).*

[59] See, eg, the Land Acquisition Appeals Board, constituted under s 19 of the Land Acquisition Act 1966; the National Council on Problem Gambling, which is constituted under the Casino Control Act 2006 and hears appeals from the Committee of Assessors relating to exclusion orders or visit limits on gambling-related premises which have been imposed on a person upon the application of a family member; and the Reviewing Tribunal constituted under the Foreign Interference (Countermeasures) Act 2021 ('FICA'), which hears appeals against orders issued by the Minister to combat hostile information campaigns under the FICA.

[60] B Thompson, 'The Place of Judicial Review in the Administrative Justice System' (2015) 4 *Juridical Review* 417, 427; Cane (n 35) 6–7. The distinction between 'legality' and 'merits' is fraught with difficulty. However, while courts are forced to confront this issue, the baggage of the legality/merits distinction applies with arguably less force in the deliberations of tribunals (unless the governing legislation specifically sets boundaries to the tribunal's jurisdiction). See, for further discussion of the legality/merits distinction, S Jhaveri, 'Revisiting Taxonomies and Truisms in Administrative Law in Singapore' (2019) *Singapore Journal of Legal Studies* 351; K Chng, 'Form and Substance in Singapore Constitutional and Administrative Law' (2020) 15(2) *Asian Journal of Comparative Law* 363; BJ Ong, 'The Unmeritorious 'Legality'/'Merits' Distinction in Singapore Administrative Law' (2021) 16(1) *Asian Journal of Comparative Law* 1.

[61] M Groves and G Weeks, 'Tribunal Justice and Politics in Australia: The Rise and Fall of the Administrative Appeals Tribunal' (2023) 97 *ALJ* 278, 278.

from the courts by helping to resolve disputes which would otherwise be channeled through the courts via judicial review applications.[62] Where disputes are not capable of being channeled via the courts, tribunals also have the potential to create a sense of access and redress for individuals who might otherwise be left with an unaddressed grievance.

Beyond providing access to administrative justice, the tribunals also form an important component of the accountability framework, acting as part of a system of checks on government power and in sometimes critical areas of impact. For example, the Reviewing Tribunal under the Foreign Interference (Countermeasures) Act 2021, hears appeals against ministerial directions made to restrict 'harmful' foreign online communications activity.[63] The directions enable the government to obtain necessary information to determine if there is any ongoing 'hostile information campaign' and contain the spread of and impact of harm caused by such a campaign. Examples of such directions include directions to internet intermediaries to take down the content, suspend or disable accounts to ensure that content is not viewable in Singapore. The difficult balance the government is striking in issuing directions is between the important objective of destabilisation of local politics against the impact on freedom of information and freedom of expression. The Reviewing Tribunal, chaired by a sitting Supreme Court Judge, is empowered to overrule the Minister on appeal by a recipient of directions. The tribunal in this context provides not only an access to justice resource but also a mode of accountability and check on powerful Ministerial powers in an area of high impact.

Accordingly, focusing on the nature of a tribunals' powers – and whether they are 'judicial' in nature or come structurally within the judicial branch – is an overly narrow approach to understanding the broader placement of tribunals within the constitutional separation of powers landscape in Singapore. The tribunals identified above – whether identified as exercising 'judicial power' or not – exercise the checks and balances functions of courts. The separation of powers framework needs to be expanded to absorb tribunals into an expanded framework. The discussion in the preceding section concluded that, while structurally and de jure, administrative tribunals are not positioned under the 'judiciary' or seen as 'exercising judicial power' under the Constitution, they do, de facto, exercise power which bears a close resemblance to the accountability powers of the courts but as they are institutionally distinct and not considered part of the courts under the Constitution – they need to have their own distinct recognition.

The separation of powers framework has been the subject of extensive scrutiny and criticism as it becomes increasingly clear that it lacks the dimensions and depth to deal with the real contemporary complexity of government.[64]

[62] ibid.

[63] Foreign Interference (Countermeasures) Act 2021, ss 94–99.

[64] See, eg, A Kavanagh, 'The Constitutional Separation of Powers' in D Dyzenhaus and M Thoburn (eds), *Philosophical Foundations of Constitutional Law* (Oxford University Press, 2016) and D Bilchitz

This chapter is not the place to engage with that debate: rather it proceeds on the basis that the analysis above has demonstrated its specific deficiency in the Singapore context with respect to administrative tribunals. And it looks at the outcropping of those criticisms elsewhere – namely, the suggestion that there exists a fourth or additional branch of government that needs to be captured in constitutional thought.

Concerns with the inadequacy of the traditional tripartite separation of powers elsewhere have led to calls to increase the number of branches. These additional branches have been referred to using various nomenclature: the fourth branch,[65] integrity branch,[66] regulatory branch, knowledge branch,[67] guarantor branch[68] to name a few. Administrative law and justice – which would include tribunals – typically come within discussions on the integrity branch.[69] Discussions of these additional branches is not without criticism.[70] Nevertheless, it is hoped that this chapter kickstarts a discussion on how this body of literature may have unique insights for the Singapore context. The chapter has proceeded on the assumption that focusing more squarely on the function of tribunals in Singapore opens the door for a broadening of the concept of the separation of powers and a recognition that, beyond the tripartite framework embedded in the text of the Constitution, there are other institutions performing the critical constitutional function of exercising checks and balance on power.[71]

and D Landau, *The Evolution of the Separation of Powers: Between the Global North and the Global South* (Edward Elgar, 2018).

[65] See M Tushnet, *The New Fourth Branch: Institutions for Protecting Constitutional Democracy* (Cambridge University Press, 2021).

[66] B Ackerman, 'The New Separation of Powers' (2000) 113 *Harvard Law Review* 633.

[67] VC Jackson, 'Knowledge Institutions in Constitutional Democracies: Preliminary Reflections' (2021) 7 *Canadian Journal of Comparative and Contemporary Law* 156.

[68] T Khaitan, 'Guarantor (or the so-called 'Fourth Branch' Institutions' in J King and R Bellamy (eds), *The Cambridge Handbook of Constitutional Theory* (Cambridge University Press, 2023).

[69] JJ Spigelman, 'The Integrity Branch of Government' (2004) 78 *Australian Law Journal* 724; J McMillan, 'Rethinking the Separation of Powers' (2010) 38 *Fed L Rev* 423, 438–41.

[70] T Khaitan, 'Guarantor (or the so-called 'Fourth Branch' Institutions' in J King and R Bellamy (eds), *The Cambridge Handbook of Constitutional Theory* (Cambridge University Press, 2023).

[71] This constitutional place and role of the tribunals is made explicit in other jurisdictions: most prominently, India – see Part XIVA of the Constitution of India.

16

Administrative Tribunals in the Pursuit of Administrative Justice in South Africa

HUGH CORDER*

'Justice afraid is justice denied. A bold constitution, such as we need in South Africa, will require bold judges. Hopefully, the constitution will be natural justice writ large, not small, enforced by judges with a vision that is broad, not narrow.'

Albie Sachs[1]

'... [I]n South Africa the superior courts have always played a crucial role in supervising the activities of administrative agencies. More remarkable is that, in spite of the introduction of a range of other safeguards since 1994, judicial review has retained its traditional prominence. Indeed ... judicial supervision of governmental action has become ... more prominent than in the past.'

Cora Hoexter[2]

The Context

By way of introduction, and given his strong South African roots, it is appropriate to note Lord Steyn's much-quoted remark at the outset of this chapter: 'In law, context is everything.'[3]

The invitation to write this contribution on administrative tribunals in the South African legal system has unlocked a period of bitter-sweet reflection. The

* I would like to record my great appreciation of the research assistance of Jenna Maujean, and the critical comments of Cora Hoexter and the very constructive reviewers. Remaining errors are mine.

[1] Preface to H Corder *Empowerment and Accountability: Towards Administrative Justice in a Future South Africa* (SA Constitution Studies Centre, 1991) xvii.

[2] C Hoexter and G Penfold, *Administrative Law in South Africa* (3rd edn, Juta, 2021) 83.

[3] See *R (Daly) v Secretary of State for the Home Department* [2001] 2 AC 532, 548 at [28].

essence of this reminiscent evaluation is encapsulated in the two quotations with which this piece begins. Albie Sachs is well known, at least, to most lawyers in the Commonwealth and beyond, for his role as an anti-apartheid activist, a key contributor in the debates leading to the drafting of the constitutional democracy which has prevailed since 1994 and as an important member of the first bench of the Constitutional Court of South Africa from 1994 to 2008. His judicial vision was both bold and broad. Cora Hoexter is the leading academic within the field of administrative law in the country, her views widely cited by the courts, and she has been involved in the development of the administrative justice landscape at every significant moment since 1994.

The 30 years which separate the quotations have witnessed the most extraordinary triumphs for both the human spirit and the establishment of the rule of law, mixed with times of despondency and despair. Indeed, the breakthrough in the political impasse and the rapidity with which progress was made were scarcely believable for most of those who had resisted injustice through the law during the bleak decades of legislated racism and economic exploitation leading up to this political revolution. In addition, the period from 1990 to 2000 was overwhelmingly characterised by the heady sense that anything was possible, that the exercise of public power in the state could be remade in the transformative vision of the values so powerfully expressed in the opening words of the Constitution of 1996,[4] and that lessons could be learned from other legal systems far and wide. Given the persistent abuse of power which marked the public administration under colonialism and apartheid, radical reform and renewal of the systems and processes for review of administrative action were a particular priority.

As a young professor whose primary focus of teaching and research was administrative law, I was greatly privileged to be involved in every significant step along this path of exploration and renewal. The details are not important, but the following aspects need to be noted:

(a) the urgent need for administrative law reform was abundantly clear to those most influential in the post-apartheid legal order who gathered in Cape Town in February 1993 to consider changes that needed to be made;[5]
(b) the transitional Constitution of 1993 (which came into force in late April 1994) already included a right to administrative justice;[6]

[4] Section 1 sets out the founding values of the South African constitutional democracy. Its significance is reflected in the fact that a 75% majority of the National Assembly is required for its amendment.

[5] See the published proceedings of that conference in Bennett et al (eds), *Administrative Law Reform* (Juta, 1993) also in the 1993 volume of *Acta Juridica*.

[6] See the Constitution of the Republic of South Africa Act 1993 (SA) s 24. For a discussion of this process see L du Plessis and H Corder, *Understanding South Africa's Transitional Bill of Rights* (Juta, 1994) 165–70.

(c) after some controversy, such a right was also included in the 'final' Constitution,[7] which required statutory supplementation within three years;[8] and
(d) within six years, almost all of the most important items highlighted as key to the process of reform had been achieved, at least on paper.[9]

The agenda for reform had been set in 1993 at the Breakwater Conference referred to in point (a) above. At its conclusion the assembled participants adopted the *Breakwater Declaration*,[10] which identified areas of agreement as well as 'areas requiring further consideration', first among which was 'the need for and design of administrative appeals, internal or external ….'[11]

Given these milestones in the development of a 'new' administrative law to assist in the achievement of an acceptable level of administrative justice in the 'never again' spirit[12] of much of the constitution-and lawmaking of the time, the account of the state of the administrative tribunal landscape which follows, makes for disconcerting reading. In particular, the complete failure to establish a framework within which those 'tribunals' which exist can both function more efficiently and in an integrated fashion, such as is the case in several comparative jurisdictions, must count as a major disappointment. Add to this the reality, as Hoexter states so clearly at the outset of this chapter, that (superior-court) judicial review of administrative action has, if anything, gained a greater share of the administrative justice field than before, and the failure is all the more dismal. Perhaps the 'boldness' of the judicial leadership (as advocated by Sachs above) given by the Constitutional Court in pushing the boundaries of review has had something to do with this. In doing so, the Court has relied on the Constitutional right, but this stance has come at some cost to the courts, both in terms of workload[13] and legitimacy.[14]

[7] Constitution of the Republic of South Africa (1996) s 33. The full text appears below.

[8] Achieved in the form of the Promotion of Administrative Justice Act 2000 (SA). For a review of the drafting of this statute, see C Hoexter, 'The Future of Judicial Review in South African Administrative Law' (2000) 117 *South African Law Journal* 484.

[9] For a review of this process see the proceedings of a conference convened to consider progress in H Corder and L van de Vijver (eds), *Realising Administrative Justice* (SiberInk, Cape Town, 2002). An overview provided in Chapter 1, H Corder, 'Reviewing review: Much achieved, much more to do'.

[10] See Bennett (n 5) 18–20.

[11] ibid 19, point III(i).

[12] See the remarks of President Mandela at his inauguration on 10 May 1994. See www.sanews.gov.za/south-africa/read-nelson-mandelas-inauguration-speech-president-sa. It is worth noting that Australia referred to the 'new' administrative law in the 1970s, albeit in a radically different social context.

[13] The superior courts are increasingly unable to meet the demands placed on their services. See, eg, the *Reserved Judgments Reports* produced by the Office of the Chief Justice of South Africa at the beginning of each judicial term: www.judiciary.org.za/index.php/judiciary/reserved-judgment-reports.

[14] The insistence of the courts in holding the executive and legislature to the constitutional limits of their powers had embroiled the judiciary in unseemly public controversy. For an account of this development, see M Le Roux and D Davis, *Lawfare: Judging Politics in South Africa* (Jonathan Ball, 2019) and H Corder and C Hoexter, '"Lawfare" in South Africa and Its Effects on the Judiciary' (2017) 10 *African Journal of Legal Studies* 105.

Against this contextual backdrop, I hope in what follows to provide a picture of the administrative-appeals terrain as it exists currently, by providing a short history, an account of the many opportunities for reform, none of which was used, leaving this area of administrative law essentially unchanged. The conclusion is that this may be assessed collectively as a 'wasted opportunity'; but perhaps one hoped in the early 1990s for too much progress, too complete a process of renewal and reform.

The History

Judicial review of administrative action provided one of the very few lawful means of challenging some of the worst injustices of apartheid, from at least 1948 till the dawn of democracy in 1990.[15] This was achieved through the courts, even on the basis of a narrow conception of the ultra vires doctrine as its foundation under the (English) common law and even while subject to judicial policy which could be described at best as 'cautious' and at worst as 'executive-minded'. Several accounts of the 'politics of the judiciary'[16] demonstrate the patchy judicial record in the exercise of its review power, yet it clearly worked sufficiently well to keep alive in the minds of many the desirable potential of the courts as a means to check the exercise of public power.[17]

While the dominant and most effective mode of regulating the exercise of public power was clearly judicial review, other mechanisms of administrative review were established in a relatively haphazard, ad hoc manner. After canvassing various types and forms of 'appeal' available, which depended on the existence of a record of the original decision-making process, the procedural and decisional powers and record of the appellate authority, and so on, Baxter[18] tried to make sense of the landscape in the mid-1980s by identifying 'revision courts', 'review boards' and 'appeal boards'.[19] He went further in his attempted systematisation of the relative profusion of such tribunals by the identification of six types of appellate bodies,[20] being the departmental Minister,[21] departmental officials,

[15] Two magisterial texts in English dominate the study of administrative law in South Africa: L Baxter, *Administrative Law* (Juta, 1984) and C Hoexter, *Administrative Law in South Africa* (three editions: 2007, 2012 and 2021, the last with Penfold, see note 3). Baxter's entire work demonstrates the myriad ways in which judicial review of administrative action both functioned and failed to keep the exercise of public power within some limits of fairness, mainly outside the political realm; Hoexter focuses overwhelmingly (see 13–15 of her second edition) on the post-apartheid era, eg, summarising the miserable record of the previous decades.

[16] Prominent among them are A Sachs, *Justice in South Africa* (Chatto-Heineman, 1973), J Dugard, *Human Rights and the South African Legal Order* (Princeton University Press, 1978), H Corder *Judges at Work* (Juta, 1984) and C Forsyth, *In Danger for Their Talents* (Juta, 1985).

[17] See the persuasive account of J Meierhenrich, *The Legacies of Law: Long-run Consequences of Legal Development in South Africa, 1652-2000* (CUP, 2008).

[18] See Baxter (n 15) 255–63.

[19] ibid 256.

[20] ibid 263ff.

[21] Of which there were in one study shown to be 34 instances.

supervisory agencies, representative bodies, appellate boards or committees, and special courts.[22] He concluded his treatment with a plea for greater order within the field, against a wistful summary analysis of the Australian administrative appeals system, then in its first innovative decade.[23]

The type of interest which fell within the jurisdiction of such appellate tribunals will sound familiar to most administrative lawyers in the Commonwealth,[24] matters such as property valuations, rent controls, transportation licensing, town planning schemes, worker compensation awards, even atmospheric pollution (which seems counterintuitively progressive for the apartheid regime, given that the authorising Act of Parliament dated from 1965). However, at least three areas where the exercise of administrative discretion was both reviewable in a court and appealable to a board were untypical and emblematic of one of the foundation stones of apartheid, legalised racism: residential 'group areas' for people of different 'races',[25] urban influx control imposed by law on 'black' citizens (the 'pass laws'),[26] and the act of classifying people by race itself.[27] With this range of administrative appeal avenues in place by the end of apartheid, the concept of administrative appeals (or 'merits review' as it is sometimes called) was certainly firmly in place and broadly accepted as a desirable element of the 'administrative review' firmament. However, its ad hoc and uncoordinated nature as well as the fact that some of the activity took place in a highly contested and unjust area of public governance made it an undervalued and unattractive area for research and reform. One must add to this the fact that the period 1970 to 1990 witnessed the growth and then dominance of a 'laager mentality'[28] which characterised every aspect of governmental activity. This militated against openness to the influence, let alone implementation, of the progressive developments within the area of administrative tribunals which was such a prominent feature of many other jurisdictions within the Commonwealth at that time, including Australia, Canada, India, Malaysia and Singapore, not to mention the United Kingdom.[29] However, the fundamental political shift which accompanied the end of apartheid provided substantial potential for thoroughgoing analysis and change, most particularly in the area of administrative appeals. It was thus abundantly clear, once the future of constitutional governance in a post-apartheid South Africa was being negotiated,

[22] Examples of the last were courts to consider income tax assessments, water access and rights, compensation for expropriation of property, restrictive trade practices, and questions relating to patents: Baxter (n 15) 267.

[23] Baxter (n 15) 267–72.

[24] ibid 256–9.

[25] See LR Dison and I Mahomed, *Group Areas and their Development* (Butterworths, 1960).

[26] See H Corder, 'The Right of Africans to remain in Urban Areas' (1977) *Responsa Meridiana* 213.

[27] See BR Bamford, 'Race Reclassification' (1967) 84 *South African Law Journal* 37–42 for a sample of the appeal and review measures available.

[28] In the pioneering sense of drawing the wagons into a circle to keep out all intrusions, the 'total onslaught'.

[29] For a contemporary overview of such developments see H Corder, *Empowerment and Accountability Towards Administrative Justice in a Future South Africa* (Centre for Constitutional Studies, 1991), especially 12–83.

that the scope, structure, processes, and remedies making up the review of administrative action broadly should receive careful attention and robust resolution.

The Opportunities

To this end, the 1990s witnessed feverish activity among lawyers and politicians in almost every part of the legal system and the administration of justice: it was as though the end of formal apartheid through the law triggered the release of reservoirs of pent-up energy both nationally and among interested parties abroad.[30] This is not the place for a detailed account of the many initiatives which focused on administrative law reform,[31] but it is vital to note those aspects of it which are relevant to the current state of administrative tribunals.

The South African Law Commission

While Baxter had at various points in his leading text drawn attention to progressive developments comparatively, and while Wiechers[32] had referred to alternative approaches to the review of administrative action, the first formal initiative in the reform process came from the South African Law Commission (SALC), the official law-reform body within the Department of Justice, and as early as 1986. It issued a Working Paper for comment in August 1986, and another one late in 1991.[33] This last took account of comments received on the first paper, but also the Commission's interim report on 'group and human rights', effectively the (futile) attempt by the ailing apartheid regime to steal a march on the bill of rights debate by crafting an instrument which emphasised group rights.[34] The 'main aim of the investigation [was] to determine whether the [then] situation regarding appeals was satisfactory', as well as to determine whether the grounds of judicial review of administrative action were an 'effective means of controlling the

[30] Among the many accounts of this process, one of the most comprehensive is H Ebrahim, *The Soul of a Nation: Constitution-Making in South Africa* (OUP, 1998); another account of particular relevance is R Spitz with M Chaskalson, *The Politics of Transition: A Hidden History of South Africa's Negotiated Settlement* (Wits University Press, 2000).

[31] For a summary account, see H Corder 'Reviewing Review: Much Achieved, Much More to Do' in H Corder and L van de Vijver (eds), *Realising Administrative Justice* (Siber Ink, 2002) ch 1.

[32] The leading text in Afrikaans *Administratiefreg* (2nd edn, 1984) was written by Marinus Wiechers, who had completed doctoral studies in France, and thus brought a European continental stance to bear on several aspects of his treatment of South African administrative law. The dominant judicial approach remained however determinedly 'common-law' albeit frozen in time.

[33] See the final Report of the South African Law Commission Project 24, *Investigation into the Courts' Powers of Review of Administrative Acts* (November 1992). Available at: www.justice.gov.za/salrc/reports/Report-Prj024-ReviewAdministrativeActs-1992.pdf.

[34] Where the group would inevitably have coincided almost completely with 'race classification'. SALC Report (n 33) 1.

legality of such acts in a modern state'.[35] The unspoken subtext was naturally the fundamental change that had taken place in the political sphere from early February 1990 through the freeing up of political activity, the release of political prisoners, and the return of exiles.

The Report marks a significant moment in the process of reform of administrative law because of the seriousness with which the Commission investigated the viability and structure of administrative appeals. After dutifully summarising the distinctions between review and appeal as they had developed through case law over much of the preceding century, reaching the unremarkable conclusion that there were 'very real distinctions' between appeal and review, being chiefly that an appeal was concerned with a reconsideration of the merits while a review was concerned 'primarily with the legality or regularity of the decision',[36] the Commission devoted considerable attention to the existing landscape of administrative appeals within South Africa. The Report contains probably the most complete list of instances where an appeal lies from an administrative act or decision, some of which remain in place despite the changed constitutional and political context.

Starting with statute-based appeals direct to the superior courts, the Report listed 36 Acts of Parliament which provided for such appeals.[37] This is followed by a similar listing of provision for appeals to government Ministers (54);[38] to departmental officials (9);[39] to 'administrative tribunals', noting that such tribunals enjoyed a range of names, such as board, appeal body, appeal tribunal, appeal committee, review board, and court of review (17);[40] to representative bodies (3);[41] to supervisory agencies (3);[42] to special courts (6);[43] and to 'other administrative bodies' (10).[44] Thus there was at that stage a total of 137 administrative appellate routes available in law.

I have reproduced the complete list of the various categories of appeal created by statute because one of the central features of administrative appeals in South Africa was, and remains, the wide variation and inconsistency in nomenclature, jurisdiction, and function which existed at that time; whether this picture has changed is clearly a question that needs to be addressed in this current assessment of administrative tribunals, and will be undertaken below. Given our central focus on 'tribunals', it is worth noting the type of issue which fell for

[35] ibid 3.

[36] ibid 19–20. An additional issue mentioned was the importance of the giving of reasons for administrative action, as well as the compilation of a record of the preceding process.

[37] ibid 22–7.

[38] ibid 27–34.

[39] ibid 34–6.

[40] ibid 36–41.

[41] ibid 41–2.

[42] ibid 42–3.

[43] ibid 43–7.

[44] ibid 47–9.

(re)decision before tribunals, being military pensions, stock exchanges, financial markets, the certification of medicines, censorship of publications, air pollution, social work and welfare, fund-raising activities, merchant shipping, and building standards.[45] The issues reserved for reconsideration by 'special courts' were the promotion of economic competition, labour relations and health and safety at work, income tax, patent registration, and rights to water, primarily for agricultural purposes.[46] These are certainly matters of some public importance, which are likely to mirror similar focal areas in comparative jurisdictions.

The Report then turned its attention to criticism of the state of affairs: this came down to one point, that the 'system' was entirely ad hoc and incoherent. Having been urged to introduce the kind of changes made in kindred jurisdictions, the Commission undertook a superficial consideration of the state of administrative tribunals in Australia,[47] the United Kingdom,[48] France,[49] the Netherlands,[50] West Germany,[51] Zimbabwe,[52] and New Zealand.[53] It thereafter reviewed the benefits and drawbacks of the following types of administrative appeal avenues as found in such jurisdictions: a separate system of administrative courts; an advisory body; an administrative appeal tribunal or court; and an administrative division of the superior court.[54]

After detailing several of the comments received by it on its earlier working papers, which reflected views both in favour of and against a shift to one of these models, the Commission spent some time reflecting on a proposal that I had made.[55] After extensive research during a period of sabbatical leave in 1991, the major part of which was spent in Australia, I had proposed the adoption of the General Administrative Appeals Tribunal model, the establishment of a body akin to the Administrative Review Council, legislative initiatives in the area of openness of government, human rights and similar commissions, and so on, underpinned by statutory measures, as the outcome of a wholesale reordering of the appeals tribunal field in South Africa. However, recognising the resource, human and political constraints and uncertainty of the time, I proposed a thin-end-of-the-wedge[56] start to the process, with the institution of two new appeals tribunals. These would focus on two issues of major political importance then (and now): the regulation of police powers and access to land. If the work of these new tribunals succeeded,

[45] ibid 39–40.
[46] ibid 34–6.
[47] ibid 51–64.
[48] ibid 64–8.
[49] ibid 69–76.
[50] ibid 76–9.
[51] ibid 79–83.
[52] ibid 83–6.
[53] ibid 86–8.
[54] ibid 95–102.
[55] ibid 102–4. The proposals were essentially the product of the report entitled *Empowerment and Accountability*, note 1.
[56] I did not call it that at the time.

I argued, the foundation would be laid for the wholesale re-ordering of the system which I had proposed. Needless to say, the Commission rejected this approach. Its words are worth citing in full because they epitomise the general view prevalent in the public administration and among government lawyers still today:[57]

> The Commission remains of the view that it is doubtful that the adoption of a piecemeal approach … would be viable at this stage of constitutional change … when it is difficult to determine the practical difficulties that would be involved with regard to geographical considerations concerning the most appropriate areas in which to locate the seats of the tribunal, the constitution of such a tribunal, the availability of persons with the requisite expertise, and the possible costs that would be involved.

I mention this only because the manner in which the SALC rejected my proposal demonstrates the unpersuasive reasoning employed in reaching its very disappointing recommendation 'that the present system of appeals should be retained, that no provision should be made for a general right of appeal to the [Supreme Court] against administrative decisions, and that reform should rather be effected … to judicial review, that is the extension of the grounds for … review.'[58] There was naturally great uncertainty and the stakes were abnormally high in taking any risks at that fraught period of constitutional and political transition. As a result, one can have some empathy with the caution or timidity of the Commissioners. However, had the rest of the negotiating process been characterised by such a conservative approach, South Africa is very unlikely to be enjoying the progressive framework for public governance which it does, despite manifold shortcomings and failures of implementation. The truth is that, despite further attempts to bring about change in the field of administrative tribunals, the situation today is essentially as it was in 1991.

The Breakwater Conference

This setback did not, however, deter the cohort driving administrative law reform, as can be seen in the Breakwater Conference programme and *Declaration* of February 1993.[59] I have noted above the identification of 'the need for and design of administrative appeals' as one of the important matters identified in the *Declaration* as needing urgent attention, but of greater significance was Govender's contribution to the proceedings, entitled 'Administrative Appeals Tribunals'.[60] After considering the broad background to reform in this area in the UK and singling out the special income tax courts, the (Natal provincial) Town Planning Board and pensions appeals to the Minister as exemplary of the spectrum of

[57] SALC (n 33) 3.12.33, p 104.
[58] ibid 3.12.38, p 106.
[59] Note 5.
[60] See K Govender, *Administrative Law Reform* (Juta, 1993) 76–87.

administrative appeals cluttering the field in South Africa,[61] Govender adopted the recommendation of the Franks Committee[62] and identified openness, fairness and impartiality as being essential qualities for any effective system of tribunals.[63] He then proceeded to spell out what steps would be needed to realise the vision of a co-ordinated, integrated and fair system of appeals tribunals, relying both on the Franks recommendations as well as Baxter's espousal of the Australian Administrative Appeals Tribunal (AAT) model, incidentally also proposing a piecemeal approach as a realistic means of managing the exigencies of the context. The issue of confronting the necessity for and structure and processes of administrative appeals tribunals was thus placed firmly on the reform table again, especially as almost every significant and influential politician, lawyer, and future judge was present among the almost one hundred participants in the conference.

The Transitional Constitution

The adoption of the transitional/interim Constitution[64] in late 1993 marked a major breakthrough in the advancement of the administrative justice cause. The background to the negotiations on this issue[65] bore testimony to the significance of the Breakwater Conference in preparing the ground politically and in ensuring that certain key negotiators were already persuaded of the need for the inclusion of a set of rights to administrative justice. While the need was widely accepted, the precise formulation of these rights was much less so, involving substantial and long political negotiations. The outcome was as follows:

> Every person shall have the right to—
> (a) lawful administrative action where any of his or her rights or interests is affected or threatened;
> (b) procedurally fair administrative action where any of his or her rights or legitimate expectations is affected or threatened;
> (c) be furnished with reasons in writing for administrative action which affects any of his or her rights or interests unless the reasons for such action have been made public; and
> (d) administrative action which is justifiable in relation to the reasons given for it where any of his or her rights is affected or threatened.

Although Namibia had adopted a set of duties imposed on its public officials along similar lines in its Bill of Rights,[66] this marked the first time that positive rights

[61] ibid 78–83.
[62] Emanating from the United Kingdom, *The Report of the Committee on Administrative Tribunals and Enquiries* (Cmnd 218, London HMSO: 1957).
[63] Govender (n 60) 83.
[64] Constitution of the Republic of South Africa (1993).
[65] For an account of these aspects, see Du Plessis and Corder (n 6) at 165–70.
[66] See the *Constitution of Namibia* (1990) art 18.

of this nature were accorded to individuals in a national constitution, and it set a trend in the constitutional reform movement which characterised that decade and the next.[67] A crucial companion right of access to information[68] was also included at this stage. Perhaps of greater significance to the discussion of administrative tribunals was section 22, access to court, as follows: 'Every person shall have the right to have justiciable disputes settled by a court of law or, *where appropriate, another independent and impartial forum*' (my emphasis). This last element was deliberately included in order to widen the scope of possible remedial action for any 'justiciable dispute', including an administrative act or decision. As we will see, the platform established by this interim provision was built on in the 'final' Constitution.

Breakwater II

Informal momentum continued to be exerted in the cause of administrative law reform. Just over three years later, a smaller and less high-profile group of lawyers gathered at the same venue to consider the theme of 'Controlling Public Power in Southern Africa'. Papers were presented[69] by leading academics and practitioners from a wide range of African countries, including Kenya, Zimbabwe, Malawi and Botswana, and by prominent academics from the UK[70] and the United States of America.[71] Significantly, papers were also given by a member of the Mandela Cabinet[72] and the first Public Protector (ombud) of South Africa,[73] attention was given to the potential role in achieving administrative justice of bodies outside the judiciary[74] and the importance of the companion to administrative justice, the right of access to information, as well as practical matters such as the accessibility of administrative review, including through public interest litigation. The most direct attention to administrative tribunals was given by D D Ntanda Nsereko, who reported that, in Botswana, administrative tribunals fell into two broad categories: those that made initial decisions and those that heard appeals.[75] Once more, the typical areas that fell within the tribunals' jurisdiction were rental agreements, town planning, censorship, taxation, public transport and trade disputes.

[67] See, eg, the Constitutions of Malawi (1994) art 43, Kenya 2010 art 70, and Zimbabwe 2013 art 68.

[68] Constitution of the Republic of South Africa 1993 (SA), s 23.

[69] The proceedings were published in H Corder and T Maluwa (eds), *Administrative Justice in Southern Africa* (Department of Public Law, University of Cape Town 1997).

[70] Patrick Birkinshaw, Paul Craig and Jeffrey Jowell.

[71] Cass Sunstein.

[72] Professor Kader Asmal, one of the leading figures in the generation of the bill of rights.

[73] (Now Judge) Selby Baqwa.

[74] Govender set out a persuasive case for the role of the Human Rights Commission here: see K Govender chapter 9 in Corder and Maluwa (n 69) from 129 to 141.

[75] See Corder and Maluwa ibid at ch 7 'Controlling Executive Power in Southern Africa: The Role of the Courts and Administrative Tribunals', especially at 113–15.

The Final Constitution

The inclusion of a right to administrative justice continued to provoke controversy in the negotiations around the final Constitution, because it was difficult to argue that it was counted among the 'universally accepted fundamental rights' of which the Constitutional Principles spoke.[76] In the end it was emphatically endorsed that (emphasis added):

(1) Everyone has the right to administrative action which is lawful, reasonable and procedurally fair.
(2) Everyone whose rights have been adversely affected by administrative action has the right to be given written reasons.
(3) National legislation must be enacted to give effect to these rights and must—
 (a) provide for the review of administrative action by a court *or, where appropriate, an independent and impartial tribunal*;
 (b) impose a duty on the state to give effect to the rights in subsections (1) and (2); and
 (c) promote an efficient administration.

Pending the drafting and adoption of the envisaged legislation, this right was suspended for a period of three years and the language of the interim right remained enforceable. It is significant, however, that 'reasonableness' had now been included as a ground of review[77] and more so for present purposes, that the language used in the interim right of access to courts was now directly incorporated in the right to 'just administrative action', as section 33 was now styled. Indeed, the right of access to court[78] in the final Constitution once again encompassed the right to a 'fair public hearing before a court or, where appropriate, another independent and impartial tribunal or forum'. It seemed, thus, that the envisaged legislation should address the matter of providing a framework and processes for a relatively coherent and stable system of administrative tribunals as an integral part of giving expression to the rights and 'promoting an efficient administration'.

The Promotion of Administrative Justice Act

Many of those who had argued for bringing a degree of order and system to the administrative review terrain had referred favourably to the positive effects of Parliamentary legislation which added flesh to the skeleton of any constitutional

[76] See Principle II in Sch 4 to the 1993 Constitution, the mandatory framework for the negotiations about the final Constitution, justiciable by the Constitutional Court, which had the final say as to whether they had been complied with.

[77] This had been a major sticking point in the 1993 negotiations and its inclusion substantially widened the grounds of review.

[78] Section 34.

rights, as well as a standing national advisory body which would monitor developments in this area of the law and propose amendments and innovations as the need arose. Prime among the precedents cited was the wholesale transformation of the Australian administrative review system the foundation stones of which – the general AAT, the Administrative Review Council, the Administrative Decisions (Judicial Review) Act 1977 (Cth) and the Federal Court 1976 (Cth) – were laid through purposeful government policy during the 1970s.[79]

The SALC had ventured into this terrain in the draft Bill which it appended to its 1992 report, but confined its attention only to the revision of the judicial review sphere in that it proposed a process and timelines for the giving of reasons for administrative action as well as a codification of the grounds of review. After the adoption of the interim Constitution, the new Minister of Justice requested the Commission in 1994 to weigh up whether its proposed draft passed constitutional muster in light of the protection accorded in it to the rights of access to court and to administrative justice. In response, the Commission produced a further slightly amended version of its proposed bill, styled the Judicial Review (Act).[80] These recommendations must have played a role in the thinking of the post-apartheid government in insisting first that the right to administrative justice be 'downgraded' to the status of legislation, but then, as a negotiating compromise, to retain the right but insist on its supplementation through legislation and anticipating a justifiable limitation in its scope in the process, as we have seen in section 33 above.

The process of drafting the required legislation then arose. Despite being aware of the necessity to meet the three-year limit within which any such legislation would have to be signed into law,[81] the Minister of Justice took until the end of 1998 to appoint a 'Project Committee' (PC)[82] of the SALC to draft a bill, consult extensively, then produce a final version for passage into legislative form through Parliament. The PC produced a draft bill for comment by the end of January 1999; after extensive consultations including hearings in four cities as well as a gathering in England of experts chiefly from Commonwealth countries, a final draft was sent to Parliament by August 1999. The Promotion of Administrative Justice Act 2000 (SA) ('PAJA'), as it is called, was passed by Parliament in late January 2000 and received assent from the President (as Head of State) the day before the expiry of the three-year period.

[79] These developments were widely praised both in Australia and abroad. For their early impact in South African debates see Baxter (n 15) 268–72; Corder (n 1) 24–45; and the SALC (n 33) 51–64.

[80] See South African Law Commission, *Investigation into the Courts' Powers of Review of Administrative Acts Supplementary Report* (Project 24, October 1994). Two versions of the proposed bill were provided, in Annexures A and B.

[81] Failing which the provisions of s 33 would have been implementable unrestricted, which might well have caused confusion and resistance.

[82] Styled the Project Committee on Administrative Law, Project 115, the PC was convened by a senior barrister complemented by three academics, among whom were Hoexter and the author, assisted by junior counsel as researcher.

While the provisions of the PAJA have tested lawyers and judges on numerous occasions, most notably the extensive and perplexing definition given in s 1 to the gatekeeping concept of 'administrative action',[83] they are relevant for present purposes for only one reason: their failure decisively to guide the future structure and processes of the administrative appeals avenue for review of administrative conduct.[84] The PC had all along included in its proposed bill a chapter[85] dealing with the establishment, functions, activities, staffing, financing, and reporting obligations of an Administrative Review Council (ARC), an unashamedly borrowed title. The PC proposed that between eight and 13 members be appointed to the ARC,[86] whose envisaged mandate was to investigate and recommend to the Minister several further changes and revisions of the administrative review field to enhance access, accountability, efficiency, and openness of government. The PC adopted this strategic route because its members realised that insufficient preparatory work had been done to allow for firm proposals for such areas of development and reform, which would no doubt have been used as a political counterargument had it made its proposals more definite.

It is clear from the record that the matter of administrative appeals was foremost in urgency and importance in the mind of the PC. So, clause 17 (Functions of the Council) read as follows:

> '… [T]he Council must:—
>
> (a) Inquire into the law and practice relating to
>
> (i) internal complaints procedures;
> (ii) internal administrative appeals; and
> (iii) …,
>
> and make its first recommendations to the Minister … within two years after the … commencement of this Act ….
>
> (b) ….
> (c) inquire into the appropriateness of establishing:—
>
> (i) independent and impartial tribunals, in addition to the courts, to review administrative action; and
> (ii) specialised administrative tribunals, including a tribunal with general jurisdiction over all organs of state[87] or a number of organs of state, to hear and determine appeals against administrative action, and make its first recommendations to the Minister … within two years of the commencement of this Act.'

[83] See, eg, the critical analysis in L Wolff 'In Search of a Definition for Administrative Action' (2017) 33 *South African Journal on Human Rights* 314.

[84] The best critical account of the drafting process and its disappointing outcome is provided by C Hoexter, 'The Future of Judicial Review in South African Administrative Law' (2000) 117 *South African Law Journal* 484.

[85] Administrative Justice Bill, ch 5, PC 115.

[86] ibid cl 16. Chaired by a nominee of the Chief Justice, with several other members serving *ex officio*, it was proposed that between three and eight 'suitably qualified' additional members should serve.

[87] The reader may be perplexed by this phrase, which was present already in the work of the SALC under apartheid. For what it is worth, it is now a fixture in the Constitution, enjoying its own definition,

Parliament was not persuaded by this proposal. Together with another important innovation proposed by the PC,[88] the necessity of the substance of this proposal was relegated to the discretionary authority of the Minister to 'make regulations'. Section 10(2) of the PAJA authorises the Minister to make regulations relating to—

> (a) the establishment, duties and powers of an advisory council to monitor the application of this Act and to advise the Minister on … (iii) the appropriateness of establishing independent and impartial tribunals, in addition to the courts, to review administrative action and of specialised administrative tribunals, including a tribunal with general jurisdiction over all organs of state or a number if organs of state, to hear and determine appeals against administrative action …

Although voices were raised at the time against this demotion of the importance of bringing some semblance of order and system to the area of administrative appeals, the government held fast to its stance. The discretionary nature of this power is accentuated by the language of section 10(1), which leaves the Minister no room to avoid the responsibility: the Minister 'must' make regulations relating to four sets of procedures being, importantly, those to promote and govern the right to procedural fairness, the holding of public inquiries and notice-and-comment procedures, and requests for reasons.[89] Despite at least a moral obligation to act in the area of administrative appeals, if not a very strong pragmatic reason to do so, there has been no movement in the intervening 23 years. Given the general decline in ministerial commitment to anything approaching the fair and efficient advancement of administrative justice over this period, and the substantially decreased appetite for any innovation in the public administration that will shake things up (and cost money), the likelihood of the Minister's initiating reform of the administrative tribunals sphere must be close to zero.

Continuing Attention

Despite the setback embodied in the failure of the PAJA to address the status of administrative appeals, many appellate bodies continue to exist and to discharge an important function in the administrative justice firmament, as we shall see.[90]

as follows (s 239): '(a) any department of state or administration in the national, provincial or local sphere of government; or (b) any other functionary or institution – (i) exercising a power or performing a function in terms of the Constitution …; or (ii) exercising a public power or performing a public function in terms of any legislation, but does not include a court or a judicial officer.' The effect of this has been substantially to widen the scope of application of administrative review, especially as this type of language has also been employed in the definition of 'administrative action' in the PAJA, s 1.

[88] That there should be a wholesale review of Rules and Standards applicable in the public administration, changes made as a result, and that the making of new rules and standards should be subject to a different process in the future: see Chapter 4.

[89] The Minister has done so: see the Regulations on Fair Administrative Procedures of 31 July 2002, in GN R1022 *GG* 23674.

[90] See below.

Academic and civil society pressure in support of reform of the administrative appeals terrain likewise continues to make itself felt from time to time. An international conference held at the University of Cape Town in 2006 brought together administrative lawyers from across the Commonwealth, with papers focusing on both comparative as well as country-specific studies.[91] The most relevant chapter in the published proceedings critically catalogued the burgeoning of administrative tribunals in India.[92] In this account, Datar referred to both successes and shortcomings, and concluded on the following cautionary note:[93]

> Great care has to be taken when creating new tribunals. The character of the dispute to be resolved, the law that has to be applied, the degree of specialisation that is necessary, and the qualifications of members who will preside over these tribunals are extremely important factors. The over-crowding of the courts cannot be used as an excuse to create tribunals that are ill-equipped to resolve disputes and dispense justice.

Two academic treatises have also traversed the field of administrative tribunals in South Africa. A decade after the coming into force of the PAJA,[94] Armstrong completed a substantial LLM thesis entitled *Administrative Justice and Tribunals in South Africa: A Commonwealth Comparison*,[95] in which she surveyed the field of administrative tribunals and weighed up the damaging effects of their fractured and incoherent nature and the burdens that this was placing on the superior courts in increasingly having to countenance applications for judicial review. The constitutionalisation of 'reasonableness' as a ground of review[96] had effectively widened the scope available to the courts for at least a partial consideration of the merits of administrative action, if only to test its validity in terms of its rationality and proportionality.[97]

While recognising that much energy and financial investment would have to go into establishing a general appellate tribunal, Armstrong pointed to the substantial costs incurred by government in defending executive and administrative action in litigation, as well as the damaging effects on the achievement of administrative justice as the result of the absence of an administrative tribunal system. She focused on Australia and England as her comparators, and reached the conclusion that:[98]

> The English and Australian models indicate a few important trends which need to be applied universally to ensure a sustained tribunal reform and a system which provides

[91] See H Corder (ed), *Comparing Administrative Justice across the Commonwealth* (Juta, 2006) – also published as 2006 *Acta Juridica*.

[92] Arvind Datar, 'The Tribunalisation of Justice in India' in Corder, ibid 288–302.

[93] ibid 301–2.

[94] Although signed into law in February 2000, the Act came into force only in November 2000.

[95] G Armstrong, *Administrative Justice and Tribunals in South Africa: A Commonwealth Comparison* (thesis presented for the LLM degree at the University of Stellenbosch, 2011, supervised by Professor Geo Quinot).

[96] In s 33(1).

[97] For a comprehensive treatment of the current state of this part of administrative law, see Hoexter and Penfold (n 2) ch 6.

[98] Armstrong (n 95) 3.

> a higher level of administrative redress than the over-burdened and institutionally inept courts currently do. These include co-operation among government departments and tribunals; open and accountable systemic change; the need for supervision and evaluation of the whole of administrative law by an independent and competent body; and ultimately a focus on the needs of users of state services.

Armstrong identified the following attributes which all tribunals should manifest:[99]

> Firstly, they should have the ability to make final, legally enforceable decisions. Secondly, they should be independent from any departmental branch of government. Thirdly, the nature of the hearings conducted in tribunals should be both public and of a judicial nature, while not necessarily subject to the stringent formalities of a court of law. Fourthly, tribunal members should be in possession of specific expertise, in the field of operation of the tribunal as well as judicial expertise. Fifthly, there should be a duty on tribunals to give clear reasons for their decisions, and lastly that there should be a right of appeal to a higher court on disputes regarding points of law.

Armstrong concluded[100]

> The need for sustained systematic reform in South Africa is one that cannot be ignored. Tribunals offer a valuable alternative to judicial review for the resolution of administrative disputes, and the value of a comprehensive and coherent structure for the establishment and administration of tribunals is apparent from the above discussion. Furthermore, the tribunal systems of Australia and England have demonstrated how the effective creation and continued use of comprehensive tribunal structures contributes firstly to cost reduction and secondly to ease the administrative burden on courts who are not suited to cure large-scale administrative error.

Armstrong makes a strong, indeed almost incontestable, case for substantial reform of the field of administrative tribunals, a recommendation reached also by Baboolal-Frank in her doctoral thesis in early 2019.[101] After setting the scene broadly, and reviewing both the historical development and current regulatory regime of administrative tribunals in South Africa,[102] Baboolal-Frank examines the jurisdiction and activities of five such bodies: the Companies Tribunal, National Consumer Tribunal, Water Tribunal, Competition Tribunal, and Rental Housing Tribunal.[103] She evaluates them all against a number of criteria, being cost-effectiveness, speed of resolution of matters brought to them, their promotion of the rule of law, the extent to which their procedures are simplified, and their informality and flexibility. She further isolates certain features evident in most of them, such as not requiring legal representation, the openness of their operations, their susceptibility to judicial review, the inadequacy of their remedial

[99] ibid 57.
[100] ibid 194.
[101] R Baboolal-Frank, *A critical analysis of tribunals in South Africa to create a harmonised tribunal system*. (Thesis presented for the LLD degree at the University of Pretoria, 2019 supervised by Drs Curlewis and Adeleke.).
[102] ibid chs 1 to 3.
[103] ibid ch 4.

enforcement, the specificity of the grounds of their jurisdiction, and so on.[104] In conclusion, she recommends that a unified South African Tribunal System be established, with three tiers on a provincialised basis, with unified rules of procedure, effective enforcement mechanisms, and an emphasis on alternative dispute resolution, among other things.[105]

It is thus clear that the urgent need for rationalisation and structure still confronts the administrative tribunal terrain in South Africa, and that the governing authorities ought to be well aware of this. Perhaps, like so many other aspects of the post-apartheid experience, expectations in this regard were too high, and those advocating the strong shift to administrative justice should be content with what they did achieve, remarkable as it was. This was especially the case, given the almost breathtaking ease and far-reaching extent of the rest of the administrative-law reform movement from 1993 to 2000. It certainly seems that the window has closed on establishing the unified system of administrative tribunals that so many have advocated, especially given the many other areas of great concern within the administration of justice currently.

Given the deliberate and cynical hollowing out of the prosecution service during the terms in office of President Zuma (2009 to 2017), and the painfully slow process of restoring its personnel, capacity, and efficacy, it seems churlish to campaign for a general administrative appeals tribunal as a national priority. The opportunity to achieve this was manifestly present; it has been wasted so far, whether for all time remains to be seen. Many administrative tribunals continue to function, however, and this chapter continues with a high-level review of the most active and significant among them, all of which have been established since 1994. This may be a sign that potential yet exists for more thorough-going reform.

The Reality

Administrative tribunals in South Africa take many forms, function in a myriad ways, and have radically varying levels of work-load, efficiency, and effectiveness.[106] Most of the 'administrative appeals' avenues which were identified almost 40 years ago by the SALC have been disestablished through the repeal of the enabling legislation, although some of the most significant bodies remain, and others have been replaced by similar appellate bodies. A cursory scan reveals the following picture: of the 36 statute-based appeals to the ordinary courts, only a dozen remain;[107] of the 52 appeals to government Ministers, only 12 remain;[108] of the eight appeals

[104] ibid 131–4.

[105] ibid 194–9.

[106] See the description of the SALC in its Report referred to in the text at nn 38–45 above.

[107] For example, in terms of the Mineral Technology Act 1989 (SA), s 15(6) and the Patents Act 1988 (SA), s 76.

[108] Mainly in education and agriculture. See, eg, the Agricultural Pests Act 1983 (SA), s 11(2) and the Education Affairs Act 1988 (SA), ss 44 and 56(3).

to departmental officials, only three remain;[109] of the 17 'administrative tribunals', seven remain;[110] none of the appeals to 'representative bodies' or to 'supervisory agencies' remains intact; and only two of the nine appeals to 'other bodies' remain in place.[111] Most significantly, the appeal avenue to 'special courts' continues in prominence, chiefly in the areas of economic competition, labour relations, taxation, patents, and rights to water, unsurprisingly given the nature of the national economy and the scarcity of the last resource.

Before focusing on just four tribunals, it is useful to note the overall pattern of (often post-apartheid-established) administrative appellate bodies, admirably reflected in the work of Hoexter and Penfold.[112] So we find examples of 'internal appeals from decisions of a tribunal or official to a superior departmental official or the Minister' in areas such as the environment[113] and tertiary education;[114] appeals to a national control body in several professional areas;[115] appeals to a specially created tribunal, such as in town planning and licensing matters;[116] appeals to specialist courts, generally presided over by a judge, such as in taxation, economic competition, and election disputes; and appeals to ordinary courts such as already mentioned above. The authors conclude their brief discussion of the current state of this area of administrative justice as follows:[117]

> Little has changed over the decades. We still have a large number of fragmented and disparate appellate tribunals and mechanisms. While some of these function efficiently enough, Baxter's (*reference omitted*) lament of 1984 remains true: there is still no 'coherent system' of administrative appeals in [South Africa]. Furthermore, since not even the first of the steps [needed] has been taken, the prospects for reform in this area seem as remote as ever.

Against the background of this bleak but accurate assessment I aim, in this section, to reflect on those newly created tribunals which enjoy the highest profile in the administrative justice system.

The Council for Conciliation, Mediation and Arbitration

The characteristics and benefits of administrative tribunals seem particularly relevant in the modern labour relations sphere where interest representation, expedition, fairness and efficiency are essential attributes of dispute resolution.

[109] Such as in terms of the Alienation of Land Act 1981 (SA), s 22 (2)(b).
[110] Such as in terms of the Social Work Act 1978, s 25 and the Merchant Shipping Act 1951 s 274.
[111] In the medical research and scientific research areas.
[112] Hoexter and Penfold (n 2) 87–88.
[113] National Environmental Management Act 1998 (SA), s 43.
[114] Higher Education Act 1997 (SA), s 64.
[115] Such as the Landscape Architectural Profession Act 2000 (SA), s 33 and the Engineering Profession Act 2000 (SA), s 33.
[116] For example, under the Films and Publications Act 1996 (SA), s 20.
[117] See Hoexter and Penfold (n 2) 93.

The post-apartheid government moved swiftly to remake the statutory framework[118] within which the fraught employer-worker relationship[119] was situated. Dispute resolution mechanisms are dealt with in detail in Chapter VIIA of the Labour Relations Act (LRA) which establishes the Commission for Conciliation, Mediation and Arbitration (CCMA), which in many ways exemplifies within a vital economic sector the potential for creating a coherent administrative tribunal which could comfortably take its place within a comprehensive administrative tribunal system.

As is evident from its name, the CCMA provides dispute resolution mechanisms in respect of almost all forms of workplace conflict, attempting where possible to resolve matters through conciliation and mediation failing which, in arbitration proceedings. In many respects, I would suggest that the CCMA represents much of what could have been achieved by a purposeful revision of the administrative tribunal landscape post-apartheid. It is efficiently run, has regional offices throughout the country, is able to handle a high volume of workplace disputes relatively inexpensively, and has achieved a 'clean audit', indeed turning in a slight surplus in its operations.[120] Some headline statistics tell this story: in the 2022/23 financial year, its almost 1,000 staff considered almost 185,000 cases; its overall dispute-settlement rate sat at 75%; almost all conciliation matters were completed within 23 days and arbitration awards were rendered within 14 days; and 42 000 new 'users' entered its doors.[121] Appeal and review from the CCMA lie to the purpose-created Labour Court,[122] whose decisions are, in turn, appealable to the Labour Appeal Court headed by its own Judge President.[123] These courts are regarded as being part of the broader superior-court structure of the country and the presiding judges are appointed in the same way as all other such judges.

In general, the employment relations field in post-apartheid South Africa has been marked by much less conflict and instability than in the decades leading to 1994, in particular. Much of the credit for this better state must be taken by the CCMA and specialised labour courts, primarily due to the integrated and dedicated manner in which the sub-system as a whole functions. This again emphasises the disappointment expressed throughout this chapter at the failure to widen this type of reform since 1994.

[118] Four Acts of Parliament comprise this framework, chief among them the Labour Relations Act 1995 (SA).

[119] Now governed broadly by s 23 of the Constitution of 1996, which sets out the labour relations rights.

[120] For a detailed overview, see the latest (2022/3) Annual Report. Available at: www.ccma.org.za/wp-content/uploads/2023/10/CCMA-2022-23-ANNUAL-REPORT-2.pdf#index.

[121] ibid Financial year at a Glance, at 8–9.

[122] LRA Chapter VII D.

[123] LRA Chapter VII E.

The Competition Tribunal

The second positive experience in establishing an administrative tribunal after 1994 is to be seen in the performance of the Competition Tribunal. At the end of apartheid, the shareholdings on the Johannesburg Stock Exchange reflected an oligopolistic concentration of wealth in a few small corporations, and the Mandela government set about tackling this socio-economic problem by the adoption of the Competition Act.[124] A summary of what this Act set out to achieve is provided in a review published[125] to mark the first decade of the structures set up in terms of it, as follows:

> The Competition Act of 1998, which came into force on 1 September 1999, reflected the commitment of South Africa's first democratic government to strengthen the competition regime in the context of the country's highly concentrated economy. The Act made provisions to establish the Competition Commission, whose main responsibility would be investigating mergers and anti-competitive conduct, and the Competition Tribunal to rule on most cases. The Competition Appeal Court was also established. The mandate of the Competition Appeal Court is to consider any appeal of a decision or review that the Competition Tribunal has made, or confirm, amend or set aside a decision or an order that is the subject of appeal or review by the Competition Tribunal.

By the time that this review was published, the over-concentration of wealth had remarkably disappeared as a problem,[126] and the Commission and the Tribunal were able to devote their attention to proposed mergers and acquisitions in the corporate sphere. The Tribunal[127] has the following chief functions:[128] after a matter is referred to it, it may:

(a) grant an exemption from a relevant provision of this Act;
(b) authorise a merger, with or without conditions, or prohibit a merger;
(c) adjudicate in relation to any conduct prohibited in terms of Chapter 2 or 3, by determining whether prohibited conduct has occurred and if so, impose a remedy provided for in Chapter 6; or
(d) grant an order for costs in terms of section 57.

The Tribunal functions as follows, in its own words[129] as a 'referee in balancing the interests of various stakeholders (government, business, workers and consumers) when deciding cases before it'. The statistics provided in its latest annual report

[124] 89 of 1998.
[125] South African Competition Commission, *Unleashing Rivalry: Ten years of enforcement by the South African competition authorities 1999–2009* (2009) 1.
[126] An overview of how this was achieved is provided in *Unleashing Rivalry* ibid 2–7.
[127] Established in terms of the Act, s 26.
[128] ibid s 27.
[129] Competition Tribunal, *Integrated Annual Report* (2022/23) 12.

reflects the immense strides made by this tribunal in its 25 years of activity, as follows:[130]

> Mergers … 199 cases heard (25.15% increase compared to … the previous year). 165 orders issued (17.86% [annual] increase), 117 reasons issued (24.46% [annual] increase), 99 mergers were decided, 37 were approved with conditions (32 of these with public interest conditions), 1 merger was prohibited. Total transaction value for mergers was R4 063 606 305 025. Total amount for penalties imposed was R40 441 341, 50% of penalties imposed was for cartel conduct. The highest penalty was imposed … (R15 700 000) for colluding with competitors to fix prices, allocating customers and engaging in bid rigging in the construction sector.

This sector of quasi-judicial conduct is overseen by the Competition Appeal Court (CAC), which is staffed on a part-time basis by superior-court judges appointed in the normal course of the functions of the Judicial Service Commission.[131] The CAC has benefited from being headed by a single Judge President[132] throughout its first 20 years of existence, which has lent stability and great expertise to its judgments. The activities of the Commission, Tribunal, and CAC have in turn stimulated the provision of tertiary-level education in competition law and the election of many young legal professionals to devote their time to specialisation in the field. The fact that this system functions under the auspices of a government department separate from the Ministry of Justice[133] may account to some extent for the general success of this administrative tribunal and its associated bodies.

The Rental Housing Tribunal

Adequate housing for South Africa's growing population has always been a problem, masked for decades by residential apartheid, which meant that the enfranchised and their representatives in Parliament were scarcely concerned about the living conditions under which the vast majority existed. This naturally changed radically after 1994 and Parliament turned its attention to a fair means of regulating a portion of this market, through an administrative tribunal established[134] at about the same time as the Competition Tribunal. This is the Rental Housing Tribunal (RHT) which is established in each of the nine provinces of the country on the initiative of the relevant Member of the Executive Committee (the MEC, effectively the provincial executive authority)[135] and which must do all that is necessary to carry out the functions set out in the Act.[136]

[130] ibid 22.
[131] Constitution, s 178.
[132] Judge Dennis Davis of the Western Cape Division of the High Court.
[133] The Department of Trade and Industry.
[134] Through the Rental Housing Act 1999 (SA).
[135] By virtue of the authority granted in the Rental Housing Act 1999 (SA), s 7.
[136] ibid s 8.

These functions essentially govern the relationship between tenants and landlords, by altering the common law and the law of contract to a certain extent.[137]

Complaints lodged with a RHT may be mediated but also adjudicated, and the effect of such an award is equivalent to the judgment of a Magistrate's Court (the name given to the network of 'lower courts' in the country).[138] The RHT in each province has exclusive jurisdiction[139] over all 'unfair practices'[140] in the rental housing market, the hearings held by it have many of the trappings of a lower court, and its order is regarded as final and binding, unless taken on review to the high court.[141] Each RHT must report to its MEC within four months of the end of each financial year.[142] The most recent report of the RHT (established in 2001) of one of the most populous and best governed provinces, the Western Cape,[143] illustrates the scale and nature of complaints brought to its attention. Here one reads that the four commissioners (supplemented by two part-timers) of the RHT received 2552 complaints during the year, the vast majority of which concerned the failure to refund deposits, unlawful notices to vacate, and the failure to pay rent.[144] Somewhat surprisingly, just fewer than 5% of the complaints related to unlawful eviction,[145] which might reflect the significant statutory regulation of the housing market.[146] The RHT renders its services without charge.

This report reflects a small but important social service provided to often vulnerable residents through an administrative tribunal structure.

The National Consumer Tribunal

The South African population has always reflected gross disparities of wealth, primarily along 'race' lines until 1994 but increasingly less so since the establishment of a constitutionally democratic system. Sadly, the wealth inequality index has widened since 1994, and the country now finds itself the most unequal in the world.[147] As a result, many people rely on credit for their daily subsistence, which makes the fair regulation of this market a critical element of the social compact between government and the citizenry.

[137] See SI Mohamed, 'The Judicial Functions of the Provincial Rental Housing Tribunals' (2005) 9(4) *LexisNexis Butterworths Property Law Digest* 2–4.
[138] See the RHA, s 13(13).
[139] ibid s 13(9).
[140] As defined in regulations issued under the RHA, s 15.
[141] ibid s 13(3).
[142] ibid s 12(3).
[143] See the Western Cape, *Rental Housing Tribunal Annual Report 2022/23*.
[144] ibid 13. 'Other' complaints made up almost 21% of the total.
[145] ibid.
[146] Notably, the *Prevention of Illegal Eviction from and Unlawful Occupation of Land Act* 1998 (SA) and the *Consumer Protection Act* 2008 (SA).
[147] There are many studies which indicate this. One such is 'Inequality in South Africa since 1960'. Available at: www.eh-exhibition.uni-bayreuth.de/en/cs/South-Africa/index.html.

To this end, Parliament has adopted the National Credit Act 2005 (SA) ('NCA') and the Consumer Protection Act 2008 (SA) ('CPA'). The NCA is extensive in its scope, seeking to regulate the activities of the consumer credit industry in all aspects of its operation, including laying down policy, the content of agreements, conditions for the collection of debt, repayment of credit, debt enforcement and dispute settlement,[148] in the last of which the National Consumer Tribunal (NCT) plays a critical role. The NCT is established in Chapter 2 Part B of the NCA as a tribunal of record with national jurisdiction, whose decisions (of a single member of the Tribunal) have the status of an order of a High Court,[149] are appealable to a panel of three members of the Tribunal, and are reviewable and appealable in turn to a High Court with jurisdiction.[150] Any matter of dispute within the consumer credit industry is amenable to the NCT's jurisdiction, usually after consideration by the National Credit Regulator.[151]

The CPA, in turn, provides in great detail for the protection of the following statutory rights for all consumers:[152] to equality, to privacy, to choose, to disclosure of information, to fair and responsible marketing, to fair and honest dealing, to fair just and reasonable terms and conditions, to fair value, good quality and safety, and to accountability (from the providers/suppliers). To regulate and enforce these rights and correlative duties the Act establishes the office of the National Consumer Commission (NCC)[153] to which complaints may be referred,[154] which is in turn empowered to enforce the resolution of a dispute, acting if necessary, together with the NCT.[155]

How is this elaborate system working? In the 2022/23 financial year[156] the NCT

> … finalised 27,889 debt re-arrangement applications … with a turnaround time of 29,15 days. … Gone are the days of a bygone era, … where imprisonment could follow for failing to pay debts. Instead, consumers can repay their debts dignifiedly through debt counselling, particularly in the unsecured lending market. … *Non-debt re-arrangement applications* During the reporting year, the NCT received 210 non-debt re-arrangement applications … It finalised 191 cases and issued final judgments with a turnaround time of 17,43 days. … The NCT is contributing to building a new South African consumer jurisprudence by delivering high-quality judgments. During the reporting year, only nine final judgments were reviewed or appealed in the High

[148] NCA, chs 3–6.
[149] ibid s 152(1).
[150] ibid s 148.
[151] For a more extensive overview of the powers and scope of work of the NCT see T Woker, 'A Critical Examination of the Role that the National Consumer Tribunal Plays in Debt Relief with Suggestions for Reform'. Available at: www.up.ac.za/media/shared/Legacy/sitefiles/file/47/327/lawclinicdraftpapersfromconference/tanyawokerdraft.pdf.
[152] Detailed in Chapter 2.
[153] CPA, s 85.
[154] ibid s 76(1)(a).
[155] ibid s 99.
[156] See the Annual Report of the NCT. Available at: www.thenct.org.za/wp-content/uploads/2023/11/2022-2023-NCT-Annual-Report.pdf.

> Court Three [internal] appeals and reviews were finalised during the reporting year. One was withdrawn and two were deemed as dismissed.

This represents a reasonable level of activity in the circumstances, but perhaps more significant is the growing awareness among consumers of the rights and remedies at their disposal, in the face of mounting indebtedness nationally.

Having reviewed summarily the authority and activities of four significant administrative tribunals created since 1994, we must determine whether the bleak assessment of this space which has characterised what appears above still holds. More specifically, does the establishment of these new tribunals which are frequently to be found in common-law jurisdictions nurture optimism for a much wider process of reform?

The Future

I have, in this chapter, endeavoured to provide a critical account of the state of the law and practice in respect of administrative appeals tribunals in South Africa. There are two central features of this account: the relatively unchanged state of the governing characteristics of the administrative appeals field in South African law over the past 40 years and the circumstances which led to wasting a tailor-made opportunity, on several occasions, to remake, modernise, and radically improve it during this period. In particular, the failure to establish an integrated, appropriately resourced, and well-managed system of tribunal activity is a clear and avoidable shortcoming.

However, all is not lost as some of the administrative appeals tribunals function relatively efficiently in delivering administrative justice to the citizenry, particularly in those areas where legislative innovation has introduced structures which reflect progressive thinking in other jurisdictions.[157] Nevertheless, given the generally laudable advances which have been achieved in post-apartheid administrative review through the courts,[158] the lack of movement in non-court review and appeal is striking. The danger naturally exists by contrast that the relatively beneficial experience of judicial review through the superior courts will lead to such an increase in this form of litigation as to overwhelm the courts and expose the judiciary to unwarranted yet damaging attacks on their independence and resourcing.[159]

Almost 40 years ago Dean speculated[160] on whether South African administrative law justified characterisation as a 'dismal science', concluding that this was in large measure an accurate assessment. I would argue that the broader field of

[157] Such as the tribunals discussed above.
[158] Which are comprehensively and graphically recounted throughout Hoexter and Penfold (n 2).
[159] See the references to works on lawfare (n 14).
[160] WHB Dean, 'Our Administrative Law: A Dismal Science?' (1986) 2 *South African Journal of Human Rights* 164.

administrative justice today should be described much less negatively, largely due to the elevation to the status of constitutional right of the necessity for the accountable exercise of public power and performance of public functions, and the complementary facilitation of the realisation of such rights through the PAJA. The exception to this claim lies in the incoherent area of administrative tribunals. The fact that the tumultuous but greatly progressive decade after 1994 has been succeeded by ever rising levels of governmental failure and corruption should, I would argue, not be seen as fatal to continuing agitation for the completion of the reform agenda. Many of those who have lived through the events described above retain a resilient commitment to finish the journey, and the socio-political context may change. That the recreation of the form and substance of administrative appeals through a tribunal structure remains unachieved should act as an inspiration for those active in the field – there is work yet to be done.

17

Ireland's Distinct Constitutional Vision: The 'Administration of Justice' in Quasi-Judicial Bodies

FIONA DONSON, DARREN O'DONOVAN AND AISLING RYAN*

Introduction

> Ireland stands out as having no political or ideological forces at play on policy approaches to the role of statutory dispute resolution bodies.[1]

Irish tribunals are numerous, but largely overlooked in terms of analysis and media attention, often only being discussed where scandals catapult them into national attention. The development of such bodies has arisen incrementally and largely haphazardly within a small constitutional space. As a result, administrative tribunals in Ireland are plagued by procedural issues, lack of resources and an atypical, complex constitutional framework. Their processes fail to adequately vindicate the rights of individual users who are required to bring claims to these bodies that emerge from the ashes of political crises, with limited reflection or engaged research on their nature and purpose.

The development of Ireland's tribunal bodies has been marked by distinctive anxieties that arise from the Constitution. Article 34.1 provides that 'justice shall be administered in courts', and judicial understandings of resulting separation of powers doctrine has resulted in sharp scrutiny of the boundary between administrative and judicial bodies. Article 37.1 does countenance the existence of such bodies, expressly mandating that they exercise only 'limited functions and powers

* This research was funded by The Traveller Equality and Justice Project and the European Union's Rights, Equality and Citizenship Programme (2014–2020) under Grant Agreement Number 963353–TEJP – REC-AG-2020 / REC-RDIS-DISC-AG-2020 for the period of January 2021–September 2023.

[1] K Mulvey (2011, March 10). 'All changes changed utterly – New times, new engagements and new solutions: How the employment relationship is changing'. Nineteenth John Lovett Memorial Lecture, University of Limerick. At the time of this lecture, Kieran Mulvey was Chief Executive of the Labour Relations Commission and Director General of the Workplace Relations Commission.

of a judicial nature'. Irish tribunal bodies have thus often had to sail through vexed constitutional waters, with the possibility of litigation arguably having a chilling effect on innovation. As we will discuss in this chapter however, the recent landmark Supreme Court case of *Zalewski v Workplace Relations Commission* [2021] IESC 24 may provide the stimulus for greater future reforms. In charting the fundamental restraints upon and requirements applying to tribunal work in Ireland, the Supreme Court has delivered greater certainty on what is permissible and possible. The Irish tribunal system may, at last, be poised to shift from defensive creation of limited, isolated bodies towards a more confident and consolidated vision of merits review.

Administrative Tribunals in Ireland: Distinct Anxieties and Silences

Defining a tribunal is fraught with difficulty, however Hogan, Morgan and Daly provide the following definition for the Irish context:

> Before going further, we ought to mention the commonly accepted definition of the term "tribunal". It is a body, independent of the Government or any other entity but at the same time not a court, which takes decisions affecting individual rights, according to some fairly precise (and usually legal) guidelines and by following a regular and fairly formal procedure.[2]

As this indicates, there has been no clear debate or policy on the development of an underlying system of tribunals in Ireland. Rather they have been created to meet the exigencies of the moment, in response to financial and legitimacy crises, increasing demand on the court system as the administrative state has grown, or sector specific attempts to improve access to justice. In Ireland, the term 'tribunal' is often used interchangeably with 'quasi judicial body', which reflects how their identity is often shaped by contrasts with the courts and judicial methodologies.

The majority of Irish tribunals fall within the 'court substitute' model, operating in the public law sphere and dealing with significant legal issues.[3] Harlow and Rawlings highlight two main justifications for establishing such tribunals: 'expertise' and their role as 'small claim courts' – that is overflow machinery to handle disputes assumed to be of small financial value or liable to generate a mass of claims likely to swamp the courts.[4] These rationalisations certainly mark out much of Ireland's approach in so far as we can indicate there has been one. The benefits of expert adjudication involving specialist knowledge in relation to complex legal

[2] G Hogan, DG Morgan and P Daly, *Administrative Law in Ireland*, 5th edn (Roundhall, 2019) at para 6.11.

[3] ibid at para 6.21.

[4] C Harlow and R Rawlings, *Law and Administration* (Cambridge University Press, 2021) at p 546.

and factual matters are acknowledged in institutional design. Such bodies include mental health tribunals, international protection appeals, planning appeals and social welfare appeals. Tribunals also operate in other fields such as equality and employment law where the state has chosen to create a tribunal to implement parts of the legal scheme.

To date the mosaic of tribunals within the Irish system has never been mapped and there is often little distinction made between different forms of tribunal – whether first instance adjudication, appeal bodies, bodies intersecting with Ombuds roles and bodies with policy formulation responsibilities. This lack of clarity is made all the more complex given the variety of names and lack of consistency around their choice. Terms such as Board/*Bord*, Commission, Tribunal and Ombudsman are used without, it seems, much regard to the individual meaning of such terms. Most confusing is perhaps the *Garda Síochána Ombudsman Commission* which combines Ombudsman and Commission to stand as a particular example of an independent investigative body dealing with complaints made by members of the public concerning the conduct of individual police officers.

The prevailing small claim courts vision has driven a profusion of appeals bodies. Ireland fits the international trend whereby tribunals grow more popular as the volume and complexity of decisions increases, and the administrative state widens and deepens. A distinctive stress is, however, laid upon bodies' ability to deal with disputes swiftly and at a cost saving. Conversely, each tribunals' funding and continued existence depends upon the priority accorded to the particular issues it deals with. There has been no drive to create a centralised tribunal system in like manner to Australia. This diversity has often led to instability, with some appeals bodies targeted in the 'bonfire of the quangos', the streamlining of government bodies which occurred after the country's economic collapse in 2008.[5] When the time came to identify key bodies to reorganise or downsize, it is unsurprising that some quasi-judicial bodies were in the firing line. In particular, the Department of Finance announced a plan to 'rationalise the industrial relations structure' of the state, merging a number of tribunal bodies from the employment sector and equality law.

The pragmatic accretion of isolated, sector-specific tribunal bodies in Ireland has resulted in a lack of visibility of their output. They are perceived as managing one-off disputes, increasingly through mediation and other private forms of settlement. Their possible contribution as early warning mechanisms for issues around legal interpretation and their work's normative effect on frontline decision-making has not been assessed. The decisions of many bodies are not publicly available.[6] This lack of visibility has adverse consequences for the normative effect, a flaw recently warned against by Australia's Royal Commission into

[5] M Murphy and J Hogan, 'Reflections on Post-bailout Policy Analysis in Ireland' (2020) 68(4) *Administration* 145–60, at 151.

[6] Recommendation 20.4 of that Royal Commission is that all decisions of Australia's federal administrative appeals tribunal which address significant issues of law or policy should be published.

the Robodebt Scheme.[7] Even one of the most developed appeals bodies, the International Protection Appeals Tribunal, embarked on a slow journey towards publication of its decisions. Prior to 2006, lawyers representing asylum applicants were barred from accessing copies of previous decisions made by the then Refugee Appeals Tribunal. In the case of *Opesyitan & others v The Refugee Appeals Tribunal*,[8] the Supreme Court overturned this practice, finding publication was required by the constitutional protection of fair hearing. It also underlined the importance of equality of arms between the parties by criticising the practice whereby presenting officers of the relevant statutory body – the Refugee Commissioner – *were* forwarded copies of the decisions. The Supreme Court stressed the value of consistency in decision-making, in particular in the relation to the interpretation of country-of-origin information. The fact the issue had to be litigated, however, points to a lack of reflection upon the normative, standard setting role of tribunals. It embodies how even specialist tribunals are not positioned as models for frontline decision-making, but as residual dispute resolution mechanisms. There is also a risk that a rigid imposition of judicial type approaches may stifle innovation or accessibility at the coalface.

As we will discuss throughout the chapter, Irish tribunals' work has often only gained prominence beyond their users if their procedures misfire or raise constitutional tension. Ireland has yet to undertake an equivalent of the Franks Committee on Tribunals and Inquiries or the Leggatt Report in the United Kingdom.[9] It has not adopted a unified framework or structure for the operation of tribunals. They are not viewed as contributing to a broader vision or system of an administrative justice system, as has been the case with the Australian Administrative Appeals Tribunal. Their work has been complicated by uncertain constitutional status and bounded by a cultural dynamic which juxtaposes their operation with that of the courts.

As the next section of the chapter discusses, the pursuit of economical and efficient tribunal decision-making has come into sharp tension with a central and often overriding theme within Irish administrative law – that of fair procedure. The recent Supreme Court decision in *Zalewski v Workplace Relations Commission*[10] focused in part on the constitutional law question of whether the Workplace Relations Commission (WRC) was administering justice and thus occupying a role that the Irish Constitution reserves for the courts. It embodies how the Irish Constitution offers a narrow and highly conditional constitutional gap for tribunal work. In a jurisdiction where support for tribunals has hinged upon their ability to offer cheaper, more accessible procedures, the case offers both firm limits upon, and a roadmap for, future development.

[7] Royal Commission into the Robodebt Scheme – Final Report – Volume 2 [2023] AURoyalC 3 (7 July 2023) at p 564.

[8] *Opesyitan & others v The Refugee Appeals Tribunal* [2006] IESC 53.

[9] Sir O Franks, (1957) Report of the Franks Committee on Administrative Tribunals and Inquiries (1957) Cmnd 218. Sir A Leggatt, Tribunals for Users, One System, One Service: Report of the Review of Tribunals, (HMSO 2001).

[10] *Zalewski v Workplace Relations Commission* [2021] IESC 24 [Hereinafter '*Zalewski*'.].

Situating Tribunals in the Irish Constitutional Context: 'The Administration of Justice' versus 'Administrative Justice'

In *Zalewski* the constitutionality of the arrangements for resolving workplace disputes was challenged. As noted already in this chapter, the WRC was established under the Workplace Relations Act 2015 as part of austerity measures. It consolidated a number of bodies (Labour Relations Commission, the National Employment Rights Authority, the Equality Tribunal, the Employment Appeals Tribunal and the Labour Court's first instance functions) into one overarching Tribunal. The body has a number of responsibilities including the resolution of industrial relations disputes, adjudication of employment and equality complaints, and the provision of workplace relations information. The development of the body as a wide-ranging Commission with a number of roles is symptomatic of the diverse expectations that can be placed on Irish tribunals.

Zalewski focused upon the adjudicatory function carried out by the Commission and the resultant question as to whether the power granted to it should have instead been designated for a court. The facts of the case offer a particularly stark example of how badly things can go wrong procedurally. It is perhaps unsurprising that the case resulted in significant reflections on the nature and quality of tribunal decision-making by the members of the Supreme Court of Ireland.

The applicant had brought a claim for unfair dismissal to the WRC under the Unfair Dismissals Act 1977. The parties to the dispute made written submissions and provided documentation, although the initial hearing was adjourned because a witness was unable to attend. When the parties attended the WRC for a subsequent hearing a few months later they were informed that a decision had already been made. The published decision that followed rejected the applicant's claim. However, the determination included a number of very significant errors:

> It contained a series of inaccuracies. It gave the impression to any reader that a hearing had taken place, where both sides had been given the opportunity of presenting their case. This was simply incorrect. It alleged the appellant had failed to file documentation. This, too, was incorrect. It was not simply that the decision contained errors concerning some aspects of a claim. That can happen. More seriously, it purported to give a full decision based on events and evidence which had simply never taken place at all.[11]

At first sight this appears to be entirely a matter of fair procedure and could have solely engaged what was primarily to become the second question raised by the case. The applicant, however, chose to query not only the process by which the WRC operated but also its fundamental position within the Constitution.[12]

[11] ibid per MacMenamin J, dissenting judgment at para 11.

[12] See P Daly, 'The Administration of Justice in Administrative Tribunals: Zalewski v. Adjudication Office' [2021] IESC 24 (Article 37.1)' (2023a) Administrative Law Matters Blog. Available at:

The Supreme Court was asked to consider a central constitutional question in Ireland: to what extent and in what circumstances can tribunals be said to be carrying out a constitutionally impermissible administration of justice? The second question in the case – considered later – whether the statutory framework adequately vindicated the procedural rights of a complainant before the WRC under the Constitution and the European Convention on Human Rights.

Central to the first question are two articles of the Irish Constitution. Article 34.1 requires that:

> Justice shall be administered in courts established by law by judges appointed in the manner provided by this Constitution, and, save in such special and limited cases as may be prescribed by law, shall be administered in public.

The State argued in the case that the Commission was not carrying out such power, and even if it was, it could be saved by the subsequent constitutional provision of Article 37.1. This clause provides that:

> Nothing in this Constitution shall operate to invalidate the exercise of limited powers and functions of a judicial nature, in matters other than criminal matters, by any person or body of persons duly authorised by law to exercise such functions and power, notwithstanding that such person or such body of person is not a judge or a court appointed or established as such under this Constitution.

The concept of the 'administration of justice' therefore underpins the operation of tribunals in Ireland. Do such bodies, applying as they do fairly precise sets of legal rules to settle decisions, and often undertaking adjudication on individual rights, administer justice? And what may be said to fall within the boundary of 'limited powers and functions of a judicial nature' and thus be permitted?

Prior to *Zalewski*, the long-agreed approach within Ireland to Article 34.1 was to be found in the case of *McDonald v Bord na gCon*.[13] In that case, relating to the operation of the Irish Greyhound Board, the Supreme Court had set out a list of five indicia of judicial power:

1. A dispute or controversy as to the existence of legal rights or a violation of the law.
2. The determination or ascertainment of the rights of parties or the imposition of liabilities or the infliction of a penalty.
3. The final determination (subject to appeal) of legal rights or liabilities or the imposition of penalties.

www.administrativelawmatters.com/blog/2023/10/18/the-administration-of-justice-in-administrative-tribunals-zalewski-v-adjudication-office-2021-iesc-24-article-37-1/; and T Hickey, '*Zalewski* and the Future of Irish Public Law' (2024) 87 *Modern Law Review* 466.

[13] *McDonald v Bord na gCon* [1965] IR 217.

4. The enforcement of those rights or liabilities or the imposition of a penalty by the court or by the executive power of the State which is called in by the court to enforce its judgment.
5. The making of an order by the court which, as a matter of history, is an order characteristic of courts in this country.

Despite its 'canonical' status on this question[14] this test was not without criticisms. Of particular concern was its circular nature: 'it seeks to identify what *should* be treated as a judicial function by reference to what *is* or *has been* treated as a judicial function'.[15]

On the specific facts of *Zalewski*, all members of the Supreme Court concluded that the WRC was indeed administrating justice and so fell within Article 34.1. The body made 'binding determinations on legal disputes between private parties according to law. That, in itself, is normally a core business of the courts'.[16] In addition, the WRC could compel witnesses, gave opportunities to parties to be heard and present evidence and the decision of the adjudicator was binding on the parties. The court concluded therefore that framework by which the WRC operated created:

> a machinery for the determination and decision by an independent body of complaints seeking relief, as a matter of law, and which permits the adjudication officer to make a binding decision on such complaint which can be enforced against the losing party. In these respects, the process is indistinguishable from the determination of a legal dispute before a court.[17]

The court therefore concluded that the first three criteria had been met. On the fifth criteria, O'Donnell J. rejected the argument of the State that the WRC was able to provide relief that was novel and went beyond that normally available under the common law. He found that 'the form of order made by a decision pursuant to the [Workplace Relations] 2015 Act is a final order determining the dispute and awarding redress of a kind known to the courts'.[18]

The question of compliance with the *McDonald v Bord na gCon* test therefore hinged on the fourth category regarding enforcement of rights. The 2015 Act provided for parties to apply to the District Court – a court of local and summary jurisdiction within Ireland – for enforcement proceedings. A previously available appeal to the Circuit Court, of higher status than the District Court, had been abolished in 2015. The District Court had a very limited discretionary space to alter the adjudicators award. Where satisfied the appropriate time had passed

[14] O'Donnell J in *Zalewski* (n 10) at para 75.
[15] Daly, 'The Administration of Justice in Administrative Tribunals: Zalewski v. Adjudication Office' (n 12) quoting Doyle, et al, 2008 at p 2020.
[16] O'Donnell J (n 10) at para 98.
[17] ibid.
[18] ibid.

without the employer complying with the order the court shall 'without hearing the employer or any evidence … make an order directing the employer to carry out the decision in accordance with its terms' under section 43(1) of the Act. The practical result, according to the Supreme Court, was that the determination of the Adjudication Officer was final and binding.

Given the Court had concluded the WRC fell within Article 34.1 of the Constitution as administering justice, the next question arising was whether the body could be 'saved' under Article 37. As noted earlier, this clause seeks to allow some space for administrative decision-makers to exercise some powers and functions which are of a judicial character. As Daly notes, it is 'remarkable' that the Irish courts have spent so little time considering this provision.[19] The case of *Re Solicitors Act 1954*[20] considered whether a professional disciplinary body could be created in order to regulate solicitors without judicial involvement. Despite the judiciary offering some scope to create such disciplinary structures, a defensive approach was taken in the aftermath of the case. A judicial role was embedded in such professional decision-making regimes, demonstrating as Daly notes 'a reluctance to test the limits of the courts' interpretation of the Constitution.'[21] As we argue later in this chapter, sensitivity to the 'chilling effect' of potential litigation has been seen in the state's legislative response to *Zalewski* and separation of powers issues generally.[22]

Zalewski is now the leading authority on the extent of the saver provision, in particular the meaning of the word 'limited' in Article 37. It sketches, for the first time, a vision of constitutionally 'proofed' administrative bodies which do not trammel upon the distinctive position of the judiciary. O'Donnell J concluded that the exemption in Article 37 needed to be read broadly. In determining whether the Tribunal's work was sufficiently 'limited' a range of matters should be taken into account. These included the Tribunal's subject-matter, the remedies available to it, enforceability of remedies and the availability of appeal.[23]

In relation to the WRC specifically, the court found that a number of elements to its powers that spoke to its operations being 'limited' in nature. It was 'limited by subject matter to those areas of employment law specifically identified in the Act'.[24] In addition, there were limitations on the awards which might be made and enforced which is complimented by the equally limited capacity of the District Court to substitute an order of reinstatement with compensation. Further, WRC decisions were subject to appeal with these being available as of right. The court also noted that judicial review was ultimately available to challenge a decision

[19] See Daly (n 12).

[20] *Re Solicitors Act 1954* [1960] IR 239.

[21] P Daly, 'The Irish Courts and the Administrative State' in Farrell and Howlin (eds), *The Oxford Handbook of Irish Politics*, (2019) Available at: https://ssrn.com/abstract=3398963 at p 6.

[22] F Donson and D O'Donovan, *Law and Public Administration in Ireland*, (Dublin, Clarus Press, 2015) at para 16.04.

[23] O'Donnell J (n 10), para 116.

[24] ibid.

of the Commission. Considering all these components together, the majority concluded that the WRC could be 'saved' from a finding of unconstitutionality based on Article 37.1.

Beyond the specifics of the case, the Supreme Court set out a revised approach to how Articles 34 and 37 operated. The position of administrative bodies has been provided with a firmer footing constitutionally. O'Donnell J recognised the need to more clearly situate the Court's understandings of Articles 34 and 37 within the modern context of administrative state:

> The great expansion in the role of the State in the 20th century, and the transfer by the legislature of functions, which previously might have been considered to be matters for the executive branch alone, to newly-created statutory bodies, and the concurrent general expansion of the power of judicial review of administrative action, has meant that the boundaries of law's empire, as it were, extend much further than might have been contemplated in 1922 or 1937. Looked at functionally, therefore, rather than from the perspective of legal theory, the decisions of the courts in this field have tended to a pragmatic outcome in which the assignment of the administration of justice to the judicial branch has not operated to hinder these developments, even if that has not been achieved by reasoning which … is not always necessarily intellectually satisfying or elegant, although, in that regard, it must be said that the approach of the case law is firmly in line with international comparators.[25]

Reflecting on the Article 34.1 checklist approach, as had operated under *McDonald v Bord na gCon*, O'Donnell J concluded it was not helpful when understood as that – a checklist. The courts should instead recognise Article 34.1 as requiring them to set out what the judiciary must do, and what other bodies can do. Judges should not focus their attention on five disparate elements and not on the broader purpose of the constitutional provision:

> The treatment of the criteria in McDonald as a checklist which must be minutely and precisely complied with risks missing the wood from the trees. It also encourages an approach to drafting that could remove proceedings from the field of the administration of justice because of some small, and in truth insignificant, deviation from the checklist. That would be a triumph of form over substance.[26]

Ultimately, the majority of courts did not abandon the *McDonald v Bord na gCon test* but rather placed it within a more contextual space allowing the courts to reflect on the specifics of the body, the overarching purpose it has and its field of operation. As Hickey notes, *Zalewski*:

> … might be understood 'as emphasising the importance of the existing jurisdiction of the courts', and as meaning that 'any provision subtracting from that jurisdiction, or creating parallel jurisdiction which might render the courts' traditional jurisdiction defunct, is one which should be closely scrutinised by the courts for compatibility with the Constitution.[27]

[25] ibid at para 90.
[26] ibid para 91.
[27] See Hickey (n 12) 480, quoting O'Donnell (n 10) at para 95.

Importantly, the court also did not give carte blanche to tribunals to operate within this broadened constitutional space as they wished. The *Zalewski* challenge would throw up another key constitutional question which has been at the heart of administrative bodies and judicial review in Ireland – that of procedure.

Procedural Protections – The Judicialisation of Public Administration?

Linked with the separation powers issue in *Zalewski* were the factual questions relating to the procedural rules and operation of the WRC. Some of these reflected the less formal and more inquisitorial approach to tribunal decision-making. The facts of the case, however, went well beyond a more administrative form of operation and were rooted in serious failings. These were not necessarily or even evidently systemic, but allowed the court the opportunity to reflect on what procedures should be adopted within the defined constitutional space of administrative justice it had just laid down. Specifically, four challenges arose:

1. Adjudication Officers were not required to have legal qualifications, experience or training;
2. Evidence at hearings was not taken under oath;
3. The WRC procedures did not provide for cross examination of witnesses;
4. The proceedings were held 'otherwise than in public'.

These procedural flaws, the applicant argued, violated his personal constitution rights to fair procedure. Hickey has noted that with the constitutional revision undertaken by the court in *Zalewski* comes with a need to ensure that such bodies operate appropriately:

> [I]f Article 37.1 is now going to bark for the administrative state, then it is going have to bite for the constitutional state as well. If it is now to represent the pillar supporting non-judicial bodies that administer justice of the kind having profound effects on the fundamental interests of individuals, then it must also ensure that that justice is administered in ways that do not undermine the constitutional rights of those individuals.[28]

Central to this is the particular status of procedural rights within the Irish legal system. Unlike other jurisdictions where fair procedure is a rebuttable common law presumption[29] in Ireland the principles have a constitutional basis rooted in Article 40.3.1° requirement that the state shall 'protect … from unjust attack' the personal rights of the citizen.

[28] Hickey (n 12) at p 11.
[29] Donson and O'Donovan (n 22) at para 10.01.

Tribunals have often been praised for offering a more accessible, efficient and economical approach to dispute resolution.[30] It has been assumed that bodies such as the WRC are able to be accessed without legal representation. The lack of legal aid to support legal representation before bodies such as these embedded within the system the idea that such tribunals should be navigable without specialised representation.

In *Zalewski*, O'Donnell J directly acknowledges the potential value of policies underlying the establishment of tribunals such as the WRC which can provide relatively informal and efficient dispute resolution. Indeed, it is in this context that he rejects the first procedural complaint – that adjudicators should be legally trained:

> Courts and lawyers do not have a monopoly on fact-finding or even on law's application, and cannot claim infallibility in either respect.[31]

There is a tension here, however, that arises as other aspects of tribunal procedures become more court like. The increasing use of legal representatives in tribunal settings inevitably brings with it increased formalisation of the proceedings. For applicants and respondents able to afford representation this has benefits; for those who cannot, they are in danger of experiencing inequality of arms and inaccessible processes. While the *Zalewski* requirements apply only to those bodies which are involved in the administration of justice, a risk of broader chilling effects accompanies the judgment.

Genn, in her seminal work on tribunals in the UK, asks whether procedural informality might be a benefit or a trap for applicants.[32] The idea that tribunals such as the WRC are accessible without legal representation involves assumptions about accessibility, formality and any particular individual's ability to navigate legal, factual and procedural terrain. However, we have already noted that a key motivation for diverting legal issues into such bodies is one of cost. As systems become more formal, and take on more court style procedures, there is an ever increasing need to ensure equality of arms for parties in accessing legal representation.

Although the Supreme Court rejected the first procedural ground raised by *Zalewski*, the court then noted that the 'standard of justice administered under Article 37 cannot be lower or less demanding than the justice administered in courts under Article 34'.[33] This statement underlines that, for the Irish constitutional order, administrative bodies must deliver certain fundamental protections. O'Donnell J stressed that:

> [T]he function being performed and the power being exercised must comply with the fundamental components of independent, impartiality, dispassionate application of

[30] B McCabe, 'Perspectives on Economy and Efficiency in Tribunal Decision-Making' (2016) 85 *AIAL Forum* 40.

[31] O'Donnell (n 10) at para 13.

[32] H Genn, 'Tribunals and Informal Justice' (1993) 56 *MLR* 393, at 393.

[33] O'Donnell (n 10) at para 138.

> the law, openness, and, above all, fairness, which are understood to be the essence of the administration of justice.[34]

This statement of principle signals a process of judicial interrogation and oversight into institutional design, case handling and procedural fairness. Will debates over the extent of formal procedural protections required encrust and complicate the operation of future tribunal bodies in Ireland?

Returning to the specific pleadings in *Zalewski*, the Supreme Court concluded that there was a presumption that justice will be administered in public. As a result, the blanket statutory ban on hearings being held in public that had been operating at the time of the case was found to be unconstitutional.[35] In addition, the court found that the WRC should have the necessary powers for it to be able to act in accordance with court-like standards. Specifically, this included an ability to require evidence to be taken under oath including the related enforcement power of prosecution for providing false evidence. This was described by the court as being 'an important part of ensuring that justice is done in cases where there is serious and direct conflict of evidence'.[36] In addition, the court noted the importance of cross-examination of witnesses.[37]

MacMenamin J in his dissent raised particular concerns about the dangers of inconsistent practice that might arise between individual hearings where a clear procedure was not adopted across the WRC system. He therefore argued for adopting binding procedural rules to underpin the Commission's operation:

> Earlier this judgment noted that the WRC has not adopted any rules of procedure by statutory instrument. This, too, creates undesirable uncertainty, which arose in this case. Where significant issues are at stake, such as employment, parties are entitled to know, in advance, the rules of procedure to be applied prior to embarking on a hearing. This did not occur. This is not to say that the full range of fair procedures would be necessary in every case, but, in this one, they were necessary. In a case where there is a conflict of evidence, a person entrusted with making decisions or determinations which may affect someone's life, must make clear to the parties, from the outset, the scope of procedures which will apply in that given case. Such procedures are necessary for the administration of justice.[38]

The majority of the court, however, specifically allowed for the fact that tribunals need a degree of flexibility in their procedures.[39] There is an inherent danger of over formalisation arising from the judgment. Irish tribunals seem set on a process of accelerated reform from a relatively informal culture into a mandatory, formal court-like approach. While this, in itself, may not be problematic in terms of the

[34] ibid.
[35] ibid at paras 141–42.
[36] ibid at para 144.
[37] ibid at para 146.
[38] ibid at para 139.
[39] ibid at para 137.

principle, surrounding systems of access to justice such as legal aid will also need to be adapted to meet the challenge.

In the aftermath of *Zalewski* the Irish state passed the Workplace Relations (Miscellaneous Provisions) Act 2021 which embedded key components of the judgment into a formal structure. Thus, evidence may be given on oath or affirmation. So the judgment of the court by which the court noted swearing an oath as being 'an important part of ensuring that justice is done in cases where there is serious and direct conflict of evidence'[40] has subsequently become standard required practice while the WRC has adopted a presumption of public hearings.[41] Indeed, the revised scheme for the WRC appears to fall within the risk free drafting approach of adopting procedural rules as standard even where the court had noted that they are to be used in the most serious of cases.

What is not clear to date is how far *Zalewski* is flowing out beyond the confines of the operation of its own tribunal – the WRC – and into other bodies. While the decision has been widely cited in cases there is limited evidence of the decision being applied to strike down decisions on judicial review. At the legislative level, signs are emerging of the wider impact. When the Central Bank (Individual Accountability Framework) Act 2023 was first published, discussions arose around its compliance with *Zalewski*.[42] The Act provided for a change to the Central Bank's administrative sanction procedure. Under the process, where there is a finding that a company has committed a 'prescribed contravention' of financial services requirements the Central Bank is required to make an application to the High Court for confirmation of the decision 'as soon as practicable'. This then embeds a judicial component into the procedure thus protecting it from Article 34. In addition, the Act requires changes to enhance procedural fairness and constitutional protections within the process including separating out investigative functions and decision-making functions. In some senses, the fact that this was regarded as a necessary change post-*Zalewski* perhaps underlines the limited engagement previously in the design of such processes given the significant danger of blending roles and potential bias claims within such systems while also being symptomatic of the state's over-cautious legislative response to judicial decisions. Maher and Mulholland[43] also note that 'similar adjustments are under consideration

[40] ibid at para 144.

[41] C Bracken, 'Comparative Approaches to the Enforcement of the Race Directive 2000/43/EC in Ireland' (2024) Traveller Equality & Justice Project Report (forthcoming) at para 34. Bracken notes that the WRC has adopted guidance on 'special circumstances' which would permit private hearings which includes medical conditions, the involvement of minors or issues of a sensitive natures such as arise in sexual harassment cases. See www.workplacerelations.ie/en/publications_forms/procedures_employment_and_equality_complaints.pdf, accessed 5 January 2024.

[42] D Maher and N Mulholland, 'Central Bank (Individual Accountability Framework) Bill: The Zalewski Judgement – A catalyst for change', (2022) Matheson Insights. Available at: www.matheson.com/insights/detail/central-bank-(individual-accountability-framework)-bill-the-zalewski-judgement---a-catalyst-for-change, accessed: 5 January 2024.

[43] ibid.

in relation to the Competition and Consumer Protection Commission and the Financial Services and Pensions Ombudsman'. Recent regulations relating to the Social Welfare Appeals Office expressly allow applicants to request an oral hearing in their matter.[44]

Lack of Independence and Effective Organisational Design

It is clear the *Zalewski* ruling has applied a distinct regulatory stimulus to the current and future operation of tribunals. We believe it is likely to stimulate the first true census of, and reflection on, standard operating procedures in tribunals in Ireland. Government will be required to take stock and, for the first time, survey the existing landscape against fresh, systemic requirements.

While it seems obvious that tribunals should be independent of government or other entities, this has not been the case in practice. Social security appeals in Ireland are heard by the Social Welfare Appeals Office, an office that is part of the Department of Social Protection. Appeals officers are appointed by the Minister and there is a perception that the appeals office is not sufficiently independent from other sections of the Department.[45] Local authority housing decisions are heard by internal appeals officers. The Residential Tenancies Board (RTB) is an appeals body responsible for first instance decisions (made by adjudicators) and tribunal decisions (made by tribunal members). Discussions regarding the need for *formal* independence, might also prompt overdue reflection upon indicia of effective, functional independence such as security of tenure and adequate resourcing. To date much reliance has been placed on wording which references independence – the 'independent adjudicator' – but which, in reality, provide little or no framework to ensure the practical implementation of this.[46]

The challenges of implementing *Zalewski* at the coalface cannot be underestimated. There is a lack of research even on the people who sit on Irish administrative tribunals. The pre-requisite qualifications and expertise vary hugely from tribunal to tribunal, and the ongoing training varies contextually too. Some tribunal members are employees of government departments or administrative tribunals, and others are fee paid independent contractors. For some practitioners, tribunal adjudication work is becoming less desirable as a career option due to the perceived inadequacy of the current daily rates. For example, Residential

[44] Minister for Social Protection, Social Welfare (Appeals) Regulations 2023. Available at: https://assets.gov.ie/252112/d7ae4fbf-ac41-4fcd-83e7-704e7c20b4b1.pdf.

[45] Free Legal Advice Centre, 'Not Fair Enough: Making the case for reform of the social welfare appeals system', (Dublin: FLAC, 2012). Available at: www.flac.ie/assets/files/pdf/not_fair_enough_final.pdf, accessed 5 January 2024.

[46] See, eg, the Workplace Relations Commission Act 2015, s 40(8) which states that: 'An adjudication officer shall be independent in the performance of his or her functions.'

Tenancy Board adjudicators are paid a flat fee of €616 per day for three hearings,[47] which provides only for the actual day of adjudications and does not include any additional preparatory period for cases or time for writing adjudication reports and determination orders. WRC external adjudicators are paid a daily rate of €525, although they can also receive sanction for one write-up day for every three days of hearings. There has been no increase since 2017 and frustration among external adjudicators is growing in relation to rates of pay, as well as lack of security of tenure and increased workload.[48] Similarly, a 2021 International Protection Tribunal Members survey shows the issue of fees arising in the immigration context. Anonymous quotations from Tribunal members in the report included the following: 'The fees currently payable to Tribunal members do not reflect the amount of work undertaken on average per file.' 'The fee also fails to reflect the significant emotional challenge inherent in the role' and 'The work is barely worth doing financially if assessed on an hourly rate. The researching and study of country-of-origin information can take days to properly assimilate … I think most of us feel that the amount of work that we have to do and the standard we have to achieve is under estimated and unappreciated by the Department of Justice.'[49] Tribunal adjudication is a responsible and onerous position, it is essential that tribunal members are well trained professionals, suited to adjudication work, and can devote sufficient time to considering cases before them.

There is also, disappointingly, evidence of significant underperformance in existing appeal bodies. An Bord Pleanála is the statutorily independent planning body responsible for deciding appeals on planning decisions. The body was traditionally afforded with the highest levels of deference from the judiciary.[50] This deferential attitude has, however, been all but eroded over the past 30 years, with poor decision making and management practices damaging the reputation of and trust in the body. Public controversies have led to an ongoing 'whole of institution' scoping review. The categories included in its Terms of Reference speak to the significant maladministration currently under investigation: conflicts of interest and objective or actual bias; statutory declarations; allocation of files; amendments to inspectors' reports; communication with external parties outside of formal statutory of administrative channels.[51] In 2023, the former Deputy Director of An Bord Pleanála, Paul Hyde, received a two-month sentence for breach of planning

[47] Residential Tenancies Board, 'Annual Report and Accounts 2022'. Available at: www.rtb.ie/images/uploads/forms/RTB_Annual_Report_2022_English.pdf at p 52.

[48] E Malone, 'Workplace Relations Commission adjudicators unhappy over pay and conditions', *The Irish Times* (24 April 2023). Available at: www.irishtimes.com/business/work/2023/04/24/workplace-relations-commission-adjudicators-unhappy-over-pay-and-conditions/.

[49] Department of Justice, 'End to End Review of International Protection Process: IPAT Members' Survey Report' (Stationery Office 2021) at pp 14–15. Available at: www.irishimmigration.ie/wp-content/uploads/2021/10/IPAT-Members-survey-report.pdf, accessed 5 January 2024.

[50] *O'Keeffe v An Bord Pleanála* [1993] 1 IR 39.

[51] An Bord Pleanála, 'Terms of Reference for investigation by Lorna Lynch SC' (2023). Available at: www.pleanala.ie/getmedia/d646ffe3-349b-4a4b-a55c-cdc91de4849a/Terms-of-reference-External-Scoping-Investigation-ABP.pdf?ext=.pdf, accessed 5 January 2024.

laws. Speaking in court during the sentencing hearing, Judge James McNulty noted: 'What makes these offences so serious is that the work of An Bord Pleanála is quasi judicial' and '[i]t is at the high end of quasi judicial'.[52] Hyde successfully appealed the custodial sentence on the basis of its severity with Cork Circuit Court increasing the sentence length to three months, but suspended it in full, while also imposing fines totalling €6,000.[53]

Given the role which planning issues played in Ireland's economic collapse in 2008, the body was amongst the highest profile tribunals in the state. This visible breach of trust has been a blow to public confidence in administrative decision-making outside the courts. It is perhaps, then, not surprising that an overhaul of the planning system in proposed in the current Planning and Development Bill 2023 which will include a new name for the planning tribunal – An Coimisiún Pleanála – to be run by a Chief Planning Commissioner and employing 14 commissioners.[54]

A perplexing paradox that emerges post-*Zalewski* is how tribunals can continue to offer distinctive benefits, when they are expected to be court-like in key aspects of procedure. They are also being called upon to navigate this tension in circumstances where legal aid is not available for the parties. There is an urgent need to think systematically and holistically about why we have these administrative bodies, what they do, and why what they do is different from judicial decision-making. While it raises significant challenges, *Zalewski* should at least bring to an end the quietism and anxiety that surrounded the status of tribunal work. This traditional discomfort in classifying or describing tribunal adjudication reflected Ireland's complex, atypical constitutional framework.

This in part flows from the separation of powers under the Irish Constitution, and a formalist adherence to the strict division between concepts that are often nebulous. As Cane observes:

> The concepts of legislative, executive and judicial functions are extremely abstract. Their abstraction partly explains why it has been found very difficult to provide robust accounts of the distinctive nature of various functions and of the differences between them. It also explains why the prefix 'quasi' is sometimes added particularly to the terms 'legislative' and 'judicial': the prefix typically indicates that the speaker senses a distinction between the real thing and the imitation, but cannot pinpoint it with confidence.[55]

[52] N Baker, 'Former deputy chair of An Bord Pleanála Paul Hyde handed two-month jail sentence', *The Irish Examiner* (30 June 2023). Available at: www.irishexaminer.com/news/courtandcrime/arid-41173816.html.

[53] P Sheehy, 'Former ABP deputy chair Paul Hyde wins sentence appeal', RTÉ (15 November 2023). Available at: www.rte.ie/news/ireland/2023/1115/1416640-paul-hyde-appeal/, accessed 5 January 2024.

[54] T Meskill, 'An Bord Pleanála to be renamed as part of changes under draft bill', RTÉ (26 January 2023). Available at: www.rte.ie/news/politics/2023/0126/1351996-draft-planning-development-bill/, accessed 5 January 2024.

[55] P Cane, *Administrative Tribunals and Adjudication* (Hart Publishing, 1st edn published 2009, paperback 2010) at p 140.

Jurisprudence of the Irish courts traditionally leant towards a strong conception of separation of powers, with jurists such as Hardiman J propounding 'the primal constitutional position of the doctrine'.[56] However, some jurists understand the doctrine in more malleable terms. Writing extra-judicially, Mr Justice Fennelly notes: 'the constitutional scheme does not, however, establish a rigid system of exclusive powers of the legislative, executive and judicial branches, within their proper spheres'.[57] The fallout from *Zalewski* will see a welcome wave of reflection upon the relationship between quasi-judicial and administrative decision making, and what distinguishes one from the other.[58]

The disparate, ad hoc nature of administrative tribunals in Ireland has contributed to a disorganised and opaque systems of administrative decision-making. Individuals are also forced to navigate appeals systems without legal representation, as civil legal aid is generally not available for tribunal-level matters. The current legal aid scheme excludes administrative bodies and quasi-judicial tribunals, with the exception of the International Protection Appeals Tribunals. Ironically, the applicant in *Zalewski* was awarded full costs for his High Court and Supreme Court actions but was statute barred from receiving any costs or legal aid funding in relation to the WRC case that prompted the litigation.[59] The result has been significant, ongoing access to justice issues with many individuals lacking the knowledge, capacity, or confidence to represent themselves before administrative tribunals. Inequality of arms between the parties are common at oral hearings, and parties who do elect for legal representation, will bear the cost regardless of the outcome.

There are also significant rule of law issues arising from the lack of public awareness of what tribunals 'do', and how you can bring an appeal before the relevant administrative tribunal. For instance, the 'Summary of the submissions received to the 2021 Public Consultation on the Review of the Equality Acts' (published in June 2023),[60] highlighted widespread public misunderstanding of which body is responsible for equality law matters. The relevant body – the WRC – was found to not commonly be understood by the public as hearing equality and discrimination cases. The report noted that there was 'significant confusion for persons, wishing to take a claim related to equality in accessing goods and

[56] Mr Justice Fennelly, 'The Courts and the Doctrine of Separation of Powers in the Irish Constitution' in E Carolan (ed), *Judicial Power in Ireland* (Institute of Public Administration, 2018) at p 48, citing Hardiman J in *Sinnott v Minister for Education* [2004] 2 IR 545, 702.

[57] Mr Justice Fennelly, ibid at p 49.

[58] Hickey (n 12).

[59] C Connolly, and K Liddy-Cormican, 'A recent Irish Supreme Court decision in the context of adjudication of workplace disputes may have implications for a wide range of decision-making bodies' (2021). Available at: www.addleshawgoddard.com/en/insights/insights-briefings/2021/litigation/decision-making-by-quasi-judical-bodies---the-implications-of-zalewski/.

[60] Department of Children, Equality, Disability, Integration and Youth, 'Summary of the submissions received to the 2021 Public Consultation on the Review of the Equality Acts' (June 2023). Available at: www.gov.ie/en/press-release/cafb4-minister-ogorman-publishes-report-on-the-submissions-to-the-public-consultation-on-the-review-of-the-equality-acts/.

services, in understanding that complaints about discrimination outside of the workplace must go to body with the word 'workplace' in its title.'

The lack of organisational design has contributed to complex appeals pathways. The England and Wales Law Commission outlines how there are four broad pillars of administrative justice: internal mechanisms of redress; external non-court avenues of redress (public inquiries and tribunals); ombudsmen; and the courts.[61] Ireland cannot neatly compartmentalise different pathways of redress due to the way in which the different complaint mechanisms have evolved, and how many tribunals are not independent of government departments.

In some areas of administration, there is no tribunal in place to hear appeals, and challenges to decisions are instead channelled into the courts system. For example, if a party wishes to appeal a first instance Equal Status Acts decision, the appeal is to the Circuit Court whereas a decision relating to a claim made under the Employment Equality Acts is appealed to the non-judicial Labour Court. This causes confusion in circumstances where both original decisions are made at first instance in the WRC. Certain decisions made by the Competition and Consumer Protection Commission are appealed to the High Court. Decisions made by the Financial Services and Pensions Ombudsman (FPSO) are appealed to the High Court. The FPSO has both investigatory and adjudicatory functions under statute, so both ombud and tribunal functions are housed within the same body.

Nason notes that 'the design and form of administrative justice oversight varies considerably depending on the context' and that 'modern administrative justice systems are ultimately characterized by multiple different pathways by which doing justice is perceived in a range of guises'.[62] Tribunals are a key oversight mechanism, but in the Irish context we tend to muddle different oversight mechanisms together, or as outlined above, rely entirely on the courts to provide oversight of first instance decision making. The manner in which tribunal adjudication has been set up in Ireland has led to a proliferation of bodies across the administrative state. Some of these tribunals make an extremely low number of decisions annually. This begs the question as to whether there could be 'grouping' of functions, reducing cost through pooling of resources and expertise.

Access to Justice and Normative Effect in the Irish Tribunal System

Amongst the most damaging impacts of the opacity of Ireland's system is an absence of policy reflection upon how these bodies deliver for their users or

[61] The Law Commission, Administrative Redress: Public Bodies and the Citizen (2010). Available at: https://s3-eu-west-2.amazonaws.com/lawcom-prod-storage-11jsxou24uy7q/uploads/2015/03/lc322_Administrative_Redress.pdf.

[62] S Nason, 'Oversight of Administrative Justice Systems' in M Hertogh, R Kirkham, R Thomas and J Tomlinson, (eds) *The Oxford Handbook of Administrative Justice* (OUP 2022), 155–76 at 173.

contribute to improved frontline decision-making in government departments. Research into the experiences of tribunal users is extremely limited, with surveys undertaken indicating that 'satisfaction' within tribunal outcomes and experience seemed to be heavily dependent upon the substantive outcome of a decision.[63] The sole prevailing tool for measuring impact remains the internal 'customer service surveys' which can provide only a limited insight into the overall operation of such bodies. Such views are often informed by the outcomes of complaints rather than the experience of access to justice.[64]

The question of whether appeals bodies have a normative effect upon departmental practices is also under-studied. One can, however, point to key areas where successful appeals rate trends have been concerningly high. The 2022 Social Welfare Appeals Office Annual Report records that 24,267 appeals were finalised in 2022; 12,654 (52.1%) of the appeals finalised had a favourable outcome for the appellant.[65] Looking back ten years, to the same year of the highly critical FLAC report discussed below, the 2012 SWAO Annual Report states that of the 32,558 appeals finalised in 2012, 16,417 (50.4%) had a favourable outcome for the appellant. These are unacceptably high numbers of revised decisions, likely indicative of poor first instance decision-making and information-gathering practices.

In 2021, the Comptroller and Auditor General called for the department to undertake a range of actions to improve the quality of its first instance decision-making.[66] It recommended that it should 'carry out periodic reviews of successfully appealed cases where no new or additional material information was provided' on the basis that 'these reviews could assist the Department in learning from the cases determined by appeals officers and in improving the quality of decisions made by its deciding officers in determining claims'.[67] Often high rates of successful appeal are attributed to the failure of individuals to provide sufficient information to ground their claims. The Comptroller and Auditor General called for the department to assess the administrative burden it was imposing upon people with disability in particular. It further required the department to 'examine the application process and related guidance for schemes which are medically or social and care needs assessed in order to ensure claimants are able to supply all necessary information to assess eligibility when they are making a claim'.[68] The Department was also asked to 'review its current procedures so as to ensure that all claimants are informed clearly of the reason(s) for refusal of claims'.[69]

[63] R Murphy, D McGuinness, E Bainbridge, L Brosnan, M Keys, H Felzmann, K Murphy, B Hallahan, A Higgins and C McDonald, 'Service Users' Experiences of Mental Health Tribunals in Ireland: A Qualitative Analysis' (2017) *Irish Journal of Psychological Medicine* 34(4) 233–42. Available at: https://doi.org/10.1017/ipm.2017.11.

[64] ibid.

[65] Social Welfare Appeals Office, 'Annual Report 2022' at p 20. Available at: https://assets.gov.ie/267678/fa47277b-b0f6-42cd-b9f9-7844d552961c.pdf.

[66] Comptroller and Auditor General of Ireland, 'Chapter 10: Management of Social Security Appeals' in *Report on the Accounts of Public Services 2020* (Stationery Office, 2021).

[67] ibid at para 10.60, Recommendation 10.4.

[68] ibid Recommendation 10.5.

[69] ibid Recommendation 10.1.

Recent regulations reforming the Appeals Office functioning have offered limited, tacit recognition of negative dynamics. Article 5 of the Social Welfare (Appeals) Regulations 2023 provides for a 'feedback loop' between the Social Welfare Appeals Office and the Department of Social Protection. The Chief Appeals Officer is empowered provide feedback and guidance to the Minister and to Department staff on what they view as appropriate interpretation of statutory provisions. This is a rare instance of an Irish appeals body being tasked with uplifting first instance decision-making. While community legal centres welcomed this when consulted on the regulations, they also noted the importance of moving to a stronger system of publication of appeals decisions. A 2023 report entitled 'Transparency and Consistency within the Social Welfare Appeals Process' argued that 'a publicly available online database of the SWAO could provide additional and significant assistance in the resolution of cases and in the appeal process'.[70] It argued that decisions which clarify a point of law or involve a statutory interpretation should be prioritised for publication. Currently, Community Law & Mediation – a community law centre – offer the only database compiled by social sector organisations and advocates and dependent upon consent by their clients.

The new feedback mechanism, however, also serves to highlight abiding tensions regarding the independence of the Social Welfare Appeals Office itself. The Minister for Social Protection appoints the Chief Appeals Officer, Deputy Chief Appeals Officers and Appeals Officers. The Social Welfare Appeals Office is part of the Department of Social Protection. There is no essence of an independent review mechanism and, as Daly notes, in *Zalewski* the court demonstrated an 'insistence on putting administrative independence on a constitutional footing'.[71] As far back 2012, the Free Legal Advice Centre published a report highly critical of the Social Welfare Appeals Office, noting 'the appeals system is failing those whom it is intended to serve and that the basic rights of access to social welfare, to fair procedures and to an effective remedy are not available as needed'.[72] It set out detailed reform recommendations regarding first instance and appellate decision-making on social security decisions, and the need for an independent tribunal.

In recent years, tribunals in Ireland are promoting mediation over adjudication as a form of dispute resolution. In October 2022, the RTB implemented a policy change whereby mediation was introduced as the 'primary default route for resolving disputes'.[73] This was done on the basis of the Housing for All 2021 Plan, whereby the government seeks to resolve disputes earlier on, without recourse to adjudication or tribunal processes. Similarly, the WRC has recently introduced a

[70] Age Action, Community Law and Mediation, Cross Care, Disability Federation of Ireland, Joint Submission to the public Consultation on Changes to the Social Welfare Appeals Regulations (2023) at p 4. Available at: https://communitylawandmediation.ie/wp-content/uploads/2023/06/Submission-to-the-public-consultation-on-changes-to-the-Social-Welfare-Appeals-Regulations-19-May-2023.pdf.

[71] Daly (n 12).

[72] FLAC (n 45).

[73] Residential Tenancies Board, 'Annual Report and Accounts 2022' (n 47).

new mediation model, seeking to resolve unfair dismissal claims through mediation. It reports a 30% increase in both parties agreeing to mediation. While we agree that '[a]ssisting amicable resolution is effective',[74] we have concerns that the current move to a 'default' mediation is being done as a cost-saving measure, without reflection on whether the relevant dispute is suitable for the parties involved, particularly where parties are navigating administrative justice systems. Hare argues that 'access to legal resources and representation are necessary for tenants to effectively represent themselves in mediation'.[75]

In circumstances where there is no legal aid available for cases before the WRC or RTB, empirical research is urgently needed to investigate the rise of tribunal mediations, taking account of intersecting societal structures that impact on participation. Is mediation forming a central part of tribunal work because it is effective and fair, or because it is cheap? There are significant power imbalances at play, particularly between employer and employee, and landlord and tenant, that require careful consideration before embracing mediation in these contexts. The Irish tribunal sector would benefit from an oversight body, such as the Administrative Justice Council, to begin the process of collecting and analysing data, with a view to feeding into future reform projects. At present, we do not even have a strong research cluster in the area, akin to the UK Administrative Justice Institute, perhaps, in part, due to the predominance of constitutional theory in public law discourse.[76]

A final significant issue facing access to justice in tribunal administration concerns the enforcement of decisions following inter-party disputes. Writing in the context of the RTB, the *Dublin Inquirer* reports that there is a perception that awards and damages are left unpaid following the issuing of determination orders.[77] The RTB's Strategy Statement 2023–2025 Public Consultation report acknowledges this concern regarding non-compliance with determination orders and introduced 'a pilot Order Enforcement Facilitation Project', aiming to prevent parties needing to enforce determination orders through the courts, instead attempting to resolve non-compliance through a facilitated mediation.[78] While we welcome the issue of enforcement being addressed, there must be concern over how seriously tribunal decisions are being taken by parties. Significant rights and entitlements are adjudicated on across the tribunal sector in Ireland, but it is sidelined in public law discourse. Enforcement of tribunal decisions was presented

[74] C Hodges, 'Delivering Administrative Justice: Implications for System Design' in Hertogh, Kirkham, Thomas and Tomlinson (n 45) 177–202 at 190.

[75] R Hare, 'Mitigating Power Imbalance in Eviction Mediation: A Model for Minnesota' (2020) *Law and Inequality: A Journal of Theory and Practice* 38(1) 135–64.

[76] Donson and O'Donovan (n 22).

[77] L Neylon, 'Landlord and Tenants Ignore RTB Rulings Too Often, Board Members Worry', *Dublin Inquirer* (8 February 2023). Available at: https://dublininquirer.com/2023/02/08/landlords-and-tenants-ignore-rtb-rulings-too-often-board-members-worry/.

[78] Residential Tenancies Board, 'RTB Statement of Strategy 2023–2025 Public Consultation Report' Available at: www.rtb.ie/images/uploads/forms/RTB_Strategy_2023-2025_consultation_%28WEB%29.pdf.

as an area in need of reform in the Irish Human Rights and Equality Commission's submission to the equality legislation review. IHREC, submits that the enforcement of decisions of the WRC (first instance body) and Labour Court (appeal body) 'should be more expansive'.[79]

The role of the Ombud is underexplored here. This could be a suitable body to drive enforcement and monitor trends across different administrative tribunals. Thomas argues that ombuds are well positioned to complement individual redress mechanisms, and to provide a depth and breadth of scrutiny that individual decision redress mechanism cannot.[80] While appeals bodies are often focused upon the services users who present before them for adjudication, there is a much wider community whom they also serve. These are the *prevented* users of tribunals: individuals who gain the benefit of appeals rulings through transformed first instance processes. Systems which are aimed at efficiency need to ensure their work is communicated, studied and reflected upon. Effective dispute resolution also needs to aim for the prevention of future disputes through transformed frontline relationships. Ireland's appeal bodies have unfortunately limited platforms, tools and resources to pursue such systemic impacts.

Conclusion: Reform and Future Directions

Reform of administrative tribunals in Ireland is long overdue. Due to the disparate nature of tribunal/quasi-judicial functions and powers across public administration, a challenge will be identifying where to start. The absence of a centralised body with responsibility for training, research, data collection, and reform proposals for tribunals, exacerbates the problems explored above because no one has a holistic view of the field. Individual tribunals are concerned with immediate problems within their sector. There is a failure to weave the threads together as part of the wider fabric of administrative justice.[81] The *Zalewski* case illustrates the reactive, rather than proactive, nature of any change to tribunal powers and structure in the Irish administrative state. A significant limitation is the tendency towards looking at administrative problems with a constitutional spyglass, honing in on the big constitutional issues, but ignoring the interrelated and connected web of administrative justice issues. We previously observed:

> While there have been extensive constitutional convention debates proposing referenda to reform the state's constitutional framework, these have largely failed to address

[79] Irish Human Rights and Equality Commission, 'Submission on the Review of the Equality Acts', (July 2023). Available at: www.ihrec.ie/app/uploads/2023/07/Submission-on-the-Review-of-the-Equality-Acts.pdf.

[80] R Thomas, 'The Northern Ireland Public Services Ombudsman's Report into Personal Independence Payment and Collective Administrative Justice (Pt 1)' (2023) 30 *Journal of Social Security Law* 143.

[81] M Doyle and N O'Brien, *Reimagining Administrative Justice: Human Rights in Small Places*, (Palgrave Pivot 2020).

> questions of administrative justice. This emphasis on the constitutional to the detriment of the administrative is extremely disappointing, as while it may be said that we have a constitutional vocabulary of rights and values, we have not yet formed an effective administrative and inter-institutional grammar for their delivery.[82]

There are seeds of reform on the horizon, with a renewed interest in the area following *Zalewski* and a growing body of scholarship on administrative tribunals.[83] It is likely that multiple tribunals are operating in a manner that may be inconsistent with *Zalewski*, with many tribunal hearings taking place in private, without provision for Court-like practices.

The Irish Law Reform Commission's Fifth Programme of Law Reform was approved by government in March 2019. The first listed project is the reform of 'Non-Court Adjudicative Bodies and Appeals to Court'. The Commission has yet to move to consultation stage to date. The project aims to 'examine the case for a reformed system, including the approach to evidential matters and simplifying the avenues of appeal to the courts from such bodies'.[84] It is likely that *Zalewski* has raised a host of unforeseen issues for the Commission to consider. It is not clear why the Commission is targeting the very broad class of 'non-court adjudicative bodies', as opposed to 'quasi-judicial bodies' or 'administrative tribunals'. It is likely that any public body with a decision-making function could be described as a 'non-court adjudicative body'. The Law Reform Commission discontinued several of its law reform projects in 2023, but the reform of non-court adjudicative bodies survived the cull.[85] However, no further information as to the reason for the delay in progressing projects has been made publicly available.

Any consultation by the Commission is likely to attract significant interest from a wide range of stakeholders. Further reflection on the purpose of administrative tribunals, what sets them apart from different types of decision-making and why, is required to ensure that any proposals are specific, implementable, and user focused. Time is of the essence for, as this chapter demonstrates, significant reform is needed to Irish administrative tribunals to ensure rights are vindicated and public resources are effectively utilised.

[82] Donson and O'Donovan (n 22) at para 16.09.

[83] BM Barry, 'Workplace Dispute Resolution in Ireland at a Crossroads: Challenges and Opportunities' (2021) 66 *The Irish Jurist* 44.

[84] Law Reform Commission, Fifth Programme of Law Reform, LRC 120-2019 at p 3.

[85] Law Reform Commission, Rationalisation of Fifth Programme of Law Reform (2023). Available at: www.lawreform.ie/press-room/rationalisation-of-fifth-programme-of-law-reform.1123.html.

INDEX

Introductory Note

References such as '178–79' indicate (not necessarily continuous) discussion of a topic across a range of pages. Wherever possible in the case of topics with many references, these have either been divided into sub-topics or only the most significant discussions of the topic are listed. Because the entire work is about 'administrative tribunals', the use of this term (and certain others which occur constantly throughout the book) as an entry point has been restricted. Information will be found under the corresponding detailed topics. Cross-references in a form such as 'courts *see also individual courts*' direct the reader to headings in a particular class (e.g. in this case 'Supreme Courts') rather than a specific '*individual courts*' entry.

www.ingramcontent.com/pod-product-compliance
Ingram Content Group UK Ltd.
Pitfield, Milton Keynes, MK11 3LW, UK
UKHW041853301225
466524UK00002B/4

9 781509 966905